Richard Chapple

A
DOSTOEVSKY
DICTIONARY

ARDIS

Ardis Publishers
2901 Heatherway
Ann Arbor, Michigan 48104

Library of Congress Cataloging in Publication Data

Chapple, Richard L., 1944-
  A Dostoevsky dictionary.

  Includes index.
  1. Dostoevsky, Fyodor, 1821-1881—Dictionaries,
indexes, etc. I. Title.
PG 3328.A09C5   891.73'3   82-18514
ISBN 0-88233-616-9

Table of Contents

To Suzanne
Larissa, Marika, Michael,
Allyson, Ashley, Lindsay

Preface

A reader's companion to Fyodor Mikhaylovich Dostoevsky (1821-81) will enable both novices and experts to gain a deeper appreciation of one of the world's great artists and thinkers. Dostoevsky's characters and literary allusions are catalogued alphabetically by work, and an exhaustive index is provided to enable the reader to familiarize himself with individual characters, note the significance of allusion, and study topics in their totality. Each form of a character's name is given and cross referenced to the full name so that the typical confusion of English readers unfamiliar with the Russian patronymic system will be alleviated.

The transliteration of Russian into English follows System I as found in J. Thomas Shaw, *The Transliteration of Modern Russian for English-Language Publications* (Madison: University of Wisconsin Press, 1967) with the exception that "ks" is substituted for "x." Certain names have also been changed to reflect more normalized French or German spelling.

The *Dictionary* is based on F.M. Dostoevsky, *Complete Works in Thirty Volumes* (Moscow: Nauka, 1972-), the new authoritative Soviet edition which is still in the process of publication.

POOR FOLK (BEDNYE LYUDI) 1846

AKSENTY MIKHAYLOVICH. A civil servant who works in the same office with **MAKAR DEVUSHKIN**. They discuss the virtues of HIS EXCELLENCY together.

AKSENTY OSIPOVICH. In an anecdote cited by MAKAR DEVUSH-KIN, an individual who has a difference of opinion with one PYOTR PETROVICH. The two succeed in settling the matter quietly and amicably. DEVUSHKIN cites this incident in contrast to his row with an OFFICER who has offended VARVARA. His attempt to defend VARVARA's honor results in the OFFICER's throwing him from his room.

AKSINYA. FYODORA's sister-in-law.

ANNA FYODOROVNA. A very distant relative of the DOBROSYO-LOVS who assumes care of VARVARA and her mother following DOBROSYOLOV's death. She poses a threat to VARVARA's relationship with MAKAR DEVUSHKIN by arranging a marriage to BYKOV, and despite her professions of Christian charity her ostensibly good deeds torment those involved. Her activities and means of livelihood are a mystery to VARVARA's circle. She occupies herself with arranging marriages, fixing dowries, and manipulating those who are in her debt by reason of guilt, indiscretion, or circumstance. An example of her management is the unequal marriage of a lovely young woman to ZAKHAR POKROVSKY, whose professed son is a tutor in ANNA FYODOROVNA's home. The defenseless and virtuous VARVARA perceives her as an evil and imminent threat to her happiness.

THE BEE [PCHELKA]. *The Northern Bee (Severnaya pchela),* a conservative St. Petersburg newspaper, published 1825-64 by Faddey Venediktovich Bulgarin (1789-1859) and Nikolay Ivanovich Grech (1787-1867). In a vibrant mood after getting the one hundred rubles from HIS EXCELLEN-CY, DEVUSHKIN goes shopping and even reads a copy of *THE BEE.*

BRAMBEUS. Baron BRAMBEUS, pseudonym of Osip Ivanovich Sen-kovsky (1800-58), Russian author and journalist. He edited *Library for Reading (Biblioteka dlya chtenia)* and wrote articles and stories that appealed to the conservative and less well-educated reader. DEVUSHKIN alludes to a civil servant who lives in the same boarding house, who is so well-read that he is able to discuss HOMER, BRAMBEUS, and others.

1

DEVUSHKIN, only recently exposed to literature, demonstrates a novice's naiveté and poor taste in placing HOMER alongside BRAMBEUS.

BYKOV. ZAKHAR POKROVSKY's former benefactor and PETENKA's natural father. He provides POKROVSKY's first wife with a dowry and establishes PETENKA in school and later in ANNA FYODOROVNA's home as a tutor. His relationship with ANNA FYODOROVNA endures despite mutual dislike. He considers her to be a base woman but acknowledges his own baseness, particularly in their dealings with SASHA. With ANNA FYODOROVNA's complicity he courts VARVARA with the admitted primary purpose of providing himself with an heir. He thus looms as a sexual threat to innocence and a bothersome hindrance to VARVARA's naive and comfortable relationship with DEVUSHKIN. His distaste for books, revulsion for romanticism, and quick temper make him the brutish dullard suggested by his name (BYKOV denotes bull or ox), and he contrasts markedly with the helpless romantics, VARVARA and DEVUSHKIN.

MADAME CHIFFON [SHIFON]. The woman to whom VARVARA sends DEVUSHKIN to see to the details of her wedding to BYKOV.

"THE CRANES OF IBYCUS" ["IVIKOVY ZHURAVLI"]. "Die Kraniche des Ibycus," a ballad written in 1797 by Friedrich Schiller (1759-1805), German dramatist, poet, and historian noted for his romantic idealism. The ballad establishes the legend of Ibycus, a Greek lyric poet, who was slain on a journey to Corinth and whose murderers were exposed by a flock of cranes with which the poet had felt comfort and companionship. The ballad was translated as "IVIKOVY ZHURAVLI" by Vasily Andreevich Zhukovsky (1783-1852) in 1813. DEVUSHKIN notes that "THE CRANES OF IBYCUS" is one of the three pieces he has read prior to his interest in literature gained through VARVARA.

MAKAR ALEKSEEVICH DEVUSHKIN. A poor copy clerk of forty seven who has spent thirty years copying documents. His life has been one of isolation, unhappiness, and lack of companionship. A distant relative of VARVARA, he takes lodgings near her in order to guard her interests and to offer her protection. He is impoverished, has had little education, and frequently apologizes to VARVARA for his inability to express himself elegantly in the numerous letters they exchange. His several allusions to his old age encourage rebuttals from VARVARA in whom, as is gradually made evident, he has more than a fatherly interest. He is very solicitous of her reputation and in order to avoid provoking rumors is unwilling to meet her in her quarters. He practices self-denial and devotes his meager resources largely to VARVARA in the form of occasional gifts of candy and money. His pride makes him defensive about his low post, and he alternately boasts of his humble nature and modest virtue and laments that he is nothing and hardly even exists. He begins to take an interest in literature and attends literary evenings at the home of RATAZYAEV, who tolerates him because DEVUSHKIN copies some of his manuscripts. VARVARA's notion to take a position as a governess greatly upsets him, and he sees himself being abandoned, just as SAMSON VYRIN is in PUSHKIN's *THE STATIONMASTER*. Poverty is the main barrier between them and happiness, and DEVUSHKIN discourses on the feelings of poor people, their pride, and their great shame before others. His perpetual fear that HIS EXCELLENCY will see him at work in his poverty-ridden condition is finally realized, but HIS EXCELLENCY is so touched when a button falls from DEVUSHKIN's coat during an interview that he gives him one hundred rubles. DEVUSHKIN feels that this gift makes life livable, and he even more strongly opposes VARVARA's notion of becoming a governess and her possible marriage to BYKOV. He objects that they could no longer write letters and that he would be alone. VARVARA ultimately commissions him to arrange the details of her marriage to BYKOV, and thereafter he succumbs to disjointed thoughts of suicide, self-pity, and buying her presents.

DOBROSYOLOV. VARVARA's father. After losing his job, he goes tó St. Petersburg to put his finances in order, but worries and failures weigh upon him and destroy both his character and his health. Death comes quickly thereafter.

DOBROSYOLOVA. VARVARA's mother, who, as her husband's affairs become increasingly difficult, becomes increasingly ill with consumption. DOBROSYOLOV's death leaves her impoverished, and she and VARVARA are taken in by ANNA FYODOROVNA. Trying to extricate herself from this situation, she works hard to gain her own means, but this prideful attempt destroys her fragile health and she dies.

VARVARA ALEKSEEVNA DOBROSYOLOVA (VARENKA). An orphan who lives in dire circumstances with FYODORA. Her days are spent in worrying about her future, suffering because of poverty, contemplating an undesired proposal of marriage from BYKOV, and writing letters to MAKAR DEVUSHKIN. She sends DEVUSHKIN her diary, which chronicles her life to the present and thus provides the background information for the novel. She had moved to St. Petersburg at age twelve and experienced the city's debilitating effects. Following her father's death she and her mother move in with ANNA FYODOROVNA, a distant relative. She recalls in the diary her association with POKROVSKY, a tutor retained by ANNA FYODOROVNA, and her discovery of books through him. She becomes infatuated with him, has romantic visions, and ultimately nurses him as he dies of consumption. Knowing that VARVARA is in difficult circumstances following her mother's death, ANNA FYODORO-VNA pressures her to move back with her and promises to make BYKOV behave properly in his courting her. Not wanting to do this, VARVARA seeks a position as a governess to be more independent, but is discouraged by DEVUSHKIN, who depends upon her emotionally. She supports DE-VUSHKIN's new interest in literature, and *THE OVERCOAT* and *THE STATIONMASTER* become leitmotifs of their relationship and their individual characters. Her desperate position and poor health prompt her to muse about the past, and she longs to return to the country and recover childhood. Wanting to extricate herself from her circumstances and seeing no other way to accomplish it, she marries BYKOV and has DEVUSHKIN do much of the detailed wedding preparations. Her farewell letter to him expresses her love and indebtedness and an awareness of his true feelings for her.

DUNYASHA. The heroine of PUSHKIN's *THE STATIONMASTER*, who abandons her possessive father, SAMSON VYRIN, for personal happiness in St. Petersburg. DEVUSHKIN perceives himself in the role of VYRIN and VARVARA as DUNYASHA. He also praises the verisimilitude of the story and compares the fictional heroine with TEREZA.

HIS EXCELLENCY [YEGO PREVOSKHODITELSTVO]. The head of the department in which DEVUSHKIN works, who is perceived by him as an object of great fear and respect. DEVUSHKIN's fears of being noticed in his poverty are countered when HIS EXCELLENCY gives him one hundred rubles and a handshake when his button falls off during an interview.

FALDONI. The servant of DEVUSHKIN's LANDLADY. He is a coarse individual, who refuses to serve DEVUSHKIN when he is behind in his rent and who continually abuses TEREZA. FALDONI and TEREZA as antagonists are parodies of the main characters, Thérèse and Faldoni, found in the sentimental *Lettres de deux amants habitant Lyon (Letters of Two Lovers Living in Lyon)*, written in 1783 by Nicolas Germain Léonard (1744-93).

FROLOVNA. As VARVARA reminisces of her childhood, she recalls listening to the mysterious fairy tales of her nurse ULYANA and being frightened by the sound of FROLOVNA's spinning wheel.

FYODOR FYODOROVICH. After reading *THE OVERCOAT*, DEVUSHKIN is furious because of the similarity between himself and the central character Akaky Akakievich and wonders how FYODOR FYODOROVICH could have permitted such a book to be printed.

FYODORA. VARVARA's gossipy, talkative, and impoverished companion, who frequently brings her word of DEVUSHKIN's activities. Exposed through FYODORA's reports, DEVUSHKIN typically issues denials or at least justifications.

GLASHA. An actress that DEVUSHKIN once pursued in youthful infatuation.

GORSHKOV. An unemployed, shy, sickly father of three, who lives with his wife and children in the same house with DEVUSHKIN. He is in abject poverty after having lost his job because of his superior's misappropriation of money. He has been judged innocent of involvement in the affair but has not as yet received financial settlement from the court. He expects favorable judgment to come any day to vindicate his honor, name, and his children, and he is much more concerned with his honor than with the money. When the favorable ruling arrives, he is overcome and dies. DEVUSHKIN compares him to SAMSON VYRIN as he generalizes on the universality of *THE STATION-MASTER*.

GORSHKOV. GORSHKOV's youngest child, a son who is still nursing.

PETYA GORSHKOV (PETENKA). GORSHKOV's oldest child, an emaciated son of nine who dies during their difficult times.

GORSHKOVA. GORSHKOV's once pretty wife, whose whole person reflects their poor circumstances.

GORSHKOVA. GORSHKOV's six year old daughter.

HOMER [GOMER]. Ancient Greek poet to whom are attributed the *Iliad* and the *Odyssey*. He is known for his broad, epic visions and proportions. DEVUSHKIN asserts that he knows a well-read civil servant who can comfortably discuss HOMER, BRAMBEUS, and others. His placing HOMER alongside BRAMBEUS is ironic and a product of his naiveté.

IVAN THE FOOL [IVANUSHKA DURACHOK]. A figure of Russian folklore who always succeeds despite his being labeled a fool. DEVUSHKIN laments that IVAN THE FOOL can find happiness in the world while VARVARA cannot.

IVAN PROKOFIEVICH. See IVAN PROKOFIEVICH ZHELTOPUZ.

PAUL DE KOCK [POL DE KOK]. French novelist (1793-1871), noted for his vivid portrayal of Parisian life. His work was considered too explicit by certain Russian critics in the 1840s. DEVUSHKIN wants to send VARVARA some books, but not those of PAUL DE KOCK, whom he considers too realistic. He is not comfortable with the new graphic tendencies in literature that came to be grouped in the Natural School.

KUCHUM. The last Siberian Khan, who battled local tribesmen, Ivan IV, and YERMAK in the sixteenth century before being finally deposed. He then lived by robbery and vandalism until his death at the hands of rival tribesmen. In RATAZYAEV's romantic work *YERMAK and ZYULEYKA*, KUCHUM is identified as the father of ZYULEYKA.

LANDLADY [KHOZYAYKA]. A slovenly, ill-tempered woman who rents space to DEVUSHKIN. She continually shouts at TEREZA, berates DEVUSHKIN for nonpayment of rent, and spreads stories about him and VARVARA.

THE LITTLE BELLRINGER [MALCHIK, NAIGRAVSHY RAZNYE SHTUCHKI NA KOLOKOLCHIKAKH]. *Le Petit Carillonneur*, a novel in four volumes written by François Guillaume Ducray-Duminil (1761-1819) in 1809. DEVUSHKIN notes that *THE LITTLE BELLRINGER* is one of the three pieces he has read prior to his interest in literature gained through VARVARA.

LOVELACE [LOVELAS]. The seducer in *Clarissa, or the History of a Young Lady*, written in 1748 by Samuel Richardson (1689-1761). The novel enjoyed wide popularity in Russia. A letter from DEVUSHKIN to VARVARA is misplaced and finds its way to one of RATAZYAEV's literary evenings. To the great discomfort of DEVUSHKIN the letter is read and mocked, and he is quickly dubbed LOVELACE. Upon their reconciliation RATAZYAEV explains to DEVUSHKIN that being called a LOVELACE is not an insult but a kind of compliment.

MARKOV. A man recommended by YEMELYAN IVANOVICH to DEVUSHKIN as a possible source of money. DEVUSHKIN makes a long journey in the rain to see him, only to be refused a loan because he has no pledge.

MASHA. The granddaughter of DEVUSHKIN's former landlady, from whom he rented for twenty years prior to his moving closer to VARVARA.

MATRYONA. ANNA FYODOROVNA's cook.

NASTASYA. A cleaning woman mentioned by FYODORA.

NOAH [NOY]. As recorded in Genesis 6-10, the Old Testament patriarch whom Jehovah commanded to build an ark prior to the destruction of the earth by flood. In the ark NOAH saved his family together with specimens of each kind of animal. DEVUSHKIN describes the crowded conditions of his boarding house as being like NOAH's ark.

PRINCE V.F. ODOEVSKY. Vladimir Fyodorovich ODOEVSKY (1803-69), Russian writer of fantastic tales whose story *The Living Corpse (Zhivoy mertvets)*, written in 1839, provides the epigraph to *Poor Folk*. See "OH, THESE STORYTELLERS!"

OFFICER [OFITSER]. A man who once lived in the same house with DEVUSHKIN and who issues an insulting proposition to VARVARA. DEVUSHKIN goes to him to defend VARVARA's honor but is summarily thrown out.

"OH, THESE STORYTELLERS!" ["OKH UZH ETI MNE SKAZO-CHNIKI!"]. The first line of a passage cited from Vladimir ODOEVSKY's *The Living Corpse (Zhivoy mertvets)* that is used as the epigraph to the novel. The passage playfully laments that writers do not write anything useful but only uncover all sorts of things. The narrator of the passage claims that he would prohibit such writing. The words comically forecast DEVUSHKIN's attitude toward *THE OVERCOAT* and the opinion of many about the graphic realism of the new Natural School.

THE OVERCOAT [SHINEL]. A short story written by Nikolay Vasilievich Gogol (1809-52) in 1842 which deals with the theft of a new overcoat from an impoverished and ridiculous copy clerk named Akaky Akakievich. VARVARA recommends *THE OVERCOAT* to DEVUSHKIN, who reacts strongly against it and considers it an insult to people like himself. He asserts that all have different capabilities, that copy clerks like he and Akaky

Akakievich also have a divinely ordained place, and that the things they do should not be subject to insult. DEVUSHKIN adds that had he written the story, he would have provided a happy ending rather than let Akaky die unnoticed and unloved.

PRINCE P-Y. Upon the death of PRINCE P-Y, his heirs turn DOBRO-SYOLOV out of his job, whereupon he takes his family to St. Petersburg to try to put his financial affairs in order.

PEGASUS [PEGAS]. Winged horse of Greek mythology. DEVUSHKIN feels exhilarated over his relationship with VARVARA, but he notices that at work he is surrounded by the same papers and old ink spots and wonders why he mentally rode PEGASUS in his excitement.

PELAGEYA ANTONOVNA. In one of RATAZYAEV's inane anecdotes, loyally repeated by DEVUSHKIN, it is noted that PELAGEYA AN-TONOVNA wears her petticoat inside out.

PETENKA. See PETYA GORSHKOV.

PETENKA. See PETENKA POKROVSKY. ZAKHAR PETROVICH POKROVSKY refers to his professed son with this term of endearment.

PETRUSHA. See PETENKA POKROVSKY. ZAKHAR PETROVICH POKROVSKY refers to his professed son with this term of endearment.

PICTURE OF MAN [KARTINA CHELOVEKA]. A work of idealistic psychology and philosophy published in 1834 by Aleksandr Galich, a Lyceum instructor of Aleksandr PUSHKIN. DEVUSHKIN mentions that this is one of the three things that he has ever read prior to his interest in literature acquired through VARVARA.

PETENKA POKROVSKY (PETRUSHA). BYKOV's natural son, a poor student whom BYKOV establishes in school and then in a position as a tutor in ANNA FYODORVNA's home. BYKOV undertakes his patronage following an irreparable conflict between the boy and his stepmother. As a tutor POKROVSKY has charge of VARVARA and her cousin SASHA. He is excitable and in poor health because of consumption. His collection of rare books stimulates VARVARA's interest in literature, and the two become fast friends bound by interests, position, infatuation, and the emotions of growing up. This relationship endures until he dies of his illness, unwilling to believe until the last that he is dying.

ZAKHAR PETROVICH POKROVSKY. PETENKA POKROVSKY's timid, small, awkward, and perpetually embarrassed familial father. He has been under the protection of BYKOV and was married for the first time under the direction of ANNA FYODOROVNA. After his first wife died, he married a merchant's daughter, who rent the life of the family asunder. She dominates and torments him until he totally lets himself go, and the only human characteristic he retains is love for PETENKA, who is delivered from his stepmother by BYKOV. He worships PETENKA but visits him infrequently because he knows that PETENKA cannot tolerate him. The big event of his life is collaborating with VARVARA to buy PETENKA the collected works of PUSHKIN for his birthday, and VARVARA generously allows him to present the gift himself. The death of PETENKA overwhelms him, and he madly strives to preserve PETENKA's books from ANNA FYODOROVNA, who wants to sell them to pay for the final arrangements.

PROKOFY IVANOVICH. In one of RATAZYAEV's inane anecdotes, loyally repeated by DEVUSHKIN, IVAN PROKOFIEVICH ZHELTO-PUZ bites the leg of PROKOFY IVANOVICH.

PUSHKIN. Aleksandr Sergeevich PUSHKIN (1799-1837), the leading Russian writer of his time, who is widely regarded as the father of modern Russian literature. VARVARA and ZAKHAR PETROVICH POKROV-SKY buy PETENKA an edition of PUSHKIN's collected works for his birthday.

PYOTR PETROVICH. One of the people from whom DEVUSHKIN unsuccessfully tries to borrow money. He totally ignores DEVUSHKIN when it is obvious that he has no pledge. In an anecdote cited by DEVUSHKIN, PYOTR PETROVICH has an argument with one AK-SENTY OSIPOVICH, but the two of them settle it quietly and in private. DEVUSHKIN appreciates this kind of diplomacy, since his own experience with the OFFICER results in his being thrown from his apartment when he attempts to defend VARVARA's honor.

RATAZYAEV. An economically successful writer who invites DEVUSH-KIN to his literary evenings, probably only because DEVUSHKIN copies his manuscripts. DEVUSHKIN shows VARVARA two examples of RATAZYAEV's writing, *Italian Passions (Italyanskie strasti)* and *YER-MAK and ZYULEYKA,* both of which are filled with extreme emotions, melodrama, and romantic clichés. RATAZYAEV holds a dim view of *THE STATIONMASTER* and mentions that writers now are concentrating on description, an allusion to the techniques of the Natural School of the 1840s.

SASHA. VARVARA's cousin, who is also an orphan and who also lives with ANNA FYODOROVNA.

SHAKESPEARE [SHEKSPIR]. William SHAKESPEARE (1564-1616), the most celebrated of English dramatists and one of the giants of world literature. When DEVUSHKIN fears that RATAZYAEV is planning to write a satire about his involvement with VARVARA, he condemns all books and literature as a craft. He insists that even SHAKESPEARE is nonsense, since everything is written to make fun of people.

SMELSKY. See VLADIMIR SMELSKY.

VLADIMIR SMELSKY. The hero in RATAZYAEV's absurdly romantic *Italian Passions.*

SNEGIRYOV. A guard where DEVUSHKIN works who refuses to let him use a government brush to clean his coat. This provokes DEVUSHKIN to bemoan that he is worth nothing in life.

SODOM. As recorded in Genesis 18-19 of the Old Testament, a city which together with Gomorrah was destroyed by Jehovah because of its wickedness. The term has come to mean wickedness or chaos. DEVUSHKIN calls the house he lives in and the people who live there a veritable SODOM.

THE STATIONMASTER [STANTSIONNY SMOTRITEL]. One of Aleksandr PUSHKIN's *THE TALES OF BELKIN,* which VARVARA gives DEVUSHKIN to read. In the story DUNYASHA abandons her father SAMSON VYRIN and runs away with an officer to St. Petersburg. DEVUSHKIN marvels at how true to life the story is and feels a personal kinship with it, first when VARVARA contemplates taking a job as a governess and second when she marries BYKOV and leaves.

THE TALES OF BELKIN [POVESTI BELKINA]. Five tales, *The Shot (Vystrel), The Storm (Metel), The Undertaker (Grobovshchik), THE STATIONMASTER,* and *Mistress Into Maid (Baryshnya-Krestyanka),* written by Aleksandr PUSHKIN in 1830. DEVUSHKIN praises their faithfulness to life, and particularly values *THE STATIONMASTER* because he senses that he shares SAMSON VYRIN's fate.

TEREZA. The servant of DEVUSHKIN's LANDLADY who is the courier of his correspondence with VARVARA. She is a good, humble girl who is continually abused by the LANDLADY and FALDONI. DEVUSHKIN compares her to DUNYASHA in *THE STATIONMASTER.* TEREZA and FALDONI as antagonists are parodies of the main characters, Thérèse and Faldoni, found in the sentimental *Lettres de deux amants habitant Lyon (Letters of Two Lovers Living in Lyon),* written in 1783 by Nicolas Germain Léonard (1744-93).

TIMOFEY IVANOVICH. A civil servant in DEVUSHKIN's department.

ULYANA. VARVARA's nurse, who used to tell her and the other children frightening fairy tales.

COUNTESS V. RATAZYAEV boasts that he attends all of the COUNTESS V's receptions.

VARENKA. See VARVARA ALEKSEEVNA DOBROSYOLOVA.

VLADIMIR. SEE VLADIMIR SMELSKY.

SAMSON VYRIN. The abandoned father in Aleksandr PUSHKIN's *THE STATIONMASTER,* whose daughter DUNYASHA runs away with an officer to St. Petersburg. His love for his daughter is possessive, and he cannot conceive that she could be happy apart from him. Unable to come to terms with the situation, he drinks himself to death. DEVUSHKIN compares VYRIN to many poor people he knows, particularly to GORSHKOV, and feels a personal link with him in that he feels himself abandoned by VARVARA.

YEFIM AKIMOVICH. A bully and tease who torments DEVUSHKIN at work.

YEMELYA. See YEMELYAN ILYICH.

YEMELYAN ILYICH (YEMELYA). A former civil servant in DEVUSHKIN's department who encourages him to defend VARVARA's honor to the OFFICER who made suggestive remarks to her.

YEMELYAN IVANOVICH. Together with DEVUSHKIN the oldest clerk in the department. He is usually the person DEVUSHKIN talks to at work.

YERMAK. YERMAK Timofeevich, Cossack ataman (d. 1585) who fought KUCHUM for control of Siberia. He becomes the hero of RATAZYAEV's ridiculous and passionate *YERMAK and ZYULEYKA.*

YEVSTAFY IVANOVICH. One of DEVUSHKIN's superiors, who summons him to see HIS EXCELLENCY after he makes a copying error.

ZAKHAR PETROVICH. See ZAKHAR PETROVICH POKROVSKY.

IVAN PROKOFIEVICH ZHELTOPUZ. In one of RATAZYAEV's inane anecdotes, loyally repeated by DEVUSHKIN, IVAN PROKOFIEVICH ZHELTOPUZ bites the leg of PROKOFY IVANOVICH.

ZINAIDA. The heroine in RATAZYAEV's absurdly romantic *Italian Passions.*

ZYULEYKA. Heroine of RATAZYAEV's ridiculous and passionate *YERMAK and ZYULEYKA.*

THE DOUBLE (DVOYNIK) 1846

ALEKSEICH. OLSUFY IVANOVICH's servant.

ALFRED. As GOLYADKIN SENIOR waits for KLARA OLSUFIEVNA outside her home, under the impression that he will whisk her away to a romantic idyll with him, he ponders that she will probably try to give him some sort of signal that she is ready to leave. He then recalls a novel he read in which the heroine gives the hero ALFRED a signal by means of a red ribbon.

ANDREY FILIPPOVICH. GOLYADKIN SENIOR's immediate supervisor at work and VLADIMIR SEMYONOVICH's uncle. His encounters with GOLYADKIN SENIOR's mental abberrations produce in him fear, wonder, and finally disgust.

ANTON ANTONOVICH. See ANTON ANTONOVICH SETOCHKIN.

THE BASSAVRYUKOVS. Party guests of GOLYADKIN SENIOR's superior.

BELSHAZZAR [VALTASAR]. Babylonian king from 550 to 539 B.C. As recorded in Daniel 5 in the Old Testament, his elaborate feast is interrupted by a hand writing on the wall, prophesying the demise of his kingdom. KLARA OLSUFIEVNA's birthday party is described by the author as something akin to BELSHAZZAR's feast.

OLSUFY IVANOVICH BERENDEEV. A wealthy official who has been a benefactor to GOLYADKIN SENIOR. SENIOR's strange behavior and desire to win the hand of KLARA OLSUFIEVNA finally alienate him.

BERENDEEVA. OLSUFY IVANOVICH's wife.

KLARA OLSUFIEVNA BERENDEEVA. OLSUFY IVANOVICH's daughter, upon whom GOLYADKIN SENIOR has marriage designs.

BARON BRAMBEUS. Pseudonym of Osip Ivanovich Senkovsky (1800-58), Russian author and journalist. He edited *Library for Reading (Biblioteka dlya chtenia)* and wrote articles and stories that appealed to the conservative and less well-educated reader. In an expansive mood GOLYADKIN SENIOR tells GOLYADKIN JUNIOR many details about St. Petersburg life and culture, including BARON BRAMBEUS.

BRYULLOV. Karl Pavlovich BRYULLOV (1799-1852), eminent Russian painter about whose masterpiece, *The Last Day of Pompei (Posledny den Pompei)*, GOLYADKIN SENIOR tells GOLYADKIN JUNIOR.

PRINCESS CHEVCHEKHANOVA. A guest at a party given by OLSUFY IVANOVICH.

DEMOSTHENES [DEMOSFEN]. The greatest of Greek orators (c.a. 383-322 B.C.). The author muses about the poem he would write about KLARA OLSUFIEVNA's birthday dinner if he only had the ability of a HOMER or a PUSHKIN. The first thing he would describe would be the expectant silence, akin to the eloquence of DEMOSTHENES, with which the guests await the first toast to KLARA OLSUFIEVNA.

ÉMIGRÉ FALBALA. The mistress of a school in Aleksandr PUSHKIN's narrative poem *Count Nulin (Graf Nulin)*, written in 1825. GOLYADKIN SENIOR attributes KLARA OLSUFIEVNA's rejection of him at her birthday party to those who have been responsible for her upbringing. He feels that she should have been reared at home instead of at a school operated by some kind of ÉMIGRÉ FALBALA.

FAUBLAS [FOBLAZ]. Central character of the novel *Les amours du chevalier de Faublas (The Amours of the Knight of Faublas)*, written by Jean Baptiste Louvet de Couvray (1760-97) in 1787-90. GOLYADKIN JUNIOR derisively refers to GOLYADKIN SENIOR as the ribald FAUBLAS because of SENIOR's alleged relationship with KAROLINA IVANOVNA.

FEDOSEICH. A paunchy porter in GOLYADKIN SENIOR's department.

GERASIMYCH. See YEMELYAN GERASIMOVICH.

GOLYADKIN JUNIOR [MLADSHY]. See YAKOV PETROVICH GOLYADKIN JUNIOR.

GOLYADKIN SENIOR [STARSHY]. See YAKOV PETROVICH GOLYDKIN SENIOR.

GOLYADKIN THE SECOND [GOLYADKIN VTOROY]. See YAKOV PETROVICH GOLYADKIN JUNIOR.

THE NEW MR. GOLYADKIN [NOVY GOSPODIN GOLYADKIN]. See YAKOV PETROVICH GOLYADKIN JUNIOR.

THE OTHER MR. GOLYADKIN [DRUGOY GOSPODIN GOLYADKIN]. See YAKOV PETROVICH GOLYADKIN JUNIOR.

YAKOV PETROVICH GOLYADKIN JUNIOR (GOLYADKIN JUNIOR, JUNIOR, GOLYADKIN THE SECOND, THE OTHER MR. GOLYADKIN, THE NEW MR. GOLYADKIN, YAKOV PETROVICH, YASHA). GOLYADKIN SENIOR's double. He appears on a miserable November St. Petersburg night to GOLYADKIN SENIOR, with whom he shares name and physical appearance. His initially meek and solicitous bearing are very pleasing to SENIOR. He relates his history of privation and poverty and asks for SENIOR's patronage. After he secures work in SENIOR's department, his personality becomes the mirror-image of SENIOR's—aggressive, ingratiating, conniving, and daring. He curries and quickly gains the favor of his superiors, moves in their social circles, and in effect replaces SENIOR in the department, thereby relegating him to the status of a nonentity. He taunts and torments SENIOR as the embodiment of SENIOR's paranoia and bids him a betraying farewell as the disturbed SENIOR is taken to an asylum.

YAKOV PETROVICH GOLYADKIN SENIOR (GOLYADKIN SEN-IOR). A mediocre and self-satisfied civil servant who is tormented by paranoia and schizophrenia. His behavior is erratic and aberrational, ranging from forays to KLARA OLSUFIEVNA, in whom he has a romantic interest, to extravagant shopping splurges which never quite materialize. After being evicted from KLARA OLSUFIEVNA's birthday party and being assured that he is no longer welcome in the home of his former benefactor OLSUFY IVANOVICH, he encounters his double GOLYADKIN JUNIOR on a cold and miserable St. Petersburg November eve. A timid man who is yet constantly aware of appearance and whose thought processes are never stable, he has been advised by his doctor KRESTYAN IVANOVICH RUTENSHPITS to change his life style and his character. The appearance of JUNIOR is an ironic sequel to the doctor's advice. He initially sees in JUNIOR a kindred spirit, a little man who has suffered as he has, but JUNIOR's aggressive, mocking, and ingratiating behavior quickly destroys SENIOR's life, SENIOR's sermons on being meek and knowing one's place notwithstanding. His condemnation of behavior like that exhibited by JUNIOR rings helpless and a bit envious. His final aberration is a letter from KLARA OLSUFIEVNA, who wants him to take her away to a romantic idyll. While waiting outside OLSUFY IVANOVICH's house, he is seen, brought into the house with some compassion, and then dispatched to an asylum under the direction of RUTENSHPITS.

HOMER [GOMER]. Ancient Greek poet to whom are attributed the *Iliad* and the *Odyssey*. He is known for his broad, epic visions and proportions. The author mentions that had he the talent of a HOMER or a PUSHKIN, he would describe the triumphant scene at KLARA OLSUFIEVNA's birthday dinner.

IVAN SEMYONOVICH. On the day that GOLYADKIN SENIOR does not go to work, IVAN SEMYONOVICH is put in his chair.

JESUIT [IEZUIT]. The Society of Jesus, a religious order for Roman Catholic men founded by Ignatius Loyola (1491-1556) in 1534. The society is known for scholarship and missionary zeal and has been accused of secrecy and intrigue. GOLYADKIN SENIOR sits outside OLSUFY IVANOVICH's house trying to decide whether to try to enter. His mind turns to the JESUITS, to whom he attributes the credo that the end justifies the means. Despite the fact that he considers all JESUITS to be fools, this credo prompts him to try to enter the house.

JUNIOR. See YAKOV PETROVICH GOLYADKIN JUNIOR.

KAROLINA IVANOVNA. The German lady with whom GOLYADKIN SENIOR takes his meals. JUNIOR spreads rumors that rather than pay his bills, SENIOR has led her to believe that he will offer her his hand in marriage.

KLARA OLSUFIEVNA. See KLARA OLSUFIEVNA BERENDEEVA.

KRESTYAN IVANOVICH. See KRESTYAN IVANOVICH RUTEN-SHPITS.

KRYLOV. Ivan Andreevich KRYLOV (1769-1844), the most important Russian writer of fables, whose works have become Russian classics. In pondering how he should respond to JUNIOR's mocking and threatening behavior, SENIOR decides to be patient and to let the situation resolve itself. This removes a great weight from him, and he recalls the gist of KRYLOV's "The Little Box" ("Larchik"), written in 1808, in which a mechanic tries to open a box that has no lock. He struggles long and gets into a sweat before finally giving up, whereupon the box opens of its own accord. SENIOR takes solace from this and hopes that the troubles with JUNIOR will simply work themselves out.

LOUISA [LUIZA]. Character in the popular novel *A Tale of the Adventures of the English Lord George and of the Brandenburg Margravine Frederika Louisa Together with the History of the Former Turkish Vizier Martsimiris and the Sardinian Queen Terezia (Povest o priklyuchenii angliiskogo milorda Georgia i o brandenburskoy margrafine Frederike Luize s prisovokupleniem k odnoy istorii byvshego turetskogo vizirya Martsimirisa i sardinskoy korolevny Terezii),* written by Matvey Komarov (ca. 1730-1812) in 1782. GOLYADKIN SENIOR, after sitting outside OLSUFY IVANOVICH's house for some time trying to decide whether to try to attend the ball, for some reason recalls LOUISA and MARTSIMI-RIS from a book he once read.

MANNA FROM HEAVEN [MANNA NEBESNAYA]. As recorded in Exodus 16 in the Old Testament the food miraculously supplied to the Israelites in the wilderness. GOLYADKIN SENIOR refers to GOLYAD-KIN JUNIOR's life history as MANNA FROM HEAVEN because he feels that he has found a kindred spirit who has suffered as he has.

MARTSIMIRIS. See LOUISA.

SERGEY MIKHEEV. The guard in GOLYADKIN SENIOR's department who delivers his letter of dismissal.

MUHAMMAD [MUKHAMMED]. In Arabic "the praised one," a name adopted by the founder of Islam (570-632). GOLYADKIN SENIOR and JUNIOR become fast friends one evening, and SENIOR talks expansively about many things, including MUHAMMAD.

GENERAL NEDOBAROV. One of PETRUSHKA's former employers.

THE NORTHERN BEE [SEVERNAYA PCHELA]. A conservative St. Petersburg newspaper, published 1825-64 by Faddey Venediktovich Bulgarin (1789-1859) and Nikolay Ivanovich Grech (1787-1867). GOLYADKIN SENIOR tells JUNIOR about *THE NORTHERN BEE* as part of his lengthy talk on St. Petersburg life.

OLSUFY IVANOVICH. See OLSUFY IVANOVICH BERENDEEV.

OSTAFIEV. A clerk in GOLYADKIN SENIOR's department.

GRISHKA OTREPIEV. A monk who posed as Ivan the Terrible's son Dmitry, allegedly murdered by Boris Godunov (1552-1605) so that he could ascend to the throne. With the help of Polish forces OTREPIEV, also called the Pretender and False Dmitri, conquered and ruled Russia from 1605 to 1606. GOLYADKIN SENIOR vows that JUNIOR, a pretender in his own right, will not get away with what GRISHKA OTREPIEV did.

PALAGEYA SEMYONOVNA. An aged aunt of GOLYADKIN JUNIOR.

COLONEL PEREBORKIN. One of PETRUSHKA's former employers.

PETRUSHA. See PETRUSHKA.

PETRUSHKA (PETRUSHA, PYOTR). GOLYADKIN SENIOR's valet, who is sour, gruff, frequently drunk, and treats his master with little respect. As SENIOR's madness worsens, PETRUSHKA leaves to work for KAROLINA IVANOVNA.

PISARENKO. A clerk in GOLYADKIN SENIOR's department.

POLICE GAZETTE [POLITSEYSKIE VEDOMOSTI]. A reference to the *St. Petersburg City Police Gazette (Vedomosti S.-Peterburgskoy gorodskoy politsii)*, which was issued in St. Petersburg from 1839 through 1917. A police officer alludes to the paper when he questions GOLYADKIN SENIOR's strange behavior and dishevelled appearance in a pub.

PUSHKIN. Aleksandr Sergeevich PUSHKIN (1799-1837), the leading Russian writer of his times, who is widely regarded as the father of modern Russian literature. The author mentions that had he the talent of PUSHKIN or HOMER he would describe the triumphant scene at KLARA OLSUFIEVNA's birthday dinner.

PYOTR. See PETRUSHKA.

JEAN JACQUES ROUSSEAU [ZHAN-ZHAK RUSSO]. French philosopher, social reformer, and writer (1712-78), who exerted the pivotal influence on the developing romantic sensibility. While waiting outside OLSUFY IVANOVICH's house to meet KLARA OLSUFIEVNA and take her away to a romantic idyll, GOLYADKIN SENIOR muses about how wives should treat husbands. He feels theirs would be an austere, practical relationship since the sentimental era of ROUSSEAU has passed.

KRESTYAN IVANOVICH RUTENSHPITS. The doctor who advises GOLYADKIN SENIOR to change his character and mode of life. It is he who accompanies SENIOR to the asylum and becomes transformed in SENIOR's eyes into a hellish, threatening figure. RUTENSHPITS' first name and patronymic are likely based upon Khristian Ivanovich Gibner, the doctor in *The Inspector General (Revizor)*, a play written in 1836 by Nikolay Vasilievich Gogol (1809-52).

SEMYON IVANOVICH. A deceased clerk whose position in the department is assumed by GOLYADKIN JUNIOR.

SEMYONYCH. A servant castigated by GERASIMYCH.

SENIOR. See YAKOV PETROVICH GOLYADKIN SENIOR.

ANTON ANTONOVICH SETOCHKIN. The babbling godfather of KLARA OLSUFIEVNA, who works with GOLYADKIN SENIOR.

SIAMESE TWINS [SIAMSKIE BLIZNETSY]. Chang and Eng (1811-74), who were exhibited around Europe and America. ANTON ANTON-

OVICH alludes to the SIAMESE TWINS as he tries to assuage GOL-YADKIN SENIOR's concern about JUNIOR.

GENERAL STOLBNYAKOV. One of PETRUSHKA's former employers.

SUVOROV. General Aleksandr Vasilievich SUVOROV (1729-1800), Russian field marshall and the most celebrated Russian military man of his time. GOLYADKIN SENIOR notes that even great men have done silly things and insists that SUVOROV once crowed like a cock.

PRINCE SVINCHATKIN. One of PETRUSHKA's former employers.

NESTOR IGNATIEVICH VAKHRAMEEV. A guard in GOLYADKIN SENIOR's department who ceases their friendship because of SENIOR's relations with KAROLINA IVANOVNA, the conduct of PETRUSHKA, and other atrocities on which he refuses to elaborate.

VILLÈLE [VILLEL]. Jean Baptiste Guillaume Joseph VILLÈLE (1773-1854), conservative Royalist French political leader. GOLYADKIN SENIOR sits for some time outside OLSUFY IVANOVICH's house trying to decide whether he should try to attend the ball. He suddenly recalls a thought of VILLÈLE that everything will come of its own accord if only one has the gumption to wait. He takes some solace in this, but ultimately enters KLARA OLSUFIEVNA's birthday celebration anyway under the more aggressive credo of the JESUITS.

VLADIMIR SEMYONOVICH. ANDREY FILIPPOVICH's nephew, whom GOLYADKIN SENIOR views as a rival for the hand of KLARA OLSUFIEVNA. SENIOR is certain that VLADIMIR SEMYONOVICH is spreading rumors about his involvement with KAROLINA IVANOVNA to damage his chances with KLARA OLSUFIEVNA.

YAKOV PETROVICH. See YAKOV PETROVICH GOLYADKIN JUNIOR and YAKOV PETROVICH GOLYADKIN SENIOR.

YASHA. See YAKOV PETROVICH GOLYADKIN JUNIOR. GOLYADKIN SENIOR refers to JUNIOR as YASHA, a term of endearment, when he feels that he has found a kindred spirit.

YEMELYAN GERASIMOVICH (GERASIMYCH). OLSUFY IVANOVICH's elderly valet.

YEVSTAFY. KAROLINA IVANOVNA's former servant.

MISTER PROKHARCHIN (GOSPODIN PROKHARCHIN) 1846

ANDREY YEFIMOVICH. A colleague of MISTER PROKHARCHIN.

AVDOTYA. One of USTINYA FYODOROVNA's lodgers.

DEMID VASILIEVICH. A clerk in the department where MISTER PROKHARCHIN works.

FEVRONYA PROKOFIEVNA. Mentioned as someone a clerk might marry since married clerks seem to fare better in all respects.

KANTAREV. One of USTINYA FYODOROVNA's lodgers.

KATERINA. A puppet. In a delirious moment MISTER PROKHARCHIN imagines that his corner is on fire, and he attempts to flee. He is quickly subdued by his fellow lodgers, who put him to bed as a puppeteer lays his PULCINELLA down by his PETRUSHKA, KATERINA, and other characters.

MARK IVANOVICH. One of USTINYA FYODOROVNA's lodgers. He is a well-read and intelligent man who gets into a heated exchange with MISTER PROKHARCHIN over the latter's stubbornly noncommunicative ways.

NAPOLEON. NAPOLEON I Bonaparte (1769-1821), emperor of France following the French Revolution and temporary conqueror of much of Europe. Disturbed at MISTER PROKHARCHIN's stubborn silence and aloofness, MARK IVANOVICH asks him if he thinks that he is a NAPOLEON for whom alone the world was created.

OKEANOV. One of USTINYA FYODOROVNA's lodgers, who is likely MISTER PROKHARCHIN's favorite. It is he who exposes ZIMOVEY-KIN and REMNYOV as they search MISTER PROKHARCHIN's belongings for anything of value.

OPLEVANIEV. One of USTINYA FYODOROVNA's lodgers.

PETRUSHKA. The main character of Russian folk theater and puppet shows, who is much like PULCINELLA and Punch. In a delirious moment MISTER PROKHARCHIN imagines that his corner is on fire, and he tries to flee. He is quickly subdued by his fellow lodgers, who put him to bed as a puppeteer lays his PULCINELLA down by his PETRUSHKA, KATERINA, and other characters.

PORFIRY GRIGORIEVICH. An official who provides ZIMOVEYKIN with a position when the latter appeals to him.

PREPOLOVENKO. One of USTINYA FYODOROVNA's lodgers, a modest and good man.

MISTER PROKHARCHIN. See SEMYON IVANOVICH PROKHARCHIN.

SEMYON IVANOVICH PROKHARCHIN (MISTER PROKHARCHIN, SEMYON IVANOVICH, SENKA, SENYA). A humble middle-aged clerk of Spartan habits who lives with several others in the home of USTINYA FYODOROVNA. He does not mix well with anyone because of deliberate self-deprivation and poverty and because of a militant insistence upon his privacy. The focal points of his privacy are an old trunk, which he keeps securely locked even though it contains only a few old rags, and his battered mattress. His rejection of ambition and pleasures and acceptance of poverty seem absolute. He takes seriously a rumor that the chancery in which he works will be closed, and the thought of being even poorer and losing his job drives him onto the streets, where he takes up with ZIMOVEYKIN, a disreputable character whom no one trusts. When he finally returns to his lodgings, he is beset by fever and hallucinations. Despite the helpful intentions of his fellow lodgers, he increasingly withdraws into himself and excuses his behavior by reason of his poverty. This withdrawal results in death. When his body is found, his mattress is discovered to be full of money, and his body is grotesquely contorted off the bed as the lodgers search to see just what and how much is hidden there.

PULCINELLA. A coarse, unscrupulous comic character from the Italian folk theater *Commedia dell'Arte* who is related to the Russian PETRUSHKA and the English Punch. See PETRUSHKA.

REMNYOV. An unscrupulous comrade of ZIMOVEYKIN.

SEMYON IVANOVICH. See SEMYON IVANOVICH PROKHARCHIN.

SENKA. See SEMYON IVANOVICH PROKHARCHIN. A familiar name with which ZIMOVEYKIN addresses MISTER PROKHARCHIN.

SENYA. See SEMYON IVANOVICH PROKHARCHIN. A familiar name with which ZIMOVEYKIN addresses MISTER PROKHARCHIN.

SUDBIN. One of USTINYA FYODOROVNA's lodgers.

USTINYA FYODOROVNA (USTINYUSHKA). MISTER PROKHARCHIN's landlady. She has simple tastes and deems MISTER PROKHARCHIN her favorite because of his modest habits. After his death, when it is discovered that he had means, she complains that he took advantage of her by calling her the familiar USTINYUSHKA and appealing to her charity.

USTINYUSHKA. See USTINYA FYODOROVNA.

YAROSLAV ILYICH. A man whom USTINYA FYODOROVNA claims she could have married. It is he who, upon MISTER PROKHARCHIN's death, goes through his last effects and discovers his money.

ZIMOVEYKIN. A reprehensible character and exemplar of bad habits. His tales of woe enable him to obtain a position from PORFIRY GRIGORIE-VICH and lodgings from USTINYA FYODOROVNA. Once his character comes to light he is dismissed from both. He takes up with MISTER PROKHARCHIN when the latter is depressed by the rumor that his job may be lost and briefly leads him astray. Both he and REMNYOV are caught rummaging around MISTER PROKHARCHIN's bed, and each quickly accuses the other of being a thief.

ZINOVY PROKOFIEVICH. One of USTINYA FYODOROVNA's lodgers, whose desire is to gain access to high society. His suggestion that MISTER PROKHARCHIN is hiding money in his chest provokes a violent rebuttal.

A NOVEL IN NINE LETTERS (ROMAN V DEVYATI PISMAKH) 1847

ANNA MIKHAYLOVNA. PYOTR IVANYCH's wife, who leaves him for YEVGENY NIKOLAEVICH. Before running away with him, she makes him deliver to her all of the love letters that he had received from TATYANA PETROVNA during the affair he had with her.

CHISTOGANOV. One of the many people PYOTR IVANYCH visits in his search for IVAN PETROVICH.

DON QUIXOTE OF LA MANCHA *[DON-KIKHOT LAMANCHSKY]*. *El Ingenioso Hidalgo DON QUIXOTE DE LA MANCHA (The Ingenious Gentleman DON QUIXOTE OF LA MANCHA)*, a novel written by Miguel de Cervantes (1547-1616) in two parts in 1605 and 1615. One of the premier works of world fiction, the novel chronicles Don Quixote's obsession with knight errantry and visionary idealism. TATYANA PETROVNA had lent the novel to ANNA MIKHAYLOVNA, but when the families quarrel, it is summarily returned.

IVAN ANDREICH. An acquaintance of PYOTR IVANYCH who encounters him at the club in his perpetual search for IVAN PETROVICH.

IVAN IVANYCH. See IVAN IVANYCH TOLOKONOV.

IVAN PETROVICH. A friend of PYOTR IVANYCH who spends most of his time trying to find him. The frustration of the futile search, compounded by the influence of YEVGENY NIKOLAEVICH, who is having or has had affairs with the wives of both men, creates a rift between the two. The rift is particularly deep because IVAN PETROVICH introduced YEVGENY NIKOLAEVICH into the PYOTR IVANYCH family and because each thinks that the other is avoiding him. He finally learns that his wife TATYANA PETROVNA has had an affair with YEVGENY NIKOLAEVICH, that she vows never to forget him, and that the child she is carrying may not be his own.

KARL FYODORYCH. The doctor who predicts that STEPAN ALEKSEICH's wife will not live long.

PAVEL SEMYONYCH. See PAVEL SEMYONYCH PEREPALKIN.

PAVEL SEMYONYCH PEREPALKIN. One of the many people PYOTR IVANYCH visits in search of IVAN PETROVICH.

PYOTR IVANYCH. A friend of IVAN PETROVICH who spends most of his time trying to find him. The sickness of his aunt, misinformation about each's whereabouts, and never quite being in the right place at the right time necessitate that their contact with each other be through the mail. He objects to YEVGENY NIKOLAEVICH's too frequent visits and asks IVAN PETROVICH to tactfully mention something since it was he who introduced YEVGENY NIKOLAEVICH into their home. He ultimately receives a letter from his wife ANNA MIKHAYLOVNA, who indicates that she is running away with YEVGENY NIKOLAEVICH.

SEMYON ALEKSEICH. His home is the point of departure for PYOTR IVANYCH's search for IVAN PETROVICH.

SIMONEVICH. A friend of both IVAN PETROVICH and PYOTR IVANYCH.

SLAVYANOV. His home becomes the scene of another missed rendezvous of IVAN PETROVICH with PYOTR IVANYCH.

STEPAN ALEKSEICH. PYOTR IVANYCH's uncle. The sickness and ultimate death of his wife YEVFIMIA NIKOLAEVNA results in IVAN PETROVICH and PYOTR IVANYCH's again missing connections.

TATYANA. See TATYANA PETROVNA.

TATYANA PETROVNA. IVAN PETROVICH's wife of three months. She has had a lengthy affair with YEVGENY NIKOLAEVICH and vows never to forget him.

IVAN IVANYCH TOLOKONOV. An acquaintance of IVAN PETROVICH.

WOE FROM WIT [GORE OT UMA]. An immensely popular play in verse, written 1822-24 by Aleksandr Sergeevich Griboedov (1795-1829). The play portrays the social and amorous failures of a progressive in backward society. PYOTR IVANYCH is assured that he will find IVAN PETROVICH attending *WOE FROM WIT* at the Aleksandrysky Theater, but such is not the case and the two miss each other again.

YEVFIMIA NIKOLAEVNA. PYOTR IVANYCH's aunt. Her sickness and ultimàte death cause PYOTR IVANYCH to miss a rendezvous with IVAN PETROVICH.

YEVGENY NIKOLAEVICH (YEVGENY NIKOLAICH). A young man who has affairs with both ANNA MIKHAYLOVNA and TATYANA PETROVNA. He is forced to give all of his love letters from TATYANA PETROVNA to ANNA MIKHAYLOVNA before she agrees to run away with him.

YEVGENY NIKOLAICH. See YEVGENY NIKOLAEVICH.

POLZUNKOV 1846

"AND THE SMOKE OF THE FATHERLAND IS SWEET AND PLEA-SANT TO US!" ["I DYM OTECHESTVA NAM SLADOK I PRIYA-TEN!"]. A line from "The Harp" ("Arfa"), a poem written by Gavriil Romanovich Derzhavin (1743-1816) in 1798. The line is also cited in *Woe From Wit (Gore ot uma),* a play written by Aleksandr Sergeevich Griboedov (1795-1829) in 1822-24. When POLZUNKOV relates how FEDOSEY NIKOLAICH bribes him to remain silent about the stolen money, the theme of loyalty to the fatherland arises, and he cites this line of verse.

MIKHAYLO MAKSIMYCH DVIGAYLOV. A retired soldier about whom POLZUNKOV digresses during his story about FEDOSEY NIKO-LAICH.

FEDOSEY NIKOLAICH. The man about whom POLZUNKOV relates a story at a party. He bribes POLZUNKOV and treats him as a future son-in-law in order to avoid exposure to a government inspector for a deficit in MATVEEV's accounts. When POLZUNKOV solicitously returns the bribe money, FEDOSEY NIKOLAICH quickly dismisses him, indicates that he is moving, and insists that he never wants to see him again.

ST. MARY OF EGYPT [MARYA YEGIPETSKAYA]. Russian Orthodox saint. After a life of profligacy in Egypt she made a vow to devote herself to mortification of the flesh and penance in the wilderness, where she gained prophetic powers and sanctity. POLZUNKOV swears by her name.

MARYA FEDOSEEVNA (MASHA, MASHENKA). FEDOSEY NIKO-LAICH's daughter. She is regarded as POLZUNKOV's intended in order to prevent his implicating FEDOSEY NIKOLAICH in financial wrongdoing. Her tears, valued by POLZUNKOV, are ultimately discovered to be for a military regiment leaving town rather than for him.

MARYA FOMINISHNA. Wife of FEDOSEY NIKOLAICH.

MASHA. See MARYA FEDOSEEVNA.

MASHENKA. See MARYA FEDOSEEVNA.

MATVEEV. The superior of both FEDOSEY NIKOLAICH and POL-ZUNKOV. FEDOSEY NIKOLAICH fears that the large deficit in MAT-VEEV's accounts may be ascribed to him.

MIKHAYLO MAKSIMYCH. See MIKHAYLO MAKSIMYCH DVI-GAYLOV.

OSIP MIKHAYLYCH. See OSIP MIKHAYLYCH POLZUNKOV.

OSIP MIKHAYLYCH POLZUNKOV. A buffoon and an insignificant little man who leaps atop a chair at a party and volunteers to tell a story about FEDOSEY NIKOLAICH and about how he himself almost married. He relates how FEDOSEY NIKOLAICH, in order to avoid being exposed as a thief, treated him ingratiatingly, bribed him, and implied that his daughter MARYA FEDOSEEVNA was his intended. He falls prey to the family's sugary treatment of him and their appeals to his loyalty and conscience. After he returns the bribe money to help FEDOSEY NIKO-LAICH in the event that he is implicated in the deficits in MATVEEV's accounts, POLZUNKOV is fired and excluded from the family.

SOFRON (SOFROSHKA). POLZUNKOV's servant.

SOFROSHKA. See SOFRON.

THE LANDLADY (KHOZYAYKA) 1847

ALEKSANDR IGNATYICH. A young man who out of curiosity goes to observe MURIN's mystical powers and who leaves very disturbed and frightened.

ALYOSHA. KATERINA's intended at the time she goes away with MURIN. He locates her some time later and persuades her to go away with him. On the evening this is to occur, MURIN himself decides to leave and asks ALYOSHA to take him and KATERINA in his boat. They encounter a storm and MURIN and ALYOSHA come to argue and struggle, but the resolution of their conflict, as reported by KATERINA, is not given.

DOMNA SAVVISHNA. ORDYNOV's former landlady. Her leaving St. Petersburg necessitates his finding another room.

KATERINA (KATERINUSHKA, KATYA). An attractive twenty year old who is married to MURIN, a much older man. After her father perishes under strange circumstances in a fire at MURIN's factory, KATERINA goes away with MURIN. She is an unstable girl who professes to love her shame, frequently changes moods, demonstrates erratic behavior, and spends long hours crying, praying, and listening to MURIN read from holy books. She refers to her husband as a wizard with mystical powers but professes not to fear him. When ORDYNOV moves near them, she is immediately drawn to him. Agonizing hours are spent telling ORDYNOV about her life and placing MURIN and ORDYNOV in conflict over her. Their romance is as confused as her mental state and concludes when ORDYNOV takes another room and she and MURIN move back to the Tatar region whence they came.

KATERINUSHKA. See KATERINA.

KATYA. See KATERINA.

KOSHMAROV. The owner of the building in which MURIN, KATERINA, and ORDYNOV live and the leader of a ring of thieves that is ultimately exposed.

ILYA MURIN. A tall, bearded old man whose pallor and burning eyes suggest a disturbed condition. He was once wealthy but through varying circumstances has lost most of his wealth and has become something of an ascetic. His eccentricity and mystical leanings are amplified by his devotion to religious books, long prayers, and penance. The reasons for his penance are never categorically given. It is rumored that he is to blame for the death of a young merchant that he loved, and he states that his very union with KATERINA is frought with transgression. He resents ORDYNOV's romantic association with KATERINA and even brandishes a pistol at him, but later states that if it had not been ORDYNOV it would have been someone else because of KATERINA's mental condition. Seemingly by evil and mystical power he mocks and repels ORDYNOV's weak attempt upon him with a knife. Acquaintances view this same power as the thread that holds KATERINA to him. He promises ORDYNOV that he will pray for him but looks at him with obvious malice. After ORDYNOV moves out he takes KATERINA back to his home in the Tatar region.

OLSUFY. An acquaintance of YAROSLAV ILYICH.

VASILY MIKHAYLOVICH ORDYNOV. A quiet young man who devotes himself to science after he completes his schooling. He encounters KATERINA and MURIN in a church and is so taken by her that he follows them home and takes a room next to them. His tormented rapture romantically increases as he listens to KATERINA's life story, and he comes into conflict with MURIN to the point that they threaten each other with weapons. After the episode in which he raises a knife against MURIN and is overcome with seemingly demonic laughter, he moves in with SPIESS and immediately falls ill. He loses interest in life, broods about KATERINA, and feels inclined to mysticism and prayer. The news that MURIN and KATERINA have moved puts an end to this segment of his life.

PUSHKIN. Aleksandr Sergeevich PUSHKIN (1799-1837), the leading Russian writer of his time, who is regarded as the father of modern Russian literature. (1) YAROSLAV ILYICH mentions that he has read all of PUSHKIN and finds an astounding depiction of men's passions and parallels with his own disillusionment with life. (2) YAROSLAV ILYICH discusses with ORDYNOV MURIN's mystical powers and recalls that PUSHKIN made mention of a similar situation in his works. He likely has reference to *The Queen of Spades (Pikovaya dama),* written in 1834, in which Hermann, the avaricious protagonist, is seemingly given the way to win at cards in a nocturnal vision.

STENKA RAZIN. Stepan Timofeevich RAZIN (ca. 1630-71), leader of rebel peasants in the Peasant War of 1670-71, who was ultimately captured and put to death. ORDYNOV awakes from a delirium and senses that he hears folk tales being related, among them one dealing with STENKA RAZIN.

SEMYON PAFNUTYCH. YAROSLAV ILYICH's personal doctor, whom he recommends to ORDYNOV.

SERGEEV. YAROSLAV ILYICH's servant.

SPIESS [SHPIS]. A poor German who lets a room to ORDYNOV.

TARASOV. An acquaintance of YAROSLAV ILYICH.

TINCHEN [TINKHEN]. SPIESS' daughter.

VILM YEMELYANOVICH. An acquaintance of YAROSLAV ILYICH.

YAROSLAV ILYICH. ORDYNOV's devoted friend. He takes ORDYNOV's advice to drop some of his friends, read, and be of use to society. He ultimately becomes quite disenchanted with people and life and assumes a practical and more realistic orientation toward matters. It is he who serves as the source of ORDYNOV's information about MURIN before and after the interlude with KATERINA.

A FAINT HEART (SLABOE SERDTSE) 1848

ARKADY IVANOVICH. See ARKADY IVANOVICH NEFEDEVICH.

ARKASHA. See ARKADY IVANOVICH NEFEDEVICH.

ARKASHENKA. See ARKADY IVANOVICH NEFEDEVICH.

ARTEMIEVA. LIZA's mother.

LIZAVETA MIKHAYLOVNA ARTEMIEVA (LIZA, LIZANKA). An animated, naive and sentimental girl who is very much in love with VASYA. Following his hospitalization for madness, she marries someone else but tearfully and romantically remembers the past.

ESPER IVANOVICH. An acquaintance of ARKASHA and VASYA.

MADAME LEROUX [LERU]. Owner of a store in which VASYA shops for a present for LIZA.

MANON LESCAUT. Heroine of *Les Aventures du Chevalier des Grieux et de MANON LESCAUT (The Adventures of the Knight des Grieux and of MANON LESCAUT)*, written in 1731 by Antoine François Prévost (1697-1763). She and her lover endure a life of passion and deceit while attempting to build a life together. Their efforts ultimately fail when MANON dies in the New World while in flight from a duel and still more deception. Her lover then turns to penance after returning to France. The cap that VASYA wants to buy for LIZA is in the style of MANON LESCAUT.

LIZA. See LIZAVETA MIKHAYLOVNA ARTEMIEVA.

LIZANKA. See LIZAVETA MIKHAYLOVNA ARTEMIEVA.

LIZAVETA MIKHAYLOVNA. See LIZAVETA MIKHAYLOVNA ARTEMIEVA.

MASHA. MAVRA's cat.

MAVRA. A servant in the home in which VASYA and ARKASHA live.

ARKADY IVANOVICH NEFEDEVICH (ARKASHA, ARKASHEN-KA). VASYA's good-natured friend who tries to help him through his ordeal of copying YULIAN MASTAKOVICH's documents. Following VASYA's madness he perceives St. Petersburg in a fantastic vein and seems to understand that it is the peculiar environment of the city acting upon a sensitive and unstable nature that drives VASYA mad.

PETENKA. See PETYA.

PETYA (PETENKA). LIZA's brother.

SASHKA. PETYA's friend.

VASILY PETROVICH SHUMKOV (VASENKA, VASYA, VASYUK, VASYUTKA). An effusive, sentimental, somewhat physically deformed young man who is planning to marry LIZA. Their livelihood will be derived from the copying he does for YULIAN MASTAKOVICH. He feels the absolute necessity of copying six thick notebooks on time even though the deadline is only two days hence. His helplessness and instability drive him alternately to copy furiously and to waste time by paying unnecessary calls on various people. This self-imposed pressure drives him to madness, and he is hospitalized. All involved are touched and amazed that such a state of mind could be reached over the unnecessary.

SKOROKHODOV. A man alluded to by ARKADY IVANOVICH.

SKOROPLYOKHIN. VASYA wants to do a good job in copying for YULIAN MASTAKOVICH whose standards of work are much higher than those of SKOROPLYOKHIN.

VASENKA. See VASILY PETROVICH SHUMKOV.

VASYA. See VASILY PETROVICH SHUMKOV.

VASYUK. See VASILY PETROVICH SHUMKOV.

VASYUTKA. See VASILY PETROVICH SHUMKOV.

YULIAN MASTAKOVICH. The person who supplies VASYA with copying and is the source of his income. He is ultimately very touched by VASYA's insanity and the fact that quite unimportant copying could drive a man mad.

ANOTHER MAN'S WIFE AND THE HUSBAND UNDER THE BED
(CHUZHAYA ZHENA I MUZH POD KROVATYU) 1848

ALEKSANDR DEMYANOVICH. LIZA's husband, who returns home when IVAN ANDREICH and the YOUNG MAN are under LIZA's bed. He is heavy, elderly, and suffers from hemorrhoids, which ailment occupies most of his conversation with his wife. Upon discovering IVAN ANDRE-ICH under the bed, he is driven to hysteria by IVAN ANDREICH's ridiculous explanations and the idea that he too may have a wife.

AMI (AMISHKA). LIZA's dog, which IVAN ANDREICH strangles under the bed.

AMISHKA. See AMI.

ANNUSHKA. One of the ladies that IVAN ANDREICH and TVOROGOV examine outside the apartment building in search of GLAFIRA PETROVNA.

BOBYNITSYN. The gentleman who has taken GENERAL POLOVITSYN's former apartment and who is seeing GLAFIRA PETROVNA secretly.

DON JUAN [DON-ZHUAN]. A legendary profligate cavalier who functions as the main character of several works of fiction and music. IVAN ANDREICH is ironically referred to as DON JUAN as he lies under LIZA's bed.

FEDOSEY IVANOVICH. A friend who recommends a remedy for ALEKSANDR DEMYANOVICH's hemorrhoids.

THE GENTLEMAN IN THE RACCOON COAT [GOSPODIN V YENOTAKH]. See IVAN ANDREEVICH SHABRIN. As he confronts TVOROGOV waiting outside the apartment building, IVAN ANDREICH refuses to identify himself and is identified only by what he wears.

GLAFIRA. See GLAFIRA PETROVNA SHABRINA.

GLAFIRA PETROVNA. See GLAFIRA PETROVNA SHABRINA.

HAMLET [GAMLET]. Central character of *HAMLET, Prince of Denmark,* a tragedy written about 1601 by William Shakespeare (1564-1616). The play chronicles HAMLET's revenge for the slaying of his father. When IVAN ANDREICH bursts into the opera house so forcefully, the conductor half expects to see him brandishing a knife à la HAMLET.

IVAN ANDREEVICH. See IVAN ANDREEVICH SHABRIN.

IVAN ANDREICH. See IVAN ANDREEVICH SHABRIN.

IVAN ILYICH. See IVAN ILYICH TVOROGOV.

JEAN. See IVAN ANDREEVICH SHABRIN. GLAFIRA PETROVNA addresses IVAN ANDREICH with the sugary appellations JEAN and KOKO when he and her former lover TVOROGOV accost her leaving BOBYNITSYN's apartment.

KAPROV. When GLAFIRA PETROVNA is caught leaving BOBYNIT-SYN's apartment by her husband and TVOROGOV, she calmly introduces BOBYNITSYN to them and explains that they met at KAPROV's ball.

PAUL DE KOCK [POL DE KOK]. French novelist (1793-1871) noted for his graphic portrayal of Parisian life. (1) IVAN ANDREICH mentions that his wife enjoys the easy, self-indulgent style of life typical of PAUL DE KOCK and complains that the novelist is partially to blame for his marital predicament. (2) It is noted that SOFYA OSTAFIEVNA is sly and always has a copy of PAUL DE KOCK under her pillow.

KOKO. See IVAN ANDREEVICH SHABRIN. GLAFIRA PETROVNA addresses IVAN ANDREICH with the sugary appellations JEAN and KOKO when he and her former lover TVOROGOV accost her leaving BOBYNITSYN's apartment.

PRINCE KOROTKOUKHOV. After being discovered under LIZA's bed, IVAN ANDREICH speaks very ingratiatingly to ALEKSANDR DEM-YANOVICH and tells him that he reminds him of PRINCE KOROT-KOUKHOV.

LIZA. ALEKSANDR DEMYANOVICH's pretty, young wife, whose dog AMI is strangled by IVAN ANDREICH under her bed.

LOVELACE [LOVELAS]. The seducer in the novel *Clarissa; or the History of a Young Lady*, written in 1748 by Samuel RICHARDSON. The author ironically refers to IVAN ANDREICH under LIZA's bed as LOVELACE. When he is exposed, IVAN ANDREICH attempts to explain his presence and insists that he could not be a LOVELACE or LIZA's lover.

MAKAR. IVAN ANDREICH is hit by a falling note at the opera and decides that the rendezvous mentioned therein likely involves his wife. He complains that everything is happening to him and recalls a proverb involving poor MAKAR, a generalized person who is perpetually out of luck and in trouble.

PANAFIDIN. ALEKSANDR DEMYANOVICH mentions to LIZA upon his return home that the PANAFIDIN girls have a Nuremburg doll.

PAVEL IVANOVICH. ALEKSANDR DEMYANOVICH returns home from a game of preference at the home of PAVEL IVANOVICH.

GENERAL POLOVITSYN. A friend of IVAN ANDREICH, GLAFIRA PETROVNA, and TVOROGOV, whose apartment is taken by BOBYNI-TSYN.

PRASKOVYA ZAKHARIEVNA. A servant in ALEKSANDR DEM-YANOVICH's house.

PRINCHIPE. The author notes that he is nervous at operas because he is constantly afraid that the ladies' opera glasses will fall upon someone's head. Sensing that such an observation is out of place in a book, he vows to send it to one of the practical columns of a newspaper that contains such things as PRINCHIPE's recommendations for getting rid of beetles and cockroaches.

PUZYRYOV. A friend of IVAN ANDREICH at whose house he meets PRINCE KOROTKOUKHOV.

RICHARDSON. Samuel RICHARDSON (1689-1761), English novelist known for his sentimental novels in which virtue triumphs. IVAN ANDREICH, in trying to explain himself to ALEKSANDR DEMYANO-VICH when caught under LIZA's bed, pleads that he is not LIZA's lover, since that is for people like RICHARDSON. He quickly corrects himself from RICHARDSON to LOVELACE.

RINALDO RINALDINI. Adventuresome robber hero of *RINALDO RINALDINI, der Räuberhauptmann (RINALDO RINALDINI, the Robber Chief)*, written in 1799 by the German writer Christian August Vulpius (1762-1827). IVAN ANDREICH notes that his being discovered under LIZA's bed and taken for a bandit is somewhat like the adventures of RINALDO RINALDINI.

IVAN ANDREEVICH SHABRIN (THE GENTLEMAN IN THE RAC-COON COAT, IVAN ANDREICH, JEAN, KOKO). The betrayed husband of GLAFIRA PETROVNA. While waiting outside of BOBY-NITSYN's apartment building for her, he meets TVOROGOV, who is performing the same vigil, questions him closely, and solicits his aid. IVAN

ANDREICH poses as the friend of a betrayed husband, insists that he is a bachelor and lover himself, and refuses to identify himself. He and TVOROGOV ascend to the apartment in question and encounter GLAFIRA PETROVNA leaving, whereupon they accept her introductions, pretend not to know each other, and part company. His next pursuit begins at the opera when he is hit upon the head by a note requesting a rendezvous. Since his wife is seated above him, he assumes that the note involves her and hurries to the address given. He blunders into the wrong apartment following A YOUNG MAN, whom he suspects of being involved in the affair. When he hears the footsteps of the husband ALEKSANDR DEMYANOVICH coming home to his wife LIZA, he crawls under the bed only to find the YOUNG MAN, who admits to having entered the wrong apartment on the way to his rendezvous. The two have much the same vague exchange that TVOROGOV and IVAN ANDREICH had outside the apartment. IVAN ANDREICH refuses to identify himself, insists that he is not a betrayed husband, and demands respect for his status and age. He strangles LIZA's dog AMI when the animal discovers him under the bed and is thereby exposed. His explanations and self-justification produce near hysteria in ALEKSANDR DEMYANOVICH and LIZA, who release him. He goes home to find GLAFIRA PETROVNA suffering from a toothache, and she demands an explanation for his tardiness and the carcass of AMI in his pocket.

GLAFIRA PETROVNA SHABRINA. IVAN ANDREICH's wife, who has been seeing both TVOROGOV and BOBYNITSYN. It is her betrayal that sends IVAN ANDREICH on his journeys and places him in ridiculous situations. She handles her husband and her lovers very well and always emerges unscathed.

SKORLUPOV. When GLAFIRA PETROVNA comically introduces TVOROGOV to IVAN ANDREICH as they confront her leaving BOBY-NITSYN's apartment, she notes that she met TVOROGOV at a ball at the SKORLUPOV residence.

SOFYA OSTAFIEVNA. When IVAN ANDREICH questions TVORO-GOV about whether he knows anyone in the apartment building they are both watching, TVOROGOV mentions that he knows one SOFYA OSTAFIEVNA.

IVAN ILYICH TVOROGOV (THE YOUNG MAN IN THE WINTER COAT). A young man who has been having an affair with GLAFIRA PETROVNA. Initially referred to only as THE YOUNG MAN IN THE

WINTER COAT, he is standing outside an apartment building awaiting a rendezvous with GLAFIRA PETROVNA. While waiting he meets IVAN ANDREICH, GLAFIRA PETROVNA's husband, who is also looking for her. Neither of them identifies himself, and TVOROGOV becomes very disturbed at IVAN ANDREICH's strange behavior. They finally enter the building together and go to BOBYNITSYN's apartment, where they encounter her. TVOROGOV's attempts to have a quick explanation with her fail, and he and IVAN ANDREICH pretend not to know each other.

A YOUNG MAN [MOLODOY CHELOVEK]. The dandy with whom IVAN ANDREICH finds himself under LIZA's bed. He had entered the wrong apartment on his way to a rendezvous and was closely followed by IVAN ANDREICH, who thought that GLAFIRA PETROVNA was the end of the YOUNG MAN's pursuit. When IVAN ANDREICH is discovered under the bed, the YOUNG MAN escapes unobserved out of the apartment, presumably to continue his quest.

THE YOUNG MAN IN THE WINTER COAT [MOLODOY CHELO-VEK V BEKESHE]. See IVAN ILYICH TVOROGOV.

THE HONEST THIEF (CHESTNY VOR) 1848

AGRAFYONA. The cook, cleaning lady, and all-round servant of the narrator. When she suggests that he take in a border, ASTAFY moves in.

ALEKSANDR FILIMONOVICH. The gentleman whom ASTAFY served for a time.

ALEKSANDROV. The thief, who takes the narrator's winter coat, initially comes to his apartment asking for a civil servant named ALEKSANDROV.

ANTIP PROKHORYCH. YEMELYA, who usually talks of trivia, notes that ANTIP PROKHORYCH married the cabby's widow.

ASTAFY. See ASTAFY IVANOVICH.

ASTAFY IVANOVICH (ASTAFY IVANYCH, ASTAFY). A retired soldier who comes to board with the narrator after having lived with YEMELYA for a time. The theft of the narrator's winter coat prompts ASTAFY to relate the story of YEMELYA, whom he dubs an honest thief.

ASTAFY IVANYCH. See ASTAFY IVANOVICH.

BOSOMYAGIN. ASTAFY once lived in a room let by BOSOMYAGIN.

FEDOSEY IVANYCH. YEMELYA considers approaching FEDOSEY IVANYCH about a job.

KOSTOPRAVOV. A doctor whom ASTAFY consults when YEMELYA becomes ill.

VLAS. A bartender mentioned by YEMELYA.

YEMELYA. See YEMELYAN ILYICH.

YEMELYAN ILYICH (YEMELYA, YEMELYANUSHKA, YEMEL-YUSHKA). A good, gentle, and meek person who has been put out of employment because of his drinking. He becomes attached to ASTAFY and follows him wherever he moves until he is taken in and cared for. When ASTAFY's breeches turn up missing, YEMELYA is suspected, but continually denies having taken them. After a lengthy drinking bout he leaves, but returns within the week haggard, blue, ill, and determined never to drink again. He admits that he stole the breeches, tells ASTAFY to sell his coat when he dies, and then soon thereafter dies.

YEMELYANUSHKA. See YEMELYAN ILYICH.

YEMELYUSHKA. See YEMELYAN ILYICH.

THE CHRISTMAS TREE AND THE WEDDING (YOLKA I SVADBA) 1848

BOY [MALCHIK]. The son of FILIPP ALEKSEEVICH's governess, a poor widow. When YULIAN MASTAKOVICH interrupts his play with the GIRL and frightens her, the BOY defends her and in turn is pursued and abused by YULIAN MASTAKOVICH.

FILIPP ALEKSEEVICH. He and his wife give a Christmas party at which YULIAN MASTAKOVICH meets the little GIRL. Both he and his wife dote on YULIAN MASTAKOVICH in the hope that he will use his influence to help the BOY. The suggestions are refused because of the BOY's defense of the frightened little GIRL.

GIRL [DEVOCHKA]. An eleven year old guest at a Christmas party given by FILIPP ALEKSEEVICH. She has a large dowry and because of this is singled out by YULIAN MASTAKOVICH, who interrupts her play with the BOY and frightens her. Because of his importance her parents dote on YULIAN MASTAKOVICH and subsequently encourage his visits to their home. Five years later the two are married, much to the GIRL's chagrin.

YULIAN MASTAKOVICH. An important official who at a Christmas party becomes very interested in an eleven year old GIRL with a very large dowry. He mentally calculates the projected value of the dowry when she will be of marriageable age and begins to pursue her. She is frightened and is defended by a BOY whom YULIAN MASTAKOVICH subsequently abuses and refuses to help. Five years later he marries the GIRL, having calculated exactly what the dowry would be worth at that time.

WHITE NIGHTS (BELYE NOCHI) 1848

BARANNIKOV. The owner of the house in which the narrator lives.

THE BARBER OF SEVILLE [SEVILSKY TSIRYULNIK]. *Barbière di Siviglia,* an opera written by Gioacchino Antonio Rossini (1792-1868) in 1816, based upon a comedy *Le Barbier de Séville,* written in 1775 by Pierre Augustin Caron de Beaumarchais (1732-99). The work chronicles the clever efforts of the barber Figaro to marry a Spanish nobleman to ROSINE, the girl of the nobleman's dreams. THE YOUNG LODGER invites NASTENKA and her GRANDMOTHER to attend a performance of THE BARBER OF SEVILLE with him.

BATTLE OF BERYOZINA [SRAZHENIE PRI BERYOZINE]. The site of a defeat of Napoleon's forces by the Russian army in 1812 which was instrumental in driving the French from Russia. THE DREAMER tells

NASTENKA that he sometimes dreams of the BATTLE OF BERYO-ZINA.

"BRENDA." The title of a ballad written by Ivan Ivanovich Kozlov (1799-1840) in 1834. The ballad tells of the frustrated love of a young man for BRENDA, his whisking her away on his horse, and their death in a turbulent river. THE DREAMER is probably referring to this ballad when he tells NASTENKA that he sometimes dreams of BRENDA.

CLEOPATRA [KLEOPATRA]. CLEOPATRA VII (69-30 B.C.), the last Macedonian queen of Egypt, famed for her consorts with Julius Caesar and Marc Antony. THE DREAMER mentions to NASTENKA that he sometimes dreams about CLEOPATRA and her lovers.

DANTON. Georges Jacques DANTON (1759-94), one of the leaders of the French Revolution who lost his life because of conflict with Maximilien Robespierre (1758-94). THE DREAMER tells NASTENKA that he sometimes dreams about DANTON.

EFFIE DEANS [YEVFIA DENS]. Female protagonist in *The Heart of Midlothian,* a novel written by Sir WALTER SCOTT in 1818. She has an illegitimate child, marries her betrayer, and upon his death retires to a convent. THE DREAMER indicates to NASTENKA that he sometimes dreams of EFFIE DEANS.

THE DREAMER [MECHTATEL]. A young man of twenty six who has spent eight years in St. Petersburg. He spends his life dreaming, has no real friends, has never had any female company, is shy, and is in love with the ideal girl of his dreams. His dreams center on characters from books and people involved in romantic deeds. When speaking he uses long phrases, numerous romantic allusions, verbose and stilted expressions, and expresses fine sensibilities. On his way home from wandering about the city he saves NASTENKA from a man who is trying to grab her and immediately tells her about himself and his dream world. They agree to meet the next night, and he spends a sleepless but ecstatic interlude. As they meet he explains the essence of life as a dreamer but agrees with NASTENKA that he has wasted his life. Despite falling in love with her he tries to help her locate THE YOUNG LODGER, the object of her own romantic vision. When this search seemingly fails, he and NASTENKA agree to spend their lives together and make plans for the future. On the way home from this discussion, however, they meet THE YOUNG LODGER, and NASTENKA quickly goes to him. THE DREAMER notices that everything around him suddenly looks older and worse than usual, and he imagines that he will be in the same condition several years hence. He mentally wishes NASTENKA well and is thankful for the moments of bliss that were his because of her.

FYOKLA. GRANDMOTHER's deaf servant girl. On one occasion NASTENKA ties FYOKLA to her GRANDMOTHER so that she herself can move about more freely.

"THE GODDESS OF FANTASY" ["BOGINYA FANTAZII"]. THE DREAMER mentions ZHUKOVSKY's "THE GODDESS OF FANTASY" as he tells NASTENKA about his life as a dreamer. He likely has reference to ZHUKOVSKY's poem "My Goddess" ("Moya boginya"), written in 1809, which sings the praises of imagination and fantasy. The poem is an adaptation of "Meine Göttin" ("My Goddess"), written in 1780 by Johann Wolfgang von Goethe (1749-1832).

GRANDMOTHER [BABUSHKA]. NASTENKA's grandmother, a blind, aged woman who lives in the past and tries to care for her orphaned granddaughter. Because of her sightlessness she ties NASTENKA to her so that she can watch over her.

HOFFMANN [GOFMAN]. Ernst Theodore Amadeus HOFFMANN (1776-1822), German author known primarily for his fantastic tales. THE DREAMER mentions to NASTENKA that he sometimes dreams of friendship with HOFFMANN.

HUS [GUS]. Jan HUS (1369-1415), Bohemian religious reformer and rector of the University of Prague, who was tried and burned at the stake for advocating reformed theology. THE DREAMER mentions to NASTENKA that he sometimes dreams of HUS' being tried before the Catholic prelates.

IVAN VASILIEVICH. IVAN IV the Terrible (1530-84), tsar of Russia from 1533 until his death. He consolidated the Russian empire under Moscow and became known for his ferocity toward his enemies and alternate periods of sensuality and piety. THE DREAMER tells NASTENKA that he sometimes dreams of IVAN VASILIEVICH's capturing Kazan after a lengthy battle in 1552.

IVANHOE [IVANGOE]. An historical novel written in 1819 by Sir WALTER SCOTT. The novel chronicles IVANHOE's chivalrous winning of Lady Rowena and his ultimate prosperity, parallel with Richard I's triumph as Norman king of England. NASTENKA mentions to THE YOUNG LODGER that of all the books he gives her to read she likes *IVANHOE* and those of PUSHKIN best.

"THE LITTLE HOUSE IN KOLOMNA" ["DOMIK V KOLOMNE"]. A narrative poem written by Aleksandr PUSHKIN in 1830. The work is a bantering piece of fun which deals with the hiring of a new cook by the daughter of a widow. The cook demands no wage but proves to be terribly inefficient and is eventually discovered by the widow to be a man dressed as a woman. THE DREAMER tells NASTENKA that he sometimes dreams of "THE LITTLE HOUSE IN KOLOMNA."

MASHENKA. A friend of NASTENKA whose move to Pskov leaves NASTENKA essentially friendless and even more literally tied to her GRANDMOTHER.

MATRYONA. The cook and cleaning woman in the house in which THE DREAMER lives. Her dullness and lack of imagination effectively contrast with his dream world.

CLARA MAWBRAY [KLARA MOVBRAY]. Heroine of *St. Ronan's Well,* published in 1824 by Sir WALTER SCOTT. She is forced to marry an illegitimate imposter who seeks her fortune, and she later dies as she flees from him. THE DREAMER indicates to NASTENKA that he sometimes dreams about CLARA MAWBRAY.

"MINNA." "Mina," a romance written in 1818 by Vasily ZHUKOVSKY. The poem records the lyric return of the writer to a pastoral, romantic setting. When THE DREAMER tells NASTENKA that he sometimes dreams of "MINNA," he likely has this verse in mind.

NASTENKA. A seventeen year old orphan who lives with her blind GRANDMOTHER. She is kept tied to her GRANDMOTHER because of the latter's sightlessness, and she spends her days reading and sewing. A YOUNG LODGER moves in with them and opens up to NASTENKA the world of literature and the theater. She falls in love with him and is ready to go away with him, but is dissuaded by assertions of poverty and promises that he will return in a year with the means to marry her. Toward the end of the year's wait she is saved from a man at night in the street by THE DREAMER, whom she comes to love and whom she enlists to help find THE YOUNG LODGER. When the search is apparently fruitless, she declares her love (or at least her gratitude that is turning into love) for THE DREAMER because he loves her, is noble, and because she is abandoned. As they make enthusiastic plans for a future life together, she sees THE YOUNG LODGER approaching, and quickly leaves THE DREAMER to join him. She later writes THE DREAMER a letter pledging to remember him because of the constancy of her heart and asking for his love because she is worthy of it.

"OR WAS HE MADE IN ORDER//TO BE IF JUST ONE MOMENT//CLOSE TO YOUR HEART?" ["IL BYL ON SOZDAN DLYA TOGO,//CHTOBY POBYT KHOTYA MGNOVENIE//V SOSEDSTVE SERDTSA TVOEGO?"]. Slightly inaccurate rendering of lines from "The Flower" ("Tsvetok"), a poem written by IVAN TURGENEV in 1843. With little change to the English translation, the original reads "Znat, on byl sozdan dlya togo,//Chtoby pobyt odno mgnovenie//V sosedstve serdtsa tvoego." The lines serve as the epigraph to *White Nights* and allude to the passing relationship of THE DREAMER and NASTENKA.

PUSHKIN. Aleksandr Sergeevich PUSHKIN (1799-1837), the greatest Russian writer of his time who is regarded as the father of modern Russian literature. NASTENKA observes to THE YOUNG LODGER that of all the books he has given her to read she likes *IVANHOE* and those of PUSHKIN best.

ROBERT. *ROBERT le Diable (ROBERT the Devil),* an opera written in 1831 by Giacomo Meyerbeer (1791-1864). THE DREAMER mentions to NASTENKA that he sometimes dreams of the dead rising in the opera *ROBERT.*

ROSINE. In *THE BARBER OF SEVILLE* the young woman whom Figaro the barber helps the Spanish nobleman to court. When THE YOUNG LODGER suggests to GRANDMOTHER and NASTENKA that he take them to a performance of the opera, GRANDMOTHER notes that she once played ROSINE in a home theatrical. Later, as THE DREAMER consents to try to deliver a letter to THE YOUNG LODGER from NASTENKA, he and she both recall ROSINE and the plot of the opera.

ST. BARTHOLOMEW'S NIGHT [VARFOLOMEEVSKAYA NOCH]. A massacre of the Huguenots by Parisian Catholics which began on St. Bartholomew's Day, 24 August 1572. THE DREAMER tells NASTENKA that he sometimes dreams of ST. BARTHOLOMEW'S NIGHT.

WALTER SCOTT [VALTER SKOTT]. English historical novelist (1771-1832). THE YOUNG LODGER sends NASTENKA and her GRAND-MOTHER several novels by WALTER SCOTT to read. The GRAND-MOTHER is concerned about their romantic content and about the possibility that love notes may be concealed within them.

SOLOMON. As THE DREAMER and NASTENKA become acquainted and eagerly share impressions, he notes that he feels like the spirit of King SOLOMON, which has been released from a thousand-year captivity. THE DREAMER probably has in mind the tale from *A Thousand and One Nights* in which the prophet Alla Suleiman (SOLOMON) binds the genie, only to have it ultimately released.

IVAN TURGENEV. IVAN Sergeevich TURGENEV (1818-83), a major Russian novelist who stands with Tolstoy and Dostoevsky as a giant of his age. His novels examine the personal lives and intellectual considerations of the Russian nobility. The epigraph to the novel is an inexact citation from one of his early poems: "OR WAS HE MADE IN ORDER//TO BE IF JUST ONE MOMENT//CLOSE TO YOUR HEART?"

COUNTESS V—A-D—A. THE DREAMER mentions to NASTENKA that he sometimes dreams about poetry readings at the home of COUN-TESS V—A-D—A. He probably has in mind Yekaterina Romanovna Vorontsova-Dashkova (1743-1810), president of the Russian Academy of Sciences, who founded the journal *The Companion of Lovers of the Russian Word (Sobesednik lyubiteley rossyskogo slova)* and who was a patroness of the arts.

DIANA VERNON. The heroine of *Rob Roy,* written by Sir WALTER SCOTT in 1818. Overcoming religious differences, she married her intended with the help of the outlaw Rob Roy, who conquers evil and overcomes all obstacles. THE DREAMER mentions to NASTENKA that he sometimes dreams of DIANA VERNON.

THE YOUNG LODGER [MOLODOY ZHILETS]. A young man who takes a room from the GRANDMOTHER. He is embarrassed to see them tied together and the manner in which they live and introduces them to literature and the theater. When he leaves for Moscow, he rejects NASTEN-KA's pleas to accompany him because of his poverty but promises to return in a year with the means to marry her. Upon his return, NASTENKA quickly abandons THE DREAMER, and they leave together.

ZHUKOVSKY. Vasily Andreevich ZHUKOVSKY (1783-1852), prominent Russian poet and translator. THE DREAMER refers to "THE GODDESS OF FANTASY" of ZHUKOVSKY as he tells NASTENKA about his life as a dreamer.

NETOCHKA NEZVANOVA 1849

ALEKSANDR (SASHA). One of PRINCE KH—Y's children and KATYA's younger brother.

ALEKSANDRA MIKHAYLOVNA. The daughter of PRINCESS KH—AYA by her first marriage. She is twenty two, affectionate, gentle, and suffers from the memory of an affair she had with S.O. and from the cool treatment she receives from her husband PYOTR ALEKSANDROVICH. She cannot live without her husband, yet her memories make every word and action around him guarded, and the two are very much unequal. After KATYA and PRINCESS KH—AYA go to Moscow to care for SASHA during his illness, ALEKSANDRA MIKHAYLOVNA takes NETOCHKA to live with her and assumes her education. Her relationship to NETOCHKA as mother, sister, and confidante decreases over the years because of her torment, failing health, and NETOCHKA's growing up, yet they remain close. When NETOCHKA discovers the love letter from S.O. and tries to stem PYOTR ALEKSANDROVICH's anger, she and ALEKSANDRA MIKHAYLOVNA defend each other before him in a scene of innuendo and accusation. Her husband's allusions to her previous affair cause her to faint and damage her health still further. At the conclusion doctors regard her condition as serious.

ALEKSEY NIKIFORYCH. A musician who accuses YEFIMOV of being implicated in the death of the Italian musician who had interested YEFIMOV in the violin. After making the accusation he falls ill and dies of brain fever and insanity.

ANNETA. See ANNA NEZVANOVA.

B. A violinist from whom NETOCHKA learns the biography of her stepfather YEFIMOV. He is a German who through methodical hard work has become a good violinist. YEFIMOV becomes a parasite on him, but B. is patient, gives him good advice for success, and later tries to help him establish his career. A close friend of ALEKSANDRA MIKHAYLOV-NA's family, he is one of the few people to visit her.

CAESAR. According to B., YEFIMOV's motto was "aut CAESAR, aut nihil" ("either CAESAR or nothing"), the motto of Cesare Borgia (1476-1507), whose meteoric career and sudden demise were based in the politics of the papacy. YEFIMOV wants to be the greatest violinist in the world or nothing, and like Borgia he becomes nothing.

CERBERUS [TSERBER]. In Greek mythology, the ferocious three-headed dog that guards the entrance to the infernal regions. When a bulldog saves SASHA's life as he is about to drown, the family rejoices and decides to keep the dog and give it a place of honor. In trying to think of a name for the dog, the family considers CERBERUS, but ultimately decides upon SIR JOHN FALSTAFF.

CORNEILLE [KORNEL]. Pierre CORNEILLE (1606-84), French dramatist and a prime shaper of the French classical theater. He is a favorite writer of MADAME LEOTARD, and she actively defends him.

D. An Italian who functions as NETOCHKA's voice teacher.

FALSTAFF. See SIR JOHN FALSTAFF.

SIR JOHN FALSTAFF (FALSTAFF, FALSTAFKA, CERBERUS, FRIKSY, HECTOR). Comic character in *Henry IV, Parts One and Two* (1597-98) and *The Merry Wives of Windsor* (1597-1601) by William Shakespeare (1564-1616). He is characterized by self-indulgence, braggadocio, buffoonery, and vice. The bulldog who rescues SASHA from drowning is kept by the family, given the name of SIR JOHN FALSTAFF after consideration of names such as CERBERUS and HECTOR, and is generally given the run of the house. The dog loves no one and is extremely independent.

FALSTAFKA. See SIR JOHN FALSTAFF.

FORTINBRAS. Prince of Norway in *Hamlet, Prince of Denmark*, written in 1601 by William Shakespeare (1564-1616). He becomes king of Denmark following Hamlet's death. During his unsuccessful career the aspiring but inept dancer KARL FYODORYCH earns only background parts, such as a member of FORTINBRAS' retinue.

FRIKSY. SIR JOHN FALSTAFF's pedestrian name prior to his saving SASHA from drowning and his adoption by the family.

HECTOR [GEKTOR]. In Homer's *Iliad* the noblest of Trojan chieftains, who is ultimately slain by Achilles. When a bulldog saves SASHA from drowning, the family is so grateful that it decides to keep the dog and give it a place of honor. In trying to think of a name for the dog, the family considers HECTOR, but ultimately decides upon SIR JOHN FALSTAFF.

IVANHOE [IVANGOE]. A novel written in 1819 by Sir WALTER SCOTT. The novel chronicles IVANHOE's chivalrous winning of Lady Rowena and his ultimate prosperity, parallel with Richard I's triumph as Norman king of England. When NETOCHKA turns sixteen, ALEKSANDRA MIKHAYLOVNA determines that she needs to read *IVANHOE*. By means of a secret key to the library NETOCHKA had read the book some time previously.

JACOPO [DZHAKOBO]. *JACOPO Sannazzaro,* a play written in 1834 by Nestor Vasilievich Kukolnik (1809-68), popular Russian romantic playwright. The play is based upon the life of the Italian poet of the same name, who lived 1456-1530. NETOCHKA recalls how her stepfather YEFIMOV and KARL FYODORYCH used to get together and complain that their talents were not recognized. She remembers a play they discover in which some JENARO or JACOPO laments about his fate as an artist and worries about his recognition and talent. As she recalls, the play ends unhappily and thus parallels the fate of YEFIMOV and KARL FYODORYCH.

JENARO [DZHENARO]. See JACOPO.

KARL FYODORYCH. See KARL FYODOROVICH MEYER.

KATENKA. See KATYA.

KATYA (KATENKA). PRINCE KH—Y's daughter, who is the same age as NETOCHKA. She is fun-loving and athletic, and because of NETOCHKA's quiet nature has little interest in her. Later her extreme pride and vanity put a barrier between the girls. KATYA attempts to humiliate NETOCHKA to gain superiority and in general wants to dominate people and control situations. Her relationship with NETOCHKA becomes one of physical and emotional love and hate, and she has a nervous collapse under the strain. Her behavior becomes obnoxious and erratic and she even introduces FALSTAFF into her aunt's quarters, thereby perpetrating chaos and a scandal. She ultimately has a full reconciliation with NETOCHKA, during which she acknowledges that she shunned her because she feared that NETOCHKA was better than she and that her father cared for NETOCHKA more. She leaves NETOCHKA when she and her mother go to Moscow to care for an ill SASHA, and the two are never reunited.

PRINCESS KH—AYA [KNYAGINYA KH-AYA]. PRINCE KH—Y's wife. She initially wants to love NETOCHKA and be a mother to her, but quickly tires of her and despairs of her possible influence on KATYA. When the two girls become involved, she sees to it that they see less of each other. She is very devoted to SASHA and hence to FALSTAFF, who saved his life. She takes KATYA with her to Moscow when informed of SASHA's illness and becomes emotionally dependent upon her daughter because of SASHA's condition.

PRINCESS KH—AYA [KNYAZHNA KH—AYA]. PRINCE KH—Y's aged aunt who lives on the top floor of his house. She had previously lived in a convent and maintains a strict, quiet order in her domain. Her moving into the house usurps FALSTAFF's place of honor, and the two become mortal enemies. Her equanimity is destroyed when KATYA in a moment of emotional instability sends FALSTAFF into her quarters.

PRINCESS KH—AYA [KNYAZHNA KH—AYA]. A sister to the COUNTESS L. and to the aged PRINCESS KH—AYA. Each of the sisters maintains an active link with the aristocratic past and holds to form and propriety, but they are incapable of getting along with one another.

PRINCE KH—Y [KNYAZ KH—Y]. YEFIMOV's former benefactor, who still tries to help him and who takes in his stepdaughter NETOCHKA when her mother dies and YEFIMOV flees. He is very solicitous of NETOCHKA and countermands his wife in order to see that KATYA behaves properly and that the girls get along with each other.

COUNTESS L. A widow in failing health who takes in her sister, the PRINCESS KH—AYA, who formerly lived with PRINCE KH—Y, to live with her in Moscow.

LA FONTAINE [LAFONTEN]. Jean de LA FONTAINE (1621-95), a prolific French writer, most noted for his fables and tales. Most of KATYA's study of French under MADAME LEOTARD involves reading LA FONTAINE.

MADAME LEOTARD [LEOTAR]. An active, perceptive woman who is retained by PRINCE KH—Y to teach KATYA, and subsequently NE-TOCHKA, French. She monitors the relations of the girls, and when they become too involved, she is persuaded that such a relationship cannot be for the best. When the KH—Y family moves to Moscow, she becomes part of ALEKSANDRA MIKHAYLOVNA's household. Her particular fetish is her favorites from French literature and culture, and while normally an unassuming woman, she warmly defends CORNEILLE, ROUSSEAU, RACINE, and VOLTAIRE.

KARL FYODOROVICH MEYER (KARL FYODORYCH). A German who comes to Russia to pursue a career in ballet, but who dances so poorly that he becomes only an extra. He becomes attached to YEFIMOV, and the two enjoy commiserating with each other about being unrecognized talents and enduring a sad fate. He often comes to YEFIMOV's lodgings to dance and get the family's opinion, but his sensitive nature is usually crushed by YEFIMOV, who besmirches him and the art of ballet. It is noteworthy that the name KARL MEYER also appears in *History of the Village of Goryukhino (Istoria sela Goryukhina)* by Aleksandr Sergeevich Pushkin (1799-1837). Pushkin's Karl Meyer is the director of a school.

MOTHER [MATUSHKA]. NETOCHKA's mother, an unhappy woman who out of poverty had married an old clerk. She later marries YEFIMOV out of love, but quickly recognizes that he has married her for money. She then takes any kind of work she can get to support the family. The hard work damages her already delicate health, but after several years of suffering she still loves YEFIMOV and shows him every consideration. On the evening that YEFIMOV attends S—TS' concert and seals his fate, she dies alone, very worried about what will happen to NETOCHKA.

NASTYA. The nurse in PRINCE KH—Y's household.

NATALYA. An old woman who accompanies NETOCHKA to her music lessons.

NETOCHKA. See ANNA NEZVANOVA.

ANNA NEZVANOVA (NETOCHKA, ANNETA). YEFIMOV's step-daughter. Her recollections of life center on her love for and defense of YEFIMOV. She later realizes that this love was pity and an almost motherly feeling. YEFIMOV uses her feelings to get her to steal some money from her MOTHER so that he can attend S—TS' concert. When the theft is discovered, she remains silent to protect him. After her MOTHER dies, she leaves with YEFIMOV. When he flees from her, she chases him, falls unconscious, and awakes in PRINCE KH—Y's home, where a new life begins, consonant with her childhood fantasies of wealth and a large house. She is very ill and nervous, and a home concert by S—TS prompts her to imagine him as YEFIMOV's murderer and sends her into another lengthy period of illness. When she meets KATYA, she wants nothing more than to please her and be friends. She is hurt when KATYA's pride initially prevents their closeness, but her devotion to and love for KATYA remain constant. When KATYA takes FALSTAFF into PRINCESS KH—AYA's apartments, NETOCHKA assumes responsibility and guilt, and the two become fast friends. SASHA's illness prompts KATYA and her mother to go to Moscow and thus separates the girls, and NETOCHKA goes to live with ALEKSANDRA MIKHAYLOVNA, who takes NETOCHKA's development into her own hands and encourages discovery and learning. Much learning takes place secretly after NETOCHKA finds a key to PYOTR ALEKSANDROVICH's library, and she avidly reads books, particularly novels. One day she discovers a farewell love letter from S.O. to ALEKSANDRA MIKHAYLOVNA in one of the books and comes to understand ALEKSANDRA MIKHAYLOVNA's constant and unconcealed suffering. PYOTR ALEKSANDROVICH finds her with the letter and becomes furious, and NETOCHKA in order to divert his attention invents an affair of her own. Following a heated exchange between husband and wife, NETOCHKA bitterly denounces PYOTR ALEKSANDRO-VICH for his motives and actions.

S.O. NETOCHKA finds a farewell love letter from S.O. to ALEK-SANDRA MIKHAYLOVNA, in which is expressed her hopeless attempt to raise S.O. to her level and the suffering she endures because of him. The point is made that they are sinless before PYOTR ALEKSANDROVICH, and the note concludes with S.O.'s praising her innocence and the purity of her intentions. See OVROV.

OVROV. PRINCE KH—Y's representative from Moscow, who comes to stay with PYOTR ALEKSANDROVICH. Immediately after NETOCH-KA attacks PYOTR ALEKSANDROVICH for his treatment of ALEK-SANDRA MIKHAYLOVNA, OVROV asks to speak with her. The proximity of scenes and the fact that OVROV's name begins with "o" suggests the possibility that he may be the author of the note.

PYOTR ALEKSANDROVICH. ALEKSANDRA MIKHAYLOVNA's husband, who maintains a strained relationship with her because of her past indiscretions. He affects sullenness and moral superiority, both results of his vanity and jealous egotism. His finding NETOCHKA with the love letter from S.O. to his wife brings the situation to a focus and exposes his vain resentment of his wife. After his wife's tears and defense of NETOCHKA, NETOCHKA accosts him in his den, and showing him the contents of the letter, berates his conduct to his wife and exposes his motives.

RACINE [RASIN]. Jean RACINE (1639-99), French classical dramatist. A favorite writer of MADAME LEOTARD, whom she actively defends.

JEAN JACQUES ROUSSEAU [ZHAN-ZHAK RUSSO]. French philosopher, social reformer, and writer (1712-78), who exerted the pivotal influence on the developing romantic sensibility. PRINCE KH—Y's uncomplimentary reference to ROUSSEAU draws a warm retort from MADAME LEOTARD, who is always willing to defend her favorites.

RUBICON [RUBIKON]. The small river separating ancient Italy from the province allocated to Julius Caesar. When Caesar crossed the river with his army, against the orders of Pompey and the senate, an irreversible step had been taken. KATYA arranges to have FALSTAFF cross the RUBICON into PRINCESS KH—AYA's apartments, an area totally forbidden to the dog.

S—TS. A visiting French concert violinist, whose concert YEFIMOV begs and literally steals to be able to attend. The concert proves to be the demise of YEFIMOV, who realizes that he is not the great violinist that he thinks he is. When an ill NETOCHKA sees his concert at PRINCE KH—Y's, she thinks that S—TS is her father's murderer and lapses into another illness.

ST. RONAN'S WELL [SEN-RONANSKIE VODY]. A novel written by Sir WALTER SCOTT in 1823. The novel tells of the attempts of an illegitimate imposter to marry Clara Mawbray for her fortune. *ST. RONAN'S WELL* is the only book by SCOTT in PYOTR ALEK-SANDROVICH's library which NETOCHKA has not read. In it she finds the love letter from S.O. to ALEKSANDRA MIKHAYLOVNA.

SASHA. See ALEKSANDR.

Sir WALTER SCOTT [VALTER SKOTT]. English historical novelist (1771-1832). As part of her education NETOCHKA reads SCOTT's novels *IVANHOE* and *ST. RONAN'S WELL.*

SODOM. As recorded in Genesis 18-19 of the Old Testament, a city which together with Gomorrah was destroyed by Jehovah because of its wickedness. The term has come to mean wickedness and chaos. When MADAME LEOTARD discovers that she has left NETOCHKA in a cold room all night, there is a great bustle of confusion to get her out, a veritable SODOM.

THERSITES [FERSIT]. A physically deformed, foul-mouthed character in Homer's *Iliad.* The narrator compares YEFIMOV to THERSITES.

VOLTAIRE [VOLTER]. Pen name of François Marie Arouet (1694-1778), noted French satirist, philosopher, and historian. He is a favorite of MADAME LEOTARD that she actively defends.

YEGOR PETROVICH YEFIMOV (YEGOR, YEGORKA, YEGORUSH-KA). NETOCHKA's stepfather. As a young man he becomes friends with a roguish Italian musician whose mysterious death bequeaths to YEFIMOV a violin. He becomes totally obsessed with the instrument, wants to become famous and has illusions of grandeur. He claims that the very devil has hold of him through the Italian, the violin, and music. He attaches himself to the German violinist B. but succumbs to apathy, vice, pride, and drunkenness. Even though he marries NETOCHKA's MOTHER for money, he remains destitute and tells all who will listen that his marriage has ruined his talent and that he will never play again until his wife dies. He enjoys tormenting her and takes all of the money she makes. B. locates him a job but his pretentious and unbearable behavior alienates everyone, and he gains the reputation of a mindless buffoon. He comes to think that he is talented but persecuted by fate and intrigues, and in this he shares moments with KARL FYODORYCH, an equally frustrated and incompetent dancer. Hearing of an upcoming concert by the renowned violinst S—TS, he has NETOCHKA try to steal money from her MOTHER so that he can go. He is finally given a ticket by PRINCE KH—Y and B., but returns from the concert pale and shattered in his fantasies that he is a capable violinist. He finds his wife dead in bed and plays a grotesque dirge over her body on a violin that emits only moans and anguish. He leaves with NETOCHKA, but flees from her in a fit of derangement. He is taken to the hospital, where he dies under the influence of the devastating truth learned at the concert.

YEGOR. See YEGOR PETROVICH YEFIMOV.

YEGORKA. See YEGOR PETROVICH YEFIMOV.

YEGORUSHKA. See YEGOR PETROVICH YEFIMOV.

THE LITTLE HERO (MALENKY GEROY) 1857

BAAL [VAAL]. A Semitic term for lord or possessor that became localized for several deities, most notably the Canaanite BAAL and Babylonian Bel. The narrator notes that such people as MONSIEUR M. are so vain as to consider themselves BAAL or MOLOCH.

BEATRICE [BEATRICHE]. Heroine of William SHAKESPEARE's *MUCH ADO ABOUT NOTHING*. Despite renouncing all men, she is ultimately united with BENEDICK, with whom she had previously engaged in a constant battle of wit and repartee. The relationship of THE BLONDE and THE YOUNG MAN is turbulent, and she is referred to as BEATRICE.

BENEDICK [BENEDIKT]. The self-assured and witty nobleman of William SHAKESPEARE's *MUCH ADO ABOUT NOTHING*. Despite renouncing women, he is ultimately united with BEATRICE, with whom he had previously engaged in a constant battle of wit and repartee. The relationship of THE BLONDE and THE YOUNG MAN is turbulent, and he is referred to as BENEDICK.

THE BLONDE [BLONDINKA]. A spoiled young beauty, worshipped by her husband as an idol. Attending an extended holiday on T—V's estate, she engages in witty battles and sarcastic repartee with THE YOUNG MAN, MONSIEUR M., and even THE LITTLE HERO, whom she catches admiring her beautiful shoulders. Her tongue is sharp and is a reflection of her vanity and will. She ultimately makes peace with THE LITTLE HERO following his harrowing ride on TANCRED and becomes quite solicitous of him.

BLUEBEARD [SINYAYA BORODA]. The villain of *Barbe-bleue (BLUE-BEARD),* written in 1697 by Charles Perrault (1628-1703). He murders his wives when they disobey his orders not to open a door, behind which, unbeknownst to them, are the bodies of previous wives. In their sarcastic exchange it seems that THE BLONDE's intent is to make MONSIEUR M. appear as BLUEBEARD.

DELORGES [DELORZH]. Knightly hero of "Der Handschuh" ("The Glove"), a ballad written by Friedrich Schiller (1759-1805) in 1797. THE LITTLE HERO is called DELORGES and TOGENBURG after his brave and harrowing ride on TANCRED.

FALSTAFF. Sir John FALSTAFF, comic character in William SHAKE-SPEARE's *Henry IV, Parts One and Two* (1597-98) and *The Merry Wives of Windsor* (1597-1601), who is characterized by self-indulgence, braggadocio, buffoonery, and vice. MONSIEUR M. is compared by the narrator to both FALSTAFF and TARTUFFE.

ILYA MUROMETS. One of the knightly heroes of the Russian folk epos. T—V notes that TANCRED is so hard to ride that the only appropriate rider would be ILYA MUROMETS.

THE LITTLE HERO [MALENKY GEROY]. An eleven year old boy who is sent to T—V's estate for an extended holiday and who narrates the tale. He becomes enchanted by a beautiful BLONDE with whom he comes into conflict when she finds him admiring her shoulders. THE BLONDE draws him into her sarcastic verbal games with MONSIEUR M. and THE YOUNG MAN, and she embarrasses him by announcing that he is in love with MADAME M. When THE BLONDE insults everyone for failure to ride TANCRED, he leaps upon the horse in a chivalric gesture to defend MADAME M. His harrowing ride earns the admiration of all, and he is dubbed a knight and a hero and called DELORGES and TOGENBURG. His final act of chivalry occurs when he finds and returns a farewell love letter from N—OY to MADAME M. He places the note in a bouquet and feigns sleep so that MADAME M. can take it. The new feelings of embarrassment and empathy that he feels for himself and others help him to grow up.

MADAME M. (NATALIE). THE BLONDE's cousin and the wife of MONSIEUR M. She is a sensitive, meek, loving person who is very ill at ease around her husband, partially because she is in love with N—OY. She is distraught when she loses N—OY's farewell love letter, and is greatly relieved when THE LITTLE HERO chivalrously makes it available to her in a bouquet. After reading the letter, she seems happily reconciled to her fate.

MONSIEUR M. The jealous and proud husband of MADAME M. He is extremely vain, is fond of expressing great sympathy for mankind, and enjoys speculating upon the proper course of philanthropy. He indulges in an ego-produced war of words and wit with THE BLONDE and is thoroughly exposed.

MOLOCH [MOLOKH]. The name of a Canaanite deity to whom first-born children were sacrificed. The narrator notes that such people as

MONSIEUR M. are so vain as to consider themselves BAAL or MO-
LOCH.

*MUCH ADO ABOUT NOTHING [MNOGO SHUMA IZ PUSTYA-
KOV].* A comedy written by William SHAKESPEARE about 1598 which
portrays the war between, and ultimate reconciliation of, the sexes. The
narrator comments that the exchanges between THE BLONDE and THE
YOUNG MAN are similar to those of BEATRICE and BENEDICK in
MUCH ADO ABOUT NOTHING.

N—OY. A guest at the T—V estate who is having a love affair with
MADAME M. It is his farewell love letter that THE LITTLE HERO
returns to a grateful MADAME M.

NATALIE. See MADAME M.

R. A noted artist who is directing the theatrical production at T—V's estate.

SCRIBE [SKRIB]. Augustin Eugène SCRIBE (1791-1861), prolific French
writer of spirited, farcical plays. The play presented on T—V's estate during
the holiday is one of SCRIBE's comedies.

SHAKESPEARE [SHEKSPIR]. William SHAKESPEARE (1564-1616),
the most eminent of English dramatists. He is mentioned as the writer of
MUCH ADO ABOUT NOTHING, in which the exchanges between
BEATRICE and BENEDICK are compared to those between THE
BLONDE and THE YOUNG MAN.

T—V. A relative of THE LITTLE HERO who invites him to an extended
holiday in the country. He is a veteran of the hussars who keeps TANCRED
to recall past exploits.

TANCRED [TANKRED]. T—V's as yet unbroken horse, which is named
for a Norman soldier and crusader (d. 1112). THE BLONDE's sarcastic
remarks about people's being afraid to ride TANCRED and her allusions to
THE LITTLE HERO's being in love with MADAME M. prompt the boy
to ride the horse. The hectic ride earns for THE LITTLE HERO the
admiration of all.

TARTUFFE [TARTYUF]. Central character of a comedy of the same
name written by Molière (1622-73) in 1664. He is characterized by scheming
and religious hypocrisy. MONSIEUR M. is compared by the narrator to
both FALSTAFF and TARTUFFE.

"THEY SOW NOT, NEITHER DO THEY REAP" ["NE ZHNUT I NE SEYUT"]. A partial rendering of Matthew 6:26 in the New Testament in which Jesus admonishes His followers to take no concern for their lives, food, or clothing. Jesus uses the birds as an example of those who are fed by God even though "THEY SOW NOT, NEITHER DO THEY REAP." As THE LITTLE HERO enjoys nature and prepares a bouquet in which to return the note from N—OY to MADAME M., he is entertained by a concert of birds, which he terms those who "SOW NOT, NEITHER DO THEY REAP."

TOGENBURG. The hero of a ballad "Ritter TOGENBURG" ("The Knight TOGENBURG"), written by Friedrich Schiller (1759-1805) in 1797. THE LITTLE HERO is called DELORGES and TOGENBURG after his brave and harrowing ride on TANCRED.

THE YOUNG MAN [MOLODOY CHELOVEK]. A guest on T—V's estate who is in love with THE BLONDE. Their exchanges are full of sarcasm, usually originating with THE BLONDE. When he cannot bring himself to mount TANCRED to accompany THE BLONDE, she hurls sarcastic abuse at him and offers him her horse. THE LITTLE HERO's riding the horse brings the verbal punishment of THE YOUNG MAN to a temporary halt.

UNCLE'S DREAM (DYADYUSHKIN SON) 1859

AFANASY MATVEICH. See AFANASY MATVEICH MOSKALYOV.

AGLAYA MIKHAYLOVNA. MOZGLYAKOV's aunt.

AKULINA PANFILOVNA. A friend to whom FARPUKHINA hurries to share her gossip.

ALHAMBRA [ALGAMBRA]. A palace and fortress built by Moorish kings at Granada, Spain, in the thirteenth century. When MARYA ALEKSANDROVNA tries to persuade ZINA to marry PRINCE K., she notes that with the prince's money ZINA could send her sickly lover VASYA to the ALHAMBRA.

ANNA MATVEEVNA. PRINCE K., who has difficulty remembering names, refers to ANNA NIKOLAEVNA ANTIPOVA as ANNA MATVEEVNA.

ANNA NIKOLAEVNA. PRINCE K., who has difficulty remembering names, refers to MARYA ALEKSANDROVNA MOSKALYOVA as ANNA NIKOLAEVNA. This is particularly galling to MARYA ALEKSANDROVNA since she and ANNA NIKOLAEVNA are mortal enemies.

ANNA NIKOLAEVNA. See ANNA NIKOLAEVNA ANTIPOVA.

ANNA VASILIEVNA. PRINCE K., who has difficulty remembering names, refers to ANNA NIKOLAEVNA ANTIPOVA as ANNA VASILIEVNA.

NIKOLAY VASILIEVICH ANTIPOV. Husband of ANNA NIKOLAEVNA ANTIPOVA.

ANNA NIKOLAEVNA ANTIPOVA. A local socialite who competes with her sworn enemies, MARYA ALEKSANDROVNA and NATALYA DMITRIEVNA, for social supremacy. After MARYA ALEKSANDROVNA's embarrassment over PRINCE K.'s retracted proposal to her daughter ZINA and her subsequent loss of prestige, ANNA NIKOLAEVNA and NATALYA DMITRIEVNA become fast friends.

ANTIPOVNA. PRINCE K., who has trouble remembering names, refers to MARYA ALEKSANDROVNA as ANTIPOVNA. This upsets her because ANNA NIKOLAEVNA ANTIPOVA is her sworn enemy.

ANYUTKA. One of ANNA NIKOLAEVNA's servants, who is sent to MARYA ALEKSANDROVNA's house to inquire about PRINCE K.

ATHANASE. MARYA ALEKSANDROVNA refers to her husband AFANASY MATVEICH with the French ATHANASE.

BEETHOVEN [BETKHOVEN]. Ludwig van BEETHOVEN (1770-1827), eminent German composer noted primarily for his symphonies. PRINCE K. claims that he was acquainted with BEETHOVEN abroad, but then wonders if it might have been another German.

BORODUEV. MOZGLYAKOV's godfather. He rescued MOZGLYAKOV's late father from financial ruin after he had gambled away government money.

BUMSTEIN [BUMSHTEYN]. When ZYABLOVA offers to retrieve ZINA's love letter for money, MARYA ALEKSANDROVNA pawns her clasp with BUMSTEIN to get the needed two hundred rubles.

LORD BYRON [LORD BAYRON]. George Gordon BYRON (1788-1824), English romantic poet who created the "Byronic Hero," a defiant, brooding young man obsessed by some mysterious past sin. PRINCE K. insists that he remembers BYRON well, that they were good friends, and that BYRON danced at the CONGRESS OF VIENNA.

CASANOVA [KAZANOVA]. Giacomo Girolamo CASANOVA de Seingalt (1725-98), Italian adventurer who, after being expelled from a seminary, led a scandalous life as a charlatan and lover. PRINCE K. asks MOZGLYAKOV if he has read CASANOVA's *MEMOIRES*.

CONGRESS OF VIENNA [VENSKY KONGRESS]. A congress held in 1814-15 by European powers after Napoleon I's first abdication in order to resolve national boundaries. PRINCE K. claims that LORD BYRON danced at the CONGRESS OF VIENNA, but subsequently decides that it was rather a Pole, who, though a cook, passed himself off as a count.

DUMAS [DYUMA]. Alexandre DUMAS (1802-70), known as DUMAS père, French novelist and dramatist whose prolific output popularized melodramatic historical romances. When PRINCE K. insists that his proposal to ZINA was only a dream, MARYA ALEKSANDROVNA, very upset, asks him if he is trying to act like one of the French court fops as portrayed in the novels of DUMAS.

SOFYA PETROVNA FARPUKHINA. An evil-tempered, vengeful scandalmonger of fifty, who has been excluded from the homes of ANNA NIKOLAEVNA and NATALYA DMITRIEVNA. She naturally gravitates to their enemy MARYA ALEKSANDROVNA, whom she keeps informed about the efforts of the other two women to gain the favors of PRINCE K. When PRINCE K. tries to extricate himself from his proposal to ZINA by insisting that it was a dream, FARPUKHINA exposes all of the involved intrigues and machinations as made known to her by ZYABLOVA.

FATHERLAND NOTES [OTECHESTVENNYE ZAPISKI]. Literary and political monthly published in St. Petersburg 1839-84. It contained some of the best literature of the day and advocated progressive social ideas, but was forcibly closed because of too liberal editorial policies. VASYA dreams of publishing the greatest poem in the world in *FATHERLAND NOTES*.

FELISATA MIKHAYLOVNA. Attends the social gathering at which MARYA ALEKSANDROVNA makes public PRINCE K.'s proposal to ZINA and PRINCE K. insists that it was only a dream.

FELISATA YAKOVLEVNA. PRINCE K., who has difficulty remembering names, refers to FELISATA MIKHAYLOVNA as FELISATA YAKOVLEVNA.

FEOFIL. PRINCE K.'s coachman, who overturns the carriage on the way to visit MISAIL. PRINCE K. upbraids him for wanting to take his life but later decides to forgive him.

FERLAKUR. Proper name manufactured from the French expression "faire la cour," to pay court to someone. When PRINCE K. insists that his proposal to ZINA was only a dream, MARYA ALEKSANDROVNA angrily asks him if he is trying to act like some kind of FERLAKUR.

FET. Afanasy Afanasievich FET (1820-92), Russian lyric poet noted for his melodic verse on love and nature. MOZGLYAKOV describes a sunset in rather pedestrian terms, but vainly finds in his words something elegaic and much like FET.

FLORIAN. Jean Pierre Claris de FLORIAN (1755-94), French writer best known for his positive, although bland fables. MARYA ALEKSANDROVNA strongly objects to ZINA's intent to marry VASYA and states that such an idea is worthy only of FLORIAN and his romantic shepherds and shepherdesses.

FONVIZIN. Denis Ivanovich FONVIZIN (1745-92), Russian satirical dramatist, who exposed the boorish mores of the semieducated gentry. MARYA ALEKSANDROVNA flatters PRINCE K. by telling him that he should become a writer and promises that he would become another FONVIZIN, GOGOL, or GRIBOEDOV. The statement is ironic, since a new FONVIZIN would describe people like MARYA ALEKSANDROVNA.

PRINCE GAVRILA. See PRINCE K.

GOGOL. Nikolay Vasilievich GOGOL (1809-52), popular Russian writer noted for his tragicomic exposing of human foibles. He was viewed by progressive critics as the fountainhead of the Natural School and credited with critically describing reality with the intent of social reform. MARYA ALEKSANDROVNA flatters PRINCE K. by encouraging him to become a writer and promising that he would become another FONVIZIN, GOGOL, or GRIBOEDOV. The irony is that she would likely find herself depicted in the work of a new GOGOL.

GRIBOEDOV. Aleksandr Sergeevich GRIBOEDOV (1795-1829), Russian dramatist known for his satirical masterpiece *Woe From Wit (Gore ot uma),* which exposed the foibles of the semieducated gentry. MARYA ALEK-SANDROVNA flatters PRINCE K. by encouraging him to become a writer and promising that he would become another FONVIZIN, GOGOL, or GRIBOEDOV. Ironically, she herself would likely be a target for GRIBOEDOV.

MADAME GRIBUSIE. Ironic manufactured name from *grib* (mushroom) connoting an old hag. ZYABLOVA notes that she has let herself go, has lost all imagination and ambition, and now resembles a MADAME GRI-BUSIE.

GRISHKA. One of the servants who attends AFANASY MATVEICH in his exile in the country.

HEINE [GEYNE]. Heinrich HEINE (1797-1856), German romantic poet, journalist, and satirist. As MOZGLYAKOV relates his experience of finding PRINCE K.'s overturned carriage, he notes that he was about to pass by the scene but adds that humanitarianism, which sticks its nose everywhere, prompts him to investigate. He comically attributes this definition of humanitarianism to HEINE.

THE HUSBAND COMES IN THE DOOR, AND THE WIFE GOES TO TVER [MUZH V DVER, A ZHENA V TVER]. A vaudeville by the anonymous A.I.V. which first appeared in St. Petersburg in 1845. When PRINCE K. discovers that MARYA ALEKSANDROVNA and AFAN-ASY MATVEICH live apart, he recalls this vaudeville with the help of MOZGLYAKOV.

HYDRA [GIDRA]. A multiheaded monstrous serpent of Greek myth-ology. MARYA ALEKSANDROVNA views her plight—PRINCE K.'s assertion that his proposal to ZINA is only a dream and the resultant delight of the women of Mordasov—as a HYDRA which she must attack forcefully. Her best machinations fail, however, and she and her family leave Mordasov.

IVAN IVANOVICH. MARYA ALEKSANDROVNA's attorney.

IVAN PAKHOMYCH. PRINCE K.'s valet, who is in charge of his elaborate toilet.

MADAME JARNY [ZHARNI]. FARPUKHINA mentions that she graduated from a very proper school directed by MADAME JARNY. She adds that the dances she did there were always proper, unlike those which NATALYA DMITRIEVNA makes SONECHKA and MASHKA perform for PRINCE K.

JESUIT [IEZUIT]. The Society of Jesus, a religious order for Roman Catholic men founded by Ignatius Loyola (1491-1556) in 1534. The society is known for scholarship and missionary zeal and has been accused of secrecy and intrigue. ZINA feels that her mother MARYA ALEKSANDROVNA intrigues like a JESUIT in the scheme to marry her to PRINCE K.

PRINCE GAVRILA K. A senile gentleman, good at heart, but with some substantial eccentricities. Age has not been particularly kind to him, and he needs to be carefully assembled every day: wig, wooden leg, glass eye, etc. This necessitates a long and elaborate toilet. Because of a sudden inheritance, he is beset both by ladies who profess to find him enchanting and heirs who consider putting him in an asylum because of his senility and because they fear that he will spend all of the money. These factors drive him to live a virtual hermit's life, watched over by STEPANIDA MATVEEVNA, who has total run of his estate. On one occasion when she is away he determines to visit a clergyman friend MISAIL, but the journey is marred when his carriage overturns, and he finds himself taken by MOZGLYAKOV to the home of MARYA ALEKSANDROVNA. There he exhibits his personality, found charming by all of the ladies: he has trouble remembering names, reminisces about everything from LORD BYRON to the CONGRESS OF VIENNA, and talks in detail about his hemorrhoids. MARYA ALEKSANDROVNA successfully extracts a proposal from PRINCE K. to her daughter ZINA so that she may share in the fortune. PRINCE K. realizes that he cannot marry and allows MOZGLYAKOV, who has designs on ZINA himself, to convince him that the proposal was only a dream. When he maintains that it was a dream at the announcement party, a terrible furor begins, and several women denounce him, making allusions to his weak mentality and false parts. MOZGLYAKOV then removes him to a hotel, where he dies three days later.

KALLIST STANISLAVICH. An acquaintance of MARYA ALEKSAN-DROVNA, from whom she obtains information about VASYA.

KANT. Immanuel KANT (1724-1804), German philosopher who attempted to define the limits of rational understanding. PRINCE K. likens his pompous and sometimes verbose servant TERENTY to KANT.

KATERINA PETROVNA. One of the women who comes to the home of MARYA ALEKSANDROVNA to see PRINCE K. and hear of the proposal.

KUROCHKIN. FARPUKHINA notes that KUROCHKIN once courted her.

LAUZUN [LOZYON]. Antonin de LAUZUN (1633-1723), French social and political leader. He was a favorite of Louis XIV and was noted for his amorous exploits. MARYA ALEKSANDROVNA, in trying to convince PRINCE K. that his proposal to the much younger ZINA will be accepted, cites the example of LAUZUN as an older man who won the hearts of younger women.

LAVRENTY. One of PRINCE K.'s servants, who is comically accused of having designs on his life.

LIBRARY FOR READING [BIBLIOTEKA DLYA CHTENIYA]. St. Petersburg monthly, published 1834-65 under the editorship of Osip Ivanovich Senkovsky (1800-58). In trying to show ZINA that VASYA is unworthy of her, MARYA ALEKSANDROVNA refers to his wretched verse that *LIBRARY FOR READING* publishes out of pity.

LOUISA [LUIZA] KARLOVNA. One of the women who comes to the home of MARYA ALEKSANDROVNA to see PRINCE K. and hear of the proposal to ZINA.

MARYA. Heroine of "Poltava," a narrative poem written by Aleksandr Sergeevich Pushkin (1799-1837) in 1829. The work chronicles Peter the Great's defeat of Sweden's King Charles XII and the love of MARYA for the much older Cossack hetman MAZEPA. MARYA ALEKSANDROV-

NA, in trying to convince PRINCE K. that his proposal to the much younger ZINA will be accepted, cites the example of MARYA, who fell in love with the older MAZEPA.

MARYA ALEKSANDROVNA. See MARYA ALEKSANDROVNA MOSKALYOVA.

MASHKA. An orphan in the home of NATALYA DMITRIEVNA. NATALYA DMITRIEVNA forces MASHKA and her own daughter SONECHKA to dance in short skirts, using a lot of kicking, in front of PRINCE K. in hope of winning him over.

MATRYOSHKA. A servant of FELISATA MIKHAYLOVNA.

MAZEPA. Ivan MAZEPA (1644-1709), Cossack hetman who deserted Peter the Great to fight for Sweden's King Charles XII. He is a main figure in "Poltava," a narrative poem written by Aleksandr Sergeevich Pushkin (1799-1837) in 1829. See MARYA.

MEMOIRES [MEMUARY]. *MEMOIRES de Jacques CASANOVA de Seingalt, écrits par lui-même (The MEMOIRS of Jacques CASANOVA de Seingalt Written by Himself)*, a work of twelve volumes published between 1826 and 1838. PRINCE K. asks MOZGLYAKOV if he has read the *MEMOIRES*, the record of CASANOVA's licentious exploits.

MEMOIRES DU DIABLE. Les *MEMOIRES DU DIABLE (MEMOIRS of a Devil)*, an adventure novel written by Melchior Frédéric Soulié (1800-47) in 1838. MARYA ALEKSANDROVNA expects scandals in society in general and in the marriage of PRINCE K. to ZINA in particular, but she hopes that the scandals will be grandiose, such as those found in *MEMOIRES DU DIABLE* and *MONTE CRISTO*.

MISAIL. A clergyman friend of PRINCE K. PRINCE K. is journeying to see him when his carriage overturns. The mishap results in his being rescued by MOZGLYAKOV, whisked off to MARYA ALEKSANDROVNA's, and involved in an intrigue to get him to marry ZINA.

MITYA. See MITYA MOSKALYOV.

MONTE CRISTO [MONTE-KRISTO]. Le *Comte de MONTE CRISTO (The Count of MONTE CRISTO)*, a romantic novel written by Alexandre DUMAS père in 1844 that chronicles the false imprisonment, escape, and revenge of Edmond Dantès. See *MEMOIRES DU DIABLE*.

AFANASY MATVEICH MOSKALYOV (ATHANASE). The intimidated husband of MARYA ALEKSANDROVNA. He has just been deprived of his job by a government inspector who cites his general inability and mental deficiency. Since MARYA ALEKSANDROVNA married him for his money, his unemployment results in a quick exile out of Mordasov into the country. He is summoned by his wife only to invite PRINCE K. to the country and is then dismissed. After PRINCE K. extricates himself from the proposal to ZINA and MARYA ALEKSANDROVNA loses her place of dominance in Mordasov society, the entire MOSKALYOV family leaves. Sometime later after ZINA's marriage, MARYA ALEKSANDROVNA lives with her son-in-law, but there is no mention of AFANASY MATVEICH, who has probably been abandoned.

MITYA MOSKALYOV. MARYA ALEKSANDROVNA's deceased son, for whom VASYA was engaged as a teacher.

MARYA ALEKSANDROVNA MOSKALYOVA. The first lady of Mordasov society and the worst scandalmonger in town. She dominates others, and irrespective of events has managed to maintain her position. She marries AFANASY MATVEICH largely for his income, and when he loses his job, she dispatches him to separate quarters in the country. She competes with the other women in town for the attention of PRINCE K., and after rejecting MOZGLYAKOV's suggestion that PRINCE K. be married to ZYABLOVA, determines to marry him to her own daughter ZINA. To do this she placates MOZGLYAKOV, who wants to marry ZINA himself, with promises that he can have ZINA after PRINCE K. dies and convinces ZINA that with PRINCE K.'s money she could perhaps restore the health of VASYA, the young teacher she is in love with. She also insists that a match with VASYA would be totally beneath ZINA. To cover up their relations as best she can she pays ZYABLOVA to recover a love letter from ZINA to VASYA, which is in circulation among her enemies. She manipulates PRINCE K. by having ZINA sing for him and then flattering him into a proposal. PRINCE K. ultimately frees himself from the proposal by claiming that it was a dream, whereupon FARPUKHINA exposes the intrigue to all, including MARYA ALEKSANDROVNA's enemies. A lusty row ensues, and MARYA ALEKSANDROVNA's position of dominance in Mordasov society is forever shattered. The whole family leaves, and MARYA ALEKSANDROVNA ultimately comes to live with ZINA and her new husband, likely having abandoned AFANASY MATVEICH along the way.

ZINAIDA MOSKALYOVA. See ZINAIDA AFANASIEVNA MOSKALYOVA.

ZINAIDA AFANASIEVNA MOSKALYOVA (ZINA, ZINOCHKA).
MARYA ALEKSANDROVNA's pretty, well-educated, and independent daughter, who at twenty three is still not married, largely because of rumors circulating about her relationship with VASYA, the tutor of her late brother MITYA. Her romantic nature had resulted in a romance with the poor teacher, and she promises never to marry anyone else despite MARYA ALEKSANDROVNA's protestations. Overcoming strong moral objections on ZINA's part, MARYA ALEKSANDROVNA convinces her to orchestrate and accept a proposal from PRINCE K. She is swayed principally by MARYA ALEKSANDROVNA's suggestions that she could use PRINCE K.'s money to better VASYA's health. When the intrigues and scandal become too sordid, ZINA admits everything and then escapes to VASYA, who is terminally ill with self-induced consumption. They talk of his romantic foolishness, and she renews her pledge never to marry. After the family moves, ZINA marries a wealthy general, who becomes a governor. She becomes proud and haughty and dances only with generals.

PAVEL ALEKSANDROVICH MOZGLYAKOV (PAUL, POL). A very distant relative of PRINCE K. who refers to him as uncle. He is a pretentious dandy of twenty five whose modern ideas are funneled through an inadequate mind and expressed with inappropriate verbosity. When he finds PRINCE K.'s carriage overturned, he delivers his uncle to MARYA ALEKSANDROVNA, proposes to ZINA, and suggests that the prince be married to ZYABLOVA. With ZYABLOVA's help he eavesdrops on MARYA ALEKSANDROVNA's intrigues with ZINA and is placated only by promises of future marriage to ZINA. His contentment is short-lived, however, as he ponders the realities of the situation, and after being attacked by dogs, he becomes bent on doing something rash. He convinces PRINCE K. that his proposal was only a dream, but during the ensuing scandal he admits his baseness to everyone. Following PRINCE K.'s death he renews his proposal to ZINA but insists that they would have to be married secretly and immediately leave town. He is quickly rebuffed and leaves for St. Petersburg, where he experiences still further failures in matrimony and career.

COUNTESS NAINSKAYA. PRINCE K. cites her as the only one who could rival ZINA in beauty, and comically adds that she married her French cook and died thirty years ago.

NAPOLEON (NAPOLEON BONAPARTE). NAPOLEON I BONAPARTE (1769-1821), emperor of France following the French Revolution and temporary conqueror of much of Europe. (1) MARYA ALEKSAN-

DROVNA is compared by her enemies to NAPOLEON. The narrator notes that NAPOLEON became a bit giddy when he assumed power and that the supporters of the deposed monarchy attributed this to the fact that NAPOLEON was not of high birth. MARYA ALEKSANDROVNA experiences no such giddiness in her high place, however. (2) PRINCE K. mentions that some people think that he looks like NAPOLEON BONA-PARTE.

NASTASYA PETROVNA. See NASTASYA PETROVNA ZYABLOVA.

NASTASYA VASILIEVNA. PRINCE K., who has difficulty remembering names, mistakenly refers to MARYA ALEKSANDROVNA as NASTASYA VASILIEVNA.

NATALYA DMITRIEVNA. See NATALYA DMITRIEVNA PASKUDINA.

NATASHKA. FARPUKHINA irreverently refers to NATALYA DMITRIEVNA as NATASHKA, partially because she has been excluded from her home.

NIKITA. MARYA ALEKSANDROVNA's cook.

THE NORTHERN BEE [SEVERNAYA PCHELA]. A conservative St. Petersburg newspaper published 1825-64 by Faddey Venediktovich Bulgarin (1789-1859) and Nikolay Ivanovich Grech (1787-1867). The narrator states that he admires MARYA ALEKSANDROVNA a great deal and wants to write a panegyric to her in the form of a letter to a friend, according to the models that were published in newspapers like *THE NORTHERN BEE*. The models in question were feuilletons written by Bulgarin and Grech.

NATALYA DMITRIEVNA PASKUDINA (NATASHKA). One of MARYA ALEKSANDROVNA's mortal enemies. She has her own designs on PRINCE K. and has her daughter SONECHKA and an orphan MASHKA dance for him in short skirts with a lot of kicking. After MARYA ALEKSANDROVNA's demise, she becomes fast friends with ANNA NIKOLAEVNA, another former enemy.

SONECHKA PASKUDINA (SONKA). NATALYA DMITRIEVNA's fifteen year old daughter, who is made to dance an immoral dance in a short skirt in front of PRINCE K. to further her mother's designs.

PAUL. See PAVEL ALEKSANDROVICH MOZGLYAKOV.

PAVEL ALEKSANDROVICH. See PAVEL ALEKSANDROVICH MOZGLYAKOV.

PINETTI. Italian magician popular in Europe in the eighteenth century. The narrator compares MARYA ALEKSANDROVNA to PINETTI because of her skill in intrigue.

POL. See PAVEL ALEKSANDROVICH MOZGLYAKOV.

PRASKOVYA ILYINISHNA. One of the women who comes to MARYA ALEKSANDROVNA's home to see PRINCE K. and hear of the proposal.

PRINCE PYOTR DEMENTYICH. PRINCE K. once played cards with him.

SEMYON. MOZGLYAKOV's coachman.

SHAKESPEARE [SHEKSPIR]. William SHAKESPEARE (1564-1616), the most eminent of English dramatists. MARYA ALEKSANDROVNA frequently uses SHAKESPEARE as a term of reproach: (1) she attributes MOZGLYAKOV's ridiculous new ideas, such as freeing the serfs, to his reading SHAKESPEARE; (2) she attributes the dreaminess and romanticism of ZINA, VASYA, and MOZGLYAKOV to SHAKESPEARE; (3) she attempts to show how limited VASYA's knowledge is by saying that he knows only SHAKESPEARE and that if ZINA married VASYA, all they would have to look forward to would be reading him; (4) she refers to VASYA as SHAKESPEARE and fears that he will suddenly appear and ruin her intrigues for ZINA's marriage to PRINCE K. On his deathbed VASYA bitterly recalls his wasted life of dreams and alludes to his reading SHAKESPEARE with ZINA.

PRINCE SHCHEPETILOV. A relative of PRINCE K. who comes to Mordasov following PRINCE K.'s death to see to final arrangements.

SIDOR. A former servant of PRINCE K. who escapes from him in Europe and becomes a dandy.

SOFRON. MARYA ALEKSANDROVNA's driver.

SOFYA PETROVNA. See SOFYA PETROVNA FARPUKHINA.

SONECHKA. See SONECHKA PASKUDINA.

SONKA. See SONECHKA PASKUDINA. FARPUKHINA refers to SONECHKA with the pejorative SONKA as she describes the dance that her mother forced her to perform in front of PRINCE K.

STEPANIDA MATVEEVNA. PRINCE K.'s confidante, who operates his estate and cares for him. When she goes to Moscow to see a sick friend, PRINCE K. becomes bored and leaves to visit MISAIL, thus beginning his adventure with MARYA ALEKSANDROVNA.

STRAUSS [SHTRAUS]. Johann STRAUSS (1825-99), Austrian composer and conductor noted for his waltzes. In trying to persuade MOZGLYAKOV to accede to the intrigue of marrying PRINCE K. to ZINA, MARYA ALEKSANDROVNA assures him that ZINA will be his in the future, and she paints the picture of their reunion at a ball to the accompaniment of music by STRAUSS.

SUSHILOV. MARYA ALEKSANDROVNA spreads the rumor that SUSHILOV visits ANNA NIKOLAEVNA continually.

TERENTY. PRINCE K.'s pompous and rather stupid servant.

VASENKA. See VASYA.

VASYA (VASENKA). A poor poet, hired as MITYA MOSKALYOV's tutor. He and ZINA are both of a romantic nature and quickly fall in love. He lives a life of dreams, pride, romanticism, and vanity, and spends much of his time reading SHAKESPEARE. Despite MARYA ALEKSANDROVNA's protestations, he and ZINA correspond, but he becomes angry on one occasion and gives one of ZINA's letters to ZAUMSHIN to be placed in the gossip mill. When he and ZINA argue over this incident, he becomes piqued and determines to commit suicide. The method chosen is to deliberately contract consumption so that ZINA will suffer from guilt and will come to his deathbed to beg forgiveness. He repents of his romantic idiocy but does so too late to prevent ZINA's parting with him at his deathbed.

COUNTESS ZALIKHVATSKAYA. FARPUKHINA boasts that she ate at the home of COUNTESS ZALIKHVATSKAYA.

ZAUMSHIN. The person to whom VASYA gives one of ZINA's love letters for gossipy circulation. He shows the letter to a number of people, particularly to NATALYA DMITRIEVNA, since she is one of MARYA ALEKSANDROVNA's mortal enemies.

ZINA. See ZINAIDA AFANASIEVNA MOSKALYOVA.

ZINAIDA AFANASIEVNA. See ZINAIDA AFANASIEVNA MOS-KALYOVA.

ZINOCHKA. See ZINAIDA AFANASIEVNA MOSKALYOVA.

NASTASYA PETROVNA ZYABLOVA. A distant relative of MARYA ALEKSANDROVNA who lives with her and who revels in gossip and scandal. She spends much of her time eavesdropping on critical conversations and is fully updated on the scope of the intrigues to marry PRINCE K. to ZINA and to placate ZINA and MOZGLYAKOV. She recovers ZINA's love letter for MARYA ALEKSANDROVNA for money, but vows to make her presence felt when she overhears MARYA ALEKSANDROVNA's true opinion of her. She enlists MOZGLYAKOV in the eavesdropping and angrily tells FARPUKHINA everything. FARPUKHINA then exposes everyone and everything during the scandal caused by PRINCE K.'s insistence that he dreamed his proposal.

THE VILLAGE OF STEPANCHIKOVO (SELO STEPANCHIKOVO) 1859

ADELAIDA. VIDOPLYASOV tells SERGEY that he is wearing a tie the color of ADELAIDA because it is a noble foreign name. He would not call the color AGRAFYONA because any peasant woman could be named that.

AFANASY MATVEICH. YEGOR's uncle.

AGAFYA TIMOFEEVNA. See AGAFYA TIMOFEEVNA KRAKHOT-KINA.

AGRAFYONA. See ADELAIDA.

AKULINA PANFILOVNA. YEGOR's grandmother.

ALEKSANDRA YEGOROVNA. See ALEKSANDRA YEGOROVNA ROSTANYOVA.

ALEXANDER THE GREAT [ALEKSANDR MAKEDONSKY]. Emperor ALEXANDER III of Macedon (356-323 B.C.), who conquered the civilized world, extended Greek civilization into the East, and ushered in the Hellenistic Age. In tirading about what and how writers should write, FOMA insists that they should portray peasants with such virtues that even ALEXANDER THE GREAT would be jealous. Later in a fit of pique FOMA attacks both CAESAR and ALEXANDER THE GREAT, minimizes and ridicules their accomplishments, and states that anyone could have done the same.

ANDRON. YEGOR's cook, who fails in his attempt to teach his nephew FALALEY grammar.

ANFISA PETROVNA. See ANFISA PETROVNA OBNOSKINA.

ANNA NILOVNA. See ANNA NILOVNA PEREPELITSYNA.

ARKHIP. See ARKHIP KOROTKY.

ARKHIPUSHKA. See ARKHIP KOROTKY.

ASMODEY. The lame devil in *Le Diable Boiteux (The Lame Devil)*, a novel written in 1709 by Alain René Le Sage (1668-1747), who takes pleasure in exposing human ugliness. ASMODEY could also refer to the demon in Hebrew lore, especially in the apocryphal book of *Tobit*. His task is to drive asunder newly wedded couples. FOMA tirades about looking over the world for a man to love, and finding FALALEY unacceptable, he says that he would rather love ASMODEY.

STEPAN ALEKSEICH BAKHCHEEV. YEGOR's neighbor, a forty five year old landowner who served with him in the hussars. He encounters SERGEY while both are having repairs made to their carriages and informs the latter about FOMA and all the happenings on YEGOR's estate. He is quite overweight, enjoys demeaning those whom he considers learned, and usually seems angry at someone. He leads the expedition in pursuit of OBNOSKIN and TATYANA and completes the rescue. Despite his previous feelings about FOMA, he becomes his devoted follower and often begs his forgiveness. He proposes to PRASKOVYA ILYINICHNA, YEGOR's sister, but is refused because she deems it her duty to stay with the family. The author indicates that he intends to discuss BAKHCHEEV in more detail in another story.

BEDLAM. Derived from the St. Mary of Bethlehem religious house in London that was converted into a hospital for lunatics in 1402. The term connotes confusion or a madhouse. After a conversation with VIDOPLYA-SOV about the color of his tie, which is said to be ADELAIDA rather than AGRAFYONA, SERGEY notes that the whole situation is like BEDLAM.

BENEDICTINES [BENEDIKTINTSY]. Roman Catholic religious order founded by St. Benedict of Nursia (ca. 480-547), which is aimed at the sanctification of its members. YEGOR observes that he has read about monastic orders in novels such as those by RADCLIFFE and asks if the BENEDICTINES are such an order.

"BLACK COLOR" ["CHYORNY TSVET"]. "BLACK COLOR, Dark Color" ("CHYORNY TSVET, mrachny tsvet"), a popular romance of the middle nineteenth century whose author is unknown. FOMA elaborates about how he was concerned about NASTYA's fate and the moral implications of her involvement with YEGOR. He piously notes that because of their relationship his whole soul was in a blackness, but not like that of the song "BLACK COLOR."

BOROZDNA. Ivan Petrovich BOROZDNA (1803-58), a minor Russian poet. FOMA expands on literature and cites poets who are not writing the moral and uplifting things that they should. PUSHKIN, LERMONTOV, and BOROZDNA are singled out as examples.

BARON BRAMBEUS. Pseudonym of Osip Ivanovich Senkovsky (1800-58), who edited *Library for Reading (Biblioteka dlya chteniya)* and who wrote articles and stories that appealed to the conservative and less well-educated reader. (1) The narrator notes that FOMA's novel would receive attention only by a critic such as BARON BRAMBEUS in his own journal. *Library for Reading* did in fact review minor works and minor writers in a humorous light. (2) VIDOPLYASOV observes that he should change his name because it does not sound sufficiently noble and delicate. He fears that when he publishes his poetry, critics like BARON BRAMBEUS will attack him because of his name.

BURTSOV. Aleksey Petrovich BURTSOV (d. 1813), a hussar officer noted for his reveling and escapades. He is mentioned in the verse of Denis Vasilievich Davydov (1784-1839), whose writing celebrates military life. MIZINCHIKOV notes that when he was in the army he often played the role of BURTSOV.

CAESAR [TSEZAR]. Julius CAESAR (100-44 B.C.), Roman general, statesman, and orator who after a distinguished military career, forcibly assumed the role of emperor. FOMA attacks both CAESAR and ALEXANDER THE GREAT, minimizes their accomplishments, and states that anyone could have done the same.

CLITUS [KLIT]. Boyhood friend of ALEXANDER THE GREAT who saved the emperor's life at Granicus and was subsequently murdered by him in 328 B.C. following a drunken quarrel at a banquet. In minimizing the greatness and accomplishments of CAESAR and ALEXANDER THE GREAT, FOMA notes that the latter killed the virtuous CLITUS.

THE CONTEMPORARY [SOVREMENNIK]. Literary and political journal founded by Aleksandr PUSHKIN in 1836. It achieved its greatest influence after 1847 under the editorship of Nikolay Alekseevich Nekrasov (1821-78), when it published the best writers and was a vocal advocate of liberal politics. Its increasingly liberal political bent subsequently drove many writers away and eventually resulted in its forcible closing in 1866. SASHA indicates that the verses ILYUSHA recites at FOMA's birthday party were written by KUZMA PRUTKOV in *THE CONTEMPORARY*.

CAPTAIN COOK [KAPITAN KUK]. James COOK (1728-99), English navigator and explorer. He discovered islands in the South Pacific and was murdered by natives in Hawaii in revenge for a flogging. When BAKHCHEEV recounts to SERGEY FOMA's activities at YEGOR's estate, he notes that affairs are in a turmoil, just as with CAPTAIN COOK.

THE CORRESPONDENT [PEREPISCHIK]. "Letters of an Out-of-Town Subscriber to the Editor of *THE CONTEMPORARY* About Russian Journalism" ("Pisma inogorodnogo podpischika v redaktsiyu *SOVREMENNIKA* o russkoy zhurnalistike") were written by Aleksandr Vasilievich Druzhinin (1824-64), author and critic, and published unsigned in *THE CONTEMPORARY* in 1849 and the early 1850s. In discussing the poverty of most literature, past and present, FOMA states that his favorite among the new writers is THE CORRESPONDENT.

CUPID [KUPIDON]. The god of love in Roman mythology. He is the son of Venus and Mercury, and is the counterpart of the Greek Eros. (1) YEGOR notes that FOMA is an authentic artist at penmanship and that he makes all kinds of beautiful forms, uses colors, and draws CUPIDS. (2) SERGEY notes that TATYANA's mania stems from CUPID and the desire for an ideal love.

DASHA. The gardener's daughter on YEGOR's estate. When OBNOSKIN is found in the garden with a woman at night, YEGOR wonders if the woman is DASHA.

DIEGO. See "THE SIEGE OF PAMBA."

DIOGENES [DIOGEN]. Greek Cynic philosopher (ca. 400-325 B.C.). He lived an ascetic life and conducted a sarcastic daylight search with a lantern to find an honest man. FOMA tirades about how he wants to love man but finds no one to love. He compares his search to that of DIOGENES and insists that he cannot love anyone until he finds that man.

ELIJAH THE PROPHET [ILYA PROROK]. As recorded in I Kings 17-21 and II Kings 1-2 in the Old Testament, a prophet who called down fire from heaven in a contest with the priests of Baal and who was carried into heaven instead of tasting death. (1) ILYUSHA is named after ELIJAH (ILYA) and preparations are made to celebrate his name day. A jealous FOMA insists that the same day is his birthday and he demands to be honored. (2) When a violent storm parallels YEGOR's expulsion of FOMA from the house, several appeal to ELIJAH to calm the elements.

ESSBUKETOV. VIDOPLYASOV pompously feels the need to change his name to something more fashionable and considers the name ESSBUKE-TOV, which he noted on a bottle of French pomade.

FALALEY. A naive, simple-hearted peasant boy of sixteen who is attached to YEGOR's house mostly because of his handsome appearance. He is a favorite of YEGOR, his late wife, and his mother, and as a consequence FOMA resents him. FOMA continually tries to catch him dancing the "KAMARINSKY" so that he can expose its immoral character and thereby cast reflections on YEGOR. FALALEY's frequent dreams about a white ox infuriate FOMA, who insists that he dream of something more noble.

FATHERLAND NOTES [OTECHESTVENNYE ZAPISKI]. Literary and political monthly published in St. Petersburg 1839-84. It contained some of the best literature of the day and advocated progressive social ideas, but was closed forcibly because of too liberal editorial policies. YEGOR, a devotee of things scholarly largely because of his ignorance, feels that *FATHERLAND NOTES* contains the best scholarship.

FEVRONIA. BAKHCHEEV mistakenly refers to TATYANA IVANOVNA as FEVRONIA. There are at least two possible sources for BAKHCHEEV's ostensible slip. (1) Yevfrosinia, the wife of David Yurievich, Prince of Murom. Prior to his assuming ruling power, Yevfrosinia cured him of an illness, and he married her in spite of her peasant background. At the end of their lives they took monastic vows with the names of Pyotr and FEVRONIA and died together in 1228. (2) A fourth century Christian martyr who was tortured to death for her refusal to marry for money.

FOMA. See FOMA FOMICH OPISKIN.

FOMA FOMICH. See FOMA FOMICH OPISKIN.

FOMKA. See FOMA FOMICH OPISKIN. BAKHCHEEV disgustedly calls FOMA by the unflattering FOMKA when they have a disagreement.

FORGET-ME-NOT [NEZABUDOCHKA]. *FORGET-ME-NOT, A Ladies' Album Comprised of the Best Articles of Russian Poetry (NEZABUDOCHKA, Damsky albom, sostavlenny iz luchshikh statey russkoy poezii)* was published in St. Petersburg in 1852 and contained verse from several Russian poets. In discussing modern literature's failings FOMA notes that he read one of the selections from this almanac but prefers the work of THE CORRESPONDENT.

FROL SILIN. A tale by Nikolay KARAMZIN, first published in 1791. The story extolls the exploits of FROL SILIN, a noble, sensitive, hard-working landowner who helps peasants in times of stress and goes about doing good. (1) SERGEY refers to his uncle YEGOR as FROL SILIN because of his generosity. (2) When FOMA discusses the work of KARAMZIN at length, he singles out *FROL SILIN* as the work for which he respects the author.

GAVRILA. See GAVRILA IGNATYICH.

GAVRILA IGNATYICH. YEGOR's valet and close friend of SERGEY. FOMA insists that he learn French.

GOGOL. Nikolay Vasilievich GOGOL (1809-52), popular Russian writer noted for his tragicomic exposing of human foibles. He was viewed by progressive critics as the fountainhead of the NATURAL SCHOOL and credited with critically describing reality with the intent of social reform. FOMA characterizes GOGOL as a light-minded writer who nevertheless comes up with thoughts very much to the point, and he ascribes to him the thought that unhappiness is sometimes the mother of virtue. This bit of philosophizing occurs when FOMA returns to YEGOR's estate following his brief exile. The figure of FOMA was intended by Dostoevsky to parody certain attributes of GOGOL's character, particularly his vanity and sense of a divine mission.

DON PEDRO GOMEZ [DON PEDRO GOMETS]. See "THE SIEGE OF PAMBA."

GRIGORY (GRISHKA). BAKHCHEEV's elderly valet, who is not averse to talking back to his master.

GRISHKA. See GRIGORY.

GRISHKA. See GRIGORY VIDOPLYASOV. He is sometimes taunted as GRISHKA by the young boys on YEGOR's estate.

HAMLET [GAMLET]. *HAMLET, Prince of Denmark* (1601), a tragedy by William SHAKESPEARE which chronicles HAMLET's revenge for the murder of his father. FOMA laments how his entire soul suffered as he worried about NASTYA's virtue at the mercy of YEGOR's unbridled passions. He invites people to read *HAMLET* to understand how he suffered.

HETMAN BURYA [ATAMAN BURYA]. *HETMAN BURYA, or the Transvolga Volunteers (ATAMAN BURYA, ili Volnitsa Zavolzhskaya),* an adventure novel with a pseudohistorical subject written by D. Presnov in 1835. The narrator notes that FOMA has written a novel similar to the raft of romantic, adventurous historical novels popular in the 1830s, such as *HETMAN BURYA.*

HISTORY [ISTORIA]. *HISTORY of the Russian State (ISTORIA gosudarstva Rossyskogo),* a twelve volume history of Russia by Nikolay KARAMZIN, generally written from the point of view of autocracy. The first eleven volumes were published 1816-24, and the uncompleted twelfth volume appeared posthumously in 1829. In FOMA's discourse on KARAM-

ZIN he notes that he does not respect the writer for his *HISTORY* but rather for *FROL SILIN.*

ILYUSHA. See ILYA YEGOROVICH ROSTANYOV.

ILYUSHKA. See ILYA YEGOROVICH ROSTANYOV.

IVAN IVANOVICH. See IVAN IVANOVICH MIZINCHIKOV.

IVAN IVANYCH. See IVAN IVANOVICH MIZINCHIKOV.

IVAN YAKOVLICH. IVAN Yakovlevich Koreysha (1780-1861), a famous Moscow holy fool who was viewed by his devotees as having prophetic powers. The influence that FOMA comes to wield over YEGOR's mother and the other women of GENERAL KRAKHOTKIN's household is compared to that wielded by IVAN YAKOVLICH and other creatures of his type.

SAINT JAMES OF COMPOSTELLO [SANKTO YAGO KOMPOS-TELLO]. The New Testament apostle JAMES, whose body was supposedly removed to COMPOSTELLO in the ninth century and who is the patron saint of Spain. In "THE SIEGE OF PAMBA" read by ILYUSHA at his name day, the nineteen remaining soldiers leave Pamba and hail SAINT JAMES and their leader DON PEDRO GOMEZ.

JESUITS [IEZUITY]. The Society of Jesus, a religious order for Roman Catholic men founded by Ignatius Loyola (1491-1556) in 1534. The society is known for scholarship and missionary zeal and has been accused of secrecy and intrigue. (1) SERGEY asks YEZHEVIKIN if he has ever heard of the JESUITS, likely with the intent of telling an anecdote. (2) When SERGEY insults FOMA in the disagreement over GAVRILA's speaking French, YEZHEVIKIN himself refers to an anecdote about JESUITS. The intent is to apply the deception and rigidity attributed to JESUITS to FOMA.

JOURNAL DES DEBATS [ZHURNAL DE DEBA]. *Journal of Débates,* French political newspaper founded in 1789. (1) When FOMA attacks SERGEY as a pseudo-scholar, he mentions the *JOURNAL DES DEBATS,* thereby implying that SERGEY reads it and is involved with progressive thought. (2) SERGEY compares FOMA's lengthy and pompous expositions of his own virtues to ten pages of small print in the *JOURNAL DES DEBATS.*

JUDAS [IUDA]. As recorded in the New Testament, JUDAS Iscariot, the apostle who betrayed Jesus by identifying Him to Roman soldiers in exchange for thirty pieces of silver. Foma refers to the money YEGOR offers him to leave as JUDAS' pieces of silver.

"KAMARINSKY." A native peasant song and dance used by Mikhail Ivanovich Glinka (1804-57) for his *Kamarinskaya*. FOMA objects to the peasant-like and inelegant sentiments of the "KAMARINSKY" and tries to put a stop to it. He is particularly anxious to catch FALALEY singing and dancing so that he can use it as a pretext to demean YEGOR.

KARAMZIN. Nikolay Mikhaylovich KARAMZIN (1766-1826), a writer and historian who sought to infuse Westernisms into the literary language to make it more like the language of the aristocracy. His fiction sought to express the noble and virtuous and was a product of the Sentimental movement, while his *HISTORY* is generally pro-autocracy. FOMA evaluates KARAMZIN and his work in a lengthy harangue and concludes that he respects him only for *FROL SILIN*.

KATYA. See KATYA ROSTANYOVA.

THE KHOLMSKY FAMILY [SEMEYSTVO KHOLMSKIKH]. *THE KHOLMSKY FAMILY, Some Characteristics of the Mores and Life Style, Family and Personal, of Russian Nobles (SEMEYSTVO KHOLMSKIKH, Nekotorye cherty nravov i obraza zhizni, semeynoy i odinokoy, russkikh dvoryan)*, a lengthy novel, first published in 1832 by D.N. Begichev (1786-1855). YEZHEVIKIN mentions *THE KHOLMSKY FAMILY* when referring to his own large family, now somewhat of a liability since he has not held a position for eight years.

PAUL DE KOCK [POL DE KOK]. French novelist (1793-1871) noted for his vivid descriptions of Parisian life. FOMA tries to conceal the fact that he reads PAUL DE KOCK, since such novels are not consistent with FOMA's pompously virtuous image.

KORNOUKHOV. YEGOR relates an anecdote in which he meets KORNOUKHOV in the theater and points out three homely women to him. The women turn out to be KORNOUKHOV's cousin, sister, and wife.

ARKHIP KOROTKY (ARKHIPUSHKA). A peasant who repairs BAKHCHEEV's carriage. He has a brief discussion with FOMA, who treats him and all peasants condescendingly.

KOROVKIN. YEGOR, who admires anyone who knows virtually anything about science, invites KOROVKIN, who knows something about the railroad, to his estate after having met him on his travels. His arrival is anxiously anticipated by YEGOR, but he arrives drunk and makes a minor scene. KOROVKIN is so embarrassed by his drunken performance that he quickly leaves the next morning without informing anyone.

GENERAL KRAKHOTKIN. An atheist, free-thinker, and misanthrope who marries YEGOR's widowed mother and who continually abuses and laughs at her. Shortly before his death he suddenly turns pious and comes under the influence of FOMA, from whom he begs forgiveness. His new leaf is incomplete, however, as he continues to violently resent "saints" such as YEGOR and PRASKOVYA ILYINICHNA.

AGAFYA TIMOFEEVNA KRAKHOTKINA. YEGOR's mother, an evil woman beset by age and loss of mental powers. She marries GENERAL KRAKHOTKIN, squeezes from her new status everything she can, and is surrounded by a bevy of hangers-on. Despite YEGOR's goodness to her, she attacks him for marrying instead of caring for her. She then moves in with him, accompanied by her retinue, to test his devotion. She cannot live without FOMA and begs for his return when he is evicted by YEGOR. Following YEGOR's marriage to NASTYA, her life becomes somewhat calmer, and she dies three years later.

KUROPATKINA. In one of YEGOR's anecdotes an actress who runs away with ZVERKOV, a cavalry captain, without doing her performance.

KUZMA. YEGOR's barber.

LERMONTOV. Mikhail Yurievich LERMONTOV (1814-41), the foremost Russian romantic poet and novelist, who perished in a duel. FOMA expands on literature and cites poets who are not writing the moral and uplifting things that they should. PUSHKIN, LERMONTOV, and BOROZDNA are singled out as examples.

THE LIBERATION OF MOSCOW [OSVOBOZHDENIE MOSKVY]. *Prince Pozharsky and the Nizhny Novgorod Citizen Minin, or THE LIBERATION OF MOSCOW in 1612 (Knyaz Pozharsky i nizhegorodsky grazhdanin Minin, ili OSVOBOZHDENIE MOSKVY v 1612 godu),* an historical adventure novel written in 1840 by Ivan Glukharyov. The narrator notes that FOMA has written a novel similar to the raft of romantic, adventurous historical novels popular in the 1830s, such as *THE LIBERATION OF MOSCOW.*

"LIBERTY-EQUALITY-FRATERNITY" ["LIBERTE-EGALITE-FRATERNITE"]. "LIBERTE-EGALITE-FRATERNITE," one of the mottoes of the French Revolution during the turbulent decade 1789-99. When YEGOR introduces SERGEY as a learned man, FOMA responds by sarcastically repeating "LIBERTY-EQUALITY-FRATERNITY" and alluding to the *JOURNAL DES DEBATS.*

LOMONOSOV. Mikhail Vasilievich LOMONOSOV (1711-65), Russian scholar, poet, and rhetorician who was instrumental in forming the literary language and rules of poetry. His own verse is rather heavy and ornate, and he specialized in the ode. YEGOR anticipates that his son ILYUSHA will probably recite something solemn from LOMONOSOV as he performs on his name day. ILYUSHA responds by reciting "THE SIEGE OF PAMBA."

LUCULLUS [LUKULLA]. Wealthy Roman officer (110-57 B.C.) who is noted for his devotion to luxury and self-indulgence. Following FOMA's death the narrator recalls his pomp, fantasy, and LUCULLUS-like indulgence in caprice.

MACHIAVELLI [MAKIAVEL]. Niccolo MACHIAVELLI (1469-1527), Florentine statesman and political philosopher most famous for *Il Principe (The Prince),* written in 1517, in which he advocated pragmatic, direct politics. In discoursing on the limitations of learned men, FOMA states that a person like MACHIAVELLI, MERCADANTE, or himself could go unnoticed before the ostensibly learned.

MALANYA. A maid at YEGOR's estate who is famed as a teller of tales.

MARFA THE MAYOR [MARFA POSADNITSA]. MARFA THE MAYOR, *or the Subjugation of Novgorod (MARFA POSADNITSA, ili pokorenie Novgoroda),* a tale written in 1803 by Nikolay KARAMZIN. In FOMA's discourse on KARAMZIN he observes that he does not respect the writer for *MARFA THE MAYOR,* but rather only for *FROL SILIN.*

MARTYN. Identified by FALALEY as a house servant. FALALEY eats a pie with gusto and states that he throws it down just as MARTYN does soap. FOMA is horrified at the use of such an expression in noble society and cross-examines FALALEY to tears.

MATRYONA. A pleasant young servant girl whom VIDOPLYASOV intends to marry until FOMA dissuades him.

MATVEY ILYICH. When VASILIEV flees from MATVEY ILYICH, he hides in BAKHCHEEV's carriage.

MATVEY NIKITICH. One of YEGOR's progenitors who was supposedly executed by PUGACHYOV.

MERCADANTE [MERKADANTE]. Saverio MERCADANTE (1795-1870), Italian composer of opera. In discoursing on the limitations of so-called learned men, such as SERGEY, FOMA states that a person like MACHIAVELLI, MERCADANTE, or himself could go unnoticed by the ostensibly learned.

MITYUSHKA. YEGOR's postilion, who plays the tambourine in a peasant orchestra.

IVAN IVANOVICH MIZINCHIKOV (IVAN IVANYCH). YEGOR's second cousin, who comes to live with him even though the two are not acquainted. He is twenty eight, heavily in debt, and retired from the hussars. His quiet and agreeable nature is deliberately affected, because financially he needs to continue living with YEGOR. In order to extricate himself from his heavy debts and care for his nineteen year old sister he determines that he needs at least one hundred thousand rubles. To get the money he plans to marry TATYANA IVANOVNA. He perceives such a marriage as a noble and virtuous gesture, but considers it obvious that the two would not live together. He offers to sell his idea to SERGEY for fifty thousand rubles, but later laments that he told OBNOSKIN about his plan and senses that he and his mother will try to beat him to TATYANA IVANOVNA. His study of agriculture prompts him to abandon his plans of marriage, and YEGOR secures him a position as foreman for a local nobleman. He is very successful, retires, buys his own estate, and sends for his sister, who takes over the housekeeping.

THE MUFF [TYUFYAK]. A story published in 1850 by Aleksey Feofilaktovich Pisemsky (1820-81). The tale, which launched Pisemsky's career, chronicles the demise of an awkward, naive, incapable young man who proceeds from mistake to mistake until he dies from drink. At a tea with hostile unfamiliar people SERGEY feels just like a muff and is prompted to ask those present whether they have read *THE MUFF.*

THE MYSTERIES OF BRUSSELS [BRYUSSELŠKIE TAYNY]. An imitation of *The Mysteries of Paris (Les Mystères de Paris)*, written in 1843 by Eugène Sue (1804-57), who is best known for his sensational romances. *THE MYSTERIES OF BRUSSELS,* translated and published anonymously in St. Petersburg in 1847, was one of a number of works which attempted to share in the success of *The Mysteries of Paris.* As FOMA tirades on literature OBNOSKINA meekly suggests that current writers also write well and cites *THE MYSTERIES OF BRUSSELS* as an example.

NARZAN. The free-flowing source of mineral water in the Russian city of Kislovodsk. In praising THE CORRESPONDENT, FOMA lauds him as a veritable NARZAN of wit, a free-flowing and seemingly inexhaustible source.

NASTASYA YEVGRAFOVNA. See NASTASYA YEVGRAFOVNA YEZHEVIKINA.

NASTENKA. See NASTASYA YEVGRAFOVNA YEZHEVIKINA.

NASTYA. See NASTASYA YEVGRAFOVNA YEZHEVIKINA.

NATURAL SCHOOL [NATURALNAYA SHKOLA]. A literary movement in Russia arising in the 1840s under the influence of socially-minded critics who advocated the critical and truthful (natural) presentation of reality with the aim of social improvement. Low characters and explicit detail became common. The weight of responsiblity was on the system rather than the individual, who despite his station in life and negative traits could retain positive characteristics. In discussing with YEGOR the concept that even in the vilest of men there is good, SERGEY alludes to the NATURAL SCHOOL.

NOAH [NOY]. As recorded in Genesis 6-10, the Old Testament patriarch whom Jehovah commanded to build an ark prior to the destruction of the earth by flood. In the ark NOAH saved his family together with specimens of each kind of animal. (1) When YEGOR is asked to participate in an examination, he asks questions of the calibre of who was NOAH. (2) YEGOR's household with its many hangers-on and visitors is described as being as full as NOAH's ark.

PAVEL SEMYONYCH OBNOSKIN (PAVLUSHA, POL). A bland twenty five year old, who with his mother ANFISA PETROVNA is a guest at YEGOR's estate. MIZINCHIKOV's plan for marrying TATYANA IVANOVNA for her money is put into operation by OBNOSKIN and his mother, who abduct her from the estate. When BAKHCHEEV, SERGEY, and others apprehend them, OBNOSKIN becomes very shy and disoriented and blames the whole affair upon his mother.

ANFISA PETROVNA OBNOSKINA. OBNOSKIN's mother, a toothless, fat widow who likes to be chic, drop names, use French, and make eyes. She and her son engineer the abduction of TATYANA IVANOVNA from YEGOR's estate so that OBNOSKIN can marry her for her money. When they are caught, she viciously attacks everyone and vows revenge.

OLD AND NEW RUSSIA [STARAYA I NOVAYA ROSSIYA]. A Note on *OLD AND NEW kUSSIA in its Political and Civil Relations (Zapiska o drevney i novoy Rossii v yeyo politicheskom i grazhdanskom otnosheniakh),* an essay written in 1811 by Nikolay KARAMZIN, but published in complete form only in 1870. In FOMA's discourse on KARAMZIN he observes that he does not respect the writer for *OLD AND NEW RUSSIA,* but only for *FROL SILIN.*

OLEANDROV. VIDOPLYASOV pompously feels the need to change his name to something more fashionable and elegant and considers the name OLEANDROV.

FOMA FOMICH OPISKIN (FOMA, FOMKA). A petty, useless, vile, and incredibly vain individual who serves GENERAL KRAKHOTKIN as a reader. His vanity is a defense against his previous failures and humiliations in life. He willingly lowers himself and plays the buffoon for the General, but dominates his wife, YEGOR's mother, and all of her retinue. He exerts a mystical influence over them, much like holy fools such as IVAN YAKOVLICH and piously reads holy books, attends services, and prophesies. When he correctly evaluates the relationship of YEGOR and his mother and sees what kind of a person YEGOR is, he assumes total control of the household following GENERAL KRAKHOTKIN's death. Ascendancy in the house would never have been his were it not for YEGOR's generous and passive personality. He informs YEGOR that after he instructs them in the proper ways, he will go to Moscow and publish a journal, entertain thousands at his lectures, write a divinely commissioned book that will be the salvation of Russia, and ultimately enter a monastery to pray. These details are intended to allude to and parody Nikolay GOGOL. His instructions in the house are an exercise in vanity and domination: he insists on being addressed as Your Excellency, claims that his birthday is on ILYUSHA's name day and demands to be honored, teaches the peasants French, torments FALALEY because he dances ignoble peasant dances and dreams of unelevated things, discourses at length upon nobility in literature, and condescendingly treats YEGOR and SERGEY as uninformed twits. FOMA's tyranny is absolute until he oversteps a barrier that moves the meek YEGOR to action. When he exposes YEGOR's relationship with NASTYA and suggests that NASTYA has become debauched, YEGOR physically throws him out of the house into a raging storm. Prompted by the pleadings of his mother and the rest of FOMA's retinue, YEGOR brings back to the house a frightened FOMA who laments how he suffered worrying about NASTYA's virtue at the mercy of YEGOR's unbridled passions. Declaring rather conveniently that he is now convinced of the purity of their love, FOMA makes everyone happy by approving their marriage. He also allows himself to be persuaded to remain in the house and accepts everyone's apologies for the insults he endured. His ascendency in the house assured, his tirades of personal praise become longer and more pompous, but in other ways he mellows because of AGAFYA TIMOFEEVNA's death and because NASTYA will not permit YEGOR to be demeaned. His final passing prompts loud mourning from his followers.

ORPHEUS [ORFEY]. In Greek mythology, a fabulous musician whose talents were such that he retrieved his slain wife from Hades. He ultimately lost her again, renounced other women, and was torn to bits by the angry and frustrated women whom he shunned. His body fragments were buried at Mt. Olympus with the exception of his head, which became an oracle. FOMA compares himself to ORPHEUS and vows to tame the mores at Stepanchikovo not through music but through forcing all to learn French.

PAVEL SEMYONYCH. See PAVEL SEMYONYCH OBNOSKIN.

PAVLUSHA. See PAVEL SEMYONYCH OBNOSKIN.

ANNA NILOVNA PEREPELITSYNA. An incredibly spiteful and evil person who is the leading member of AGAFYA TIMOFEEVNA's retinue. Her bile is directed principally toward YEGOR, whom she maliciously attacks when it becomes evident that she has no hope of marrying him. After AGAFYA TIMOFEEVNA's death, she remains in the house to try to attach herself to TATYANA IVANOVNA and her money, but failing that, she marries a local civil servant. He marries her because he mistakenly thinks that she has money, and their life together with his six children is a disaster.

PETRARCH [PETRARKA]. Francesco PETRARCA (1304-74), Italian poet and scholar who was a major force in the development of the Renaissance, Humanism, and European culture. As FOMA explains his suffering and fear for NASTYA at the mercy of the passionate YEGOR, he notes that he was reminded of PETRARCH's statement that innocence is often only a step away from destruction. This is a sentimental vulgarization of the sentiments of PETRARCH's "Era il giorno ch'al sol si scolararo" ("It was the morning of that blessed day whereon the sun in pity veiled his glare"), which expresses the author's defenselessness before the onslaught of love on a Good Friday.

POL. See PAVEL SEMYONYCH OBNOSKIN.

GENERAL POLOVITSYN. ANFISA PETROVNA OBNOSKINA, who likes to drop names, mentions that she knew GENERAL POLOVITSYN in St. Petersburg.

PRASKOVYA ILYINICHNA. See PRASKOVYA ILYINICHNA ROSTANYOVA.

KUZMA PRUTKOV. Fictional creation of Count Aleksey Konstantinovich Tolstoy (1817-75) and three cousins surnamed Zhemchuzhnikov. Under this pseudonym they published humorous verse and other writings between 1851 and 1884. PRUTKOV is a conservative, self-satisfied clerk who enjoys dealing in platitudes but whose verse is largely nonsense. The poem that ILYUSHA recites on his name day and FOMA's ostensible birthday is "THE SIEGE OF PAMBA" by PRUTKOV.

PUGACH. See PUGACHYOV. GAVRILA refers to PUGACHYOV colloquially as PUGACH.

PUGACHYOV (PUGACH). Yemelyan Ivanovich PUGACHYOV (1743-75), Russian Cossack who led an uprising against Catherine the Great in 1773 while posing as her late husband Peter III. He was ultimately captured and executed. GAVRILA mentions that his father remembers PUGACHYOV.

PUSHKIN. Aleksandr Sergeevich PUSHKIN (1799-1837), the leading Russian writer of his time, who is regarded as the father of modern Russian literature. (1) FOMA expands on literature and cites poets who are not writing the moral and uplifting things that they should. LERMONTOV,

BOROZDNA, and PUSHKIN are singled out as examples. (2) At FOMA's birthday party ILYUSHA reads a poem by KUZMA PRUTKOV, and YEGOR comments that he knows PUSHKIN, but is not familiar with PRUTKOV. (3) SERGEY listens as FOMA addresses the peasants and thoroughly confuses them with subjects he knows nothing about. SERGEY is reminded of an anecdote related by PUSHKIN in *Table-Talk* about a father who boasts to his four year old son that he is such a brave father that the tsar loves him. SERGEY observes that the father hardly needs a listener for such a speech and notes that the bewildered peasants listen to FOMA in the same way.

PYKHTIN. In YEGOR's anecdote about KORNOUKHOV, the latter's sister marries PYKHTIN.

PYTHAGORAS [PIFAGOR]. Greek philosopher and mathematician (ca. 582-507 B.C.) to whom the Pythagorean theorem of geometry is attributed. He also delved into mysticism and theorized on the transmigration of souls. As FOMA labors over a mathematics problem, he sketches the breeches of PYTHAGORAS three times before he is satisfied.

RADCLIFFE [RADKLIF]. Ann RADCLIFFE (1764-1823), English novelist known for her tales of horror in the convention of the Gothic novel. YEGOR mentions that he has read about monks and monastic orders in the work of RADCLIFFE. He probably has in mind *The Italian, or the Confessional of the Black Penitents* (1797) which features a villainous monk.

ILYA YEGOROVICH ROSTANYOV (ILYUSHA, ILYUSHKA). YE-GOR's eight year old son. His name day observance is marred by FOMA's insistence that it is his birthday and that he too should be honored. To commemorate the occasion ILYUSHA reads "THE SIEGE OF PAMBA."

SERGEY ALEKSANDROVICH ROSTANYOV (SERGEY, SERGEY ALEKSANDRYCH, SERYOZHA, SERGE). The narrator of the story. He is YEGOR's nephew and an orphan who has been raised and provided for by YEGOR. YEGOR invites him to come to Stepanchikovo to marry NASTYA, his children's governess. When he arrives, meets NASTYA, and suggests this to her, his vanity is pricked as she quickly dismisses the idea as nonsense. He then spends his time meeting the other people at the estate, reporting what they do, giving evaluations of them, and then reporting their fate following the conclusion of the story.

YEGOR ILYICH ROSTANYOV (YEGOR, YEGORUSHKA). A retired forty year old hussar colonel, who is the nicest and most generous man imaginable. YEGOR is comically naive and ignorant of the arts and sciences and values very highly those who know anything at all about them. He endures many insults from his mother but remains devoted to her and is anxious for her to move in following the death of her second husband GENERAL KRAKHOTKIN. He always finds a way to think that he is guilty, to believe the insults heaped upon him, and to praise those who condemn him. His mother and FOMA convince him that he is coarse, ignorant, and egotistical, and he readily agrees that FOMA has been sent from God to save him and teach him to control his passions. He is completely convinced of FOMA's high qualities, and without a person like YEGOR, FOMA's tyranny would be impossible. He is in love with NASTYA, his children's governess, and since FOMA and his mother are conspiring to marry him to TATYANA IVANOVNA, he sends for his nephew SERGEY to marry NASTYA and care for her. He responds aggressively to his situation only when FOMA casts aspersions upon NASTYA's virtue. YEGOR throws FOMA out of the house and agrees to accept him back only if he apologizes to NASTYA. After he retrieves FOMA, who pompously joins his hand with NASTYA's, YEGOR returns to his praises of FOMA and apologizes for his own conduct and baseness. After marriage he is totally devoted to NASTYA and acquiesces to her every wish.

ALEKSANDRA YEGOROVNA ROSTANYOVA (SASHENKA, SASHA, SASHURKA). YEGOR's pretty fifteen year old daughter, who is the only one to provide any opposition to FOMA. She begs her father to no avail to defend himself and not to submit to such as FOMA. She ultimately marries a fine young man.

KATYA ROSTANYOVA. YEGOR's late wife.

PRASKOVYA ILYINICHNA ROSTANYOVA. YEGOR's meek sister, who looks after GENERAL KRAKHOTKIN until his death and then stays with YEGOR to care for him. She refuses a proposal from BAKHCHEEV because she considers it her duty to remain with her family.

GENERAL RUSAPYOTOV. YEGOR's former commander. FOMA is so insulted by the attention RUSAPYOTOV receives when he pays a call on YEGOR that he insists that he too be referred to as Your Excellency.

SASHA. See ALEKSANDRA YEGOROVNA ROSTANYOVA.

SASHENKA. See ALEKSANDRA YEGOROVNA ROSTANYOVA.

SASHURKA. See ALEKSANDRA YEGOROVNA ROSTANYOVA.

SERGE. See SERGEY ALEKSANDROVICH ROSTANYOV.

SERGEY. See SERGEY ALEKSANDROVICH ROSTANYOV.

SERGEY ALEKSANDRYCH. See SERGEY ALEKSANDROVICH ROSTANYOV.

SERYOZHA. See SERGEY ALEKSANDROVICH ROSTANYOV.

SHAKESPEARE [SHEKSPIR]. William SHAKESPEARE (1564-1616), the most eminent of English dramatists. (1) FOMA discourses about how he worries about the fate of NASTYA's virtue at the mercy of YEGOR's unbridled passions. He suggests that SHAKESPEARE's *HAMLET* be consulted as an illustration of how he suffers. (2) FOMA notes that he considers the future a deep, dark abyss, at the bottom of which is a crocodile, and he incorrectly attributes the image to SHAKESPEARE. The source of the allusion appears to be *Atala,* a novel written by François René de Chateaubriand (1768-1848) in 1801, in which a North American Indian comments that even the purest of hearts is like the calm source of a stream at the bottom of which is a crocodile.

"THE SIEGE OF PAMBA" ["OSADA PAMBY"]. A humorous poem by KUZMA PRUTKOV, first published in *THE CONTEMPORARY.* The poem is quoted by ILYUSHA at his name day and FOMA's birthday celebration with a few departures from the original. The work chronicles the nine year siege of a Moorish bastion by DON PEDRO GOMEZ, who allows his men only milk. His nine thousand soldiers are reduced to nineteen, and it is decided to abandon the siege, but to rejoice that their vow to consume nothing but milk was never broken. The chaplain DIEGO mumbles that he would have vowed to eat nothing but meat and drink nothing but wine, and DON PEDRO rewards him with just that because of his gallant jesting. DON PEDRO's approach to the siege has certain parallels with YEGOR's quixotic character.

FROL SILIN. See *FROL SILIN.*

SODOM. As recorded in Genesis 18-19 of the Old Testament, a city which together with Gomorrah was destroyed by Jehovah because of its wickedness. The term has come to mean wickedness and chaos. The expulsion of FOMA during a terrible storm and YEGOR's mother's begging for his return are described by SERGEY as a virtual SODOM.

SONS OF LOVE, OR THE RUSSIANS IN 1104 (SYNOVYA LYUBVI, ILI RUSSKIE V 1104 GODU). The narrator observes that FOMA has written a novel derivative of the raft of romantic, adventurous historical novels popular in the 1830s, such as *SONS OF LOVE, OR THE RUSSIANS IN 1104.* With this title SERGEY may have in mind novels written by Mikhail Nikolaevich Zagoskin (1789-1852), such as *Yury Miloslavsky, or the Russians in 1612 (Yury Miloslavsky, ili Russkie v 1612 godu),* written in 1829 or *Roslavlev, or the Russians in 1812 (Roslavlev, ili Russkie v 1812 godu),* written in 1831.

STEPAN ALEKSEICH. See STEPAN ALEKSEICH BAKHCHEEV.

TALLEYRAND [TALEYRAN]. Charles Maurice de TALLEYRAND-Périgord (1754-1838), French statesman who helped to restore the Bourbon monarchy following the defeat of Napoleon I and who represented his country at the Congress of Vienna. YEGOR and SERGEY discuss the situation at Stepanchikovo, and YEGOR notes that one has to be cunning and diplomatic around the house à la TALLEYRAND.

TANTSEV. VIDOPLYASOV is convinced that he needs to change his name to something more noble and elegant and considers TANTSEV.

TATYANA IVANOVNA. An orphan who grows up in poverty and turns to dreams and imagination to find happiness and her ideal of love. Gradually her reason and mind weaken. When she comes into a large inheritance, she is sure that her ideal will soon arrive, but she is pursued by men because of her money, and her reason completely fails. She is thirty five, pale, and has a very good heart. FOMA and YEGOR's mother want to marry her to YEGOR, and MIZINCHIKOV has designs on her, but it is OBNOSKIN and his mother who abduct her in order to marry into her money. When their flight is intercepted, she gladly returns to Stepanchikovo. Upon her death some of her money goes to NASTYA, while the remainder goes toward the education of orphan girls.

VALENTIN IGNATYICH TIKHONTSOV. According to YEZHEVIKIN, an acquaintance who gains a rank and becomes a scoundrel at the same time.

TRISHIN. An acquaintance of YEZHEVIKIN.

TYULPANOV. VIDOPLYASOV is convinced that he needs to change his name to something more noble and elegant and considers TYULPANOV.

ULANOV. VIDOPLYASOV is convinced that he needs to change his name to something more noble and elegant and considers ULANOV.

VALENTIN IGNATYICH. See VALENTIN IGNATYICH TIKHONTSOV.

VASILIEV. A runaway peasant who is discovered in BAKHCHEEV's carriage. He confesses that he is fleeing a village which is about to be given to FOMA.

VERNY. See GRIGORY VERNY.

GRIGORY VERNY. VIDOPLYASOV adopts this name in his search for a more noble and elegant name.

GRIGORY VIDOPLYASOV (GRISHKA, ESSBUKETOV, OLEAN-DROV, TANTSEV, TYULPANOV, ULANOV, GRIGORY VERNY). YEGOR's lackey, who, FOMA insists, is learned. He dresses in the latest style, is fashionably pale, and affects delicacy, subtlety, and a high opinion of his personal worth. Since coming under FOMA's influence he becomes increasingly snobbish and writes poetry, which he dedicates to FOMA. Much of his energy is devoted to changing his name, which he considers insufficiently noble and elegant and which he fears will be ridiculed by critics like BARON BRAMBEUS when he publishes his poetry. He appeals to MIZINCHIKOV and SERGEY for aid through an example of his writing called "VIDOPLYASOV's Lament," which is so ornate as to be practically unintelligible. It is rumored that he eventually is committed to an insane asylum, where he dies.

VOLTAIRE [VOLTER]. Pen name of François Marie Arouet (1694-1778), noted French satirist, philosopher, and historian. His name connotes a free-thinking approach to issues and philosophy. In a quasi-literary discussion BAKHCHEEV complains that all writers are followers of VOLTAIRE. YEGOR defends him as a fine writer who exposed prejudice and comically asserts that he was not a Voltairian at all.

"WHEN FROM THE DARKNESS OF DELUSION" ["KOGDA IZ MRAKA ZABLUZHDENYA"]. A poem by Nikolay Alekseevich Nekrasov (1821-78) published in 1846. The work features the theme of the regeneration of the fallen woman and the stimulation of elevated human feelings. SERGEY in trying to show YEGOR that there is good in the most vile men, quotes this well-known line of verse.

YEGOR. See YEGOR ILYICH ROSTANYOV.

YEGOR ILYICH. See YEGOR ILYICH ROSTANYOV.

YEGORUSHKA. See YEGOR ILYICH ROSTANYOV.

YEMELYA. One of the peasants who repairs BAKHCHEEV's carriage.

YEVDOKIM. One of BAKHCHEEV's servants.

YEVGRAF LARIONYCH. See YEVGRAF LARIONYCH YEZHEVIKIN.

YEVGRAF LARIONYCH YEZHEVIKIN. A self-styled scoundrel and buffoon who willingly demeans himself to fulfill those roles. He has not had a position in eight years because of his sarcastic tongue and lives in poverty with his eight children, supported exclusively from his daughter NASTYA's income. His status in life is a result of his pride, and even after NASTYA's marriage to YEGOR, he will accept money only from her.

NASTASYA YEVGRAFOVNA YEZHEVIKINA (NASTYA, NASTEN-KA). YEVGRAF LARIONYCH's daughter, who supports his large family and who suffers at his antics. She serves as the governess for YEGOR's children and has fallen in love with him. When their marriage appears blocked by FOMA and YEGOR's mother, she considers entering a convent and quickly refuses SERGEY's offer of marriage. After FOMA magnanimously joins her with YEGOR following his brief banishment, she mellows FOMA substantially, since she will not tolerate his demeaning YEGOR. Following their marriage she and YEGOR become totally devoted to each other. She frequently reads saints' lives and is inclined toward a poverty-level Christian life.

ZEPHYR [ZEFIR]. In classical mythology, the west wind. In the excitement following FOMA's magnanimous joining together of NASTYA and YEGOR there is a great bustle of activity, and TATYANA IVANOVNA's actions around BAKHCHEEV are compared to a ZEPHYR.

ZUY. One of the peasants repairing BAKHCHEEV's carriage.

ZVERKOV. In one of YEGOR's anecdotes he is a cavalry captain who runs away with the actress KUROPATKINA.

THE INSULTED AND INJURED (UNIZHENNYE I OSKORBLYONNYE) 1861

ABBADDONA A novel by the journalist and critic Nikolay Alekseevich Polevoy (1796-1846), published in 1834. The hero of the novel is a composite of romantic clichés. IKHMENEV observes that he learned that writers are pale and dreamy romantics from reading *ABBADDONA*.

"ACH, DU LIEBER AUGUSTIN" ["O MEYN LIBER AVGUSTIN"]. Popular German song. MASLOBOEV ruefully claims that the cousin to whom HEINRICH sent his letters and diaries likely understood only the parts about the moon, "ACH, DU LIEBER AUGUSTIN," and WIELAND.

ADAM. As recorded in Genesis 1 in the Old Testament, the first man on earth who dwelt in the Garden of Eden. VALKOVSKY relates a story about a civil servant who loses his mind in Paris, removes his clothing to look like ADAM, and exposes himself to people. VALKOVSKY notes that he gets the same thrill by sticking out his tongue at SCHILLERS at the proper moment.

ADAM IVANYCH. See ADAM IVANYCH SCHULZ.

AGASHA. Goddaughter of MARYA VASILIEVNA. She conveys information to ANNA ANDREEVNA about NATASHA.

MADAME ALBERT. KATYA's French companion.

ALEKSANDR PETROVICH. The literary entrepreneur through whom VANYA publishes and to whom he is in debt.

ALEKSANDRA SEMYONOVNA (SASHENKA). MASLOBOEV's common-law wife, who helps to care for NELLI when she is ill. She becomes close to NELLI and has her best interest at heart.

ALEKSANDRINA. A French woman whom VALKOVSKY introduces to his son ALYOSHA. The boy quickly begins an affair with her.

ALEKSEY MIKHAYLOVICH. ALEKSEY MIKHAYLOVICH Romanov (1629-76), second tsar of the Romanov dynasty that ruled Russia from 1613 to 1917. His own rule extended from 1645 to his death. ANNA ANDREEVNA, in an attempt to demonstrate the superiority of her daughter NATASHA over KATYA, states that her genealogy, the SHUMILOV line, traces itself back to ALEKSEY MIKHAYLOVICH. Her assertion is not substantiated in fact.

ALEKSEY PETROVICH. See ALEKSEY PETROVICH VALKOVSKY.

ALEXANDER THE GREAT [ALEKSANDR MAKEDONSKY]. Emperor Alexander III of Macedon (356-323 B.C.), who conquered the civilized world, extended Greek civilization into the East, and ushered in the Hellenistic Age. See "ALEXANDER THE GREAT WAS A HERO, EVERYONE KNOWS THAT, BUT WHY BREAK CHAIRS?"

"ALEXANDER THE GREAT WAS A HERO, EVERYONE KNOWS THAT, BUT WHY BREAK CHAIRS?" ["ONO KONECHNO, ALEKSANDR MAKEDONSKY GEROY, NO ZACHEM ZHE STULYA LOMAT?"]. Words of the mayor Skvoznik-Dmukhanovsky in the first scene of *The Inspector General (Revizor)*, a play written in 1836 by Nikolay GOGOL. The mayor comments on the history teacher's enthusiasm for his subject, but questions why he must become so excited, even over ALEXANDER THE GREAT, that he breaks chairs. When VANYA reads his novel about the poor civil servant to NATASHA and her mother, ANNA ANDREEVNA, though touched, looks at him as much as to say "ALEXANDER THE GREAT WAS A HERO, EVERYONE KNOWS THAT, BUT WHY BREAK CHAIRS?" She reacts this way in order to maintain her coolness to VANYA as a suitor for NATASHA.

ALPHONSE AND DALINDA [ALFONS I DALINDA].ALPHONSE AND DALINDA, or the Magic of Art and Nature (ALFONS I DALINDA, ili volshebstvo iskusstva i natury), a sentimentally moralizing tale published in *CHILDREN'S READING* in 1787. VANYA reminisces about how he and NATASHA read this story together in a romantic setting under a tree on their favorite bench.

ALNASKAR. ALNASKAROV, a retired midshipman in the comedy *Castles in the Air (Vozdushnye zamki),* written in 1818 by Nikolay Ivanovich Khmelnitsky (1789-1846). IKHMENEV, who retired from the hussars after losing most of what he had at cards, compares himself to ALNASKAR.

ALYOSHA. See ALEKSEY PETROVICH VALKOVSKY.

ANDRON TIMOFEICH. BUBNOVA threatens to send for ANDRON TIMOFEICH, a police officer, when VANYA tries to defend NELLI from her. BUBNOVA, NELLI's guardian, is intent on beating her for returning home late.

ANNA ANDREEVNA. See ANNA ANDREEVNA IKHMENEVA.

ANNA NIKOLAEVNA. VALKOVSKY mistakenly refers to NATASHA (NATALYA NIKOLAEVNA) as ANNA NIKOLAEVNA. The mistake is indicative of the depth of his interest in her.

ANNA TRIFONOVNA. See ANNA TRIFONOVNA BUBNOVA.

ANNUSHKA. See ANNA ANDREEVNA IKHMENEVA.

ARKHIPOV. A fifty year old bankrupt debauchee who is dubbed both JUDAS and FALSTAFF by MASLOBOEV. Most of his time is spent in helping SIZOBRYUKHOV waste a second inheritance. When he tries to take advantage of the thirteen year old NELLI at BUBNOVA's, he is roundly beaten by MITROSHKA, who has come to hate both him and SIZOBRYUKHOV.

ASTAFIEV. When VANYA meets IKHMENEV standing before NATASHA's door, vascillating about whether to knock, the proud IKHMENEV explains that he is looking for the clerk ASTAFIEV.

AZORKA. NELLI's mother's dog. Following her death the dog is taken by grandfather SMITH and serves as one of the last memories of his daughter. SMITH himself dies shortly after the dog.

B. A literary critic, who, though enthralled with VANYA's first novel, subsequently criticizes him. The possible allusion is to the influential critic Vissarion Grigorievich Belinsky (1811-48), who enthusiastically received Dostoevsky's first novel *Poor Folk* in 1846, but who was quite cool to *The Double,* published later in 1846, and to his subsequent work.

COUNT BARABANOV. In praising MITROSHKA, MASLOBOEV states that MITROSHKA is so adept that he could pass himself off as a COUNT BARABANOV in the English club.

FRIEDRICH BARBAROSSA [FRIDRIKH BARBARUSA]. FRIED-RICH I, surnamed BARBAROSSA (red beard) (1123?-1190), King of Germany and Holy Roman Emperor (1152-1190), who helped to unite Germany and fought to subjugate Italy. MASLOBOEV mentions that when he is drunk, he sometimes imagines himself as a HOMER, DANTE, or FRIEDRICH BARBAROSSA.

BEETHOVEN [BETKHOVEN]. Ludwig van BEETHOVEN (1770-1827), eminent German composer noted primarily for his symphonies. KATYA in playing BEETHOVEN's *Third Symphony* discovers that all of her emotions in her involvement with ALYOSHA and NATASHA are expressed by the music.

"A BEGGAR—THE DESCENDANT OF AN ANCIENT LINE" ["GOL-YAK—POTOMOK OTRASLI STARINNOY"]. A line from the poem "The Princess" ("Knyaginya"), published in 1856 by Nikolay Alekseevich Nekrasov (1821-78). The poem tells the tale of a beautiful and powerful Russian princess who leads an indifferent and abusive life until she falls hopelessly in love with a French doctor. He takes her money and torments her, and she dies poor and forgotten, leaving behind an impoverished estate. Her descendant must accordingly enter society as "A BEGGAR—THE DESCENDANT OF AN ANCIENT LINE." VANYA mentions that the impoverished young VALKOVSKY entered society in this manner.

BEZMYGIN. The head of a group of young progressive thinkers. The group counts as members both LEVENKA and BORENKA, from whom ALYOSHA gets his new ideas.

"THE BLIZZARD IS CALMED; THE PATH IS LIT" ["ULEGLASYA METELITSA; PUT OZARYON"]. A line from the poem "The Little Bell" ("Kolokolchik"), published in 1854 by Yakov Petrovich Polonsky (1819-98). The poem relates the subsiding of a storm and a woman's waiting for her love to return. As NATASHA waits to discuss with VANYA her relationship with ALYOSHA, she recalls this and several other lines from the same poem that she and VANYA once read together.

BORENKA. A young progressive thinker from whom ALYOSHA gets his modern ideas. The name seems to be taken from *Woe From Wit (Gore ot uma),* a comedy written by Aleksandr Sergeevich Griboedov (1795-1829) in 1822-24. In the comedy Levon (cf. LEVENKA) and BORENKA are members of the respected English Club and contrast markedly with ALYOSHA's young liberal friends.

BOYHOOD [OTROCHESTVO]. The second part (1854) of an autobiographical trilogy written by Count Lev Nikolaevich Tolstoy (1828-1910) between 1852 and 1857. ALYOSHA suggests to NATASHA that they read both *BOYHOOD* and *CHILDHOOD* because they are so good.

BRUDERSCHAFT [BRUDERSHAFT]. To demonstrate VALKOVSKY's debauchery MASLOBOEV concocts a narrative using fictitious names in which he chronicles one of VALKOVSKY's escapades abroad. The narrative features a daughter who runs away with her lover, is jilted, has a baby, and then lives with a platonic lover. The names MASLOBOEV provides for the platonic lover are a comic verbal exercise in German and include BRUDERSCHAFT, PFEFFERKUCHEN, FRAUENMILCH, and FEUERBACH.

ANNA TRIFONOVNA BUBNOVA. A fat, coarse procuress. She becomes NELLI's guardian and continually curses and abuses her despite efforts by VANYA to protect her. VANYA finally succeeds in freeing NELLI, but not until after BUBNOVA attempts to make her available to ARKHIPOV.

JULIUS CAESAR [YULY TSEZAR]. Roman general, statesman, and orator (100-44 B.C.), who after a distinguished military career forcibly assumed the role of emperor. ALYOSHA indicates that he attended a seance and summoned the spirit of JULIUS CAESAR.

ADMIRAL CHAINSKY. A colloquial term referring to a glass of tea *(chay).* When MASLOBOEV meets his friend VANYA after a lengthy separation, he invites him into a restaurant for a talk. He indicates to VANYA that he is a drinker and will have time to down ADMIRAL CHAINSKY, several kinds of wine, and whatever else he can think of.

CHILDHOOD [DETSTVO]. The first novel (1852) of an autobiographical trilogy written by Count Lev Nikolaevich Tolstoy (1828-1910) between 1852 and 1857. ALYOSHA suggests to NATASHA that they read both *CHILDHOOD* and *BOYHOOD* because they are so good.

CHILDREN'S READING [DETSKOE CHTENIE]. *CHILDREN'S READING For the Heart and the Mind (DETSKOE CHTENIE dlya serdtsa i razuma)*, the first Russian children's journal, published 1785-89 by Nikolay Ivanovich Novikov (1744-1818). VANYA reminisces about how he and NATASHA once took a copy of CHILDREN'S READING, sat on their favorite bench, and read *ALPHONSE AND DALINDA*.

THE CORRESPONDENT [PEREPISCHIK]. "Letters of an Out-of-Town Subscriber to the Editor of *The Contemporary* About Russian Journalism" ("Pisma inogorodnogo podpischika v redaktsiyu *Sovremennika* o russkoy zhurnalistike") were written by Aleksandr Vasilievich Druzhinin (1824-64), author and critic, and published unsigned in *The Contemporary* in 1849 and the early 1850s. VANYA notes that THE CORRESPONDENT has reviewed his work, neither praising nor condemning it, but commenting that it appears to be laboriously produced.

CUPID [KUPIDON]. The god of love in Roman mythology. He is the son of Venus and Mercury and is the counterpart of the Greek Eros. ANNA ANDREEVNA has a picture of NATASHA in the guise of CUPID painted by a vagabond artist.

DANTE [DANT]. DANTE Alighieri (1265-1321), Italian poet who was the first prominent writer to write in Italian. One of the greatest of world writers, he is known principally for *The Divine Comedy.* MASLOBOEV mentions that when he is drunk he sometimes imagines that he is HOMER, DANTE, or FRIEDRICH BARBAROSSA.

DERZHAVIN. Gavriil Romanovich DERZHAVIN (1743-1816), the greatest Russian poet of the eighteenth century, who is known primarily for his odes. IKHMENEV is distressed that NATASHA is romantically linked with VANYA because he is a writer and is not planning a more practical career. VANYA and NATASHA try to mollify him by asserting that writing is an honorable profession and that DERZHAVIN was rewarded handsomely for his work.

DON QUIXOTE [DON KIKHOT]. The hero of *El Ingenioso Hidalgo DON QUIXOTE de la Mancha (The Ingenious Gentleman DON QUI-*

XOTE of la Mancha), a novel written by Miguel de Cervantes (1547-1616) and published in 1605 and 1615. One of the premier works of world fiction, the novel chronicles DON QUIXOTE's obsession with knight errantry and visionary idealism. MASLOBOEV complains to VANYA about BUBNO-VA, but asks VANYA not to consider him a DON QUIXOTE, a crusader against evil.

DORFBARBIER. *THE VILLAGE BARBER,* a German humor magazine published in Leipzig since 1844 and known since 1852 as *Der Illustrierte DORFBARBIER (The Illustrated VILLAGE BARBER).* ADAM IVAN-YCH SCHULZ is reading this magazine when he notices JEREMIAH SMITH staring at him. SCHULZ take offense,and the embarrassed old man dies not long after.

DUSSOT [DYUSSO]. The owner of a French restaurant in St. Petersburg. The intoxicated ARKHIPOV and SIZOBRYUKHOV suggest to MAS-LOBOEV and VANYA that they accompany them to DUSSOT's.

THE EMPRESS [IMPERATRITSA]. Catherine the Great (1729-96), who ruled Russia from 1762 to her death. IKHMENEV despairs that his daughter NATASHA is romantically involved with VANYA because the latter is a writer and plans no other career. VANYA and NATASHA attempt to comfort him by pointing out that writing is an honorable profession, that SUMAROKOV held the rank of general, that DER-ZHAVIN was rewarded handsomely, and that THE EMPRESS herself paid a visit to LOMONOSOV. Catherine visited his home and laboratory in 1764.

FALSTAFF [FALSTAF]. Sir John FALSTAFF, who appears as a comic character in *Henry IV, Parts One and Two* (1597-98) and *The Merry Wives of Windsor* (1597-1601) by William Shakespeare (1564-1616). He is characterized by self-indulgence, braggadocio, buffoonery, and vice. MAS-LOBOEV refers to ARKHIPOV as both a JUDAS and a FALSTAFF.

FEDOSYA TITISHNA. A repulsive woman who is sometimes with BUBNOVA.

FEUERBACH [FEYERBAKH]. Ludwig FEUERBACH (1804-72), Ger-man philosopher who analyzed religion from the psychological and anthropological point of view. See BRUDERSCHAFT.

KATERINA FYODOROVNA FILIMONOVA (KATYA). The seventeen year old stepdaughter of COUNTESS ZINAIDA FYODOROVNA, who conspires with VALKOVSKY to marry KATYA to ALYOSHA. She has a substantial dowry, and both VALKOVSKY and the countess sense that it would be very easy to get the money after the marriage. She is not pretty, but has a good heart, is a thinker, and has a passion for good and justice. Under the promptings of LEVENKA and BORENKA, she has promised to give a million rubles for the benefit of society, and the two young men are already arguing about how best to spend the money. She falls in love with ALYOSHA, but also highly respects NATASHA with whom he is living. She and NATASHA meet and agree that ALYOSHA loves KATYA more and will eventually be hers alone. They also agree that they both love him because he is a child and because they feel sorry for him.

FILIPP. See FILIPP FILIPPOVICH MASLOBOEV.

FILIPP FILIPPOVICH. See FILIPP FILIPPOVICH MASLOBOEV.

FILIPP FILIPPYCH. See FILIPP FILIPPOVICH MASLOBOEV.

FRAUENMILCH [FRAUENMILKH]. See BRUDERSCHAFT.

GAVARNI. Paul GAVARNI (1804-66), popular French illustrator and lithographer, who achieved his greatest notoriety by illustrating the works of Romantic writers, in particular the fantastic stories of E.T.A. HOFFMANN. VANYA observes that SMITH and his dog AZORKA look like something out of HOFFMANN illustrated by GAVARNI.

GOETHE [GYOTE]. Johann Wolfgang von GOETHE (1749-1832), German poet, playwright, novelist, and scientist, who is one of the giants of world literature. IKHMENEV banters about how all writers look pale, much like GOETHE. He has categorized GOETHE as a Romantic and linked him with the image of the writer that he found in *ABBADDONA*.

GOGOL. Nikolay Vasilievich GOGOL (1809-52), popular Russian writer known for his tragicomic exposing of human foibles. He was viewed by progressive critics as the fountainhead of the Natural School and credited with critically describing reality with the intent of social reform. (1) MASLOBOEV mentions that among his failures in life is an article he wrote on GOGOL. (2) ALYOSHA relates how at a seance he calls up the spirit of

JULIUS CAESAR. While under this influence a pencil of its own volition writes the word "get drenched!" ("obmokni!"), which, ALYOSHA notes, is also found in GOGOL. He has in mind the dramatic fragment *The Lawsuit (Tyazhba)* in which an ill landlady mistakenly writes "obmokni." (3) In attempting to give credence to his profession as a writer and to his role as a possible husband for NATASHA, VANYA cites the success of GOGOL, who chose writing instead of a more formal career. IKHMENEV then observes that GOGOL was sent a lot of money each year when he was abroad. (4) When ALYOSHA tells NATASHA and VANYA that VAL-KOVSKY has given him permission to marry NATASHA, he acts so dignified and youthfully proud that the other two cannot restrain their laughter. The narrator notes that they become so amused that they are like GOGOL's midshipman, who roared with laughter at the slightest provocation. The midshipman referred to is Petukhov in *The Marriage (Zhenitba)*, written in 1842.

HAMLET [GAMLET]. HAMLET, Prince of Denmark, a tragedy written by William Shakespeare (1564-1616) in 1601. (1) VALKOVSKY relates an anecdote to VANYA about a mad French civil servant, who takes off his clothes and exposes himself a la ADAM. Following this, the clerk majestically vanishes like the ghost in *HAMLET.* The ghost referred to is HAMLET's murdered father, who appears to his son, names his brother Claudius as the murderer, and asks HAMLET to seek revenge. (2) VALKOVSKY mentions a fool who philosophized to the extent that he determined that the best thing in life was hydrocyanic acid. He suspects that VANYA, being a writer and a romantic, will probably explain away the fool as a HAMLET in the depths of depression. HAMLET indeed played the fool for a time in order to expose Claudius.

HEINRICH [GENRIKH]. See HEINRICH SALZMANN.

HISTORY [ISTORIA]. HISTORY of the Russian State (ISTORIA gosudarstva Rossyskogo), a twelve volume history of Russia by Nikolay KARAMZIN, generally from the point of view of autocracy. The first eleven volumes were published 1816-24, and the uncompleted twelfth volume appeared posthumously in 1829. ANNA ANDREEVNA, anxious to demonstrate the superiority of her daughter NATASHA over KATYA as a fiancee for ALYOSHA, traces the noble lineage of the IKHMENEV and SHUMILOV lines and insists that documents to this effect can be found in KARAMZIN's *HISTORY.* The contention is unsupported by fact.

HOFFMANN [GOFMAN]. Ernst Theodor Amadeus HOFFMANN (1776-1822), German author primarily known for his fantastic tales. VANYA observes in his narration that SMITH and his dog AZORKA look like something out of HOFFMANN illustrated by GAVARNI.

HOMER [GOMER]. Ancient Greek poet to whom are attributed the *Iliad* and the *Odyssey*. He is known for his epic visions and proportions. MASLOBOEV mentions that when he is drunk he sometimes imagines that he is HOMER, DANTE, or FRIEDRICH BARBAROSSA.

NIKOLAY SERGEICH IKHMENEV. A simple, noble, and good man who is naive and romantically inclined. After serving for a time in the hussars and losing almost everything at cards, he retires and marries ANNA ANDREEVNA. He then goes to work for VALKOVSKY and comes to love the latter's son ALYOSHA. He and VALKOVSKY have a rift when IKHMENEV is accused of being a thief and his daughter NATASHA is rumored to be having an affair with ALYOSHA. This situation causes IKHMENEV to become involved in a lengthy litigation to defend himself. He has raised VANYA, an orphan, in his home, but objects to VANYA's desire to marry NATASHA because he wants to make writing his profession. IKHMENEV does not hold literature in high regard and feels that VANYA needs more of a career before marriage. His whole life comes apart when NATASHA leaves to go live with ALYOSHA, and he becomes morose, quick-tempered, and difficult to be with. He weeps at night but maintains a severe exterior, and even though he hungers for NATASHA's return, he wants her to return alone and repentant. His pride precludes his forgiving, and he considers his daughter debauched and deserving of curses and punishment. When the litigation goes badly and NATASHA remains with ALYOSHA, he determines to challenge VALKOVSKY to a duel. VALKOVSKY refuses the challenge and then condescendingly and cynically gives IKHMENEV money, even though he wins the suit. This further damages IKHMENEV's pride, and he vows never to forgive NATASHA. He then turns to NELLI and wants her to come live with him and ANNA ANDREEVNA to replace NATASHA. NELLI condemns his actions because she has seen the same situation destroy her grandfather SMITH and her mother, who had run away with VALKOVSKY. Under NELLI's influence there is a reconciliation of father and daughter, and IKHMENEV subsequently devotes himself entirely to NATASHA. NELLI becomes very close to the family and is expected to leave with them when IKHMENEV assumes a new position, but her untimely death makes him inconsolable and very ill.

ANNA ANDREEVNA IKHMENEVA (ANNUSHKA). IKHMENEV's poor but proud wife. She becomes enchanted by VALKOVSKY and encourages her husband to go to work for him. When NATASHA and ALYOSHA become romantically linked, she is eager to demonstrate NATASHA's superiority over her wealthy rival KATYA, and she takes great pains to inform others of the noble heritage of the IKHMENEV and SHUMILOV (her maiden name) families. She is crushed when NATASHA leaves to live with ALYOSHA but quickly forgives her and hungers for news of her. The situation gradually undermines her health and mind, and even though NATASHA returns, ANNA ANDREEVNA is but a shadow of her former self.

NATALYA NIKOLAEVNA IKHMENEVA (NATALYA NIKOLAV-NA, NATASHA, NATASHENKA, NATASHECHKA). IKHMENEV's only daughter, who comes to love two men. She is very touched by VANYA's writing and accepts his proposal of marriage. Their wedding is postponed at the insistence of her parents, who want to see whether VANYA will ever have a successful career. Sometime later she confides to VANYA that she is going to live with ALYOSHA. She indicates that she loves VANYA's goodness and his heart but that she loves ALYOSHA to insanity and knows that if she is not with him constantly, he will forget her. Even the torment she endures from ALYOSHA gives her happiness, and despite her jealousy she always forgives his exploits with other women. She comes to hate VALKOVSKY and his machinations because he tries to manipulate ALYOSHA's affections and influence him to marry KATYA. She bitterly refuses VALKOVSKY's consent to allow ALYOSHA to marry her, because she knows that even that is an attempt to drive him to KATYA. She and KATYA eventually meet and determine that ALYOSHA will certainly be KATYA's and that they both love him because he is a pitiable child. NATASHA also admits that she enjoys suffering and relishes forgiving ALYOSHA for his involvement with other women. The more guilty ALYOSHA is, the better. After parting with ALYOSHA, she returns to her parents to ask their forgiveness and enters the apartment just as they are preparing to come to her for reconciliation. When IKHMENEV's new position requires a relocation, she dreads to part with VANYA, who remains faithful to her throughout. She seems convinced that she and VANYA could have been happy together forever.

IVAN ALEKSANDRYCH. An undertaker who lives in BUBNOVA's house and who helps NELLI and her mother.

IVAN KARLOVICH. The German foreman on VALKOVSKY's estate, who is dismissed for theft.

IVAN PETROVICH (VANYA). The twenty five year old narrator, who grows up as an orphan in IKHMENEV's home. While there he falls in love with NATASHA and proposes, but his offer is rejected by her parents because he is a writer with no other visible career. Following this disappointment he moves into the apartment of the recently deceased JEREMIAH SMITH, where he hopes to continue his writing. While there he meets NELLI, who is searching for her grandfather SMITH, and thereafter his time is divided between consoling NATASHA, reporting her movements and emotions to ANNA ANDREEVNA, and becoming increasingly involved in NELLI's life. He essentially moves from character to character, is privy to the unraveling of the mystery of NELLI, her mother, and VALKOVSKY, and he is party to the resolution of NATASHA's affair with ALYOSHA and her reconciliation with her family. He also provides a sounding board for VALKOVSKY, who explains his real desires and motives to the shocked VANYA. He is left behind as the IKHMENEVS leave, but NATASHA's eyes tell him wistfully that they could have been happy together. In many ways VANYA is the analogue of Dostoevsky himself. VANYA had wanted a large room by himself so that he could pace back and forth while he wrote, and it is known that Dostoevsky liked to pace while writing. VANYA's first novel, received with much praise particularly by the critic B. (likely a reference to Belinsky), deals with a young man who dies (Pokrovsky), an old man (Makar Devushkin), and a young girl (Varenka) involved in a situation that turns out badly, and it could easily be construed to be *Poor Folk*. VANYA's subsequent work is not greeted with the same enthusiasm and may parallel the cool reception accorded *The Double.*

IVAN VASILIEVICH THE TERRIBLE [IVAN VASILIEVICH GROZ-NY]. Tsar IVAN IV of Russia (1530-84). He nominally assumed the throne at age three and ruled until his death. IVAN consolidated the Russian empire under Moscow and became known for his ferocity toward his enemies and his alternate periods of sensuality and piety. ANNA ANDREEVNA, wanting to show NATASHA's superiority over KATYA as a possible fiancee for ALYOSHA, traces the noble lineage of both the IKHMENEV and SHUMILOV lines and insists that the former can be traced back to IVAN VASILIEVICH THE TERRIBLE.

JESUIT [IEZUIT]. The Society of Jesus, a religious order for Roman Catholic men founded by Ignatius Loyola (1491-1556) in 1534. The society is known for scholarship and missionary zeal and has been accused of secrecy and intrigue. ALYOSHA praises his father VALKOVSKY's ability to merely look at people and thereby ascertain their thoughts. He muses that this is probably why VALKOVSKY is called a JESUIT. The rumor subsequently circulates that VALKOVSKY has actually become a JESUIT, and ANNA ANDREEVNA and others eagerly spread it.

JOSEPHINA [ZHOZEFINA]. One of the women with whom ALYOSHA has an affair while he is living with NATASHA.

MADAME JOUBERT (JOUBERTA) [ZHUBER, ZHUBERTA]. When very drunk KARP VASILYICH breaks MADAME JOUBERT's large English pier-glass in Paris.

JOUBERTA. See MADAME JOUBERT.

JUDAS [IUDA]. As recorded in the New Testament, JUDAS Iscariot, the apostle who betrayed Jesus by identifying Him to Roman soldiers in exchange for thirty pieces of silver. MASLOBOEV refers to both ARKHI-POV and VALKOVSKY as JUDAS.

PRINCESS K. ALYOSHA's elderly godmother, who because of her wealth and social standing is in a position to insure his career and success in life. She loves dogs, and ALYOSHA wins her over by teaching her dog MIMI to extend its paw.

KARAMZIN. Nikolay Mikhaylovich KARAMZIN (1766-1826), writer and historian who infused Westernisms into the literary language to make it more like the language of the aristocracy. His fiction sought to express the noble and virtuous and was a product of the Sentimental movement, while his *HISTORY* is generally pro-autocracy. ANNA ANDREEVNA insists that documents proving the noble lineage of the IKHMENEV and SHUMILOV families can be found in KARAMZIN's *HISTORY*. This however is unsubstantiated by fact. She is anxious to demonstrate her daughter NATASHA's superiority over her rival KATYA.

KARP VASILYICH. SIZOBRYUKHOV relates at BUBNOVA's that when he and KARP VASILYICH were in Paris, the latter when quite drunk broke a large English pier-glass at the home of MADAME JOUBERT.

KATERINA FYODOROVNA. See KATERINA FYODOROVNA FI-LIMONOVA.

KATYA. See KATERINA FYODOROVNA FILIMONOVA.

COUNTESS KHLYOSTOVA. To illustrate VALKOVSKY's debauchery MASLOBOEV concocts a narrative using fictitious names in which he chronicles one of VALKOVSKY's escapades abroad. The narrative features a daughter who runs away with her lover, is jilted, has a baby, and then lives with a platonic lover. MASLOBOEV notes that the influential opinions of people like COUNTESS KHLYOSTOVA and BARON POMOYKIN prevent the marriage of the lover to the seduced daughter. The name of COUNTESS KHLYOSTOVA is probably taken from *Woe From Wit (Gore ot uma),* a comedy written between 1822-24 by Aleksandr Sergeevich Griboedov (1795-1829).

KLUGEN. The owner of the large house in which JEREMIAH SMITH rents a wretched apartment. This is the same apartment which VANYA takes following SMITH's death.

KOLOTUSHKIN. The owner of a house in which NATASHA rents a room.

FYODOR KARLOVICH KRIEGER [KRIGER]. A frequenter of MIL-LER's confectionary shop who offers to stuff JEREMIAH SMITH's dead dog AZORKA.

LAZARUS [LAZAR]. As recorded in Luke 16:19-31 in the New Testament, a beggar who pleads daily at the gate of the rich man and who ultimately unlike the rich man receives an eternal reward. The name has become part of a fixed expression in Russian, meaning to bemoan one's fate. A drunken VALKOVSKY, upset with the whole situation about NELLI's mother, bemoans the situation à la LAZARUS and almost admits to MASLOBOEV his personal involvement.

LENOCHKA. See YELENA.

LEVENKA. A young progressive thinker from whom ALYOSHA gets his modern ideas. See BORENKA.

THE LIBERATION OF MOSCOW [OSVOBOZHDENIE MOSKVY]. *Prince Pozharsky and the Nizhny Novgorod Citizen Minin,* or *THE LIBERATION OF MOSCOW IN 1612 (Knyaz Pozharsky i nizhegorodsky grazhdanin Minin, ili OSVOBOZHDENIE MOSKVY v 1612 godu),* an historical adventure novel written in 1840 by I. Glukharyov. After listening to VANYA read his novel, IKHMENEV notes that he has at home *THE LIBERATION OF MOSCOW,* a much more elevated piece of writing.

LOMONOSOV. Mikhail Vasilievich LOMONOSOV (1711-65), Russian scholar, poet, and rhetorician who was instrumental in forming the literary language and rules of poetry. His own verse is rather heavy and ornate, and he specialized in the ode. When VANYA, NATASHA, and IKHMENEV discuss the validity of writing as a career as opposed to something more stable, VANYA cites the example of the visit of the EMPRESS herself to LOMONOSOV's home and laboratory in 1764.

MARYA VASILIEVNA. A woman living in VALKOVSKY's house, who conveys information about NATASHA to her mother ANNA ANDRE-EVNA through AGASHA and MATRYONA.

FILIPP FILIPPOVICH MASLOBOEV (FILIPP, FILIPP FILIPPYCH). An old school chum of VANYA who has had a life of failures and bad conduct and who seems to VANYA to be one of the many half-dead people of Russia. He has been hired by VALKOVSKY to trace NELLI's mother, and his search unravels the mystery of NELLI and her relationship to VALKOVSKY. MASLOBOEV is the source of the background information about all characters except the IKHMENEV family, and because of this VANYA has extensive contact with him.

MATRYONA. The IKHMENEV's devoted maid, who periodically conveys to ANNA ANDREEVNA information about NATASHA.

MAVRA. A servant woman at the disposal of NATASHA.

MEPHISTOPHELES [MEFISTOFEL]. The demon-like tempter in the various versions of the Faust legend. When VANYA first sees AZORKA, he senses that the dog is unlike others and that in it is concealed something fantastic and bewitched, like some MEPHISTOPHELES in the form of a dog. In GOETHE's *Faust* MEPHISTOPHELES first appears as a black poodle.

MILLER. The owner of the confectionary shop which JEREMIAH SMITH frequents.

MIMI. PRINCESS K.'s dog, which ALYOSHA teaches to extend its paw. The wealthy and influential socialite, a dog lover, is captivated by ALYOSHA's feat and will see to his career and success in life.

MINNA. One of the women with whom ALYOSHA has an affair while he is living with NATASHA.

MITROSHKA. An antagonist of ARKHIPOV and SIZOBRYUKHOV who rescues NELLI from ARKHIPOV's advances at BUBNOVA's house.

MOLIERE [MOLIER]. Pen name of Jean Baptiste Poquelin (1622-73), who became the foremost French comic dramatist. He has few rivals in the comic exposition of human foibles. When MASLOBOEV extracts a bribe from BUBNOVA, he comments "Je prends mon bien, où je le trouve" ("I take my profit where I find it") and attributes the words to MOLIERE. He adds that only in this is he anything like MOLIERE.

MON—REVECHE [MON-REVESH]. A French émigré from whom ANNA ANDREEVNA gets her education.

N. NATASHA wonders why VANYA stays up nights to write and hurries to complete his work when a writer like N. writes only one work in ten years.

COUNT N. An older man with means and connections for whom VALKOVSKY occasionally procures young women like NATASHA. IKHMENEV pursues VALKOVSKY to the home of COUNT N. in order to challenge him to a duel.

COUNT NAINSKY. VALKOVSKY's influential relative, who assists him with his career and who assumes the upbringing of ALYOSHA for a time.

NATALYA NIKOLAEVNA. See NATALYA NIKOLAEVNA IKHMENEVA.

NATALYA NIKOLAVNA. See NATALYA NIKOLAEVNA IKHMENEVA.

NATASHA. See NATALYA NIKOLAEVNA IKHMENEVA.

NATASHECHKA. See NATALYA NIKOLAEVNA IKHMENEVA.

NATASHENKA. See NATALYA NIKOLAEVNA IKHMENEVA.

NELLI. See YELENA.

NELLICHKA. See YELENA.

CORNELIUS NEPOS [KORNELY NEPOT]. Roman historian and biographer (ca. 100-25 B.C.). MASLOBOEV reminisces with VANYA about how they used to study CORNELIUS NEPOS in school.

ST. NICHOLAS [NIKOLAY UGODNIK]. The bishop of Myra, who died about 345 A.D. BUBNOVA insists that she assumed guardianship of NELLI following her mother's death because of a desire to be noble and serve ST. NICHOLAS. Her saintliness extends to beating NELLI and trying to involve her in prostitution.

NIKOLAY. See NIKOLAY SERGEICH IKHMENEV.

NIKOLAY SERGEICH. See NIKOLAY SERGEICH IKHMENEV.

NOAH [NOY]. As recorded in Genesis 6-10, the Old Testament patriarch whom Jehovah commanded to build an ark prior to the destruction of the earth by flood. In the ark NOAH saved his family together with specimens of each kind of animal. The large house divided into several apartments in which JEREMIAH SMITH lives is compared to NOAH's ark.

THE NORTHERN DRONE [SEVERNY TRUTEN]. Comically mistaken reference to *The Northern Bee (Severnaya pchela)*, a conservative St. Petersburg newspaper published 1825-64 by Faddey Venediktovich Bulgarin (1789-1859) and Nikolay Ivanovich Grech (1787-1867). IKHMENEV begins to read the critical articles of B. and to warmly criticize B.'s enemies who write in *THE NORTHERN DRONE. The Northern Bee* did in fact attack Belinsky and the Natural School during the 1840s.

PFEFFERKUCHEN [FEFERKUKHEN]. See BRUDERSCHAFT.

MADEMOISELLE PHILEBERTE. VALKOVSKY asks VANYA if he would like to be introduced to MADEMOISELLE PHILEBERTE late some night.

POLICHINELLO [POLISHINEL]. A variant of Pulcinella, the coarse, unscrupulous comic character from the Italian folk theater *commedia dell' arte* who is related to the Russian Petrushka and the English Punch. As VALKOVSKY reveals to VANYA the extent of his debauchery, cynicism, and manipulations, VANYA describes his tone as that of POLICHINELLO.

BARON POMOYKIN. See COUNTESS KHLYOSTOVA. It is noteworthy that the name POMOYKIN is also found in Nikolay GOGOL's comedy *The Marriage (Zhenitba),* completed in 1842.

PRASKOVYA ANDREEVNA. ANNA ANDREEVNA's sister. She has a niece named YELENA who is also nicknamed NELLI.

PUSHKIN. Aleksandr Sergeevich PUSHKIN (1799-1837), the leading writer of his time, who is regarded as the father of modern Russian literature. VANYA tries to convince IKHMENEV of the validity of writing as a profession so that he can seriously be regarded as NATASHA's fiance, and he cites PUSHKIN as an example of a successful writer. IKHMENEV, who distrusts literature in general and poetry in particular, acknowledges that PUSHKIN may have been great, but he wrote only verse.

PYOTR ALEKSANDROVICH. See PRINCE PYOTR ALEKSANDROVICH VALKOVSKY.

PRINCE R. NATASHA, competing with KATYA for ALYOSHA's affections, suggests to VANYA that since he frequents the home of PRINCE R., he might try to become acquainted there with COUNTESS ZINAIDA FYODOROVNA, KATYA's stepmother, and find out all he can about KATYA.

ROSLAVLEV. *ROSLAVLEV, or the Russians in 1812 (ROSLAVLEV, ili Russkie v 1812 godu),* historical romance published in 1831 by Mikhail Nikolaevich Zagoskin (1789-1852). After listening to VANYA's novel about the poor clerk, IKHMENEV notes that it would have been nice to have had a more interesting hero or perhaps something historical such as is found in *ROSLAVLEV* or *YURY MILOSLAVSKY.*

ROTHSCHILD [ROTSHILD]. A family of internationally known German-Jewish bankers who helped to finance several European nations in the nineteenth century. ALYOSHA explains to his father VALKOVSKY that even though they are titled nobility they are not really princes, because they have no great wealth. He adds that ROTHSCHILD is now the most important prince because of his wealth.

S. NATASHA wonders why VANYA stays up nights to write and hurries to complete his work. She fears that he will damage his health and his talent by working like that and cites the example of S., who produces one work every two years.

MARQUIS DE SADE [MARKIZ DE SAD]. Donatien Alphonse François DE SADE (1740-1814), prolific French writer who spent a good deal of his life in prison as punishment for his sexual escapades and for writing licentious books. His name has become synonymous with depravity, particularly torturing the object of love. VALKOVSKY discusses an affair he had with a woman who was so voluptuous that even the MARQUIS DE SADE could have learned some things from her.

HEINRICH SALZMANN [GENRIKH ZALTSMAN]. The platonic lover of NELLI's mother who lives with her in Europe until his death. All the time they are together he sends letters and diaries to another woman, a cousin, who maintains her love for him throughout. It is through these documents that MASLOBOEV unravels the mystery of NELLI, her mother, and VALKOVSKY.

SAPHIR [SAFIR]. Moritz Gottlieb SAPHIR (1795-1858), German humorist and writer. VANYA notes that the Germans who gather at MILLER's confectionary shop sometimes exchange a joke or a witticism from the noted German humorist SAPHIR.

SASHENKA. See ALEKSANDRA SEMYONOVNA.

SCHILLER [SHILLER]. Johann Christoph Friedrich von SCHILLER (1759-1805), German dramatist, poet, and historian noted for his romantic idealism. (1) In MASLOBOEV's fictionalized account of VALKOVSKY's escapade abroad the platonic lover of the seduced and abandoned girl is said to be a poetic brother of SCHILLER. As the two travel together about Europe, they often read SCHILLER together. (2) VALKOVSKY accuses VANYA of being some kind of SCHILLER, since even though VANYA has lost NATASHA to ALYOSHA, he remains close friends with them and even tries to insure the success of their relationship. (3) VALKOVSKY admits that he hates the naiveté and pastorals of the eternally young followers of SCHILLER, loves to torment them and enjoys sticking his tongue out at them at the proper moment. (4) VALKOVSKY refers to the entire situation involving NATASHA and ALYOSHA as characteristic of SCHILLER. (5) In VALKOVSKY's escapade abroad the girl he seduces steals money from her father and gives it to him. After he abandons her, he keeps the money in order to enhance the suffering he believes she desires. He determines to accommodate her SCHILLERIAN nature.

ADAM IVANYCH SCHULZ [SHULTS]. A merchant from Riga who comes to MILLER's confectionary. He becomes upset when JEREMIAH

SMITH stares at him. He is unaware that the old man comes to the shop daily to sit, listen, and look. SMITH becomes very confused and agitated when SCHULZ objects, and both he and the dog die shortly thereafter.

SCRIBE [SKRIB]. Augustin Eugène SCRIBE (1791-1861), prolific French writer of spirited, farcical plays. When ALYOSHA decides to become a writer, he envisions his first novel based upon one of SCRIBE's comedies.

SEMYON. See SEMYON VALKOVSKY.

ANNA ANDREEVNA SHUMILOVA. Maiden name of ANNA ANDREEVNA IKHMENEVA.

STEPAN TERENTYICH SIZOBRYUKHOV. A dissolute young man who is wasting his second inheritance with the help of ARKHIPOV.

IVAN SKORYAGIN. A tailor who three years ago made VANYA's only frock coat.

JEREMIAH SMITH [IEREMIA SMIT]. An Englishman who marries a Russian wife. His daughter, NELLI's mother, takes his money and runs away with VALKOVSKY to Europe. He never forgives her, and even though he sees NELLI often and is kind to her, he avoids contact with his daughter. After her death, he quite loses his mind and makes NELLI beg for him in the streets. He begins to come daily to MILLER's confectionary with his deceased daughter's dog AZORKA, sits for a time, stares, and leaves. On one occasion SCHULZ, unfamiliar with his routine, becomes offended at his stares and complains. AZORKA dies on the spot, and SMITH dies shortly thereafter.

THE SMITH GIRL [SMITIKHA]. JEREMIAH SMITH's daughter, who takes his money and runs away to Europe with VALKOVSKY. She is quickly jilted but has a daughter NELLI by him. She travels in Europe with a platonic friend named HEINRICH and stays with him until he dies. Upon returning to Russia she makes attempts to be reconciled with her father and suffers because of her guilt toward him. Her attempts fail, and she dies of consumption without her father's love. She leaves a letter with NELLI to be given to VALKOVSKY after her death in which she refuses to forgive him and demands that he do something for NELLI.

STEPAN. A waiter in the restaurant where MASLOBOEV reminisces with VANYA and exposes VALKOVSKY.

STEPAN TERENTYICH. See STEPAN TERENTYICH SIZOBRYU-
KHOV.

SUMAROKOV. Aleksandr Petrovich SUMAROKOV (1718-77), Russian
dramatist and poet who was instrumental in the reform of the literary
language and in establishing Classicism in Russia. In answer to IKHME-
NEV's concern that VANYA's desire to be a writer reflects lack of ambition
and impracticality, VANYA cites the example of SUMAROKOV, who held
the rank of general.

TALLEYRAND [TALEYRAN]. Charles Maurice de TALLEYRAND-
Périgord (1754-1838), French statesman who helped to restore the Bourbon
monarchy following the defeat of Napoleon and who represented his
country at the Congress of Vienna. When VANYA accuses VALKOVSKY
of robbing SMITH's daughter of the money she stole from her father,
VALKOVSKY responds by calling him a TALLEYRAND. He implies that
through his diplomacy and intrigues VANYA has found out about the
whole affair.

TOLSTOY. Count Lev Nikolaevich TOLSTOY (1828-1910), eminent
Russian writer and thinker. ALYOSHA and VANYA agree to use the
familiar grammatical forms instead of the formal ones when speaking with
each other, but ALYOSHA has trouble remembering. His forgetfulness
reminds him of a similar occurrence in the writings of TOLSTOY where two
young people agree to use the familiar form but have so much trouble
remembering that they avoid pronouns altogether. The scene he recalls
occurs in *CHILDHOOD.*

ALEKSEY PETROVICH VALKOVSKY (ALYOSHA). VALKOVSKY's
naive, spoiled son, whom he sends to IKHMENEV in the country so he can
learn values, discipline, and practicality. The project fails and he remains
weak, naive, egotistical, and impractical—still very much a child. When
VALKOVSKY tries to arrange an advantageous marriage for him to
KATYA, ALYOSHA rebels and asks NATASHA to come live with him.
He acts on impulse and self-interest, and if NATASHA is not with him
continually, he quickly finds someone else. While they live together he
constantly asserts that he is not worthy of NATASHA, that they will get
married soon, and that he might even go to work to support them. Debts
and other women take up his time instead of work, however, and their
relationship becomes one of betrayal and confession. After meeting
KATYA, whom his father wants him to marry because of her large dowry,
ALYOSHA finds himself caught between NATASHA and KATYA, and he

irretrievably inclines toward the latter, who is more able to fill the activity and intellectual vacuum in his personality than is NATASHA. During his romantic crisis, he dabbles in the progressive ideas of the younger generation and fashionably and unconvincingly denounces his father's generation. He finally writes NATASHA a confused and tormented letter in which he implies farewell, and it is clear that despite all of his vows to the contrary he will marry KATYA.

PRINCE PYOTR ALEKSANDROVICH VALKOVSKY. A forty year old widower and representative of St. Petersburg high society. He moves to the country on an estate next to IKHMENEV, befriends him because he thinks he can use him, and hires him to be the foreman of his estate. His prosperous estate is the result of his first marriage to a woman he married for her money. Following her death he goes abroad with the daughter of JEREMIAH SMITH and convinces her to take her father's money. He takes the money, abandons her pregnant with NELLI, and returns to his active social life in St. Petersburg. Some provincial scandalmongers send him word that ALYOSHA, whom he sent to the country to learn some values, is having an affair with NATASHA and that IKHMENEV is misusing the estate funds. Litigation ensues, and even though he later realizes that IKHMENEV is innocent, he decides to ruin him. Afraid that ALYOSHA will do something rash, he forbids him to see NATASHA and concentrates on arranging a marriage with KATYA, the wealthy step-daughter of COUNTESS ZINAIDA FYODOROVNA, with whom he is having an affair. He and the countess are certain that they can get the money after the marriage. When ALYOSHA and NATASHA begin to live together, he ostensibly gives the arrangement his blessing, but orchestrates events to allow ALYOSHA extensive contact with KATYA. Before the resolution of his son's marriage he has a lengthy discussion with VANYA in which he exposes his true self. He relates to VANYA instances of his debauchery, his love of pleasure, his hatred for idealism and things reminiscent of SCHILLER, and his belief in ego, status, and money. After ALYOSHA seems safely in love with KATYA, he tries to procure NATASHA for COUNT N. His employment of MASLOBOEV to trace SMITH's daughter results in his exposure as NELLI's father and in the suggestion that he and NELLI's mother were actually married for a time.

SEMYON VALKOVSKY. VALKOVSKY's brother.

VANYA. See IVAN PETROVICH.

VOLODKA. To illustrate VALKOVSKY's debauchery MASLOBOEV narrates a story to VANYA using fictionalized names in which a daughter runs away with her lover, is jilted, has a baby, and then lives with a platonic lover. The name given to the child is VOLODKA, and MASLOBOEV calls it both a son and a daughter.

WIELAND [VILAND]. Christoph Martin WIELAND (1733-1813), German novelist, poet, editor, and translator. The cousin, who patiently loves HEINRICH and who receives all his letters and diaries, in MASLOBOEV's opinion understands only those parts about the moon, "ACH, DU LIEBER AUGUSTIN," and WIELAND.

YELENA (NELLI). A niece of PRASKOVYA ANDREEVNA who is also nicknamed NELLI.

YELENA (LENOCHKA, NELLI, NELLICHKA). The product of a brief liaison between VALKOVSKY and THE SMITH GIRL, who has suffered extensively in life. Following her mother's death she is taken in by BUBNOVA, who abuses her and plans to turn her to prostitution. For a time she passively accepts her beatings from BUBNOVA, but after MITROSHKA rescues her from ARKHIPOV's advances, she goes to live with VANYA. Despite better living conditions, her health continues to deteriorate because of her emotional condition and because of a heart ailment that would respond to the quiet and calm that she seldom experiences. She is a proud girl of almost fourteen who enjoys suffering, deliberately seeks it, and whose ego responds to injury and injustice. This state of mind causes her to flee VANYA several times and to beg in the street. She ultimately becomes close to the IKHMENEV family, and her relating the story of her mother and grandfather SMITH to IKHMENEV softens his heart enough to provoke his reconciliation with NATASHA. Dreams of her sordid past life, her tormented awareness of VALKOVSKY as her father, and an epileptic seizure weaken her progressively until she dies. Before she dies she asks VANYA to deliver her mother's letter of reproach to VALKOVSKY and indicates that she too does not forgive him.

YELISEEV. Proprietor of a popular delicatessen. NATASHA prepares a fine meal and orders wine from YELISEEV in anticipation of a reconciliation with ALYOSHA.

YURY MILOSLAVSKY. *YURY MILOSLAVSKY, or the Russians in 1612 (YURY MILOSLAVSKY, ili Russkie v 1612 godu),* a historical romance published in 1829 by Mikhail Nikolaevich Zagoskin (1789-1852).

After listening to VANYA's novel about the poor clerk, IKHMENEV notes that it would have been nice to have had a more interesting hero or perhaps something historical such as is found in *ROSLAVLEV* or *YURY MILOSLAVSKY.*

COUNTESS ZINAIDA FYODOROVNA. KATYA's stepmother, who conspires to marry her to ALYOSHA and then to somehow get her money. She is having a liaison with VALKOVSKY and would like to make KATYA's marriage conditional upon her own to VALKOVSKY. She is about twenty eight, pleasure loving, flippant, egocentric, and involved with VALKOVSKY because of the potential for gain as well as for passion.

NOTES FROM THE HOUSE OF THE DEAD (ZAPISKI IZ MYORTVOGO DOMA) 1860

A—CHUKOVSKY. A Polish political prisoner.

A—V. A moral QUASIMODO who has been exiled because of several false accusations he made in an effort to get money to support his debauchery. In prison he continues his life as an informer, mostly against M., in order to ingratiate himself with the MAJOR. His toadying succeeds in getting him a commission to paint the MAJOR's portrait, but it is ultimately discovered that his talent is not that of another BRYULLOV and he is dismissed. He finally plots an escape together with KULIKOV and KOLLER but is captured and flogged.

GENERAL ABROSIMOV. A prominent local figure who is staging a theatrical presentation in the town. The convicts are certain that their amateur productions will be as good.

AKIM AKIMYCH. One of the prisoners from the nobility that the rest of the prisoners generally dislike. He has been sentenced for the murder of a prince and appears quite indifferent and resigned to being in prison permanently. He is naive and extremely pleasant, and despite his noble heritage he learns every imaginable trade in prison.

AKSYONOV. A typical convict who on one occasion has a pleasant conversation with SMEKALOV, the former commander of the camp whom all the prisoners respected.

AKULINA KUDIMOVNA (AKULKA). ANKUDIM TROFIMYCH's daughter. Her parents beat her morning and night for supposedly having caroused with FILKA MOROZOV, who spreads rumors about her. After her marriage to SHISHKOV, it is discovered that she is innocent of FILKA's charges, but SHISHKOV continues the beatings because of his fear of FILKA. When FILKA goes into the army, she forgives him his slander and admits that she loves him, whereupon SHISHKOV murders her.

AKULKA. See AKULINA KUDIMOVNA.

ALEKSANDR (ALEKSANDRA). A Kalmyk who is called by the feminine ALEKSANDRA by the other prisoners. He is condemned to four thousand strokes for killing his superior officer and claims that he endures the punishment only because he has been beaten with regularity since youth. He decides to be baptized into the Russian Orthodox Church to see if his sentence would be lightened, but this ruse fails, and at night he dreams only of being beaten.

ALEKSANDR PETROVICH. See ALEKSANDR PETROVICH GOR-YANCHIKOV.

ALEKSANDRA. See ALEKSANDR.

ALEY. See ALEY SEMYONYCH.

ALEY SEMYONYCH. The youngest of three Tatar brothers in the camp who have been exiled for robbery. He is naive, sincere, sympathetic, soft-hearted, and good. He and GORYANCHIKOV, who teaches him Russian, bunk together and become very close.

ALMAZOV. The sour and sober supervisor of the upper-class prisoners in the alabaster workings. He intensely dislikes the nobility.

ANKUDIM TROFIMOVICH. A wealthy and well-respected man of seventy who has two children, VASYA and AKULINA, by his second wife MARYA STEPANOVNA. He and his wife regularly beat AKULINA when FILKA MOROZOV spreads rumors that he has been having an affair with her.

ANTIPKA. A prisoner.

VASILY ANTONOV. A prisoner in the civilian division. Despite his malicious personality and tall, powerful frame, he quickly backs down during an altercation with PETROV.

ANTONYCH. An old toothless prisoner.

AREFIEV. A prisoner who borrows a book on COUNTESS LAVALLIER by DUMAS from an adjutant and then lends it to PETROV.

B. A frail and sickly prisoner from the nobility. He expresses his hatred for his fellow prisoners, whom he refers to as brigands.

B—M. A Polish political prisoner, an older man who makes a very disagreeable impression. He is an expert painter who is used to paint the officials' houses. The MAJOR is particularly impressed by him.

B—SKY. One of the Polish political prisoners.

BABAY. A Lezghi tribesman who has a butting contest with VASKA, the camp goat.

SASHA BAKLUSHIN. A prisoner of the special division who is one of the nicest and liveliest of the convicts. He becomes very involved in and excited about the theatricals that he hopes to help stage for Christmas. He relates to GORYANCHIKOV the story of his imprisonment: he falls in love with LOUISA, a German girl who wants to marry him but who is finally persuaded by her aunt to marry SCHULZ, an older but wealthy watchmaker. When SCHULZ dares the enraged BAKLUSHIN to shoot him, he obliges.

BELKA. One of the camp dogs. It had once been run over and its spine curves inward. The dog is very submissive and reacts joyfully when shown any attention and affection by GORYANCHIKOV, who is the only prisoner or guard to do so. BELKA is ultimately killed by other dogs.

BRINVILLIERS [BRENVILIE]. Marie Madeleine d'Aubray, Marquise de BRINVILLIERS (1630-76), infamous French criminal who poisoned her victims and enjoyed seeing them suffer. When GORYANCHIKOV discusses the beatings and punishment administered in the camp, he comments that there were once those who plied their trade with the enjoyment of the MARQUIS DE SADE and BRINVILLIERS.

BRYULLOV. Karl Pavlovich BRYULLOV (1799-1852), Russian artist noted for his portraits. The MAJOR thinks that A—V is an artist like BRYULLOV and commissions him to do his portrait.

BULKIN. A small, slight prisoner who suddenly follows VARLAMOV around the camp on Christmas Day, never having had anything to do with him previously. VARLAMOV's every word is met with BULKIN's retort that it is a lie and the insistence that he stop lying.

ISAY FOMICH BUMSTEIN [BUMSHTEYN]. A thin, feeble, vain Jew of fifty who is the camp pawnbroker and usurer and who has most of the prisoners in his debt. He enjoys gaining the attention of the other prisoners through his Sabbath ritual.

COUNT BUTYLKIN. VARLAMOV states that even though he was once drunk and indifferent like COUNT BUTYLKIN (Count Bottle), the girls were quite fond of him.

MITRY BYKOV. One of SHISHKOV's acquaintances. He delivers a message to ANKUDIM TROFIMOVICH during SHISHKOV's negotiations to marry AKULINA.

CHEKUNDA. One of the bakers who comes to sell not only baked goods but herself to the prisoners. She is described as the filthiest girl in the world.

CHEKUNOV. A soldier from the disciplinary battalion who tries to ingratiate himself with GORYANCHIKOV in the hospital. He waits on GORYANCHIKOV with zeal because he thinks that he has money.

CHEREVIN. A cold and conceited member of the disciplinary battalion, about fifty years of age. He has a wife named OVDOTYA, whom he beat severely when he caught her with a lover.

CHRIST [KHRISTOS]. Jesus CHRIST, in Christian teachings the Son of God. GORYANCHIKOV ponders about those who administer punishment to the prisoners and who seem to revel in the thrill of pain and domination. Such people enjoy this tyranny even though according to the law of CHRIST they are brothers to those whom they beat.

CONVERSATION PETROVICH [RAZGOVOR PETROVICH]. See SAVELIEV.

ROBINSON CRUSOE [ROBINZON KRUZE]. The hero of *The Life and Strange Surprising Adventures of ROBINSON CRUSOE, of York, Mariner,* written in 1719-20 by Daniel Defoe (1660-1731). He is ship-wrecked and wanders about an island for years before being able to return to England. A little peasant who is in the service of GENERAL KUKUSHKIN has a passion for wandering and could have been another ROBINSON CRUSOE.

DON JUAN [DON-ZHUAN]. A legendary profligate cavalier who functions as the main character of several works of fiction and music. Central to the several versions of the legend is the statue of a dead man who accepts DON JUAN's invitation to dinner. In most versions DON JUAN is taken to hell. One of the theatricals that the prisoners stage, *KEDRIL THE GLUTTON,* is somewhat like DON JUAN in that devils take the baron and his servant to hell at the conclusion.

DRANISHNIKOV. An engineer soldier.

THE DUCHESS DE LA VALLIERE [GERTSOGINYA LAVALIER]. LA DUCHESSE DE LA VALLIERE, a novel written in 1804 by Stephanie Felicite de Genlis (1746-1830), in which the life of a favorite of King Louis XIV is portrayed. A young educated convict is mentioned as having read this or something very much like it.

DUMAS [DYUMA]. Alexandre DUMAS (1802-70), known as DUMAS pere, French novelist and dramatist whose prolific output popularized melodramatic historical romances. PETROV naively asks GORYAN-CHIKOV if DUMAS' book about the COUNTESS DE LA VALLIERE is true, and he seems quite satisfied with the response that it is probably fiction. DUMAS mentions her in his novel *The Viscount of Bragelonne (Le Vicomte de Bragelonne),* published in 1847.

DUTOV. A soldier exiled to the camp for two years. He is a terrible braggart and an exceptional coward who in order to postpone a second exile brutally attacks an officer.

DVUGROSHOVAYA. One of the bakers who comes to the camp to sell not only baked goods but also herself to the prisoners. She is described as being beyond all description.

DYATLOV. The prison clerk. In reality it is he who operates the camp, and he exerts a strong influence even over the MAJOR.

FEDKA. An executioner.

FEDKA. A valet.

FILATKA. One of the roles in the prison production of *FILATKA AND MIROSHKA—RIVALS*. BAKLUSHIN, who plans to play this part himself, boasts that the role will be played in such a style as not seen even in the St. Petersburg theaters.

FILATKA AND MIROSHKA—RIVALS [FILATKA I MIROSHKA SOPERNIKI]. *FILATKA AND MIROSHKA—RIVALS, or Four Suitors and One Bride (FILATKA I MIROSHKA SOPERNIKI, ili Chetyre zhenikha i odna nevesta),* a popular Russian vaudeville of the 1830s written by Pyotr Grigorievich Grigoriev (1807-54).

FILKA. See FILKA MOROZOV.

COLONEL G. A mad prisoner tells GORYANCHIKOV that he was to receive two thousand stripes but now will avoid the punishment because the daughter of COLONEL G. is in love with him and has taken up his case.

G—V. See G—KOV.

G—KOV (G—V). A lieutenant colonel who commands the garrison and the camp before the MAJOR assumes charge. The prisoners love and respect him as a father. Pursuant to the change of command he has a heated exchange with the MAJOR, who is a much different person than he.

GAVRILKA. A tramp who is an accomplice in the murder of six Kirghiz tribesmen for which LOMOV is innocently sent to prison. In prison he and LOMOV get into a fight and LOMOV stabs him.

GAZIN. The strongest of the prisoners. He makes extra money as a wine dealer, drinks up all the money he takes in, and when drunk becomes extremely violent. To suppress his violence several prisoners beat him into unconsciousness, but GAZIN is so strong that the next morning he is fully recovered. He makes a horrifying impression on others, and it is said that he likes to kill children.

GLINKA. Mikhail Ivanovich GLINKA (1804-57), the first important Russian composer. The prisoners note that it would be nice if GLINKA could hear the convict orchestra play his *KAMARINSKAYA*.

GNEDKO. The camp's sorrel horse, the third in line by that name.

GOGOL. Nikolay Vasilievich GOGOL (1809-52), popular Russian writer known for his tragicomic exposing of human foibles. He was viewed by progressive critics as the fountainhead of the Natural School and credited with critically describing reality with the intent of social reform. GORYANCHIKOV notes that ISAY FOMICH reminds him of YANKEL in GOGOL's *TARAS BULBA*.

ALEKSANDR PETROVICH GORYANCHIKOV. A noble exiled for killing his wife in their first year of marriage in a fit of jealousy. In exile he lodges with an older woman, her consumption-ridden daughter, and the latter's illegitimate daughter KATYA, to whom he gives lessons. He is quiet and unsociable and goes out only to give lessons to GVOZDIKOV's daughters in exchange for a pittance. He becomes friends only with KATYA, and it is evident that that was also his wife's name. He is very concerned about how the prisoners, mostly peasants and soldiers, will treat him, and senses that the only one who loves him is SHARIK, one of the prison dogs. When he dies, he leaves behind a lot of written material in which he describes the prisoners and prison life. In his writing he is concerned about the prisoners both as types and as individuals, and he is not averse to making moral judgments. The narrator has ostensibly found the manuscript and hereby offers it to the public in the form of *Notes From the House of the Dead.*

GRIGORY PETROVICH. A company commander who is killed by SIROTKIN, a recruit who cannot bear military service.

GRISHKA TYOMNY KABAK. Two prisoners argue over whether GRISHKA TYOMNY KABAK (loosely, a murky pub or pigsty) is the nickname of the executioner FEDKA.

IVAN IVANOVICH GVOZDIKOV (IVAN IVANYCH). The father of five daughters, all with high aspirations, who secures GORYANCHIKOV to give them lessons. The narrator who presents GORYANCHIKOV's writing to the public first meets him at GVOZDIKOV's home.

HERCULES [GERKULES]. Mythical Greek hero of fabulous strength. NURRA, a Lezghi tribesman imprisoned for robbery, is proportioned like HERCULES, while OSIP, who cooks for GORYANCHIKOV, is described as a seven year old HERCULES.

ISA. ALEY, the Moslem Tatar, and GORYANCHIKOV read the New Testament together. ALEY enjoys the SERMON ON THE MOUNT and thinks that ISA (Jesus CHRIST) is a great prophet.

ISAY. See ISAY FOMICH BUMSTEIN.

ISAY FOMICH. See ISAY FOMICH BUMSTEIN.

IVAN IVANYCH. See IVAN IVANOVICH GVOZDIKOV.

IVAN MATVEICH. An officer who helps to supervise the prisoners' work.

IVAN SEMYONYCH. See IVAN SEMYONYCH SHISHKOV.

IVANOV. A prisoner who plays the role of the landowner's wife in one of the prison theatricals.

JESUIT [IEZUIT]. The Society of Jesus, a religious order for Roman Catholic men founded by Ignatius Loyola (1491-1556) in 1534. The society is known for scholarship and missionary zeal and has been accused of secrecy and intrigue. GORYANCHIKOV notes that M—TSKY is as adroit as a JESUIT in dealing with people.

K—CHINSKY. An educated Polish political prisoner.

KAMARINSKAYA. A composition for symphony orchestra adapted from a peasant song and dance by Mikhail GLINKA. (1) The convict orchestra plays this number and wishes that GLINKA himself could be there to hear it. (2) When the lunatic OSTROZHSKY gets carried away, GORYANCHIKOV notes that he dances with *KAMARINSKAYA* gestures.

KAMENEV (KORENEV). GORYANCHIKOV mentions that he once saw KAMENEV, a famous bandit chieftain who committed many atrocities. He adds however that GAZIN is somehow worse. KAMENEV is also referred to by the author as KORENEV. In exile KAMENEV teaches GORYANCHIKOV how to put on and take off his underclothing around the leg irons.

KATYA. The illegitimate granddaughter of the woman with whom GORYANCHIKOV lodges. She and he become friends.

KEDRIL. The lead role in *KEDRIL THE GLUTTON,* one of the prisoners' theatricals. The role is played by POTSEYKIN.

KEDRIL THE GLUTTON [KEDRIL OBZHORA]. One of the prisoners' theatricals, it is part of the folk theater and a published text is not extant.

KHAVROSHKA. One of the bakers who comes to sell not only baked goods but also herself to the prisoners.

KIRILL. No one is quite sure why the central figure of *KEDRIL THE GLUTTON* is called KEDRIL instead of the more naturally Russian KIRILL.

KOBYLIN. LUKA KUZMICH's stupid but friendly bunk mate.

KOLLER. A Polish guard and officer who escapes together with A—V and KULIKOV. He is captured, flogged, and sent to another camp.

KORENEV. See KAMENEV.

KOSHKIN. In the prisoners' theatricals he plays a Brahmin in a musical pantomime.

GENERAL KUKUSHKIN. Some beggars observe to SHAPKIN and YEFIM that they are in the service of GENERAL KUKUSHKIN, that is, they live in the forest (where the cuckoo sings) as tramps.

KULIKOV. A dignified prisoner of consequence and the camp veterinarian. He loses most of his trade to YOLKIN and then escapes with A—V and KOLLER only to be captured and flogged.

KULTYAPKA. A dog brought into the camp as a puppy by GORYAN-CHIKOV. NEUSTROEV kills it and uses the fur to line his boots.

KVASOV. A notorious liar and gossip whom none of the prisoners believes.

COUNTESS DE LA VALLIERE [GRAFINYA LAVALIER]. PETROV asks GORYANCHIKOV if DUMAS' book about the COUNTESS DE LA VALLIERE is fact or fiction. DUMAS mentions her in his novel *The Viscount of Bragelonne (Le Vicomte de Bragelonne)*.

LEPORELLO. The valet of Don Giovanni in *Don Giovanni,* an opera written by Wolfgang Amadeus Mozart (1756-91) in 1787. The opera is an adaptation of the DON JUAN legend. According to GORYANCHIKOV, KEDRIL, a servant in the prisoners' theatrical *KEDRIL THE GLUTTON,* possesses some of the same attributes of LEPORELLO.

LOMOV. A stupid and quarrelsome prisoner from a family of peasants made rich by illegal means, who has been imprisoned unjustly for the murder of six Kirghiz tribesmen. He gets into a brawl with GAVRILKA, who actually took part in the murders, over the favors of a disgusting girl. LOMOV stabs GAVRILKA and is eagerly punished by the MAJOR, who had unsuccessfully tried to extort a bribe from him.

LOUISA [LUIZA]. The German girl with whom BAKLUSHIN falls in love and because of whom he murders SCHULZ. She married SCHULZ for money and security even though she loves BAKLUSHIN.

LUCHKA. See LUKA KUZMICH.

LUKA KUZMICH (LUCHKA). A small, vain prisoner who has been sentenced for murdering a major. He is proud of his crime and enjoys talking about it. He is difficult to get along with and treats his bunk mate KOBYLIN with contempt.

M. One of the prisoners. A—V informs on him most of all, largely because he is everything that A—V is not. M. warns GORYANCHIKOV to be leery of PETROV.

M—TSKY. A Polish political prisoner. He becomes more bitter the longer he is incarcerated and frequently indicates to GORYANCHIKOV how much he hates his fellow prisoners, whom he calls brigands. His mother successfully petitions for his release, and he moves into town and secures a position.

MAJOR [MAYOR]. The head of the prison camp garrison. He is a drunken, cruel man who considers the prisoners his enemies and punishes them for the slightest offense, for example, not sleeping on their right side. He extorts bribes when possible and seems to love only his dog TREZOR-KA. He is finally arrested, tried, removed from his post, and ultimately descends to poverty.

MAJOR [MAYOR]. The prisoner who shaves the men's heads, thereby saving them a torturous trip to the prison barbers. He is for some reason called MAJOR.

MAKHNI-DRALO. See SHAPKIN.

MAMETKA. A Tatar prisoner.

MARTYNOV. An older prisoner and a former hussar. He is hotheaded, restless, and a natural leader.

MARYA STEPANOVNA. ANKUDIM TROFIMYCH's second wife, who bears him VASYA and AKULINA. She and her husband regularly beat AKULINA when FILKA falsely accuses her of having an affair with him.

MARYASHA. One of the bakers who comes to sell not only baked goods but also herself to the prisoners.

"THE MEMORY IS FRESH BUT HARDLY TO BE BELIEVED" ["SVEZHO PREDANIE, A VERITSYA S TRUDOM"]. A line from the comedy *Woe From Wit (Gore ot uma),* written 1822-24 by Aleksandr Sergeevich Griboedov (1795-1829). GORYANCHIKOV discusses punishment at length and mentions ZHEREBYATNIKOV and his evident relish for punishment. He muses that in the not too distant past, where "THE MEMORY IS FRESH BUT HARDLY TO BE BELIEVED," there were others like ZHEREBYATNIKOV.

MIKHAIL VASILYICH. See MIKHAIL VASILYICH SMEKALOV.

MIKHAYLOV. A convict suffering from consumption who is in the hospital with GORYANCHIKOV. He dies a horrible death while still bound by his fetters.

MIKHAYLOV. GORYANCHIKOV cites examples of those who are sentenced to exile but who induce someone to take their place. A certain MIKHAYLOV retains his freedom in this manner, while SUSHILOV agrees to come in another's place.

MIKITA. See MIKITA GRIGORIEVICH.

MIKITA GRIGORIEVICH (MIKITA, MIKITA GRIGORYICH). An older widower to whom ANKUDIM TROFIMYCH wants to marry AKULINA. When FILKA MOROZOV boasts that he has been carrying on with AKULINA, MIKITA rejects a possible marriage because of the disgrace.

MIKITA GRIGORYICH. See MIKITA GRIGORIEVICH.

MIKITKA. A prisoner.

MIROSHKA. One of the characters in the theatrical *FILATKA AND MIROSHKA—RIVALS* performed by the prisoners.

MITKA. A prisoner.

MITROFAN STEPANYCH. SHISHKOV's uncle.

FILKA MOROZOV. A young man whose deceased father had been in business with ANKUDIM TROFIMYCH. He demands money from the business as his right and then goes on a binge and spreads false rumors that he has had an affair with AKULINA. He sells himself to go into the army in the place of another and uses the money to continue his debauchery. Before he leaves for the service he bows before AKULINA, confesses his love, and begs her forgiveness. SHISHKOV, AKULINA's husband, is so petrified and frustrated by the experience that he kills AKULINA and is sent to the prison camp.

NAPOLEON. Charles Louis NAPOLEON Bonaparte (1808-73), who became NAPOLEON III. He was chosen president of the French Republic in 1848 and later declared himself emperor in 1852. He was deposed in 1871 following defeat in the Franco-Prussian War. PETROV questions GOR-YANCHIKOV about NAPOLEON and wonders if he is related to the Napoleon of 1812. The two are indeed distantly related.

NASTASYA IVANOVNA. A widow who lives in the town where the prison camp is located. She makes a practice of helping the prisoners even though she is poor.

NETSVETAEV. One of the convict actors, who plays a country gentleman in one of the theatricals.

NEUSTROEV. A prisoner who kills the dog KULTYAPKA and uses the skin to line some boots.

NEVALID PETROVICH. An invalid prisoner.

NOZDRYOV. A comic character in *Dead Souls (Myortvye dushi),* a novel written in 1842 by Nikolay GOGOL. He is characterized by his coarse gaiety, bullying, and drinking. GORYANCHIKOV notes that ZHEREB-YATNIKOV has NOZDRYOV's rolling, loud laughter.

NURRA. A Lezghi tribesman imprisoned for robbery. His behavior in prison is perfect; he never steals, always says his Islamic prayers, and is liked by everyone. He exerts himself to make GORYANCHIKOV feel at home.

ONUFRIEV. A prisoner who teases VARLAMOV about his girl and ardently defends his own.

ORLOV. A runaway soldier and infamous bandit. He is an extraordinary villain who is guilty of many murders, including those of children and the aged. He is sentenced to several lashes and is brutally beaten with the first installment but quickly mends because of his indomitable will. He eagerly awaits complete recovery so that he can finish his lashes and then escape. GORYANCHIKOV tries to find a hint of remorse or repentance in him but finds none and is simply laughed at. ORLOV dies after his second brutal beating.

OSIP. A gentle, kind prisoner who is no worse than people in free society. His only fault seems to be his interest in smuggling wine. AKIM AKIMYCH recommends him to GORYANCHIKOV, who engages him as his cook.

OSTROZHSKY. A dignified sixty year old Pole who was sentenced in 1830, the year of the Polish revolt. During his years in prison he has become the overseer of a brickyard. He goes mad when he is under investigation and is brought into the hospital ward in which GORYANCHIKOV is being treated. There he produces a general feeling of depression and hopelessness.

VANKA OTPETY. One of the convict actors, who loses the part of the country gentleman to NETSVETAEV.

OVDOTYA. CHEREVIN's wife, who is caught with a lover and beaten.

PETROV. A convict in the special section who threatens to kill the MAJOR because of some additional punishment imposed. He has no trade, seemingly lives a life of leisure, and is regarded by M. as the most desperate of all. He begins to visit GORYANCHIKOV and to discuss literature, current events, and the facts of general education. His questions often reflect naivete and misinformation, but he is always satisfied with GORYAN-CHIKOV's answers. After a time he begins to steal from GORYANCHI-KOV, almost unintentionally, and feels no remorse at all. There is something about him that is frightening, and the malicious and powerful ANTONOV quickly backs down from him in a brief altercation.

PETROVICH. The prisoners ascribe the name PETROVICH to a peasant they ridicule.

STEPAN FYODOROVICH POMORTSEV. SKURATOV has POMOR-TSEV fix his shoes on one occasion and is very satisfied with the job.

POTACHIVAY. One of the tramps who is caught breaking into a rich man's house with SHAPKIN and YEFIM.

POTSEYKIN. The prisoner who plays KEDRIL in the prison performance of *KEDRIL THE GLUTTON.* He does an excellent job.

PROKOFIEV. A prisoner.

QUASIMODO [KVAZIMODO]. The deformed bell ringer in *The Hunch-back of Notre Dame (Notre-Dame de Paris),* a novel written by Victor Hugo (1802-85) in 1831. GORYANCHIKOV states that A—V is a moral QUASIMODO because of his continual denunciations and warped outlook on life.

RASTORGUEV. A prisoner who is given extra punishment by the MAJOR following an abortive mutiny over food.

THE RED SEA [CHERMNOE MORE]. As recorded in Exodus 14 of the Old Testament, the sea through which Moses led the children of Israel out of Egypt. At his command the sea parted to allow them to pass, but then closed in upon their Egyptian pursuers. ISAY FOMICH continually chants a seemingly wordless song and insists that it is the same song that the Children of Israel sang when they crossed THE RED SEA.

ROMAN. A silent and solid fifty year old peasant prisoner.

MARQUIS DE SADE [MARKIZ DE SAD]. Donatien Alphonse Fran-çois DE SADE (1740-1814), prolific French writer who spent a good deal of his life in prison as punishment for his sexual escapades and for writing licentious books. His name has become synonymous with depravity, particularly torturing the object of love. When GORYANCHIKOV discusses the beatings and punishment administered in the camp, he comments that there were once those who plied their trade with the enjoyment of the MARQUIS DE SADE and BRINVILLIERS.

SASHA. See SASHA BAKLUSHIN.

SAVELIEV. A prisoner who is called CONVERSATION PETROVICH by IVAN MATVEICH because he talks instead of working.

SCHULZ [SHULTS]. An older, wealthy watchmaker who wants to marry LOUISA, the woman BAKLUSHIN loves. In an argument he dares BAKLUSHIN to shoot him and is summarily shot and killed.

SERMON ON THE MOUNT [NAGORNAYA PROPOVED]. CHRIST's sermon, recorded principally in Matthew 5-8 in the New Testament, in which He teaches the essence of the new Gospel and the fulfilment of the Mosaic Law. ALEY and GORYANCHIKOV read the SERMON ON THE MOUNT together, and ALEY is impressed with ISA and with the doctrine of forgiving one's enemies.

SH. BAKLUSHIN relates how SH. gives the MAJOR a verbal dressing down, to the great amusement of the convicts.

SHAPKIN. A convict in the hospital ward with GORYANCHIKOV who complains that the worst pain is having one's ears pulled. He relates how his ears were pulled by a police captain who caught him and others breaking into a rich man's house. He tells the officer when caught that his name is MAKHNI-DRALO.

SHARIK. One of the camp dogs.

SHILKIN. A convict who makes stoves and does plastering. KULIKOV, A—V, and KOLLER go out of the prison with him ostensibly to help him plaster. When the three leave and are gone for a time, he reports them in order to remove suspicion from himself and to avoid punishment. The escape fails, and they are all caught and flogged.

IVAN SEMYONYCH SHISHKOV. A shallow, whimsical prisoner of thirty who is sentenced for the murder of his wife. He relates his tale to CHEREVIN on one occasion in the prison hospital. He and FILKA

MOROZOV once caroused together, and SHISHKOV recalls how he even beat his poverty-stricken mother to get money to support his debauchery. Despite FILKA's slander that he had slept with AKULINA, SHISHKOV marries her for her money and ultimately learns of her innocence. He beats her in spite of her innocence because he fears FILKA and because FILKA makes fun of him. When AKULINA and FILKA part with declarations of love and forgiveness, SHISHKOV kills her.

SIROTKIN. A quiet, gentle prisoner of twenty three who has been sentenced for murdering his company commander. He had been forcibly recruited but hated the service and tried to commit suicide. When suicide failed he killed his company commander.

SKURATOV. A buffoon disliked by his fellow prisoners because of his absence of reserve and dignity.

MIKHAIL VASILYICH SMEKALOV. The commander of the camp before the MAJOR. His fairness and friendship are recalled fondly by the prisoners.

SOKOLOV. A runaway soldier and vicious murderer.

SOLOMONKA. A wretched Jewish prisoner.

STEPAN DOROFEICH (STYOPKA). A prisoner who has an argument on Christmas Day with one who claims that he owes him money.

STYOPKA. See STEPAN DOROFEICH.

"THE SUN IS SETTING" ["SOLNTSE NA ZAKATE"]. "THE SUN IS SETTING," the Time is Gone" ("SOLNTSE NA ZAKATE, vremya na utrate"), a song written by S. Mitrofanov in 1799, which became very popular in a folk variant. During the theatricals some prisoners sing this song as part of their comic repertoire.

SUSHILOV. A pitiable but good man who becomes GORYANCHIKOV's servant. He took another's place and sentence, but is belittled by his fellow prisoners because he got so little for it. He is very hurt when GORYAN-CHIKOV suggests that he is serving him for money, even though he does need the money to repay a debt to ANTON VASILIEV.

T—VSKY. A prisoner of the nobility who gains the peasants' respect.

TARAS BULBA. A short novel published in 1835 by Nikolay GOGOL, which deals with the involvement of a Cossack family in a war against the Poles. ISAY FOMICH reminds GORYANCHIKOV of the Jew YANKEL in *TARAS BULBA*.

TOCHI NE ZEVAY. One of the tramps caught breaking into the rich man's house with SHAPKIN and YEFIM claims that his name is TOCHI NE ZEVAY.

TOPOR. One of the tramps caught breaking into the rich man's house with SHAPKIN and YEFIM claims that his name is TOPOR (ax).

TREZORKA. The MAJOR's dog, which he loves very much.

USTYANTSEV. A prisoner who out of fear of corporeal punishment drinks vodka laced with snuff in order to contract consumption.

VANKA-TANKA. An attractive girl who becomes involved with KULIKOV. She aids him, A—V, and KOLLER in their unsuccessful attempt to escape.

VARLAMOV. A clever, good-natured convict from the special division who takes up with a beggar woman.

ANTON VASILIEV. A prisoner who demands payment of a debt from SUSHILOV. SUSHILOV serves GORYANCHIKOV in hope of making the money.

VASKA. The camp goat. When the MAJOR discovers his existence, he orders it executed.

VASKA. See VASYA.

VASYA (VASKA). A prisoner.

VASYA. ANKUDIM TROFIMYCH's son.

VLASOV. A person who lives in the same town as SHISHKOV.

YANKEL. A greedy, servile, and flattering Jewish character in Nikolay GOGOL's *TARAS BULBA*. ISAY FOMICH reminds GORYANCHIKOV very much of YANKEL.

YASHKA. A soldier who marries so that he can sell his wife to support his drinking. FILKA MOROZOV makes the same suggestion to SHISHKOV with respect to AKULINA.

YEFIM. A tramp who unsuccessfully tries to break into a rich man's house with SHAPKIN.

YEROSHKA. A convict who becomes disgusted with camp food and wants to make a complaint.

YOLKIN. A shrewd Siberian peasant and a charlatan who becomes a successful veterinarian in camp and takes most of KULIKOV's business.

ZH—KY. One of the Polish prisoners, a good-natured old man who had been a mathematics professor. His continual prayers earn the respect of the prisoners.

ZHEREBYATNIKOV. A tall, fat lieutenant who laughs like NOZDRYOV and who particularly enjoys superintending floggings. He is fond of punishment and treats it as an art.

GENERAL ZIBERT. When KVASOV is accused of not knowing any generals, he responds that he knows GENERAL ZIBERT.

ZVERKOV. A prisoner, who has anxiously awaited the arrival of the baker women-prostitutes, asks them upon arrival if they have visited the ZVERKOVS.

A NASTY AFFAIR (SKVERNY ANEKDOT) 1862

AKIM PETROVICH. See AKIM PETROVICH ZUBIKOV.

CUP OF GALL AND VINEGAR [CHASHA ZHELCHI I OTSTA]. As recorded in Matthew 27:34 in the New Testament, the drink given to Jesus on the cross. When PRALINSKY intrudes upon the wedding party, it is evident that more and better liquor must be purchased. PSELDONIMOV is totally without money and has to beg some from his mother-in-law. She gives him the money together with some humiliation and tyranny, and PSELDONIMOV is made to drink the CUP OF GALL AND VINEGAR in exchange for the favor.

DREAM BOOK [SONNIK]. *DREAM BOOK of Contemporary Russian Literature (SONNIK sovremennoy russkoy literatury)*, a humorous book of dream interpretations, published 1855-57 by the poet Nikolay Fyodorovich Shcherbina (1821-69). The book explains how to interpret dreams using the literary personalities of the day. Ivan Kostenkinych mentions the book at the wedding party and notes that if one dreams of PANAEV, one will surely spill coffee on his shirt.

EMERANCE [EMERANS]. An acquaintance of PRALINSKY who rejects going to visit him on foot because of the hard St. Petersburg pavement.

THE FIREBRAND [GOLOVESHKA]. The reference is probably to *The Spark (Iskra)*, a popular satirical journal published 1859-73 and edited by Nikolay Aleksandrovich Stepanov (1807-77) and Vasily Stepanovich Kurochkin (1831-74). One of the guests at the wedding party works for *THE FIREBRAND* and keeps himself properly aloof and dignified in the face of the general merrymaking, drinking, and dancing.

FOKIN. An unclear reference, probably to a dancer popular in St. Petersburg at the time. At the wedding party a medical student dances with ferocious abandon, like FOKIN, hoping to impress KLEOPATRA SEM-YONOVNA.

GOGOL. Nikolay Vasilievich GOGOL (1809-52), popular Russian writer known for his tragicomic portrayal of human foibles. He was viewed by progressive critics as the fountainhead of the Natural School and was credited with critically describing reality with the intent of social reform. PRALINSKY muses about whether he should intrude on PSELDONI-MOV's wedding party and imagines that if he did he would be seated beside the most important guest there—some relative, retired captain with a red nose, or some other original character as found in the work of GOGOL.

HARUN-AL-RASHID [GARUN AL-RASHID]. Known as Aaron the Upright (764-809), the fifth caliph of Arabia from 785 until his death, who according to legend took evening strolls around Bagdad where he became familiar with the life of his subjects. He was idealized as a ruler in *A THOUSAND AND ONE NIGHTS*, in which all things wondrous are attributed to him. The narrator notes that PRALINSKY descends upon the wedding party much as HARUN-AL-RASHID did in his journeys about Bagdad.

IVAN ILYICH. See IVAN ILYICH PRALINSKY.

IVAN KOSTENKINYCH. A young, handsome guest at the wedding party, who mentions the new literary *DREAM BOOK.*

KLEOPATRA SEMYONOVNA. A guest at the wedding party whom a medical student tries to impress with his dancing. The student feels that she is worth all risks.

KRAEVSKY. Andrey Aleksandrovich KRAEVSKY (1810-89), Russian journalist and publisher, who published *Fatherland Notes.* At the wedding party it is mentioned that a *NEW LEXICON* is being produced and that KRAEVSKY will be writing many of the articles. This provokes responses of dismay among some of the younger guests, who allude to KRAEVSKY's ignorance and incapability. There was in fact opposition to KRAEVSKY's involvement with the project, and he edited only the first volume.

MIKHEY. NIKIFOROV's coachman.

MLEKOPITAEV. A terrible tyrant and drunkard who has lost the use of his legs and who spends his time drinking vodka and being evil. He keeps several female relatives around his house just to torment them and decides to marry his daughter to PSELDONIMOV because all of the women are against it and because he wants a son-in-law to dominate.

MLEKOPITAEVA. MLEKOPITAEV's wife, a vicious woman who enjoys tyrannizing MADAME PSELDONIMOV. When the makeshift wedding bed collapses after the party, she takes her daughter away into her own room.

MLEKOPITAEVA. The seventeen year old, skinny, pale, and rather homely daughter of MLEKOPITAEV whom he is marrying to PSEL-DONIMOV. She is evil and obnoxious and makes it very clear to PSELDONIMOV that she would rather have married an officer she knows.

NEW LEXICON [NOVY LEKSIKON]. At the wedding party it is observed that a *NEW LEXICON* is coming out under the editorship of KRAEVSKY. The young discussants have reference to a new edition of the *Encyclopedic*

Dictionary (Entsiklopedichesky slovar), of which KRAEVSKY edited only the first volume and which ceased publication with the sixth volume.

NEW WINE AND NEW BOTTLES [NOVOE VINO I NOVYE MEKHI]. As recorded in the New Testament (Matthew 9:17, Mark 2:22, and Luke 5:37-38), Jesus' sermon that new wine is placed in new bottles rather than in old weakened ones to avoid breakage and loss of the wine. PRALINSKY discusses his theory of humanity to one's fellowmen with SHIPULENKO and NIKIFOROV and insists that the aristocracy would break down under the strain of humane relations with clerks, peasants, and others below them. PRALINSKY sarcastically draws a parallel with putting NEW WINE IN NEW BOTTLES.

STEPAN NIKIFOROVICH NIKIFOROV. A sixty five year old bachelor official who achieves his ambition of getting his own fine home. He even invites two guests, SHIPULENKO and PRALINSKY, to a housewarming, contrary to his habit of never having guests. He has remained single because he is an egotist who loves comfort and isolation.

PANAEV. Ivan Ivanovich PANAEV (1812-62), Russian writer and journalist. At the wedding party some of the young people discuss a new literary *DREAM BOOK* that has been published, in which dreams involving literary personalities are comically interpreted. IVAN KOSTEN-KINYCH mentions that if one dreams about PANAEV, one will surely spill coffee on his shirt.

PORFIRKA. See PORFIRY PETROVICH PSELDONIMOV.

PORFIRY. See PORFIRY PETROVICH PSELDONIMOV.

PORFIRY PETROVICH. See PORFIRY PETROVICH PSELDONI-MOV.

IVAN ILYICH PRALINSKY. A forty three year old bachelor and newly appointed general, who hopes for a wealthy bride commensurate with his own wealthy and titled family. He likes to talk and play the part of the confirmed liberal. At a house warming for NIKIFOROV he preaches humanity to one's inferiors and allows that peasants and clerks are people too. When his carriage is not ready after the housewarming, however, he denounces his coachman, TRIFON, threatens punishment, and decides to walk home to teach him a lesson. On the way home he muses about humanity, love of one's fellows, and individual worth. When he happens upon the wedding party of PSELDONIMOV, one of the clerks who works in his chancery, he muses about how he would be accepted if he walked in and how subtly he would show them his position and the distance between them and himself. He determines to enter just to show that the nobility can adapt to the new times of reform. His arrival makes everyone including himself uneasy, and he realizes that he has made a disastrous mistake. Because of his discomfort he resents all those present, particularly PSELDONIMOV, and asks him why his name is not PSEVDONIMOV (pseudonym). His uneasiness evolves into hatred, and his feelings are compounded by the fact that he gets quite drunk. He has an altercation with a young worker for *THE FIREBRAND*, who exposes his egocentric motives for intruding upon the party, but he cannot extricate himself from the situation because his drunkenness makes him quite ill. He is placed upon the marriage bed to spend the night and quickly and ashamedly leaves in the morning. His shame produces suffering as he imagines that everyone knows of his escapade, and he avoids the chancery for eight days, afraid of what people will say and think. When he has sufficient courage to return, he is greatly relieved to see that he is still treated the same and especially that PSELDONIMOV has asked for a transfer. Strict measures seem suddenly more necessary than humanity, and he realizes that he did indeed break down as NIKIFOROV had suggested would be the case, when the aristocracy is forced to associate with those socially and economically beneath them.

PORFIRY PETROVICH PSELDONIMOV (PORFIRKA, PSELDO-NIMUSHKA). An impoverished clerk who works in PRALINSKY's chancery for ten rubles per month. He agrees to marry MLEKOPITAEVA for money. The marriage brings him four hundred rubles and a wooden house, for which he is willing to endure the tyranny and torment of the MLEKOPITAEV family. When PRALINSKY intrudes upon his wedding party and becomes drunk and sick, he relinquishes the marriage bed to him so that he can spend the night. A makeshift wedding bed is arranged, but after it collapses, the bride goes to her mother's room to spend the night. The affair convinces him that he needs a transfer out of PRALINSKY's chancery, and he is promised a position by SHIPULENKO.

MADAME PSELDONIMOVA. PSELDONIMOV's forty five year old mother, who eagerly caters to PRALINSKY when he intrudes upon the wedding party. She is tyrannized by the MLEKOPITAEV family.

PSELDONIMUSHKA. See PORFIRY PETROVICH PSELDONIMOV.

SEMYON IVANOVICH. See SEMYON IVANOVICH SHIPULENKO.

SEMYON IVANYCH. See SEMYON IVANOVICH SHIPULENKO.

SHEMBEL. PRALINSKY worries about what SHEMBEL will think when he hears that PRALINSKY was at PSELDONIMOV's wedding party.

SEMYON IVANOVICH SHIPULENKO (SEMYON IVANYCH). An important official who attends NIKIFOROV's housewarming together with PRALINSKY. In response to PRALINSKY's liberal prattle about being humane to one's inferiors, he insists that the aristocracy simply will break down trying to do such a thing.

SHUBIN. PRALINSKY worries about what SHUBIN will think when he learns that PRALINSKY was at PSELDONIMOV's wedding party.

SODOM. As recorded in Genesis 18-19 of the Old Testament, a city which together with Gomorrah was destroyed by Jehovah because of its wickedness. The term has come to mean wickedness and chaos. The atmosphere of the MLEKOPITAEV home in general and of the wedding party in particular is described as a virtual SODOM.

STEPAN NIKIFOROVICH. See STEPAN NIKIFOROVICH NIKIFOROV.

A THOUSAND AND ONE NIGHTS [TYSYACHA ODNA NOCH]. A collection of Eastern tales, originally written in Arabic and arranged in its current form in the fifteenth century. The stories are related one per night without climax by Scheherazade to her husband in order to postpone her execution. A hanger-on at the MLEKOPITAEV house, a German woman, relates to MLEKOPITAEV stories from *A THOUSAND AND ONE NIGHTS.*

TRIFON. PRALINSKY's coachman. When he does not have the carriage ready on time, PRALINSKY walks home in order to punish him. It is on this walk that he discovers PSELDONIMOV's wedding party and intrudes upon it.

VARLAM. SHIPULENKO's coachman.

AKIM PETROVICH ZUBIKOV. A department chief in PRALINSKY's chancery who attends PSELDONIMOV's wedding party. PRALINSKY views him as a godsend, since he is then able to converse with someone more on his own level.

NOTES FROM UNDERGROUND (ZAPISKI IZ PODPO-LYA) 1864

ALEXANDER THE GREAT [ALEKSANDR MAKEDONSKY]. Emperor Alexander III of Macedon (356-323 B.C.), who conquered the civilized world, extended Greek civilization into the East, and ushered in the Hellenistic Age. APOLLON has the vanity that only ALEXANDER THE GREAT should have.

ANAEVSKY. A. Ye. ANAEVSKY (1788-1866), author of miscellany who was the target of journalistic humor because of the caliber of his work. As the UNDERGROUND MAN philosophizes about man's will and perversity throughout the ages, he notes that some may find the history of man majestic and alludes to the COLOSSUS OF RHODES as an example. He observes that ANAEVSKY has written that some commentators think that the COLOSSUS was man-made, while others speculate that it arose from nature.

ANTON ANTONYCH. See ANTON ANTONYCH SETOCHKIN.

APOLLON. A former tailor who lives with the UNDERGROUND MAN, nominally as his servant, for seven rubles per month. He is a pedant with the vanity only an ALEXANDER THE GREAT should have, who treats everyone despotically and condescendingly. He tyrannizes his "master," generally makes his own rules about what he will and will not do, and acts as though the completion of every task is the rendering of a great favor. In fact he does little, but does enjoy pompously reading the PSALTER aloud. His pride precludes his ever asking the UNDERGROUND MAN for his salary, and his silent, cold stare produces the money from his unwilling master.

ATTILA [ATILLA]. The king of the Huns (d. 453). He is notorious for his attacks upon Europe during the final stages of the Roman Empire and for his cruelty and vandalism. In raving about man's perversity throughout the ages, the UNDERGROUND MAN mentions ATTILA and STENKA RAZIN and compares them to the more bloodthirsty barbarians of the present day who go unnoticed in civilized society because they are so prevalent.

AUSTERLITZ [AUSTERLITS]. The scene of a battle in 1805 at which NAPOLEON inflicted a heavy defeat on the combined Russian and Austrian forces. In his frequent dreams of the sublime and the beautiful the UNDERGROUND MAN muses vainly that he would go forth to teach new ideas and would defeat the retrogrades at AUSTERLITZ.

BORGHESE [BORGEZE]. A wealthy Italian family close to the papacy and influential in Roman life. The UNDERGROUND MAN's romantic reveries into the sublime and beautiful involve many fantasies, including a ball for all of Italy at the villa BORGHESE. The villa was controlled at that time by Camillo BORGHESE (1775-1832), who was married to NAPOLEON THE GREAT's sister Pauline.

BUCKLE [BOKL]. Henry Thomas BUCKLE (1821-62), English historian known chiefly for his *History of Civilization in England.* The UNDERGROUND MAN attacks the theory put forth by many thinkers that man rationally seeks his own good. He attacks BUCKLE's view that with civilization man gradually becomes better and less prone to war and cites the example of the NAPOLEONS to disprove it.

CHURKIN. When the UNDERGROUND MAN restyles his wardrobe in anticipation of bumping into the OFFICER on Nevsky Prospect, he buys new black gloves and a hat from CHURKIN.

CLEOPATRA [KLEOPATRA]. CLEOPATRA VII (69-30 B.C.), the last Macedonian queen of Egypt, famed for her consorts with Julius Caesar and Marc Antony. In discussing the farce of civilization and the reality of man's perversity, the UNDERGROUND MAN notes CLEOPATRA's penchant for sticking gold pins into her servants' breasts and the great enjoyment she derived from it.

COLOSSUS OF RHODES [KOLOSS RODOSSKY]. A gigantic statue of Helios, the Greek sun god, on the island of Rhodes. It was completed about 280 B.C. to commemorate the successful defense of the island and is regarded as one of the Seven Wonders of the World. The UNDERGROUND MAN notes the perversity of man throughout the ages but

acknowledges that some may find the history of man majestic and cites the
COLOSSUS OF RHODES as an example.

CRYSTAL PALACE [KHRUSTALNY DVORETS]. A project of the
English architect Sir Joseph Paxton (1803-65) which served as the main
pavilion at the London World Fairs of 1851 and 1862. It was viewed in the
1860s as a symbol of the economic and social ideals of the utopian socialists.
Dostoevsky himself saw the structure while abroad. As the UNDER-
GROUND MAN muses about the perversity of man's history and about the
hopelessness of efforts to plan rationally man's utopia on earth, he notes
that the laws of economics, mathematics, and other sciences will make life
very boring. With the development of these laws, he asserts, the CRYSTAL
PALACE will be built, a symbol of the success of man's reason. The
UNDERGROUND MAN finds the sequence of events leading to the
CRYSTAL PALACE both troubling and boring. The allusion to the palace
also has application to *What is to be Done? (Chto delat?),* a novel published
in 1863 by Nikolay Gavrilovich Chernyshevsky (1828-89) in which an
idealistic young socialist dreams of the impending paradise in the form of a
CRYSTAL PALACE in which the socialist community will live.

PRINCE D. One of the fashionable social lions seen strolling on Nevsky
Prospect.

PRINCESS D—AYA. FERFICHKIN, SIMONOV, TRUDOLYUBOV,
and ZVERKOV, even though they have never seen her, discuss the rare
beauty and grace of PRINCESS D—AYA at the dinner in ZVERKOV's
honor.

FATHERLAND NOTES [OTECHESTVENNYE ZAPISKI]. Literary
and political monthly published in St. Petersburg 1839-84. It contained
some of the best literature of the day and advocated progressive social ideas
but was forcibly closed because of too liberal editorial policies. The
UNDERGROUND MAN writes a story denouncing the OFFICER who so
damages his ego and sends it to *FATHERLAND NOTES,* but it is rejected.

FERFICHKIN. One of the friends who plans a farewell dinner for
ZVERKOV.

THE FLOOD [VSEMIRNY POTOP]. As recorded in Genesis 6-8 in the
Old Testament, the inundation which Jehovah sent upon the earth to
remove all of the wicked. Only Noah and his family were saved by means of
the ark. The UNDERGROUND MAN notes that ever since THE FLOOD

right up to SCHLESWIG-HOLSTEIN man has been characterized by perversity.

GE. Nikolay Nikolaevich GE (1831-94), Russian artist. In complaining about his lack of identity, the UNDERGROUND MAN wishes that he could be called something, even if it were only lazy. Such an identity would make him happy, and he would gladly praise GE's painting and also the article "TO ONE'S SATISFACTION" because he loves the sublime and the beautiful.

GOGOL. Nikolay Vasilievich GOGOL (1809-52), popular Russian writer known for his tragicomic portrayal of human foibles. He was considered by progressive critics to be the fountainhead of the Natural School and was credited with critically exposing reality with the intent of social reform. After the UNDERGROUND MAN's ego-shattering experience with the OFFICER, he laments that the OFFICER is not the kind of man who would fight a duel, but rather a man like GOGOL's PIROGOV, who likes simply to complain to the powers that be.

HEINE [GEYNE]. Heinrich HEINE (1797-1856), German romantic poet, journalist, and satirist. The UNDERGROUND MAN notes that HEINE once commented that true autobiographies do not exist because men lie about themselves. He gleefully notes that such a generalization applies also to ROUSSEAU.

KAGAN. A bird referred to by Siberian exiles as recorded by Dostoevsky in his *Siberian Notebook (Sibirskaya tetrad)*. The UNDERGROUND MAN sarcastically observes that when all of the rational laws of nature are in effect and everything is mathematically determined, this bird of paradise will undoubtedly come too.

KOLYA. A wealthy young prince who is a friend of ZVERKOV.

KOSTANZHOGLO. Konstantin KOSTANZHOGLO, the ideal landowner in the uncompleted second volume of Nikolay GOGOL's *Dead Souls (Myortvye dushi)*. The UNDERGROUND MAN insists that Russian romantics are not inherently so ridiculous as their Western European counterparts and that their ideals were provided for them by critics and publicists who lauded KOSTANZHOGLO and PYOTR IVANOVICH.

LERMONTOV. Mikhail Yurievich LERMONTOV (1814-41), the foremost Russian romantic writer, who perished in a duel. As the proud but shunned UNDERGROUND MAN pursues FERFICHKIN, SIMONOV, TRUDOLYUBOV, and ZVERKOV to the brothel following the unsuccessful dinner in ZVERKOV's honor, his imagination runs rampant. He envisions a duel with ZVERKOV, a Siberian exile, forgiveness, shooting into the air instead of taking ZVERKOV's life when he has the chance, and other similar romantic situations. When his mind returns to reality, he realizes that all he had envisioned was borrowed from SILVIO and from LERMONTOV's *MASQUERADE.*

LIZA. A twenty year old prostitute who assumes her trade at the instigation of her parents. She receives the UNDERGROUND MAN when he follows FERFICHKIN, SIMONOV, TRUDOLYUBOV, and ZVERKOV to the brothel after the dinner in ZVERKOV's honor. Under the influence of his speech about love, family, and her likely ultimate fate as a prostitute, LIZA agrees to come to the UNDERGROUND MAN, who will become her savior. Before he leaves her, she shows him a letter from a medical student who declares his love for her in elevated, flowery, and sincere tones. When she comes to the UNDERGROUND MAN's miserable quarters and sees him as a most unlikely deliverer, she understands his situation, state of mind, and unhappiness. When he abuses her and has her physically, she sees that he is incapable of love and desires only to dominate. She then leaves his underground for a very uncertain future.

MANFRED. The central figure of the dramatic poem *MANFRED,* written by the English romantic poet Lord Byron (1788-1824) in 1817. He sells himself to the devil and lives in splendid and proud solitude without any human sympathies. The UNDERGROUND MAN dreams of being wealthy, giving all his means to mankind as a sacrifice, and then confessing all of his sins. He views such acts as part of the sublime and the beautiful, which he claims to worship, and also as things that MANFRED would do.

MASQUERADE [MASKARAD]. A romantic play written 1835-36 by Mikhail LERMONTOV. The play chronicles the fate of Arbenin, a romantic egotist, who poisons his wife when he suspects that she has betrayed him and who goes insane when he learns of her innocence. See LERMONTOV.

NAPOLEON THE GREAT [NAPOLEON VELIKY]. NAPOLEON I Bonaparte (1769-1821), emperor of France following the French Revolution and temporary conqueror of much of Europe. (1) The UNDERGROUND MAN disputes the idea of BUCKLE that time and civilization temper man and make him less prone to war, and he cites the examples of

NAPOLEON THE GREAT and THE CURRENT NAPOLEON to show that wars are still in vogue and that men are still perverse. (2) The UNDERGROUND MAN in one of his confrontations with APOLLON stands before him with arms folded à la NAPOLEON.

THE CURRENT NAPOLEON [NAPOLEON TEPERESHNY]. Charles Louis NAPOLEON Bonaparte (1808-73), who became NAPOLEON III. He was chosen president of the French Republic in 1848 and declared himself emperor in 1852. He was deposed in 1871 following France's debacle in the Franco-Prussian War. See NAPOLEON THE GREAT.

NEKRASOV. Nikolay Alekseevich NEKRASOV (1821-78), Russian poet and editor prominent in radical literature. His poetry exhibits a concern for socially moral values and liberal ideals. He edited both *The Contemporary* and *FATHERLAND NOTES.* An extract from his poem "WHEN FROM THE DARKNESS OF DELUSION" begins the second part of *Notes From Underground.*

OFFICER [OFITSER]. When the UNDERGROUND MAN happens upon an altercation in a pub, he eagerly enters the fray, hoping to be thrown out of the window, thereby being noticed and becoming somebody. A tall OFFICER who is in the middle of the row simply picks the UNDER-GROUND MAN up and sets him aside as if he were a fly or did not exist at all. The OFFICER then becomes an object of revenge for the shattered ego of the UNDERGROUND MAN, who buys new clothes and tries to bump into him on the street without giving ground.

OLIMPIA. As FERFICHKIN, SIMONOV, TRUDOLYUBOV, and ZVERKOV travel to the brothel following the farewell dinner, ZVERKOV claims that OLIMPIA is his once they arrive.

PIROGOV. Character in Nikolay GOGOL's story *Nevsky Prospect,* written in 1835. He is an officer and self-styled cavalier who pursues a German woman for her favors only to be roundly beaten by her enraged husband. Rather than challenge the irate husband to a duel, PIROGOV complains to the police and to his commanding officer. The UNDER-GROUND MAN laments that the OFFICER who shattered his ego is not the kind who would fight a duel but rather a man like GOGOL's PIROGOV.

PODKHARZHEVSKY. A wealthy hussar whom FERFICHKIN, SI-MONOV, TRUDOLYUBOV, and ZVERKOV discuss at their dinner. They try to determine how much he makes.

PSALTER. The Biblical book of Psalms. APOLLON enjoys pompously reading it aloud.

PYOTR IVANOVICH. PYOTR IVANOVICH Aduev, the practical and pragmatic uncle who aids in the socialization of his romantic, idealistic nephew in *A Common Story (Obyknovennaya istoria)*, a novel written by Ivan Aleksandrovich Goncharov (1812-91) in 1844. The UNDERGROUND MAN singles out PYOTR IVANOVICH and KOSTANZHOGLO as examples of ideals that have been foisted on the Russian romantics by critics and publicists.

STENKA RAZIN. Stepan Timofeevich RAZIN (ca. 1630-71), leader of the rebelling peasants in the Peasant War (1670-71), who was ultimately captured and put to death. In complaining about man's perversity throughout history the UNDERGROUND MAN mentions ATTILA and STENKA RAZIN and compares them with the more bloodthirsty barbarians of the present day who go unnoticed in civilized society because they are so prevalent.

ROUSSEAU [RUSSO]. Jean Jacques ROUSSEAU (1712-78), French author, philosopher, and political theorist. The UNDERGROUND MAN notes that HEINE once commented that true autobiographies do not exist because men lie about themselves. ROUSSEAU, therefore, also lied. He has reference to ROUSSEAU's *Confessions,* written between 1766 and 1770, but published only posthumously.

GEORGE SAND [ZHORZH ZAND]. Pen name of Amantine Lucie Aurore Dupin Dudevant (1804-76), French author who wrote romantic works examining free love, humanitarian reforms, nature, and rustic manners. The UNDERGROUND MAN imagines how he will be LIZA's savior, how she will fall at his feet to declare her love, and how he will speak with the delicacy of a GEORGE SAND.

"TO ONE'S SATISFACTION" ["KAK KOMU UGODNO"]. An article written in 1863 by Mikhail Yevgrafovich Saltykov (1826-89), noted Russian novelist, satirist, and editor, sympathetically responding to a painting by the artist Nikolay GE. The UNDERGROUND MAN selfservingly notes that if he were something in life, he would be glad to praise many things because of his devotion to the sublime and the beautiful. Among those things he would praise would be GE's painting and Saltykov's article about it.

SCHLESWIG-HOLSTEIN [SHLEZVIG-GOLSHTEYN]. Two contiguous duchies of Denmark that became objects and pretexts of European power struggles in the nineteenth century. The UNDERGROUND MAN notes that man has exhibited constant perversity from THE FLOOD down to the period of SCHLESWIG-HOLSTEIN. He also cites the conflict that arose there as another example of the failure of BUCKLE's thesis that increased civilization results in a diminished inclination toward war.

ANTON ANTONYCH SETOCHKIN. The UNDERGROUND MAN's department head, from whom he borrows money to replace the collar on his coat in anticipation of bumping into the OFFICER. He chooses a more fashionable German beaver collar to replace the old raccoon one.

SHAKESPEARE [SHEKSPIR]. William SHAKESPEARE (1564-1616), the most eminent of English dramatists. At ZVERKOV's farewell dinner FERFICHKIN, SIMONOV, TRUDOLYUBOV, and ZVERKOV unanimously and magnanimously agree that SHAKESPEARE is immortal.

SILVIO. The central figure of *The Shot (Vystrel)*, a short story written by Aleksandr Sergeevich Pushkin (1799-1837) in 1830. Having had his pride damaged by a wealthy young count who refused to treat a duel seriously, SILVIO sacrifices everything for revenge. When the count marries and becomes more attached to life, SILVIO determines to reconvene the duel. He is satisfied when he sees the count's fear and embarrassment in front of his bride, and he magnanimously wastes his shot in a gesture that shows the count that he could have taken his life. See LERMONTOV.

SIMONOV. A school acquaintance of the UNDERGROUND MAN whom he sees periodically. Together with FERFICHKIN and TRUDOLYUBOV he plans a farewell dinner for ZVERKOV and reluctantly consents to permit the UNDERGROUND MAN to attend. He lends the UNDERGROUND MAN the money to follow them to the brothel after the dinner.

TRUDOLYUBOV. One of the friends who plans a farewell dinner for ZVERKOV.

UNDERGROUND MAN [PODPOLNY CHELOVEK]. The narrator of the story. He is an orphan who is placed in a school by relatives. At school he feels that he is despised for his poverty, and he comes to hate his schoolmates and to seek their torment. There is only one boy who can reasonably be called his friend and the UNDERGROUND MAN desires only to dominate him. This desire to dominate and a masochistic desire for suffering extend into his adult years. He gets a job in a chancery but has no friends, avoids and even hates people, and alternately puts people above himself and himself above them. When he happens upon a brawl in a pub one evening, he immediately enters hoping at least to be thrown out of the window, thereby gaining attention and becoming an individual. He is regarded however as a nonentity by an OFFICER who simply picks him up and sets him aside away from the fray. His ego is crushed and he determines to revenge himself upon the OFFICER. To prepare for his moment of glory he gets a new wardrobe and then frequents the Nevsky Prospect where after several passes and several days he finally brushes against the OFFICER in walking past him. He is elated with his victory in not yielding ground to the OFFICER and returns home so thrilled in his revenge that he sings Italian arias. He vegetates in his vanity and daily humdrum until he visits SIMONOV and finds him, FERFICHKIN, and TRUDOLYUBOV planning a farewell party for ZVERKOV. He invites himself to attend and is perversely glad that no one wants him to come. At the dinner he proudly pouts as they ignore him and then anxiously seeks their friendship. When the four decide to go to a brothel, he borrows money from SIMONOV and follows them. On the way he fantasizes from the point of view of SILVIO and *MASQUERADE* and exposes his dream world to the reader. At the brothel he is received by LIZA, and he is glad that he appears objectionable and grotesque to her. He becomes enchanted by the game of domination but also by a sincere response to something higher, and imposes upon LIZA a lengthy lecture about love, family, and the fate of prostitutes. She is won over by his ideas and rhetoric and agrees to come to him. He soon resents his sentimentality and his invitation and considers it more important to justify himself before SIMONOV and the others. He fears that LIZA will come to him and see how he lives, and that as a result he will no longer be a hero to her, yet he also fantasizes that he is her saviour, who will magnanimously accept her love and gratitude. Throughout all of these events he is in perpetual conflict with his servant APOLLON, whose will and vanity surpass even his own. When LIZA does come, sees how he lives, and is witness to his unsuccessful attempt to dominate APOLLON, he determines that she will pay for her knowledge, and therefore her superiority over him. He suffers because he is no longer a hero and sobs bitterly. When she commiserates with him, he resents that she is now the heroine. In order to revenge himself and regain dominance he has LIZA sexually and then pays her. He is distressed at her leaving but justifies his behavior and acknowledges his inability to love. Some years later he receives a modest inheritance and retires to his underground, where he deliberately lives in squalid conditions. He then writes these notes in which he chronicles the major events of his life and philosophizes about the necessity of freedom of choice, the limits and general failure of man's reason, suffering, and his own inactivity.

VANYUKHA. In the UNDERGROUND MAN's lecture to LIZA about love, family, and the fate of prostitutes he notes that some VANYUKHA will likely help bury LIZA's consumption-ridden body some day.

WAGENHEIM [VAGENGEYM]. The surname of several St. Petersburg dentists. The UNDERGROUND MAN philosophizes about how a toothache can bring one pleasure and notes that the sufferer and all kinds of WAGENHEIMS are very much at the mercy of teeth and the laws that they obey.

"WHEN FROM THE DARKNESS OF DELUSION" ["KOGDA IZ MRAKA ZABLUZHDENYA"]. A poem by Nikolay NEKRASOV written in 1845, part of which begins the second part of *Notes From Underground* and two lines of which introduce the ninth chapter of the second part. The poem deals with the regeneration of the fallen woman through the aid of the man that loves her. The UNDERGROUND MAN sees himself in the role of the hero and savior who delivers the grateful woman from the error of her ways, but his failure with LIZA demonstrates the general impotence of the naive and egocentric romantic vision.

ZVERKOV. A school acquaintance of the UNDERGROUND MAN. FERFICHKIN, SIMONOV, and TRUDOLYUBOV arrange a farewell dinner in his honor on the occasion of his going to the provinces as an officer. He was always considered to be a cut above his schoolmates, even though a poor student, and the UNDERGROUND MAN resents ZVERKOV's vanity, self-satisfaction, and success.

THE CROCODILE (KROKODIL) 1865

AFIMYA. See AFIMYA SKAPIDAROVA.

ANDREY ALEKSANDROVICH. See ANDREY ALEKSANDROVICH KRAEVSKY. IVAN MATVEICH notes that people justifiably compare ANDREY ALEKSANDROVICH with ALFRED DE MUSSET, the French romantic poet. The two in reality have nothing in common, and the comparison is ironic.

ANDREY OSIPYCH. YELENA IVANOVNA considers appealing to ANDREY OSIPYCH for money to buy the crocodile so that IVAN MATVEICH can be freed.

BOREL. The proprietor of an expensive St. Petersburg restaurant specializing in elegant fare. In reporting the story of IVAN MATVEICH's being swallowed by a crocodile, the newspaper *THE SHEET* distorts the account completely and observes that the gourmet N., probably tiring of the fare at BOREL's restaurant, ate the crocodile alive.

DIOGENES [DIOGEN]. Greek Cynic philosopher (ca. 400-325 B.C.). He lived an ascetic life and gained notoriety by conducting a search with a lantern in daylight to find an honest man. IVAN MATVEICH feels that his new career from inside the crocodile will be to become a DIOGENES, a SOCRATES, or a combination of both, to benefit mankind.

ENCYCLOPEDIC DICTIONARY [ENTSYKLOPEDICHESKY SLO-VAR]. A standard Russian reference work, a new edition of which was begun by KRAEVSKY in 1861. KRAEVSKY edited only the first volume, after which he relinquished the editorship under pressure. The new edition stopped publication with the sixth volume. IVAN MATVEICH informs his wife YELENA IVANOVNA that in order for her to have the breadth of knowledge she needs to complement his future brilliant career inside the crocodile, she must study KRAEVSKY's *ENCYCLOPEDIC DICTIONARY*.

FOURIER [FURIE]. François Marie Charles FOURIER (1772-1837), French reformer and economist whose utopian theories became very chic in Russia. He envisioned a society in which economic activity would be carried out by groups of people living together in communal environments called phalanxes. IVAN MATVEICH anticipates that as he teaches visitors his new economic theory from his vantage point inside the crocodile, he will become a new FOURIER.

GARNIER-PAGES [GARNIE-PAZHESS] (GARNIER-PAGESISHKA). Louis GARNIER-PAGES (1803-78), French political leader who participated in the Revolutions of 1830 and 1848 and who held numerous elective and appointive positions. IVAN MATVEICH envisions his future brilliant career inside the crocodile and insists that he is as important as GARNIER-PAGES, whom he refers to with the familiar GARNIER-PAGESISHKA.

GARNIER-PAGESISHKA [GARNIE-PAZHESISHKA]. See GARNIER-PAGES.

THE GERMAN [NEMETS]. The owner of the crocodile KARLCHEN, who swallows IVAN MATVEICH. He is far more worried about his animal than about IVAN MATVEICH and warns YELENA IVANOVNA that she will have to pay for KARLCHEN if he is cut open to free her husband. He is ecstatic when he hears IVAN MATVEICH's voice from inside the animal, because he can then charge a larger admission and more people will come to see the attraction.

IGNATY PROKOFYCH. A capitalist who talks of nothing but economics. He advocates enticing foreign capital and even selling all of Russia if need be. He is also in favor of building up the bourgeoisie and of making the peasant work.

IVAN MATVEICH. A vain pseudo-intellectual who is swallowed by a crocodile. He is initially concerned about what his superiors will say and about getting money to buy the animal so that he can be freed, but his thoughts soon turn to the brilliant career that he will have inside the beast. He envisions contriving new theories of economics, of becoming a new FOURIER, of being an oracle to the many important people who will come see him, and of being greatly admired and respected. He is sure that YELENA IVANOVNA will be admired because she is his wife, and he wants her to establish a salon in which she can entertain those who come to see him. Food does not concern him, and he professes to be content with his great ideas. Freedom is also not important, since intelligent races prefer order. While he anticipates becoming a new DIOGENES or SOCRATES, he does express some uneasiness over the literary critics and satirical newspapers.

KARLCHEN [KARLKHEN]. The crocodile that swallows IVAN MATVEICH

ANDREY ALEKSANDROVICH KRAEVSKY. Russian journalist and publisher (1810-89), who published *Fatherland Notes*. IVAN MATVEICH tells YELENA IVANOVNA that in order to be the kind of wife she needs to be to complement his future brilliant career, she must study KRAEVSKY's *ENCYCLOPEDIC DICTIONARY* to be able to talk about everything.

LAVROV. Pyotr Lavrovich LAVROV (1823-1900), Russian social thinker and philosopher, who was one of the theoreticians and leaders of revolutionary populism. He sometimes gave public lectures in the arcade in St. Petersburg. SEMYON SEMYONYCH tells YELENA IVANOVNA not to make a scene in the arcade simply over IVAN MATVEICH's being swallowed by the crocodile, since LAVROV may be giving a lecture.

LESSEPS. Ferdinand Marie de LESSEPS (1805-94), French diplomat and engineer who built the Suez Canal. In reporting IVAN MATVEICH's mishap with the crocodile, the newspaper *THE SHEET* so distorts the story that it reports that the gourmet N. ate a live crocodile. The article also gives some background on crocodile eating and states that LESSEPS and his party found crocodile feet a delicacy.

LUKA ANDREICH. A friend of TIMOFEY SEMYONYCH.

LUKYANOV. In *THE VOICE* version of the story of the crocodile swallowing IVAN MATVEICH, the merchant LUKYANOV is castigated for not keeping his stairs in repair, thereby causing AFIMYA SKAPIDAROVA to fall and break her leg.

ALFRED DE MUSSET [ALFRED DE MYUSSE]. French poet, novelist, and dramatist (1810-57), who is known for his literary romanticism and for his stormy love affair with George Sand. IVAN MATVEICH observes that ANDREY ALEKSANDROVICH (KRAEVSKY) is properly considered the Russian ALFRED DE MUSSET. The equation of the journalist with the romantic writer is quite ironic.

N. *THE SHEET* reports that the famous gourmet N. ate the crocodile alive while he was dickering with the GERMAN over a price. This story is somehow journalistically derived from KARLCHEN's swallowing IVAN MATVEICH.

NIKIFOR NIKIFORYCH. IVAN MATVEICH loses some money one evening at the home of NIKIFOR NIKIFORYCH.

"OHE, LAMBERT! OU EST LAMBERT, AS-TU VU LAMBERT?" "Oh, Lambert! Where is Lambert; have you seen Lambert?" Comic French expression designed to create a humorous effect. The phrase serves as the epigraph to the story and alludes to the disappearance of IVAN MATVEICH.

PHARAOH [FARAON]. The Hebraic term indicating the kings of Egypt. IVAN MATVEICH refers to the crocodile as a resident of the kingdom of PHARAOH and feels that perhaps even the ancient PHARAOHS knew the Italian word "crocodillo," which comes from the French root "croquer," which means "to eat." IVAN MATVEICH's pseudoscientific etymological exercise parallels his expectations of a brilliant career.

PROKHOR SAVVICH. A colleague of SEMYON SEMYONYCH.

ST. PETERSBURG NEWS [ST. PETERBURGSKIE IZVESTIA]. The reference is to the *St. Petersburg Record (St. Peterburgskie vedomosti).* IVAN MATVEICH states that in order for YELENA IVANOVNA to complement his brilliant future she must read the editorials in the *ST. PETERSBURG NEWS* and compare them daily with *THE VOICE.*

SEMYON SEMYONYCH. The narrator of the story, a friend, co-worker, and distant relative of IVAN MATVEICH. Once IVAN MATVEICH is inside the crocodile, SEMYON SEMYONYCH admits that he never could tolerate him and his vain, condescending air. He also admits his interest in YELENA IVANOVNA, but tries to mask it as the interest of a father.

THE SHEET [LISTOK]. The narrator probably has in mind *The Petersburg Sheet; A Newspaper of City Life and Literature (Peterburgsky listok; Gazeta gorodskoy zhizni i literatury),* a daily newspaper founded in 1864. This paper carries an item about IVAN MATVEICH and the crocodile on the day following the incident but somehow reports only that the famous gourmet N. ate the crocodile alive. The article further suggests that crocodiles could become the basis of a Russian industry for food, clothing, etc.

AFIMYA SKAPIDAROVA. In *THE VOICE* account of the crocodile's swallowing IVAN MATVEICH, much of the attention is directed toward exposing the merchant LUKYANOV, whose stairs are in such disrepair that AFIMYA SKAPIDAROVA fell on them and broke her leg.

SOCRATES [SOKRAT]. Greek teacher of wisdom (ca. 470-399 B.C.), who is known through the writings of Plato, Aristotle, and Xenophon. He taught that virtue was knowledge, and is credited with formulating the SOCRA-TIC method of teaching by using questions and answers. He was tried in Athens for impiety and corrupting youth, was sentenced to death, and took his own life by drinking hemlock. IVAN MATVEICH feels that his future career in the crocodile is to become another DIOGENES or SOCRATES for the benefit of mankind.

SODOM. As recorded in Genesis 18-19 of the Old Testament, a city which together with Gomorrah was destroyed by Jehovah because of its wickedness. The term has come to mean wickedness and chaos. When IVAN MATVEICH is swallowed by the crocodile, the situation is described as a veritable SODOM.

SON OF THE FATHERLAND [SYN OTECHESTVA]. A St. Petersburg daily, founded in 1862, specializing in politics, science, and literature. TIMOFEY SEMYONYCH observes that since he is not in authority he can do nothing for IVAN MATVEICH's predicament inside the crocodile. He insists that he speaks as a son of the fatherland and not as *SON OF THE FATHERLAND*.

STEPANOV. Nikolay Aleksandrovich STEPANOV (1807-77), satirical artist and caricaturist, who edited and published the satirical journals *The Spark (Iskra)* and *The Alarm Clock (Budilnik)*. SEMYON SEMYONYCH feels that if YELENA IVANOVNA makes a scene over the incident of IVAN MATVEICH's being swallowed by the crocodile, she may draw the attention of STEPANOV.

WILLIAM TELL [VILGELM TELL]. The legendary national hero and popular leader of Switzerland. For his refusal to declare allegiance to Austria he was condemned to shoot an apple from his son's head. His successful shot resulted in imprisonment, but the peasantry liberated him, and he led his country to independence from Austria in the fourteenth century. IVAN MATVEICH had intended to go to Switzerland for a visit, to the homeland of WILLIAM TELL.

"THOUGH THE HOUSES ARE NEW, THE CONVENTIONS ARE OLD" ["DOMA NOVY, NO PREDRASSUDKI STARY"]. Words from *Woe From Wit (Gore ot uma)*, a play written by Aleksandr Sergeevich Griboedov (1795-1829) in 1822-24. The lines are spoken by the main protagonist Chatsky, a frustrated idealist. *THE VOICE* version of the

IVAN MATVEICH-crocodile story cites this line to assert that society has not progressed very far. To illustrate the assertion the reporter uses the examples of a fat man who crawls into the mouth of a poor crocodile and of LUKYANOV, who does not repair his stairs and causes AFIMYA SKAPIDAROVA to fall.

THE TIMES [TEYMS]. *The London Times.* IGNATY PROKOFICH states that *THE TIMES* insists that Russia's economic problem is that it has no bourgeoisie or proletariat.

TIMOFEY SEMYONYCH. A person to whom SEMYON SEMYON-YCH appeals for money to buy the crocodile so that IVAN MATVEICH can be rescued. TIMOFEY SEMYONYCH refuses and insists that IVAN MATVEICH's trouble arises from his progressive views and too much education. He finds IVAN MATVEICH's desire to go abroad suspect and thinks that the stay inside the crocodile might do him good. TIMOFEY SEMYONYCH discusses capital and the necessity of attracting foreign investment and adds that IVAN MATVEICH should feel proud to have so increased the value of a foreign crocodile.

YEVGENIA TUR. Pseudonym of Yelizaveta Vasilievna Salias de Turne-mir (1815-92), Russian writer and author of publicistic articles, who maintained a fashionable and popular salon for writers and scholars. IVAN MATVEICH envisions YELENA IVANOVNA's maintaining a large salon to entertain the many important people who will come to visit him and learn from him while he is inside the crocodile. He makes the comparison that if ANDREY ALEKSANDROVICH can justifiably be called the Russian ALFRED DE MUSSET, then his wife will be called the Russian YEVGENIA TUR. The fact that YEVGENIA TUR is Russian seems to escape IVAN MATVEICH.

THE VOICE [GOLOS]. Newspaper edited by ANDREY ALEKSAN-DROVICH KRAEVSKY. The narrator continually refers to the publica-tion as *VOLOS (THE HAIR)* as a pun on *GOLOS.* (1) IVAN MATVEICH tells YELENA IVANOVNA that to be the kind of wife she needs to be to complement his future brilliant career inside the crocodile, she must read the editorials in the *ST. PETERSBURG NEWS* and compare them daily with *THE VOICE.* (2) When *THE VOICE* reports the story of IVAN MAT-VEICH and the crocodile, it states that a fat man crawled into a poor crocodile. This incident is extended into a social commentary about man's lack of progress, and a supporting example is drawn from the merchant LUKYANOV, whose failure to repair his stairs results in AFIMYA

SKAPIDAROVA's falling and breaking her leg.

VOLOS. See *THE VOICE.*

YELENA IVANOVNA. IVAN MATVEICH's beautiful wife. Following IVAN MATVEICH's trip into the crocodile she finds the idea that she is something of a widow quite interesting, and she takes to admiring herself in mirrors and flirting. She categorically refuses to join her husband inside the crocodile and wonders if a divorce would be appropriate. The idea of maintaining a salon for the many important people who will come to see IVAN MATVEICH intrigues her, and she immediately begins to plan for a new wardrobe.

THE GAMBLER (IGROK) 1866

ALBERT. An officer whom BLANCHE sees periodically in Paris.

ALEKSEY IVANOVICH (ALEXIS). The narrator of the story, a gambler who views roulette as his only salvation. He is a twenty five year old university graduate and a member of the nobility who is attached to THE GENERAL's family as a teacher. He endures a master-slave relationship with POLINA, THE GENERAL's stepdaughter; he hopelessly loves her and would do anything for her, yet he also hates her and could sometimes kill her. To show POLINA that he will do her biddng, he creates a scene with the BARONESS WURMERHELM by impudently approaching her and offering to be her servant. The stunt results in his being fired by THE GENERAL. Appeals to abandon his pursuit of the joke are ineffective until he finally heeds POLINA's demand to drop the matter. Following his dismissal THE GENERAL, DE GRIEUX, and BLANCHE beg him to prevent TARASEVICHEVA, an elderly relative whose money THE GENERAL desperately needs, from losing her vast wealth at roulette. He attaches himself to her but is unable to prevent her losing everything that she brought with her. Thereafter, contrary to his previous experience, he wins big at roulette and makes a fortune. He presents the money to POLINA who spends the night with him but then throws the money in his face and leaves. Angry and subdued, he retaliates by going to Paris with BLANCHE, who promises him a month of riotous living. BLANCHE goes through all of the money, frequently calls him a fool, and finally leaves him to marry THE GENERAL. His life then becomes an endless round of roulette, debts, and poverty. ASTLEY locates him and reports that POLINA loves him but forecasts that he will be ruined and will spend the rest of his life at roulette. He decides to prove to POLINA that he is a man, but his actions are limited to musing about how he could change his fate by winning at roulette.

ALEXIS. See ALEKSEY IVANOVICH.

AMALCHEN [AMALKHEN]. In discussing the German way of obtaining capital, as opposed to his own method of trying to win at roulette, ALEKSEY IVANOVICH notes that all is sacrificed to pass down resources to the eldest son. The son in turn cannot marry AMALCHEN until he has accumulated enough money. They finally marry when he is forty, she thirty five, and the money secure.

ANTONIDA VASILIEVNA. See ANTONIDA VASILIEVNA TARA- SEVICHEVA.

APOLLO BELVEDERE [APOLLON BELVEDERSKY]. A statue of Apollo, the Greek sun god, originally done by the Athenian sculptor Leochares in the fourth century B.C. A copy now stands in the Vatican Museum. ALEKSEY IVANOVICH tells ASTLEY that while POLINA respects ASTLEY, her heart will belong to DE GRIEUX, who is like an APOLLO BELVEDERE compared with the businesslike and calm AST- LEY.

MISTER ASTLEY. A wealthy Englishman who is in love with POLINA and who spends time and money doing her bidding and helping THE GENERAL and ALEKSEY IVANOVICH. POLINA flees to him after her night with ALEKSEY IVANOVICH, and she uses ASTLEY to keep herself informed about him. He aids ALEKSEY IVANOVICH financially, but identifies him as a ruined man with no hope of regeneration.

COUNT B. After ALEKSEY IVANOVICH wins a fortune at roulette, he is given the hotel rooms formerly occupied by COUNT B.

BALAKIREV. Ivan Aleksandrovich BALAKIREV (1699-1763), notorious source of anecdotes, whose exploits were published in a popular book. ALEKSEY IVANOVICH wonders if POLINA needs him at all or simply as a buffoon like BALAKIREV.

BARBERINI. Aristocratic Italian family which wielded great influence in Rome and around the papacy through the seventeenth century. ASTLEY reports to ALEKSEY IVANOVICH that BLANCHE cavorted with a Polish count with an Italian historical name something like BARBERINI. The Pole quickly abandons BLANCHE when she loses heavily at roulette, and he leaves her with all their accumulated bills.

MADAME BLANCHARD. Marie BLANCHARD (1778-1819), wife of Jean Pierre Blanchard, a pioneering balloonist, who herself ascended many times. When ALEKSEY IVANOVICH bets all that he has on one roulette turn and anxiously awaits the result, he feels what MADAME BLANCHARD must have felt.

BLANCHE. See BLANCHE DE COMINGES.

CLEOPATRE. One of the impressive women who attend the lavish parties given by ALEKSEY IVANOVICH and BLANCHE in Paris.

BLANCHE DE COMINGES (MADEMOISELLE ZELMA, BLANCHE DU PLACET). A French woman of twenty five whose desire is to live well, be wealthy, and gain the status of a general's wife. She begins her quest by attaching herself to a Polish count, BARBERINI, but he quickly leaves her when she sustains heavy gambling losses. When she asks BARON WURMERHELM to place a bet for her, his wife the BARONESS is so enfuriated that BLANCHE is forced to leave town. Thereafter she does not gamble herself but lends her money at interest to those who do. She views THE GENERAL as a way to both become wealthy and to gain the title she desires, but she deserts him when TARASEVICHEVA, the source of his future fortune, loses heavily at roulette. She then attaches herself to PRINCE NILSKY, whom she drops when she learns that all he wants is a loan to play roulette. When she learns that ALEKSEY IVANOVICH has won a fortune, she invites him into her boudoire and provocatively invites him to come to Paris with her. She demands fifty thousand francs in exchange for a month of fun. She gets much more and comes to "love" him during their brief spree because he lets her see other men and spend as she wishes. When THE GENERAL arrives in Paris, she makes good use of him socially and finally marries him when it is learned that TARASEVICHEVA is very ill and that he will get all of her money. When THE GENERAL himself dies, she inherits everything.

MADAME DE COMINGES. A woman who functions as BLANCHE's mother for social necessity and effect.

CORNEILLE [KORNEL]. Pierre CORNEILLE (1606-84), French dramatist and a prime shaper of the French Classical theater. When BLANCHE
challenges ALEKSEY IVANOVICH to accompany her to Paris following
his winning a fortune at roulette, they exchange lines from CORNEILLE's
play *Le Cid* written in 1637. The play deals with the classic conflict of love
and duty, with love finally gaining ascendence. See "MON FILS, AS-TU
DU COEUR? TOUT AUTRE..."

"ET APRES LE DELUGE!" "And after, the deluge!" adaptation of a reply
to King Louis XV (1710-74) of France following the defeat of the French
and Austrian armies by Frederick the Great of Prussia in 1757 during the
Seven Years War. The remark is attributed to Madame de Pompadour
(1721-64) who is reputed to have said "Après nous le déluge" ("After us the
deluge"). After ALEKSEY IVANOVICH wins a fortune at roulette,
BLANCHE offers him a Parisian fling with her for a month or more so long
as the money lasts. She concludes the description of her offer with the phrase
"ET APRES LE DELUGE!"

MISTER FEADER [FIDER]. MISTER ASTLEY's information about
BLANCHE comes from MISTER FEADER, who took BLANCHE out of
town after she had been abandoned by BARBERINI and had offended
BARONESS WURMERHELM.

FEDOSYA. The nurse of THE GENERAL's children.

FYODOR. TARASEVICHEVA's lackey.

THE GENERAL. A pathetic widower of fifty five who is hopelessly in love
with BLANCHE. He is in severe financial straits and has mortgaged his
estate and everything he has to DE GRIEUX, his business partner. His only
hope to prevent DE GRIEUX from taking over everything is his aged aunt
TARASEVICHEVA, from whom he stands to inherit a great deal. When
TARASEVICHEVA herself arrives in Europe and begins to gamble and
lose heavily, he appeals to ALEKSEY IVANOVICH to minimize her losses.
After his aunt loses everything that she brought, he appeals to her for money
in the name of his debts, his love for BLANCHE, and their family name, but
is promptly refused. The refusal causes both BLANCHE and DE GRIEUX
to abandon him. When BLANCHE and ALEKSEY IVANOVICH sub-
sequently leave for Paris, he has an attack and acts as if he has lost his mind.
He meekly follows BLANCHE to Paris and becomes totally dependent
upon her. BLANCHE finally marries him when it is clear that his aunt is
very ill and that he will inherit everything, and he becomes very happy. He

dies shortly thereafter of a stroke, thus leaving BLANCHE the fortune and title she desires.

GINZE [GINTSE]. When ALEKSEY IVANOVICH sinks into debt and despair and desperately needs a job and money, he serves as GINZE's valet.

DE GRIEUX [MARKIZ DE GRIE]. THE GENERAL's business partner who holds a mortgage on everything that THE GENERAL has. He informs POLINA, who has been his mistress, that he plans to sell THE GENERAL's indebted holdings but will leave a bit that she can recover from him through a lawsuit. His name is probably taken from *Les Aventures du Chevalier des Grieux et de Manon Lescaut (The Adventures of the Knight des Grieux and of Manon Lescaut),* written by Antoine François Prévost (1697-1763) in 1731.

HOPPE [GOPPE]. ALEKSEY IVANOVICH possibly has in mind a banking company in Amsterdam. He discusses the way Germans gradually accumulate wealth by scrimping and passing it on to the eldest son, in contrast to the impatient schemes of Russians. In several generations in such a German family there will emerge a BARON ROTHSCHILD or a HOPPE and Company.

HORTENSE. BLANCHE promises to introduce ALEKSEY IVANO-VICH to HORTENSE in Paris.

KARL. The lackey on ALEKSEY IVANOVICH's floor of the hotel.

KATERINA. POLINA's late mother.

PAUL DE KOCK [POL DE KOK]. French novelist (1793-1871) noted for his graphic portrayals of Parisian life. ALEKSEY IVANOVICH reads his novels, which he cannot tolerate, in German translation when he is in the depths of poverty, debt, and compulsive gambling.

LISETTE. One of the impressive women who attend the lavish Paris parties given by BLANCHE and ALEKSEY IVANOVICH.

LOVEL. MISTER ASTLEY is an official of the LOVEL and Company sugar corporation.

MARFA. TARASEVICHEVA's maid.

MARYA FILIPPOVNA. A member of THE GENERAL's household.

MEMOIRS [ZAPISKI]. The *MEMOIRS* of General Vasily PEROVSKY, in which is recorded among many other things the cruelty of the retreating French army as it left Russia during the War of 1812. ALEKSEY IVANOVICH discusses with a disbelieving Frenchman the atrocities perpetrated by the French upon the Russians in the War of 1812. He suggests that he read General PEROVSKY's *MEMOIRS* to verify his statements.

MEZENTSOV. A dinner guest of THE GENERAL.

MISHA. One of THE GENERAL's children, who with his inheritance from TARASEVICHEVA goes to study in London.

"MON FILS, AS-TU DU COEUR? TOUT AUTRE..." "My son, have you courage? Every other...," lines from CORNEILLE's *Le Cid.* When BLANCHE challenges the suddenly wealthy ALEKSEY IVANOVICH to accompany her to Paris, they exchange these lines.

LA GRANDE DUCHESSE DE N. When TARASEVICHEVA comes to Europe to gamble, she takes the suite that was occupied by LA GRANDE DUCHESSE DE N.

NADENKA. See NADYA.

NADYA (NADENKA). One of THE GENERAL's children, who uses her share of TARASEVICHEVA's money to go to London to study.

PRINCE NILSKY. A Russian nobleman commonly in the company of THE GENERAL and his group. When TARASEVICHEVA loses heavily at roulette, BLANCHE ignores THE GENERAL and attaches herself to PRINCE NILSKY. She quickly drops him, however, when she discovers that all he wants is a loan to play roulette.

OPINION NATIONALE. Parisian political daily published 1859-79. ALEKSEY IVANOVICH reads slanderous statements about Russia in *OPINION NATIONALE.*

PAULINE. See POLINA ALEKSANDROVNA.

LORD PEABROOK [PIBROK]. A cousin of MISTER ASTLEY.

PEROVSKY. General Vasily Alekseevich PEROVSKY (1794-1857), Russian military figure whose *MEMOIRS* chronicle the horrors perpetrated upon the Russians by the retreating French army during the War of 1812. ALEKSEY IVANOVICH discusses with a disbelieving Frenchman the atrocities of the French army during the War of 1812. He suggests that the Frenchman read excerpts from PEROVSKY's *MEMOIRS* to verify his assertions.

DU PLACET. BLANCHE's real surname.

POLINA. See POLINA ALEKSANDROVNA.

POLINA ALEKSANDROVNA (PAULINE, POLINA, PRASKOVYA). The extremely proud stepdaughter of THE GENERAL, who is using ALEKSEY IVANOVICH to gamble for her in hope of making money. She is caught among three men: DE GRIEUX, who has been her lover, ASTLEY, whom she respects, and ALEKSEY IVANOVICH, with whom she has a stormy love-hate relationship. She tortures ALEKSEY IVANO-VICH, who also both loves and hates her, and enjoys exercising her dominance over him. She makes him cause a scene with the BARONESS WURMERHELM to test his devotion and to give her some amusement. When he brings back his large earnings to her, she declares her hate for him and compares him to DE GRIEUX in trying to buy her. She suddenly becomes affectionate, reflects upon his servile deeds for her, and spends the night with him, only to throw the money in his face the next morning and run to ASTLEY. After she gets her inheritance from TARASEVICHEVA, she travels to Switzerland but maintains surveillance on ALEKSEY IVANOVICH because she retains her love for him.

POTAPYCH. TARASEVICHEVA's old butler.

PRASKOVYA. See POLINA ALEKSANDROVNA. POLINA is called PRASKOVYA by TARASEVICHEVA.

RACINE [RASIN]. Jean RACINE (1639-99), French Classical dramatist. In trying to define the French condition and character from the Russian point of view to MISTER ASTLEY, ALEKSEY IVANOVICH cites the example of RACINE, who typifies refinement and elegance of form in literature.

BARON ROTHSCHILD [ROTSHILD]. A family of Jewish bankers who dominated European finance in the nineteenth century. The ROTHS-

CHILD referred to in *The Gambler* is likely James (1792-1868), who controlled the French branch of the banking empire. (1) ALEKSEY IVANOVICH discusses the way Germans accumulate wealth by scrimping and then passing it down to the eldest son. In several generations under such a system there emerges a BARON ROTHSCHILD or a HOPPE. (2) ALEKSEY IVANOVICH muses that in gambling avarice is relative and that what for ROTHSCHILD is petty for him is a fortune.

DE SAGO SAGO. After she marries THE GENERAL, BLANCHE cannot pronounce her new surname and offers DE SAGO SAGO as an approximation.

ANTONIDA VASILIEVNA TARASEVICHEVA. THE GENERAL's seventy five year old aunt whose death is anxiously awaited so that her money can relieve him of his financial crisis. She suddenly arrives in Roulettenburg with her entire retinue at the same hotel in which THE GENERAL is staying and confronts him, DE GRIEUX, and the rest, with their telegrams inquiring about her death and expressing interest in an inheritance. She accuses THE GENERAL of robbing from his own children and vows to disinherit him. Despite ALEKSEY IVANOVICH's efforts she loses all the money she brought with her at roulette. While gambling she is perpetually attended by a series of fawning Poles who attempt to rob her. She then returns to Moscow, somewhat tempered, and admits that she has been a fool. She finally passes on, and her money filters down to THE GENERAL and his children.

THERESE-PHILOSOPHE. The heroine of the erotic novel *THERESE-PHILOSOPHE, ou Mémoires pour servir à l'histoire de D. Dirrag et de M-lle Eradice (Therese the Philosopher, or Memoirs Serving as a History of D. Dirrag and Mademoiselle Eradice)*, which was published anonymously in 1748. HORTENSE is referred to as THERESE-PHILOSOPHE in her immediate circle.

TIMOFEY PETROVICH. An acquaintance of POLINA who sends word from St. Petersburg that her grandmother TARASEVICHEVA is likely dying.

BARON WURMERHELM [VURMERGELM]. A tall, thin German of forty five. When ALEKSEY IVANOVICH accosts his wife and offers to be her servant, he is offended and considers the young man crazy.

BARONESS WURMERHELM [VURMERGELM]. The short and extremely fat wife of BARON WURMERHELM. To test ALEKSEY IVANOVICH's devotion and to get a good laugh, POLINA has him approach the BARONESS WURMERHELM, address her in French, and offer to be her servant in hopes that her husband will beat him with his walking stick.

ZAGORYANSKY. After she marries THE GENERAL, BLANCHE cannot pronounce her new surname and offers ZAGORYANSKY as an approximation.

ZAGOZIANSKY. After she marries THE GENERAL, BLANCHE cannot pronounce her new surname and offers ZAGOZIANSKY as an approximation.

ZAZHIGIN. A family that is part of TARASEVICHEVA's household in Russia.

MADEMOISELLE ZELMA. A name used by BLANCHE during her escapade with BARBERINI.

CRIME AND PUNISHMENT (PRESTUPLENIE I NAKAZANIE) 1866

ABRAHAM [AVRAAM]. As recorded in Genesis 12-25, an Old Testament patriarch who was led by Jehovah out of Ur of the Chaldees into another land so that he could worship properly. Jehovah made a covenant with him to the effect that ABRAHAM would become a great nation that would bless the world. After recovering from an illness in Siberia, RASKOLNIKOV goes out to work and is impressed by the vast plains and the impression of freedom and expanse that they convey. He ponders that this is how it must have looked at the time of ABRAHAM.

ACHILLES [AKHILLES]. In Greek mythology, the king of the Myrmidons. He is the hero of Homer's *Iliad* and the prototype of manly valor and beauty whose only vulnerable spot is his heel. SVIDRIGAYLOV refers to the guard before whom he commits suicide as ACHILLES because of his helmet, which strikes him as something that ACHILLES would wear.

AFANASY IVANOVICH. See AFANASY IVANOVICH VAKH-RUSHIN.

AFANASY PAVLYCH. See AFANASY PAVLYCH DUSHKIN.

AFROSINYUSHKA. The woman who attempts to drown herself while RASKOLNIKOV is standing on the bridge. She is quickly rescued.

THE AGE [VEK]. A St. Petersburg literary and political weekly published 1861-62. SVIDRIGAYLOV alludes to an article in *THE AGE* which castigates a woman who gave a provocative public reading of "EGYPTIAN NIGHTS."

ALEKSANDR GRIGORIEVICH. See ALEKSANDR GRIGORIE-VICH ZAMYOTOV.

ALEKSEY SEMYONYCH. A worker in SHELOPAEV's office who attempts to deliver the money that PULKHERIA ALEKSANDROVNA sends to RASKOLNIKOV. The delivery is delayed because RASKOLNI-KOV is delirious.

ALLAH [ALLAKH]. Arabic name for the Supreme Being. RASKOLNI-KOV envisions MUHAMMAD mounted warlike atop a horse, eager to obey the word of ALLAH. He considers himself a louse in comparison with the MUHAMMAD of such a vision.

ALMA. Crimean river which was the scene of a defeat for the Russian army during the Crimean War in 1854. PORFIRY PETROVICH discusses with RASKOLNIKOV various strategies of capturing a criminal. Much of the interchange uses the analogy of military campaigns, and the battle at ALMA is mentioned.

ALYONA IVANOVNA. A heartless and cruel pawnbroker of sixty, who lives with her half-sister LIZAVETA IVANOVNA, whom she keeps in virtual servitude. She demands exorbitant rates of interest from desperate people and sends most of the money to a monastery for prayers for her soul. She is brutally murdered with an ax by RASKOLNIKOV, who uses her to test his theory of ordinary and extraordinary people.

ALYOSHKA. The younger of the two workmen who are repainting the murdered ALYONA IVANOVNA's flat. RASKOLNIKOV meets him when he returns to the scene of his crime.

AMALIA FYODOROVNA. See AMALIA FYODOROVNA LIPPE-WECHSEL.

AMAL-IVAN. See AMALIA FYODOROVNA LIPPEWECHSEL. AMALIA FYODOROVNA refers to herself as AMAL-IVAN in a comic approximation of the Russian patronymic.

AMALIA LUDWIGOVNA [LUDVIGOVNA]. See AMALIA FYODOROVNA LIPPEWECHSEL. KATERINA IVANOVNA deliberately refers to AMALIA FYODOROVNA as AMALIA LUDWIGOVNA to irritate her and call attention to her German background.

ANDREY SEMYONOVICH. See ANDREY SEMYONOVICH LEBE-ZYATNIKOV.

ANISKA. The seamstress on the SVIDRIGAYLOV estate. When MAR-FA PETROVNA "appears" to her husband SVIDRIGAYLOV for the third time after her death, she is wearing a new green dress and comments that ANISKA cannot make a dress as good as the one she is wearing.

ARKADY IVANOVICH. See ARKADY IVANOVICH SVIDRIGAY-LOV.

AVDOTYA ROMANOVNA. See AVDOTYA ROMANOVNA RAS-KOLNIKOVA.

AZTECS [ATSTEKI]. An Indian tribe that dominated much of Mexico at the time of the Spanish conquest of 1519-21 under Hernando Cortez (1485-1547). When RASKOLNIKOV searches the papers for reports of his murders, he notices an article on two AZTEC midgets, BARTOLA and MASSIMO, who are being exhibited in St. Petersburg.

B—N. A doctor whom PORFIRY PETROVICH consults and who recommends that he quit smoking. B—N is likely a reference to Dr. Sergey Petrovich Botkin (1832-89), whom Dostoevsky himself consulted.

BABUSHKIN. A civil servant from whom RAZUMIKHIN rents his apartment.

BACCHUS [BAKHUS]. In Roman mythology the god of wine. SVID-RIGAYLOV is particularly coarse with DUNYA, as she serves as governess on his estate, when he is under the influence of BACCHUS.

BAKALEEV. LUZHIN finds DUNYA and PULKHERIA ALEKSAN-DROVNA a room in a building owned by BAKALEEV when they arrive in St. Petersburg.

BARTOLA. A female midget, who, with a male counterpart named MASSIMO, was exhibited in St. Petersburg in 1865. They were billed as direct descendants of the AZTECS. When RASKOLNIKOV searches the papers for reports of his murders, he comes across an article on the AZTECS BARTOLA and MASSIMO.

BELINSKY. Vissarion Grigorievich BELINSKY (1811-48), Russian literary critic and journalist. He wrote for both *Fatherland Notes* and *The Contemporary* and insisted that literature realistically expose the seamy side of life with the intent of social reform. He was the first and most eminent of the so-called Radical Critics, and his ideas were important in the development of the Natural School. LEBEZYATNIKOV claims that he has developed further than most radicals because he rejects more and insists that he would argue even with BELINSKY if he were alive.

BERG. A balloonist and a developer of St. Petersburg entertainment attractions. SVIDRIGAYLOV observes that BERG is in the city making balloon ascensions and will take people up for a fee.

PRINCESS BEZZEMELNAYA. KATERINA IVANOVNA mentions that the PRINCESS BEZZEMELNAYA saw her dance at a ball and praised her.

BIBLE [YEVANGELIE]. A collection of books organized into the Old Testament, a religious history from Adam through the twelve tribes of Israel, with emphasis on Judah, and the New Testament, the life and ministry of JESUS CHRIST. (1) SONYA and LIZAVETA IVANOVNA enjoy reading the BIBLE together. (2) After RASKOLNIKOV discovers that he loves SONYA, he takes her BIBLE, which he has kept under his pillow, and wonders if he can make SONYA's ideals his own.

BUKH. RASKOLNIKOV's former landlord.

CAPITOLIUM [KAPITOLIA]. One of the hills on which ancient Rome was built and a center of religion and politics. RASKOLNIKOV admits to DUNYA that he has spilled blood, but he insists that it is the same blood for which men have been crowned in CAPITOLIUM and called benefactors of mankind. Julius Caesar and other Roman emperors were so rewarded after successful military expeditions.

CHEBAROV. An official to whom ZARNITSYNA assigns RASKOLNI-KOV's letter of IOU. He convinces her to press the matter with RASKOL-NIKOV in hope of recovering the debt and finally sells the note to RAZUMIKHIN.

CINQ SOUS. Five Cents, a popular French song sung by beggars. When KATERINA IVANOVNA takes herself and her children into the streets to beg and show what a noble family has been driven to, she determines to sing *CINQ SOUS.*

CONFESSIONS. *Les CONFESSIONS,* the autobiography of Jean Jacques ROUSSEAU, written 1766-70. It was published posthumously in 1781 and 1788. KHERUVIMOV wants RAZUMIKHIN to translate excerpts from the second part of *CONFESSIONS* so that he can publish it. He is interested in such a venture because he heard that ROUSSEAU was rather like RADISHCHEV.

THE CRAFTSMAN [MESHCHANIN]. A fifty year old lower middle class worker who suddenly comes to RASKOLNIKOV and calls him a murderer. He is outside the building in which ALYONA IVANONVA lives when RASKOLNIKOV returns to the scene of the murders and acts very strangely. Because of this he suspects RASKOLNIKOV of the murders and informs PORFIRY PETROVICH. When PROFIRY PETROVICH inter-rogates RASKOLNIKOV in his office, he has THE CRAFTSMAN waiting behind a door prepared to make a denunciation. The plan is foiled however when NIKOLAY rushes into the office and confesses. THE CRAFTSMAN subsequently comes to RASKOLNIKOV and asks forgiveness for his accusation.

CRYSTAL PALACE [KHRUSTALNY DVORETS, PAL DE KRIS-TAL]. A project of the English architect Sir Joseph Paxton (1803-65) which served as the main pavillion at the London World Fairs of 1851 and 1862. It was viewed in the 1860s as a symbol for the economic and social ideals of the utopian socialists. Dostoevsky himself saw the structure while abroad. In 1862 there was opened in St. Petersburg a restaurant by the same name. The restaurant is mentioned on occasion in the movements of both RAZU-MIKHIN and RASKOLNIKOV.

CYRUS THE GREAT [KIR PERSIDSKY]. The founder of the Persian Empire (d. 529 B.C.), who conquered neighboring lands and permitted the exiled Jews to rebuild Jerusalem. MARMELADOV tries to give SONYA some education and tells her about world history, but he stops with CYRUS THE GREAT.

DARWIN [DARVIN]. Charles Robert DARWIN (1809-82), English naturalist who originated the theory of evolution by natural selection. The theory aroused a storm of protest from fundamentalist theoreticians and remains an area of controversy. LEBEZYATNIKOV refrains from explaining DARWIN to LUZHIN when the latter becomes increasingly sarcastic with him.

DARYA FRANTSEVNA. A woman who once tried to lure SONYA into prostitution.

NIKOLAY DEMENTIEV (MIKOLAY, MIKOLKA, NIKOLKA, NIKOLASHKA). A painter who together with MITREY is painting an apartment in the building in which ALYONA IVANOVNA lives. He and MITREY get into a good-natured scuffle when MITREY rubs some paint on him, and NIKOLAY chases him down the stairs and out of the building. This permits RASKOLNIKOV to flee the scene of his crime and briefly hide in the room they are painting. RASKOLNIKOV had torturously been waiting in ALYONA IVANOVNA's flat while KOKH and PESTRYAKOV tried to get in. When the two realize that something is wrong and momentarily slip downstairs for help, RASKOLNIKOV leaves the flat and hides in the painted room. He then escapes from the building when a group of men led by KOKH and PESTRYAKOV comes to investigate ALYONA IVANOVNA's apartment. NIKOLAY finds some earrings that RASKOLNIKOV had dropped in the room, pledges them with DUSHKIN for some drinking money, and goes on a binge. He later confesses to the murders and interrupts PORFIRY PETROVICH's interrogation of RASKOLNIKOV. NIKOLAY, according to PORFIRY PETROVICH, is young, impressionable, has a vivid imagination, and is part of a schismatic religious sect. He theorizes that NIKOLAY's attempt to hang himself and his confession to the murders are attempts to submit himself to suffering.

"THE DISGRACEFUL DEED OF *THE AGE*" ["BEZOBRAZNY POS-TUPOK *VEKA*"]. The title of an article by women's rights advocate

Mikhail Larionovich Mikhaylov (1826-65), written against an article appearing in *THE AGE. THE AGE* article had attacked a public reading of PUSHKIN's "EGYPTIAN NIGHTS" by a woman. Mikhaylov responded by attacking the conservatism express in *THE AGE.*

DMITRY (MITREY, MITKA). A painter who together with NIKOLAY is painting an empty flat in the building in which ALYONA IVANOVNA lives. His wiping paint on NIKOLAY results in a friendly scuffle that permits RASKOLNIKOV to escape from the building following the murders. See NIKOLAY DEMENTIEV.

DMITRY PROKOFYICH. See DMITRY PROKOFYICH RAZUMI-KHIN.

DOBROLYUBOV. Nikolay Aleksandrovich DOBROLYUBOV (1836-61), Russian journalist and literary critic who emphasized the social usefulness of literature. He was one of the Radical Critics, a follower of BELINSKY, and literary editor of *The Contemporary.* LEBEZYAT-NIKOV claims that he has developed further than other radicals because he rejects more and that he would argue even with DOBROLYUBOV if he were alive.

DU HAST DIAMANTEN UND PERLEN. *You Have Diamonds and Pearls,* a romance written in 1824 by Franz Schubert (1797-1828), the noted Austrian composer, to the words of a song written by the German author Heinrich Heine (1797-1856). KATERINA IVANOVNA sings this song in delirium on her deathbed.

DUKLIDA. A prostitute to whom RASKOLNIKOV gives some change for a drink.

DUNECHKA. See AVDOTYA ROMANOVNA RASKOLNIKOVA.

DUNYA. See AVDOTYA ROMANOVNA RASKOLNIKOVA.

AFANASY PAVLYCH DUSHKIN. A pub owner who accepts earrings from NIKOLAY DEMENTIEV in exchange for a drink. He becomes convinced that NIKOLAY is the murderer of ALYONA IVANOVNA and LIZAVETA.

DUSSOT [DYUSSOT]. The owner of a fashionable St. Petersburg restaurant. SVIDRIGAYLOV, who has steadily lost interest in everything, mentions this restaurant as one of the many places in which he no longer has any interest.

DYRKA. A character in Nikolay GOGOL's play *The Marriage (Zhenitba),* completed in 1842. PORFIRY PETROVICH mentions DYRKA as one who would believe anything he was told. PORFIRY PETROVICH likely has in mind the character Petukhov, who is quite gullible.

"EGYPTIAN NIGHTS" ["YEGIPETSKIE NOCHI"]. A narrative poem written in 1835 by Aleksandr PUSHKIN. SVIDRIGAYLOV alludes to a woman's provocative public reading of this work that precipitated a controversy over women's emancipation.

FEDOSYA. The cook in the home of SVIDRIGAYLOV's young fiancee.

FEDYAEV. Operator of a clothing store.

FILIPP (FILKA). SVIDRIGAYLOV's servant, who commits suicide because of his master's torments. After his death he "appears" to SVID-RIGAYLOV when the latter calls for his pipe.

FILIPP. A lackey who served SVIDRIGAYLOV in a restaurant.

FILKA. See FILIPP.

FOURIER [FURIE]. François Marie Charles FOURIER (1772-1837), French reformer and economist whose socialist theories became very chic in Russia. He envisioned a society in which economic activity would be carried out by groups of people living together in a communal environment called a phalanx. LEBEZYATNIKOV refrains from explaining FOURIER's ideas to LUZHIN because LUZHIN becomes increasingly sarcastic about LEBEZYATNIKOV personally and about some of the new ideas.

GENERAL CONCLUSION OF THE POSITIVIST METHOD [OB-SHCHY VYVOD POLOZHITELNOGO METODA]. A collection of scientific essays translated into Russian in 1866. LEBEZYATNIKOV recommends this book and particularly the articles by PIDERIT and WAGNER to the KOBYLYATNIKOVS.

GERTRUDA KARLOVNA. See GERTRUDA KARLOVNA RESS-LICH.

GOGOL. Nikolay Vasilievich GOGOL (1809-52), popular Russian writer noted for his tragicomic portrayal of human foibles. He was viewed by BELINSKY and others as the fountainhead of the Natural School and credited with critically describing reality with the intent of social reform. PORFIRY PETROVICH praises GOGOL above all other writers for his sense of the comic and the playful.

GOLGOTHA [GOLGOFA]. The hill near Jerusalem where JESUS CHRIST was crucified. RASKOLNIKOV is convinced that DUNYA plans to marry LUZHIN in a sacrificial gesture to help him, and he ponders how hard it must have been for her to come to such a decision. He compares her determination to be self-sacrificial to the difficulty of ascending to GOLGOTHA.

GOSPEL OF JOHN [YEVANGELIE IOANNOVO]. The last of the four gospels, which are the first four books of the New Testament. It was probably written sometime between 80-95 A.D. by the apostle JOHN. At his request SONYA reads RASKOLNIKOV the story of LAZARUS' being raised from the dead from the GOSPEL OF JOHN.

HENRIETTE [GENRIET]. A guest at the home of LOUISA IVANOVNA who is struck by another rowdy guest. Following the row LOUISA IVANOVNA is compelled to explain it all at police headquarters.

A HUSSAR LEANING ON HIS SABRE [GUSAR NA SABLYU OPIRAYAS]. A popular song based upon "The Parting" ("Razluka"), a poem written by Konstantin Nikolaevich Batyushkov (1787-1855) in 1815 and set to music by Matvey Yurievich Vielgorsky (1794-1866). When KATERINA IVANOVNA takes her family into the streets to sing and beg, following MARMELADOV's death and the abortive funeral dinner, she determines that they will not sing *A HUSSAR LEANING ON HIS SABRE*.

ILYA PETROVICH (POROKH). A proud young lieutenant who works in police headquarters and who is referred to as POROKH ([gun-] powder). When RASKOLNIKOV comes to confess the murders, ILYA PETRO-VICH will hardly let him speak and prefers to talk about literature and his own personal worth. RASKOLNIKOV determines to confess to ILYA PETROVICH because of his intolerable vanity, and the confession shocks him greatly.

IN THE HEAT OF THE DAY, IN A VALLEY IN DAGHESTAN [V POLDNEVNY ZHAR, V DOLINE DAGESTANA]. A popular romance based upon the words of "The Dream" ("Son"), a poem written in 1841 by Mikhail Yurievich Lermontov (1814-41). In a delirium on her deathbed KATERINA IVANOVNA sings lines from this song, which deals with the final communication of a dying soldier with his love far away.

IVAN AFANASIEVICH. The official who gives MARMELADOV another chance at a job, despite his history of irresponsibility and drunkenness.

IVAN THE GREAT [IVAN VELIKY]. IVAN III (1440-1505), grand prince of Moscow who established Muscovite independence from the occupying Tatar forces and who unified northern Russia into a single state under his rule. RAZUMIKHIN discusses with RASKOLNIKOV and PORFIRY PETROVICH the role that environment plays in crime and opposes the notion that it plays a substantial role. He objects to the logic they use to explain criminals by their surroundings and insists that by the same logic he can show that PORFIRY PETROVICH has white eyelashes simply because IVAN THE GREAT was thirty five sazhens tall (about seventy five meters!).

IVAN IVANOVICH. IVAN IVANOVICH KLOPSTOCK.

IVAN MIKHAYLYCH. KATERINA IVANOVNA's father, who, she insists, was almost governor.

IZLER. Ivan Ivanovich IZLER, popular St. Petersburg figure who operated a mineral water resort outside the city. When RASKOLNIKOV searches the newspapers for reports of his murders, he notes an item about IZLER.

JESUIT [IEZUIT]. The Society of Jesus, a religious order for Roman Catholic men founded by Ignatius Loyola (1491-1556) in 1534. The society is known for scholarship and missionary zeal and has been accused of secrecy and intrigue. RASKOLNIKOV reflects on DUNYA's betrothal to LUZHIN and her apparent self-sacrificial motives, and he muses that people tend to accept fixed formulas of action such as those prescribed by the JESUITS. Only by following these formulas can virtue be obtained.

JESUS CHRIST [IISUS KHRISTOS]. In Christian teaching, the Son of God. At his request SONYA reads to RASKOLNIKOV the account from the GOSPEL OF JOHN wherein JESUS CHRIST raises LAZARUS from the dead.

JOHANN [IOGAN]. In her perpetual argument with KATERINA IVAN-OVNA over their respective fathers and heritages AMALIA IVANOVNA insists that she had a very important father in Berlin by the name of JOHANN.

JOUVEN [ZHUVEN]. French glovemaker. LUZHIN wears a pair of gloves made by JOUVEN.

KAPERNAUMOV. A lame man with a speech impediment, whose wife and children have the same handicaps. SONYA takes a room with the family after she is evicted from MARMELADOV's quarters because of her prostitution.

KAPERNAUMOVA. KAPERNAUMOV's wife, who in addition to being lame and having a speech impediment is also a bit deaf.

KARL. The yardkeeper of the house in which LOUISA IVANOVNA lives. He is struck by her rowdy guest.

KATERINA IVANOVNA. See KATERINA IVANOVNA MARME-LADOVA.

KATYA. An eighteen year old singer who sings for SVIDRIGAYLOV in the pub in exchange for money and wine. She kisses his hand when she is asked to leave.

KEPLER. Johannes KEPLER (1571-1630), German astronomer who helped to establish the validity of the Copernican concept that the sun was the center of the solar system and that the planets orbited about it. In explaining his theory of ordinary and extraordinary people, RASKOLNI-KOV cites KEPLER as an example of one who had the right to overstep bounds to make his discoveries available to society.

KHARLAMOV. RAZUMIKHIN mistakenly notes that KHARLAMOV is RASKOLNIKOV's former landlord.

KHERUVIMOV. A book dealer for whom RAZUMIKHIN is translating. He wants RAZUMIKHIN to translate part of ROUSSEAU's *CONFES-SIONS* because he understands that ROUSSEAU is much like RA-DISHCHEV.

IVAN IVANOVICH KLOPSTOCK [KLOPSHTOK]. An official who refuses to pay SONYA for the shirts she makes him because he claims that the collars are the incorrect size. The official ironically bears the name of Friedrich Gottlieb Klopstock (1724-1803), an important German poet.

KNOP. The owner of a clothing store in St. Petersburg. After LUZHIN is dismissed as DUNYA's suitor, he ruefully complains that had he given DUNYA and her mother money for their necessities and for all kinds of rubbish from KNOP and the English store, the rift between them would not have occurred.

KOBELEV. RAZUMIKHIN notes that the St. Petersburg address bureau lists RASKOLNIKOV, but, ironically, not General KOBELEV.

KOBYLYATNIKOVA. A middle-aged woman who with her unmarried daughter comes to St. Petersburg to check on her late husband's pension. They take lodgings in AMALIA IVANOVNA's flat, but avoid the MARMELADOVS and refuse to attend his funeral dinner because of SONYA's prostitution.

KOKH. A large, important man who comes to see ALYONA IVANOVNA immediately after RASKOLNIKOV has murdered her and LIZAVETA. RASKOLNIKOV locks the door to the apartment from the inside and waits while KOKH and a student named PESTRYAKOV wonder why the door is not answered, yet is locked from the inside rather than the outside. When the two go to get help, RASKOLNIKOV slips out and escapes.

KOLKA. See KOLYA.

KOLYA (KOLKA). KATERINA IVANOVNA's six year old son and the youngest of her children. He is petrified when his mother takes them into the street to sing, dance, and beg.

KOZEL. A wealthy German metal craftsman who owns the house in which the MARMELADOVS live.

KRYUKOV. An official who witnesses the brawl between NIKOLAY and MITREY following the murders.

LAVIZA IVANOVNA. See LOUISA IVANOVNA. Because of her German accent she is jokingly called LAVIZA IVANOVNA by ILYA PETROVICH and the policemen to whom she explains the row in her house.

LAZARUS [LAZAR]. As recorded in Luke 16:19-31 in the New Testament, a beggar who pleads daily at the gate of a rich man and who ultimately, unlike the rich man, receives an eternal reward. RASKOLNIKOV determines that he must make the most of his poverty and illness and feign LAZARUS the beggar in order to avoid the suspicion of PORFIRY PETROVICH, who already suspects him of the murders.

LAZARUS [LAZAR]. As recorded in John 11 in the New Testament, the brother of MARY and MARTHA of Bethany, who was raised from the dead by JESUS CHRIST. (1) When RASKOLNIKOV explains to RAZUMIKHIN and PORFIRY PETROVICH his theory of ordinary and extraordinary people, he notes that he believes in the literal raising of LAZARUS from the dead. (2) RASKOLNIKOV asks SONYA to read him the account of LAZARUS' being raised from the dead from the GOSPEL OF JOHN. (3) After RASKOLNIKOV discovers his love for SONYA, he takes the BIBLE from which SONYA read him the story of LAZARUS and wonders if he can make SONYA's ideals his own.

ANDREY SEMYONYCH LEBEZYATNIKOV. A caricature of the progressive thinker, who rejects the past and the arts in favor of the present, science, and utility. He is rather stupid and intellectually vulgar and is the kind of person who debases any good idea. His pronouncements are a catalogue of satirized new ideas: (1) he insists that he has developed further because he has rejected more and would even argue with BELINSKY and DOBROLYUBOV if they were alive; (2) he refuses to attend the funeral dinner in honor of MARMELADOV in order to object to and expose superstition; (3) he wishes that his parents were alive so that he could protest to them; (4) he insists that the environment is everything and that man is nothing; (5) he approves of SONYA's prostitution as a social protest and tries to "educate" her into an affair with him; (6) he insists that whatever is useful is noble and that cleaning refuse pits is better than PUSHKIN or RAPHAEL; and (7) he rejects lawful marriage but muses that if he ever did get married, he would bring his wife a lover so that she would not only love him but also respect him. He shares his lodgings with LUZHIN, who quickly finds him to be simple-minded in the extreme. His presence in the flat enables him to expose LUZHIN's plot to make SONYA appear as a thief and to effectively ruin any hope that LUZHIN entertains of making DUNYA his wife.

LEWES [LYUIS]. George Henry LEWES (1817-78), English scientific writer, novelist, playwright, and critic. LEBEZYATNIKOV convinces SONYA to read LEWES' *PHYSIOLOGY of Common Life.*

LIDA (LIDOCHKA, LYONA, LYONYA). KATERINA IVANOVNA's seven year old daughter, who becomes very afraid when she is made to dance and sing in the streets.

LIDOCHKA. See LIDA.

AMALIA FYODOROVNA LIPPEWECHSEL [LIPPEVEKHZEL] (AMALIA LUDWIGOVNA, AMAL-IVAN). A disorderly, foolish, and quarrelsome German, who is MARMELADOV's landlady. She is forever arguing with KATERINA IVANOVNA about whose father is more eminent and whose heritage is more noble. At the funeral dinner for MARMELADOV, for which she provides utensils and a kitchen, she becomes upset at KATERINA IVANOVNA's haughtiness and inserts a comment about how important her father was. A terrible row ensues, and she evicts KATERINA IVANOVNA and the children.

THE LITTLE FARM [KHUTOROK]. A popular song based upon a poem written by Aleksey Vasilievich Koltsov (1809-42) in 1839 and set to music by Ye. Klimovsky. (1) As RASKOLNIKOV listens to MARMELADOV relate his life story in the pub, he hears the strains of *THE LITTLE FARM* sung by a young boy accompanied by an organ grinder. (2) When KATERINA IVANOVNA takes her children into the street to sing, dance, and beg, she refuses to let her son KOLYA sing *THE LITTLE FARM* because she does not consider it noble enough.

LIVINGSTONE [LIVINGSTON]. David LIVINGSTONE (1813-73), English medical missionary and African explorer who wrote vivid accounts of his travels and discoveries. When RASKOLNIKOV comes to confess to the murders, ILYA PETROVICH prefers to talk about literature and asks him if he has read LIVINGSTONE's work.

LIZAVETA IVANOVNA. A half-sister of ALYONA IVANOVNA, who keeps her in virtual servitude. She is tall, shy, humble, and about thirty five. She and SONYA are very close and like to read the BIBLE together. Her shy and loving manner makes her agreeable to practically anything, and at the time of her death she is pregnant though unmarried. RASKOLNIKOV murders her when she happens into the apartment following the murder of her sister.

LOUISA [LUIZA] IVANOVNA (LAVIZA IVANOVNA). While RASKOLNIKOV waits at the police station to answer for not paying his rent, LOUISA IVANOVNA, a comical German woman, is brought in because of a drunken disturbance. She explains away the whole situation by blaming a rowdy guest over whom she had no control "in her noble home."

PYOTR PETROVICH LUZHIN. A haughty, rather sullen, and wealthy gentleman of forty five who is a distant relative of MARFA PETROVNA. His education is limited, but he fancies himself a devotee of new and progressive ideas. He is vain and enjoys talking and being listened to. He has always envisioned marrying a poor and much younger girl who would regard him as her savior. With this in mind he courts DUNYA, who agrees to marry him. When DUNYA and her mother come to St. Petersburg, he fails to meet them and arranges very poor accommodations for them. He himself has taken lodgings with LEBEZYATNIKOV because it is cheap and because he wants to find out whether there is anything in the progressive ideas of the younger generation that threatens his budding career. Before going to see DUNYA, he pays a visit to RASKOLNIKOV, who is very upset that DUNYA would sacrifice herself to marry such a man. He mentions to RASKOLNIKOV the philosophy that one should love oneself most, since everything is grounded in self-interest, and he is subsequently insulted and dismissed. Irate over the insult, he requests a meeting with DUNYA and her mother by themselves to discuss RASKOLNIKOV's behavior toward him and his propensity to give away the money his mother sends him. The family insists that RASKOLNIKOV be present at the meeting, and LUZHIN leaves in a rage after his motives are exposed. He values his money above all else but wonders if the affair would have gone better had he given DUNYA and her mother something to spend. When MARMELADOV dies, he sees an opportunity to discredit RASKOLNIKOV through SONYA. Under the pretext of doing something for the bereaved family, he gives SONYA ten rubles, but conceals a one hundred ruble note in her pocket. When he tries to expose her as a thief at the funeral dinner, he is himself exposed by LEBEZYATNIKOV, who watches him conceal the money in SONYA's pocket. His final hope gone, LUZHIN leaves the house.

LYCURGUS [LIKURG]. A legendary legislator who is credited with reforming Sparta in the sixth century B.C. into a stern and disciplined state. In explaining his theory of ordinary and extraordinary people, RASKOL-NIKOV cites the example of lawgivers such as LYCURGUS, SOLON, MUHAMMAD, and NAPOLEON, who were all criminals in that they introduced a new law and destroyed the old. He insists that these people were superior to their fellow-men and had the right to do whatever they did. PORFIRY PETROVICH then questions RASKOLNIKOV about what the effect will be on his system if someone suddenly thinks that he is a new MUHAMMAD or LYCURGUS.

LYONA. See LIDA.

LYONYA. See LIDA.

GENERAL MACK [MAK]. Karl MACK (1752-1828), Austrian field-marshall who participated in the struggle against NAPOLEON in the War of 1812. PORFIRY PETROVICH discusses with RASKOLNIKOV various tactics of capturing criminals and makes several comparisons with military history and maneuvers. He mentions the Austrian high command, which had NAPOLEON captured on paper but whose plans resulted in GENERAL MACK's surrendering his entire army.

MADONNA. Mary, the mother of JESUS CHRIST. SVIDRIGAYLOV tells RASKOLNIKOV that he wrote about RAPHAEL's MADONNA in the album of Mrs. PRILUKOVAYA. RAPHAEL painted several MADONNAS, the most noted of which is probably the SISTINE MADONNA (1518).

MALBOROUGH S'EN VA-T-EN GUERRE. Malborough is Gone to War, a popular European song that became a children's favorite in Russia. The song deals with the military journeys of the Duke of Marlborough (1650-1722), noted English statesman and military commander. When KATERINA IVANOVNA takes her children into the streets to sing, dance, and beg, following MARMELADOV's death, she ponders what numbers they will do. She rejects *MALBOROUGH S'EN VA-T-EN GUERRE,* even though she notes that it is sung in all aristocratic homes.

MANGOT [MANGO]. A Frenchman who taught KATERINA IVANOVNA French.

MARFA PETROVNA. See MARFA PETROVNA SVIDRIGAYLOVA.

SEMYON ZAKHAROVICH MARMELADOV (SEMYON ZAKHARYCH). An unemployed civil servant who has a history of failing to hold positions because of his drinking. He is SONYA's natural father and has rather recently married KATERINA IVANOVNA, a widow with three children. He willingly accepts the blame for the plight of his family and for SONYA's prostitution, and he enjoys the suffering he experiences through drinking and acknowledging his own baseness. His reemployment exults KATERINA IVANOVNA, but he suddenly takes all of the family resources and goes on a binge. During his caper he meets RASKOLNIKOV in a pub and spares no self-incriminating details in relating his life story. He intimates in his story that he will be saved by God in the end because he does not count himself worthy. RASKOLNIKOV takes him home to his family where MARMELADOV revels in the beating and denunciation he receives from KATERINA IVANOVNA. He is ultimately struck by a carriage as he crosses a street in a drunken stupor and begs the forgiveness of KATERINA IVANOVNA and SONYA as he dies. His life is a constant exercise in deliberately seeking self-debasement and suffering because of his low estimation of himself.

KATERINA IVANOVNA MARMELADOVA. MARMELADOV's wife. She is an officer's daughter who attended a fine school and who retains memories of dancing at graduation and receiving a medal and a letter. Because of subsequent events she lives in the past and relishes these memories, which become exaggerated through time and pride. She marries an officer for love but is given a life of card playing and beatings until he dies. Left with three small children in extreme circumstances, she marries MARMELADOV, who gradually ruins the family with his drinking. When MARMELADOV is killed, she curses him for leaving the family helpless but insists upon holding an elaborate funeral dinner to show that she is as good and noble as other people. The dinner is a failure since only a few Poles and some rabble from the street attend, and it becomes a scandal as the focal point of the ongoing battle between KATERINA IVANOVNA and her landlady AMALIA IVANOVNA. The two women argue perpetually over whose father and heritage are superior, and they almost come to blows at the dinner. The argument is intensified by the presence of SONYA and LUZHIN's attempt to prove her a thief, and KATERINA IVANOVNA vows to take her children into the streets to find truth and justice. She physically accosts her late husband's superior and then forces the children to sing, dance, and beg to demonstrate to all how a noble family has been brought to ruin. She ultimately collapses on the street and shortly thereafter dies of the consumption that her mode of life had inflicted upon her.

SOFYA SEMYONOVNA MARMELADOVA (SONYA, SONECHKA, SOFYA IVANOVNA). MARMELADOV's child-like eighteen year old daughter, who engages in prostitution to help support KATERINA IVANOVNA and the children. She is characterized by an active sisterly love, a deep faith in God, and a willingness to bear others' burdens. She is hesitant to share her faith with RASKOLNIKOV because she senses that he is unworthy, yet she desires to help him and consents to read him her favorite BIBLICAL passage, the raising of LAZARUS. The death of her father provides LUZHIN with an opportunity to discredit RASKOLNIKOV through SONYA, and he tries to make it appear that she has stolen money from him. LUZHIN's plot and motivation are exposed by LEBEZ-YATNIKOV and RASKOLNIKOV, but she remains largely an outcast and is shunned by many. After the scene with LUZHIN, RASKOLNIKOV comes to her and confesses the murders of ALYONA IVANOVNA and LIZAVETA. She insists that he kiss the earth, bow to the people, and accept suffering so that he can expiate his sin, and she vows to help insofar as she can. She gives him her cross and follows him to the police station, where her presence gives him the strength to confess. With money given her by SVIDRIGAYLOV she accompanies RASKOLNIKOV to Siberia, where she is treated rudely by RASKOLNIKOV but loved and revered by the prisoners from among the common people. RASKOLNIKOV discovers that he loves her when she becomes ill, and she is thrilled with the prospect of further building his faith.

MARTHA [MARFA]. The sister of LAZARUS, who is raised from the dead. SONYA reads RASKOLNIKOV the account of LAZARUS, in which MARTHA is mentioned.

MARY [MARYA]. The sister of LAZARUS, who is raised from the dead. SONYA reads RASKOLNIKOV the account of LAZARUS, in which MARY is mentioned.

MASSIMO. A male midget, who with a female counterpart named BARTOLA, was exhibited in St. Petersburg in 1865. They were billed as direct descendants of the AZTECS. When RASKOLNIKOV searches the newspapers for reports of his murders, he comes across an article on the AZTECS BARTOLA and MASSIMO.

MATVEY. A peasant in RASKOLNIKOV's dream about the horse that is beaten to death.

MIKOLKA. See NIKOLAY DEMENTIEV.

MIKOLKA. In RASKOLNIKOV's dream, the drunken MIKOLKA gleefully beats his horse to death, when it cannot pull a cart overloaded with men.

MITKA. See DMITRY.

MITREY. See DMITRY.

MOSCOW RECORD [MOSKOVSKIE VEDOMOSTI]. A broadly circulated Moscow daily. ZAMYOTOV mentions to RASKOLNIKOV that he read in the *MOSCOW RECORD* about the capture of a ring of counterfeiters.

MUHAMMAD [MAGOMET]. In Arabic "the praised one," a name adopted by the founder of Islam (570-632). In explaining his theory about usual and unusual people RASKOLNIKOV cites the examples of lawgivers like LYCURGUS, SOLON, MUHAMMAD, and NAPOLEON, who were all criminals in that they introduced new laws and destroyed the old. He insists that these men were superior to their contemporaries and had the right to do all that they did. PORFIRY PETROVICH wonders aloud what could happen in RASKOLNIKOV's system if someone suddenly thinks that he is another LYCURGUS or MUHAMMAD. Later in the conversation RASKOLNIKOV indicates that he does not consider himself a MUHAMMAD or NAPOLEON.

NAPOLEON. NAPOLEON I Bonaparte (1769-1821), emperor of France following the French Revolution and temporary conqueror of much of Europe. (1) See LYCURGUS. (2) RASKOLNIKOV indicates to PORFIRY PETROVICH that he does not consider himself to be another MUHAMMAD or NAPOLEON. (3) PORFIRY PETROVICH drily tells RASKOLNIKOV that all in Russia now consider themselves NAPOLEONS. (4) ZAMYOTOV challengingly intimates to RASKOLNIKOV that it was a future NAPOLEON who killed ALYONA IVANOVNA. (5) As he castigates himself and his actions RASKOLNIKOV bitterly compares NAPOLEON with his pyramids and WATERLOO to the disgusting old ALYONA IVANOVNA with her chest of pledges under her bed. (6) RASKOLNIKOV ruefully contemplates the anomaly of NAPOLEON under ALYONA IVANOVNA's bed as he increasingly questions his own status as a superior person. (7) PORFIRY PETROVICH discusses with RASKOLNIKOV various tactics of apprehending criminals and makes many comparisons with military history and maneuvers. He recalls the Austrian high command, which had NAPOLEON captured on paper during the War of 1812 but eventually surrendered the entire army of GENERAL MACK to him. (8) After discussing catching criminals in terms of military tactics, PORFIRY PETROVICH observes that perhaps he should have had a military career. He notes that he would not have become a NAPOLEON but perhaps could have been a major. (9) RASKOLNIKOV admits to SONYA that he murdered in order to be a NAPOLEON. (10) RASKOLNIKOV wonders whether NAPOLEON would have murdered an old woman like ALYONA IVANOVNA if that were his only road to glory. He decides that NAPOLEON would indeed have murdered her. (11) RASKOLNIKOV disgustedly tells SONYA that if he has to think for days how NAPOLEON would have acted that it is clear that he is not a NAPOLEON. (12) When SVIDRIGAYLOV explains RASKOLNIKOV's crime to DUNYA, he notes that her brother was enchanted by NAPOLEON.

NASTASYA. See NASTASYA PETROVNA.

NASTASYA NIKIFOROVNA. See NASTASYA PETROVNA. RAZUMIKHIN mistakenly refers to NASTASYA PETROVNA as NASTASYA NIKIFOROVNA.

NASTASYA PETROVNA (NASTASYA, NASTASYUSHKA, NASTENKA, NASTASYA NIKIFOROVNA). A talkative, good-natured country woman who is ZARNITSYNA's only servant. She often feeds RASKOLNIKOV and is very considerate of him.

NASTASYUSHKA. See NASTASYA PETROVNA.

NASTENKA. See NASTASYA PETROVNA.

NATALYA YEGOROVNA. See NATALYA YEGOROVNA ZARNITSYNA.

NEW JERUSALEM [NOVY IERUSALIM]. An exalted Jerusalem descending from God Himself, as recorded by John in the Book of Revelation in the New Testament. The coming of the NEW JERUSALEM is synonymous with the coming of an earthly paradise. In discussing his theory of ordinary and extraordinary people RASKOLNIKOV insists that they have equal rights to exist and will be in conflict until the time of the NEW JERUSALEM.

NEWTON [NYUTON]. Sir Isaac NEWTON (1642-1727), English mathematician and natural philosopher who was one of the great geniuses of history. His discoveries include the method of fluxions, the composition of light, and the law of gravity. In explaining his theory of ordinary and extraordinary people RASKOLNIKOV notes that NEWTON was one who had the right to overstep bounds to make his discoveries available to society.

NIKODIM FOMICH. A police inspector who is quite compassionate toward RASKOLNIKOV.

NIKOLASHKA. See NIKOLAY DEMENTIEV.

NIKOLAY. See NIKOLAY DEMENTIEV.

NIKOLKA. See NIKOLAY DEMENTIEV.

NIL PAVLYCH. A worker at police headquarters.

NOAH [NOY]. As recorded in Genesis 6-10, the Old Testament patriarch whom Jehovah commanded to build an ark prior to the destruction of the earth by flood. In the ark NOAH saved his family together with specimens of each kind of animal. ZAMYOTOV calls the building in which ALYONA IVANOVNA lives a NOAH's ark with many compartments to emphasize how difficult it was to see the escaping murderer.

"NOW A CERTAIN MAN WAS SICK, NAMED LAZARUS, OF BETHANY..." ["BYL ZHE BOLEN NEKTO LAZAR, IZ VIFA-NII..."]. The beginning of John 11:1 in the New Testament, which contains the account of JESUS CHRIST's raising LAZARUS from the dead. SONYA reads the account to RASKOLNIKOV at his request. The verses actually quoted in the novel are John 11:1, 19-27, 32-45.

"OU VA-T-ELLE LA VERTU SE NICHER?" "Who would expect to find virtue there?" the words attributed to Moliere, who made the statement when a beggar asked if he had made a mistake in giving him a gold coin. When RASKOLNIKOV objects to SVIDRIGAYLOV's debauched anecdotes, SVIDRIGAYLOV, who knows that RASKOLNIKOV murdered the women, cynically comments about virtue, using this quotation.

PALMERSTON. Henry John Temple PALMERSTON (1784-1865), English statesman who was twice prime minister. RAZUMIKHIN comically refers to one of the hats he buys for RASKOLNIKOV as PALMERSTON.

PARASHA. A beautiful but stupid servant girl whom SVIDRIGAYLOV uses sexually on his estate. DUNYA demands that he stop molesting her.

PASHENKA. See PRASKOVYA PAVLOVNA ZARNITSYNA.

PERIODIC SPEECH [PERIODICHESKAYA RECH]. See *WEEKLY SPEECH.*

PESTRYAKOV. The student who comes to see ALYONA IVANOVNA immediately after she has been murdered. He and KOKH stand outside her locked door and wonder what could be wrong, while RASKOLNIKOV waits breathlessly inside. When he and KOKH leave briefly to get help, RASKOLNIKOV escapes.

PETRUSHKA. The main character of Russian folk theater and puppet shows, who is much like the Italian Pulchinella and the English Punch. He is a coarse, unscrupulous comic character. When she takes her children into the street to sing, dance, and beg, KATERINA IVANOVNA proudly states that she does not perform some PETRUSHKA, but rather sings noble romances.

PHYSIOLOGY [FIZIOLOGIA]. *PHYSIOLOGY of Common Life,* a work published by George Henry LEWES in 1860. LEBEZYATNIKOV persuades SONYA to read LEWES' *PHYSIOLOGY* in an effort to properly educate her.

PIDERIT. Theodor PIDERIT (1826-82), Russian physiologist. LEBEZ-YATNIKOV recommends the book *GENERAL CONCLUSION OF THE POSITIVIST METHOD* and especially the articles by PIDERIT and WAGNER to the KOBYLYATNIKOVS. The article by PIDERIT in the book is "The Mind and the Spirit. An Essay on Physiological Psychology for all Thinking Readers" ("Mozg i dukh. Ocherk fiziologicheskoy psikhol-ogii dlya vsekh myslyashchikh chitateley").

POCHINKOV. RAZUMIKHIN rents lodgings in a house owned by POCHINKOV.

POKOREV. A fellow student who gave RASKOLNIKOV ALYONA IVANOVNA's address in the event that he ever needed money.

POLECHKA. See POLINA MIKHAYLOVNA.

POLENKA. See POLINA MIKHAYLOVNA.

POLINA MIKHAYLOVNA (POLENKA, POLYA, POLECHKA). KA-TERINA IVANOVNA's oldest child, a daughter of about ten. Like the other children, she lives a miserable existence and is very frightened when her mother takes them into the streets to sing, dance, and beg.

POLYA. See POLINA MIKHAYLOVNA.

PORFIRY PETROVICH. A distant relative of RAZUMIKHIN, about thirty five years of age, who is the chief detective of the local police. He quickly suspects that RASKOLNIKOV may be guilty of the murders of ALYONA IVANOVNA and LIZAVETA and pursues him in a thorough psychological way. He spends much time with RASKOLNIKOV discussing the latter's theory of ordinary and extraordinary people, the psychology of the criminal, and ways of apprehending the criminal. The cat and mouse environment produced by these exchanges drives RASKOLNIKOV into a frenzy. He sets up a situation in which he intends to expose RASKOL-NIKOV through the denunciation by THE CRAFTSMAN, but the trap is foiled by NIKOLAY DEMENTIEV, who bursts into PORFIRY PETRO-VICH's office and confesses to the murders. Undaunted, PORFIRY PETROVICH pays a personal visit to RASKOLNIKOV, explains why he thinks that NIKOLAY confessed, and indicates that RASKOLNIKOV is unquestionably the murderer. He urges him to confess so that his sentence will be lighter and so that he will have life to look forward to.

POROKH. See ILYA PETROVICH.

POTANCHIKOV. PULKHERIA ALEKSANDROVNA expresses concern that RASKOLNIKOV leaves his sick bed to bustle about the city. She cites the example of POTANCHIKOV, a friend of her late husband, who left his sick bed in similar circumstances, in a fever, and stumbled into a well to his death.

PRASKOVYA PAVLOVNA. See PRASKOVYA PAVLOVNA ZARNI-TSYNA.

PRILUKOVA. SVIDRIGAYLOV relates that he wrote about RAPHA-EL's MADONNA in PRILUKOVA's album.

PULKHERIA ALEKSANDROVNA. See PULKHERIA ALEKSAN-DROVNA RASKOLNIKOVA.

PUSHKIN. Aleksandr Sergeevich PUSHKIN (1799-1837), the leading writer of his age who is widely regarded as the father of modern Russian literature. (1) Prior to RASKOLNIKOV's dream about the horse that is beaten to death, the author notes that on occasion dreams are so vivid and strange that they cannot be recreated while awake even by a PUSHKIN or a TURGENEV. (2) LEBEZYATNIKOV lauds the virtues of natural science and utilitarianism as opposed to art and beauty and insists that the cleaning of refuse pits is more noble and elevated than the work of RAPHAEL or

PUSHKIN. (3) LUZHIN argues with LEBEZYATNIKOV about the validity of lawful marriage and indicates that he insists upon a proper marriage so that he will not be a cuckold and raise other men's children. LEBEZYATNIKOV considers the use of the term cuckold to be an allusion to PUSHKIN, whose wife made his life difficult through her coquetry. The situation eventually developed into a duel in which PUSHKIN was fatally shot.

PYOTR PETROVICH. See PYOTR PETROVICH LUZHIN.

RADISHCHEV. Aleksandr Nikolaevich RADISHCHEV (1749-1802), an outstanding poet of the eighteenth century whose liberal views on government and serfdom incurred the ire of Catherine the Great, who exiled him to Siberia. KHERUVIMOV wants RAZUMIKHIN to translate excerpts of the second part of ROUSSEAU's *CONFESSIONS,* since he heard that ROUSSEAU was rather like RADISHCHEV.

RAPHAEL [RAFAEL]. Raffaelo Sanzio (1483-1520), Italian painter who is one of the great artists in history. He was the leading exponent of the Renaissance conception of human nobility and is best known for his MADONNAS. (1) SVIDRIGAYLOV tells RASKOLNIKOV that he wrote about RAPHAEL's MADONNA in PRILUKOVA's album. (2) LEBEZYATNIKOV, in advocating the new ideas of utilitarianism, insists that cleaning refuse pits is more noble and elegant than the work of RAPHAEL or PUSHKIN. (3) SVIDRIGAYLOV, who has become engaged to a fifteen year old girl, describes his fiancee's face as being much like RAPHAEL's MADONNA.

RODION ROMANOVICH RASKOLNIKOV (RODION ROMAN-YCH, RODION, RODKA, RODYA, RODENKA). The handsome, proud son of PULKHERIA ALEKSANDROVNA, who lives in St. Petersburg in dire poverty. He ceases to give lessons as a livelihood and remains in his coffin-like room, where he indulges in his vanity and his reason. This isolation and rationality produce a theory of ordinary and extraordinary people. The extraordinary are virtual supermen who have the right to overstep bounds and transgress law. LYCURGUS, MUHAMMAD, and NAPOLEON are viewed as such superior people. He determines to prove this theory in his own life by murdering an old pawnbroker to see if he too is a superman. He murders ALYONA IVANOVNA and also her sister LIZAVETA when the latter chances upon the scene, and he begins an odyssey filled with painful doubts about his superiority and with desires to both test himself and to suffer. His bizarre theory is contrasted to an impulsive generosity that prompts him instinctively, counter to his reason, to help people and give away what little money he has. These qualities bring him into contact with the MARMELADOV family, and particularly with SONYA, who is his spiritual antithesis and whom he regards as the embodiment of mankind's suffering. When he receives word that his sister DUNYA is about to marry the wealthy LUZHIN, he is convinced that it is a self-sacrificial gesture to help him, and he proudly determines to reject it. His insistence brings out the worst in LUZHIN, who is exposed and dismissed from relations with the family. His crime brings him into contact with PORFIRY PETROVICH, a police detective who immediately suspects him and whose psychological pursuit drives RASKOLNIKOV into a frenzy. This pursuit compounds his sufferings and near-confessions but also accentuates his pride, rationality, and his inability to love. While in the process of unmasking LUZHIN, he comes into contact with SVIDRI-GAYLOV, whose debauchery and extreme rationality have brought him to a final crisis in life. SVIDRIGAYLOV observes that he and RASKOL-NIKOV have much in common. This comment symbolically places RASKOLNIKOV between SONYA and SVIDRIGAYLOV, the embodiments of good and evil, and RASKOLNIKOV's suffering is further intensified. He finally confesses his murders to SONYA, but suffers only because he is a louse instead of a man rather than because he has sinned. SONYA insists that he reunite himself with the Russian people and Russian soil, confess, and accept punishment. This counsel is combined with a visit from PORFIRY PETROVICH, who also advises him to confess, and with a conviction that he is a failure as a superman, RASKOLNIKOV confesses. He continues to reject the idea that he has sinned or committed a crime and pridefully accepts only his own weakness for, which he determines to suffer. His sentence is light because of his confession, accounts of his helping others, and the chic new theory of temporary insanity, and he is exiled to Siberia. There he suffers from injured pride and is hated by the prisoners from the common people, who regard him as an atheist and an alien. His regeneration begins only when SONYA, who follows him into exile, becomes ill, and he realizes that he loves her. This newly found capacity to love changes his entire outlook, and he determines to try to make SONYA's thoughts and convictions his own. The author cautions that such a new life will not be won easily.

AVDOTYA ROMANOVNA RASKOLNIKOVA (DUNYA, DUNECH-KA). RASKOLNIKOV's beautiful and proud sister. She works on SVIDRIGAYLOV's estate as his children's governess and is compelled frequently to refuse his advances. She stands as a moral force before him and fruitlessly tries to rehabilitate him. After RASKOLNIKOV becomes destitute and the whole family is in dire circumstances, she determines to marry the wealthy LUZHIN largely as a means to help her family. When her brother actively opposes the match and she sees what LUZHIN really is, she dismisses his attentions, admitting that she had been enticed by his money but insisting that she had not realized what sort of a person he was. Still desiring to help RASKOLNIKOV, she agrees to meet SVIDRIGAYLOV, who entices her with information about RASKOLNIKOV's crime. SVID-RIGAYLOV promises to save her brother if she will be his. She weakly defends herself with a gun, but quickly realizes that she cannot kill even him and finds herself helpless. Her pleas that she could never love him or give herself willingly secure her release. She sees RASKOLNIKOV before he goes to confess and pledges him love and support. She accepts RAZU-MIKHIN's offer of marriage, and the two conduct a vigil over her brother's progress in Siberia.

PULKHERIA ALEKSANDROVNA RASKOLNIKOVA. RASKOLNI-KOV's mother, who at forty three is still pretty, gentle, shy, and submissive. She worries about her son from afar, sends him money that she cannot really spare, and finally comes with DUNYA to St. Petersburg to help him. His agitated condition and refusal to submit to his intuitive self torture her, particularly when he announces that he is leaving them. She rationalizes that there is much she does not understand about his budding career as a great thinker, and she constantly studies his article about ordinary and extraordinary people. Her concern develops into a nervous disorder verging on insanity, which finally takes her life. In a delirium prior to death she says things that indicate that she knows much more than she admits about her son's situation and condition.

RASSUDKIN. LUZHIN mistakenly refers to RAZUMIKHIN as RAS-SUDKIN when he temporarily forgets his name. The root of both names means "reason."

DMITRY PROKOFYICH RAZUMIKHIN (RASSUDKIN, VRAZU-MIKHIN). A friend of RASKOLNIKOV who is expansive and verbose yet genuine and good almost to a fault. He spends most of his time taking care of RASKOLNIKOV's interests and, after they arrive in St. Petersburg, of the interests of DUNYA and her mother. A distant relative of PORFIRY PETROVICH, he introduces RASKOLNIKOV to him, thereby initiating the cat and mouse exchange between detective and criminal. After the final break between the RASKOLNIKOVS and LUZHIN, he vows to devote himself to them, partially because of his romantic interest in DUNYA. Following RASKOLNIKOV's exile, he marries DUNYA, returns to the university to finish his studies, and plans in a few years to move to Siberia to be with RASKOLNIKOV and SONYA.

GERTRUDA KARLOVNA RESSLICH [RESSLIKH]. A German acquaintance of SVIDRIGAYLOV who rents an apartment next to KAPERNAUMOV. She lets part of her apartment to SVIDRIGAYLOV, who is able to listen through the wall to RASKOLNIKOV's confession to SONYA. He uses that information to get DUNYA to agree to meet him.

RODENKA. See RODION ROMANOVICH RASKOLNIKOV.

RODION. See RODION ROMANOVICH RASKOLNIKOV.

RODION ROMANYCH. See RODION ROMANOVICH RASKOLNIKOV.

RODKA. See RODION ROMANOVICH RASKOLNIKOV.

RODYA. See RODION ROMANOVICH RASKOLNIKOV.

ROMEO. The male lead in the tragedy *ROMEO and Juliet* written by William Shakespeare (1564-1616) in 1596. He is sentimental, romantic, and ultimately commits suicide when he thinks that Juliet is dead. RASKOLNIKOV, anxious to remove suspicion of the murders from himself and to present a jovial appearance when he meets PORFIRY PETROVICH, calls RAZUMIKHIN ROMEO with respect to his feelings for DUNYA just as they enter PORFIRY PETROVICH's quarters. The name-calling enables him to enter in a spirit of levity.

ROUSSEAU [RUSSO]. Jean Jacques ROUSSEAU (1712-78), French author, philosopher, and liberal political theorist. KHERUVIMOV wants RAZUMIKHIN to translate part of ROUSSEAU's *CONFESSIONS,* since he has heard that ROUSSEAU is rather like RADISHCHEV.

RUBINSTEIN [RUBINSHTEYN]. Anton Grigorievich RUBINSTEIN (1829-94), Russian pianist and composer. RAZUMIKHIN flatters ZOSIMOV by telling him that he is a master at the piano and plays like RUBINSTEIN. He uses this approach to try to get ZOSIMOV to spend some time with PRASKOVYA PAVLOVNA so that he can be free to do some other things.

SCHILLER [SHILLER]. Johann Christoph Friedrich von SCHILLER (1759-1805), German dramatist, poet, and historian noted for his romantic idealism. (1) RASKOLNIKOV refers to his mother PULKHERIA ALEK-SANDROVNA as a beautiful soul, like SCHILLER, who always thinks the best of people. He has reference to her optimistic impression of LUZHIN and of DUNYA's proposed marriage to him. (2) PORFIRY PETROVICH visits RASKOLNIKOV, identifies him as the murderer, and urges him to confess so that his sentence will be lighter and his life will still be before him. He admits that RASKOLNIKOV may consider him a SCHILLER for expressing such sentiments. (3) When RASKOLNIKOV is apalled at SVIDRIGAYLOV's anecdotes about his debauched antics with women and particularly young girls, SVIDRIGAYLOV notes that it is very ironic that RASKOLNIKOV should be objecting in the name of virtue and refers to him as a SCHILLER. (4) SVIDRIGAYLOV says of RASKOLNIKOV that the SCHILLER in him is perpetually confused and embarrassed.

SCHLESWIG-HOLSTEIN [SHLEZVIG-GOLSHTEYN]. Two contiguous duchies of Denmark that became objects and pretexts of European power struggles in the nineteenth century. RASKOLNIKOV muses that DUNYA would not sacrifice her moral freedom for all of SCHLESWIG-HOLSTEIN, let alone LUZHIN, and concludes that she is sacrificing herself for him and the family by planning marriage to LUZHIN.

SEMYON SEMYONOVICH. See SEMYON SEMYONOVICH SHEL-OPAEV.

SEMYON ZAKHAROVICH. See SEMYON ZAKHAROVICH MAR-MELADOV.

SEMYON ZAKHARYCH. See SEMYON ZAKHAROVICH MAR-MELADOV.

SEVASTOPOL [SEVASTOPL]. A city and port in the Crimea which was the object of an eleven-month siege in 1854-55 by the French and English during the Crimean War. The Russians finally retired after the city was destroyed. PORFIRY PETROVICH discusses with RASKOLNIKOV various ways of capturing criminals and makes comparisons with military maneuvers and battles. During this explanation he mentions SEVASTO-POL.

SHARMER. A St. Petersburg tailor mentioned by RAZUMIKHIN.

PRINCE SHCHEGOLSKOY. KATERINA IVANOVNA claims that she danced the mazurka with PRINCE SHCHEGOLSKOY and that he wanted to propose, but she refused, since she loved another.

SEMYON SEMYONOVICH SHELOPAEV. A merchant through whom PULKHERIA ALEKSANDROVNA sends money to RASKOLNIKOV.

SHIL. When he returns to the scene of the murders, RASKOLNIKOV tells a group outside ALYONA IVANOVNA's building that he lives in a building owned by SHIL.

SISTINE MADONNA [SIKSTINSKAYA MADONNA]. The most famous of the MADONNAS painted by RAPHAEL. It was completed in 1518. SVIDRIGAYLOV mentions that he finds the face of his fifteen year old fiancee much like that of RAPHAEL's MADONNA. He adds that the face of the SISTINE MADONNA strikes him as fantastic and somewhat like a mournful holy fool.

SODOM. As recorded in Genesis 18-19 in the Old Testament, a city which together with Gomorrah was destroyed by Jehovah because of its wickedness. The term has come to mean wickedness and chaos. MARMELADOV refers to the relationship of his family with AMALIA IVANOVNA as SODOM.

SOFYA IVANOVNA. See SOFYA SEMYONOVNA MARMELADOVA. RAZUMIKHIN mistakenly refers to SONYA as SOFYA IVANOVNA.

SOFYA SEMYONOVNA. See SOFYA SEMYONOVNA MARMELADOVA.

SOLON. Greek statesman and poet (ca. 640-558 B.C.) who is regarded as the founder of Athenian democracy. In explaining his theory of ordinary and extraordinary people RASKOLNIKOV cites the example of lawgivers such as LYCURGUS, SOLON, MUHAMMAD, and NAPOLEON, who were all criminals in that they introduced new laws and destroyed the old. He insists that their superiority to other men gave them the right to overstep bounds to accomplish what they did.

SONECHKA. See SOFYA SEMYONOVNA MARMELADOVA.

SONYA. See SOFYA SEMYONOVNA MARMELADOVA.

ARKADY IVANOVICH SVIDRIGAYLOV. A wealthy landowner of about fifty who is characterized by rationality and debauchery. He is married to MARFA PETROVNA, who bought him out of debtor's prison and who holds a document over his head to make him behave. While DUNYA is engaged as his children's governess, he falls in love with her and vows to do anything if she will be his. His advances are repelled, and DUNYA attempts to reform him, particularly after he molests the servant girl PARASHA. After the death of his wife, he inherits a large estate but also endures three visitations from his dead wife and one from his servant FILKA, both of whom SVIDRIGAYLOV had abused. He follows DUNYA and her mother to St. Petersburg to continue his pursuit of her and takes a room with GERTRUDA KARLOVNA RESSLICH, whose young relative some years earlier had hanged herself after presumably being sexually used by him. From the vantage point of this apartment he overhears RASKOLNIKOV's confession to SONYA and decides to use it to see DUNYA. Promising news of her brother he attracts her into the isolated apartment and has her totally at his mercy when she is unable to defend herself with a pistol. When he learns that she can never love him or give herself willingly to him, he releases her. She represents for him a final chance to live, since his previous excesses have destroyed his interest in life and brought him to a terminal crisis. He takes a room in a run-down hotel and dreams of a mouse, a young girl who committed suicide from shame, and a five year old who becomes a prostitute. The next morning he shoots himself in front of a soldier after informing him that he is going to America. His life is characterized by excesses of passion and reason, which control him. He proposes that Eternity is akin to a bathhouse in the country full of spiders, and his face becomes a mask devoid of feeling. He observes to RASKOLNIKOV that they are very much alike, and he may represent the end result of the path RASKOLNIKOV follows. To a large extent the difference between the two is evident in their relations with DUNYA and SONYA respectively and in the fact that SVIDRIGAYLOV has fallen further. He does not continually play the villain, however. He takes care of KATERINA IVANOVNA's children financially, assumes the cost of her final arrangements, gives SONYA money to accompany RASKOLNIKOV to Siberia, and gives his fifteen year old fiancee much money, yet there perpetually seems to be something ulterior in his actions. Throughout he represents one possibility of RASKOLNIKOV's future.

MARFA PETROVNA SVIDRIGAYLOVA. A distant relative of LU-ZHIN and a wealthy landowner who buys the younger SVIDRIGAYLOV out of debtor's prison and marries him. She holds incriminating documents over his head during their marriage until she feels that she can trust him.

When she feels that DUNYA as her children's governess is trying to have an affair with SVIDRIGAYLOV, she angrily dismisses her and denounces her all over the city. When her husband admits his guilt, she travels the same route to correct her denunciation and even organizes public readings of a letter of refusal that DUNYA had sent to SVIDRIGAYLOV. She ultimately dies of a stroke and appears to her husband three times in aberrant vision.

SVIRBEY. A distant relative of SVIDRIGAYLOV whom, he states proudly, he has never bored.

TEREBYOVA. A progressive acquaintance of LEBEZYATNIKOV who leaves her parents to join a commune.

TIT VASILYICH. The older of the two workmen who are repainting ALYONA IVANOVNA's apartment following the murders.

TURGENEV. Ivan Sergeevich TURGENEV (1818-83), Russian novelist known for his poetic prose and portrayals of the personal and intellectual lives of the nobility. Prior to RASKOLNIKOV's dream of the horse being beaten to death, the author notes that sometimes dreams are so vivid and strange that they cannot be recreated while awake even by a PUSHKIN or a TURGENEV.

AFANASY IVANOVICH VAKHRUSHIN. A friend of PULKHERIA ALEKSANDROVNA's late husband, from whom she borrows money to send to RASKOLNIKOV.

VARENTS. An acquaintance of LEBEZYATNIKOV who abandons her husband and two children to form a commune with another man. She writes her former husband and states that she will never forgive him for not telling her about communes.

VASYA. PULKHERIA ALEKSANDROVNA is appalled at the way RASKOLNIKOV is dressed when she visits his poverty-ridden room, and she notes that VASYA, VAKHRUSHIN's errand boy, is better dressed.

VRAZUMIKHIN. RAZUMIKHIN's real surname, which no one ever uses.

VYAZEMSKY. Owner of a St. Petersburg building containing pubs and rooms used by the dregs of society. SVIDRIGAYLOV observes to

RASKOLNIKOV that in the past he used to sleep there.

WAGNER [VAGNER]. Adolph Wagner (1835-1917), German economist. LEBEZYATNIKOV recommends the book *GENERAL CONCLUSION OF THE POSITIVIST METHOD* and the articles therein by PIDERIT and WAGNER to the KOBYLYATNIKOVS. The article by WAGNER is "Consistency in Apparently Arbitrary Human Actions" ("Die Gesetz-mässigkeit in den scheinbar willkürlichen menschlichen Handlungen").

WATERLOO [VATERLOO]. A village near Brussels at which the European allies defeated NAPOLEON in 1815 and ended his second attempt to expand the French empire. RASKOLNIKOV bitterly compares the grandeur of NAPOLEON and WATERLOO to the disgusting ALY-ONA IVANOVNA and her case of pledges beneath her bed. He views the striking difference as an indication that perhaps he is not a superman at all.

WEEKLY SPEECH [YEZHENEDELNAYA RECH]. RASKOLNIKOV submits his article on crime and supermen to *WEEKLY SPEECH*, but the journal ceases publication and merges with *PERIODIC SPEECH*, which publishes the work. The references could be to the newspaper *Russian Speech (Russkaya rech)*, which ceased publication in 1861 and merged with the *Moscow Herald (Moskovsky vestnik)*.

YUSHIN. A merchant who rents rooms in the BAKALEEV building. LUZHINA engages a room from him for DUNYA and her mother.

ALEKSANDR GRIGORIEVICH ZAMYOTOV. A stylish young clerk at police headquarters. He meets RASKOLNIKOV by chance in the CRYS-TAL PALACE restaurant shortly after the murders, and the agitated RASKOLNIKOV practically confesses to him. He ultimately leaves his job with the police and quarrels with everyone in the process.

ZARNITSYN. PRASKOVYA PAVLOVNA's late husband.

NATALYA YEGOROVNA ZARNITSYNA. The homely and sickly daughter of PRASKOVYA PAVLOVNA, who likes to give to beggars and constantly dreams of going to a convent. RASKOLNIKOV intends to marry her and discusses with her his theory and his plan to test it through murder. She strongly objects to such ideas but dies of typhus before they can be married. RASKOLNIKOV later suspects that he was drawn to her because she was sickly.

PRASKOVYA PAVLOVNA ZARNITSYNA (PASHENKA). RASKOL-NIKOV's landlady, who after the death of her daughter seeks to recover the credit she has extended to him. She is a chubby widow of forty who is shy and rather stupid and who can listen to a man talk for hours about literally anything. Her only reactions to any lecture are smiles and sighs.

ZEUS [ZEVES]. The supreme god of the ancient Greeks. After RASKOL-NIKOV receives his mother's letter informing him of DUNYA's relationship with LUZHIN and of their upcoming trip to St. Petersburg, he mentally accuses DUNYA of acting like ZEUS in organizing people's lives. He feels manipulated by her seeming self-sacrifice in marrying LUZHIN.

ZIMMERMAN [TSIMMERMAN]. A St. Petersburg manufacturer and seller of hats. (1) RASKOLNIKOV owns a hat by ZIMMERMAN. (2) When RASKOLNIKOV goes into police headquarters to ILYA PETRO-VICH to confess the murders, ILYA PETROVICH observes that he bought his wife a hat from ZIMMERMAN.

ZOSIMOV. The proud, pretentious, but competent doctor who attends RASKOLNIKOV during his illness and who enjoys impressing DUNYA with his ability.

THE IDIOT (IDIOT) 1868

ADELAIDA. See ADELAIDA IVANOVNA YEPANCHINA.

ADELAIDA IVANOVNA. See ADELAIDA IVANOVNA YEPAN-CHINA.

AFANASY IVANOVICH. See AFANASY IVANOVICH TOTSKY.

AGASHKA. A female acquaintance of KELLER.

AGLAYA. See AGLAYA IVANOVNA YEPANCHINA.

AGLAYA IVANOVNA. See AGLAYA IVANOVNA YEPANCHINA.

ALEKSANDR. Tsar ALEKSANDR I (1777-1825), who ruled Russia 1801-25 and who fought against NAPOLEON in the War of 1812. IVOLGIN asserts that when he was NAPOLEON's page as a boy in 1812, he used to watch NAPOLEON cry and moan at night because of his strained relations with ALEKSANDR. IVOLGIN adds that he begged NAPOLEON to make up with ALEKSANDR and even to ask for his forgiveness.

ALEKSANDRA. See ALEKSANDRA IVANOVNA YEPANCHINA.

ALEKSANDRA IVANOVNA. See ALEKSANDRA IVANOVNA YEPANCHINA.

ALEKSANDRA MIKHAYLOVNA. IVOLGIN takes MYSHKIN to meet his friend SOKOLOVICH, but the result is a confused odyssey of knocking on wrong doors and being unable to find the right address. IVOLGIN knocks at the door of KULAKOV and is told that neither ALEKSANDRA MIKHAYLOVNA nor MARYA ALEKSANDROVNA is at home.

ALEKSASHA. See ALEKSASHA LIKHACHYOV.

ALEKSEY. A valet in the YEPANCHIN home whom MYSHKIN treats as an equal.

ALLAH [ALLAKH]. Arabic name for the Supreme Being. MYSHKIN discusses the moment of bliss experienced prior to an epileptic seizure and as an example cites MUHAMMAD, who during a seizure saw all the realms of ALLAH.

ANDREEV. ROGOZHIN is sent by his father to pay ANDREEV a debt, but uses the money to buy NASTASYA FILIPPOVNA some earrings. His father becomes furious and ROGOZHIN is forced to flee the house.

ANFISA ALEKSEEVNA. See ANFISA ALEKSEEVNA ORDYNT-SEVA.

ANISYA. LEBEDEV's deceased sister and DOKTORENKO's mother.

ANNA FYODOROVNA. IVOLGIN mentions ANNA FYODOROVNA in connection with SOKOLOVICH, whom he takes MYSHKIN to meet. She is quite likely SOKOLOVICH's wife.

ANNENKOV. Pavel Vasilievich ANNENKOV (1812-87), Russian literary critic who advocated, at different times in his career, the social responsibility of literature and art for art's sake. LEBEDEV, when he discovers that YEPANCHIN does not have PUSHKIN's works in his house, offers to sell the YEPANCHINS his edition of PUSHKIN edited by ANNENKOV.

D'ANTHES [DANTES]. Georges Charles D'ANTHES (1812-95), the adopted son of the Dutch envoy in St. Petersburg. He became involved with PUSHKIN's wife and ultimately killed the writer in a duel. AGLAYA discusses duels and how to fire pistols with MYSHKIN, since she fears that MYSHKIN may be challenged for defending NASTASYA from an officer. MYSHKIN mentions during their discussion that D'ANTHES probably gave PUSHKIN his fatal wound accidentally.

ANTICHRIST [ANTIKHRIST]. Biblical term referring to a man of sin who denies the Father and the Son and whose disturbing presence presages the Second Coming of CHRIST and the end of the world. LEBEDEV admits to NIL ALEKSEEVICH that he is a professor of ANTICHRIST since he knows the APOCALYPSE so well. MYSHKIN insists that the Roman Catholic Church preaches ANTICHRIST.

ANTIP. See ANTIP BURDOVSKY.

APOCALYPSE [APOKALIPSIS]. In the New Testament the Revelation of St. John, which outlines the end of the world and the Final Judgment. (1) LEBEDEV reports to MYSHKIN that NASTASYA FILIPPOVNA reacts violently when he preaches to her from the APOCALYPSE. (2) AGLAYA asks LEBEDEV to tell her about the APOCALYPSE, but IVOLGIN strongly responds that what she would hear from LEBEDEV would be charlatanism. (3) LEBEDEV's young son tells MYSHKIN that the star WORMWOOD which will poison the fountain of waters as mentioned in the APOCALYPSE is, according to his father, the network of railroads in Europe. MYSHKIN doubts the boy but promises to check with LEBEDEV as soon as he can to determine if that is what he teaches. (4) IPPOLIT wonders what the "sources of life" are that are alluded to in the APOCALYPSE and whether the sun is the source of life. IPPOLIT has reference to the water of life and the tree of life which, according to the Revelation, will replace the sun as the source of life. (5) After impatiently listening to LEBEDEV expound on the APOCALYPSE, IVOLGIN notes that GRIGORY SEMYONOVICH BURMISTROV is an authentic expounder of the book. (6) Before IPPOLIT reads his literary explanation to those assembled at MYSHKIN's birthday celebration, he observes that an angel in the APOCALYPSE announces that there will be no more time. He therefore feels that he must read "My Indispensable Explanation" before it is too late. (7) LEBEDEV discusses the APOCALYPSE with his superior, NIL ALEKSEEVICH, who dies shortly thereafter. LEBEDEV takes credit for predicting the death. He had told NIL ALEKSEEVICH that he is a professor of ANTICHRIST because he knows the APOCALYPSE so well.

"APRES MOI LE DELUGE!" "After me the deluge!" rather vain adaptation of a reply to King Louis XV of France (1710-74) following the defeat of the French and Austrian armies by Frederick the Great of Prussia in 1757 during the Seven Years War. The remark is attributed to Madame de Pompadour who is reputed to have said "Après nous le déluge" ("After us the deluge"). IPPOLIT subtitles "My Indispensable Explanation," "A-PRES MOI LE DELUGE!"

ARAMIS. One of the famous trio in *The Three Musketeers (Les Trois Mousquetaires),* a novel written by Alexandre Dumas, père (1802-70) in 1844. ARAMIS wears black, is sober, and frequently vows to enter a monastery. IVOLGIN refers to himself, YEPANCHIN, and NIKOLAY LVOVICH MYSHKIN as ATHOS, PORTHOS, and ARAMIS respectively.

ARCHIVE [ARKHIV]. Russian *ARCHIVE (RUSSKY ARKHIV),* historical-literary journal published 1863-1917. MYSHKIN gives IVOLGIN a copy of *ARCHIVE* so that he might read an article of interest. He reads the article and argues at length with LEBEDEV about it.

ARDALION ALEKSANDROVICH. See ARDALION ALEKSANDRO ICH IVOLGIN.

ARDALION ALEKSANDRYCH. See ARDALION ALEKSANDRO-VICH IVOLGIN.

ARMANS. A woman that LEBEDEV met through LIKHACHYOV.

ATHOS [ATOS]. One of the famous trio in *The Three Musketeers (Les Trois Mousquetaires),* a novel written by Alexandre Dumas, père (1802-70) in 1844. He is gallant and gentlemanly in all respects. IVOLGIN refers to himself, YEPANCHIN, and NIKOLAY LVOVICH MYSHKIN as A-THOS, PORTHOS, and ARAMIS respectively. It is noteworthy that he reserves the most gallant, ATHOS, for himself.

B—N. A doctor who IPPOLIT claims told him that he has only about two weeks to live. He later admits that he has never seen B—N, and the diagnosis really comes from a fellow student KISLORODOV. Doctor B—N could likely be a reference to Doctor Sergey Petrovich Botkin (1832-89), whom Dostoevsky himself consulted.

BABETTE. See VARVARA ARDALIONOVNA IVOLGINA.

BACCHUS [VAKKH]. In Roman mythology the god of wine. IVOLGIN sings a song of war and BACCHUS to LEBEDEV, who later describes IVOLGIN as an ardent devotee of BACCHUS.

BAKHMUTOV. A student acquaintance of IPPOLIT. He tries to make friends with IPPOLIT but fails inasmuch as IPPOLIT considers him an enemy because of his wealth, intelligence, and good disposition. When IPPOLIT returns a lost wallet to a former doctor who is in dire straits because of intrigues, he determines to take up his cause. He contacts BAKHMUTOV, whose uncle PYOTR MATVEEVICH BAKHMUTOV has the final word in the doctor's petition, and urges him to intercede with his uncle. BAKHMUTOV agrees to ask his uncle about the affair, and the doctor is ultimately vindicated and launched again in his career.

PYOTR MATVEEVICH BAKHMUTOV. An important official who at the instigation of his nephew BAKHMUTOV issues a favorable decision on a petition from an impoverished country doctor. See BAKHMUTOV.

FILIPP ALEKSANDROVICH BARASHKOV. An impoverished land-owner who lives near TOTSKY's large country estate. He goes mad and dies when his miserable estate and his wife are lost in a fire. His daughter NASTASYA FILIPPOVNA and another daughter, who subsequently dies, are taken in by TOTSKY after the tragedy.

NASTASYA FILIPPOVNA BARASHKOVA (NASTYA). A beautiful, haughty, and proud woman whose life is dominated by pride and suffering. After her mother perishes in a fire and her father goes mad and also dies, she is taken in by TOTSKY, a neighboring landowner, who sees that she gets an excellent education but who uses her sexually. The experiences with TOTSKY crush her feeling of self-worth, and thereafter she actively seeks suffering and debasement. Her cynical debasement is focussed in marriage. TOTSKY and YEPANCHIN want her to marry GANYA so that TOTSKY can consider himself free to marry ALEKSANDRA IVANOVNA YE-PANCHINA. She responds by selling herself to the highest bidder and involving ROGOZHIN and MYSHKIN in the contest for her hand. The two men represent respectively to debasement and compassionate love, and her vacillation between the two reflects her inner struggles. She utterly dismisses GANYA as a suitor because he wants only her money. To humiliate him she throws the money ROGOZHIN uses to purchase her into a fire and tells GANYA that it is his if he will grovel to remove it. She is drawn mostly to ROGOZHIN, since living with him reinforces her feeling that she is the most fallen and guilty of creatures even though she is certain that he will ultimately kill her. MYSHKIN's happiness is important to her, and she attempts to make a match for him with AGLAYA. When the two women clash because of pride and vanity, NASTASYA FILIPPOVNA forces MYSHKIN, who loves them both in his own way, to choose between them and orders him to stay with her. When he complies, she immediately insists on a wedding and is very jealous over his concern for AGLAYA. Just as she is to enter the church for the wedding ceremony, she sees ROGOZHIN in the crowd and runs away with him. Her frequent presentiments of death are shortly thereafter realized when ROGOZHIN stabs her in the heart.

BARON DE BAZANCOURT [BAZANKUR]. Jean Baptiste DE BAZANCOURT (1767-1830), French general who actively participated in the NAPOLEONIC campaigns. In IVOLGIN's fantastic tale of his service as a young page of NAPOLEON, he claims that he becomes a page to replace BARON DE BAZANCOURT, who died when NAPOLEON entered Moscow in 1812.

PRINCESS BELOKONSKAYA. AGLAYA's godmother and an elderly friend of YELIZAVETA PROKOFIEVNA YEPANCHINA. She is a tyrant with much social influence. She introduces YEVGENY PAVLOVICH into the YEPANCHIN family hoping that he will marry AGLAYA. When she is consulted as to the advisability of marrying AGLAYA to MYSHKIN, she determines after meeting him that he should not be considered as AGLAYA's intended.

SOFYA BESPALOVA. At FERDYSHCHENKO's instigation at NASTASYA FILIPPOVNA's birthday celebration it is agreed that all will relate the worst thing that they have ever done. In TOTSKY's account of his worst transgression he relates a tale of SOFYA BESPALOVA, who is to attend ANFISA ALEKSEEVNA ORDYNTSEVA's birthday ball carrying a bouquet of white camelias. When ANFISA ALEKSEEVNA hears of this, she has a great desire to have a bouquet of red camelias. PETYA VORKHOVSKOY, who has a crush on ANFISA ALEKSEEVNA, is anxious to secure the flowers for her and conducts a desperate search. He finally hears that TREPALOV has red camelias and rushes to him only to discover that TOTSKY arrived first so that he could present the flowers to ANFISA ALEKSEEVNA. PETYA becomes ill with disappointment and then goes to war in the Crimea, where he is killed by the Turks. TOTSKY's tale is related nervously in the presence of NASTASYA FILIPPOVNA, whom he has wronged so blatantly.

BIBLE [SVYASHCHENNOE PISANIE]. A collection of books organized into the Old Testament, a religious history from Adam through the twelve tribes of Israel with emphasis on Judah, and the New Testament, the life and ministry of Jesus CHRIST. After his wife dies LEBEDEV takes to drink and while drunk reads his orphans the BIBLE at night.

BISKUP. An acquaintance of ROGOZHIN who helps him raise the money to "buy" NASTASYA FILIPPOVNA. In an attempt to humiliate YEV-GENY PAVLOVICH, NASTASYA FILIPPOVNA loudly shouts to him from a carriage that she and ROGOZHIN will help him work out his nasty situation with BISKUP, a likely reference to YEVGENY PAVLOVICH's debts.

BOURDALOUE [BURDALU]. Louis BOURDALOUE (1632-1704), a JESUIT and one of the most popular preachers at the time of Louis XIV. KELLER observes that BOURDALOUE would not be merciful to such as he but that MYSHKIN was and judged his confession humanely. He has reference principally to the fact that he can get money from the generous and suddenly wealthy MYSHKIN.

BURDOVSKY. The father of ANTIP BURDOVSKY. His wife had a dowry through the benevolence of PAVLISHCHEV, and he used the money to begin a business. He was deceived, turned to drink, and died while still a young man.

ANTIP BURDOVSKY. A dishevelled and cocky twenty two year old and one of the young progressive thinkers who like to reject everything but their own interest. After MYSHKIN receives a sizable inheritance, DOK-TORENKO, IPPOLIT, KELLER, and BURDOVSKY come to him and demand money for BURDOVSKY as the illegitimate son of PAVLISH-CHEV. PAVLISHCHEV in fact had supported BURDOVSKY exten-sively while he was still living. They insist that since MYSHKIN received much money from PAVLISHCHEV, even though he was not his son, then MYSHKIN should share his wealth with BURDOVSKY, who is PAV-

LISHCHEV's son. BURDOVSKY supports with some difficulty his poverty-ridden, sickly mother, but finally refuses to accept MYSHKIN's money in a very vain and haughty manner. MYSHKIN correctly perceives him as innocent and easily deceived and manipulated by others, particularly by his attorney CHEBAROV. BURDOVSKY ultimately writes to MYSHKIN to thank him for helping his mother and to indicate that he has broken with CHEBAROV and DOKTORENKO, but he retains his absolutist and vain approach to life.

GRIGORY SEMYONOVICH BURMISTROV. After impatiently listening to LEBEDEV expound on the APOCALYPSE, IVOLGIN mentions that BURMISTROV was a real declaimer of the book.

CATHERINE [IMPERATRITSA YEKATERINA]. Empress CATHERINE the Great (1729-96), who ruled Russia from 1762 until her death. Her reign marked an increase in contact with the West. In IVOLGIN's amusing tale of his service as NAPOLEON's page, he notes that when NAPOLEON entered Moscow in 1812 and saw CATHERINE's portrait in the palace, he commented that she was a great woman.

CHARRAS [SHARRAS]. Jean Baptiste CHARRAS (1810-65), French political figure and historian who authored *Histoire de la campagne de 1815, Waterloo (History of the Campaign of 1815, Waterloo).* MYSHKIN mentions CHARRAS' book about WATERLOO and notes the obvious glee of the writer in NAPOLEON's defeat.

CHEBAROV. A lawyer who is engaged by BURDOVSKY to help him get part of MYSHKIN's inheritance. BURDOVSKY poses as PAVLISHCHEV's illegitimate son with the support of DOKTORENKO, KELLER, and IPPOLIT. MYSHKIN discovers that CHEBAROV is a rogue who is using the naive young "new people" to further his own aims.

CHERNOSVITOV. Rafail Aleksandrovich CHERNOSVITOV (1810-?), a member of the Petrashevsky Circle, a group of young liberals to which Dostoevsky belonged, who was exiled in 1849 for involvement with socialist ideas. In exile he manufactured and wrote about artificial legs. LEBEDEV insists that he has a wooden leg made by CHERNOSVITOV.

CHETYI-MINEI. An ecclesiastical calendar containing lives of saints and martyrs. ROGOZHIN mentions that his mother reads her *CHETYI-MINEI* continually.

CHOPIN [SHOPEN]. Frédéric CHOPIN (1810-49), the outstanding pianist and composer for piano in the Romantic era. IVOLGIN tries to take MYSHKIN to meet SOKOLOVICH, but knocks on the wrong door. When informed that MARYA ALEKSANDROVNA and ALEKSANDRA MIKHAYLOVNA are not at home, IVOLGIN asks that the servants convey to them his hope that all they dreamed about on Thursday evening listening to CHOPIN will be realized!

CHRIST [KHRISTOS]. Jesus CHRIST, in Christianity the Son of God. (1) At the home of YEPANCHIN MYSHKIN discusses capital punishment and the horrible finality of the guillotine in comparison to the thread of hope in other forms of execution. He notes that CHRIST Himself spoke of such agony in Gethsemane and that one should not treat man in such a way. (2) MYSHKIN mentions a woman who told him that the joy of a mother at a child's first smile is like the joy of God at a repentant sinner. He adds that this was the message of CHRIST. (3) YELIZAVETA PROKOFIEVNA YEPANCHINA condemns BURDOVSKY, IPPOLIT, DOKTORENKO and others of the progressive new generation for not believing in CHRIST. (4) IPPOLIT mentions that he saw a painting of CHRIST in ROGOZHIN's house. (5) IPPOLIT notes the majesty of CHRIST's calling LAZARUS forth from the dead in comparison with the impact of HOLBEIN's picture of CHRIST. (6) In one of NASTASYA FILIPPOVNA's letters to AGLAYA, through which she tries to encourage AGLAYA to marry MYSHKIN, she mentions how she would paint CHRIST. She envisions Him staring thoughtfully into the distance, with His hand resting on a child looking intently at Him. (7) In a tirade against the Roman Catholic Church MYSHKIN asserts that the church has gone beyond atheism in that it teaches a distorted concept of CHRIST. (8) MYSHKIN insists that the Roman Catholic Church has replaced CHRIST with itself. (9) SAVELIEV wants to purchase ROGOZHIN's copy of HOLBEIN's painting of CHRIST.

"THE CLOUD" ["TUCHA"]. A fable by Ivan KRYLOV written in 1815 in which a proud and heavily-laden cloud passes benignly over the parched earth and rains heavily into the ocean. Proud of its fine storm, the cloud is rebuked by the mountain for having done no good at all. In KELLER's sarcastic article about MYSHKIN's inheriting a fortune he notes that the money descends upon MYSHKIN as in KRYLOV's "THE CLOUD." The implication is that it should have descended elsewhere.

COLUMBUS [KOLUMB]. Christopher COLUMBUS (1451-1506), Italian navigator who under the flag of Spain made four voyages to the Americas.

He is credited with discovering the New World in 1492 on his first voyage. (1) IPPOLIT asserts that COLUMBUS was happy not when he discovered America but rather when he was in the process of discovering it. (2) The author discusses ordinary men who desire to be original but are not and seemingly can never be. The suffering they experience over trying to think of something to discover, however, matches the authentic pangs of discovery of a COLUMBUS or GALILEO. (3) MYSHKIN compares the discovery of the New World by COLUMBUS to the discovery of Russia by Russians themselves. The discovery of Russia is equivalent to the discovery of the regeneration of man.

CONSTANT [KONSTAN]. CONSTANT Wairy (1778-1845), a favorite valet of NAPOLEON. In IVOLGIN's fantastic story of his service with NAPOLEON as a page he claims that CONSTANT had been sent by NAPOLEON with a letter to JOSEPHINE and hence was not with NAPOLEON in Moscow.

LA DAME AUX CAMELIAS. The Lady of the Camelias, a novel by Alexandre DUMAS which he published in 1848 and later reworked into a popular play under the same title. As TOTSKY relates his story of the worst thing he has ever done, he notes that the novel *LA DAME AUX CAMELIAS* was very popular in society and probably was the pretext for the desire of the ladies for camelias. See SOFYA BESPALOVA.

GEORGE DANDIN [ZHORZH DANDEN]. Central character of a play of the same name written by MOLIERE in 1668. In discussing ordinary people the author notes that society is full of people like GEORGE DANDIN and PODKOLYOSIN, who have provided names for the mediocre people that are seen daily. He admits that not every husband cries out at every step "TU L'AS VOULU, GEORGE DANDIN!" but many husbands shout out after the honeymoon or even the day after the wedding. DANDIN's shout results from his wife Angélique's betrayal and the comic support she receives from her high society parents. He is an average man bound in an average situation.

DANILOV. A.M. DANILOV, a nineteen year old student and member of the nobility who murdered a pawnbroker and his servant woman in 1866 and who was exiled to a labor camp in 1867. (1) MYSHKIN discusses the younger generation with YELIZAVETA PROKOFIEVNA and assures her that people like GORSKY and DANILOV are exceptions in society. (2) IPPOLIT, a member of the set that YELIZAVETA PROKOFIEVNA ridicules, discusses some of the new ideas of the young progressives.

YEVGENY PAVLOVICH notes that their ideas seem to lead toward the notion that might is right, and he insists that the distance between that notion and the actions of DANILOV and GORSKY is not far at all.

DARYA. At NASTASYA FILIPPOVNA's birthday celebration FERDYSHCHENKO suggests that each guest relate the worst thing he ever did. In his own account FERDYSHCHENKO notes that while in the home of SEMYON IVANOVICH ISHCHENKO he stole three rubles from SEMYON IVANOVICH's daughter MARYA SEMYONOVNA. FERDYSHCHENKO allows the servant girl DARYA to be blamed for the theft and says that she was dismissed the very next day.

DARYA ALEKSEEVNA. A guest at NASTASYA FILIPPOVNA's birthday celebration who later entertains her at her dacha.

DAVOUT [DAVU]. Louis Nicolas DAVOUT (1770-1823), French marshall and minister of war during NAPOLEON's second attempt at a French empire in 1815. In his amusing tale of his service as a page with NAPOLEON, IVOLGIN notes that one of his few formal duties was to accompany NAPOLEON on rides. He insists that when they rode out DAVOUT and ROUSTAN usually went with them. IVOLGIN asserts that DAVOUT was NAPOLEON's closest adviser on many things, for example, the idea to adopt Russian Orthodoxy and release the serfs in order to rally the Russian people behind him and the idea to fortify themselves in the Kremlin for the winter, but he also notes that NAPOLEON usually took his advise instead of that of DAVOUT.

DEAD SOULS [MYORTVYE DUSHI]. A novel by Nikolay GOGOL which chronicles the attempt of Chichikov to buy deceased serfs from an array of grotesque landowners. The first volume was published in 1842, and GOGOL envisioned sequels in which the rakish hero would be reformed. IVOLGIN laments, "WHERE IS MY YOUTH, WHERE IS MY FRESHNESS," and questions KOLYA about the source of the words. KOLYA responds that they are from GOGOL's *DEAD SOULS*.

VLADIMIR DOKTORENKO. The son of LEBEDEV's sister ANISYA and one of the new younger generation who reject everything except their own interests. He locates himself in his uncle LEBEDEV's house and refuses to leave until he is given money. Together with BURDOVSKY, KELLER, and IPPOLIT he accosts MYSHKIN and demands that BURDOVSKY as the illegitimate son of PAVLISHCHEV receive part of MYSHKIN's inheritance. He then refuses to accept money from MYSHKIN and adopts a very self-righteous and absolutist stance. Of all the new generation he is the most intolerable and doctrinaire.

DON JUAN [DON-ZHUAN]. A legendary profligate who has an unscrupulous obsession for pursuing women. PRINCE N., who attends the party at the YEPANCHIN home at which MYSHKIN is presented to society, is compared to DON JUAN.

DON QUIXOTE OF LA MANCHA [DON-KIKHOT LAMANCHSKY]. *El Ingenioso Hidalgo DON QUIXOTE DE LA MANCHA (The Ingenious Gentleman DON QUIXOTE OF LA MANCHA),* a novel by Miguel de Cervantes (1547-1616) published 1605 and 1615. One of the premier works of world literature, the novel chronicles DON QUIXOTE's obsession with knight errantry and visionary idealism. (1) AGLAYA receives a note from MYSHKIN and places it in a copy of *DON QUIXOTE OF LA MANCHA.* As she comes to know MYSHKIN's personality, this coincidence strikes her as very amusing. (2) AGLAYA compares MYSHKIN with PUSHKIN's "THE POOR KNIGHT" and observes that "THE POOR KNIGHT" is quite like DON QUIXOTE but is more serious.

COUNTESS DU BARRY [GRAFINYA DYUBARRI]. Marie Jeanne DU BARRY (1743-93), adventuress and mistress of King Louis XV of France until his death in 1774. She dominated the king and his court and wielded much influence in society until she was guillotined during the French Revolution in 1793. LEBEDEV admits that after he read of her life he prayed for the peace of her soul and the souls of sinners like her.

DUMAS FILS [DYUMA-FIS]. Alexandre DUMAS (1824-95), French novelist and dramatist known as DUMAS the son. In TOTSKY's story of the worst thing he ever did, DUMAS FILS is mentioned as the author of *LA DAME AUX CAMELIAS.*

"THE EAST AND SOUTH ERE LONG HAVE BEEN PORTRAYED " **["VOSTOK I YUG DAVNO OPISAN"].** A slightly adjusted quotation from the poem "The Journalist, the Reader and the Writer" ("Zhurnalist, chitatel i pisatel"), written in 1840 by Mikhail LERMONTOV. The original reads "VOSTOK I YUG DAVNO OPISANY," with no change in the translation. When ALEKSANDRA IVANOVNA asks MYSHKIN for a suggestion as to what she might paint, she observes in verse that "THE EAST AND SOUTH ERE LONG HAVE BEEN PORTRAYED."

"LES EXTREMITES SE TOUCHENT". "Extremes meet," words of Blaise Pascal (1623-62), French scientist, philosopher, religious thinker, and writer. The quotation is taken from his *Pensées sur la réligion et sur quelques autres sujets (Thoughts on Religion and Certain Other Subjects).* IPPOLIT characterizes his relationship with ROGOZHIN as "LES EXTREMITES SE TOUCHENT."

FAMUSOV. Comically conservative landowner in *Woe From Wit (Gore ot uma),* a comedy in verse written by Aleksandr Sergeevich Griboedov (1795-1829) in 1822-24. YEVGENY PAVLOVICH challengingly asserts that all of the pronouncements of the so-called Russian socialists are taken from the writings of Russian landowners even before FAMUSOV.

FEDOSEEV. A business acquaintance of YEPANCHIN.

FERDYSHCHENKO. A bawdy and indecent buffoon who rents a room from IVOLGIN. He is thirty, filthy, unpleasant looking, and is kept as part of NASTASYA FILIPPOVNA's retinue largely to torment people. On his first meeting with MYSHKIN he warns him never to lend him money because he will never pay it back and adds that he does not intend to pay for his room. He tries to impress people with his originality and gaiety but is seldom successful, and he privately questions whether one can live with a name like FERDYSHCHENKO. At NASTASYA FILIPPOVNA's birthday celebration he suggests that each guest relate the worst thing he has ever done. His own account chronicles his theft of three rubles from MARYA SEMYONOVNA ISHCHENKO for which the servant girl DARYA is severely reprimanded and dismissed.

FILIPP ALEKSANDROVICH. See FILIPP ALEKSANDROVICH BARASHKOV.

FILISOVA. A small, sharp-featured woman of forty in whose house NASTASYA FILIPPOVNA rents rooms.

FYODOR. One of YEPANCHIN's domestic servants.

GALILEO [GALILEY]. GALILEO Galilei (1564-1642), Italian physicist, philosopher, and astronomer whose discoveries include Jupiter's satellites and sun spots. The author discusses ordinary men who desire to be original but who are not, such as GANYA and PTITSYN. He notes that the suffering such people endure in trying to think of something to discover and be original is equivalent to the pains of discovery of a COLUMBUS or GALILEO.

GANECHKA. See GAVRILA ARDALIONOVICH IVOLGIN.

GANKA. See GAVRILA ARDALIONOVICH IVOLGIN.

GANYA. See GAVRILA ARDALIONOVICH IVOLGIN.

GAVRILA ARDALIONOVICH. See GAVRILA ARDALIONOVICH IVOLGIN.

GAVRILA ARDALIONYCH. See GAVRILA ARDALIONOVICH I-VOLGIN.

GLASHA. See AGLAYA IVANOVNA YEPANCHINA.

STEPAN GLEBOV. STEPAN Bogdanovich GLEBOV (ca. 1672-1718), the lover of PETER the Great's first wife. He was tortured to death for a conspiracy against PETER and for his liaison with the tsar's wife, who had been sent to a convent. As IPPOLIT discusses his imminent death with MYSHKIN, he recalls the death of STEPAN GLEBOV and expresses the conviction that he can die just as nobly.

GOGOL. Nikolay Vasilievich GOGOL (1809-52), popular Russian writer noted for his tragicomic portrayal of human foibles. He was viewed by progressive critics as the fountainhead of the Natural School and credited with critically describing reality with the idea of social reform. (1) YEVGENY PAVLOVICH asserts that Russian literature is not really Russian, with the exceptions of LOMONOSOV, PUSHKIN, and GOGOL. (2) As the author discusses the mass of average people in society as exemplified by GEORGE DANDIN and PODKOLYOSIN, he praises GOGOL, the creator of PODKOLYOSIN, for providing a name and a label for mediocre people. (3) As the author continues his discussion of the mediocre, he mentions those characterized by a base naiveté and idiotic self-assurance and can think of no better example than GOGOL's PIROGOV. (4) IVOLGIN laments, "WHERE IS MY YOUTH, WHERE IS MY FRESHNESS," and asks KOLYA for the source of the quotation. KOLYA indicates that it is found in GOGOL's *DEAD SOULS*.

GORSKY. Vitold GORSKY, an eighteen year old student from the nobility who in 1868 murdered six members of the ZHEMARIN family. While serving in the family as the tutor of ZHEMARIN's son, he planned the murders with exactitude. (1) MYSHKIN discusses the younger generation with YELIZAVETA PROKOFIEVNA and assures her that people like DANILOV and GORSKY are exceptions in society. (2) IPPOLIT, a member of the set that YELIZAVETA PROKOFIEVNA so ridicules, discusses some of the new ideas of the young progressives. YEVGENY PAVLOVICH notes that their ideas seem to lead toward the notion that might is right and that the distance from such an idea to the actions of DANILOV and GORSKY is not far at all.

GRIGORY SEMYONOVICH. See GRIGORY SEMYONOVICH BURMISTROV.

GRISHA. See KAPITON ALEKSEEVICH YEROPEGOV.

ABBAT GURO. A JESUIT under whose influence PAVLISHCHEV embraces Roman Catholicism and becomes a JESUIT himself.

HAMLET [GAMLET]. Central character of *HAMLET, Prince of Denmark*, a tragedy written by William Shakespeare (1564-1616) in 1601. At MYSHKIN's birthday celebration LEBEDEV notes that the conversation will be on contemporary themes with questions and answers rather like HAMLET's "TO BE OR NOT TO BE."

HISTORY [ISTORIA]. HISTORY of the Russian State (ISTORIA gosudarstva Rossyskogo), a twelve volume history of Russia by Nikolay KARAMZIN, generally from the point of view of autocracy. The first eleven volumes appeared 1816-24, and the uncompleted twelfth volume was published posthumously in 1829. ROGOZHIN indicates that the name MYSHKIN is probably mentioned in KARAMZIN's HISTORY.

HISTORY [ISTORIA]. HISTORY of Russia from Antiquity (ISTORIA Rossii s drevneyshikh vremyon) by Sergey SOLOVYOV, a twenty three volume history, seventeen volumes of which had been issued at the time *The Idiot* was being written. (1) MYSHKIN notices SOLOVYOV's *HISTORY* opened and marked, lying on ROGOZHIN's desk. (2) NASTASYA FILIPPOVNA informs ROGOZHIN that he should become educated and recommends that he read SOLOVYOV's *HISTORY*.

HISTORY [ISTORIA]. Probably *Weltgeschichte für das deutsche Volk (World History for the German People)*, a nineteen volume history written by Friedrich SCHLOSSER in 1844-56. PETROV asks his schoolmates KOLYA and KOSTYA to buy SCHLOSSER's *HISTORY*.

HANS HOLBEIN [GANS GOLBEYN]. HOLBEIN the Younger (1497-1543), German painter of portraits and religious works. ROGOZHIN has a copy of HOLBEIN's *Dead CHRIST* (1521), which portrays CHRIST in naturalistic detail just as He has been removed from the cross. ROGOZHIN greatly enjoys looking at it. IPPOLIT discusses the painting at length in his "Explanation."

HOLBEIN'S MADONNA [GOLBEYNOVA MADONNA]. *Madonna with the Family of the Bürgermeister Jacob Meyer,* a copy displayed in Dresden of HOLBEIN's original work, done in 1525-26. MYSHKIN notes that ALEKSANDRA IVANOVNA's face has the peculiar nuances of color found in HOLBEIN'S MADONNA.

"IMAGE OF PURE BEAUTY" ["OBRAZ CHISTOY KRASOTY"]. Inexact rendering of a phrase from the poem "To***" ("K***") written to Anna Petrovna Kern in 1825 by Aleksandr PUSHKIN. The original line is "genius of pure beauty" ("geny chistoy krasoty"). AGLAYA describes the attitude of THE POOR KNIGHT to his feminine ideal as an "IMAGE OF PURE BEAUTY."

INDEPENDANCE/INDEPENDANCE BELGE. Belgian Independence, a Brussels newspaper published 1830-1937 which reflected the political and cultural life of Western Europe. (1) IVOLGIN claims to read the newspaper regularly. (2) NASTASYA FILIPPOVNA reads the paper regularly. When IVOLGIN relates an anecdote about throwing a lady's dog out of the window after she had done the same with his cigar, she notes that she recently read this story in *INDEPENDANCE BELGE* and offers to show him the issue. (3) When IVOLGIN waits for MYSHKIN in a pub, the author notes that he reads this newspaper.

IPPOLIT. See IPPOLIT TERENTIEV.

MARYA SEMYONOVNA ISHCHENKO. In FERDYSHCHENKO's tale of the worst thing he has ever done he steals three rubles from MARYA SEMYONOVNA and allows the servant girl DARYA to be punished for it.

SEMYON IVANOVICH ISHCHENKO. MARYA SEMYONOVNA ISHCHENKO's father in FERDYSHCHENKO's account of the worst thing he ever did.

IVAN FOMICH. See IVAN FOMICH SURIKOV.

IVAN FYODOROVICH. See GENERAL IVAN FYODOROVICH YE-PANCHIN.

IVAN PETROVICH. See IVAN PETROVICH PTITSYN.

IVAN PETROVICH. An elderly relative of PAVLISHCHEV and devotee of things English who attends the social gathering at the YEPANCHIN home at which MYSHKIN is presented to society.

IVANYCH. In YELIZAVETA PROKOFIEVNA's tirade against BUR-DOVSKY, IPPOLIT, DOKTORENKO, and the other young progressives, she cites the example of a girl who grows up in a proper home but who suddenly bids her family farewell and announces that she has married some KARLYCH or IVANYCH.

GENERAL ARDALION ALEKSANDROVICH IVOLGIN (ARDA-LION ALEKSANDRYCH). A retired general who once served with YEPANCHIN. He is fifty five and likes to display his worthiness through anecdotes and elaborate tales of his accomplishments, none of which is true. Because of this need to be recognized, the poor management of his affairs, and predilection for vodka he is an acute embarrassment to his family, particularly to his proud son GANYA, and he is made to live essentially alone. At the suggestion of YEPANCHIN, MYSHKIN takes a room with IVOLGIN but is warned by NINA ALEKSANDROVNA IVOLGINA not to give her husband any money. IVOLGIN is subsequently put into debtor's prison by MARFA BORISOVNA TERENTIEVA, but is released through MYSHKIN's intercession. His life then becomes one of finding a refuge—he lives with both PTITSYN and LEBEDEV—and of trying to recover his personal worthiness. He quarrels with LEBEDEV over whose false recollections of the War of 1812 are true and then concocts a fantastic tale of his serving as NAPOLEON's page. Broken in spirit and aware of the problem he has been to his wife and family, he makes a final pathetic effort to justify himself to his son KOLYA and then dies of a series of strokes.

GAVRILA ARDALIONOVICH IVOLGIN (GAVRILA ARDALION-YCH, GANYA, GANKA, GANECHKA). The twenty eight year old son of IVOLGIN who serves as YEPANCHIN's secretary. He is very proud and thoroughly embarrassed by his family and particularly his father. He is tortured by his being ordinary and mediocre and is used by the author as an example in his discussion of the mess of unoriginal people in society. He views money as everything, and his schemes to marry AGLAYA and NASTASYA FILIPPOVNA are designed to get money so that he can overcome his mediocrity and become somebody. TOTSKY and YEPAN-CHIN encourage marriage to NASTASYA FILIPPOVNA so that TOT-SKY will be free to marry ALEKSANDRA IVANOVNA, but NAS-

TASYA FILIPPOVNA refuses the offer at MYSHKIN's suggestion. Knowing GANYA's love for money she throws the money ROGOZHIN uses to "buy" her into the fire and tells GANYA that he can have it. He refuses to move as his vanity conquers his greed, but he is so overcome with the ordeal that he faints. Even after she pulls it out of the fire herself, he refuses to accept it. The experience causes him to become quite ill and changes his outlook somewhat. He makes a final attempt to marry AGLAYA following her break with MYSHKIN but is rebuffed.

NIKOLAY ARDALIONOVICH IVOLGIN (KOLYA). IVOLGIN's thirteen year old son who is assigned by the family to take care of him. He is very sensitive to his father's behavior and pities him greatly.

NINA ALEKSANDROVNA IVOLGINA. IVOLGIN's fifty year old wife, who loves him but suffers a great deal because of his behavior. She has an insulted look and life has not been kind to her. She strongly objects to NASTASYA FILIPPOVNA's behavior and suggests to YEPANCHIN that she not be permitted to associate with his daughters.

VARVARA ARDALIONOVNA IVOLGINA (VARYA, VARKA, BABETTE). IVOLGIN's twenty three year old daughter. She is counted among the usual and ordinary by the author and marries the very average PTITSYN. She is decisive and opinionated and suggests that NASTASYA FILIPPOVNA be thrown out of their house. When GANYA struggles with her over this matter, she spits in his face.

JESUIT [IEZUIT]. The Society of Jesus, a religious order for Roman Catholic men founded by Ignatius Loyola (1491-1556) in 1534. The society is known for scholarship and missionary zeal and has been accused of secrecy and intrigue. (1) IPPOLIT derisively refers to MYSHKIN as having a JESUIT-like soul. (2) When KAPITON ALEKSEICH RADOMSKY commits suicide at an advanced age and leaves a lot of money to YEVGENY PAVLOVICH, NASTASYA FILIPPOVNA reacts cynically and sarcastically. YEPANCHIN suspects that she probably considers the whole affair reminiscent of the JESUITS. (3) Under the influence of the JESUIT ABBAT GURO, PAVLISHCHEV converts to Catholicism and becomes a JESUIT. MYSHKIN expresses horror and great disappointment at the news. (4) MYSHKIN expresses the opinion that because of his passionate nature a Russian would undoubtedly become a JESUIT if he converted to Catholicism.

JOSEPHINE [ZHOZEFINA]. Marie Joséphe Rose Tascher de la Pagerie (1763-1814), NAPOLEON's wife, whom he divorced in 1809 when an heir could not be produced. In his tale of service as NAPOLEON's page IVOLGIN notes that CONSTANT was not with, NAPOLEON in Moscow in 1812 because he had been sent with a letter to JOSEPHINE.

JUDAS [IUDA]. As recorded in the New Testament, JUDAS Iscariot, the apostle who betrayed CHRIST to Roman soldiers in exchange for thirty pieces of silver. ROGOZHIN, who notes how easily GANYA can be bought, refers to him as JUDAS.

JUPITER OF OLYMPUS [YUPITER OLIMPYSKY]. Supreme deity of Roman mythology who corresponds to the Greek Zeus. OLYMPUS is the home of the Greek gods. YEPANCHIN reverently regards a dignitary who has long been his benefactor as JUPITER OF OLYMPUS and feels guilty if he ever deigns to think of himself as his equal.

COUNTESS K. IVAN PETROVICH, after mentioning that PAVLISH-CHEV converted to Catholicism and became a JESUIT, notes that COUNTESS K. entered a Catholic convent abroad.

KAPITAN ALEKSEEVICH. See KAPITON ALEKSEEVICH YERO-PEGOV.

KAPITON. See KAPITON ALEKSEEVICH YEROPEGOV.

KAPITON ALEKSEEVICH. See KAPITON ALEKSEEVICH YERO-PEGOV.

KAPITON ALEKSEICH. See KAPITON ALEKSEICH RADOMSKY.

KAPITOSHKA. See KAPITON ALEKSEEVICH YEROPEGOV.

KARAMZIN. Nikolay Mikhaylovich KARAMZIN (1766-1826), writer and historian who sought to infuse Westernisms into the Russian literary language to make it more like the language of the aristocracy. His fiction sought to express the noble and virtuous and was a product of the Sentimental movement, while his *HISTORY* is written generally from the point of view of autocracy. ROGOZHIN suggests that the name MYSH-KIN is probably found in KARAMZIN's *HISTORY*.

KARLYCH. See IVANYCH.

KARS. A city in northern Turkey that withstood a lengthy siege by Russian forces in 1855 during the Crimean War (1853-56). (1) IVOLGIN claims to have been wounded at KARS and to still carry the bullets in his chest. (2) LEBEDEV relates a tale of the early Middle Ages in which during a lengthy period of famine one man ate sixty Catholic monks. To lend credibility to his story he asks all to remember the siege of KARS and what those people endured.

KATERINA ALEKSANDROVNA. See KATERINA ALEKSANDROV-NA MYTISHCHEVA.

KATKA. See KATYA.

KATYA (KATKA). NASTASYA FILIPPOVNA's maid.

KELLER. An officer, boxer, and former member of ROGOZHIN's retinue. He is thirty and frequents young progressive circles and accompanies BURDOVSKY, IPPOLIT, and DOKTORENKO when they visit MYSH-IN to demand money for BURDOVSKY as the son of PAVLISHCHEV. He writes an insulting article against MYSHKIN and his inheritance in which he attempts to support BURDOVSKY's claim. Sometime later he comes to MYSHKIN, confesses his sins, and asks for money. When he receives some money, he praises MYSHKIN's mercy and generosity.

KHLUDYAKOV. ROGOZHIN notes that a family named KHLUDYA-KOV once lived in his family's house.

KINDER. When NASTASYA FILIPPOVNA determines to sell herself to the suitor who is the highest bidder, ROGOZHIN desperately tries to raise one hundred thousand rubles through KINDER, TREPALOV, and BISKUP.

KING OF THE JEWS [KOROL IUDEYSKY]. As recorded in the New Testament, the sarcastic appellation given to Jesus CHRIST at His crucifixion. (1) GANYA confesses to MYSHKIN his great desire to get money in order to be somebody and muses that when he has money people will call him the KING OF THE JEWS. (2) GANYA berates PTITSYN for having no ambition and for not wanting to be KING OF THE JEWS. GANYA likely has reference to becoming wealthy like ROTHSCHILD and other Jews and has no Biblical connection.

KISLORODOV. A student acquaintance whom IPPOLIT summons for a frank medical opinion of his disease. KISLORODOV, a materialist and atheist, informs IPPOLIT that he has about one month to live.

KNIF. GANYA wins extensively from KNIF at cards.

PAUL DE KOCK [POL DE KOK]. French novelist (1793-1871) noted for his graphic portrayals of Parisian life. AGLAYA tells MYSHKIN that she reads all of the forbidden books and recently read two novels by PAUL DE KOCK so that she would know everything.

KOLPAKOV. As IVOLGIN reminisces with MYSHKIN about his experiences with his father, he mentions KOLPAKOV, whom MYSHKIN's father punished so severely for theft that he died shortly thereafter. He adds that KOLPAKOV suddenly turned up alive some months later in the same company.

KOLYA. See NIKOLAY ARDALIONOVICH IVOLGIN.

VASILY VASILYICH KONEV. He informs ROGOZHIN of the death of his father.

KORALIA. A woman that LEBEDEV meets through LIKHACHYOV.

KOSTYA. See KOSTYA LEBEDEV.

KRYLOV. Ivan Andreevich KRYLOV (1769-1844), the most famous Russian author of fables, whose works have become classics. (1) In a sarcastic exchange with YEPANCHIN, FERDYSHCHENKO alludes to KRYLOV's fable "THE LION AND THE ASS" and insists that YEPAN-CHIN is the lion while he is the ass. (2) In his satirical exposé of MYSHKIN and his inheritance from PAVLISHCHEV, KELLER observes that the fortune descends upon MYSHKIN in the manner that KRYLOV portrayed in his fable "THE CLOUD," in which the cloud passes over parched earth to empty its rain into the ocean.

KULAKOV. When IVOLGIN takes MYSHKIN to meet SOKOLOVICH, he mistakenly knocks on KULAKOV's door and is told that neither ALEKSANDRA MIKHAYLOVNA nor MARYA ALEKSANDROVNA is at home.

KUPFER. In an attempt to humiliate YEVGENY PAVLOVICH, NASTASYA FILIPPOVNA shouts to him from a carriage that his debts with KUPFER have been temporarily taken care of by ROGOZHIN.

KURMYSHEV (MOLOVTSOV). A proud young officer friend of YEVGENY PAVLOVICH who becomes incensed when NASTASYA FILIPPOVNA speaks insolently to YEVGENY PAVLOVICH about his uncle's suicide and the inheritance he will receive from him. She insists that his uncle KAPITON ALEKSEICH RADOMSKY embezzled a good deal of government money. When KURMYSHEV insults her, she takes his cane and strikes him in the face. MYSHKIN attempts to prevent KURMYSHEV's physical retaliation, and rumors quickly arise that a duel will ensue. YEVGENY PAVLOVICH succeeds in disuading KURMYSHEV's revenge, however.

LACENAIRE [LASENER]. Pierre Francois LACENAIRE (1800-36), French murderer who was the center of a celebrated trial in the 1830s. The vanity and cynicism that he displayed throughout the process became celebrated in romantic society, and his posthumous *Mémoires et révélations* were very popular. When IPPOLIT's attempt at suicide fails because there is no cap in the pistol, YEVGENY PAVLOVICH observes to MYSHKIN that IPPOLIT will likely not make another attempt. He refers to him as a homegrown LACENAIRE for whom crime means nothing.

LARIONOV. In reminiscing about MYSHKIN's father, IVOLGIN notes that MYSHKIN took command of a company following the death of LARIONOV.

LAZARUS [LAZAR]. The brother of Mary and Martha, who was raised from the dead by JESUS CHRIST, as recorded in John 11 in the New Testament. IPPOLIT alludes to the majesty of CHRIST's calling LAZARUS forth from the grave and contrasts it with the picture of CHRIST by HOLBEIN which hangs in ROGOZHIN's house. The picture portrays CHRIST just having been removed from the cross and emphasizes suffering through naturalistic detail.

KOSTYA LEBEDEV. LEBEDEV's son.

LUKYAN TIMOFEEVICH LEBEDEV (LUKYAN TIMOFEICH). A buffoonish civil servant who will do anything for money and who so frequently indulges in self-debasement and confessions that MYSHKIN questions his sincerity. His desire for money and his lack of concern with the impression he makes upon others in getting it are illustrated in his encounters with ROGOZHIN and NASTASYA FILIPPOVNA. He expresses a willingness to dance, walk on his hands, or leave his family in exchange for some of ROGOZHIN's money, and when NASTASYA FILIPPOVNA throws the money ROGOZHIN uses to "buy" her into the fire and challenges GANYA to get it, LEBEDEV begs her on his knees to let him get it instead. He agrees to defend ZAYDLER, a pawnbroker who swindles a poor old woman, because he will realize more money defending him than defending the woman. Because no one respects him he willingly plays the buffoon, but he does like to expound on the APOCALYPSE because the end of the world and the Final Judgment are great levelers of men.

TIMOFEY LUKYANOVICH LEBEDEV. LEBEDEV refers to himself as TIMOFEY LUKYANOVICH instead of LUKYAN TIMOFEEVICH to MYSHKIN until corrected by his family, and he asserts that he does so in order to demean himself.

LYUBOV LEBEDEVA (LYUBOCHKA). LEBEDEV's daughter, a small baby whose birth causes her mother's death.

TANYA LEBEDEVA. LEBEDEV's daughter.

VERA LUKYANOVNA LEBEDEVA. LEBEDEV's daughter, who takes a deep personal interest in MYSHKIN and who is kept apprised of his condition abroad by YEVGENY PAVLOVICH.

YELENA LEBEDEVA. LEBEDEV's wife, who dies in childbirth.

LEGROS [LEGRO]. MYSHKIN discusses capital punishment and recalls LEGROS, a fierce criminal, who cried and begged for mercy when he was taken to the guillotine in France.

LENOCHKA. See LENOCHKA TERENTIEVA.

LEON. See PRINCE LEV NIKOLAEVICH MYSHKIN.

LERMONTOV. Mikhail Yurievich LERMONTOV (1814-41), the foremost Russian romantic writer, who perished in a duel. KOLYA IVOLGIN complains about how people act in society and singles out insults, duels, and begging forgiveness, all of which he refers to as ridiculous despotism. He notes that LERMONTOV based his play *THE MASQUERADE* on emotions such as these and that the result is silly and unnatural. KOLYA does admit, however, that LERMONTOV was quite young when he wrote the play.

"LET MERCY REIGN IN THE COURTS" ["DA TSARSTVUET MILOST V SUDAKH"]. Inexact rendering of part of the manifesto of Tsar Aleksandr II (reigned 1855-81) at the conclusion of the Crimean War in 1856, which reads "let truth and mercy reign in her [Russia's] courts" (pravda i milost da tsarstvuyut v sudakh yeyo"). After LEBEDEV decides to defend the pawnbroker ZAYDLER against the old woman he swindled, he cites these words from a noted lawgiver.

LEV NIKOLAEVICH. See PRINCE LEV NIKOLAEVICH MYSHKIN.

LEV NIKOLAICH. See PRINCE LEV NIKOLAEVICH MYSHKIN.

COUNTESS LEVITSKAYA. An elderly benefactor of YEPANCHIN is reminded that years ago he abandoned his post and ran away to Paris with COUNTESS LEVITSKAYA.

ALEKSASHA LIKHACHYOV. A friend of LEBEDEV with whom he travelled and met many people including NASTASYA FILIPPOVNA. He is now in debtor's prison.

"THE LION AND THE ASS" ["LEV DA OSYOL"]. FERDYSH-CHENKO's inaccurate reference to KRYLOV's fable "The Aged Lion" ("Lev sostarevshysya"), written in 1825. In the fable a lion becomes aged and weak and is compelled to endure the revenge of all the beasts he has tormented in the past. When the ass arrives to claim his revenge, the lion begs for death and states that anything is easier than bearing the insult of an ass. FERDYSHCHENKO sarcastically mentions this fable to YEPAN-CHIN and identifies the general as the lion and himself as the ass. His intent is to ridicule the aging YEPANCHIN, but his own identification with the ass slights him.

LIZAVETA. See YELIZAVETA PROKOFIEVNA YEPANCHINA.

LOMONOSOV. Mikhail Vasilievich LOMONOSOV (1711-65), Russian scholar, poet, and rhetorician who was instrumental in forming the literary language and rules of poetry. His own verse is rather heavy and ornate, and he specialized in the ode. YEVGENY PAVLOVICH asserts that Russian literature is not really Russian with the exceptions of LOMONOSOV,

PUSHKIN, and GOGOL.

LUKYAN TIMOFEEVICH. See LUKYAN TIMOFEEVICH LEBE-DEV.

LUKYAN TIMOFEICH. See LUKYAN TIMOFEEVICH LEBEDEV.

LYUBOCHKA. See LYUBOV LEBEDEVA.

LYUBOV. See LYUBOV LEBEDEVA.

MADAME BOVARY. Novel written in 1856 by Gustave Flaubert (1821-80) which chronicles the life of Emma Bovary from marriage to a mediocre man through adultery and the search for romantic love to misery and suicide. MYSHKIN pursues NASTASYA FILIPPOVNA after she flees just prior to their wedding and traces her to St. Petersburg, where he stops in the room in which she stayed. Inside he finds an opened copy of *MADAME BOVARY* and takes it with him. The novel presages the death she expected when she went with ROGOZHIN.

MALTHUS [MALTUS]. Thomas Robert MALTHUS (1766-1834), English political economist who proposed the theory that population increases geometrically while means of subsistence increase only arithmetically and that as a result war, disease, crime, and moral restraint are necessary curbs on population. LEBEDEV discusses humanitarianism and insists that any efforts to help mankind must have a moral base. He cites MALTHUS as an amoral humanitarian and sarcastically refers to him as a friend of mankind.

MARFA. NASTASYA FILIPPOVNA's cook.

MARFA BORISOVNA. See MARFA BORISOVNA TERENTIEVA.

MARFA NIKITISHNA. One of MYSHKIN's teachers when he was under the protection of PAVLISHCHEV.

MARIE [MARI]. A poor girl ill with consumption who lives with her aged mother in the Swiss village in which MYSHKIN is under the care of SCHNEIDER. She is seduced by a Frenchman and runs away with him only to be abandoned after a week. When she returns home she is rejected by her mother, who also turns the village against her, and she is ultimately blamed for her mother's death. MYSHKIN comes to love her in a pure, brotherly way and converts the children of the village to her and her virtues.

Through their love they are able to make her final days pleasant.

MARLINSKY. Pseudonym of Aleksandr Aleksandrovich Bestuzhev (1797 -1837), Russian author of romantic adventure novels. One of the rabble that enters NASTASYA FILIPPOVNA's apartment accompanying ROGO-ZHIN is a retired second lieutenant whom ROGOZHIN found in the street asking for a handout in the manner of MARLINSKY. Such a manner is artificial, strained, elevated, and passionate.

MARYA ALEKSANDROVNA. See ALEKSANDRA MIKHAYLOV-NA.

PRINCESS MARYA ALEKSEEVNA. In FAMUSOV's concluding monologue from *Woe From Wit (Gore ot uma)*, written by Aleksandr Sergeevich Griboedov (1795-1829) in 1822-24, he laments the problems he has had with the liberal young Chatsky and expressed concern about what PRINCESS MARYA ALEKSEEVNA will have to say regarding the whole affair. She represents the epitome of aristocratic social opinion. As IPPOLIT gives his confused explanation, he alludes to her scolding judgments as he laughingly ponders the effect his words will have.

MARYA PETROVNA. See MARYA PETROVNA SUTUGOVA.

MARYA PETROVNA. See MARYA PETROVNA ZUBKOVA.

MARYA SEMYONOVNA. See MARYA SEMYONOVNA ISHCHEN-KO.

THE MASQUERADE [MASKARAD]. A romantic play in verse written by Mikhail LERMONTOV in 1835. The play chronicles the fate of Arbenin, a romantic egotist who poisons his wife when he suspects that she has betrayed him and who goes insane when he learns of her innocence. KOLYA IVOLGIN complains that society seems to operate on high emotions, insults, and duels and that LERMONTOV based *THE MAS-QUERADE* on just such emotions. He feels that the result is silly and unnatural, but admits that LERMONTOV wrote the play when he was quite young.

MATRYONA. A servant in the IVOLGIN household.

MATRYONA. A servant mentioned by IPPOLIT who is probably attached to the TERENTIEV family.

MAVRA. One of the YEPANCHIN's domestic servants.

"THE MEMORY IS FRESH BUT HARDLY TO BE BELIEVED" ["SVEZHO PREDANIE, A VERITSYA S TRUDOM"]. A line from the comedy *Woe From Wit (Gore ot uma),* written 1822-24 by Aleksandr Sergeevich Griboedov (1795-1829). In KELLER's slanderous article about MYSHKIN's inheriting a fortune he notes that PAVLISHCHEV, simply called P., owned four thousand serfs and did nothing but loaf and live off them. Such a situation he describes with the anecdote "THE MEMORY IS FRESH BUT HARDLY TO BE BELIEVED."

MEYER. The owner of the house adjacent to IPPOLIT's lodgings. Ill with consumption, IPPOLIT spends hours looking out his window at the red brick wall surrounding MEYER's house and being depressed by its aura of finality.

"THE MIGHTY LION, TERROR OF THE FORESTS,//HAS LOST HIS STRENGTH FROM AGE" ["MOGUCHY LEV, GROZA LESOV//OT STAROSTI LISHILSYA SILY"]. Inexact rendering of the first two lines of KRYLOV's "The Aged Lion," which is mistakenly identified by FERDYSHCHENKO as "THE LION AND THE ASS." In the original the second line reads "Overtaken with age, he lost his strength" ("Postignut starostyu, lishilsya sily"). FERDYSHCHENKO quotes these two lines to YEPANCHIN as he sarcastically identifies YEPANCHIN with the lion of the fable.

MILLEVOYE [MILVUA]. Charles Hubert MILLEVOYE (1782-1816), French poet. IPPOLIT complains during his confession that MYSHKIN and the others present would rather have him recite noble verse than commit suicide. He obliges by reciting a quatrain which begins "O, PUISSENT VOIR VOTRE BEAUTE SACREE" and attributes it to MILLEVOYE.

MOLIERE. Pen name of Jean Baptiste Poquelin (1622-73) who became the foremost French comic dramatist. He likely has no rivals in the comic exposition of human foibles. In the author's discussion of the plethora of ordinary people in society he cites GEORGE DANDIN as an example and praises MOLIERE as his creator.

MOLOVTSOV. KURMYSHEV, the young officer who almost challenges MYSHKIN to a duel, is referred to as MOLOVTSOV by KELLER, who volunteers to be MYSHKIN's second.

THOMAS MORUS [TOMAS MORUS]. Latin name of Sir THOMAS MORE (1478-1535), English statesman, humanist, author, and saint. A staunch Catholic, he broke with King Henry VIII over papal supremacy in England and was executed when he would not swear to the King's superiority over foreign kings and the pope. LEBEDEV admits to baseness in many of his dealings and tells MYSHKIN to punish the heart but spare the beard. He attributes these words to MORUS, who in fact did tell his executioner to avoid his beard since it was pure and had never committed heresy.

MUHAMMAD [MAGOMET]. In Arabic "the praised one," a name adopted by the founder of Islam (570-632). MYSHKIN notes that the moment of bliss he experiences prior to an epileptic seizure must be like the moment MUHAMMAD experienced in a seizure when he saw the realms of ALLAH.

"MY NIGHT AT THE PRICE OF [YOUR] LIFE" ["TSENOYU ZHIZNI NOCH MOYU"]. Quotation from the poem about Cleopatra in Aleksandr PUSHKIN's "Egyptian Nights" (Yegipetskie nochi"), written in 1835. The poem relates how Cleopatra auctioned herself off in exchange for the life of the winner. Just prior to NASTASYA FILIPPOVNA's scheduled wedding to MYSHKIN and her flight with ROGOZHIN, several men admire her beauty. One comments that he would sell his soul for her and then quotes "MY NIGHT AT THE PRICE OF YOUR LIFE."

LEV NIKOLAEVICH MYSHKIN. IVOLGIN mistakenly refers to MYSH-KIN's father NIKOLAY LVOVICH as LEV NIKOLAEVICH.

PRINCE LEV NIKOLAEVICH MYSHKIN (LEV NIKOLAICH, LEON). A twenty six year old noble of meager circumstances who has just returned from Switzerland, where he was under the care of DR. SCHNEIDER for mental problems and epilepsy. Because of this he refers to himself as an idiot. He is the last of his line, and his illness has made him incapable of producing any children. When he arrives in Russia, he goes to the home of YEPAN-CHI, whose wife YELIZAVETA PROKOFIEVNA is a distant relative, to seek help in making his way in a new life. He becomes acquainted with AGLAYA, and after taking a room with the IVOLGINS, with NAS-TASYA FILIPPOVNA. The two women form the focal point of his life and he is characterized through his interactions with them. He comes to love them both—NASTASYA FILIPPOVNA because he has compassion for her and sees a need to build her self-concept and prevent her destruction, and AGLAYA because he has compassion for her and sees in her a new hope and a new life. He is so good and such a moral force that he seldom sees anything wrong with anything and frequently naively elevates others and lowers himself. When he receives an inheritance, naiveté prompts him to give away money to all who ask, irrespective of the justness of their request. His desire to help NASTASYA FILIPPOVNA draws him into conflict with ROGOZHIN, who attempts to murder him and stops only when MYSH-KIN has an epileptic seizure. He is ulitmately compelled to choose NASTASYA FILIPPOVNA over AGLAYA, when the former haughtily insists that he make a choice. He is motivated by a feeling that she needs him more than does AGLAYA and by the fact that she faints when it appears that he will follow AGLAYA. A wedding is arranged, but NASTASYA FILIPPOVNA, seeking debasement, suffering, and death, flees with ROGOZHIN just prior to the ceremony. His search for her leads him to ROGOZHIN's house, where he finds her corpse, stabbed through the heart and presided over by a lone droning fly. He tearfully comforts ROGOZHIN as a father would a child, but his mind snaps under the strain, and he is returned to Switzerland for more treatment. MYSHKIN is the embodiment of Christian love and kindness, but his naiveté renders his practical influence questionable. In addition to advocating morality he speaks out on the Roman Catholic Church, which he views as ANTICHRIST and as socialism masked as religion.

NIKOLAY LVOVICH MYSHKIN (NIKOLAY PETROVICH). MYSH-KIN's father.

KATERINA ALEKSANDROVNA MYTISHCHEVA. In TOTSKY's story of the worst thing he ever did he notes that ANFISA ALEKSEEVNA ORDYNTSEVA's rival in everything is KATERINA ALEKSANDROV-NA MYTISHCHEVA.

MYTOVTSOVA. IVOLGIN mistakenly asserts that NASTASYA FILIP-POVNA has lodgings with MYTOVTSOVA.

PRINCE N. A guest at the YEPANCHIN house on the evening that MYSHKIN is presented to society. He is forty five, a renowned conqueror of women's hearts, and views himself as the sun standing far above the YEPANCHINS.

NAPOLEON. NAPOLEON I Bonaparte (1769-1821), emperor of France following the French Revolution and temporary conqueror of much of Europe. (1) IPPOLIT asks his school "enemy" BAKHMUTOV to intercede with his uncle, an important official, on behalf of a poor doctor to whom

IPPOLIT returned a lost wallet. IPPOLIT is convinced that BAKH-MUTOV will not refuse him as an enemy and likens the latter's response to NAPOLEON's being forced to deal with his English conquerors. (2) AGLAYA asks MYSHKIN if he ever fantasizes about being a fieldmarshall and defeating NAPOLEON. MYSHKIN admits that his fantasies involve beating the Austrians. (3) LEBEDEV insists to IVOLGIN that he was one of NAPOLEON's pages in 1812. (4) In response to LEBEDEV's claim that he was one of NAPOLEON's pages, IVOLGIN concocts an elaborate tale in which as a young boy he becomes not only a page following the death of BARON DE BAZANCOURT, but also NAPOLEON's major advisor on critical issues. (5) IVOLGIN claims that although NAPOLEON took him as a page in order to ingratiate himself with the Russians, the emperor loved him sincerely. (6) MYSHKIN has a light beard in the style of NAPOLEON.

NASTASYA FILIPPOVNA. See NASTASYA FILIPPOVNA BARASH-KOVA.

NASTYA. See NASTASYA FILIPPOVNA BARASHKOVA.

NATALYA NIKITISHNA. One of MYSHKIN's childhood teachers on PAVLISHCHEV's estate.

NELATION [NELATON]. Auguste NELATON (1807-73), French surgeon and professor of surgery. IVOLGIN insists to MYSHKIN that during the siege of SEVASTOPOL, PIROGOV dropped everything to telegraph NELATON in Paris about the thirteen bullets in IVOLGIN's chest.

NIKIFOR. YEPANCHIN's orderly in his account of the worst thing that he ever did.

NIKOLAY ANDREEVICH. See NIKOLAY ANDREEVICH PAVLISH-CHEV.

NIKOLAY ANDREICH. See NIKOLAY ANDREEVICH PAVLISH-CHEV.

NIKOLAY ARDALIONOVICH. See NIKOLAY ARDALIONOVICH IVOLGIN.

NIKOLAY PETROVICH. When IVOLGIN tries to demonstrate how close he was to MYSHKIN's father, NIKOLAY LVOVICH, he mistakenly calls him NIKOLAY PETROVICH.

NIL ALEKSEEVICH. An official under whom LEBEDEV once worked. On one occasion LEBEDEV discusses the APOCALYPSE with him, and he dies shortly thereafter. LEBEDEV claims to have predicted his death.

NINA ALEKSANDROVNA. See NINA ALEKSANDROVNA IVOL-GINA.

NORMA. IPPOLIT's dog. In his dream it bites a hideous scorpion-like creature and is bitten in return.

NOZDRYOV. A character in Nikolay GOGOL's *DEAD SOULS* who is characterized by his coarse gaiety, bullying, and drinking. GANYA disgustedly reacts to IPPOLIT, cites his vanity and gross naiveté, and refers to him as a PIROGOV and a NOZDRYOV in a tragedy.

"NURSE, WHERE IS YOUR GRAVE?" ["NYANYA, GDE TVOYA MOGILA!"]. Citation from the third part of an unfinished poem entitled "Humor" ("Yumor"), written 1840-77 by Nikolay Platonovich Ogaryov (1813-77), Russian publicist, poet, and revolutionary exile. Prior to his first stroke IVOLGIN cites many excerpts from literature and asks his son KOLYA where they are to be found. This exercise is part of a disjointed and confused effort to justify his actions. He asks KOLYA for the source of "NURSE, WHERE IS YOUR GRAVE?" but KOLYA does not know.

PLATON ORDYNTSEV. In TOTSKY's story about the worst thing he ever did, he stops by the estate of PLATON ORDYNTSEV, where the drama of the camelias is subsequently played out.

ANFISA ALEKSEEVNA ORDYNTSEVA. PLATON ORDYNTSEV's wife in TOTSKY's account of the worst thing he ever did in his life. Under the influence of DUMAS' *LA DAME AUX CAMELIAS* ANFISA ALEKSEEVNA's birthday celebration results in a drama of camelias. See SOFYA BESPALOVA.

OSTERMAN. Andrey Ivanovich OSTERMAN, born Heinrich Johann Friedrich OSTERMAN (1686-1747), Russian political figure and diplomat. He exerted pivotal influence in both internal and external affairs until the ascension of Elizabeth I in 1741, when he was arrested and sentenced first to death and then to permanent exile. In discussing his impending death with MYSHKIN, IPPOLIT notes the noble death of STEPAN GLEBOV and determines to die just as gloriously. He also mentions the ignoble death of OSTERMAN, whose resurrection will not be particularly meaningful.

P. KELLER's veiled allusion to PAVLISHCHEV in his satirical attack on MYSHKIN and his inheritance.

PAFNUTIEVNA. A maid who serves ROGOZHIN's mother.

PAFNUTY. Founder of a hermitage in the Kostromsky District in the fourteenth century. When YEPANCHIN wants to sample the handwriting of the newly arrived MYSHKIN, the latter writes "The humble abbot PAF-NUTY affixed his signature" ("Smirenny igumen PAFNUTY ruku prilozhil") and insists that it is the signature of PAFNUTY himself.

PAPUSHIN. A bankrupt Moscow merchant whose daughter, MYSHKIN's aunt, leaves MYSHKIN a fortune.

PAPUSHIN. PAPUSHIN's wealthy brother, who leaves all of his money to his niece who subsequently leaves it to MYSHKIN.

PARFYON SEMYONOVICH. See PARFYON SEMYONOVICH RO-GOZHIN.

PARFYON SEMYONYCH. See PARFYON SEMYONOVICH ROGO-ZHIN.

PASHA. NASTASYA FILIPPOVNA's maid.

PRINCESS PATSKAYA. A woman that LIKHACHYOV introduces to LEBEDEV.

NIKOLAY ANDREEVICH PAVLISHCHEV (NIKOLAY ANDREICH). MYSHKIN's benefactor, who helps many people, including BURDOVSKY and his mother. BURDOVSKY uses this support and the claim that he is PAVLISHCHEV's illegitimate son to try to get money from MYSHKIN's inheritance. PAVLISHCHEV ultimately converts to Roman Catholicism and becomes a JESUIT to the great horror of MYSHKIN.

"PERHAPS AT MY SORROWFUL DEMISE//THE SMILE OF LOVE WILL SHINE IN PARTING" ["I MOZHET BYT, NA MOY ZAKAT PECHALNY//BLESNYOT LYUBOV ULYBKOYU PROSHCHAL-NOY"]. The concluding couplet of Aleksandr PUSHKIN's "Elegy" ("Elegia', written in 1830. IPPOLIT complains that MYSHKIN does not take him seriously and accuses MYSHKIN of ascribing these verses to him.

PETER [PYOTR]. PETER I or PETER the Great (1672-1725), tsar of Russia from 1689 until his death. His reign saw the construction of St. Petersburg and the opening of active contact with the West. In discussing how he will face death IPPOLIT selects two examples from the reign of PETER. He mentions STEPAN GLEBOV, who, though tortured and impaled, died nobly, and the diplomat OSTERMAN, whose intrigues earned him a death sentence commuted to life imprisonment.

PETROV. A schoolboy friend of KOLYA and KOSTYA who gives them some money to buy SCHLOSSER's *HISTORY*. They purchase instead a hedgehog and an ax.

PETYA. See PETYA VORKHOVSKOY.

PIROGOV. IVOLGIN explains to MYSHKIN that during the siege of SEVASTOPOL in the Crimean War PIROGOV dropped everything to telegraph to NELATON in Paris about the thirteen bullets in IVOLGIN's chest. Dostoevsky could have in mind Nikolay Ivanovich PIROGOV (1810-81), one of the greatest Russian doctors and pedagogues of the nineteenth century and the outstanding authority on battlefield surgery. PIROGOV was present during the siege of SEVASTOPOL and coordinated medical care of the wounded.

PIROGOV. A vain and cocky character in Nikolay GOGOL's story *Nevsky prospect* written in 1835. He is an öfficer and self-styled cavalier who pursues a German woman for her favors, only to be roundly beaten by her enraged husband. In discussing the ordinary and mediocre people who compose the majority of society the author mentions PIROGOV, who is characterized by a brazen naiveté and the unflinching confidence of a stupid person in himself. GANYA subsequently refers to IPPOLIT as a PIRO-GOV and a NOZDRYOV in a tragedy.

PODKOLYOSIN. The central character of Nikolay GOGOL's play *The Marriage (Zhenitba)*, published in 1842. He frantically jumps out of a window and escapes just prior tó his wedding. In discussing average people like PTITSYN, VARYA, and GANYA the author praises GOGOL for the creation of PODKOLYOSIN, who provides a name and an embodiment for the many unoriginal and mediocre people seen every day.

PODKUMOV. In trying to be nice to YEPANCHIN's benefactor, MYSH-KIN praises him for helping the student PODKUMOV and for saving the civil servant SHVABRIN from exile.

POGODIN. Mikhail Petrovich POGODIN (1800-75), Russian historian, writer, and journalist. After YEPANCHIN admires MYSHKIN's handwriting, MYSHKIN asks him if he has POGODIN's publication. He likely has in mind *Models of Ancient Russo-Slavonic Writing (Obraztsy slavyano-russkogo drevlepisania)* which was published by POGODIN in 1840-41.

THE POOR KNIGHT [BEDNY RYTSAR]. Central figure of a ballad by Aleksandr PUSHKIN written in 1829, titled by the first line, "THERE ONCE LIVED A POOR KNIGHT" ("ZHIL NA SVETE RYTSAR BEDNY"). The ballad relates the story of a knight who sees the Virgin Mary in a vision and who subsequently renounces all things to devote his life to her service. (1) AGLAYA speaks at length about THE POOR KNIGHT and quotes the ballad. She notes that he is a more serious figure than DON QUIXOTE and is characterized by the vision of an ideal and by blind devotion to it. She perceives MYSHKIN in the role of THE POOR KNIGHT and both respects and condemns him for it. (2) YELIZAVETA PROKOFIEVNA demands to know from MYSHKIN what the allusions to THE POOR KNIGHT that she has been hearing mean, but he disclaims any knowledge of the subject. (3) After AGLAYA denounces MYSHKIN for lowering himself before people to which he is superior, KOLYA shouts out THE POOR KNIGHT! AGLAYA resents MYSHKIN's debasement because her pride views it as a weakness. (4) ALEKSANDRA tells her mother, YELIZAVETA PROKOFIEVNA, that AGLAYA's behavior toward MYSHKIN is largely an extension of her making fun of him as THE POOR KNIGHT.

PORTHOS [PORTOS]. One of the famous trio in *Les Trois mousquetaires (The Three Musketeers)*, a novel written by Alexandre Dumas, père (1802-70) in 1844. PORTHOS is very strong but not overly intelligent. IVOLGIN refers to himself, YEPANCHIN, and NIKOLAY LVOVICH MYSHKIN as ATHOS, PORTHOS, and ARAMIS respectively.

SERYOZHA PROTUSHIN. When his father becomes furious over his using money intended to pay a debt to buy NASTASYA FILIPPOVNA earrings, ROGOZHIN borrows some money from SERYOZHA PROTUSHIN so that he can leave town and escape the consequences.

PROUDHON [PRUDON]. Pierre Jospeh PROUDHON (1809-65), French socialist and anarchist. He was an ardent reformer and was very critical of private property, church, and state. (1) YEVGENY PAVLOVICH comments that the ideology of people like IPPOLIT could easily stem from the right of power doctrine which he attributes to PROUDHON. (2) After listening to IPPOLIT's "My Indispensable Explanation," KOLYA observes that he would have expected such a document from a VOLTAIRE, ROUSSEAU, or PROUDHON, but for IPPOLIT to have written it was an exercise in pride and vanity.

IVAN PETROVICH PTITSYN (VANKA). A very unoriginal and ordinary young man who escapes poverty by becoming a pawnbroker. He marries VARYA following NASTASYA FILIPPOVNA's humiliation of GANYA and has the entire family move in with him.

VARVARA ARDALIONOVNA PTITSYNA. VARVARA ARDALIONOVNA IVOLGINA's married name.

"O, PUISSENT VOIR VOTRE BEAUTE SACREE." "Oh, may they see your sacred beauty," slightly inaccurate rendering of the first four lines taken from "Ode imitée de plusieurs psaumes" ("An Ode in Imitation of Several Psalms") written in 1780 by the French poet Nicolas Joseph Laurent Gilbert (1750-80) and mistakenly attributed by IPPOLIT to MILLEVOYE. IPPOLIT laments that MYSHKIN and others would rather have him recite noble verses than commit suicide, and he responds by sarcastically reciting a quatrain.

PUSHKIN. Aleksandr Sergeevich PUSHKIN (1799-1837), the leading Russian writer of his age, who is widely regarded as the father of modern Russian literature. (1) AGLAYA identifies the verses she quotes about THE POOR KNIGHT as being by PUSHKIN. (2) The YEPANCHINS do not have the works of PUSHKIN in their home, but after YELIZAVETA PROKOFIEVNA hears AGLAYA read the poem about THE POOR KNIGHT, she wants them purchased immediately. (3) LEBEDEV offers to sell his edition of PUSHKIN edited by ANNENKOV to the YEPANCHINS. (4) LEBEDEV claims that the new progressive generation of people like BURDOVSKY, DOKTORENKO, and IPPOLIT are not interested in subjects such as PUSHKIN. (5) YEVGENY PAVLOVICH insists that Russian literature is not really Russian, with the exception of LOMONOSOV, PUSHKIN, and GOGOL. (6) After MYSHKIN tries to defend NASTASYA FILIPPOVNA from KURMYSHEV's retaliation for her insults, it is rumored that KURMYSHEV will challenge MYSHKIN to a duel. AGLAYA gives MYSHKIN some instruction in duels and pistols and mentions that she would never run away from a duel. When MYSHKIN states that few people are ever killed in duels, AGLAYA counters by mentioning that PUSKHIN was fatally shot. (7) MYSHKIN recalls that he and ROGOZHIN had read PUSHKIN together and that it was evident that ROGOZHIN did not know the name of PUSHKIN nor who he was.

PYOTR ZAKHARYCH. A former colleague of LEBEDEV.

KAPITON ALEKSEICH RADOMSKY. A seventy year old gourmet and lavish socialite who suddenly commits suicide because he is discovered to have embezzled a great deal of government money. He is the uncle of YEVGENY PAVLOVICH and leaves his nephew a sizable inheritance.

YEVGENY PAVLOVICH RADOMSKY (YEVGENY PAVLYCH). A twenty eight year old officer and progressive thinker who is introduced into the YEPANCHIN household by his distant relative PRINCE SHCH. and PRINCESS BELOKONSKAYA. His acquaintance with the family results in an interest in AGLAYA, but his formal proposal is rejected. He seldom speaks seriously, and his words are usually punctuated with irony. This flippancy is carried over into his actions, and he confesses to MYSHKIN that he would like to do one absolutely noble deed in life without ulterior motive, but that he is not quite ready to do it. He endures two insults from NASTASYA FILIPPOVNA who exposes his indebtedness to BISKUP and KUPFER and his uncle's suicide and embezzlement. He vocalizes MYSHKIN's failures and explains to the prince the series of unfortunate actions in his relationship with NASTASYA FILIPPOVNA and AGLAYA. Following NASTASYA FILIPPOVNA's murder he takes an interest in MYSHKIN, returns him to Switzerland for care, and writes to VERA LEBEDEVA regularly about his condition. His most important ideological statement is his indictment of the falseness of Russian liberals and socialists who want to destroy Russia itself and not simply the old order of things.

PARFYON SEMYONOVICH ROGOZHIN (PARFYON SEMYON-YCH). A passionate man of twenty seven who is totally obsessed with NASTASYA FILIPPOVNA. He incurs his father's wrath by using money intended for payment of a debt to buy earrings for NASTASYA FILIP-POVNA, and he is compelled to flee his family. Only when his father dies does he return home to claim his inheritance and renew his pursuit of NASTASYA FILIPPOVNA. Hearing that she might marry GANYA, he offers to buy her and works feverishly to raise one hundred thousand rubles. She uses this money to humiliate GANYA and then commences a rowdy life with ROGOZHIN and his motley retinue. ROGOZHIN is forced to devote his efforts to trying to commit her to marry him, competing with

MYSHKIN for her, and pursuing her when she runs away from him. He endures torture and humiliation from her and both loves and hates her. His conflict with MYSHKIN becomes acute, and even though they exchange crosses, he attempts to murder him. He takes NASTASYA FILIPPOVNA away at her request just prior to her scheduled marriage to MYSHKIN and then murders her. He brings MYSHKIN to his house, shows him the corpse, and slips into a disconsolate and feverish agitation that results in brain fever. When he recovers he is exiled to Siberia for fifteen years.

SEMYON PARFYONOVICH ROGOZHIN. ROGOZHIN's father. He is furious when his son buys NASTASYA FILIPPOVNA earrings with the money he intends for repayment of a debt, and ROGOZHIN is so afraid that he runs away. He goes to NATASYA FILIPPOVNA and begs her to return his son's gift whereupon she throws the earrings at him. When he dies, he leaves a fortune.

SEMYON SEMYONOVICH ROGOZHIN (SEMYON SEMYONYCH, SENKA). ROGOZHIN's brother, who turns his father against him. He is elated to get all of the inheritance when ROGOZHIN is convicted of NASTASYA FILIPPOVNA's murder.

PRINCES DE ROHAN [PRINTSESSA DE ROGAN]. An ancient and noble French family. KELLER notes that MYSHKIN should be expected to marry someone like a PRINCESS DE ROHAN because of his noble lineage.

ROTHSCHILD [ROTSHILD]. A family of Jewish bankers who dominated European finance in the nineteenth century and became synonymous with great wealth. (1) In his literary explanation IPPOLIT mentions that he has no sympathy for people like SURIKOV who live in poverty, lose their families, and endure other similar hardships and deprivations. He insists that they should become like ROTHSCHILD. (2) In categorizing mediocre and ordinary people the author includes those with wealth, but not the ROTHSCHILD kind of wealth. (3) GANYA upbraids PTITSYN for having no ambition and for not wanting to be a ROTHSCHILD. PTITSYN responds that he has known for several years, since his youth, that he would never be a ROTHSCHILD and that it does not concern him in the least.

ROUSSEAU [RUSSO]. Jean Jacques ROUSSEAU (1712-78), French author, philosopher, and liberal political theorist. KOLYA comments that had VOLTAIRE, ROUSSEAU, or PROUDHON written what IPPOLIT did in his "My Indispensable Explanation" about rejection of religion and advocacy of the will, it would not have surprised him, but for IPPOLIT to write such things is an exercise in pride and ego.

ROUSTAN [RUSTAN]. NAPOLEON's valet and bodyguard (1780-1845). In IVOLGIN's incredible story of his service as NAPOLEON's page he notes that one of his few duties was to accompany NAPOLEON when he went for rides. He adds that ROUSTAN, who always slept very soundly and snored, and DAVOUT usually rode out with them.

S. A well-known atheist and scholar with whom MYSHKIN once had a conversation.

SALAZKIN. MYSHKIN receives a letter from SALAZKIN while in Switzerland informing him of the possibility of a large inheritance.

SAMSON. LEBEDEV mentions that the name of COUNTESS DU BARRY's executioner was SAMSON.

IVAN DMITRICH SAVELIEV. A merchant who desires to buy ROGOZHIN's copy of HOLBEIN's painting of CHRIST.

SAVELY. ORDYNTSEV's coachman in TOTSKY's story of the worst thing he ever did. It is SAVELY who takes TOTSKY to get the red camelias before PETYA VORKHOVSKOY can.

SCHLOSSER [SHLOSSER]. Friedrich Christoph SCHLOSSER (1776-1861), eminent German historian whose work comprises several volumes. PETROV asks his schoolmates KOLYA and KOSTYA to buy a copy of SCHLOSSER's *HISTORY*.

SCHNEIDER [SHNEYDER]. MYSHKIN's doctor in Switzerland who treats him with cold water and gymnastics.

SEMYON IVANOVICH. See SEMYON IVANOVICH ISHCHENKO.

SEMYON PARFYONOVICH. See SEMYON PARFYONOVICH RO-GOZHIN.

SEMYON SEMYONOVICH. See SEMYON SEMYONOVICH ROGO-ZHIN.

SEMYON SEMYONYCH. See SEMYON SEMYONOVICH ROGO-ZHIN.

SENKA. See SEMYON SEMYONOVICH ROGOZHIN.

SERYOZHKA. See SERYOZHKA PROTUSHIN.

SEVASTOPOL [SEVASTOPL]. A city and port in the Crimea which was the object of an eleven-month siege 1854-55 by the French and English during the Crimean War. IVOLGIN explains to MYSHKIN how during the siege of SEVASTOPOL, PIROGOV dropped everything to telegraph NELATON in Paris about the thirteen bullets in IVOLGIN's chest.

PRINCE SHCH. A progressive thirty five year old from Moscow who becomes acquainted with the YEPANCHIN family and proposes to ADELAIDA.

SHVABRIN. In trying to be nice to YEPANCHIN's benefactor, MYSH-KIN praises him for helping the student PODKUMOV and for saving the civil servant SHVABRIN from exile.

SKOPTSY. A small secretive offshoot from the Russian Orthodox Church that practiced castration in order to renounce the body. (1) ROGOZHIN notes that members of the SKOPTSY once lived in his family's house. (2) NASTASYA FILIPPOVNA observes that it would be possible for ROGOZHIN himself to join the SKOPTSY.

SODOM. As recorded in Genesis 18-19 in the Old Testament, a city which together with Gomorrah was destroyed by Jehovah because of its wicked-ness. The term has come to mean wickedness and chaos. (1) YEPANCHIN refers to the events at NASTASYA FILIPPOVNA's birthday celebration as SODOM: ROGOZHIN brings money to "buy" NASTASYA FILIP-POVNA; she throws the money in the fire and challenges GANYA to get it; and she refuses GANYA's proposal at MYSHKIN's suggestion. (2) When NASTASYA FILIPPOVNA is properly paid for by ROGOZHIN and goes away with him, TOTSKY dubs the affair SODOM.

SOKOLOVICH. IVOLGIN boasts to MYSHKIN that SOKOLOVICH is one of his friends who owes him everything, but when he tries to take MYSHKIN to meet him, he cannot find the house.

SOLOVYOV. Sergey Mikhaylovich SOLOVYOV (1820-79), Russian historian. (1) MYSHKIN notices SOLOVYOV's *HISTORY* opened and marked on ROGOZHIN's desk. (2) NASTASYA FILIPPOVNA recommends SOLOVYOV's *HISTORY* to ROGOZHIN as a way to obtain education.

COUNTESS SOTSKAYA. In TOTSKY's story of the worst thing he ever did he mentions that SOFYA BESPALOVA and COUNTESS SOTSKAYA plan to bring bouquets of white camelias to ANFISA ALEKSEEVNA ORDYNTSEVA's birthday ball. As a result the hostess jealously desires a bouquet of red camelias.

STEPAN. See STEPAN VORKHOVSKOY.

THE STOCK MARKET RECORD [BIRZHEVYE VEDOMOSTI]. Political, economic and literary newspaper issued 1861-1917 in St. Petersburg. ROGOZHIN brings the one hundred thousand rubles to buy NASTASYA FILIPPOVNA wrapped in *THE STOCK MARKET RECORD*.

IVAN FOMICH SURIKOV. An acquaintance of IPPOLIT's family whom he mentions in his "My Indispensable Explanation." SURIKOV is wretched and beset by poverty. He lost his wife because he could not buy medicine, had a child freeze to death, and saw his oldest daughter go to work to support the family. IPPOLIT blames SURIKOV for all of his problems and says that he should have become a ROTHSCHILD.

SUTUGINA. See MARYA PETROVNA SUTUGOVA.

MARYA PETROVNA SUTUGOVA (SUTUGINA). In IVOLGIN's confused story of KAPITON YEROPEGOV, MARYA PETROVNA SUTUGOVA, later called SUTUGINA, is KAPITON's wife.

"TALITHA CUMI" ["TALIFA KUMI"]. "Damsel, I say unto thee, arise," the Aramaic words that JESUS CHRIST spoke to the daughter of Jairus as He called her forth from the dead, as recorded in Mark 5:41 in the New Testament. IPPOLIT notes the majestic impression created by these words and also the raising of LAZARUS and contrasts it to HOLBEIN's picture of CHRIST, which hangs in ROGOZHIN's house. The picture portrays CHRIST just having been removed from the cross and emphasizes suffering through naturalistic detail.

TALLEYRAND [TALEYRAN]. Charles Maurice de TALLEYRAND-Périgord (1754-1838), French statesman who helped to restore the Bourbon monarchy following NAPOLEON's fall and who represented his country at the Congress of Vienna. LEBEDEV claims to MYSHKIN that he was born a TALLEYRAND and cannot understand how he remained only a LEBEDEV.

TANYA. See TANYA LEBEDEVA.

TARASOV. The name of the building in which those sent to debtor's prison are placed. IVOLGIN is sent there by TERENTIEVA and quickly makes new friends.

CAPTAIN TERENTIEV. A deceased subordinate and friend of IVOLGIN who is IPPOLIT's father.

IPPOLIT TERENTIEV. Eighteen year old member of the new generation who is terminally ill with consumption. Like his fellow progressives he professes to reject aggressively everything except his own interests. He is vain and very sensitive and is embarrassed when he shows emotion or genuine feeling. At MYSHKIN's birthday party he anxiously reads to all present "My Indispensable Explanation," which he comically and vainly subtitles "APRES MOI LE DELUGE!" In his explanation he notes that because of his illness he is restricted much of the time to looking out his window at MEYER's red brick wall and being depressed by its aura of finality and permanence. He indicates that he will commit suicide rather than simply die of his illness because suicide will be an act of will which he regards as supreme. Consonant with his set he renounces religion completely and disclaims a belief in an after-life, although he admits that it probably exists. Following the reading of his explanation and to the accompaniment of the cynicism of those present, he attempts to shoot himself. The gun misfires because of the lack of a cap, and IPPOLIT becomes hysterical and begs people to believe that he did not deliberately forget it. He deeply laments that he is dishonored forever, but he does not make another attempt on his life and lets the disease run its course. IPPOLIT is beset by the contradictions typical of his youth—zeal and naiveté: he enlists BAKHMUTOV to help a poor country doctor to whom he returned a lost wallet, yet he insists that SURIKOV is responsible for his own plight and is undeserving of help; he craves attention and acceptance, yet is too proud to seek or accept it; he praises reason, yet is emotional. IPPOLIT is also an integral figure in the novel's symbolism: he responds vividly to HOLBEIN's picture of CHRIST; he views ROGOZHIN as a symbol of evil and sees a vision of him on the evening of his discussion of evil, which he conceptualizes as a tarantula (the tarantula and ROGOZHIN are thus equated); he dreams of a terrible scorpion-like creature, symbol of generalized evil, as well as the evil of IPPOLIT's own rationalism.

LENOCHKA TERENTIEVA. MARFA BORISOVNA's eight year old daughter.

MARFA BORISOVNA TERENTIEVA. The forty year old widow of the late CAPTAIN TERENTIEV who is always heavily powdered and rouged and who has been on very friendly terms with IVOLGIN. She finally attacks IVOLGIN for wasting all her money and possessions and for leaving her nothing to feed her poor orphans, and she has him committed to debtor's prison.

TERENTYICH. When IPPOLIT returns the dropped wallet to the impoverished country doctor, he passes through the room of TERENTYICH to find the owner. TERENTYICH does little but lie and drink.

"THERE ONCE LIVED A POOR KNIGHT" ["ZHIL NA SVETE RYTSAR BEDNY"]. A ballad written by Aleksandr PUSHKIN in 1829. AGLAYA quotes the poem and equates THE POOR KNIGHT with MYSHKIN, whom she both loves and resents for his meekness and idealism.

JULES THIBAUD [ZHUL TIBO]. The children's teacher in the Swiss village in which MYSHKIN is treated by SCHNEIDER. He resents MYSHKIN's success with the children and his attitude that one should learn from children and not vice versa.

TIMOFEY FYODOROVICH. See TIMOFEY FYODOROVICH VYAZOVKIN.

"TO BE OR NOT TO BE" ["BYT ILI NE BYT"]. The phrase beginning HAMLET's monologue in William Shakespeare's tragedy of the same name. At MYSHKIN's birthday celebration LEBEDEV notes that the conversation will be on contemporary themes with questions and answers rather like HAMLET's "TO BE OR NOT TO BE."

AFANASY IVANOVICH TOTSKY. A wealthy, extremely egocentric, fifty five year old landowner with the highest of connections. After the tragedy in the BARASHKOV family, he assumes care of NASTASYA

FILIPPOVNA, provides her with an education, and returns from abroad each summer to make use of her sexually. His actions destroy her concept of self-worth, and she becomes convinced that she is the lowest of creatures. Her seeking of self-debasement is in large measure traceable to TOTSKY. When he determines to marry ALEKSANDRA YEPANCHINA, he is anxious to have NASTASYA FILIPPOVNA out of the way, and together with YEPANCHIN he tries to arrange her marriage to GANYA. He is very annoyed when she refuses GANYA's offer upon MYSHKIN's advice. At NASTASYA FILIPPOVNA's birthday celebration FERDYSHCHENKO suggests that all present relate the worst thing they have ever done. NASTASYA FILIPPOVNA is very uneasy when TOTSKY begins to relate his experience, but rather than admit his relationship with her, he relates a flaccid tale of camelias in a petty drama played out on the ORDYNTSEV estate. He ultimately does not formally propose to ALEKSANDRA, but becomes involved with a wealthy young French woman.

TREPALOV. ROGOZHIN tries desperately to raise the money he bids for NASTASYA FILIPPOVNA's hand through KINDER, TREPALOV, and BISKUP.

TREPALOV. In TOTSKY's tale of the worst thing he ever did PETYA VORKHOVSKOY discovers that TREPALOV has the red camelias that ANFISA ALEKSEEVNA so desperately wants for her birthday ball.

"TU L'AS VOULU, GEORGE DANDIN!" "You would have it so, GEORGE DANDIN!" inexact rendering of words from the concluding monologue of *GEORGE DANDIN,* a comedy written by MOLIERE in 1668. Dostoevsky changes the verb and the pronoun from the original "Vous l'avez voulu, George Dandin!" See GEORGE DANDIN.

TURGENEV. Ivan Sergeevich TURGENEV (1818-83), Russian novelist known for his poetic prose and portrayals of the personal and intellectual lives of the Russian nobility. When MYSHKIN decides to remain with NASTASYA FILIPPOVNA after she forces him to choose between her and AGLAYA, rumor mongers insist that he is a democrat who has gone mad with the nihilism described by TURGENEV. The gossips have in mind TURGENEV's novel *Fathers and Sons (Ottsy i deti), written in 1862.*

VANKA. See IVAN PETROVICH PTITSYN.

VARKA. See VARVARA ARDALIONOVNA IVOLGINA.

VARVARA ARDALIONOVNA. See VARVARA ARDALIONOVNA IVOLGINA.

VARYA. See VARVARA ARDALIONOVNA IVOLGINA.

VASILY VASILYICH. See VASILY VASILYICH KONEV.

VENUS [VENERA]. The goddess of love and beauty in Roman mythology. NASTASYA FILIPPOVNA has a statue of VENUS in her apartment.

VERA. See VERA LUKYANOVNA LEBEDEVA.

VERA ALEKSEEVNA. See VERA ALEKSEEVNA ZUBKOVA.

VERA LUKYANOVNA. See VERA LUKYANOVNA LEBEDEVA.

VILKIN. A drunken friend of FERDYSHCHENKO.

VOLTAIRE [VOLTER]. Pen name of François Marie Arouet (1694-1778), noted French satirist, philosopher, and historian. His name connotes a free-thinking approach to issues and philosophy. (1) LEBEDEV claims that disbelief in the devil is a French idea stemming largely from VOLTAIRE. (2) After listening to IPPOLIT's "My Indispensable Explanation" KOLYA notes that had VOLTAIRE, ROUSSEAU, or PROUDHON written such a document, it would not have surprised him, but for IPPOLIT to do so is an exercise in pride and will.

PETYA VORKHOVSKOY. In TOTSKY's anecdote of the worst thing he ever did, PETYA VORKHOVSKOY has a crush on ANFISA ALEK-SEEVNA ORDYNTSEVA and desperately wants to get the red camelias she desires for her birthday ball. See SOFYA BESPALOVA.

STEPAN VORKHOVSKOY. In TOTSKY's tale of the worst thing he ever did, STEPAN VORKHOVSKOY, PETYA's brother, commands a company in the Crimea, where PETYA is killed by the Turks.

TIMOFEY FYODOROVICH VYAZOVKIN. A retired colonel, a relative and friend of the late PAVLISHCHEV who supplies GANYA with two letters to help disprove BURDOVSKY's claim to be PAVLISHCHEV's illegitimate son.

PRINCE VYGORETSKY. In IVOLGIN's confused story about KAPI-TON YEROPEGOV, PRINCE VYGORETSKY is a captain who has a duel with YEROPEGOV.

WATERLOO [VATERLOO]. A village near Brussels at which the European allies defeated NAPOLEON in 1815 and ended his second attempt to expand the French empire. In a conversation with IVOLGIN, MYSHKIN mentions CHARRAS' history of the WATERLOO campaign and the author's evident glee in NAPOLEON's defeat.

"WHERE IS MY YOUTH, WHERE IS MY FRESHNESS" ["GDE MOYA YUNOST, GDE MOYA SVEZHEST"]. Slightly inexact rendering of Chichikov's lament in Nikolay GOGOL's *DEAD SOULS*. Chichikov bemoans his fate with "Oh, my youth, oh my freshness." IVOLGIN complains thus to his son KOLYA and then questions him about the source of the quotation.

WORMWOOD [POLYN]. As recorded in the eighth chapter of the Revelation of St. John in the New Testament, in the last days prior to the destruction of the earth the star WORMWOOD will fall upon a third part of the rivers and on the fountains and bring about the death of many. LEBEDEV's schoolboy son asserts that his father believes that this account in the APOCALYPSE refers to a network of railroads in Europe. LEBEDEV later denies this interpretation when confronted by IPPOLIT and the progressive viewpoint.

YELENA. See YELENA LEBEDEVA.

YELIZAVETA PROKOFIEVNA. See YELIZAVETA PROKOFIEVNA YEPANCHINA.

GENERAL IVAN FYODOROVICH YEPANCHIN. A wealthy and important retired general of fifty six who has many highly-placed friends. When MYSHKIN arrives in Russia, he appeals directly to YEPANCHIN, who offers to be of assistance. He conspires with TOTSKY to marry NASTASYA FILIPPOVNA to GANYA so that his daughter ALEK-SANDRA can marry TOTSKY. He is very perturbed when, at MYSH-KIN's suggestion, NASTASYA FILIPPOVNA refuses the match.

ADELAIDA IVANOVNA YEPANCHINA. The twenty three year old daughter of YEPANCHIN who is expected to marry PRINCE SHCH.

AGLAYA IVANOVNA YEPANCHINA (GLASHA). The twenty year old daughter of YEPANCHIN and the family favorite. She is spoiled, vain, and proud, and demonstrates her personality most completely in her relationship with MYSHKIN. She views MYSHKIN as better, more intelligent, and more noble than others and is furious when he seemingly has no pride, exhibits humility, and is continually deceived and used. Because of her frustration with him she taunts him with allusions to THE POOR KNIGHT and DON QUIXOTE and intermingles these taunts with genuine concern. She becomes very jealous of NASTASYA FILIPPOVNA when MYSHKIN is torn between the two women and continually demonstrates her immaturity and pride by alternately mocking and defending MYSHKIN. When MYSHKIN compassionately remains with NASTASYA FILIPPOVNA when she demands that he choose between her and AGLAYA, AGLAYA leaves and becomes very ill. She rejects the proposals of GANYA and YEVGENY PAVLOVICH and goes abroad, where she marries a false Polish count, becomes involved in Polish freedom organizations, and joins the Catholic Church. All of this causes a sizable rift in the family.

ALEKSANDRA IVANOVNA YEPANCHINA. YEPANCHIN's twenty five year old daughter who exudes beauty, talent, and virtue. YEPANCHIN decides to marry her to TOTSKY, but the marriage does not materialize when NASTASYA FILIPPOVNA refuses the offer of GANYA.

YELIZAVETA PROKOFIEVNA YEPANCHINA (LIZAVETA). The wife of YEPANCHIN who by birth is a Myshkina and who is distantly related to MYSHKIN. She is an enthusiastic and ardent person who dominates her husband and runs the household. She attacks the new progressive generation and exposes their vanity and atheism, yet she sympathizes with IPPOLIT and others who are ill or somehow beset. The fact that her daughters are still single and that AGLAYA shows interest in MYSHKIN, whom she does not consider to be the proper husband for AGLAYA, causes her no little concern. Her words criticizing Europe conclude the novel.

KAPITON ALEKSEEVICH YEROPEGOV (KAPITOSHKA, KAPITAN ALEKSEEVICH, KAPITON, GRISHA, YEROSHKA). IVOLGIN begins to relate an anecdote about YEROPEGOV, but becomes very confused when GANYA insists that no such person exists. He uses several different names, alternates between captain and KAPITON, and is unable to recount the story with any degree of credibility.

YEROSHKA. See KAPITON ALEKSEEVICH YEROPEGOV.

YEVGENY PAVLOVICH. See YEVGENY PAVLOVICH RADOM-SKY.

YEVGENY PAVLYCH. See YEVGENY PAVLOVICH RADOMSKY.

YEVLAMPIA NIKOLAVNA. A widow who parasitically attaches herself to the YEPANCHIN house. AGLAYA compares her perpetual concern with money to MYSHKIN's preoccupation with capital punishment and the quality of life in prison.

"YOU WILL WEAR GOLD AND HAVE A GENERAL'S RANK!" ["BUDESH V ZOLOTE KHODIT, GENERALSKY CHIN NOSIT!"]. Widespread motif of Russian lullabies. The author notes that irrespective of the children's situation in life this song is sung to them by their nannies.

ZALYOZHEV. An acquaintance of ROGOZHIN who tells him about NASTASYA FILIPPOVNA.

ZARNITSYN. In "My Indispensable Explanation" IPPOLIT expresses disgust that ZARNITSYN would permit himself to starve to death.

ZAYDLER. A moneylender who allegedly swindles a poor woman out of five hundred rubles. LEBEDEV agrees to defend him against the woman because of the prospect of making more money than he would realize by defending the woman. ZAYDLER agrees to pay him fifty rubles if he wins the case but only five if he loses.

ZEMTYUZHNIKOV. An officer whom NASTASYA FILIPPOVNA sees after she promises to marry ROGOZHIN. ROGOZHIN is sure that she does it only to belittle him.

ZHEMARIN. A merchant whose wife, mother, son, relative, and cook were murdered in 1868 by Vitold GORSKY, his son's tutor. (1) LEBEDEV questions MYSHKIN as to whether he has read in the newspapers about the ZHEMARIN murders. (2) When MYSHKIN feels compelled to visit ROGOZHIN, he ponders at length about the ZHEMARIN murders. His presentiments prove valid and his own life is spared from ROGOZHIN's knife only because of an epileptic seizure.

MARYA PETROVNA ZUBKOVA. ORDYNTSEV's neighbor in TOT-SKY's tale of the worst thing he ever did.

VERA ALEKSEEVNA ZUBKOVA. A widow and a recent aquaintance of VARYA. She supplies GANYA with a letter that helps to disprove BURDOVSKY's claim to be the illegitimate son of PAVLISHCHEV.

THE ETERNAL HUSBAND (VECHNY MUZH) 1870

ALEKSEY IVANOVICH. See ALEKSEY IVANOVICH VELCHANI-NOV.

STEPAN MIKHAYLOVICH BAGAUTOV. A friend of TRUSOTSKY who has an affair with NATALYA following her escapade with VELCHANINOV. He becomes totally captivated with her and lingers by her for five years. He dies prematurely in St. Petersburg.

DICKENS [DIKKENS]. Charles DICKENS (1812-70), widely considered the greatest English novelist. His novels expose social abuse and corruption. VELCHANINOV and TRUSOTSKY often read DICKENS to NA-TALYA.

GLINKA. Mikhail Ivanovich GLINKA (1804-57), the first important Russian composer. When TRUSOTSKY takes VELCHANINOV to meet the ZAKHLEBININ family and his fiancee NADYA, VELCHANINOV is persuaded to sing and delivers a powerful romance from GLINKA.

MITENKA GOLUBCHIKOV. A distant relative of TRUSOTSKY who moves in with him and his new wife OLIMPIADA SEMYONOVNA. His presence insures that TRUSOTSKY remains the eternal husband.

GOLUBENKO. A colonel who insults a young man and then arranges to marry the woman of his rival's heart. The young man retaliates by stabbing GOLUBENKO at his wedding.

HAYDN [GAYDN]. Franz Joseph HAYDN (1732-1809), Austrian composer who composed prolifically in many forms. When TRUSOTSKY and VELCHANINOV visit the ZAKHLEBININ family, KATYA plays a selection from HAYDN to entertain them.

JUPITER [YUPITER]. The supreme deity of Roman mythology, who corresponds to the Greek Zeus. (1) TRUSOTSKY becomes very offended when he imagines that VELCHANINOV considers him ignorant of his wife's betrayal. He accuses VELCHANINOV of considering himself a JUPITER far above the rest of mankind. (2) LOBOV notes that at home ZAKHLEBININ is simple and gay but at the department he is a virtual JUPITER.

KATERINA FEDOSEEVNA. See KATERINA FEDOSEEVNA ZA-KHLEBININA.

KATYA. A prostitute that TRUSOTSKY visits.

KATYA. See KATERINA FEDOSEEVNA ZAKHLEBININA.

KLAVDIA PETROVNA. See KLAVDIA PETROVNA POGOREL-TSEVA.

KOBYLNIKOV. A character in SHCHEDRIN's short story *For Children (Dlya detskogo vozrasta),* written in 1863. He is shunned by a group of young women in much the same way that TRUSOTSKY is excluded from the ZAKHLEBININ family. The instigator in both instances is named NADYA and is identified as being fifteen years of age. In *For Children* the young women exclude KOBYLNIKOV by claiming that he has a stomach ache. Nothing he says can prevent those present from believing the falsehood. In *The Eternal Husband* the device the girls use to exclude TRUSOTSKY on the evening he brings VELCHANINOV to visit is to claim that he has a cold and has forgotten his handkerchief. Sometime later when LOBOV notices that VELCHANINOV does not feel well, he quotes "KOBYLNIKOV HAS A STOMACH ACHE" and cynically leaves.

"KOBYLNIKOV HAS A STOMACH ACHE" ["U KOBYLNIKOVA ZHIVOT BOLIT"]. A line from SHCHEDRIN's story *For Children.* See KOBYLNIKOV.

KOKH. The doctor who treats NATALYA.

LIPOCHKA. See OLIMPIADA SEMYONOVNA.

SEMYON PETROVICH LIVTSOV. A former visitor to the TRUSOT-SKY home. He relates an anecdote about how his younger brother stabbed GOLUBENKO, a colonel who insulted him and arranged to marry the woman of his heart.

LIZA. See YELIZAVETA.

ALEKSANDR LOBOV (SASHENKA). An unbearable representative of the new generation, about nineteen years old. He informs TRUSOTSKY that he and NADYA are in love and that TRUSOTSKY should abandon his plans to marry her. He proudly announces that after he and NADYA marry, he will give her complete freedom to have affairs, obtain a divorce, or whatever she wishes. PREDPOSYLOV, another of the new generation, has taught him these progressive ideas. When he formally proposes, he receives only ZAKHLEBININ's laughter.

MARYA NIKITISHNA. A twenty three year old governess and friend of NADYA.

MARYA SYSOEVNA. A good woman who rents TRUSOTSKY a room and then provides VELCHANINOV with much information about TRU-SOTSKY and LIZA.

MASHKA. See MASHKA PROKHVOSTOVA.

MAVRA. The woman who replaces PELAGEYA as the cleaning woman in VELCHANINOV's apartment. She does next to nothing, and VEL-CHANINOV suspects that she even steals a bit.

"THE MIGHTY PATROCLUS IS DEAD/ /THE VILE THERSITES LIVES ON!" ["NET VELIKOGO PATROKLA/ /ZHIV PREZRITEL-NY FRESIT!"]. Vasily Andreevich Zhukovsky's 1828 translation of two lines from Friedrich SCHILLER's "Das Siegesfest" ("The Feast of Victory"), written in 1803. The original reads "Denn Patroklus liegt begraben,/ /Und Thersites kommt zurück!" ("For Patroclus lies buried,/ /And Thersites homeward goes!"). TRUSOTSKY quotes these lines as he visits VELCHANINOV and mentions that BAGAUTOV has died. When he pronounces THERSITES, he points to himself.

MITENKA. See MITENKA GOLUBCHIKOV.

NADENKA. See NADEZHDA FEDOSEEVNA ZAKHLEBININA.

NADEZHDA FEDOSEEVNA. See NADEZHDA FEDOSEEVNA ZA-KHLEBININA.

NADYA. See NADEZHDA FEDOSEEVNA ZAKHLEBININA.

NASTYA. A guest in the ZAKHLEBININ home.

NATALYA. See NATALYA VASILIEVNA TRUSOTSKAYA.

NATALYA VASILIEVNA. See NATALYA VASILIEVNA TRUSOTSKAYA.

OLIMPIADA SEMYONOVNA (LIPOCHKA). TRUSOTSKY's pretty, young second wife. When she is insulted by a drunken merchant, she is rescued by VELCHANINOV, who happens to be traveling by. To TRUSOTSKY's horror she invites VELCHANINOV to come stay with them for a month, but to his immense relief VELCHANINOV confides that he likely will not come. When VELCHANINOV sees her with MITENKA, who is staying with TRUSOTSKY, he assumes that she and MITENKA are having an affair and continuing to prove TRUSOTSKY to be the eternal husband.

PAL PALYCH. See PAVEL PAVLOVICH TRUSOTSKY.

PATROCLUS [PATROKL]. In Homer's *Iliad* a loyal friend of Achilles. PATROCLUS' death at the hands of Hector persuades Achilles to reenter the fighting with the Greeks againt Troy. See "THE MIGHTY PATROCLUS IS DEAD/ /THE VILE THERSITES LIVES ON!"

PAVEL PAVLOVICH. See PAVEL PAVLOVICH TRUSOTSKY.

PELAGEYA. VELCHANINOV's former servant girl in his St. Petersburg apartment, who is replaced by the useless MAVRA.

ALEKSANDR PAVLOVICH POGORELTSEV. A longtime friend of VELCHANINOV. VELCHANINOV asks him to care for LIZA for a time.

KLAVDIA PETROVNA POGORELTSEVA. POGORELTSEV's wife. Some years ago she had almost married VELCHANINOV, and she remains his friend and confidante. VELCHANINOV asks her to care for LIZA for a time.

PYOTR KUZMICH POLOSUKHIN. When VELCHANINOV becomes ill, TRUSOTSKY mentions that POLOSUKHIN has the same malady and identifies it as a liver ailment.

PREDPOSYLOV. A very affected and militant member of the young progressive generation who teaches LOBOV modern ideas about marriage. He advocates complete freedom to have affairs, secure divorces, and do whatever one may wish.

MASHKA PROKHVOSTOVA (MASHKA PROSTAKOVA). A prostitute for whom TRUSOTSKY abandons KATYA.

MASHKA PROSTAKOVA. MASHKA PROKHVOSTOVA is also referred to as MASHKA PROSTAKOVA.

THE PROVINCIAL LADY [PROVINTSIALKA]. One act comedy written by Ivan TURGENEV in 1851 in which a young wife dominates her older husband and manipulates an aging Don Juan through flattery and suggestions that he may win her favors. (1) TRUSOTSKY wryly comments that VELCHANINOV became a fixture in his house just as portrayed in *THE PROVINCIAL LADY.* (2) SEMYON SEMYONOVICH stages *THE PROVINCIAL LADY* on his estate and casts BAGAUTOV as the aging count who is amorously interested in the dominating wife, NATAL-YA as the wife, and TRUSOTSKY as STUPENDIEV, the meek husband who is vulnerable but who is not betrayed. An adjustment in casting is necessary when NATALYA demands that TRUSOTSKY be removed from the role of STUPENDIEV.

PYOTR KARLOVICH. VELCHANINOV's lawyer.

QUASIMODO [KVAZIMODO]. The deformed bellringer in *The Hunchback of Notre Dame (Notre Dame de Paris),* a novel written by Victor Hugo (1802-85) in 1831. The name connotes deformity of body and mind. In pondering TRUSOTSKY's desire to kill him VELCHANINOV pictures him as a QUASIMODO in the form of a SCHILLER. VELCHANINOV remembers how TRUSOTSKY respected his elegant ways and notes that a QUASIMODO loves aesthetics.

SASHENKA. See ALEKSANDR LOBOV.

SCHILLER [SHILLER]. Johann Christoph Friedrich von SCHILLER (1759-1805), German dramatist, poet, and historian noted for his romantic idealism. (1) VELCHANINOV refers to TRUSOTSKY as a SCHILLER in the form of a QUASIMODO. (2) When VELCHANINOV learns that TRUSOTSKY and LOBOV have drunk together and parted friends, he refers to them as poets and SCHILLERS.

SEMYON SEMYONOVICH. A wealthy landowner on whose estate TRUSOTSKY, NATALYA, and their acquaintances spend much time. TRUSOTSKY ruefully alludes to the pleasant times that he, NATALYA, and VELCHANINOV enjoyed at SEMYON SEMYONOVICH's estate.

SHCHEDRIN. Penname of Mikhail Yevgrafovich Saltykov (1826-89), Russian journalist, novelist, satirist, and political activist. When LOBOV sees that VELCHANINOV is ill, he quotes "KOBYLNIKOV HAS A STOMACH ACHE," attributes it to SHCHEDRIN, and mentions that he likes his writing.

SODOM. As recorded in Genesis 18-19 in the Old Testament, a city which together with Gomorrah was destroyed by Jehovah because of its wickedness. The term has come to mean wickedness and chaos. MARYA SYSOEVNA comments that it would be good for VELCHANINOV to place LIZA temporarily in another home to get her away from the SODOM that she endures with TRUSOTSKY.

STEPAN MIKHAYLOVICH. See STEPAN MIKHAYLOVICH BA-GAUTOV.

STUPENDIEV. The dominated and potentially easily betrayed husband in TURGENEV's *THE PROVINCIAL LADY*. TRUSOTSKY is to play the part of STUPENDIEV in a production of the play until NATALYA objects.

THERSITES [FERSIT]. A physically deformed, foul-mouthed character in the *Iliad* of Homer. TRUSOTSKY in announcing BAGAUTOV's death quotes "THE MIGHTY PATROCLUS IS DEAD//THE VILE THERSI-TES LIVES ON," and indicates that he himself is THERSITES.

NATALYA VASILIEVNA TRUSOTSKAYA. TRUSOTSKY's first wife, who to all appearances is completely devoted. She is strong-willed and intelligent, but does not hesitate to stand up for TRUSOTSKY, whom she thoroughly dominates. She also does not hesitate to take a lover and employs consecutively VELCHANINOV and BAGAUTOV. She is absolutely faithful to her lovers, whom she both torments and rewards, and she dominates them as thoroughly as she does TRUSOTSKY. VELCHANINOV is dismissed as a lover when she thinks that she is pregnant, and she subsequently orders him never to come back. Her daughter LIZA is the result of the liaison. She dies suddenly and prematurely from consumption.

**PAVEL PAVLOVICH TRUSOTSKY (PAL PALYCH, VASILY PET-
ROVICH).** The eternal husband, a type that exists seemingly only to be
married to someone like NATALYA. He is dominated by her and is
deceived with regularity. Following NATALYA's death he brings LIZA
with him on a search for VELCHANINOV to gain revenge. LIZA, the
daughter of NATALYA by VELCHANINOV, becomes the brunt of
TRUSOTSKY's frustrated and injured pride. He accuses her of not being
his daughter and threatens to commit suicide because of her. When he
allows LIZA to be temporarily taken in by the POGORELTSEVS, she is
heartbroken that he would part with her, and death quickly follows. He
confronts VELCHANINOV with his knowledge of NATALYA's affair
with BAGAUTOV, whose death he rues because he would rather have his
enemy alive, and regularly implies that he knows of VELCHANINOV's
involvement with his wife. Amidst his plans to torment VELCHANINOV,
whose elegance and capability he respects, he announces that he plans to
marry NADYA ZAKHLEBININA. Her youth and her innocence captivate
him, and he sees the possibility of regeneration. He is ultimately shunned by
NADYA and her young progressive friends, made fun of, and dismissed as a
suitor. Following this disappointment VELCHANINOV becomes ill, and
TRUSOTSKY volunteers to nurse him. He tries to kill VELCHANINOV at
night with a razor, but when he is overpowered, he leaves St. Petersburg for
good. He sends VELCHANINOV a letter that NATALYA had never
mailed, making it clear that he knows of their relationship and that LIZA is
VELCHANINOV's daughter. Some time later he marries OLIMPIADA
SEMYONOVNA, but also opens his home to MITENKA GOLUBCHI-
KOV, a distant relative. This arrangement insures that he will remain an
eternal husband. When VELCHANINOV rescues OLIMPIADA SEM-
YONOVNA from a drunken merchant, she invites him to spend a month
with them. TRUSOTSKY is horrified and is greatly relieved when
VELCHANINOV confides to him that he will not come. He worries about
how he will explain this to his wife, and it is obvious that his relationship
with her is much like his life with NATALYA.

TURGENEV. Ivan Sergeevich TURGENEV (1818-83), Russian novelist
known for his poetic prose and portrayals of the personal and intellectual
lives of the Russian nobility. TRUSOTSKY sarcastically reminisces that
VELCHANINOV became a friend of the family in much the same way that
is portrayed in TURGENEV's *THE PROVINCIAL LADY*.

VASILY PETROVICH. LOBOV mistakenly refers to TRUSOTSKY as
VASILY PETROVICH instead of PAVEL PAVLOVICH.

ALEKSEY IVANOVICH VELCHANINOV. A rather cultured, educated, and intelligent man of about thirty eight who feels old and suffers from hypochondria. His ailments stem from guilt feelings for some events in his past. His vanity is effected by reminiscences and he suddenly realizes that the source of much of his despondence is a man he met in the street. The man proves to be TRUSOTSKY, with whose wife NATALYA he had a passionate affair. NATALYA absolutely controlled him because of his desperate passion, and he comes to hate her later because of the effect she has on his vanity. When he meets LIZA, whom he suspects to be his daughter by NATALYA, he desires to love her, possibly to atone for part of his life. He arranges for her to be placed temporarily with the POGORELT-SEVS and anticipates that TRUSOTSKY will simply abandon her, thereby leaving him the chance to assume her care. LIZA's subsequent death distresses him. He agrees to accompany TRUSOTSKY to meet NADYA, TRUSOTSKY's intended, and while there sings a romance that entirely captivates her. When he shortly thereafter becomes ill, he permits TRU-SOTSKY to nurse him but regrets it when the latter tries to kill him with a razor. He overpowers him and sends him away and soon receives a letter indicating that TRUSOTSKY knows all about his involvement with NATALYA. Two years later he feels much better and has lost his hypochondria, largely because successful litigation has restored his finances. While journeying to become acquainted with a certain lady, he rescues a pretty young woman from a drunken merchant and is invited to spend a month at her estate. When she proves to be TRUSOTSKY's new wife, VELCHANINOV sees that the eternal husband has remained eternal. He calms TRUSOTSKY by confiding to him that he definitely will not come. He determines not to continue his journey to try to see the woman because he is not in the mood, but he later resents the decision.

"WHEN IN THE JOYOUS HOUR YOU OPEN YOUR LIPS"["KOGDA V CHAS VESYOLY OTKROESH TY GUBKI"]. The first of six lines cited from a romance by GLINKA based upon the words of the Polish Romantic poet Adam Mickiewicz (1798-1855) as translated into Russian in 1834. When TRUSOTSKY takes VELCHANINOV to visit the ZAKHLEBININ family and to meet his fiancee NADYA, VELCHANINOV is persuaded to sing, and he renders this passionate romance exclusively to NADYA and wins her over.

YELIZAVETA (LIZA). VELCHANINOV's daughter by NATALYA who was born eight months after NATALYA sent him away. She is tormented by TRUSOTSKY with taunts of not being his child and threats to commit suicide because of her. Despite this she loves TRUSOTSKY and this love, coupled with her pride, makes her greatly resent being sent temporarily to the POGORELTSEVS. She becomes ill because of the deep hurt and dies ten days after changing homes.

FEDOSEY PETROVICH ZAKHLEBININ. The father of eight daughters who has agreed to marry one of them, NADYA, to TRUSOTSKY.

MADAME ZAKHLEBININA. ZAKHLEBININ's wife.

KATERINA FEDOSEEVNA ZAKHLEBININA (KATYA). ZAKHLE-BININ's oldest daughter, who is twenty four.

NADEZHDA FEDOSEEVNA ZAKHLEBININA (NADYA, NADEN-KA). The fifteen year old daughter of ZAKHLEBININ who is the proposed bride of TRUSOTSKY. She commissions VELCHANINOV to return a bracelet to TRUSOTSKY and to tell him not to return because she will never be his.

COUNT ZAVILEYSKY. LOBOV hopes to participate in the operation of COUNT ZAVILEYSKY's ruined estates to make some money.

THE POSSESSED (BESY) 1871

AGAFYA. A servant girl in the new quarters LEBYADKIN occupies.

AGAFYA (AGAFYUSHKA). A servant of LIPUTIN.

AGAFYUSHKA. See AGAFYA.

AGASHA. VARVARA PETROVNA's favorite maid.

THE AGE [VEK]. A St. Petersburg literary and political weekly published 1861-62. See "*THE AGE* AND *THE AGE* AND LEV KAMBEK."

"THE AGE AND THE AGE AND LEV KAMBEK,/ /LEV KAMBEK AND THE AGE AND THE AGE" ["VEK I VEK I LEV KAMBEK, LEV KAMBEK I VEK I VEK"]. The beginning lines of some comic verse written by Dostoevsky to parody the popular issues of satirical journalism in the 1860s. When STEPAN TROFIMOVICH, at a gathering of the progressive younger generation in St. Petersburg, defends PUSHKIN as being more important than boots he is ridiculed and laughed at. His humiliation results in a semi-delirium, and he mutters these verses most of the way back to Moscow.

ALEKSEY NILYICH. See ALEKSEY NILYICH KIRILLOV.

ALEKSEY YEGOROVICH (ALEKSEY YEGORYCH). VARVARA PETROVNA's valet.

ALEKSEY YEGORYCH. See ALEKSEY YEGOROVICH.

"ALL YE THAT LABOR AND ARE HEAVY LADEN" ["VSE ETI TRUZHDAYUSHIESYA I OBREMENYONNYE"]. A partial citation from Matthew 11:28 in the New Testament, which reads "Come unto me, ALL YE THAT LABOR AND ARE HEAVY LADEN, and I will give you rest." The narrator refers to the important people of Europe as "ALL YE THAT LABOR AND ARE HEAVY LADEN" because of their devotion to KARMAZINOV. The pompous writer dotes on their adulation but regards all of them as no better than his cook.

ALYONA FROLOVNA. LIZA's nurse.

AMALIA. The fifth daughter of an important general who is a relative of VON LEMBKE. While VON LEMBKE is living with the general and trying to establish his career, he and AMALIA become interested in each other, but the romance is curtailed when she marries an elderly friend of her father.

ANCUS MARCIUS [ANK MARTSY]. The legendary fourth king of early Rome who ruled 642-617 B.C. and who established the plebeian class by bringing to Rome conquered populations. In describing the bewildering subject matter of KARMAZINOV's "MERCI" the narrator notes that in one part ANCUS MARCIUS suddenly appears out of a mist wearing a laurel wreath and moving over the roofs of Rome.

"AND THERE WAS THERE AN HERD OF SWINE FEEDING ON THE MOUNTAIN: AND THEY BESOUGHT HIM [JESUS] THAT HE WOULD SUFFER THEM TO ENTER INTO THEM" ["TUT NA GORE PASLOS BOLSHOE STADO SVINEY, I ONI PROSILI YEGO, CHTO-BY POZVOLIL IM VOYTI V NIKH"]. As cited in LUKE 8:32-36 in the

New Testament, the first words of the account of Jesus' casting the devils from the wild man in the country of the Gadarenes. When STEPAN TROFIMOVICH becomes ill during his pilgrimage to find the real Russia, he asks SOFYA to read him the account of the devils who were cast from the man possessed and permitted to enter the bodies of swine. After the reading he acknowledges that people of his generation and also those of PYOTR STEPANOVICH's generation must be purged from Russia like the devils were from the wild man. Implicit in STEPAN TROFIMOVICH's acknowledgement is that the devils have been cast from him even as they were from the wild man and that he has come to his right mind. This passage also stands as one of the epigraphs to the novel.

"AND UNTO THE ANGEL OF THE CHURCH OF THE LAODICEANS WRITE" ["I ANGELU LAODIKYSKOY TSERKVI NAPISHI"]. When STEPAN TROFIMOVICH becomes ill on his pilgrimage to find the real Russia, he asks SOFYA to read him something out of the BIBLE. She reads in the Revelation of St. John 3:14-17 the account of the lukewarm followers who will be rejected by God because of their indifference and their lack of awareness of their condition. The passage stimulates in STEPAN TROFIMOVICH a desire to improve himself.

NIKON SEMYONOVICH ANDREEV (ANDREJEFF). An eccentric local merchant who buys some timber land from STEPAN TROFIMOVICH. His delay in payment causes STEPAN TROFIMOVICH extreme grief. It is he who informs VARVARA PETROVNA that the woman kneeling before her outside the church is MARYA LEBYADKINA.

ANDREJEFF. See NIKON SEMYONOVICH ANDREEV.

ANDREY ANTONOVICH. See ANDREY ANTONOVICH VON BLÜM.

ANTICHRIST [ANTIKHRIST]. Biblical term referring to a man of sin who denies the Father and the Son and whose disturbing presence presages the Second Coming of CHRIST and the end of the world. In reviewing what STAVROGIN once taught him SHATOV recalls the assertions that the Roman Catholic Church teaches a CHRIST who submitted to the third temptation of Satan and became tied to an earthly political kingdom. Because of this the Roman Catholic Church professes ANTICHRIST and has destroyed all of the Western World.

ANTON GOREMYKA. A short novel written in 1847 by Dmitry Vasilievich Grigorovich (1822-99) which sentimentally discusses the tragedies and realities of peasant life. LIPUTIN observes that praising peasants is necessary for the new progressive movement and that even ladies of high society shed tears when reading *ANTON GOREMYKA.*

ANTON LAVRENTIEVICH. See ANTON LAVRENTIEVICH G-V.

APOCALYPSE [APOKALIPSIS, L'APOCALYPSE]. In the New Testament, the Revelation of St. John which outlines the end of the world and the FINAL JUDGMENT. (1) In discussing his planned suicide with STAVROGIN, KIRILLOV vows to stop time on earth, thereby making it become eternal and doing away with the concept of an afterlife. STAVROGIN responds that such a stoppage of time is prophesied in the APOCALYPSE. In Revelation 10:6 the angel swears by the Creator of all things that time will be no more. (2) In recalling those things that STAVROGIN once taught him SHATOV notes that reason and science are subsidiary forces to the spirit of life and the rivers of living water. He adds that it is prophesied in the APOCALYPSE that the rivers of living water will be dried up. He likely has reference to Revelation 8:10-11, in which is projected the fatal pollution of a third part of the rivers through the star Wormwood, which falls from the heavens. (3) KIRILLOV reads FEDKA the APOCALYPSE at night and FEDKA enjoys it very much. (4) In condemning PYOTR STEPANOVICH and lauding KIRILLOV, FEDKA explains that KIRILLOV is a philosopher and that he has explained the creation of things and their imminent fate as recorded in the APOCALYPSE. (5) When STEPAN TROFIMOVICH on his pilgrimage to find Russia requests that SOFYA read him something from the BIBLE, she turns to the prophecy that those who are neither hot nor cold but who are lukewarm will be cast out as recorded in Revelation 3:14-17. She identifies this as coming from the APOCALYPSE. See "AND UNTO THE ANGEL OF THE CHURCH OF THE LAODICEANS WRITE."

ARINA PROKHOROVNA. See ARINA PROKHOROVNA VIRGINSKAYA.

ARTEMY PAVLOVICH. See ARTEMY PAVLOVICH GAGANOV.

"AT NIGHT I WANDER WITH NO HOME/ /BY DAY WITH BREAKNECK SPEED" ["NOCHYU DUYU BEZ NOCHLEGA,/ / DNOM ZHE, VYSUNUV YAZYK"]. Slightly inaccurate rendering of lines from "In Memory of the Artist Orlovsky" ("Pamyati zhivopistsa Orlovskogo"), written in 1838 by Prince Pyotr Andreevich Vyazemsky (1792-1878). The only difference between the original and the citation is the use of "you wander" ("duesh") instead of "I wander" ("duyu"). When STAVROGIN visits LEBYADKIN and discovers to his surprise that LEBYADKIN is sober and living in clean quarters, the latter responds by quoting these lines.

AVDOTYA SERGEVNA. When STEPAN TROFIMOVICH embarks on his pilgrimage to find Russia, he meets ANISIM IVANOV in a peasant village. IVANOV comments that he used to work for GAGANOV and saw STEPAN TROFIMOVICH there, often visiting the late AVDOTYA SERGEVNA. She is most probably GAGANOV's wife.

BABYLON [VAVILON]. The ancient capital of the Chaldean/Babylonian Empire which gradually diminished in importance after it fell to Cyrus the Great of Persia in 539 B.C. The term BABYLON is symbolic of wickedness and confusion. KARMAZINOV and PYOTR STEPANOVICH discuss Europe and agree that it is BABYLON in decay and that the fall of it will be great. References to the great fall of BABYLON abound in the BIBLE, and among the most prominent are Isaiah 21:9, Jeremiah 50-51, Revelation 14:8 and 18:2.

BADINGUET. The surname of a brickmason with whose name and clothes Louis Napoleon Bonaparte, the future Napoleon III, escaped the Ham Fortress in 1846. When VARVARA PETROVNA determines to marry STEPAN TROFIMOVICH to DASHA and employs her own will and his weakness and financial plight as levers, he complains that he is a virtual prisoner à la BADINGUET.

BALZAC. Honoré de BALZAC (1799-1850), noted French novelist. See *THE WOMEN OF BALZAC.*

BAZAROV. Central figure of *Fathers and Sons (Ottsy i deti),* published in 1862 by Ivan TURGENEV. BAZAROV was criticized by both radical and conservative elements, who found him a caricature and too positive a figure respectively. STEPAN TROFIMOVICH notes that BAZAROV was rejected by the progressive circles of the 1860s and refers to him as an unclear mixture of NOZDRYOV and BYRON.

"BE STILL, DESPAIRING HEART!" ["MOLCHI, BEZNADYOZH-NOE SERDTSE!"]. Inexact citation from "Doubt" ("Somnenie") a poem by Nestor KUKOLNIK. The original reads "Sleep, despairing heart!" ("Zasni, beznadyozhnoe serdtse!") LEBYADKIN laments to VARVARA PETROVNA that he has suffered greatly in life and asks her if it is possible to die from the nobility of one's soul. In this atmosphere he directs his despairing heart to be still.

BELINSKY. Vissarion Grigorievich BELINSKY (1811-48), Russian literary critic and journalist. He wrote for both *Fatherland Notes* and *The Contemporary* and insisted that literature realistically expose the seamy side of life with the intent of social reform. He was the first and most eminent of the so-called Radical Critics, and his ideas helped to stimulate the Natural School. (1) The narrator notes that STEPAN TROFIMO-VICH, fond of perceiving himself as a progressive liberal in the vanguard of thought and of concern to the government, was once mentioned almost in the same breath with CHAADAEV, BELINSKY, GRANOVSKY, and HERZEN. (2) While discussing his own fashionable skepticism toward the concept of God, STEPAN TROFIMOVICH refers to BELINSKY's letter to GOGOL in which GOGOL's belief in God and seeming abandonment of progressive ideals are attacked. STEPAN TROFIMOVICH adds that BELINSKY himself could not look for salvation amidst the rituals and ornaments of the church. (3) SHATOV attacks STEPAN TROFIMO-VICH and his generation for not knowing the people and for doing nothing for them, and he cites BELINSKY's letter to GOGOL as a good example. He adds that BELINSKY, STEPAN TROFIMOVICH, and others like them are no better than KRYLOV's *AN INQUISITIVE MAN.* (4) An ardent young schoolboy who attends a meeting of PYOTR STEPANO-VICH's socialist circle insists that ever since BELINSKY all Russia has known that the commandment to honor one's father and mother is worthless. (5) At the socialist meeting called by PYOTR STEPANOVICH a LAME TEACHER attempts to get the group to seriously consider SHIGALYOV's ideas about society. To encourage them he observes that HERZEN and BELINSKY spent a good deal of time working out the structure of future society.

THE BELL [KOLOKOL]. A biweekly revolutionary journal published in London by Aleksandr HERZEN from 1857-67. It was smuggled into Russia, where it had a large readership. *THE BELL* was very critical of the social and political order in Russia. (1) A major, a close relative of VIRGINSKY, once distributed copies of *THE BELL* and other pamphlets and proclamations even though he did not believe in them. Like many others he felt it a sin not to make them available. (2) STEPAN TROFIMO-VICH reports excitedly and proudly to the narrator that VON BLÜM has requisitioned his papers and books, among them foreign editions of HERZEN and a worn copy of *THE BELL.*

BELSHAZZAR [VALTASAR]. As recorded in Daniel 2 in the Old Testament, the king of BABYLON whose luxurious feast for his lords was interrupted by a hand writing on the wall. Daniel was called to interpret and indicated that both the king and the kingdom would fall. YULIA MIKHAYLOVNA's original idea for the holiday to benefit the local governesses was to have an elaborate champagne breakfast at which she would give many toasts. Even though this idea is rejected as extravagant, the public still dreams of such a BELSHAZZAR's feast until the very last minute.

BERESTOV. After PYOTR STEPANOVICH has murdered SHATOV and is hurrying out of town, an acquaintance promises to introduce him to BERESTOV, an important colonel.

BIBLE [PISANIE, YEVANGELIE, L'EVANGILE]. A collection of books organized into the Old Testament, a religious history from Adam through the twelve tribes of Israel with emphasis on Judah, and the New Testament, the life and ministry of Jesus CHRIST. (1) As SHATOV reviews the ideas that STAVROGIN taught him, he notes that man is not stimulated in life by reason and science but by the spirit of life and the rivers of living waters as recorded in the BIBLE. See APOCALYPSE (2). (2) DASHA insists that if she and STAVROGIN do not end up together, she will become a nurse or a seller of BIBLES. (3) KIRILLOV discusses his epileptic-like sensations with SHATOV while MARIE is in labor. He mentions that the sensations are so intense that it is like living all of one's life in a few seconds and that one must change physically to endure it. KIRILLOV adds that people should stop having children since through him mankind's goal is achieved and there is no hope for further progress. To illustrate his contention he notes that the BIBLE teaches that after the resurrection people will be as angels and will not bear children. His allusion is a distortion of Matthew 22:30 and Mark 12:25 in the New Testament, which assert that after resurrection people will not marry but will be as angels. (4) On his pilgrimage to find Russia STEPAN TROFIMOVICH buys a BIBLE from SOFYA. (5) STEPAN TROFIMOVICH offers to help SOFYA sell BIBLES and to explain the book to those who are religious but who do not understand the BIBLE. (6) During his illness on his pilgrimage STEPAN TROFIMOVICH asks SOFYA to read him anything from the BIBLE. (7) When VARVARA PETROVNA finds the ill STEPAN TROFIMOVICH on his pilgrimage to find Russia, he informs her that he plans to preach from the BIBLE the rest of his life. (8) After STEPAN TROFIMOVICH dies, VARVARA PE-TROVNA tells SOFYA that she no longer has anyone in life and may go sell BIBLES with her.

BISMARCK [BISMARK]. Prince Otto von BISMARCK (1815-98), chancellor of Prussia who through pragmatic and opportunistic politics founded the German Reich in 1871. He is noted for his conservative and adept diplomacy. (1) A frustrated STEPAN TROFIMOVICH refers to VARVARA PETROVNA as a veritable BISMARCK because of her skill in intrigue. She responds that she can detect falsehood and stupidity even without being a BISMARCK. (2) For the literary evening LYAMSHIN creates a piano number called the "Franco-Prussian War," in which he juxtaposes the "MARSEILLAISE" with "MEIN LIEBER AUGUSTIN." The narrator notes that the "MARSEILLAISE" fades out much like JULES FAVRE leaning on the bosom of BISMARCK and giving him absolutely everything.

ANDREY ANTONOVICH VON BLÜM [FON BLYUM]. A sullen German and a distant relative of VON LEMBKE who works for him in the governor's office. He makes no friends, has had no successes in life, and only VON LEMBKE ever cares for him. He persuades VON LEMBKE to search STEPAN TROFIMOVICH's room by telling him that he is sure to find the source of the provincial unrest and the radical pamphlets. YULIA MI-KHAYLOVNA does not care for him in the least. She wants to conceal his blood relationship with VON LEMBKE and would like VON BLÜM to change his first name and patronymic so that they would differ from her husband's.

BÜCHNER [BYUKHNER]. Ludwig BÜCHNER (1824-99), German physician and philosopher whose materialistic interpretation of the universe proved very controversial because of its rejection of God, the creation, religion, and man's free will. To VON LEMBKE's horror a second lieutenant attached to the regiment in his province seemingly goes crazy and bites his commanding officer. In his room are found some progressive pamphlets together with the works of VOGT, BÜCHNER, and MO-LESCHOTT.

BYRON [BAYRON]. Lord George Gordon BYRON (1788-1824), English Romantic poet who created the "Byronic Hero," a defiant, brooding young man obsessed by some mysterious past sin. (1) In discussing the rejection of TURGENEV's BAZAROV by the progressive circles of the 1860s STE-PAN TROFIMOVICH asserts that BAZAROV is an unclear mixture of NOZDRYOV and BYRON. (2) In describing the contents and mood of KARMAZINOV's pompous and hopelessly rhetorical and sentimental "MERCI" the narrator notes that the work contains a typical attack of BYRONIC melancholy.

CABET [KABET]. Etienne CABET (1788-1856), French-American utopian socialist who founded the Icarian movement and established communes based upon pacifism and communism. (1) The LAME TEACHER
at the socialist meeting called by PYOTR STEPANOVICH speaks in
support of SHIGALYOV's system for the organization of future society. He
defends the system's despotism by saying that FOURIER, CABET, and
PROUDHON also had despotic and somewhat fantastic solutions to the
future of society. (2) At the gathering of socialists that he convenes PYOTR
STEPANOVICH insists that the works of FOURIER and CABET are an
aesthetic passing of time and are like novels that can be written by the
thousands. He tries to convince them that it is time to act rather than to talk.

"CALENDARS ALWAYS LIE" ["VSYO VRUT KALENDARI"]. A line
from the play *Woe From Wit (Gore ot uma)*, written by Aleksandr
Sergeevich Griboedov (1795-1829) in 1822-24. On the morning following
LIZA's flight to STAVROGIN she observes that according to the calendar
the sun should already have risen. STAVROGIN responds that "CALEN-
DARS ALWAYS LIE" and that it is boring to live by calendars.

CANDIDE. A popular philosophical novel written in 1759 by VOLTAIRE.
The novel satirizes the naively optimistic view of life and takes direct issue
with the German philosopher Gottfried Wilhelm Leibniz (1646-1716), who
felt that this is the best of all possible worlds. The hero CANDIDE goes
from one revolting situation to another with nothing ever working out right.
On the morning following his quarrel with YULIA MIKHAYLOVNA over
PYOTR STEPANOVICH and prior to the culmination of provincial
unrest, VON LEMBKE reads a passage from *CANDIDE* to the effect that
"TOUT EST POUR LE MIEUX DANS LE MEILLEUR DES MONDES
POSSIBLES."

CAPEFIGUE [KAPFIG]. Jean Baptiste Honoré Raymond CAPEFIGUE
(1802-72), French author of several somewhat superficial and unenduring
historical works. VARVARA PETROVNA berates STEPAN TROFI-
MOVICH for giving her only CAPEFIGUE to read after she asked him to
direct her intellectual development.

CASSIUS [KASSY]. Caius CASSIUS Longinus (d. 42 B.C.), Roman
general and politician who supported POMPEY against Caesar during the
Civil War and who later instigated the plot against Caesar's life. In
describing the content of KARMAZINOV's hopelessly rhetorical and
pompous "MERCI" the narrator notes that in one section two lovers sit
together under a tree in Germany where they suddenly see CASSIUS or

POMPEY and are filled with cold ecstasy.

CHAADAEV. Pyotr Yakovlevich CHAADAEV (1794-1856), Russian philosopher whose *Lettres Philosophiques (Philosophical Letters)* discuss Russia's heritage from the past, her lamentable isolation from the West, and her mystical Christian mission. His work angered the authorities such that he was declared insane and forbidden to publish further. The narrator notes that STEPAN TROFIMOVICH, fond of perceiving himself as a progressive liberal in the vanguard of thought and of concern to the government, was once mentioned almost in the same breath with CHAADAEV, BELINSKY, GRANOVSKY, and HERZEN.

MADAME CHEVALIER [SHEVALE]. On one occasion LIZA stops at the home of MADAME CHEVALIER to get a bouquet for STEPAN TROFIMOVICH.

CHOPIN [SHOPEN]. Frédéric CHOPIN (1810-49), the outstanding pianist and composer for piano in the Romantic era. In describing typical subject matter from KARMAZINOV's pompous "MERCI" the narrator recalls that a water nymph whistles something from CHOPIN to accompany the appearance of HOFFMAN and the suspension of ANCUS MARCIUS over the roofs of Rome.

CHRIST [KHRISTOS]. Jesus CHRIST, in Christianity the Son of God. (1) STEPAN TROFIMOVICH asks his son PYOTR STEPANOVICH if he intends to offer the people caricatures like BAZAROV instead of CHRIST. (2) STAVROGIN had once taught SHATOV that the Roman Catholic Church teaches a CHRIST that succumbed to the third temptation of Satan and that as a result He cannot stand on the earth without an earthly kingdom. (3) SHATOV recalls that STAVROGIN had once quizzed him about CHRIST and the truth, posing the question that if it were proven that CHRIST and the truth were mutually exclusive, would he choose to remain with CHRIST rather than the truth. (4) When asked by STAVROGIN if he believes in God, SHATOV responds that he believes in Russia, Orthodoxy, the body of CHRIST, and a Second Coming located in Russia, and that he will come to believe in God. (5) KIRILLOV has an icon of CHRIST in his room and maintains a lamp burning in front of it. (6) At his request SOFYA reads STEPAN TROFIMOVICH the account in LUKE 8:32-36 in the New Testament of the devils who were cast from the man possessed and permitted to enter the bodies of swine. STEPAN TROFIMOVICH asserts that he can foresee the day when Russia herself will sit in her right mind at CHRIST's feet just as the wild man does in the BIBLICAL account.

CICERO [TSITSERON]. Marcus Tillius CICERO (106-43 B.C.), states-man, philosopher, and writer who was Rome's greatest orator. He was elected consul and served the Republic well but ultimately was murdered by the forces of Marc Antony. PYOTR STEPANOVICH expresses his delight over SHIGALYOV's system for the organization of future society because it produces mass slavery and spying. He notes that under such a system CICERO would have his tongue cut out, COPERNICUS would have his eyes put out, and SHAKESPEARE would be stoned to death.

"THE COCKROACH" ["TARAKAN"]. The grotesque incomplete fable which LEBYADKIN reads to VARVARA PETROVNA and other assembled guests at her home. In the fable some flies complain to JUPITER because a cockroach gets into their glass. Through the fable Dostoevsky is likely parodying "A Fantastic Tale" ("Fantasticheskaya vyskazka"), which also chronicles the plight of a cockroach in a glass. "A Fantastic Tale" was written by the poet Ivan Petrovich Myatev (1796-1844) in 1834. Myatev was noted for his parody and wit and wrote some verse in the spirit of Kuzma Prutkov.

COLUMBUS [KOLUMB]. Christopher COLUMBUS (1451-1506), Italian navigator who under the flag of Spain made four voyages to the Americas. He is credited with discovering the New World in 1492 on his first voyage. (1) LIZA reminisces about how STEPAN TROFIMOVICH told her of COLUMBUS' discovering America. (2) PYOTR STEPANOVICH tells STAVROGIN that he is nothing without him, a COLUMBUS without America. (3) After he murders SHATOV, PYOTR STEPANOVICH visits KIRILLOV to arrange for KIRILLOV's suicide and letter of confession. Since KIRILLOV feels that he becomes a god through his ultimate act of the will and is standing on virgin soil, PYOTR STEPANOVICH observes to him that he should feel like COLUMBUS.

CONSIDERANT [KONSIDERAN]. Victor Prosper CONSIDERANT (1808-93), French utopian socialist who after FOURIER's death became the leader of the utopian movement. His *Destinée Sociale (Social Destiny),* written 1834-38 is considered the most important work of the FOURIER school. When STAVROGIN sees a volume of CONSIDERANT in LIPUTIN's house, he asks him if he is a follower of FOURIER.

COPERNICUS [KOPERNIK]. Nicolaus COPERNICUS (1473-1543), Polish astronomer who laid the foundation for modern astronomy by positing the sun rather than the earth as the center of the solar system. His statement produced great scientific and theological polemics. PYOTR

STEPANOVICH is delighted with SHIGALYOV's system for the organization of future society because it produces mass slavery and spying. He notes that under such a system CICERO would have his tongue cut out, COPERNICUS would have his eyes put out, and SHAKESPEARE would be stoned to death.

CUPID [AMUR]. In Roman mythology the god of love, a counterpart to the Greek Eros. LIPUTIN becomes incensed when STAVROGIN attends his wife's birthday party, kisses her three times, and quickly leaves. He states that womanizers like STAVROGIN are nothing more than landowners with wings just like those on the ancient CUPIDS.

DARWIN [DARVIN]. Charles Robert DARWIN (1809-82), English naturalist who originated the theory of evolution by natural selection. The theory aroused a storm of protest from fundamentalist theoreticians and remains an area of controversy. The narrator describes KARMAZINOV's fiction as a process of borrowing ideas, adding antitheses, and arriving at puns. He notes that one of the subjects KARMAZINOV treats in this manner is DARWIN.

DARYA PAVLOVNA. See DARYA PAVLOVNA SHATOVA.

DASHA. See DARYA PAVLOVNA SHATOVA.

DASHENKA. See DARYA PAVLOVNA SHATOVA.

DASHKA. See DARYA PAVLOVNA SHATOVA.

DENIS DAVYDOV. DENIS Vasilievich DAVYDOV (1784-1839), Russian poet noted for his glorification of the swashbuckling hussar life of wine, women, song, and camaraderie. After LEBYADKIN scandalizes a gathering at VARVARA PETROVNA's estate by blabbering and reading some of his terrible poetry, he admits that the threshold of his passions is the hussar bottle made famous by DENIS DAVYDOV.

DERZHAVIN. Gavriil Romanovich DERZHAVIN (1743-1816), the greatest Russian poet of the eighteenth century known primarily for his odes. In illustrating his relationship to STAVROGIN and his circumstances, LEBYADKIN recites: "I am a slave, a worm but not God, and that is where I differ from DERZHAVIN." LEBYADKIN has reference to DERZHAVIN's famous ode "God" ("Bog") written in 1784, one line of which reads "I am tsar,—I'm a slave, I'm a worm,—I am God!" ("Ya tsar,—ya rab, ya cherv,—ya bog!'").

DICKENS [DIKKENS]. Charles DICKENS (1812-70), widely considered the greatest English novelist. His novels expose social abuse and corruption. STEPAN TROFIMOVICH once published a progressive journal featuring translations from DICKENS.

DMITRY MITRICH. In the excitement of VON BLÜM's search of his apartment it seems to STEPAN TROFIMOVICH that he hears the name DMITRY MITRICH mentioned. He owes STEPAN TROFIMOVICH fifteen rubles that he lost to him at cards.

DRESDEN MADONNA [DREZDENSKAYA MADONNA]. Probably *Madonna With the Family of the Bürgermeister Jacob Meyer* by Hans Holbein the Younger (1497-1543), painted in 1525-26. A copy of the work is housed in Dresden. In defending STEPAN TROFIMOVICH, VAR-VARA PETROVNA comments that he is planning to write something about the DRESDEN MADONNA.

DROZDIKHA. See PRASKOVYA IVANOVNA DROZDOVA.

IVAN IVANOVICH DROZDOV. A general and friend of VARVARA PETROVNA's late husband. While a guest at VARVARA PETROVNA's salon in St. Petersburg, he argues with a member of the young progressive generation over values and literature. As a result he, VARVARA PETROVNA, and STEPAN TROFIMOVICH are caricatured in a progressive magazine.

MAVRIKY NIKOLAEVICH DROZDOV (MAURICE). A tall, handsome, and proper officer of thirty three who is wholly devoted to LIZA, his distant relative. He becomes LIZA's constant companion, and society assumes that they are engaged. LIZA loves and respects him but is torn between him and STAVROGIN. Knowing this he visits STAVROGIN and asks him to marry LIZA if at all possible and adds that despite the fact that LIZA loves him, he is certain that she would go with STAVROGIN whenever he desires. When STAVROGIN replied that he is already married, MAVRIKY NIKOLAEVICH orders him to leave LIZA alone and threatens to kill him if he does not. When LIZA runs away to STAVRO-GIN, he does not try to restrain her but maintains a vigil outside the estate all night and into the next day until she flees the house. Reunited with her, he takes LIZA, at her insistence, to the scene of the murder of LEBYADKIN and MARYA, where they are both beaten by an angry mob of peasants. The beating proves fatal to LIZA, and MAVRIKY NIKOLAEVICH leaves the area following her death.

DROZDOVA. YULIA MIKHAYLOVNA VON LEMBKE's maiden name.

PRASKOVYA IVANOVNA DROZDOVA (DROZDIKHA). Wife of the late IVAN IVANOVICH DROZDOV and an acquaintance of VARVARA PETROVNA since her youth. VARVARA PETROVNA has always dominated her and treated her very much as an inferior. Her first marriage was to TUSHIN, a junior captain in the cavalry, by whom she gave birth to LIZA. After LIZA is beaten to death, PRASKOVYA IVANOVNA becomes very senile and childlike.

DUNDASOV. When VARVARA PETROVNA sends STEPAN TROFIMOVICH abroad for a visit, he renews his acquaintaince with DUNDASOV and his wife in Berlin.

NADEZHDA NIKOLAEVNA DUNDASOVA. DUNDASOV's wife.

ERKEL. A naive young ensign who is totally devoted to the socialist cause and to PYOTR STEPANOVICH. He, PYOTR STEPANOVICH, and TOLKACHENKO are the only ones who actively participate in murdering SHATOV. He is arrested following LYAMSHIN's confession, but does not show any contrition. The authorities pity him because of his youth and because of his aged mother, whom he supports.

ERNEST. LEBYADKIN bemoans the fact that he bears the coarse name of IGNAT instead of something like ERNEST.

ERNESTINA. Rather than the expected MINNA or ERNESTINA, VON LEMBKE marries YULIA MIKHAYLOVNA and anticipates a blissful life with her.

FALSTAFF [FALSTAF]. Sir John FALSTAFF, who appears as a comic character in William SHAKESPEARE's *Henry IV, Parts One and Two* (1597-98) and *The Merry Wives of Windsor* (1597-1601). He is characterized by self-indulgence, braggadocio, buffoonery, and vice. (1) STEPAN TROFIMOVICH attributes STAVROGIN's extreme behavior to the youth of a PRINCE HARRY who cavorts with FALSTAFF, POINS, and MISTRESS QUICKLY as portrayed by SHAKESPEARE. (2) STAVROGIN refers to LEBYADKIN as his FALSTAFF who makes everyone laugh. (3) LEBYADKIN recalls that in their days of carousing he was known as STAVROGIN's FALSTAFF.

FAUST. A play in two parts written in 1808 and 1832 by GOETHE. The play chronicles the career of FAUST, who sells his soul to Mephistopheles in exchange for the promise to comprehend all experience. The second part of the play deals with the larger experiences of history, culture, and politics and is done in a more allegorical fashion. The narrator notes that STEPAN TROFIMOVICH has written a bad poem that is quite allegorical and rather like the second part of *FAUST.*

JULES FAVRE [ZHYUL FAVR]. French political leader (1809-80), a republican and staunch opponent of Napoleon III. After the defeat and overthrow of Napoleon III in 1870 as a result of the Franco-Prussian War, FAVRE became minister of foreign affairs in the provisional government and vowed not to surrender any territory in the peace negotiations with Germany. He was compelled, however, to sign a treaty that provided for heavy indemnity payments as well as the loss of territory. He resigned his post in disgrace. See BISMARCK (2).

FEDKA. See FYODOR FYODOROVICH.

FEDKA THE CONVICT [FEDKA KATORZHNY]. See FYODOR FYODOROVICH.

FILIPPOV. The owner of a pub and a house on Epiphany (Bogoyavlens- kaya) Street in which SHATOV, KIRILLOV, and LEBYADKIN live. MARIE SHATOVA gives birth to IVAN in the house.

THE FINAL JUDGMENT [STRASHNY SUD]. In Christian tradition the final accounting of each man to God. (1) VARVARA PETROVNA tells STEPAN TROFIMOVICH that she is ready to call PRASKOVYA IVANOVNA DROZDOVA a fool at THE FINAL JUDGMENT. (2) LEBYADKIN informs VARVARA PETROVNA that he has suffered so much in life that God Himself will be surprised at THE FINAL JUDG- MENT.

FINAL TALE [POSLEDNYAYA POVEST]. LEBYADKIN claims that he has written a work which he will leave to the world much like GOGOL's *FINAL TALE* which emerged from his very soul. LEBYADKIN had in mind GOGOL's reference in his *Selected Passages From Correspondence With Friends (Vybrannye mesta iz perepiski s druzyami)* to a *FINAL TALE* which was not simply written but which sprang forth from his very soul.

VASILY IVANOVICH FLIBUSTEROV. A police officer who finds the deranged VON LEMBKE in a field picking flowers. VON LEMBKE confuses FLIBUSTEROV with filibuster *(flibustery)*, to which he attributes the commotion in town.

FOMKA. See FOMKA ZAVYALOV.

FOMUSHKA. A servant of VARVARA PETROVNA.

"FOR NOTHING IS SECRET THAT SHALL NOT BE MADE MANI-FEST" ["NICHEGO NET TAYNOGO, CHTO BY NE SDELALOS YAVNYM"]. A passage from LUKE 8:17 in the New Testament. In discussing with PYOTR STEPANOVICH the problem of who will ever know of his suicide and the reasons for it, KIRILLOV quotes the words of CHRIST, "FOR NOTHING IS SECRET THAT SHALL NOT BE MADE MANIFEST."

FOURIER [FURIE]. François Marie Charles FOURIER (1772-1837), French reformer and economist whose utopian socialist theories became very chic in Russia. He envisioned a society in which economic activity would be carried out by groups of people living together in communal environments called phalanxes. (1) STEPAN TROFIMOVICH, typical of liberals of the 1840s, once belonged to a small circle which read and translated FOURIER. (2) When STAVROGIN notices a volume by CONSIDERANT in LIPUTIN's library, he asks LIPUTIN if he is a follower of FOURIER. (3) At the meeting of socialists called by PYOTR STEPANOVICH, SHIGALYOV dismisses all social thinkers such as PLATO, ROUSSEAU, and FOURIER as dreamers, storytellers, and fools because they often contradict themselves. He then presents his own system, which is entirely contradictory. (4) At the socialist meeting a LAME TEACHER attempts to defend SHIGALYOV's system to the group by saying that FOURIER, CABET, and PROUDHON also had some despotic and fantastic solutions to the problem of the structure of future society. (5) At the same socialist meeting PYOTR STEPANOVICH argues that the works of CABET and FOURIER are nothing more than an aesthetic passing of time and are like novels that can be written by the thousands. He insists that it is time to act rather than talk. (6) PYOTR STEPANOVICH states that SHIGALYOV is a genius just like FOURIER but that SHIGALYOV is smarter and more forceful because he invented equality. The equality comes from the organization of a large slave class that spies on itself and does the bidding of a small ruling class. (7) PYOTR STEPANOVICH and LIPUTIN have a heated exchange over the merits of FOURIER, whom PYOTR STEPANOVICH dismisses as nonsense. (8) When the socialist group gathers to murder SHATOV, SHIGALYOV challengingly notes that the project does not jibe with his plan for the future organization of society and that he consequently wants no part of it. PYOTR STEPANOVICH angrily calls him a FOURIER, and SHI-GALYOV just as angrily denies it.

FRA-DIAVOLO. A comic opera completed in 1830 by Daniel François Esprit Auber (1782-1871), one of the chief creators of French comic opera. The narrator notes that as a schoolboy VON LEMBKE would on occasion make jokes, as for example when he would play the overture from *FRA-DIAVOLO* quite skillfully on his nose.

FRENZEL [FRENTSEL]. A doctor whose help SHATOV seeks when MARIE goes into labor.

"FULL OF PUREST LOVE//TRUE TO HIS SWEET DREAM" ["PO-LON CHISTOYU LYUBOVYU//VEREN SLADOSTNOY MECHTE"]. A couplet from Aleksandr PUSHKIN's ballad "There Once Lived a Poor Knight" ("Zhil na svete rytsar bedny"), written in 1829. The ballad characterizes an idealist who maintains absolute devotion to his dream. STEPAN TROFIMOVICH quotes these lines to VARVARA PETROV-NA as he threatens to leave her and everything else and embark upon a new path.

FYODOR FYODOROVICH (FEDKA, FEDKA THE CONVICT). A former house serf of PYOTR STEPANOVICH whom STEPAN TROFI-MOVICH sold into the army fifteen years prior to the action of the novel in order to cover losses at cards. He is a forty year old fugitive from Siberia who has committed many crimes including robbing a church and murdering the guard. He is the embodiment of active, physical evil. When he hints to STAVROGIN that he can be of use to him and that he would be willing to do away with the LEBYADKINS, STAVROGIN silently accedes and throws him some money into the mud. FEDKA spends a good deal of time picking up each bill. He murders LEBYADKIN and MARYA, but does not get the money he seeks because LIPUTIN had already taken it from LEBYADKIN. PYOTR STEPANOVICH had helped to orchestrate the murders by giving LEBYADKIN some money and making sure that FEDKA knew about it. When he encounters PYOTR STEPANOVICH at KIRILLOV's apartment, he both verbally and physically abuses him. He is murdered that same evening, probably by FOMKA.

FYODOR MATVEEVICH (FYODOR MATVEICH, FYODOR PETRO-VICH). Desiring to continue his pilgrimage to find Russia instead of talk with a group of peasants, STEPAN TROFIMOVICH attempts to put an end to their conversation by indicating that he must go to the village of Spasov to see one FYODOR MATVEEVICH. As he leaves, STEPAN TROFIMOVICH mistakenly refers to his ostensible target as FYODOR PETROVICH.

FYODOR MATVEICH. See FYODOR MATVEEVICH.

FYODOR PETROVICH. See FYODOR MATVEEVICH.

IVAN FYODOROV (PASHKA). VARVARA PETROVNA's late personal valet. The narrator identifies him as SHATOV's father.

ANTON LAVRENTIEVICH G—V. STEPAN TROFIMOVICH's confidant, who narrates the events of the novel. He provides the link between many of the characters and is instrumental in advancing the action as he carries information and arranges interviews.

ARTEMY PAVLOVICH GAGANOV. A powerful merchant, important social figure, and the son of PAVEL PAVLOVICH GAGANOV, whom STAVROGIN insulted. He is about thirty three, aristocratically white, well-fed, proud, excitable, and inclined toward gossip. He regularly insults STAVROGIN through letters and rumors in order to bait him into a duel so that he can avenge his father. When a duel finally materializes, he engages MAVRIKY NIKOLAEVICH, a school friend, as his second and eagerly proceeds. At the duel he becomes progressively insulted when STAVROGIN arrives on a horse rather than taking the precaution of bringing a vehicle, and when his opponent deliberately misses three shots. He leaves shattered from the experience.

PAVEL PAVLOVICH GAGANOV. A distinguished older member of a fashionable club who has the habit of boasting that he will not be led around by the nose. When he mentions this in the club one evening while STAVROGIN is there, the latter promptly grabs him by the nose and leads him about the room.

GARINA. The maiden name of BERESTOV's wife.

GLUCK [GLYUK]. Christoph Willibald von GLUCK (1714-87), Austrian composer of opera. In trying to describe the rhetorical, pompous, and sentimental content of KARMAZINOV's "MERCI" the narrator cites typical passages. Among them is a scene in which GLUCK plays an unfamiliar number on the violin while standing in the rushes.

GLUPOV. The name of the city in *History of a Town (Istoria odnogo goroda)*, written by Mikhail Yevgrafovich Saltykov (1826-89) in 1869-70. The work is the satirical history of an imaginary town (Stupidville) which draws on events and personalities from Russian history. The narrator complains that the younger generation is doing the sort of strange things that will turn their town into a GLUPOV.

GOETHE [GYOTE]. Johann Wolfgang von GOETHE (1749-1832), German poet, playwright, novelist, and scientist, who is one of the giants of world literature. (1) STEPAN TROFIMOVICH insists that he is a believer in God but is really more of a pagan like GOETHE or the ancient Greeks. (2) In order to make a good impression on KARMAZINOV, who plans to pay a visit to STEPAN TROFIMOVICH, VARVARA PETROVNA loans STEPAN TROFIMOVICH her TENIERS so that he can hang it by his portrait of GOETHE.

GOGOL. Nikolay Vasilievich GOGOL (1809-52), popular Russian writer noted for his tragicomic portrayal of human foibles. He was viewed as the fountainhead of the Natural School and credited with critically describing reality with the idea of social reform. (1) While expounding on his kind of belief in God, STEPAN TROFIMOVICH alludes to BELINSKY's letter to GOGOL in which BELINSKY attacked him for believing in God and abandoning the progressive cause. STEPAN TROFIMOVICH can imagine nothing funnier than GOGOL reading this letter. (2) SHATOV attacks STEPAN TROFIMOVICH and his generation for not understanding the people and for doing nothing for them. He states that the posture adopted by BELINSKY in his letter to GOGOL is a good example of this failure. (3) The narrator identifies KARMAZINOV as a mediocre talent when compared with PUSHKIN, GOGOL, MOLIERE, and VOLTAIRE, who wrote new and original works. (4) In a comic reaction to PRASKOVYA IVANOVNA DROZDOVA's "treatment" of himself and VARVARA PETROVNA, STEPAN TROFIMOVICH refers to DROZDOVA as an extremely provocative KOROBOCHKA out of the works of GOGOL. (5) LEBYADKIN asserts that he has written a work which he will leave to the world much as GOGOL's *FINAL TALE*.

GRANOVSKY. Timofey Nikolaevich GRANOVSKY (1813-55), Russian historian, university lecturer, and political figure. He was an active Westernizer who advocated a liberal course and opposed serfdom. (1) The narrator notes that STEPAN TROFIMOVICH, fond of perceiving himself as a progressive thinker of concern to the government, was once mentioned almost in the same breath with CHAADAEV, BELINSKY, GRANOVSKY, and HERZEN. (2) STEPAN TROFIMOVICH recalls that the last time he saw KARMAZINOV was at a dinner in GRANOVSKY's honor.

GULLIVER. Lemuel GULLIVER, a ship's physician who makes four journeys in the satirical masterpiece *Travels into Several Remote Nations of the World, by Lemuel GULLIVER*, written in 1726 by Jonathan Swift (1667-1745). The narrator compares STEPAN TROFIMOVICH to GULLIVER, who, after returning to London from the LILLIPUTIANS, still thinks that he is a giant among men. STEPAN TROFIMOVICH has for so long considered himself an important progressive thinker of concern to the government that reality makes no impact upon him.

HAMLET [GAMLET]. Central character of William SHAKESPEARE's *HAMLET, Prince of Denmark*, written in 1601. (1) LIZA reminisces about how STEPAN TROFIMOVICH once taught her about HAMLET. (2) In trying to explain STAVROGIN's behavior, VARVARA PETROVNA states that he is perhaps more like HAMLET than PRINCE HARRY, as had been suggested.

PRINCE HARRY [PRINTS GARRI]. HARRY Monmouth, also known as Prince Hal, in William SHAKESPEARE's *HENRY THE FOURTH, Parts One and Two* (1597-98). He is a boistrous youth who maintains bad company yet who matures quickly with responsibility. In *Henry the Fifth* he is a capable and sagacious king who commands respect. (1) STEPAN TROFIMOVICH attributes STAVROGIN's extreme behavior to the rowdy youth of a PRINCE HARRY who cavorts with FALSTAFF, POINS, and MISTRESS QUICKLY. (2) LIZA mentions to her mother that STEPAN TROFIMOVICH and VARVARA PETROVNA had discussed a possible connection between STAVROGIN and PRINCE HARRY.

HEECKEREN [GEKKERN]. Baron Louis Borchard Beveriwaert van HEECKEREN (1791-1884), Dutch envoy to Russia in the 1830s. His adopted son, George d'Anthès, became involved with PUSHKIN's wife and then fatally shot the writer when challenged to a duel. HEECKEREN's role in the drama was one of complicity and encouragement. When STAVRO-

GIN claims that no one had ever received a letter like the one he has received from a furious GAGANOV, KIRILLOV responds that PUSHKIN wrote a letter to HEECKEREN prior to his duel that must have been just as insulting.

HEINE [GEYNE]. Heinrich HEINE (1797-1856), German romantic poet, journalist, and satirist. In trying to describe the pompous, sentimental, and rhetorical content of KARMAZINOV's "MERCI" the narrator describes a passage of borrowed ideas in which there is BYRONIC melancholy, a grimace from HEINE, and something or other from PECHORIN.

HENRY THE FOURTH [GENRIKH IV]. *Parts One and Two,* plays by William SHAKESPEARE, written 1597-98. LIZA mentions to her mother PRASKOVYA IVANOVNA that VARVARA PETROVNA and STE-PAN TROFIMOVICH had mentioned the similarity between STAVRO-GIN and the boisterous PRINCE HARRY, who was described in *HENRY THE FOURTH.* The reference is to *Part One* in which PRINCE HARRY lives a riotous existence for a time.

HERZEN [GERTSEN]. Aleksandr Ivanovich HERZEN (1812-70), Russian journalist and political thinker. He was twice exiled for political activity and finally emigrated in 1847 and settled in London, where he published a biweekly journal *THE BELL,* which even though suppressed, enjoyed a wide readership in Russia. Through *THE BELL* he criticized the Russian social order and advocated the adoption of Western European socialism. (1) The narrator observes that STEPAN TROFIMOVICH, fond of thinking of himself as a progressive thinker of concern to the authorities, was once mentioned almost in the same breath with CHAADAEV, BELINSKY, GRANOVSKY, and HERZEN. (2) In discussing the young second lieutenant who suddenly bit his commanding officer, the narrator mentions that the young man is much like a person described with great humor by HERZEN. The narrator is likely referring to a naive young socialist whom HERZEN met in London. He gave HERZEN some money for *THE BELL* prior to embarking on a quixotic journey to found a socialist colony on the Marquesas Islands. (3) PYOTR STEPANOVICH tells VON LEMBKE that the poem "AN ILLUSTRIOUS PERSONALITY," which VON LEMBKE fears is subversive and intended to stir up the people, was written by SHATOV to promote his own cause and was not written by HERZEN as SHATOV claims. (4) In order to convince VON LEMBKE to search STEPAN TROFIMOVICH's room, VON BLÜM notes that STEPAN TROFIMOVICH's library contains RYLEEV's *THOUGHTS* and the works of HERZEN. (5) PYOTR STEPANOVICH tells SHATOV that he intends to claim that HERZEN himself wrote "AN ILLUSTRIOUS PERSONALITY" in PYOTR STEPANOVICH's album. (6) At the socialist meeting called by PYOTR STEPANOVICH, the LAME TEACHER attempts to persuade the group to seriously consider SHIGALYOV's ideas by stating that HERZEN and BELINSKY spent much time working out the structure of the future society. (7) STEPAN TROFIMOVICH excitedly and proudly reports to the narrator that VON BLÜM has requisitioned his papers and books, among them the foreign editions of HERZEN and a worn copy of *THE BELL.* (8) The narrator informs STEPAN TROFIMOVICH that he is crazy to think that he would be exiled for having the works of HERZEN. (9) STEPAN TROFIMOVICH is conviced that he will be exiled for having the works of HERZEN, a point of view that illustrates his pride and detachment from reality. (10) After reading "AN ILLUSTRIOUS PERSONALITY," LIPUTIN tells PYOTR STEPANOVICH that it is the worst poetry he has ever read and that he cannot believe that HERZEN wrote it. (11) STAVROGIN writes to DASHA that he, like HERZEN, has become a citizen of the Swiss canton of Uri, and he requests that she come there to be with him. HERZEN assumed Swiss citizenship in 1851 following his emigration from Russia.

HOFFMANN [GOFMAN]. Ernst Theodor Amadeus HOFFMANN (1776-1822), German writer known primarily for his fantastic tales. In trying to describe the rhetorical, sentimental, and pompous content and mood of KARMAZINOV's "MERCI" the narrator reports a typical scene in which HOFFMANN appears out of a mist, a water nymph whistles CHOPIN, and ANCUS MARCIUS in a laurel wreath hovers over the roofs of Rome.

HOMER [GOMER]. Ancient Greek poet to whom are attributed the *Iliad* and the *Odyssey.* He is noted for his broad, epic vision and proportions. LIZA organizes an excursion to visit SEMYON YAKOVLEVICH, a local holy oracle. When the oracle utters a not very holy obscenity to one of the women, the men burst forth in HOMERIC laughter.

L'HOMME QUI RIT. *The Man who Laughs,* a novel published in 1869 by the French novelist Victor Hugo (1802-85). The novel is a social commentary centering on an orphan Gwynplaine whose mutilated face is set in a perpetual grin. STEPAN TROFIMOVICH complains that VARVARA PETROVNA is ignoring him because she is so caught up with her son and KARMAZINOV. He shows the narrator a letter that she returned to him unanswered which he keeps in his room lying under the novel *L'HOMME QUI RIT.*

HORATIO [GORATSIO]. HAMLET's loyal friend and confidant in William SHAKESPEARE's *HAMLET, Prince of Denmark,* written in 1601. In reacting to the story of STAVROGIN's involvement with MARYA LEBYADKINA, VARVARA PETROVNA laments that her son had only a mother and no companion like HORATIO or OPHELIA.

"I DON'T NEED A NEW TALL ROOM" ["MNE NE NADOBEN NOV-VYSOK TEREM"]. First line of a quatrain from a folk song attributed to Yevdokia Fyodorovna Lopukhina, the first wife of Peter the Great, who was forcibly confined to a convent by her husband. MARYA LEBYAD-KINA sings the song to SHATOV after she mentions that her husband appeared in a dream. The lines express her intent to remain in a cell to pray and become holy.

IGRENEV. A character in VON LEMBKE's novel.

"AN ILLUSTRIOUS PERSONALITY" ["SVETLAYA LICHNOST"]. A parody of the poem "The Student" ("Student") written in 1869 by Nikolay Platonovich Ogaryov (1813-77), a collaborator of HERZEN and a noted revolutionary in his own right. The poem was used by Sergey Gennadievich Nechaev (1847-82) to give himself credibility in establishing small socialist groups in Russia, just as PYOTR STEPANOVICH tries to do. (1) PYOTR STEPANOVICH notices a copy of the poem on VON LEMBKE's desk, quotes it to him from memory, and indicates that he saw the "illustrious personality" not long ago abroad. (2) PYOTR STEPANOVICH tells VON LEMBKE that the poem was written by SHATOV to promote himself, and not by HERZEN, as SHATOV claims. (3) PYTOR STEPANOVICH indicates to SHATOV that he intends to use the poem to promote the socialist cause and will claim that HERZEN himself wrote it in his album. (4) LIPUTIN attacks the poem as the worst poetry he has ever read and adds that HERZEN could not possibly have written it.

ILYA ILYICH. One of the demonstrating workers who come to VON LEMBKE to complain of conditions at the SHPIGULIN factory.

"THE INQUISITIVE MAN" ["LYUBOPYTNY"]. A fable written by Ivan KRYLOV in 1814 which portrays a man's excursion to a new museum. He is enthralled with the insects and tiny birds to the extent that he does not notice the elephant. SHATOV insists that BELINSKY and the rest of the liberal generation are just like KRYLOV's "THE INQUISITIVE MAN," who fails to notice the elephant.

INTERNATIONALE [INTERNATSIONALKA]. An international association founded in London in 1864 under the leadership of Karl Marx and Friedrich Engels which was organized to advance socialist principles. When it could not generate the support of nationalistic trade unions, it lost influence and collapsed in the late 1870s. (1) PYOTR STEPANOVICH notes that the SHPIGULIN Factory employs five hundred workers in terrible conditions while the owners are millionaires. He feels certain that some of the factory workers must know about the INTERNATIONALE. (2) STAVROGIN states that PYOTR STEPANOVICH's socialist group has connections with the INTERNATIONALE. (3) When PYOTR STEPANOVICH takes STAVROGIN to the socialist meeting he has organized, STAVROGIN wryly comments that PYOTR STEPANOVICH probably wants to pass STAVROGIN off as a member of the INTERNATIONALE. (4) PYOTR STEPANOVICH states that in his design for the future society he wants to put the pope in charge of the Western world but adds that the pope will first have to come to terms with the INTERNATIONALE. (5) Following the debacle of YULIA MIKHAYLOVNA's fest in honor of the provincial government, most people blame the INTERNATIONALE for the troubles and insist that PYOTR STEPANOVICH is under its control.

IVAN. See IVAN SHATOV.

IVAN ALEKSANDROVICH. An elderly member of a fashionable town club.

IVAN FILIPPOVICH. PYOTR STEPANOVICH desires to use STAVROGIN as a myth around which he can rally the people and his socialist forces. He mentions the legends of the SKOPTSY but vows to start a better legend with STAVROGIN as IVAN THE TSAREVICH. He forecasts that soon people will build up visual legends comparable to the SKOPTSY legend in which IVAN FILIPPOVICH, the Lord of SABAOTH, rose into heaven in a chariot. The source of the name IVAN FILIPPOVICH is uncertain. Quite possibly, however, is that it is a combination of Danilo Filippov and Ivan Timofeevich Suslov. Filippov (d. 1700) was the founder of the Khlysty or Flagellants who declared himself to be the God of SABAOTH. He enlisted Suslov (1616-1716) into the sect, and Suslov subsequently became a "CHRIST" and helped to spread the sect and its views.

IVAN IVANOVICH. See IVAN IVANOVICH DROZDOV.

IVAN OSIPOVICH. The gentle and perhaps too lenient former governor of the province. He was a relative of VARVARA PETROVNA and had been thoroughly dominated by her. When STAVROGIN inexplicably bites his ear, he has him arrested.

IVAN PAVLOVICH. See IVAN PAVLOVICH SHATOV.

IVAN THE TSAREVICH [IVAN-TSAREVICH]. The beloved hero of several Russian folktales. He is usually the young son of an elderly tsar who endures all trials because of his virtuous qualities. All things are at his command and he invariably succeeds. PYOTR STEPANOVICH tells STAVROGIN that he wants to initiate disturbances and create legends and that he wants STAVROGIN to function as an IVAN THE TSAREVICH, a mythic figure around whom PYOTR STEPANOVICH can rally the people.

ANISIM IVANOV. A former servant of GAGANOV who is acquainted with STEPAN TROFIMOVICH and who meets him on his pilgrimage to find Russia.

JESUIT [IEZUIT]. The Society of Jesus, a religious order for Roman Catholic men founded by Ignatius Loyola (1491-1556) in 1534. The society is known for scholarship and missionary zeal and has been accused of secrecy and intrigue. (1) In discussing his belief in God STEPAN TROFIMOVICH notes that he rejects rituals and does not want to be JESUIT-like in his approach to the issue. (2) YULIA MIKHAYLOVNA refers to the wife of the marshall of the nobility as a JESUIT because of the aspersions she casts upon VON LEMBKE and YULIA MIKHAYLOVNA herself.

JOB [LE LIVRE DE JOB]. One of the books of the Old Testament which portrays the life of a righteous man who, despite great suffering and privation, retains his faith in God. In describing administrative zeal to VARVARA PETROVNA, STEPAN TROFIMOVICH cites the example of the deacon who threw an English family out of his church prior to the reading of PSALMS and JOB. The deacon according to STEPAN TROFIMOVICH was anxious to demonstrate his authority.

JULIE. See YULIA MIKHAYLOVNA VON LEMBKE.

JUPITER [YUPITER]. The supreme deity of Roman mythology who corresponds to the Greek Zeus. (1) In describing what he thinks administrative zeal is to VARVARA PETROVNA, STEPAN TROFIMOVICH cites the example of a nonentity who sells railroad tickets and who suddenly decides to preside over his affairs and demonstrates his power like some JUPITER. (2) LEBYADKIN writes a ridiculous fable entitled "THE COCKROACH" ("Tarakan") in which the flies complain to JUPITER when a cockroach gets into their glass.

COUNT K. See PRINCE K.

PRINCE K. (COUNT K.). A very important St. Petersburg personality who treats STAVROGIN as a son while in Paris.

LEV KAMBEK. LEV Loginovich KAMBEK, minor Russian journalist. See *"THE AGE* AND *THE AGE* AND LEV KAMBEK."

KAPITON MAKSIMOVICH. VIRGINSKY's relative who serves as a major in the province. He speaks out strongly against the emancipation of women and spends most of one night disputing the issue with VIRGINSKY's sister, whom he recalls cuddling as a baby.

KARMAZINOFF. See SEMYON YEGOROVICH KARMAZINOV. STEPAN TROFIMOVICH refers to him on occasion with the French pronunciation of KARMAZINOFF.

SEMYON YEGOROVICH KARMAZINOV (KARMAZINOFF). A novelist and distant relative of YULIA MIKHAYLOVNA. He is petty, vindictive, vain, and spoiled, and views himself as a great writer. The narrator refers to him as an average talent who has written himself out and who does not compare with writers like PUSHKIN and GOGOL. At YULIA MIKHAYLOVNA's literary day for the benefit of the provincial governesses he plans to read his farewell to literature entitled "MERCI" and then to abandon his pen and retire to Germany to Karlsruhe. He has lived in Karlsruhe for several years, considers himself a German, and regards the construction of a water main there more important than reforms in Russia. While in the province he tries to ingratiate himself with PYOTR STEPANOVICH because of the connections he thinks PYOTR STEPANOVICH has with the younger generation and the revolutionary movement. His reading of "MERCI" produces bewilderment. The pompous, rhetorical, sentimental, and obscure work is read at debilitating length in a very condescending manner, as if KARMAZINOV is rendering a great service. The audience is in disbelief as he makes many literary allusions, cites the great minds of Europe, and elevates himself above them all. His desperate

need for praise is met with interruptions and general confusion. KARMA-
ZINOV is intended as a parody of TURGENEV.

KARTUZOV. A periodic visitor to STEPAN TROFIMOVICH's circle.

KHRISTOFOR IVANOVICH. Even though LIZA flees to be with
STAVROGIN, she insists that she will not remain with him. She vows not to
be like KHRISTOFOR IVANOVICH, who used to come visit STAVRO-
GIN, promise to stay for only a moment, and then remain for the entire day.

ALEKSEY NILYICH KIRILLOV. An engineer of about twenty seven who
lives in poverty and spends his time thinking of God and death. He loves
children and life but prefers isolation and enjoys staying awake at night and
thinking. Like SHATOV's his ideas originate with STAVROGIN, and like
SHATOV he rethought his ideas and came to his present conclusions while
the two of them were in America seeing firsthand the conditions of the
American worker. KIRILLOV is determined to commit suicide. He
observes that man fears death because he loves life but that life is nothing but
pain and fear. He states that a new man will appear who is happy and proud
and who will not be afraid to die. This man will take his own life and will
become God because he overcomes the pain and fear of life. He defines the
God that men worship as the pain of the fear of death, and he admits that the
idea of God has tormented him all of his life. He knows that God is necessary
but also knows that He does not and cannot exist. If God exists then all will
is His, but since He does not and cannot, then will is KIRILLOV's, and he
has the obligation to demonstrate this to mankind. Suicide is the highest
demonstration of will, and he must show the way to others who are afraid to
demonstrate their will because of God. Through this process he saves
mankind and becomes Man-God, as opposed to God-Man, the act of
CHRIST becoming flesh. PYOTR STEPANOVICH plans to use KIRIL-
LOV's suicide for the promotion of himself and the revolutionary cause. In
the suicide note he has KIRILLOV claim responsibility for SHATOV's
murder in anticipation that this will divert any possible suspicion from
himself. KIRILLOV enters a darkened room, agonizes for several moments, and then shoots himself after he has signed a confession and
expressed his disgust for PYOTR STEPANOVICH.

PAUL DE KOCK [POL DE KOK]. French novelist (1793-1871) noted for
his graphic portrayals of Parisian life. (1) For appearance's sake STEPAN
TROFIMOVICH will on occasion carry a volume of TOCQUEVILLE into
the garden to study but will invariably have a concealed novel by PAUL DE
KOCK with him too. (2) In pointing out STEPAN TROFIMOVICH's

deficiencies, VARVARA PETROVNA observes that he reads only PAUL DE KOCK, does not write, plays cards, drinks, and associates with riff-raff.

"KOMARINSKY." A native peasant song and dance used by the Russian composer Mikhail Ivanovich Glinka (1804-57) for his *Kamarinskaya*. (1) STEPAN TROFIMOVICH pompously asserts that the only thing the peasants have contributed to Russia in one thousand years is the "KOMARINSKY." (2) At YULIA MIKHAYLOVNA's literary fest to benefit the provincial governesses an announcement is suddenly made about a fire at the SHPIGULIN Factory, and people rush madly outside. Many of the poorer ones remain, raid the buffet, and dance the "KOMARINSKY" without interference.

KOROBOCHKA. A female landowner in Nikolay GOGOL's *Dead Souls (Myortvye dushi)*, written in 1842. She is characterized by incredible stupidity. (1) When STEPAN TROFIMOVICH feels that PRASKOVYA IVANOVNA DROZDOVA is slighting him and VARVARA PETROVNA, he retaliates by referring to her as a provocative and evil KOROBOCHKA. (2) When the announcement of the SHPIGULIN Factory fire is made at the literary benefit for the provincial governesses, one woman cries out that the people have intentionally been gathered at the ball so that fires could be set elsewhere. Her statement is described as the natural reaction of a KOROBOCHKA.

KOROVAEV. LEBYADKIN recalls that he passed KOROVAEV some counterfeit money but fortunately did not get caught because KOROVAEV drowned in a pond while drunk.

KRAEVSKY. Andrey Aleksandrovich KRAEVSKY (1810-89), Russian journalist and publisher. Neither his intellect nor his political views were highly regarded by the progressives and liberals. KRAEVSKY is one of the topics of conversation for the fashionably progressive younger generation.

MISS KRIEGS [KRIGS]. The governess that VARVARA PETROVNA hires for DASHA.

KRYLOV. Ivan Andreevich KRYLOV (1769-1844), the most famous Russian writer of fables, whose works have become classics. (1) SHATOV insists that BELINSKY and the rest of the liberal generation are just like KRYLOV's "THE INQUISITIVE MAN," who upon visiting the museum directed all of his attention to the French socialist beetles and did not even notice the elephant. (2) When LEBYADKIN recites his coarse fable "THE

COCKROACH," he first attributes it to KRYLOV, then a friend, and finally admits that he wrote it himself. (3) LEBYADKIN notes that KRYLOV is a great writer of fables and that the Ministry of Education is planning to erect a monument in his honor.

KUBRIKOV. A sixty two year old official who attends the literary fest given by YULIA MIKHAYLOVNA to benefit the provincial governesses. When many attribute the furor surrounding the fest to the INTERNATIONALE, he states that he has been under the influence of the INTERNATIONALE for the past several months. When pressed for an explanation, he insists that he simply feels the influence with all of his senses.

KUKOLNIK. Nestor Vasilievich KUKOLNIK (1809-68), Russian poet and dramatist noted for his sentimental, patriotic tragedies. (1) The narrator observes that STEPAN TROFIMOVICH looks quite like a portrait of KUKOLNIK. (2) In describing what STEPAN TROFIMOVICH has meant to the liberal set, the narrator asserts that he has been their KUKOLNIK.

L—N. The narrator compares STAVROGIN to certain fearless and adventurous legendary figures, and he cites L—N,who participated in the Decembrist uprising of 1825, as an example. He could have reference to Mikhail Sergeevich Lunin (1787-1845), a socialist and revolutionary who following the Decembrist revolt spent the final twenty years of his life in prison and exile.

LAME TEACHER [KHROMOY]. A teacher who attends the socialist meeting called by PYOTR STEPANOVICH and who tries to persuade those assembled to seriously consider the ideas of SHIGALYOV.

THE LAY OF IGOR'S HOST [SLOVO O POLKU IGOREVE]. An epic poem of old Russian literature dating from the twelfth century. STEPAN TROFIMOVICH had once offered to give DASHA a course in the history of Russian literature but gave only a single lecture. When VARVARA PETROVNA understands that his second lecture is to cover *THE LAY OF IGOR'S HOST,* she puts a stop to his course.

IGNAT LEBYADKIN. A forty year old FALSTAFF who plays the buffoon to get money and drink. He is large, coarse, causes scenes, and alternately praises and debases himself. He moves in with the VIRGINSKY family after ARINA PROKHOROVNA announces that she prefers him to her husband, but he is "beaten" by the small VIRGINSKY and dismissed.

After this failure he removes his sister MARYA from a convent and brings her to the provincial town. He starves and beats her but hopes to capitalize on her presence to get more money from STAVROGIN, who has supported MARYA since their marriage. His character and failures in life are reflected in his coarse verse, which he values highly and with which he attempts to get recognition. He expresses his love for LIZA in verse but is quickly rebuffed, and his absurd fable about a cockroach leaves VARVARA PETROVNA bewildered. He and MARYA are ultimately murdered by FEDKA who hopes to get the money that PYOTR STEPANOVICH gave him.

MARYA TIMOFEEVNA LEBYADKINA (MARYA TIMOFEVNA, MARYA THE UNKNOWN). LEBYADKIN's thirty year old sister who is lame and mentally deficient. She has a dazed but happy expression and sits for days by herself fortune telling with cards or looking into a small mirror. STAVROGIN had married her in his youth and maintains her in a convent with a regular allowance. In the convent she practices a folk religion, viewing God and nature as unified. She often mentions her ideal husband and a deceased baby, but STAVROGIN insists that this is her imagination and that she is still a virgin. LEBYADKIN brings her into the provincial town hoping to use her to get money from STAVROGIN, and while there he beats and starves her. She views STAVROGIN with both fear and rapture but ultimately dismisses him as a poor imitation of her prince and refers to him as GRISHKA OTREPIEV, an imposter. She frequently refers to a knife and insists that STAVROGIN wants to kill her. She and LEBYAD-KIN are ultimately stabbed by FEDKA, who acts with STAVROGIN's implicit approval.

MADAME LEFEBURE. VARVARA PETROVNA recalls that PRA-SKOVYA IVANOVNA once insisted that the hussar SHABLYKIN was courting her. She eagerly adds that MADAME LEFEBURE exposed the contention as a lie.

LEMBKA. See ANDREY ANTONOVICH VON LEMBKE. VON LEMB-KE is called LEMBKA as a schoolboy.

ANDREY ANTONOVICH VON LEMBKE (LEMBKA). The new gover-nor of the province who replaces IVAN OSIPOVICH. He was educated in an exclusive school where he was a poor student who played alot of tricks. His career developed gradually and always under the direction of German superiors. When frustrated by failure, he resorts to making paper theaters and trains, and he remains childlike and dependent throughout his life. He finally marries YULIA MIKHAYLOVNA when he is thirty eight and she past forty, and her connections insure his career. Even though he likes to voice liberal ideas, he quickly comes into conflict with PYOTR STEPANO- VICH, who assumes many liberties with the governor because of the foolishness of YULIA MIKHAYLOVNA. VON LEMBKE becomes increasingly depressed and taciturn because of the progressive pamphlets found in the area and the worker unrest, and he uncharacteristically permits himself to argue with YULIA MIKHAYLOVNA. He objects to being dominated by his wife and to her relationship with PYOTR STEPANO- VICH, and this frustration coupled with worker demonstrations and the fire at the SHPIGULIN Factory causes his mind to snap.

YULIA MIKHAYLOVNA VON LEMBKE (JULIE). VON LEMBKE's wife, born a DROZDOVA and a cousin to LIZA. She marries the younger VON LEMBKE when she is in her forties and pushes him into society and advantageous connections. When VON LEMBKE becomes the governor of the province, she finds herself in a social struggle with VARVARA PETROVNA for local supremacy, and she attempts to use her planned literary fest for the benefit of the provincial governesses as a way to insure her social dominance. She is drawn to the younger progressive generation and feels that she must be close to them and treat them gently. Because of this she adopts PYOTR STEPANOVICH as her favorite, inasmuch as she is convinced that he is an oracle who has extensive mysterious ties. She views herself as the savior of the younger generation and feels assured that PYOTR STEPANOVICH is devoted to her. Even though she is anxious for VON LEMBKE to succeed, she often sides with PYOTR STEPANOVICH when the two are in conflict. When VON LEMBKE quite uncharacteristi- cally objects, she treats him coldly and silently and contributes to his mental breakdown. The narrator is careful to note that she should be blamed for much of the chaos in the province. When public opinion turns away from her following the literary fest and the ball, her thoughts turn wholly but belatedly to VON LEMBKE, who is already out of touch with reality.

LERMONTOV. Mikhail Yurievich LERMONTOV (1814-41), the fore- most Russian Romantic writer, who perished in a duel. The narrator notes that STAVROGIN disdains fear and possesses a cold and calculating spite that transcends both L—N and LERMONTOV.

"LIBERTE, EGALITE, FRATERNITE OU LA MORT!" "Liberty, equal- ity, fraternity or death!" one of the mottoes used during the French Revolution of 1789-99, modified through the addition of "OU LA MORT!" KIRILLOV writes these words under his signature on the confession he leaves prior to his suicide.

LILLIPUTIANS [LILIPUTY]. The six-inch tall people that GULLIVER encounters on one of his journeys. They are characterized not only by physical smallness but also by pettiness. The narrator compares STEPAN TROFIMOVICH to GULLIVER, who after returning to London from the LILLIPUTIANS still thinks that he is a giant among men. STEPAN TROFIMOVICH's vanity and naiveté obscure his uselessness.

LIPOUTINE. See SERGEY VASILYICH LIPUTIN. STEPAN TROFI-MOVICH on occasion refers to LIPUTIN with a French pronunciation.

SERGEY VASILYICH LIPUTIN (LIPOUTINE). An old skinflint, slanderer, and devotee of FOURIER who is part of the small liberal circle around STEPAN TROFIMOVICH. He invites STAVROGIN to his wife's birthday party after the scandal with GAGANOV, but becomes upset when STAVROGIN kisses his wife three times and then leaves. Despite his age and liberal pretensions, he is close to LEBYADKIN and the young riff-raff and takes part in their antics. He helps LEBYADKIN write the verse that is read at YULIA MIKHAYLOVNA's literary fest and orchestrates the affair so that a scandal will result. He becomes a member of PYOTR STEPANO-VICH's inner circle together with VIRGINSKY, SHIGALYOV, TOL-KACHENKO, and LYAMSHIN, but despises PYOTR STEPANOVICH because of his high-handedness. He steals the two hundred rubles from LEBYADKIN that FEDKA sought when he murdered him and considers escaping abroad. When the socialist group kills SHATOV, he takes no part and quickly flees to St. Petersburg, where he indulges in debauchery and is finally arrested. He faces his trial with optimism and remains quite obstinate.

MADAME LIPUTINA. LIPUTIN's much younger and pretty wife. At her birthday party STAVROGIN dances with her, kisses her three times, and abruptly leaves.

LISE. See LIZAVETA NIKOLAEVNA TUSHINA.

LITTRE. Emile LITTRE (1801-81), French philosopher, doctor, lexico-grapher, and political figure. In discussing his future personal triumph and the eventual success of socialism with STAVROGIN, PYOTR STEPA-NOVICH notes that when he left Russia, LITTRE's thesis that crime is insanity was in vogue. When he returns, however, crime is viewed as a rational, almost expected, and noble protest. He is convinced that this new attitude will aid his success. It would appear that Dostoevsky has inaccurately ascribed the theory that crime is insanity to LITTRE and that the source of the idea in Russia was Lambert Adolphe Jacques Quetelet (1796-1874), Belgian statistician and astronomer who applied the mathematical methods of averages and probabilities to the study of man and society. The idea that crime is insanity and that both are predictable through the laws of probability and the environment provoked a reevaluation of whether man should be punished or not.

"A LIVING MONUMENT OF CENSURE//YOU STOOD BEFORE YOUR COUNTRY,//OH,LIBERAL-IDEALIST" ["VOPLOSHCHYON-NOY UKORIZNOYU//TY STOYAL PERED OTCHIZNOYU,//LIBER-AL-IDEALIST"]. Inaccurate rendering of lines from "The Bear Hunt" ("Medvezhya okhota"), penned by Nikolay Alekseevich Nekrasov (1821-78) in 1867. The lines from the original are "You stood before your country/ /Honest of thought and pure of heart,//A living monument of censure/ /Oh, Liberal-idealist!" ("Ty stoyal pered otchiznoyu//Chesten myslyu, serdtsem chist,//Voploshchyonnoy ukoriznoyu//Liberal-idealist!"). The lines in "The Bear Hunt" are ironic praise for the aristocratic liberal who, though satirized in the past, is nonetheless still respected and loved by certain segments of society. These lines are quoted with reference to STEPAN TROFIMOVICH, the embodiment of the ineffectual liberal.

LIZA. See LIZAVETA NIKOLAEVNA TUSHINA.

LIZAVETA NIKOLAEVNA. See LIZAVETA NIKOLAEVNA TUSHINA.

LUKE [LUKA]. The third of the four Gospels in the New Testament. SOFYA reads STEPAN TROFIMOVICH the account from LUKE about the devils who were cast out of the man possessed and permitted to enter the bodies of swine.

LYAMSHIN. A liberal Jew and periodic visitor to STEPAN TROFIMO-VICH's circle who is involved with the young rogues in many of their scandalous antics. His personal tricks include putting dirty pictures in a BIBLE seller's pack. He becomes a member of PYOTR STEPANOVICH's inner circle together with LIPUTIN, VIRGINSKY, SHIGALYOV, and TOLKACHENKO. On the evening when MARIE SHATOVA is in labor SHATOV comes to him in need of money to pay for the baby. He gives SHATOV only half of the money he asks for in exchange for his pistol. He is very nervous and ill prior to SHATOV's murder and takes no part in the actual killing. After the murder he seems to lose his mind and runs screaming to the authorities, where he confesses everything and completely indicts PYOTR STEPANOVICH.

LYNCH [LINCH]. SHATOV relates some of the things he saw in America and mentions the existence of the LYNCH law, a situation in which private citizens execute punishment without the authority of law. The procedure is traced to Charles LYNCH (1736-86), Virginia planter, soldier, and public official. As presiding judge in a frontier county at the time of the breakdown of government during the period of the American Revolution, he often sentenced people in extralegal courts.

MADONNA. In Christianity the Virgin Mary, the mother of CHRIST. VARVARA PETROVNA berates STEPAN TROFIMOVICH for being high-handed with her and for thinking that she could have no thoughts or feelings of any consequence. She cites his reluctance to discuss the MADONNA with her as an example.

MAKAR. STEPAN TROFIMOVICH writes to VARVARA PETROV-NA from Berlin and uses the expression "dans le pays de MAKAR et de ses veaux" ("in the country of MAKAR and his calves"). The expression is based upon the Russian saying "kuda MAKAR telyat ne gonyal" ("where MAKAR did not drive the calves"), which indicates a place far out of the way where one would not go of his own accord. The context is often one of penal exile. STEPAN TROFIMOVICH uses the expression as a reference to the German police, who, he feels sure, are watching him.

MARFA SERGEVNA. ANISIM IVANOV, a former servant of PAVEL PAVLOVICH GAGANOV, now serves MARFA SERGEVNA, a sister of AVDOTYA SERGEVNA.

MARIE. See MARYA IGNATIEVNA SHATOVA. SHATOV usually refers to his wife as MARIE.

"LA MARSEILLAISE" ["MARSELIEZA"]. The French national anthem dating from the French Revolution. See BISMARCK (2).

MARYA. See MARYA IGNATIEVNA SHATOVA.

MARYA. A servant of VARVARA PETROVNA.

MARYA IGNATIEVNA. See MARYA IGNATIEVNA SHATOVA.

MARYA THE UNKNOWN [MARYA NEIZVESTNAYA]. See MARYA TIMOFEEVNA LEBYADKINA. When talking with VARVARA PE-TROVNA, LEBYADKIN refers to his sister as MARYA THE UN-KNOWN.

MARYA TIMOFEEVNA. See MARYA TIMOFEEVNA LEBYADKI-NA.

MARYA TIMOFEVNA. See MARYA TIMOFEEVNA LEBYADKINA.

MASHKEEVA. When SHATOV comes to ARINA PROKHOROVNA VIRGINSKAYA in the middle of the night to ask her to help MARIE deliver her baby, he is initially put off and asked to get MASHKEEVA instead.

MAURICE. See MAVRIKY NIKOLAEVICH DROZDOV. STEPAN TROFIMOVICH refers to MAVRIKY NIKOLAEVICH with the French MAURICE.

MAVRIKY NIKOLAEVICH. See MAVRIKY NIKOLAEVICH DROZ-DOV.

"MEIN LIEBER AUGUSTIN." "Ach, Du Lieber Augustin," popular German song. See BISMARCK (2).

"MERCI." KARMAZINOV writes this farewell to literature and his reading public and plans to read it at YULIA MIKHAYLOVNA's literary fest. Thereafter he plans to retire to Karlsruhe and never write again, no matter how strongly he is importuned. KARMAZINOV is intended as an analogue to Ivan TURGENEV, and "MERCI" parallels TURGENEV's *Enough (Dovolno)* published in 1865, in which he too bade farewell to literature. "MERCI" is pompous and obscure and creates a feeling of bewilderment in those who hear it.

MILLEBOYE [MILBUA]. A civil servant and friend of VON LEMBKE. After the workers of the SHPIGULIN Factory demonstrate and he has a row with YULIA MIKHAYLOVNA, VON LEMBKE recalls some of the events of his past in a feverish and disconnected manner. One memory involves youthful experiences with MILLEBOYE. The two once caught a sparrow in Aleksandrov Park and mused that one of them already had a high rank.

MINCHEN [MINKHEN]. See MINNA.

MINERVA. The Roman goddess of wisdom and patroness of the arts and trades. The narrator refers to VARVARA PETROVNA and the other women of the town as MINERVAS.

MINNA (MINCHEN). Rather than the anticipated MINNA or ERNEST-INA, VON LEMBKE marries YULIA MIKHAYLOVNA and anticipates a blissful life with her.

MOLESCHOTT [MOLESHOTT]. Jacobus MOLESCHOTT (1822-93), Dutch materialist philosopher and physiologist whose work was canonized by the young Russian radicals of the 1860s and 1870s. When a second lieutenant in his provincial regiment seemingly goes crazy and bites his commanding officer, his room is searched and in addition to some progressive pamphlets are found the works of VOGT, MOLESCHOTT, and BÜCHNER.

MOLIERE. Pen name of Jean Baptiste Poquelin (1622-73), who became the foremost French comic dramatist. He likely has no rival in the comic exposition of human foibles. The narrator evaluates KARMAZINOV as a mediocre talent who does not compare with the originality and innovativeness of PUSHKIN, GOGOL, MOLIERE, and VOLTAIRE.

PRINCE DE MONBARS [MONBAR]. LEBYADKIN complains that he was named IGNAT instead of something like ERNEST or PRINCE DE MONBARS.

MOSCOW RECORD [MOSKOVSKIE VEDOMOSTI]. A widely circulated Moscow daily. LEBYADKIN notes that VARVARA PETROVNA had published in the *MOSCOW RECORD* that their provincial town had a local charitable society.

MUHAMMAD [MAGOMET]. In Arabic "the praised one," a name adopted by the founder of Islam (570-632). KIRILLOV discusses with SHATOV the feelings of unendurable bliss and harmony that he sometimes gets. SHATOV suspects that it must be akin to pre-epilepsy and cites the example of MUHAMMAD, who talked with Allah and the prophets and traveled throughout the heavenly realms on his horse in the short time it took to steady a pitcher to prevent its falling. He reminds KIRILLOV that MUHAMMAD was an epileptic. SHATOV has reference to the Islamic legend that the angel Gabriel brushed a pitcher with his wing one night while visiting MUHAMMAD and that as MUHAMMAD steadied the pitcher he took his journey into the heavens.

NAPOLEON. NAPOLEON I Bonaparte (1769-1821), emperor of France following the French Revolution and temporary conqueror of much of Europe. YULIA MIKHAYLOVNA's white room in the governor's mansion is expensively furnished and contains furniture from the period of NAPOLEON.

NASTASIE. See NASTASYA. STEPAN TROFIMOVICH refers to NASTASYA with the French NASTASIE.

NASTASYA (STASIE, NASTASIE). STEPAN TROFIMOVICH's maid. He insists that he cannot believe in God as she does.

NATALYA PAVLOVNA. STEPAN TROFIMOVICH refers to an official who had the audacity to insult him twice and notes with glee that the same official was severely beaten when he was discovered in NATALYA PAVLOVNA's boudoire.

ST. NICHOLAS [NIKOLAY UGODNIK]. The bishop of Myra who died about 345 A.D. FEDKA admits to STAVROGIN that he robbed a church and took money and an icon of ST. NICHOLAS. When he tries to sell parts of the icon, he receives little and is told that it is adorned with plate instead of pure silver.

NICOLAS. See NIKOLAY VSEVOLODOVICH STAVROGIN. STEPAN TROFIMOVICH frequently refers to STAVROGIN by the French NICOLAS.

NIKIFOR. A character in LEBYADKIN's ridiculous fable "THE COCKROACH."

NIKODIMOV. Ostensibly a character in one of KARMAZINOV's novels. The writer boasts that through NIKODIMOV he exposed all of the faults of the Westernizers. Dostoevsky possibly refers to Panshin in TURGENEV's *A Nest of Gentlefolk (Dvoryanskoe gnezdo),* written in 1859, who comes out second best to the Slavophile Lavretsky. In "About *Fathers and Sons*" ("Po povodu *Ottsov i detey*"), written in 1869, TURGENEV noted that even though he was a confirmed Westernizer, he exposed the negative qualities of the movement in Panshin and portrayed Lavretsky as positive because that is how he viewed social conditions in the middle 1850s.

EMPEROR NIKOLAY PAVLOVICH. Tsar NIKOLAY I (1796-1855). He ruled Russia from 1825 to 1855 and was known for his rigidly military reign. KIRILLOV has a portrait of EMPEROR NIKOLAY PAVLOVICH hanging in his room.

NIKOLAY VSEVOLODOVICH. See NIKOLAY VSEVOLODOVICH STAVROGIN.

NIKOLENKA. See NIKOLAY VSEVOLODOVICH STAVROGIN.

NIKON SEMYONYCH. See NIKON SEMYONYCH ANDREEV.

NOZDRYOV. A character in Nikolay GOGOL's *Dead Souls (Myortvye dushi)*, written in 1842, who is characterized by his coarse gaiety, bullying, and drinking. (1) As he tries to explain BAZAROV's rejection by the progressive circles of the 1860s, STEPAN TROFIMOVICH insists that BAZAROV is an unclear mixture of BYRON and NOZDRYOV. (2) STAVROGIN was once fond of saying that to believe in God, one must first have a God. He often used this saying much like NOZDRYOV, who continually boasted that he had caught a rabbit by the hind legs.

OLYMPUS [OLIMP]. In Greek mythology the home of the gods. In STEPAN TROFIMOVICH's allegorical poem, which he considers to be of concern to the authorities, the TOWER OF BABEL is completed and the ruler of OLYMPUS (Zeus) jumps atop of it.

"ON TROUVE TOUJOURS PLUS DE MOINES QUE DE RAISON." "One always meets more monks than reason," inexact rendering of a comment by Blaise PASCAL in his *Lettres Ecrits à un provincial par Blaise Pascal (Letters Written to a Provincial by Blaise Pascal)* written 1656-57. The original reads "parce qu'il leur est bien plus aise de trouver des moines que des raisons" ("because it is much easier for them to find monks than reasons"). STEPAN TROFIMOVICH makes this comment in discussing the intellectual capacities of men and adds that Russians have never really said anything of consequence.

OPHELIA [OFELIA]. In William SHAKESPEARE's *HAMLET, Prince of Denmark* (1601), the object of HAMLET's romantic advances. At her father's request she spurns them. In reacting to the history of STAVROGIN's involvement with MARYA LEBYADKINA, VARVARA PETROVNA laments that her son had only a mother and no companions such as HORATIO or OPHELIA.

OTHELLO [OTELLO]. *OTHELLO, the Moor of Venice*, a tragedy by William SHAKESPEARE written about 1604. The play relates the tale of OTHELLO, who strangles his love Desdemona when he suspects her of infidelity and who then commits suicide when he learns that she is innocent. LIZA mentions that she read the first act of *OTHELLO* to her ill mother PRASKOVYA IVANOVNA.

GRISHKA OTREPIEV. A monk who posed as the slain tsarevich Dmitry, son of Ivan IV the Terrible. Dmitry was allegedly murdered by Boris Godunov so that he could become tsar. With the help of Polish forces GRISHKA, also called the Pretender, conquered and ruled Russia 1605-6. (1) MARYA LEBYADKINA asks STAVROGIN if he has read of GRISHKA OTREPIEV's being anathematized in seven cathedrals. Since 1605 OTREPIEV has been cursed by the Russian Orthodox Church. (2) MARYA LEBYADKINA rejects STAVROGIN as her ideal prince and falcon, and calls him GRISHKA OTREPIEV anathema, a pretender to the ideal.

"OVER WHOM FLASHED THE TONGUE" ["NAD KOEY VSPY-KHNUL SEY YAZYK"]. An inexact citation from Aleksandr PUSHKIN's "The Hero" ("Geroy"), written in 1830. The original reads, without change in the English translation, "Nad koim vspykhnul sey yazyk." In the poem the tongue of glory flashes over and singles out those whom it will. After her marriage to VON LEMBKE, YULIA MIKHAYLOVNA considers herself foreordained for success, and she vigorously pushes forward as one "OVER WHOM FLASHED THE TONGUE."

PASCAL [PASKAL]. Blaise PASCAL (1623-62), French philosopher, scientist, and writer. In talking with VARVARA PETROVNA about intellectual abilities, STEPAN TROFIMOVICH quotes "ON TROUVE TOUJOURS PLUS DE MOINES QUE DE RAISON" and admits that they are not his words but those of PASCAL. He adds that he himself is not a PASCAL but that Russians have never said anything anyway.

PASHKA (IVAN FYODOROV). SHATOV mentions that he is the son of STAVROGIN's serf PASHKA. Since SHATOV's patronymic is PAVLO-VICH, his father's name would have been Pavel, one diminutive form of which is PASHKA. The narrator's statement that SHATOV's father's name was IVAN FYODOROV is suspect in view of this and in view of the different surname.

FATHER PAVEL. The archpriest at the provincial town church.

PAVEL PAVLOVICH. See PAVEL PAVLOVICH GAGANOV.

"THE PEASANTS ARE COMING AND CARRYING AXES,//SOME-THING DREADFUL WILL HAPPEN" ["IDUT MUZHIKI I NESUT TOPORY,//CHTO-TO STRASHNOE BUDET"]. Rewording of an anonymous poem "Fantasy" ("Fantazia"), which appeared in *The Polar Star (Polyarnaya zvezda)* in 1861. STEPAN TROFIMOVICH quotes these lines at a meeting of his small liberal circle.

PECHORIN. The sullen, spoiled, proud, and sometimes cruel hero of Mikhail LERMONTOV's novel *A Hero of Our Time (Geroy nashego vremeni)*, published in 1841. (1) After STAVROGIN comes to MADAME LIPUTINA's birthday party, dances with her, kisses her three times, and then abruptly leaves, LIPUTIN refers to him as a PECHORIN and a lady-killer. (2) In citing typical material from KARMAZINOV's "MERCI," the narrator notes that KARMAZINOV, a borrower of ideas, includes some melancholy from BYRON, a grimace from HEINE, and something or other from PECHORIN.

ANTON PETROV. A leader of the peasant rebellions in 1861 following the freeing of the serfs. He was executed for telling the peasants that all of the land was theirs and that they did not have to pay any rent. The rebellion was quickly and ruthlessly put down by military force. Rumors of ANTON PETROV and the peasant movement around the time of the emancipation disturb STEPAN TROFIMOVICH greatly.

PETRUSHA. See PYOTR STEPANOVICH VERKHOVENSKY. STEPAN TROFIMOVICH on occasion refers to his son with this term of endearment.

PIERRE. See PYOTR STEPANOVICH VERKHOVENSKY. STEPAN TROFIMOVICH on occasion refers to his son with the French equivalent.

PLATO [PLATON]. Greek philosopher and writer (ca. 427-348 B.C.). He is noted for his dialogues that record the thinking of his teacher Socrates and also for his positing a realm of ideas and truth outside the empirical. SHIGALYOV dismisses all social thinkers such as PLATO, ROUSSEAU, and FOURIER as dreamers, storytellers, and idiots who often contradict themselves, and then he presents his own system, which is full of contradictions.

POGOZHEV. A character in one of KARMAZINOV's novels through which the writer professes to have exposed all of the faults of the Slavophile movement.

POINS [POYNS]. In William SHAKESPEARE's *HENRY IV, Part I and Part II*, the confidant of PRINCE HARRY. STEPAN TROFIMOVICH attributes STAVROGIN's extreme behavior to the youth of a PRINCE HARRY who carouses with FALSTAFF, POINS, and MISTRESS QUICKLY.

POLINKA SAKS. A novel written in 1847 by Aleksandr Vasilievich Druzhinin (1824-64). The work deals with the theme of the emancipated woman and records how a husband willingly permits his wife to join her young lover. PYOTR STEPANOVICH asks LIZA if she has read *POLINKA SAKS* following her flight to be with STAVROGIN. PYOTR STEPANOVICH makes the statement when he observes that MAVRIKY NIKOLAEVICH has maintained a vigil over the house all night.

POMPEY. Gnaeus Pompeius Magnus (106-48 B.C.), Roman general and statesman who was deposed by Julius Caesar during the civil war and was later murdered in Egypt. In describing the pompous and rhetorical "MERCI," the narrator notes a typical passage in which lovers sit under a tree in Germany and suddenly see either POMPEY or CASSIUS. They are filled with the chill of ecstasy because of the experience.

"POOR" LIZA. The heroine of the sentimental tale *Poor Liza (Bednaya Liza)*, written by Nikolay Mikhaylovich Karamzin (1766-1826) in 1792. In the tale a seduced and abandoned peasant girl commits suicide. LIZA asks STEPAN TROFIMOVICH to pray for "POOR" LIZA, an allusion to her involvement with STAVROGIN.

POTTAGE OF LENTILS [CHECHEVICHNOE VAREVO]. As recorded in Genesis 25 in the Old Testament, Esau sells his birthright to Jacob in return for bread and a POTTAGE OF LENTILS. When VARVARA PETROVNA and STEPAN TROFIMOVICH part, she disgustedly reflects on their twenty years together. STEPAN TROFIMOVICH feels that her feelings have been stimulated by others, likely PYOTR STEPANO-VICH, and asks her for what POTTAGE OF LENTILS she has sold her freedom.

PRASKOVYA IVANOVNA. See PRASKOVYA IVANOVNA DROZ-DOVA.

PRIPUKHLOV. Following SHATOV's murder and KIRILLOV's suicide, an acquaintance of PYOTR STEPANOVICH plans to introduce him to PRIPUKHLOV, a millionaire merchant.

PROKHORYCH. The main cook in the fashionable provincial club. He is to provide some of the food for YULIA MIKHAYLOVNA's literary fest in honor of the local governesses.

PROUDHON [PRUDON]. Pierre Joseph PROUDHON (1809-65), French socialist and anarchist. He was an ardent reformer and was very critical of private property, church, and state. At the socialist meeting called by PYOTR STEPANOVICH, the LAME TEACHER tries to get the group to consider seriously SHIGALYOV's ideas by stating that FOURIER, CABET, and PROUDHON also had some despotic and fantastic solutions to the problems of society's structure.

PSALMS [CES CHANTS]. One of the books of the Old Testament that contains the songs of David and others. In describing administrative zeal to VARVARA PETROVNA, STEPAN TROFIMOVICH cites the example of the deacon who threw an English family out of his church prior to the reading of PSALMS and JOB. The deacon, according to STEPAN TROFIMOVICH, was anxious to demonstrate his authority.

PUSHKIN. Aleksandr Sergeevich PUSHKIN (1799-1837), the leading Russian writer of his age, who is widely regarded as the father of modern Russian literature. (1) The verses serving as one of the epigraphs to the novel, "STRIKE ME DEAD, THE WAY IS LOST," are attributed to A. PUSHKIN. (2) STEPAN TROFIMOVICH is loudly denounced by a progressive audience when he declares that PUSHKIN is far superior to having boots. (3) The narrator characterizes KARMAZINOV as a very average writer when compared with PUSHKIN, GOGOL, MOLIERE, and VOLTAIRE, who are original and innovative. (4) When STAVROGIN comments that no one has ever received as insulting a letter as the one he received from GAGANOV prior to the duel, KIRILLOV notes that PUSHKIN wrote a vehemently insulting letter to HEECKEREN prior to his duel with d'Anthès.

PYOTR ILYICH. A member of the fashionable provincial club.

PYOTR MIKHAYLOVICH. An elderly member of the fashionable provincial club.

PYOTR STEPANOVICH. See PYOTR STEPANOVICH VERKHO-VENSKY.

PYOTR STEPANYCH. See PYOTR STEPANOVICH VERKHOVEN-SKY.

MISTRESS QUICKLY [MISTRIS KVIKLI]. The silly and gullible hostess of the Boar's Head Tavern in William SHAKESPEARE's *HENRY THE FOURTH, Part I and Part II,* written 1597-98. STEPAN TROFI-MOVICH attributes STAVROGIN's extreme behavior to the youth of a PRINCE HARRY cavorting with FALSTAFF, POINS, and MISTRESS QUICKLY.

RACHEL [RASHEL]. Elisabeth RACHEL Felix (1821-58), French tragic actress. STEPAN TROFIMOVICH insists that he would exchange all Russian peasants for one RACHEL.

RADISHCHEV. Aleksandr Nikolaevich RADISHCHEV (1749-1802), Russian writer whose liberal views on government and serfdom incurred the ire of Catherine the Great, who exiled him to Siberia. (1) The narrator notes that when liberal ideas were fashionable, STEPAN TROFIMOVICH was compared even with RADISHCHEV. (2) The narrator angrily discusses the riff-raff that surface during difficult times and cites YULIA MIKHAY-LOVNA's literary fête as an example. He singles out the LYAMSHINS, TENTETNIKOVS, and the local snivelling RADISHCHEVS.

RAPHAEL [RAFAEL]. Raffaelo Sanzio (1483-1520), Italian painter who is one of the greatest artists in history. He was the leading exponent of the Renaissance conception of human nobility and is best known for his MADONNAS. At YULIA MIKHAYLOVNA's literary fest STEPAN TROFIMOVICH discusses the difference between his generation and the younger generation and concludes that the basic difference lies in the conception of which is better—SHAKESPEARE or boots, RAPHAEL or petroleum. He defiantly insists that SHAKESPEARE and RAPHAEL are more valuable than the emancipation of the serfs, socialism, science, or anything else.

STENKA RAZIN. Stepan Timofeevich RAZIN (ca. 1630-71), leader of the rebelling peasants in the Peasant War of 1670-71 who was ultimately captured and put to death. PYOTR STEPANOVICH wants to use STAVROGIN as a mythic figure around which to rally the peasants and feels that he can successfully play the role of STENKA RAZIN.

RENAN. Ernest RENAN (1823-92), French historian, journalist, and writer. STEPAN TROFIMOVICH recalls having read RENAN's *VIE DE JESUS (Life of Jesus)* some years ago. The book appeared in 1863 and contends against the divinity of CHRIST.

ROSENTHAL. STEPAN TROFIMOVICH mistakenly refers to VON BLÜM as ROSENTHAL.

ROUSSEAU [RUSSO]. Jean Jacques ROUSSEAU (1712-78), French author, philosopher, and liberal political theorist. SHIGALYOV dismisses all social thinkers, including PLATO, ROUSSEAU, and FOURIER, as dreamers, storytellers, and veritable idiots who continually contradict themselves. He proposes his own social system, which ironically is also based on contradiction.

ROZANOV. A doctor and obstetrician attached to the provincial regiment.

RYLEEV. Kondraty Fyodorovich RYLEEV (1795-1826), poet, journalist, and leader of the Decembrist movement, which sought to establish a constitutional monarchy upon the ascension of NIKOLAY PAVLOVICH in 1825. He was hanged for his part in the uprising in 1826. His major literary work is *THOUGHTS* which expresses liberal civic and national feelings. In trying to convince VON LEMBKE to search STEPAN TROFIMOVICH's apartment, VON BLÜM notes that STEPAN TROFI-MOVICH's library contains RYLEEV's *THOUGHTS* and the works of HERZEN.

SABAOTH [SAVAOF]. A Babylonian word meaning man or army, usually found in the expression Lord of SABAOTH, the Lord of Hosts. PYOTR STEPANOVICH wants to use STAVROGIN as a mythic figure around which he can rally the people. In discussing his idea with STAVROGIN he notes the SKOPTSY legend in which IVAN FILLIPO-VICH, the Lord of SABAOTH, ascends to heaven in a chariot before the eyes of his followers. PYOTR STEPANOVICH vows to create better legends than this, with STAVROGIN functioning as IVAN THE TSAR-EVICH.

MARQUIS DE SADE [MARKIZ DE SAD]. Donatien Alphonse François DE SADE (1740-1814), prolific French writer who spent a good deal of his life in prison for his sexual escapades and for writing licentious books. His name has become synonymous with torturing the object of love and with depravity. SHATOV confronts STAVROGIN with the allegation that he was part of a depraved secret group in St. Petersburg that debauched children and that could have taught the MARQUIS DE SADE things. STAVROGIN denies only the allegation about children.

SAKS. The husband in the novel *POLINKA SAKS,* written in 1847 by Aleksandr Vasilievich Druzhinin (1824-64). He frees his wife POLINKA to go away with another man with whom she has fallen in love. When PYOTR STEPANOVICH encounters LIZA as she leaves STAVROGIN's house following their fateful night together, he alludes to MAVRIKY NIKOLAE-VICH, who has maintained a vigil over the house during the night, and recalls that in *POLINKA SAKS* the husband has his unfaithful wife arrested. SAKS in reality does no such thing and even divorces POLINKA so that she can marry Galitsky.

SALZFISCH [ZALTSFISH]. The doctor that VARVARA PETROVNA engages to minister to STEPAN TROFIMOVICH on his pilgrimage to find Russia. He indicates that there is little hope that STEPAN TROFIMO-VICH will recover from his illness.

GEORGE SAND [ZHORZH ZAND]. Pen name of Amantine Lucie Aurore Dupin Dudevant (1804-76), French writer who wrote romantic works advocating free love and humanitarian reforms and examining nature and rustic manners. (1) STEPAN TROFIMOVICH once published a journal which promoted the works and thought of GEORGE SAND. (2) As STEPAN TROFIMOVICH tries to explain what kind of a believer he is, he notes that according to one of GEORGE SAND's novels Christianity did not understand women. He probably has in mind *Lélia* (1833), which expresses aversion to social norms, including Christianity, and promotes romantic feminism. (3) In LEBYADKIN's verse, read by LIPUTIN at YULIA MIKHAYLOVNA's literary fest, the "poet" addresses the governesses and refers to them as retrogrades and GEORGE SANDS.

SCHOOLBOY [GIMNAZIST]. A young visitor to the socialist meeting called by PYOTR STEPANOVICH. He spends the evening uttering stupidities and arguing with the young VIRGINSKAYA over extreme principles.

SEMYON YAKOVLEVICH. The local holy man and oracle. He is about fifty five and is a former civil servant. He is popular and frequently sought out, and LIZA organizes an expedition of young people to go see him. As the group surrounds him, he utters an obscenity to one of the ladies and precipitates a scene.

SEMYON YEGOROVICH. See SEMYON YEGOROVICH KARMA-ZINOV.

SERGEY VASILYICH. See SERGEY VASILYICH LIPUTIN.

SERMON ON THE MOUNT [NAGORNAYA PROPOVED]. CHRIST's sermon recorded in Matthew 5-8 of the New Testament, in which He teaches the essence of the new Gospel and the fulfillment of the Mosaic Law. SOFYA reads to STEPAN TROFIMOVICH from the SERMON ON THE MOUNT.

SEVOSTYANOV. The owner of the rural home in which SEMYON YAKOVLEVICH lives. LIZA organizes an excursion to the house.

SHABLYKIN. VARVARA PETROVNA recalls that PRASKOVYA IVANOVNA once insisted that the hussar SHABLYKIN was courting her. She eagerly adds that MADAME LEFEBURE exposed the contention as a lie.

SHAKESPEARE [SHEKSPIR]. William SHAKESPEARE (1564-1616), the most eminent of English dramatists. (1) STEPAN TROFIMOVICH attributes STAVROGIN's extreme behavior to the youth of a PRINCE HARRY carousing with FALSTAFF, POINS, and MISTRESS QUICK-LY as portrayed by SHAKESPEARE. (2) LIZA notes to PRASKOVYA IVANOVNA that STEPAN TROFIMOVICH and VARVARA PETROV-NA found a similarity between STAVROGIN and PRINCE HARRY in SHAKESPEARE's *HENRY THE FOURTH.* (3) LIZA mentions that her mother knows SHAKESPEARE very well. (4) PYOTR STEPANOVICH discusses SHIGALYOV's system with STAVROGIN and notes that under such a social organization CICERO would have his tongue cut out, COPERNICUS would have his eyes put out, and SHAKESPEARE would be stoned to death. (5) While discussing KARMAZINOV's ego, the narrator refers to him and other prominent Russian writers as Russia's SHAKESPEARES, one of which even referred to himself as being great. (6) At YULIA MIKHAYLOVNA's literary fest STEPAN TROFIMOVICH discusses the difference between his generation and the younger generation and concludes that the basic difference is the conception of which is greater—SHAKESPEARE or boots, RAPHAEL or petroleum. He insists that SHAKESPEARE and RAPHAEL are more valuable than the emancipation of the serfs, socialism, science, or anything else.

SHARMER. A St. Petersburg tailoring establishment. PYOTR STEPAN-OVICH makes use of SHARMER's services at STAVROGIN's recommendation, and VON LEMBKE wears a coat made by him.

IVAN SHATOV. MARIE's child by STAVROGIN. The baby dies of exposure when MARIE runs through the streets looking for SHATOV, who she is sure has been killed.

IVAN PAVLOVICH SHATOV (SHATUSHKA). The twenty eight year old son of VARVARA PETROVNA's serf valet. He is a former pupil of STEPAN TROFIMOVICH and was expelled from the university because of a student disturbance. He then went to Europe, where he met and married MARIE, a progressive and emancipated governess who lived with him for only three weeks before leaving him for STAVROGIN. While in Europe and under the influence of STAVROGIN he abandons his socialist ideals, and following a trip to America with KIRILLOV, he adopts entirely different persuasions, all of which originate with STAVROGIN. He now indicts both the liberals and the socialists—the STEPAN TROFIMO-VICHES and the PYOTR STEPANOVICHES—as being separated from the people and not understanding them. He asserts that societies are based on the search for God, not upon reason, and each country has its own God. Russia is a nation of God-bearing people, and the Russian Orthodox Church has a missionary message for the atheistic and fallen people of Western Europe. He insists that neither an atheist nor one who is not Russian Orthodox can ever be a Russian and that one who loses ties with the people also loses God. The Roman Catholic Church, on the contrary, has fallen and teaches ANTICHRIST, much as socialism does. Even though SHATOV believes all of these premises, he does not as yet believe in God, but he vows to be able to believe in the future. Upon his return to Russia he meets STAVROGIN again and strikes him a tremendous blow at a gathering at VARVARA PETROVNA's. He subsequently admits to STAVROGIN that he struck him because of STAVROGIN's fall and evident rejection of the ideas he taught SHATOV. As they discuss the past, STAVROGIN warns SHATOV that PYOTR STEPANOVICH has arrived in town to murder him. SHATOV had been part of PYOTR STEPANOVICH's socialist circle until he rethought his persuasions, and PYOTR STEPANOVICH plans to use the threat of SHATOV's informing on the group as a pretext to kill him. PYOTR STEPANOVICH feels that the murder will bind the group solidly together under his leadership. Overcome by the deaths of LIZA and MARYA LEBYADKINA, SHATO-V considers exposing the socialist circle but is forestalled by the arrival of his wife MARIE. He is so overcome that he does not notice that she is pregnant and about to deliver a baby. Upon the birth of a son, SHATOV and MARIE have a reconciliation, and he eagerly looks forward to the future. He leaves with ERKEL to show the socialist group where he buried the organization's printing press, confident that this is the last contact he will have with them. Near the STAVROGIN estate PYOTR STEPANOVICH shoots him in the head, and his body is weighted with stones and thrown into a pond.

DARYA PAVLOVNA SHATOVA (DASHA, DASHENKA, DASH-KA). SHATOV's sister and a former pupil of STEPAN TROFIMOVICH who lives with VARVARA PETROVNA as her favorite ward. At VARVARA PETROVNA's behest she lives abroad for a time with the DROZDOVS to keep an eye on STAVROGIN. After a marriage between STAVROGIN and LIZA does not materialize and after STAVROGIN is seen with DASHA, VARVARA PETROVNA determines to marry DASHA to STEPAN TROFIMOVICH to prevent a match she does not want. DASHA apathetically agrees, but the marriage does not prove necessary or possible because STAVROGIN is already married to MARYA LEBYADKINA and STEPAN TROFIMOVICH vocally objects to being used to cover another's sins. DASHA informs STAVROGIN that when he ultimately needs her, she will be available, and that if he does not call for her, she will never marry but will become a nurse or a BIBLE seller. When he finally calls for her to come to him in Switzerland, she prepares to go with VARVARA PETROVNA, but plans are cancelled when they find his body hanging in a room at the estate.

MARYA IGNATIEVNA SHATOVA (MARIE). A very liberated twenty five year old woman who marries SHATOV in Europe and then quickly leaves him for STAVROGIN. She returns to SHATOV three years later, tired, disillusioned, bitter, and bearing STAVROGIN's child. She is defensive about SHATOV's showing her any consideration or love and rebels against his helping her, but the two have a reconciliation following the birth of a son whom she wants to name IVAN after SHATOV. On the day following SHATOV's murder she madly searches for him and discovers KIRILLOV's body. After her frenzied excursion through the streets the baby dies of exposure and MARIE becomes delirious and also dies.

SHATUSHKA. See IVAN PAVLOVICH SHATOV. MARYA LEBYAD-KINA often refers to SHATOV as SHATUSHKA.

SHIGALYOV. The brother of ARINA PROKHOROVNA VIRGINSKA-YA. He is a member of PYOTR STEPANOVICH's inner circle, along with

LIPUTIN, LYAMSHIN, VIRGINSKY, and TOLKACHENKO and is characterized by sullenness. At the socialist meeting called by PYOTR STEPANOVICH he denounces all previous social philosophers as idiots who contradict themselves and then proposes a social system which proceeds from the hypothesis of absolute freedom to the reality of absolute despotism. His system calls for a small elite to rule a massive faceless herd which will become submissive through education. At SHATOV's murder he announces that the crime does not fit in with his program and that he wants no part of it. Despite threats and denunciations from PYOTR STEPANO-VICH, he coolly leaves. Following LYAMSHIN's confession he is quickly arrested.

SHPIGULIN. A family of millionaires that operates a factory in the province. The workers labor in terrible conditions and demonstrate to get relief. These demonstrations together with the rumors of socialist activity in the province contribute to VON LEMBKE's mental breakdown. The factory is finally closed when disease erupts, but the workers are treated poorly when a settlement is concluded.

SISTINE MADONNA [SIKSTINSKAYA MADONNA]. A painting done by RAPHAEL in 1518. (1) On STEPAN TROFIMOVICH's trip abroad he discusses such topics as eternal beauty, the regeneration of man, and the SISTINE MADONNA. (2) STEPAN TROFIMOVICH tirades against PYOTR STEPANOVICH and the new generation for thinking that food for the masses is more useful than the SISTINE MADONNA. (3) When VARVARA PETROVNA mentions that STEPAN TROFIMO-VICH is planning to write something about the DRESDEN MADONNA, YULIA MIKHAYLOVNA responds that she must have in mind the SISTINE MADONNA instead. She notes that she was disappointed in the SISTINE MADONNA and found it hard to understand, and adds that KARMAZINOV agrees that it is difficult to understand. (4) As part of his final confrontation with the younger generation at YULIA MIKHAYLOV-NA's literary fest, STEPAN TROFIMOVICH plans to make the SISTINE MADONNA one of his topics. He sarcastically notes at the fest that the younger generation thinks that petroleum is more valuable than RA-PHAEL.

SKOPTSY. A small secret offshoot from the Russian Orthodox Church that practiced castration in order to renounce the body. (1) PYOTR STEPANOVICH observes that there are SKOPTSY in the province. (2) In discussing his intent to make STAVROGIN into a mythic center around which he can rally the people, PYOTR STEPANOVICH vows to manufacture better legends than those which the SKOPTSY profess.

PRINCE SLONTSEVSKY. A Polish visitor to STEPAN TROFIMO-VICH's small liberal circle who for a time is accepted on principle but then is simply not accepted at all because of his nationality.

SODOM. As recorded in Genesis 18-19 in the Old Testament, a city which together with Gomorrah was destroyed by Jehovah because of its wickedness. The word implies wickedness and chaos. PYOTR STEPANOVICH refers to the kind of life that LEBYADKIN and his sister MARYA lead as SODOM. He begs and drinks while she works and starves.

SOFYA. See SOFYA MATVEEVNA ULITINA.

SOFYA ANTROPOVNA. An elderly lady of the nobility who lives with YULIA MIKHAYLOVNA.

SOFYA MATVEEVNA. See SOFYA MATVEEVNA ULITINA.

SOLOMON. As recorded in the Old Testament, the son of David and Bathsheba, who succeeded his father as the last king of a united Israel. His reign (ca. 973-933 B.C.) was characterized by lavish spending, heavy taxation, and the building of the temple. SOLOMON gained a reputation for wisdom and the just treatment of judicial matters. (1) PYOTR STEPANOVICH states that once the new order has been instituted and STAVROGIN has brought in the new truth, they will issue a few judgments worthy of SOLOMON. (2) At YULIA MIKHAYLOVNA's literary fest for the benefit of the provincial governesses a professor gives a pompous speech in which he exposes all of Russia's faults. He sarcastically notes that, unlike in the past, the courts now issue judgments worthy of SOLOMON.

SOPHIA [SOFIA]. Cathedral of St. Sophia in Novgorod, built 1045-50. A professor speaks at YULIA MIKHAYLOVNA's literary fest for the benefit of the provincial governesses and pompously condemns all of Russia's faults. He notes sarcastically that the commemorative sphere for Russia's thousand year anniversary will be placed in Novgorod across from the old and useless SOPHIA. The reference is to a sculpture placed opposite the cathedral in 1862.

STASIE. See NASTASYA. STEPAN TROFIMOVICH occasionally refers to her with the French STASIE.

VSEVOLOD STAVROGIN. VARVARA PETROVNA's late husband and STAVROGIN's father. He is rather simple-minded, and he and VARVARA PETROVNA separate because of differences of character.

NIKOLAY VSEVOLODOVICH STAVROGIN (NICOLAS, NIKOLEN-KA). The only son of VARVARA PETROVNA, who is raised by STEPAN TROFIMOVICH because of the separation of his parents. After he finishes school and joins a swank cavalry regiment, his behavior becomes extreme and he seemingly offends for the joy of it. He precipitates two duels in which he kills one and maims another opponent and is then exiled to a punitive regiment. Upon leaving the army he returns to St. Petersburg where he associates with the dregs of society and involves himself in all manner of debauchery. While in St. Petersburg he marries MARYA LEBYADKINA because of her peculiar virtues and because of the revolting absurdity of such a marriage. He returns to the provinces and his mother and quickly precipitates three scandals: (1) he pulls PAVEL PAVLOVICH GAGANOV around by the nose, (2) kisses MADAME LIPUTINA three times at her birthday party and then abruptly leaves, and (3) bites IVAN OSIPOVICH's ear. He is arrested, becomes violently ill with a fever, and is considered by the attending doctors as not having his full faculties. Sent to Europe to recover, he becomes close to LIZA but also indulges in more physical and intellectual extremes by having an affair with MARIE SHATOVA and teaching SHATOV and KIRILLOV ideological contradictions. STAVROGIN is the source of strength and ideas for several characters. PYOTR STEPANOVICH in his socialist scheme wants to use him as a mythic figure around whom the people can gather and admits that he is nothing compared to STAVROGIN. SHATOV is taught that the Russian people are God-bearing people, that one must believe in God to be Russian, that one who loses his ties with the people also loses God, and that the Russian Orthodox Church must save Western Europe, which is under the influence of a Roman Catholic church that is identical to socialism. SHATOV feels that only STAVROGIN can bear the cross of this ideology. At the same time that STAVROGIN teaches SHATOV these concepts, he teaches KIRILLOV that God does not and cannot exist, that man's supreme will must be demonstrated, and that suicide is the supreme expression of that will. LEBYADKIN expresses his total dependence upon STAVROGIN, and FEDKA, the physical embodiment of much of the novel's metaphysical evil, receives implicit permission from STAVROGIN to kill LEBYADKIN and MARYA. Because of physical and intellectual excesses STAVROGIN becomes bored and apathetic toward life, and he instigates unintentional scandals. His humiliation of ARTEMY PAVLOVICH GAGANOV in a duel is an example of his indulging in a base deed without forethought.

MARYA LEBYADKINA's rejection of him as her prince and falcon and her perceiving him as an imposter, a GRISHKA OTREPIEV, aptly characterize his condition. Her rejection prompts his tacit instruction to FEDKA to proceed with the murders. His weakness makes his condition as described by MARYA irremediable, yet he accepts LIZA's love as a pitiable and pointless gesture at regeneration. He is aware that he does not love her and will destroy her, but permits himself to act out the drama. When she leaves him, he asks her to stay away from the scene of the LEBYADKIN murders, because he recognizes his guilt and knows that many will implicate LIZA because of her coming to him. He then leaves the country for Switzerland and sends for DASHA to come be his nursemaid, even though he knows that her love cannot resurrect him. After he vows not to commit suicide, though he likely should, he hangs himself.

VARVARA PETROVNA STAVROGINA. STAVROGIN's mother and LIZA's aunt. After her separation from her flighty husband for differences in character, she persuades STEPAN TROFIMOVICH to come live on the estate and be STAVROGIN's tutor. He remains twenty years, and she both loves and hates him as her creation. The two maintain an adolescent relationship, frequently fighting and placing demands on each other. She loves her son greatly and is anxious to believe the best, and this enables her to view his involvement with MARYA as a humanitarian gesture. She hopes to marry him to LIZA, but when they have a falling out and when STAVROGIN is seen frequently with DASHA, whom VARVARA PETROVNA sent abroad to keep an eye on him, she determines to marry DASHA to STEPAN TROFIMOVICH in order to prevent a match that she does not feel would be desirable. She explains to DASHA what a sacrifice it would be to marry an "old woman" like STEPAN TROFIMO-VICH, but promises a lot of money and secures an acceptance. When STEPAN TROFIMOVICH agrees, largely because of financial need, she is pained by jealousy, but when he ultimately objects that he is being used to cover another man's sins, she is furious and orders him out of the house, never to return. She berates him for their twenty years together, for their mutual pride and ego, for his withholding ideas from her, which stunted her development and results in her being behind YULIA MIKHAYLOVNA in their struggle for social supremacy, and for his pompous verbosity. Their separation is brief, however, and when she hears of his pilgrimage and his illness, she flies to see him. She initially abuses SOFYA, when she finds STEPAN TROFIMOVICH with her, but quickly perceives the situation and comes to respect her. As STEPAN TROFIMOVICH is dying she secures the last rites for him and is very anxious for him to profess religion Following his death she tells SOFYA that she may sell BIBLES with her since she now has no one, and she rejects the idea that she has a son. When STAVROGIN sends for DASHA from Switzerland, she determines to accompany her there, but amid preparations to leave she discovers STAVROGIN's body in a room at the estate.

THE STOCK MARKET RECORD [BIRZHEVYE]. *BIRZHEVYE vedomosti,* a political, economic, and literary newspaper issued 1861-1917 in St. Petersburg. After the fiasco at YULIA MIKHAYLOVNA's literary fest to benefit provincial governesses, PYOTR STEPANOVICH urges her to attend the ball to expose people and to clear the air of rumor. He also urges her to send the information on the events to *THE VOICE* and to *THE STOCK MARKET RECORD.*

STORIES FROM SPANISH HISTORY [RASSKAZY IZ ISPANSKOY ISTORII]. A probable reference to a series written by Timofey GRANOVSKY on topics from Spanish history. STEPAN TROFIMOVICH, somewhat for appearance's sake, mentions to VARVARA PETROVNA that he intends to read *STORIES FROM SPANISH HISTORY.*

"STRIKE ME DEAD, THE WAY IS LOST" ["KHOT UBEY, SLEDA NE VIDNO"]. The first of eight lines from Aleksandr PUSHKIN's "The Devils" ("Besy"), a poem published in 1832. The poem depicts a nobleman and his driver who become lost in a blizzard as if led astray by demons. The eight lines cited comprise one of the epigraphs to the novel and reinforce the notion that demons are responsible for the chaos in Russia and that many people are actually possessed.

NADEZHDA YEGOROVNA SVETLITSYNA. A provincial lady who had promised to take SOFYA to Spasov. When she fails to arrive, it gives STEPAN TROFIMOVICH the opportunity to provide transportation.

AVDOTYA PETROVNA TARAPYGINA. When VON LEMBKE returns to town, he confronts the demonstrating workers and uncharacteristically makes them kneel before him and even has some of them beaten. It becomes rumored that AVDOTYA PETROVNA TARAPYGINA, a collector of alms for the cemetery, views the proceedings and condemns them. It is also rumored that she is taken and dealt with by the authorities. The town starts a collection for her, but it ultimately becomes known that she does not exist.

ALYOSHA TELYATNIKOV. A civil servant and a working resident of the governor's mansion who is dismissed when VON LEMBKE becomes governor of the province.

THE TEN COMMANDMENTS [DESYAT ZAPOVEDEY]. As recorded initially in Exodus 20 in the Old Testament, the divine laws Jehovah gives to Moses. They form the basis of the Judeo-Christian ethic. At the socialist meeting called by PYOTR STEPANOVICH the young VIRGINSKAYA girl tirades on the woman question and against God. She insists that if God promises rewards for obeying law, He is immoral, and she uses as an example the commandment and promise that if man honors his parents, he will live a long life and have wealth. She militantly observes that such things are in the TEN COMMANDMENTS. The fifth commandment promises a long life in the land in return for honoring parents.

TENIERS [TENIER]. David TENIERS the Younger (1610-90), Flemish painter who excelled in peasant scenes, landscapes, and still life. VAR-VARA PETROVNA lends STEPAN TROFIMOVICH her copy of a TENIERS painting so that he can hang it by his portrait of GOETHE to impress KARMAZINOV. To try to show his independence STEPAN TROFIMOVICH puts the painting in his bureau.

TENTETNIKOV. A young liberal and enlightened landowner in the second volume of Nikolay GOGOL's *Dead Souls (Myortvye dushi)*, left incomplete at the author's death in 1852. The narrator discusses the riff-raff that surface in difficult times and cites YULIA MIKHAYLOVNA's literary fest as an example. He singles out the LYAMSHINS, TENTETNIKOVS, and the home-grown RADISHCHEVS.

THOUGHTS [DUMY]. A collection of verse and longer poems by Kondraty RYLEEV published in 1825. The selections express liberal civic and nationalistic feelings and reflect the constitutional monarchist views of the Decembrist revolutionaries. In trying to convince VON LEMBKE to search STEPAN TROFIMOVICH's room, VON BLÜM notes that STEPAN TROFIMOVICH's library contains RYLEEV's *THOUGHTS* and the works of HERZEN.

TIKHON. A former priest who because of illness lives at a local monastery. SHATOV suggests that STAVROGIN bow down to the earth and go see TIKHON so that he can right himself ideologically and spiritually.

TIME OF IGOR [IGOREVO VREMYA]. The TIME OF IGOR could refer either to Prince IGOR of Kiev (d. 945) or Prince IGOR Svyatoslavich (1150-1202) of Novgorod-Seversky. During both eras the prince solidified his own position and strengthened the princedom by warring against neighboring tribesmen. IGOR Svyatoslavich's unsuccessful campaign against the Polovtsians in 1185 became the subject of *THE LAY OF IGOR'S HOST.* In a tirade against Slavophilism and nationalism STEPAN TROFIMOVICH notes that he is not speaking about the TIME OF IGOR.

TITOV. A merchant to whom MARIE SHATOVA runs after discovering KIRILLOV's body. She herself dies later, probably in his house.

TOCQUEVILLE [TOKEVIL]. Count Alexis Charles Henri Maurice Clérel de TOCQUEVILLE (1805-59), French historian noted for his studies of the nature and operation of democracy and particularly for his *Démocratie en Amérique (Democracy in America)* written 1835-39. STEPAN TROFIMOVICH likes to go into the garden with a volume of TOCQUEVILLE and a concealed novel by PAUL DE KOCK.

"TODAY SHALT THOU BE WITH ME IN PARADISE" ["BUDESH SEGODNYA SO MNOYU V RAYU"]. As recorded in LUKE 23:43 in the New Testament, the words of CHRIST to one of the thieves who was crucified with Him. KIRILLOV mentions that the greatest man who ever lived spoke these words because He really believed in them. Yet, KIRILLOV contends, the thief found neither paradise nor resurrection, and CHRIST lived in a world of lies. KIRILLOV uses these premises as further justification of his impending suicide.

TOLKACHENKO. A member of PYOTR STEPANOVICH's inner circle together with VIRGINSKY, LYAMSHIN, LIPUTIN, and SHIGALYOV. He is a strange man of about forty who dresses poorly and knows well the dregs of society. He, ERKEL, and PYOTR STEPANOVICH are the only ones who really participate in SHATOV's murder. After LYAMSHIN's confession he is arrested, but he faces his trial with optimism and intends to defend himself.

"TOUT EST POUR LE MIEUX DAN LE MEILLEUR DES MONDES POSSIBLES." "All is for the best in this best of all possible worlds," an ironic citation from VOLTAIRE's *CANDIDE* spoken to CANDIDE by his teacher, the philosopher Pangloss. Following his midnight argument with YULIA MIKHAYLOVNA over PYOTR STEPANOVICH, VON LEMBKE reads this quote from *CANDIDE.* He subsequently encounters a worker demonstration and under the strain has a nervous breakdown as a graphic condemnation of Pangloss' ironic statement.

THE TOWER OF BABEL [VAVILONSKAYA BASHNYA]. As recorded in Genesis 11 of the Old Testament, a tower begun by the descendants of Noah by means of which they intended to reach heaven. Jehovah prevented its completion by confounding the language of the builders. In STEPAN TROFIMOVICH's allegorical poem, which he views as being of concern to the authorities, THE TOWER OF BABEL is completed and the ruler of OLYMPUS leaps out atop of it.

TURGENEV. Ivan Sergeevich TURGENEV (1818-83), Russian novelist known for his poetic prose and portrayals of the personal and intellectual lives of the Russian nobility. STEPAN TROFIMOVICH mentions that he does not understand TURGENEV at all, and he lapses into a discussion of how BAZAROV was rejected by the progressive circles of the 1860's. The figure of KARMAZINOV is intended to be a parody of TURGENEV, with whom Dostoevsky quarrelled.

NIKOLAY TUSHIN. PRASKOVYA IVANOVNA DROZDOVA's first husband and LIZA's father.

LIZAVETA NIKOLAEVNA TUSHINA (LIZA, LISE). PRASKOVYA IVANOVNA DROZDOVA's only child by her late husband NIKOLAY TUSHIN. LIZA is a tall, slender, pale girl of twenty one, who is quite proud and has a mocking and obstinate personality. While abroad she becomes romantically interested in STAVROGIN and tries to make him jealous through PYOTR STEPANOVICH. When the two men become acquainted on apparently congenial terms and STAVROGIN begins to see DASHA, LIZA is infuriated and becomes ill with a nervous disorder. She grows to both hate and love STAVROGIN and greatly resents both DASHA and MARYA LEBYADKINA, whom STAVROGIN had married. Her relationship with MAVRIKY NIKOLAEVICH, widely regarded as her intended, is also one of both love and hate. She belittles and tests his devotion to her, yet resents his willingness to serve her because she does not want him to appear absurd. This turmoil in her life effects her many good intentions and beginnings, and even though she wants very much to be good and virtuous, her pride and confusion make it difficult. She is capable of bowing in the mud and donating her diamond earrings to the church, yet she also suddenly leaves MAVRIKY NIKOLAEVICH to spend the night with STAVROGIN. Her single night with him proves disastrous for both of them. As she enters his house she calls herself a dead woman and as she leaves she notes that she cannot resurrect STAVROGIN and has no desire to be his nursemaid. She admits that her ideal in life is to go to Moscow, make visits, and entertain, and that as an aristocrat she cannot accept

STAVROGIN's nobility toward her. As she flees the house, she is anxious that she not be seen by MAVRIKY NIKOLAEVICH, who has maintained a vigil over the house all night, but when he encounters her, she kisses his hand and begs his forgiveness. Despite STAVROGIN's warnings, she insists that MAVRIKY NIKOLAEVICH take her to see the bodies of the murdered LEBYADKIN and MARYA. On the way they encounter STEPAN TROFIMOVICH leaving on his pilgrimage to find Russia, and she makes the sign of the cross over him and asks him to pray for "POOR" LIZA. Despite MAVRIKY NIKOLAEVICH's efforts, she is beaten to death at the site of the murders by a crowd that links her with FEDKA through STAVROGIN.

SOFYA MATVEEVNA ULITINA. A widow of thirty four who sells BIBLES. She meets STEPAN TROFIMOVICH on his pilgrimage to find Russia and reads him the BIBLE in his final hours.

VANYA. The coachman who takes MARYA LEBYADKINA to the church where she meets VARVARA PETROVNA.

VARVARA. See VARVARA PETROVNA STAVROGINA.

VARVARA PETROVNA. See VARVARA PETROVNA STAVROGINA.

VASILY IVANOVICH. See VASILY IVANOVICH FLIBUSTEROV.

VERKHISHINA. A widow who comes to SEMYON YAKOVLEVICH, the local holy man and oracle, to lament. She complains that when the family home burned, her children dragged her into the fire with a rope.

PYOTR STEPANOVICH VERKHOVENSKY (PYOTR STEPANYCH, PETRUSHA, PIERRE). STEPAN TROFIMOVICH's twenty seven year old son, who has been seen by his father on two occasions, at birth and prior to entering the university. When he finishes the university, he gets involved in the socialist movement, endures a trial, and then goes to Europe, where he meets STAVROGIN. He comes to the provinces to sell the estate which he inherited from his mother, unaware that the estate has been partially sold and mortgaged by his financially strapped father. He treats his father with humor and contempt and exposes the idiocy of his last twenty years with VARVARA PETROVNA. Society quickly accepts him, and he succeeds in ingratiating himself with YULIA MIKHAYLOVNA to the extent that he can take great liberties with VON LEMBKE. While in the province he organizes a socialist group composed of an inner circle of TOLKACHEN-KO, VIRGINSKY, SHIGALYOV, LYAMSHIN, and LIPUTIN and peripheral members who utter idiotic oratory and spy on each other. His intent is to use STAVROGIN as a mythic figure around which to rally the Russian people through a series of legends. He plans to leave Western Europe in the hands of the pope after the latter has come to terms with the INTERNATIONALE. To bind the small group closer to himself and to insure their loyalty he plans to have them all murder SHATOV, whom he presents to them as an informer. To solidify his own leadership he intends to circulate a poem "AN ILLUSTRIOUS PERSONALITY," which he claims was written about him by HERZEN himself. He also plans to use KIRILLOV's promised suicide to benefit the movement by having KIRIL-LOV confess to SHATOV's murder in his suicide note. In order to insure that he has time to make his plans work he dupes VON LEMBKE into believing that SHATOV is the author of the poem and the center of socialist activity. He promises to solve the matter for VON LEMBKE and even succeeds in getting from him a letter of denunciation about the socialist movement. Even though he manipulates people rather easily and has plans that can succeed, he admits that he is wholly dependent upon STAVROGIN and is nothing without him. In reality he is more a buffoon and a scoundrel than a socialist, but he is dangerous and knows no bounds. He is willing to do anything to accomplish his means and helps to orchestrate FEDKA's murder of LEBYADKIN and MARYA by giving LEBYADKIN money and letting FEDKA know about it. The murder of SHATOV is committed, but the group quickly disintegrates, and PYOTR STEPANOVICH hurriedly laves the area with his plot in shambles.

STEPAN TROFIMOVICH VERKHOVENSKY. PYOTR STEPANO-VICH's father and a once prominent liberal whose ideas both fostered the younger radical generation and now appear ridiculous to it. He is now practically forgotten, yet he features himself still dangerous in some official circles and has even convinced himself that he lives in exile. After being twice widowered, he accepts VARVARA PETROVNA's offer to be the tutor for her son. This launches a twenty year odyssey in which the two both love and hate each other yet seldom express their true feelings. The depth of their communication is evident in the fact that even though they live in the same house, he besieges her with letters. While living at the STAVROGIN estate, he maintains a small circle to which he patronizingly advocates his antiquated liberal ideas. He praises the West, uses French, notes the comparative worthlessness of the peasant, and insists that Russians have as yet done nothing. When VARVARA PETROVNA suddenly asks him to marry DASHA, he is surprised and hurt but agrees since he needs the

money. The money is the pivotal factor, since his son PYOTR STEPANO-
VICH, whom he has seen only at birth and prior to the boy's entering the
university, intends to sell the estate he inherited from his mother, unaware
that his father has already sold part of it and mortgaged the rest. After he
becomes convinced that his proposed marriage to DASHA is intended to
conceal some of STAVROGIN's indiscretions, he makes his feelings
known, and a furious VARVARA PETROVNA evicts him from the house.
She berates him for his pride and their twenty ridiculous years together but
promises to care for him financially wherever he decides to live. When VON
BLÜM shortly after his eviction requisitions his books and papers, he is
exhilarated. He gloats at being under surveillance and is convinced that he
will be exiled because of having the works of HERZEN. The narrator notes
that such a distance from reality is both charming and repulsive. On this
note of triumph he prepares for a final battle with the younger generation at
YULIA MIKHAYLOVNA's literary fest for the benefit of the provincial
governesses. In his speech he insists that SHAKESPEARE and RAPHAEL
are infinitely more valuable than the emancipation of the serfs, science, or
social reforms, and that life cannot proceed without beauty. He then
tearfully requests a reconciliation. When his pleas are met with accusations
of having sold FEDKA into the army to cover losses at cards, he vows to
abandon everything and to go on a pilgrimage to find the real Russia. On his
travels he meets SOFYA, a seller of BIBLES, and he determines to link his
life with hers and to help her sell BIBLES and to explain them to the people.
When he becomes ill, he has SOFYA read to him THE SERMON ON THE
MOUNT, the injunction in the APOCALYPSE to be either hot or cold but
not lukewarm, and the passage from LUKE about the demons who left the
man possessed and entered the bodies of swine. He sees the day that Russia
will be healed of people like himself and his son and acknowledges many of
life's mistakes. When VARVARA PETROVNA arrives, he expresses his
love for her, receives the last rites, and dies quietly much as a candle
flickering out.

VIE DE JESUS. The *Life of Jesus,* a book by Ernest RENAN, written in
1863 which faithfully chronicles the life of JESUS but denies His divinity.
STEPAN TROFIMOVICH mentions having read *VIE DE JESUS* in the
recent past.

VIRGINSKAYA. A short, chubby young student who professes to be a
nihilist. At the socialist meeting called by PYOTR STEPANOVICH she
militantly blares out radical ideas and argues with everyone. She feels very
strongly about the emancipation of women and the plight of students and
plans to devote herself to sharing in the suffering of students and arousing

them to rebellion.

ARINA PROKHOROVNA VIRGINSKAYA. VIRGINSKY's twenty seven year old progressive wife and SHIGALYOV's sister. She lives with VIRGINSKY barely a year when she tells him that she prefers LEBYAD-KIN, and she has an affair with him on principle. She is a midwife and delivers MARIE SHATOVA's baby.

VIRGINSKY. An honest, progressive idealist of thirty who is a member of PYOTR STEPANOVICH's inner circle together with LIPUTIN, LYAM-SHIN, SHIGALYOV, and TOLKACHENKO. When his wife informs him that she prefers LEBYADKIN, he tolerates his presence in the family for a time but then beats him and sends him away. His credentials as a progressive are thereby tainted, and he spends the entire night begging his wife's forgiveness. He looks for a way out of participating in SHATOV's murder and is very overcome by it. When he is arrested shortly thereafter, he is happy and relieved.

VOGT [FOKHT]. Carlos VOGT (1817-95), German naturalist who wrote extensively in many areas of science. When a second lieutenant in the provincial regiment seemingly goes crazy and bites his commanding officer, his room is searched and in addition to some progressive pamphlets are found the works of VOGT, MOLESCHOTT, and BÜCHNER.

THE VOICE [GOLOS]. A St. Petersburg newspaper edited by Andrey KRAEVSKY and circulating 1863-83. (1) A colonel is mentioned as reading THE VOICE. (2) After the fiasco at YULIA MIKHAYLOVNA's literary fest to benefit the provincial governesses, PYOTR STEPANOVICH urges her to attend the ball to expose people and to clear the air of rumors. He also urges her to send the information on the events to THE VOICE and to THE STOCK MARKET RECORD. (3) One observer of the literary quadrille performed at the ball given by YULIA MIKHAYLOVNA as part of her benefit for provincial governesses notes that the intent of the dancing seems to be to criticize THE VOICE. This passage in the novel had a real life counterpart in 1869 when a similar quadrille was held in which participants were costumed to represent the various newspapers. (4) STEPAN TROFI-MOVICH mentions to LIZA as he initiates his pilgrimage to find the real Russia that THE VOICE is in the habit of covering all of the crime that occurs throughout the country.

VOLTAIRE [VOLTER]. Pen name of François Marie Arouet (1694-1778), noted French satirist, philosopher, and historian. His name connotes a free-thinking approach to issues and philosophy. (1) The narrator refers to KARMAZINOV as an average talent when compared to PUSHKIN, GOGOL, MOLIERE, and VOLTAIRE, who were innovative and original. (2) SEMYON YAKOVLEVICH, the local holy man and oracle, sits in an old, worn armchair in the style of VOLTAIRE. (3) On the morning following his argument with YULIA MIKHAYLOVNA over PYOTR STEPANOVICH and prior to his confronting the demonstrating workers from the SHPIGULIN Factory, VON LEMBKE reads from VOLTAIRE's *CANDIDE* that "TOUT EST POUR LE MIEUX DAN LE MEILLEUR DES MONDES POSSIBLES."

"VOX POPULI VOX DEI." "The voice of the people, the voice of God," words taken from *Works and Days* by the eighth century B.C. Greek poet Hesiod. PYOTR STEPANOVICH indicates that the people are linking STAVROGIN with the murder of LEBYADKIN and his sister MARYA and quotes to him "VOX POPULI VOX DEI."

STEPAN VYSOTSKY. A local member of the nobility.

WHAT IS TO BE DONE? [CHTO DELAT?]. A novel written in 1863 by Nikolay Gavrilovich Chernyshevsky (1828-89), critic, editor, and a leader of the radical wing of literature. The novel advocates new social structures and portrays how the new progressive generation should think and act. STEPAN TROFIMOVICH reads *WHAT IS TO BE DONE?* in preparation for a final battle with the younger generation at YULIA MIKHAY-LOVNA's literary fest. He significantly notes that all of the basic ideas of the novel are distortions of those advocated by his own liberal generation.

THE WOMEN OF BALZAC [ZHENSHCHINY BALZAKA]. PYOTR STEPANOVICH observes that STAVROGIN has a book entitled *THE WOMEN OF BALZAC* in his room. The reference is likely to *Les Femmes de H. de BALZAC,* edited by Laure de Balzac Surville and published in Paris in 1851.

YELIZAVETA THE BLESSED [BLAZHENNAYA]. A woman who was in the same convent that MARYA LEBYADKINA stayed in for a time. YELIZAVETA sat in the same small room in the convent wall for seventeen years, did not wash, and endured other mortifications of the flesh.

YERMOLOV. General Aleksey Petrovich YERMOLOV (1772-1861), Russian general, commander and diplomat who served with distinction in the War of 1812 and later commanded Russian forces in the Caucasus.

LEBYADKIN claims his grandfather was killed in the Caucasus right in front of YERMOLOV himself.

"YES, IT IS TRUTH, IT IS GOOD" ["DA, ETO PRAVDA, ETO KHOROSHO"]. Distortion of "And God saw that it was good" ("I uvidel bog, chto eto khorosho"), the words of satisfaction God pronounces at the end of each day of creation as recorded in the first chapter of Genesis (verses 4, 10, 12, 18, 21, 25, 31) in the Old Testament. KIRILLOV recounts to SHATOV the feelings of unendurable joy he sometimes feels and equates these to the experience of encountering all of nature and acknowledging that it is truth. He adds that such a pronouncement would be similar to the satisfaction expressed by God at the end of each creative day.

YULIA MIKHAYLOVNA. See YULIA MIKHAYLOVNA VON LEMB-KE.

FOMKA ZAVYALOV. A local scoundrel who is rumored to have been involved in arson and in the murder of FEDKA. PYOTR STEPANOVICH accuses TOLKACHENKO of inciting him to action without his command.

ZEMIRKA. PRASKOVYA IVANOVNA's miserable old dog.

ZOSIMA. STAVROGIN visits LEBYADKIN and is surprised to find him sober and living in clean surroundings. LEBYADKIN notes that he is now living like ZOSIMA.

BOBOK 1873

AVDOTYA IGNATIEVNA. One of the corpses that IVAN IVANYCH hears talking in the cemetery. She is a society woman who is somewhat snobbish and whom no one likes. KLINEVICH reminds her that fifteen years ago she debauched him when he was only fourteen years old. She very enthusiastically welcomes KLINEVICH's suggestion that they all enjoy their new life by not lying and by being ashamed of nothing. She is most enthusiastic about being ashamed of nothing.

KATISH BERESTOVA. One of the corpses that IVAN IVANYCH hears talking in the cemetery. She continually giggles, has led a loose life, and is referred to by KLINEVICH as a monster. TARASEVICH immediately takes a lustful interest in her.

BOTKIN. Possibly Sergey Petrovich BOTKIN (1832-89), a doctor whom Dostoevsky himself consulted. The young man who was being treated by SCHULZ for a chest ailment notes that he was preparing to consult BOTKIN when he unexpectedly died. He and PERVOEDOV disagree on BOTKIN's qualifications and the fairness of his fees.

CALENDAR [KALENDAR]. Russian *CALENDAR* [*Russky KALENDAR*], a popular and widely-circulated calendar published by SUVORIN beginning in 1872. See SUVORIN.

CHARPENTIER. See YULKA CHARPENTIER DE LUSIGNAN.

YULKA CHARPENTIER DE LUSIGNAN. KLINEVICH admits that in collaboration with the Jew ZIFEL he circulated 50,000 rubles in counterfeit notes and then informed on ZIFEL to the authorities. He adds that YULKA CHARPENTIER DE LUSIGNAN escaped with the money to Bordeau.

THE CITIZEN [GRAZHDANIN]. A political and literary journal and newspaper published in St. Petersburg 1872-1914. It was founded by the writer and publicist Vladimir PetrovichMeshchersky (1839-1914) and was edited in 1873-74 by Dostoevsky, who published his *Diary of a Writer (Dnevnik pisatelya)* therein. IVAN IVANYCH vows to listen further to the corpses, obtain their biographies, and take them to *THE CITIZEN* for publication.

EK. A recently deceased young man, who finds it difficult to come to terms with his death, notes that he was being treated for a chest ailment by SCHULZ. He is told by other corpses that he should have consulted EK. When the corpses decide that they will all tell the truth and be ashamed of nothing, they are all excited about their new life and are eager to assume it. One corpse, probably the same young man, comments that now he does not want to go consult EK, since the new life sounds so appealing.

MADEMOISELLE FURY [FYURI]. KLINEVICH notes that he once took TARASEVICH to visit MADEMOISELLE FURY.

GRAND-PERE. KLINEVICH refers to TARASEVICH as GRAND-PERE (grandfather) as a comic comment on his debauchery late in life.

IVAN IVANYCH. The narrator of the tale, an unsuccessful writer who dabbles in announcements from booksellers and slogans for merchants. He is among the dregs of society and has a drinking problem. He muses defensively and at length about madness and insists that merely designating someone else as mad does not mean that the accusers are automatically either sane or intelligent. After his objections to the defining and treatment of those deemed to be mad, he observes that he has been feeling strange of late, has suffered headaches, and feels that his character is changing. He adds that he has begun to see and hear strange things, among them the word "bobok." Feeling the need to divert himself, he leaves and happens upon the funeral of a distant relative. Since he was never very welcome in their home, his pride prevents his getting involved in the proceedings, but he does remain at the cemetery to do some more musing. When he lies down near a grave, he hears the voices of the corpses in the cemetery. The corpses maintain their personalities and social status and interact just as they would were they alive. The group warmly endorses a suggestion to be totally honest about their lives and ashamed of nothing in this stage of their lives, and while they energetically attempt to convince PERVOEDOV of the merits of the idea, IVAN IVANYCH suddenly sneezes. Stoney silence immediately reigns, and IVAN IVANYCH vows to return and listen to their biographies and then to publish them in *THE CITIZEN*.

K. In musing about mental illness and mental hospitals IVAN IVANYCH cites the thought that condemning another as mentally ill does not prove that others are sane or intelligent. He disputes the thought that "K. has gone mad, thus we are now intelligent" ("K. s uma soshyol, znachit teper my umnye").

KATISH. See KATISH BERESTOVA.

BARON PYOTR PETROVICH KLINEVICH. One of the corpses that IVAN IVANYCH hears talking in the cemetery. He is very direct with others and makes a habit of exposing their secrets as well as his own. For example, he admits that he and ZIFEL circulated 50,000 rubles in counterfeit notes, after which he turned ZIFEL over to the authorities; that AVDOTYA IGNATIEVNA debauched him fifteen years ago when he was but fourteen; and that he attempted to bribe TARASEVICH in exchange for not informing on his theft of a large sum of government money. Prior to his death he managed to become betrothed to SHCHEVALEVSKAYA, a fifteen year old girl with a 90,000 ruble dowry. He wonders how he and the other corpses can seem to speak and move even though they really cannot and then suggests that in the weeks of consciousness they have remaining they all enjoy themselves, be honest, and be ashamed of nothing they have done. He notes that living and lying are synonymous, and he wants to build their new life on honesty and lack of shame. All of the corpses with the exception of PERVOEDOV, who does not want to share his life, readily agree.

KUDEYAROV. KLINEVICH announces that KUDEYAROV has recently died and is quite an exceptional person. He notes that it will be good when KUDEYAROV awakens and is able to join in their conversations.

SEMYON YEVSEICH LEBEZYATNIKOV. One of the corpses that IVAN IVANYCH hears talking in the cemetery. He is a servile court councilor who lies buried next to PERVOEDOV and who acts much like the general's lackey.

VASILY VASILIEVICH PERVOEDOV (VASILY VASILIEV). One of the corpses that IVAN IVANYCH hears talking in the cemetery. He is a major general who insists on preferential treatment and the continuation of a proper social order beyond the grave. He is the only corpse that objects to KLINEVICH's suggestion that all agree to be totally honest and ashamed of nothing in their new existence. He wants to maintain his general's status and does not want to relate his biography.

PLATON NIKOLAEVICH. One of the corpses in the cemetery. When KLINEVICH asks how it is that the corpses seem to be moving and talking even though they are not, LEBEZYATNIKOV refers him to PLATON NIKOLAEVICH, who is known as the resident philosopher. PLATON NIKOLAEVICH has expressed the opinion that man's consciousness continues to exist for a time after death.

PYOTR MATVEEVICH. IVAN IVANYCH observes that he made some money writing a panegyric to the late PYOTR MATVEEVICH.

PYOTR PETROVICH. See BARON PYOTR PETROVICH KLINE-VICH.

SCHULZ [SHULTS]. A doctor who had been treating a recently deceased young man.

SEMYON ARDALONOVICH. One of IVAN IVANYCH's acquaintances who asks him on one occasion if he is ever sober.

SEMYON YEVSEICH. See SEMYON YEVSEICH LEBEZYATNIKOV.

SHCHEVALEVSKAYA. A fifteen year old girl with a dowry of 90,000 rubles to whom KLINEVICH becomes betrothed prior to his death.

SUVORIN. Aleksey Sergeevich SUVORIN (1834-1912), Russian writer (under the pseudonym of A. Bobrovsky), critic, publisher, and theater devotee who founded the Maly Theater in St. Petersburg. IVAN IVAN-YCH finds a partially eaten sandwich on a grave and removes it in the name of propriety. He states that if the sandwich decomposes on the ground it is not sinful, but on the grave is a different matter. He notes that he should check on this matter in SUVORIN's *CALENDAR*.

TARASEVICH (GRAND-PERE). One of the corpses that IVAN I-VANYCH hears talking in the cemetery. KLINEVICH informs all that TARASEVICH embezzled 400,000 rubles in government money from his post as a privy counselor and indulged in debauchery until he died in his seventies. KLINEVICH had threatened to inform on him unless he was bribed, but TARASEVICH's death precludes this. When he becomes aware of the presence of KATISH BERESTOVA, he immediately takes a lustful interest in her.

VALLEY OF JEHOSHAPHAT [DOLINA IOSAFATOVA]. A valley east of Jerusalem named for a ninth century B.C. king of Israel. It is considered a place of judgment and a place of appeal for the deliverance of Judah and Israel. PERVOEDOV welcomes a recently deceased young man into their so-called VALLEY OF JEHOSHAPHAT and offers his services.

VASILY VASILIEV. See VASILY VASILIEVICH PERVOEDOV.

VASILY VASILIEVICH. See VASILY VASILIEVICH PERVOEDOV.

VOLOKONSKYS. KLINEVICH introduces himself to PERVOEDOV, reminds him that they met at the VOLOKONSKYS, and expresses surprise that PERVOEDOV was received at their home at all.

VOLTAIRE [VOLTER]. Pen name of François Marie Arouet (1694-1778), noted French satirist, philosopher, and historian. His name connotes a freethinking approach to issues and philosophy. IVAN IVANYCH wants to collect the *bons mots* of VOLTAIRE for publication but is afraid that they may be too bland for the public, which now regards VOLTAIRE as rather passé.

YULKA. See YULKA CHARPENTIER DE LUSIGNAN.

ZIFEL. KLINEVICH admits that in collaboration with the Jew ZIFEL he circulated 50,000 rubles in counterfeit notes and then turned ZIFEL over to the authorities.

A RAW YOUTH (PODROSTOK) 1875

ABISHAG [AVISHAGA]. As recorded in I Kings 1:2-4 (III Kings 1:2-4 in the Russian BIBLE) in the Old Testament, a young virgin brought to King DAVID by his servants to minister to him and be his concubine. The scriptures indicate that she cherished and ministered to the king but that the king knew her not. While drinking with LAMBERT, ARKADY asserts that VERSILOV's love for AKHMAKOVA cannot last because it is too emotionally charged and fleeting. He insists that such love would turn to revulsion and then asks LAMBERT if he knows the story of ABISHAG.

ACIS AND GALATEA [ASIS I GALATEYA]. *Acis et Galatée,* a painting produced by CLAUDE LORRAINE in 1657. The landscape is based upon the myth of GALATEA, a sea-nymph, who is pursued by the monster Polyphemus, or Cyclops, and who herself is in love with ACIS. The jealous Cyclops crushes ACIS to death, but GALATEA then changes her beloved into the Sicilian river that bears his name. In a dream VERSILOV sees this painting, which he has always referred to as "The Golden Age," and is again touched by Europe's Grecian roots. He is distressed to contemplate Europe's demise after the vision of the painting.

AFERDOV. A notorious gambler. ARKADY insists that he is a thief and accuses him of stealing part of his winnings on two occasions.

AGAFYA. The cook in TOUCHARD's school.

AGRAFYONA. An acquaintance of MARYA IVANOVNA.

"AGREE WHILE IN THE WAY, UNTIL THOU HAST PAID THE UTTERMOST FARTHING" ["MIRITES POKA NA PUTI, DONDEZHE NE ZAPLATITE POSLEDNY KODRANT"]. Ironic misquotation of Matthew 5:25-26, part of CHRIST's Sermon on the Mount in the New Testament. The original reads: "Agree with thine adversary quickly, while thou art in the way with him; lest at any time the adversary deliver thee to the judge, and the judge deliver thee to the officer, and thou be cast into prison. Verily I say unto thee, Thou shalt by no means come out thence, till thou hast paid the uttermost farthing" ("Miris s sopernikom tvoim skoree, poka ty yeshchyo na puti s nim, chtoby sopernik ne otdal tebya sudie, a sudya ne otdal by tebya sluge, i ne vvergli by tebya v temnitsu; Istinno govoryu tebe: ty ne vydesh ottuda, poka ne otdash do poslednego kodranta"). See BIBLE (2).

AKHMAKOV. A still youthful general who has squandered his wife's dowry through gambling and improvident living. Following a stroke he lives abroad in Ems with his second wife KATERINA NIKOLAEVNA AKHMAKOVA and a consumptive seventeen year old daughter, LIDIA, from his first marriage. He strongly objects when VERSILOV, who is living with the family through the efforts of PRINCE NIKOLAY IVANOVICH, and LIDIA discuss marriage. He dies of another stroke following his daughter's suicide.

KATERINA NIKOLAEVNA AKHMAKOVA (KATERINA NIKOLAVNA, KATYA, THE GENERAL'S WIFE, MILITRISA). AKHMAKOV's widow and the daughter of PRINCE NIKOLAY IVANOVICH. While living abroad with her ailing husband and stepdaughter LIDIA, she becomes acquainted with VERSILOV, who comes to live with them. Passion and flirtation unite them briefly, but they part bitterly, and VERSILOV's resulting hatred inspires great fear in her. Their relationship and VERSILOV's possible marriage to LIDIA create a stormy atmosphere. Her role in the novel largely centers on her emotional flight from VERSILOV and on her attempts to recover an incriminating letter she had once written about her father. On one occasion when she was nursing her father back to health following an attack, she became concerned about his erratic mental behavior and wrote to ANDRONIKOV to inquire how she could declare him incompetent without causing a scandal. When her father recovers, she becomes very concerned, inasmuch as she has been left destitute after AKHMAKOV's death and fears that her father will disinherit her should he learn of the letter. Her greatest fear is that VERSILOV has the letter and will use it against her. When ARKADY falsely assures her that KRAFT has destroyed the letter, she is greatly relieved, until VERSILOV writes her an insulting and threatening letter in which he insists that the letter still exists. This causes a rift with ARKADY, until news of MAKAR's death creates the atmosphere for a reconciliation and prompts a willingness to forgive VERSILOV. Her emotional flight from VERSILOV results in pleas for peace and calm and periodic intentions to marry BOERING. She admits that she once loved VERSILOV but now finds his intense and challenging feelings a blunt upon her own. BOERING by contrast would create a much less electric relationship, and she rejects VERSILOV's proposal. Following her refusal BOERING and BARON R. forcibly remove her father from the grasp of ANNA ANDREEVNA, and the semi-abduction indicates how closely the themes of marriage and money are linked. The letter does ultimately come back to haunt her even after her father and his money are delivered from ANNA ANDREEVNA. LAMBERT attempts to bribe her with the letter, makes vulgar allusions, and even threatens her with a revolver, but she is rescued by VERSILOV. She swoons from the ordeal and is then carried about the room in the arms of VERSILOV, who attempts a murder-suicide but succeeds only in wounding himself. After this crisis she severs relations with BOERING, escapes abroad with the PELISHCHEV family, and ultimately inherits a substantial sum from her father.

LIDIA AKHMAKOVA. AKHMAKOV's daughter by his first marriage. He is completely devoted to her. She is seventeen, consumptive, beautiful, and inclined toward fantasy. While living abroad at Ems with her father and stepmother KATERINA NIKOLAEVNA, she becomes enamoured of VERSILOV, and the two discuss marriage despite the strong opposition of her parents. She has a child by SERGEY SOKOLSKY, and the rumor widely circulates, owing principally to the efforts of STEBELKOV, that the child is VERSILOV's. She ultimately commits suicide.

ALEKSANDR SEMYONOVICH (ALEKSANDR SEMYONYCH). A young doctor who attends ARKADY and MAKAR.

ALEKSANDR SEMYONYCH. See ALEKSANDR SEMYONOVICH.

ALEKSANDRA PETROVNA. See ALEKSANDRA PETROVNA SINITSKAYA.

ALEKSEY MAKAROVICH. See ARKADY ANDREEVICH DOLGORUKY. SERGEY mistakenly refers to ARKADY as ALEKSEY MAKAROVICH, basing the patronymic on the first name of his legal father MAKAR.

ALEKSEY MIKHAYLOVICH. ALEKSEY MIKHAYLOVICH Romanov (1629-76), tsar of Russia from 1645 to his death. He was the father of PETER the GREAT. In a semidelirium ARKADY hears the ringing of a church bell that reminds him of the Church of NIKOLA in Moscow, which he says was built during the reign of ALEKSEY MIKHAYLOVICH.

ALEKSEY NIKANOROVICH. See ALEKSEY NIKANOROVICH ANDRONIKOV.

ALFONSINA KARLOVNA. See ALPHONSINE DE VERDEN.

ALFONSINKA. See ALPHONSINE DE VERDEN.

ALLAH [ALLAKH]. Arabic name for the Supreme Being. VERSILOV teaches ARKADY that it is impossible to love one's neighbor without despising him also. He insists that in the KORAN ALLAH commands the prophet to do good to the obstinate but also to pass them by. He observes that this is rather proud but nonetheless accurate. ARKADY wonders how VERSILOV can be a Christian with such ideas. There is no such passage in the KORAN.

ALPHONSINE. See ALPHONSINE DE VERDEN.

NIKOLAY SEMYONOVICH ANDREEV (DADAIS, LE GRAND DADAIS). A friend of PETYA whom ARKADY meets at LAMBERT's. He is a tall, coarse individual who has been dismissed from the army and whose behavior is unbearable. His conduct is often designed to elicit a bribe from LAMBERT in exchange for his either leaving or behaving. Life's disappointments and the fact that he has wasted his family's inheritance torment him, and he responds in part by never washing or changing clothes. He ultimately commits suicide.

ANDREY ANDREEVICH. See ANDREY ANDREEVICH VERSILOV.

ANDREY MAKAROVICH. See ARKADY ANDREEVICH DOLGORUKY. ANDREY ANDREEVICH mistakenly and ironically refers to ARKADY by VERSILOV's first name and the patronymic of MAKAR, who should have been his natural father.

ANDREY PETROVICH. See ANDREY PETROVICH VERSILOV.

ANDRIEUX. Proprietor of a house (likely of ill repute) mentioned by ALPHONSINE. He has connections with LAMBERT.

ALEKSEY NIKANOROVICH ANDRONIKOV. An acquaintance who manages some of VERSILOV's affairs. When he dies, his family remains with the VERSILOVS.

THE ANDRONIKOVS. ANDRONIKOV's family.

ANIKY. MAKAR relates to ARKADY how he visited the Bogorodsky Monastery to pay homage to the relics of the miracle-workers ANIKY and GRIGORY. It is unclear whom MAKAR has in mind, but it could be Ioaniky, who is buried in the Zaonikiev Monastery of the Vladimir Mother of God.

ANNA. See ANNA ANDREEVNA VERSILOVA.

ANNA ANDREEVNA. See ANNA ANDREEVNA VERSILOVA.

ANNA FYODOROVNA. See ANNA FYODOROVNA STOLBEEVA.

ANTON. A poor peasant, the central character in *ANTON GOREMYKA*. ARKADY wonders how VERSILOV, who ostensibly took *ANTON GOREMYKA* very seriously, could have taken SOFYA ANDREEVNA away from her husband MAKAR. He notes by comparison that in the tale ANTON loses only his horse.

ANTON GOREMYKA. A tale written by Dmitry Vasilievich Grigorovich (1822-99) in 1847. The work is a naturalistic portrayal of the privation and hardship of the peasant and focuses on the figure of ANTON, who is forced by an unsympathetic manager to try to sell his horse to pay his rent. The horse is stolen and ANTON and his family sink still deeper into a morass of hopelessness. VERSILOV reads the tale and feels that it has some influence on his decision to move to the country, where he commences a liaison with SOFYA. ARKADY observes that *ANTON GOREMYKA* and *POLINKA SAKS* had a tempering influence on the generation of the 1840s.

ANTONINA VASILIEVNA. TOUCHARD's wife.

APOCALYPSE [APOKALIPSIS]. In the New Testament the Revelation of St. John, which outlines the end of the world and the FINAL JUDGMENT. As he and ARKADY discuss the fate of nations, VERSI-

LOV expresses his opinions about economic failures and the rise of Jewish influence and power and suggests to ARKADY that he consult the APOCALYPSE.

ARINA (ARINOCHKA, RINOCHKA). A 3-4 month old baby girl that is abandoned at the home of MARYA IVANOVNA and NIKOLAY SEMYONOVICH. DARYA RODIVONOVNA, who had recently lost a baby daughter by the same name, assumes care of the child. The baby's illness and ultimate death cause ARKADY great anguish.

ARINOCHKA. See ARINA.

ARINOCHKA. The baby daughter of an old carpenter and his young wife DARYA RODIVONOVNA. She is the only child from eight years of marriage, and tragically dies.

ARKADY. See ARKADY ANDREEVICH DOLGORUKY.

ARKADY ANDREEVICH. See ARKADY ANDREEVICH DOLGORUKY.

ARKADY MAKAROVICH. See ARKADY ANDREEVICH DOLGORUKY. ARKADY is sometimes referred to by the patronymic derived from MAKAR, who is his legal father.

ARKASHA. See ARKADY ANDREEVICH DOLGORUKY.

ARKASHENKA. See ARKADY ANDREEVICH DOLGORUKY.

ARKASHKA. See ARKADY ANDREEVICH DOLGORUKY.

AVERYANOV. STEBELKOV observes that DARZAN gave a false IOU to AVERYANOV for 8000 rubles.

BALLE. When VERSILOV wins his litigation with the SOKOLSKY PRINCES, he brings home food items from the YELISEEV and BALLE establishments to celebrate.

BASHUTSKY. Pavel Yakovlevich BASHUTSKY (1771-1836), commandant of St. Petersburg during the reigns of Aleksandr I and Nikolay I. He was the brunt of several anecdotes. VERSILOV discusses popular anecdotes with ARKADY and observes that there are several about the commandant

BASHUTSKY dealing with a missing monument. One story circulated that the monument of PETER the GREAT had been stolen by Swedish agents literally under the commandant's nose.

"BEHOLD THE BRIDEGROOM COMETH" ["SE ZHENIKH GRYA-DYOT"]. Possibly an allusion to the Parable of the Ten Virgins as recorded in Matthew 25: 1-13 in the New Testament. The virgins (the church) await the arrival of the bridegroom (CHRIST) and then are awakened by these words, which form part of verse 6. The modern Russian version reads "Vot, ZHENIKH idyot," with the same translation. VERSILOV recovers from his self-inflicted wounds near Easter and sings out these words. He could be referring to his relationship to SOFYA, whom he has promised to marry, but the proximity to Easter makes possible another reading of the words in the sense that VERSILOV has recovered or by analogy risen from the dead.

BELINSKY. Vissarion Grigorievich BELINSKY (1811-48), Russian literary critic and journalist. He wrote for both *Fatherland Notes* and *The Contemporary* and insisted that literature realistically expose the seamy side of life with the intent of social reform. He was the first and most eminent of the so-called Radical Critics, and his ideas helped to stimulate the Natural School. (1) ARKADY notices that SERGEY has a volume of BELINSKY. (2) During a heated exchange with SERGEY, ARKADY touches the volume of BELINSKY and is told to leave it alone.

DUC DE BERRI. See DUKE DE BERRY.

DUKE DE BERRY [GERTSOG BERRYSKY] (DUC DE BERRI). Charles Ferdinand de Bourbon (1778-1820), the second son of King Charles X of France. He served briefly in the Russian army, commanded Parisian troups against NAPOLEON, was active in the post-NAPOLEON French government, and was assassinated by a political radical. See JAMES ROTHSCHILD (1).

BIBLE [BIBLIA, YEVANGELIE]. A collection of books organized into the Old Testament, a religious history from Adam through the twelve tribes of Israel with emphasis on Judah, and the New Testament, the life and ministry of CHRIST. (1) Under the influence of STEBELKOV's slanderous rumors, ARKADY states that VERSILOV has several illegitimate children and that when conscience and honor demand it, even a son will leave home in objection to such conduct. He adds that children traditionally leave their fathers and form their own nests and ascribes all of his thinking to the BIBLE. He likely has reference to such passages as "Therefore shall a man leave his

father and mother, and shall cleave unto his wife: and they shall be one flesh"
(Genesis 2:24). (2) A lawyer that OLYA's mother consults takes all of her
money before informing her that she does not have a case. He advises her to
settle the matter and then quotes ironically and expressively from the BIBLE
"AGREE WHILE IN THE WAY, UNTIL THOU HAST PAID THE
UTTERMOST FARTHING." (3) In reflecting upon ANNA ANDREEV-
NA, who has offered to marry him, PRINCE NIKOLAY IVANOVICH
refers to her as a BIBLICAL beauty typical of LES CHANTS DE
SALOMON. (4) While returning from MAKAR's funeral, SOFYA asks
ARKADY to read something from the BIBLE, and he responds by reading
part of LUKE.

BISMARCK [BISMARK]. Prince Otto von BISMARCK (1815-98), chancellor of Prussia, who through pragmatic and opportunistic politics founded
the German Reich in 1871. He is noted for his conservative and adept
diplomacy. (1) After ARKADY explains some of his ideas in what he fears is
a mediocre and superficial way, he asserts by way of self-justification that
ready understanding and acceptance of ideas usually is a reflection of their
poverty. He notes that BISMARCK's ideas were quickly lauded and that
BISMARCK himself was regarded as a genius, but he insists that both the
man and the ideas be reviewed after a decade to determine their actual
significance. (2) AKHMAKOVA objects to ARKADY that men do not
speak seriously with women on certain subjects. As an example she notes that
she recently spoke with SERGEY about BISMARCK and that he answered
her very condescendingly and ironically. (3) AKHMAKOVA recalls that she
and ARKADY once argued about BISMARCK and that he claimed to have
a much purer and more elevated idea than BISMARCK. (4) ALPHONSINE
complains to ARKADY that LAMBERT is a cruel person just like
BISMARCK. (5) VERSILOV discusses a photograph of SOFYA and
observes that it is very difficult to take a picture that looks just like an
individual. He adds that in a picture NAPOLEON could look stupid and
BISMARCK gentle.

BARON BOERING [BYORING]. A thirty five year old German colonel
who has an on-again off-again engagement with AKHMAKOVA. He is not
entirely acceptable as a refuge for her in her emotional flight from
VERSILOV. Because of his relationship with AKHMAKOVA he comes
into conflict with ARKADY and the VERSILOV family. On one occasion
he pushes ARKADY aside in front of AKHMAKOVA much as he would a
bothersome insect. The scene recalls an episode in *Notes From Underground,* when the Underground Man is similarly treated, and causes
ARKADY no little embarrassment. Together with BARON R. he intervenes

in the implied name of AKHMAKOVA when he forcibly removes PRINCE NIKOLAY IVANOVICH from the grasp of ANNA ANDREEVNA and he roundly insults her in the process. ARKADY abortively intercedes, a struggle ensues, and BOERING has him arrested. At the insistence of TATYANA PAVLOVNA, however, he writes a letter permitting ARKADY's release. AKHMAKOVA finally breaks off their relationship when BOERING somewhat indignantly questions some of the activities that transpire around her.

BOREL. The proprietor of an expensive St. Petersburg restaurant specializing in elegant fare. ARKADY decides to change his life-style, buys new clothes, starts to spend money, and frequents restaurants like that of BOREL.

"BORNE BY CONCOURSES OF ANGELS" ["DORI-NO-SI-MA CHIN-MI"]. Part of a Russian Orthodox song which reads in part "Yako do Tsarya vsekh podymem, angelskimi nevidimo dorinosima chinmi" ("That we may raise the King of all, with triumph BORNE by CONCOURSES OF ANGELS unseen"). See FAUST.

"BUT THE YEARS PASS BY—AND THE BEST YEARS AT THAT!" ["A GODY IDUT—I VSYO LUCHSHIE GODY!"]. Inexact rendering of a line from "It's Boring and Sad" ("I skuchno i grustno"), a poem written by Mikhail Yurievich Lermontov (1814-41) in 1840. The original reads "BUT THE YEARS PASS BY—all THE BEST YEARS" ("A GODY prokhodyat—vse LUCHSHIE GODY!"). The poem expresses frustration that there is no one for the poet to love, that passion is mindless, while eternal love is impossible, and that life is an empty, inane joke. PETYA TRISHATOV quotes these lines as he tries to explain ANDREEV's bizarre behavior. He notes that he and ANDREEV are both unhappy even though they desire to be happy, and sense that life is passing them by.

"BUT WHOSO SHALL OFFEND ONE OF THESE LITTLE ONES WHICH BELIEVE IN ME, IT WERE BETTER FOR HIM THAT A MILLSTONE WERE HANGED ABOUT HIS NECK, AND THAT HE WERE DROWNED IN THE DEPTH OF THE SEA" ["A IZHE ASHCHE SOBLAZNIT YEDINOGO MALYKH SIKH VERUYUSHCH-IKH V MYA, UNE YEST YEMU, DA OBESITSYA ZHERNOV OSELSKY NA VYI YEGO, I POTONET V PUCHINE MORSTEY"]. Citation from Matthew 18:6 in the New Testament. The more modern Russian version reads "A kto soblaznit odnogo iz malykh sikh, veruyushchikh v Menya, tomu luchshe bylo by, yesli by povesili yemu melnichny zhernov na sheyu i potopili yego vo glubine morskoy." In MAKAR's sad tale about a young boy who commits suicide, SKOTO-BOYNIKOV feels grieving guilt and quotes this with reference to himself.

BYRON [BAYRON]. Lord George Gordon BYRON (1788-1824), English romantic poet who created the "BYRONIC hero," a defiant, brooding young man obsessed by some mysterious past sin. ARKADY insists that there is nothing of BYRON in his idea—no curses, no complaints at being an orphan, no tears over his illegitimacy.

"LA CALOMNIE...IL EN RESTE TOUJOURS QUELQUE CHOSE." "Calumny—there is always something of it that remains" appears to have at least two sources. In the eighth scene of the second act of *The Barber of Seville,* a comedy written by Pierre Augustin Caron de Beaumarchais (1732-99) in 1775, are found the words "Calomniez, calomniez, il en restera toujours quelque chose" ("Slander, slander, there will always something remain"). Similar words are found in *De Dignitate et Augmentis Scientiarum (Of the Dignity and Advancement of Learning),* written by Sir Francis Bacon (1561-1626), English philospher and statesman, published in 1663. He wrote "Calumniare audacter, semper aliquid haeret" ("Slander bravely, something always remains"). When ARKADY learns that BOERING is not going to marry AKHMAKOVA, he attributes the decision to the effect of VERSILOV's scandalous letter and then quotes these words.

CELADON [SELADON]. A shepherd whose love for Astrée provides the plot for the multivolume pastoral novel *L'Astrée* written by Honoré d'Urfé (1567-1625) from 1607 until his death. CELADON is a passionate, idealistic lover who pursues Astrée with some vigor and constancy. Upon learning of OLYA's suicide, VERSILOV reflects that he may have been a bit lightminded and gay with her when he offered a position and an advance and that this may have caused her negative feelings. He indicates that he may have caused her to think that he was some kind of a wandering CELADON.

LES CHANTS DE SALOMON. Apparently the Old Testament book, The Song of Solomon, more properly referred to as the Song of Songs or Canticles, which is attributed to SOLOMON. The book may be read as a love lyric or a theological allegory of CHRIST's relationship with Israel. The title actually more closely approximates the Psalms of Solomon, 18 apocryphal psalms in Hebrew and Greek, which, though attributed to SOLOMON, are unrelated to him. In reflecting upon ANNA ANDREEVNA, who has offered to marry him, PRINCE NIKOLAY IVANOVICH comments that she is a BIBLICAL beauty worthy of LES CHANTS DE SALOMON. He quickly corrects himself and deems it more appropriate to compare her and himself to DAVID and the young woman who was to warm him in his old age.

CHARLEMAGNE [KARL VELIKY]. Known as Charles the Great and Charles I (742-814), the founder of the Holy Roman Empire. He ruled much of Western Europe and was acknowledged as Emperor of the West (800-14) and King of the Franks (768-814). See GALILEO.

CHATSKY. Aleksandr Andreevich CHATSKY, the progressive young hero of *WOE FROM WIT.* (1) ARKADY recalls that when he first met VERSILOV, he was declaiming CHATSKY's final monolog in front of a mirror, particularly the last line "A COACH FOR ME, A COACH!" (2) VERSILOV observes that once he played the role of CHATSKY in the amateur theater of ALEKSANDRA PETROVNA VITOVTOVA when ZHILEYKO became ill. (3) When ARKADY sees VERSILOV rehearse the roll of CHATSKY, he comments that VERSILOV is an authentic CHATSKY. VERSILOV responds that he questions whether ARKADY, still comparatively youthful, really knows CHATSKY already. (4) At the performance of *WOE FROM WIT* at VITOVTOVA'a estate, ARKADY is captivated by VERSILOV's performance of CHATSKY, particularly when he exclaims "A COACH FOR ME, A COACH!" VERSILOV's identification with CHATSKY emphasizes the progressive, idealistic side of his personality and accentuates the almost worshipful attitude that ARKADY cultivates toward him.

CHERNYSHEV. Aleksandr Ivanovich CHERNYSHEV (1785-1857), governmental functionary during the reign of Nikolay I who served as minister of war. As he discusses popular anecdotes with ARKADY, VERSILOV observes that several of them deal with persons at court, among them CHERNYSHEV. One such anecdote relates how CHERNYSHEV at seventy years of age changed his appearance to look thirty years old and fooled the tsar. ARKADY admits that he himself told anecdotes about CHERNYSHEV.

CHERVYAKOV. A lodger who lives near ARKADY in PYOTR IPPO-LITOVICH's apartment. He is a coarse, vain fool in ARKADY's estimation.

CHRIST [KHRISTOS, IISUS KHRISTOS]. Jesus CHRIST, in Christianity the Son of God. (1) VERSILOV alludes to the "GENEVA IDEAS" and defines them as virtue without CHRIST. (2) After an argument with his mother, ARKADY apologizes and asserts that he loves CHRIST. SOFYA responds that CHRIST will forgive all, that He is Father, and that He will shine in the densest darkness. (3) VERSILOV reports a conversation in a pub in which PYOTR IPPOLITOVICH insists that the English Parliament once reenacted the trial of CHRIST before PILATE to see how it would be conducted under current law. He notes that the jury was compelled to uphold the original verdict. (4) While recovering from an illness, ARKADY overhears someone praying to CHRIST in an adjoining room. He goes to see who it is and discovers the recently arrived MAKAR. (5) At the end of his illness and after he meets MAKAR, SOFYA blesses ARKADY with CHRIST. (6) MAKAR counsels ARKADY to pray to CHRIST for those for whom no one prays. (7) While discussing the relative merits of saving one's soul as an ascetic in the wilderness (MAKAR's point of view) and of serving humanity (ARKADY's point of view), MAKAR in order to enhance his own position quotes CHRIST, "GO AND GIVE AWAY ALL YOUR RICHES AND BECOME THE SERVANT OF ALL." (8) In MAKAR's tale the archimandrite tries to comfort SKOTOBOYNIKOV by saying that only CHRIST is perfect and that the angels serve Him.

"CHRIST ON THE BALTIC SEA" [KHRISTOS NA BALTYSKOM MORE"]. An image found in "Frieden" ("Peace"), a poem from a cycle of poems entitled *Die Nordsee (The North Sea)* written by Heinrich HEINE in 1826. The cycle is found in *Das Buch der Lieder (The Book of Songs)* published in 1827. The poem depicts the author dreamily musing at the helm of his ship and then seeing CHRIST walk over the land and the water bringing peace and expiation by means of the blood shed from His heart. VERSILOV laments the loss of the idea of God from Western Europe and notes that he has a vision of a perfect society in which everyone loves everyone else. He adds that the vision always concludes with a picture of "CHRIST ON THE BALTIC SEA" as in HEINE.

CHYORT IVANOVICH. A contrived name meant to refer to anyone derisively. It literally refers to the devil, the son of Ivan. ARKADY's admission that he lied about destroying AKHMAKOVA's letter infuriates TATYANA PAVLOVNA who accuses him of trying to revenge himself on some CHYORT IVANOVICH simply because he is illegitimate.

"A COACH FOR ME, A COACH!" ["KARETU MNE, KARETU!"]. The concluding line of CHATSKY's final monolog in *WOE FROM WIT.* Prompted by his failure in love and frustration with society and ignorant people, CHATSKY lashes out at the world and then calls for a carriage so he can leave. See CHATSKY (1,4).

COLUMBUS [KOLUMB]. Christopher COLUMBUS (1451-1506), Italian navigator who under the flag of Spain made four voyages to the Americas. He is credited with discovering the New World in 1492 on his first voyage. (1) ARKADY puts aside his retiring personality and extreme thrift and attends an auction of the effects of MADAME LEBRECHT. He compares his venture into this new world with COLUMBUS' going to discover America. (2) Prior to his finally putting his idea in writing, ARKADY draws a parallel with COLUMBUS in which he insists that had COLUMBUS told others of his goal before he actually discovered America, they would not have understood. He uses this as justification for his long silence but affirms that he does not want to equate himself with COLUMBUS.

LES CONFESSIONS [ISPOVED]. The autobiography of JEAN JACQUES ROUSSEAU, written 1766-70 and published posthumously in 1781 and 1788. Together with a rather reprehensible student ARKADY carouses and speaks vulgarities to passing women. He mentions to the student that ROUSSEAU admitted in *LES CONFESSIONS* that as a youth he was wont to expose himself to passing women.

COPERNICUS [KOPERNIK]. Nicolaus COPERNICUS (1473-1543), Polish astronomer who laid the foundation for modern astronomy by positing the sun rather than the earth as the center of the solar system. His statement produced great scientific and theological polemic. See GALILEO.

THE COVETOUS KNIGHT [SKUPOY RYTSAR]. The central figure of a short play by the same name written by Aleksandr PUSHKIN in 1830. The play is the first of the *Little Tragedies (Malenkie tragedii)* and examines the theme of avarice through the conflict between a greedy father and son. ARKADY notes that he memorized the monolog of PUSHKIN's COVETOUS KNIGHT when he was a child and adds that PUSHKIN has created no higher idea. The monolog encompasses the entire second act of the drama and reveals the father's love for money. ARKADY makes mention of this in connection with his idea that if ROTHSCHILD does the things that other men do, the whole charm of the idea will be lost.

CUPID [AMUR]. In Roman mythology the god of love, a counterpart of the Greek Eros. At the auction of MADAME LEBRECHT's effects

ARKADY buys what he refers to as the most worthless thing in the world, an album in a box decorated with swans and CUPIDS.

DADAIS. See NIKOLAY SEMYONOVICH ANDREEV. He is derisively referred to as a dodo.

"DARK-COMPLECTED, TALL, ERECT" ["SMUGLOLITS, VYSOK I PRYAM"]. Line from "Vlas," a poem written by Nikolay Alekseevich Nekrasov (1821-78) in 1854. The poem portrays Vlas, a peasant and former sinner, who views his ultimate divine punishment in a vision. He thereafter gives away all he has and goes on a pilgrimage to collect money for the erection of a church. VERSILOV uses these words to describe MAKAR.

DARYA ONISIMOVNA (NASTASYA YEGOROVNA). OLYA's mother. She is placed in STOLBEEVA's home following OLYA's suicide and cares for the child that LIDIA had by SERGEY. In the second half of the novel Dostoevsky begins to refer to her as NASTASYA YEGOROVNA.

DARYA RODIVONOVNA. The young wife of a much older carpenter who is given to drink. When ARINOCHKA, her only child after eight years of marriage, dies in infancy, she assumes the care of ARINA, the baby abandoned near MARYA IVANOVNA's kitchen.

ALEKSEY VLADIMIROVICH DARZAN. A wealthy young acquaintance of SERGEY. He, too, is a gambler and is quite notorious for his behavior, which earlier had resulted in his discharge from the army.

DAVID. Shepherd boy who succeeded Saul as King of the Hebrews, the twelve tribes of Israel, and who lived approximately 1032-962 B.C. He is celebrated as the conqueror of Goliath and as a poet and musician who wrote many of the Psalms. (1) VERSILOV compares MAKAR to URIAH and himself to DAVID in their situation with SOFYA. His reference is to the Old Testament account found in II Samuel 11-12 (II Kings 11-12 in the Russian edition) of DAVID's romance with Bathsheba. While king of the land DAVID seduced Bathsheba and then sent her husband URIAH into the heat of battle so that he might be killed. DAVID then married her but incurred the reprimand of God. (2) See LES CHANTS DE SALOMON. (3) PRINCE NIKOLAY IVANOVICH refers to ANNA ANDREEVNA as a young beauty of DAVID's old age. See ABISHAG.

DERGACHEV. A twenty five year old acquaintance of KRAFT. ARKADY attends a gathering at his apartment and vigorously debates the issue of personal freedom. He is ultimately arrested.

DERGACHEVA. DERGACHEV's wife.

DESDEMONA [DEZDEMONA]. The wife of OTHELLO, who is smothered to death by her violently jealous husband. She is innocent of any wrongdoing and is the victim of the intrigues and lust for power of IAGO. ARKADY mentions to AKHMAKOVA that VERSILOV once observed that OTHELLO did not kill DESDEMONA out of jealousy but because he had lost his ideal. ARKADY, who has idealized AKHMAKOVA, makes this comment as part of his expression of thanks to her for restoring his ideal. She apologizes to him for using him to gain information about her letter.

DICKENS [DIKKENS]. Charles DICKENS (1812-70), widely considered the greatest English novelist. His novels expose social abuse and corruption. PETYA TRISHATOV asks ARKADY if he has read DICKENS' *THE OLD CURIOSITY SHOP* and then recalls a scene in it for him.

"DIES IRAE, DIES ILLA!" "Oh day of wrath, oh that day," the first line in a Roman Catholic mass for the dead. The verse is chanted after readings from the New Testament and refers to the preliminary judgment of man prior to the FINAL JUDGMENT. See FAUST.

"THE DISCRIMINATING BRIDE" ["RAZBORCHIVAYA NEVES-TA"]. A fable written by Ivan KRYLOV in 1806. The work humorously describes a maiden who finds all potential suitors deficient because of her pride and unrealistic demands. As she becomes older, however, she quite willingly marries the first suitor, even though he is crippled. When ARKADY first meets VERSILOV, he comments that he particularly likes KRYLOV's fables. In response to VERSILOV's request to recite something from memory, he quotes "THE MAID HER SUITOR SHREWDLY EYED," the first line of "THE DISCRIMINATING BRIDE."

MADAME DOBOYNY. During a discussion of how *INDEPENDANCE* often incorrectly reports Russian names, PETYA notes that a MADAME DOBOYNY has been mentioned there.

DOLGOROWKY. See ARKADY ANDREEVICH DOLGORUKY.

PRINCE DOLGORUKY. MAKAR gloats over his surname DOL-GORUKY because there are several named PRINCE DOLGORUKY.

ARKADY comes to loathe his name because he is not a prince. The name belongs to a long line of prominent nobility.

ARKADY ANDREEVICH DOLGORUKY (ARKADY MAKAROVICH, ARKADY, ARKASHA, ARKASHENKA, ALEKSEY MAKAROVICH, DOLGOROWKY, ARKASHKA, ANDREY MAKAROVICH). The twenty year old illegitimate son of VERSILOV and SOFYA. The novel is written in the first person and comes about as a result of his desire to write his autobiography, ostensibly without literary embellishment and not intended for the praise of man. His writing is characterized by a great concern for what others will think of him, obsession with his own self-worth, naivete, and youthful idealism. He is young and immature, and these qualities both chart the course of the novel and allow him to fall victim to himself and to events that seemingly everyone except him perceives. He is sensitive about his noble name and the fact that he himself is not a prince, and suffers noticeably as almost everyone questions him about his name. His relationship with his parents is almost nonexistent, inasmuch as he is given to others to raise shortly after his birth. He sees his mother on only two or three occasions in his first twenty years of life and VERSILOV only once. This factor coupled with his lack of acquaintance with MAKAR and his illegitimacy prompt a vigorous search for self-identity and a strong desire to know and love his parents, in particular VERSILOV. His other major obsession is a search for and refinement of what he refers to as his idea. These crusades are united when VERSILOV invites him to come to St. Petersburg to join his family. VERSILOV promises him peace and quiet and the opportunity to pursue his idea. His hunger for a father and a family and his youthful immaturity create a love/hate relationship with VERSILOV. He first expands on his idea at DERGACHEV's apartment, where he contests KRAFT's assertion that Russia is a second-rate country. He then adds that his ideal is to be by himself and thereby to enjoy complete personal freedom. The feelings expressed by the progressive group that there will be a future paradise and that God must be rejected are countered by ARKADY's claims that he can serve humanity best through personal freedom and being himself. He insists that in this he really loves humanity more than these professed humanitarians do. His acquaintance with KRAFT focuses not only on the expression of ARKADY's idea but also on his quest to know VERSILOV, and he questions KRAFT about VERSILOV's life in Ems and his contemplated marriage to LIDIA AKHMAKOVA. His quest for VER-SILOV is amplified by the fact that he is in possession of the letter that AKHMAKOVA wrote to ANDRONIKOV concerning her father PRINCE NIKOLAY IVANOVICH's incapacity. The fact that she is under the impression that VERSILOV has the letter causes ARKADY to view AKHMAKOVA in a love/hate manner. He loves her as an ideal and as a victim, since he can control her by the letter, but he hates her haughty manner and enjoys the power he holds over her. When he finally puts his great idea into writing it emerges as a desire to become exactly like JAMES ROTHSCHILD. He considers the key to this goal as persistence and determination, and to test himself he eats only bread and water for a month and saves every kopeck in order to accumulate money. He considers the end result of his goal to be isolation and feels that to achieve it he also needs power. Isolation is sought because ARKADY does not care for people and proudly finds himself intellectually superior to all of them. He senses that he lowers himself whenever he praises someone and he hates those he praises. The validity and permanence of the idea is illustrated by two anecdotes that ARKADY tells about himself. At a time when he permits his idea to govern his life and perceptions, he carouses with a coarse student and scandalizes women with vulgarities. When he becomes selflessly involved in the care of ARINOCHKA, however, he forgets that his idea exists. His idea is so transparent and such a product of his proud and naive nature that to ARKADY's chagrin VERSILOV guesses the idea when they first meet in St. Petersburg. This chagrin and VERSILOV's barbs and insults fail to substantially alter ARKADY's quest for a father, and he finds himself crushed by the rumor that VERSILOV fathered a child by LIDIA. He is even willing to fight a duel with SERGEY, who reportedly slapped VERSILOV in Ems. When he meets SERGEY, ARKADY is quickly won over by him, a characteristic of his naive and impetuous manner. For the next several weeks he abandons his idea, spends most of his days and nights with SERGEY, and enters the world of restaurants, gambling, and spending money. He does not like the person he becomes in the gambling establishments, while at the same time his pride and sensitivity make him embarrassed in public. His success at gambling results in a conflict with SERGEY, who in retaliation for injured pride informs ARKADY that his sister LIZA is pregnant by him. He is stunned, but his principal response is disgust that he had not suspected and that events have made him out to be a fool. He is greatly upset whenever he appears funny and is not respected. His gambling leads him into a scandal when he accuses AFERDOV of stealing money from him, and he is evicted from the gambling establishment as a thief himself. The torment he feels stimulates reminiscences of his past, mostly his hunger for a mother, and results in his returning to her in an almost delirious condition. While recuperating there, he discovers that MAKAR is also in the apartment, and the two discuss the mysteries of God. He acknowledges believing in God but his pride and inexperience cause him to emphasize science and speak out when he should not. His illness also precipitates a crisis with AKHMAKOVA. He had told her that KRAFT had burned her incriminating letter, even though he himself retained it. This was justified in his mind by his intention to destroy the letter. While ARKADY is in a delirium and is being cared for by LAMBERT, the latter learns of the letter and begins to plot to get a bribe. ARKADY is rather flattered that he is the center of intrigue and even takes LAMBERT's offer to marry him to AKHMAKOVA seriously for a time. His love/hate relationships with both VERSILOV and AKHMAKOVA and the fact that VERSILOV and AKHMAKOVA also jostle over the incriminating letter bring the novel to its dramatic conclusion. LAMBERT, who steals the letter from ARKADY, attempts to bribe AKHMAKOVA, but is overpowered by VERSILOV, who then attempts to kill both himself and AKHMAKOVA. ARKADY, who has eavesdropped on the entire scene, struggles with him so that he succeeds only in wounding himself. Following this melodramatic episode and a life characterized by naive pride and a yearning for ideals, ARKADY maintains that a new life is opening up for him and that he has retained his idea albeit in a different form.

MAKAR IVANOVICH DOLGORUKY (MAKAR IVANOV, MAKAR IVANYCH, MAKAR, MAKARUSHKA). A former serf at the VERSILOV house and ARKADY's legal father. He is regarded by many as a local wise man and by some as a saint who is able to endure many things. At the request of her dying father he marries SOFYA when she is 18 and he 55, but he loses her to VERSILOV. After their break, MAKAR becomes a pilgrim of sorts and travels to cities and monasteries throughout Russia, maintaining throughout a periodic polite correspondence with SOFYA. When VERSILOV first approaches MAKAR about his relationship with SOFYA, he offers him money, and to VERSILOV's immense surprise, MAKAR accepts it and even insists that he receive all of it with interest. ARKADY later insists that MAKAR accepted the money because he felt that VERSILOV would leave SOFYA destitute when he dies. At the time of the novel's action MAKAR is 70 years old, a large man with thick hair and a white beard. He comes to the VERSILOV house in St. Petersburg to stay for a time because of ill health, and while there has several discussions with ARKADY. VERSILOV assesses him as a man capable of respecting himself as he is and as one who has a real feeling of dignity and personal worth. ARKADY in turn senses in him an absolutely pure heart and the absence of any pride. While staying with the VERSILOVS, MAKAR relates many tales and legends and discusses the mysteries of God with ARKADY. During his stay there he dies suddenly of heart failure.

"THE DRAGON-FLY AND THE ANT" ["STREKOZA I MURA-VEY"]. A fable written by Ivan KRYLOV in 1808. The fable portrays a dragon-fly who sings the summer away and is hence unprepared for winter. Her appeal to the more practical ant for food and shelter until spring is met with the suggestion that since she sang all summer she could now dance the winter away. VERSILOV is delighted with ARKADY's recitation of "THE DISCRIMINATING BRIDE" and comments that had he recited something on the order of "THE DRAGON-FLY AND THE ANT," he would have found it quite natural, but for a young man to recite a fable with a more mature content is highly entertaining.

DRESDEN MADONNA [DREZDENSKAYA MADONNA]. The madonna painted 1515-19 by Raffaelo Sanzio (Raphael) (1483-1520) for the Sistine Chapel and later housed in the Dresden Gallery. VERSILOV has a gravure of the DRESDEN MADONNA hanging in his living room.

DUBASOV. DARZAN indicates that DUBASOV, who always knows the latest society news, told him that KATERINA AKHMAKOVA is going to marry BOERING.

EDMUND KARLYCH. See EDMUND KARLYCH LICHTEN.

FANARIOTOVA. VERSILOV's wife, a society woman who bears him a son, ANDREY ANDREEVICH, and a daughter, ANNA ANDREEVNA, before she dies at a young age.

FANARIOTOVA. VERSILOV's wife's mother. ARKADY spends some time in her home while she is abroad. During the action of the novel ANNA ANDREEVNA lives with her.

THE FANARIOTOVS. The family into which VERSILOV marries.

FAUST. A play in two parts written 1808 and 1832 by Johann Wolfgang von Goethe (1749-1832). The play chronicles the career of Faust, who sells his soul to Mephistopheles in exchange for the promise to comprehend all experience. The second part of the play deals with the larger experience of history, culture, and politics and is done in a more allegorical fashion. PETYA TRISHATOV tells ARKADY that if he were to write an opera, he would take a theme from *FAUST.* He pictures a tormented GRETCHEN in a cathedral with a somber choir in the background singing "DIES IRAE, DIES ILLA!" Satan would tell GRETCHEN that she cannot be forgiven, and she in turn would pray a short number like some of those of

STRADELLA. She would then faint and be carried from the stage to the accompaniment of a thunderous chorus of hosannas somewhat akin to "DORI-NO-SI-MA CHIN-MI."

FERZING. In MAKAR's tale the colonel's wife who together with her daughter meets the young boy fleeing from SKOTOBOYNIKOV's house just prior to the lad's suicide.

FILIPP. A hairdresser from whom PETYA buys ANDREEV a tie.

FINAL JUDGMENT [STRASHNY SUD]. In Christian tradition the final accounting of each man to God. At one point in his life VERSILOV suddenly begins speaking of religion, demands that believers become monks, and frightens people with words about the FINAL JUDGMENT.

FOMA. In MAKAR's tale one of SKOTOBOYNIKOV's employees. SKOTOBOYNIKOV pays his employees only what he deems necessary, and on one occasion he pays FOMA less than he should. Following his conversion under the influence of the young boy's suicide and his marriage to the boy's mother, he pays FOMA what he owes him.

"FOR ME IS SUFFICIENT THE CONSCIOUSNESS OF THIS" ["S MENYA DOVOLNO SEGO SOZNANYA"]. Part of the monolog of THE COVETOUS KNIGHT, who expresses satisfaction through these words at the power he possesses because of his wealth. ARKADY pictures himself with the power and proud isolation of ROTHSCHILD, who has people flock to him regularly. He notes that he will be proud but will receive them graciously and generously. He insists, however, that petitioners will leave only with gifts and not with satiated curiosity, that is, he will give them goods but not himself. This will insure that he keeps his isolation and distance from people.

FYODOR. ARKADY complains that women promenade about the streets in improper dress with improper airs, and he observes that the streets are for IVAN and FYODOR, euphemisms for men, too.

FYOKLA. The servant girl who attends ARKADY in PYOTR IPPO-LITOVICH's apartment.

GALILEO [GALILEI]. GALILEO Galilei (1564-1642), Italian astrono-mer, mathematician, and physicist whose investigations helped lay the foundations of modern science. He anticipated some of Sir Isaac Newton's discoveries and helped to confirm COPERNICUS' view of the solar system. ARKADY mentions that he once conceived the scene of a common man addressing people such as GALILEO, COPERNICUS, CHARLE-MAGNE, NAPOLEON, PUSHKIN, and SHAKESPEARE. The common man tells them how great they all are, acknowledges his own talentlessness and illegitimacy, but insists that he is greater than they. The scene is an illustration of ARKADY's naive pride.

THE GENERAL'S WIFE [GENERALSHA]. See KATERINA NIKOL-AEVNA AKHMAKOVA.

"GENEVA IDEAS" ["ZHENEVSKIE IDEI"]. According to Dostoevsky, the ideas fashionable among socialists and progressives, including the rejection of religion, social equality, and utopian society built upon the theories of men. Dostoevsky attributed the genesis of many of the ideas to ROUSSEAU, who was born in Geneva. VERSILOV defines what he terms the "GENEVA IDEAS" as virtue without CHRIST.

GENNADY. Perhaps a sixteenth century ascetic who as a youth abandoned a wealthy family in favor of saving his soul as a monk. He ultimately moved to an island in the Kostromsky Forest and founded a monastery in 1565. MAKAR tells ARKADY a story of PYOTR VALERYANYCH in the wilderness of GENNADY.

"GO AND GIVE AWAY ALL YOUR RICHES AND BECOME THE SERVANT OF ALL" ["PODI I RAZDAY TVOYO BOGATSTVO I STAN VSEM SLUGA"]. Adaptation of the account of the rich young ruler as recorded in the New Testament. The ruler asked CHRIST what he needed to do to be saved, and after he acknowledged living the law since his youth, he was told "go and sell that thou hast, and give to the poor, and thou shalt have treasure in heaven: and come and follow me" (Matthew 19:21). The ruler was unable to part with his riches, whereupon CHRIST taught the people the necessity of putting the Kingdom of God first. The same account is found in Mark 10:21 and LUKE 18:22. MAKAR quotes these words while he and ARKADY discuss the relative merits of saving one's soul in the wilderness (MAKAR) or by serving humanity (AR-KADY).

"GOD SAID, LET THERE BE LIGHT: AND THERE WAS LIGHT" ["RECHE GOSPOD: DA BUDET SVET, I BYST SVET"]. As recorded in Genesis 1:3 in the Old Testament, the account of God providing light to the newly formed world. MAKAR looks through MALGASOV's microscope and quotes these words in amazement.

LE GRAND DADAIS. See NIKOLAY SEMYONOVICH ANDREEV. He is derisively referred to as the great dodo.

GRANZ [GRANTS]. STEBELKOV tells ARKADY that a doctor named GRANZ delivered LIDIA AKHMAKOVA's baby by VERSILOV.

"GRATTEZ LE RUSSE ET VOUS VERREZ LE TARTARE." "Scratch off a Russian and you will see a Tartar," misquotation of sentiments expressed by French statesman Joseph de Maistre (1753-1821) in his *Soirées de Saint-Petersbourg (St. Petersburg Evenings),* published in 1821. His statement "Scratch a Russian, and you will wound a Tartar" has also been identified with the Prince de Ligne and with NAPOLEON. NIKO-LAY SEMYONOVICH expresses his dismay at what he perceives to be a lack of true progressives and liberals in Russia, and he quotes this in reference to the majority of society.

GRETCHEN [GRETKHEN]. The maiden with whom Mephistopheles tempts FAUST. She gives herself to FAUST out of pure love but is unable to bear the burden of her grief and ultimately kills her child and then dies herself. A heavenly voice declares her saved rather than condemned. See *FAUST.*

GRIGORY. MAKAR relates to ARKADY how he visited the Bogorodsky Monastery to pay homage to the relics of the miracleworkers ANIKY and GRIGORY. MAKAR perhaps refers to GRIGORY Pelshemsky, who founded a monastery in 1426.

GRISHA. See GRISHA VASIN.

GUBONIN. Pyotr Ionovich GUBONIN (1825-94), prominent railroad industrialist. See KOKOREV.

HARPAGON [GARPAGON]. The miserly central character of *L'Avare (The Miser),* a comedy written by Molière (1622-73) in 1668. The plot chronicles the efforts of the miser's son and daughter to marry for love instead of money and HARPAGON's ultimate permission because of money. ARKADY cites the example of two wealthy beggars who concealed their wealth and begged in order to accumulate still more. He insists that they did not really want to become a ROTHSCHILD and that they are nothing more than HARPAGONS and PLYUSHKINS.

HECUBA [GEKUBA]. In Greek mythology the queen of Troy and the wife of Priam who was taken as a slave by Odysseus. She ultimately was transformed into the sea, where her tomb serves as a landmark for sailors. When ARKADY learns of KRAFT's suicide, he states that KRAFT was a noble man who died for an idea, for HECUBA. The allusion recalls Hamlet's words about an actor whose monolog reflects the sufferings of HECUBA.

HEINE [GEYNE]. Heinrich HEINE (1797-1856), German romantic poet, journalist, and satirist. See "CHRIST ON THE BALTIC SEA."

HERCULES [YERKUL]. Mythical Greek hero of fabulous strength. LAMBERT observes that ANDREEV is as strong as HERCULES.

HERMANN [GERMANN]. The main character in Aleksandr PUSH-KIN's *QUEEN OF SPADES*. He is beset by the fantasy of instant wealth and ultimately goes mad. On a damp, foggy morning ARKADY observes that it is the kind of morning on which HERMANN's wild dream could be portrayed. There is a parallel between ARKADY and HERMANN in their search for wealth.

HERZEN [GERTSEN]. Aleksandr Ivanovich HERZEN (1812-70), Russian journalist and political thinker. He was twice exiled for political activity and finally emigrated in 1847. He settled in London, where he published a bi-weekly journal *The Bell*, which even though suppressed, enjoyed a wide readership in Russia. Through *The Bell* he criticized the Russian social order and advocated the adoption of Western European socialism. (1) When VERSILOV acknowledges that he once left his family to go to Europe, ARKADY wonders if he went to join HERZEN to participate in his propaganda. VERSILOV comments that he was never involved in such things. (2) VERSILOV tells ARKADY how he fell in love with SOFYA while he was in Europe and then sent for her. He is relieved that ARKADY asks about her and observes that he feared that ARKADY had forgiven his conduct out of regard for HERZEN or some little conspiracy because of his presence in Europe.

HORATIUS [GORATSY]. In Roman legend a father who sent his three sons to fight against three representatives of Alba Longa to settle a dispute between that city and Rome. Only one son returned, but the victory was Rome's. When VERSILOV expresses concern about his material condition, ARKADY wonders if this is the kind of elevated idea for which a father would sacrifice his son as HORATIUS did for the idea of Rome.

VICTOR HUGO [VIKTOR GYUGO]. VICTOR Marie HUGO (1802-85), French poet, novelist, and dramatist who became the leader and most authoritative writer of the French Romantic School. See OTHELLO (3).

"I AM GOING INTO THE WILDERNESS" ["YA V PUSTYNYU UDALYAYUS"]. The first line of a popular late eighteenth century song. During an argument with ARKADY, VERSILOV states that he knows that ARKADY is beset by an idea and that the gist of it is this line. ARKADY does indeed intend to distance himself proudly from others.

IAGO [YAGO]. The villain in William SHAKESPEARE's *Othello*. He connives for advantage with no regard for anything but himself and his intrigue results in OTHELLO's murdering the innocent DESDEMONA for suspected infidelity and then taking his own life. At the conclusion of the play IAGO faces the prospect of being tortured to death for his schemes. When ARKADY tells VERSILOV about his meeting with KATERINA AKHMAKOVA, VERSILOV indicates that TATYANA PAVLOVNA may have also been in the house. This enfuriates ARKADY because it warps his idealistic vision that in this situation he is OTHELLO and VERSILOV is IAGO. ARKADY quickly discounts his dramatic comparison, however, by stating that there could be no OTHELLO in this instance, since his relations with others are much different.

"IN VINO VERITAS." "In wine is the truth," a statement proverbially referred to by Gaius Plinius Secundus, Pliny the Elder (23-79), in his *Historia Naturalis* II.XIV.141. He wrote "Vulgoque veritas iam attributa vino est" ("Now truth is commonly said to be in wine"). When drunk ARKADY ponders about marrying KATERINA AKHMAKOVA, but he later states that not even wine could justify having such thoughts. He then quotes these words to comment ironically upon himself.

INDEPENDANCE. The Brussels newspaper *INDEPENDANCE Belge (Belgian Independence)* published 1830-1937. When PETYA TRISHA-TOV observes that the *JOURNAL DES DEBATS* often makes errors in Russian names, ANDREEV corrects him by stating that it is rather the *INDEPENDANCE*.

IPPOLIT. See PYOTR IPPOLITOVICH.

IVAN. See FYODOR.

JESUIT [IEZUIT]. The Society of Jesus, a religious order for Roman Catholic men found by Ignatius Loyola (1491-1556) in 1534. The society is known for scholarship and missionary zeal and has been accused of secrecy and intrigue. (1) A disturbed OLYA complains that while SAFRONOV openly and coarsely propositioned her, VERSILOV through his offers of money and prospects for a job propositioned her like a crafty JESUIT. (2) KATERINA AKHMAKOVA becomes acquainted with ARKADY in order to get information from him about the location of the letter she wrote about her father. When ARKADY objects to being used, she apologizes, and he responds that he expected to find her to be a JESUIT but instead found only honor. (3) When VERSILOV praises him a bit, ARKADY asks him to refrain, since he suspects that the praise comes from JESUIT motivations inconsistent with truth in an effort to make ARKADY like him. (4) ARKADY reflects on the many things troubling him—VERSI-LOV, AKHMAKOVA, her letter, deception—and insists that if he did not consider everything correctly, it is because his mind was incapable rather than because he is a JESUIT. (5) LIZA counsels SERGEY on what to do to be honorable in his circumstances with STEPANOV, and she advises him not to send a letter of confession. ARKADY observes that she thought through the affair like a JESUIT. (6) ARKADY notes that when VERSILOV first met AKHMAKOVA, he considered her to be a hypocrite and a JESUIT rather than the simple, good-hearted society woman that she really is.

JOB [IOV]. Central figure of the Old Testament book of the same name who is tried mightily by Satan but who remains faithful to God despite losing everything. As a reward for his constancy he receives renewed health, a new family, and prosperity. As MAKAR reflects upon dying, he states that he is comforted in the present but still remembers the past. He observes by way of comparison that as JOB looked at his new children and received consolation, he still could not forget all that he had lost in the past.

JOSEPHINE [ZHOZEFINA]. When ARKADY discusses his dislike for women, VERSILOV notes that this is not normal and healthy. ARKADY responds with some anger that he is not going to visit some local JOSEPHINE and then come to tell VERSILOV all about it.

JOURNAL DES DEBATS. *Journal of Debates,* French political news-paper founded in 1789. PETYA TRISHATOV mentions that Russian names are often related incorrectly in the *JOURNAL DES DEBATS.* He notes this when ARKADY thinks that ANDREEV refers to him as KOROVKIN.

JUPITER [YUPITER]. The supreme deity of Roman mythology, who corresponds to the Greek Zeus. ARKADY notes that once he has power he will be content, just as JUPITER is with his thunder bolts. He notes by comparison that if a writer or a peasant woman were in JUPITER's place, the thunder would never cease.

KATERINA NIKOLAEVNA See KATERINA NIKOLAEVNA AKHMAKOVA.

KATERINA NIKOLAVNA. See KATERINA NIKOLAEVNA AKHMAKOVA.

KATYA. See KATERINA NIKOLAEVNA AKHMAKOVA.

KILYAN. A civil servant.

PAUL DE KOCK [POL DE KOK]. French novelist (1793-1871) noted for his graphic portrayals of Parisian life. PRINCE NIKOLAY IVANOVICH comments that ANNA ANDREEVNA is the young beauty of DAVID's old age but adds that PAUL DE KOCK would make a boring alcove scene out of such a circumstance and all would laugh. He adds that even though PAUL DE KOCK has talent he had no measure of taste.

KOKOREV. Vasily Aleksandrovich KOKOREV (1817-89), Russian millionaire. ARKADY notes that he would gladly sell a share of stock to make a profit even though such people as KOKOREV, GUBONIN, and POLYAKOV would advise him to hold that stock in order to make a greater profit. He insists that their mistake in taking this approach is relying on percentages rather than on constancy and determination.

KORAN. The sacred book of Islam containing the revelations of ALLAH to Muhammad (570-632), Islam's founder. See ALLAH.

KOROVKIN. ARKADY mistakenly feels that ANDREEV refers to him as KOROVKIN.

KRAFT. A delicate, quiet man of twenty six whom ARKADY meets at DERGACHEV's apartment. He has determined that Russia is a second-rate country and that it is not worth it for a Russian to live. He becomes the source of much of ARKADY's information about VERSILOV's involvement with the AKHMAKOVS at Ems. When KRAFT commits suicide, VASIN suggests that it is the logical end of reason, that is, his intellectual judgments on Russia.

KRYLOV. Ivan Andreevich KRYLOV (1769-1844), the most famous Russian writer of fables, whose works have become classics. (1) ARKADY recalls that when he lived with the ANDRONIKOVS he loved KRYLOV's fables and often memorized them. (2) See "THE DISCRIMINATING BRIDE."

KUDRYUMOV. A rather offensive and bellicose individual who is present at DERGACHEV's apartment when ARKADY debates the issue of individual freedom.

MAURICE LAMBERT. A school acquaintance of ARKADY who once tried to dominate him and frequently beat him. He is not bound by traditional morals and ethics, and this results in aberrant thoughts and behavior. It is noted, for example, that his ambition is to become wealthy and then feed dogs bread and butter while children starve and burn fuel in a field while children freeze. He also steals money from his widowed mother and threatens to cut the throat of the ABBE RIGAUD, who is involved with his mother. He keeps company with coarse individuals whom he tries to manipulate for his own ends, and while in Moscow prior to the actions of the novel he was close to a ring involved in learning compromising secrets about well-established families and then bribing them. He has come to St. Petersburg to pursue similar endeavors and for such purposes maintains ALPHONSINE and uses PETYA TRISHATOV and ANDREEV. In St. Petersburg he reopens his acquaintance with ARKADY, and on one occasion while nursing him in his apartment learns through his delirious ravings about KATERINA AKHMAKOVA's letter and about those potentially involved in a scandal. He immediately contacts ANNA ANDREEVNA and in exchange for a bribe of 30,000 rubles offers to use the letter to discredit AKHMAKOVA, thereby allowing ANNA ANDREEVNA to marry PRINCE NIKOLAY IVANOVICH and become a millionaire. To pursue his aims he gets ARKADY drunk and with ALPHONSINE's help steals the letter that ARKADY had sewn into his coat and replaces it with a piece of paper. He then gains access to TATYANA PAVLOVNA's house by bribing MARYA, has ALPHONSINE divert TATYANA PAVLOVNA and ARKADY by telling them that LAMBERT and VERSILOV are plotting to murder AKHMAKOVA, and then meets AKHMAKOVA in the house. He accosts her with the letter and threatens her with a revolver, but the melodrama is halted when VERSILOV rushes into the room and knocks LAMBERT unconscious with the revolver. The intrigue is concluded when LAMBERT simply leaves the letter in TATYA-

NA PAVLOVNA's house and then goes away without suffering any retribution. He subsequently returns to Moscow and quickly gets into some difficulty.

LAVROVSKY. When LAMBERT offers to marry him to AKHMA-KOVA, ARKADY recalls a school friend named LAVROVSKY with whom he had discussed marriage when they were 15 years of age. The two boys seriously discussed the prospect from the standpoint that the age of 15 is as good as any other.

LAW [LOU]. John LAW (1671-1729), Scottish financier in France and Louisiana. He established the Banque Général in 1716 with government guaranteed paper currency, but speculation resulted in bankruptcy. ARKADY relates the tale of LAW's scheme in Paris which created frenzied speculation. People went to all extremes to sign up for shares, but there was nothing to write on, so an enterprising hunchback volunteered his back for a price. The scheme failed but the hunchback became wealthy. ARKADY equates himself with the hunchback.

MADAME LEBRECHT [GOSPOZHA LEBREKHT]. A newspaper announcement read by ARKADY indicates that the possessions of a certain MADAME LEBRECHT are to be sold at auction. He attends and buys a worthless album in a box decorated with CUPIDS.

LEPAGE [LEPAZH]. One evening while still in TOUCHARD's school ARKADY and LAMBERT discuss LEPAGE's pistols, Cherkessian swords, and other exotica.

EDMUND KARLYCH LICHTEN [LIKHTEN]. A Moscow doctor who prescribes a linament for MAKAR's legs.

LIDIA. See LIDIA AKHMAKOVA.

"THE LIE THAT US EXALTS/IS DEARER ME THAN DARK OF PETTY TRUTHS" ["TMY NIZKIKH ISTIN MNE DOROZHE/NAS VOZVYSHAYUSHCHY OBMAN"]. Lines from "The Hero" ("Geroy"), a poem written by Aleksandr PUSHKIN in 1830. The poem is written in the form of an exchange between a poet and his friend who discuss the issue of truth. VASIN and ARKADY discuss the principle expressed in these lines, and ARKADY admits that he subscribes to the idea.

LIFE OF MARY OF EGYPT [ZHITIE MARII YEGIPETSKOY]. Any one of a number of hagiographic works dealing with a sixth century saint. After a life of profligacy in Egypt she made a vow to devote herself to mortification and penance in the wilderness, where she gained prophetic powers and sanctity. MAKAR relates this and other tales and legends to ARKADY.

LITVINOVA. VERSILOV lives in an apartment in LITVINOVA's house.

LIZA. See LIZAVETA MAKAROVNA.

LIZAVETA MAKAROVNA (LIZA, LIZOCHKA, LIZOK). ARKADY's sister. She is blonde, looks much like her mother SOFYA, and according to both her and ARKADY, is very different from her brother. She spent time abroad with VERSILOV and her mother and met SERGEY there. Since that time SERGEY pursues her, and ARKADY learns that she is pregnant by him. She has agreed to marry him after a long refusal, and ARKADY speculates that her love for SERGEY is the love of a strong person for a weak one and is linked with pride and the control of another. When SERGEY surrenders himself to the authorities because of his role in a counterfeiting scheme, LIZA forgives him everything and does all that she can to help. During this ordeal she becomes proud and somewhat distant. SERGEY becomes jealous as she visits VASIN for advice in the matter, and his concern is valid as LIZA ultimately finds it necessary to refuse a proposal from VASIN. VASIN entrusts a manuscript to her, and when SERGEY sees it, he becomes even more jealous and shows it to the authorities. VASIN is arrested as a result. Arrangements are made for LIZA to marry SERGEY in the prison, but his untimely death precludes this. Following his death she becomes very despondent. She falls, has a miscarriage, encounters poor health, and faces a rather bleak future. ARKADY ultimately characterizes her as a willing seeker of torments.

LIZOCHKA. See LIZAVETA MAKAROVNA.

LIZOK. See LIZAVETA MAKAROVNA.

CLAUDE LORRAINE [KLOD LORREN]. CLAUDE Gelée (1600-82), French painter who specialized in expansive, bright landscapes. He painted for a time in Rome under the patronage of the papacy. (1) See *ACIS AND GALATEA.* (2) VERSILOV laments the passing of the idea of God from Europe even though he himself is not a great believer. He compares the passing of this great source of strength to the grand, beckoning sun in

CLAUDE LORRAINE's picture.

LUCIA [LYUCHIA]. *LUCIA di Lammermoor,* an opera written by Italian composer Gaetano Donizetti (1797-1848) in 1835. The three act opera is based on *The Bride of Lammermoor,* a novel written by Sir Walter Scott (1771-1832) in 1819. The novel's love intrigue among Edgar, Bucklaw, and Lucy Ashton finds expression in the relationship of VERSILOV, AKHMA-KOVA, and BOERING. (1) VERSILOV takes ARKADY into a miserable pub and observes that he is sometimes so bored that he visits such places which feature among other things smoke, billiards, and an aria from *LUCIA.* (2) After VERSILOV and ARKADY discuss ANNA AN-DREEVNA's possible marriage to PRINCE NIKOLAY IVANOVICH, he decides to request music from *LUCIA* because he likes the solemnity of its dreariness. (3) In a confused state of mind ARKADY muses that VERSILOV may be sitting in a pub listening to *LUCIA* and thereafter may go kill BOERING.

LUKE [LUKA]. The third of the four Gospels in the New Testament written by a physician and early follower of CHRIST. On the way home following MAKAR's funeral, SOFYA asks ARKADY to read something from the BIBLE, and he responds by reading a chapter from LUKE.

LUKERYA. VERSILOV's cook.

"THE MAID" ["NEVESTA-DEVUSHKA"]. While ARKADY recites "THE DISCRIMINATING BRIDE," VERSILOV summons TATYANA PAVLOVNA to listen. ARKADY again recites, but refers to the work as "THE MAID."

"THE MAID HER SUITOR SHREWDLY EYED" ["NEVESTA-DE-VUSHKA SMYSHLYALA ZHENIKHA"]. ARKADY recites this line from KRYLOV to the great amusement of VERSILOV. See "THE MAID HER SUITOR SHREWDLY EYED,/THERE IS NO CRIME IN THAT."

"THE MAID HER SUITOR SHREWDLY EYED,/THERE IS NO CRIME IN THAT" ["NEVESTA-DEVUSHKA SMYSHLYALA ZHENI-KHA,/TUT NET YESHCHYO GREKHA"]. The first two lines of KRYLOV's "THE DISCRIMINATING BRIDE." VERSILOV is delighted when ARKADY recites these lines and comments how striking it is for a boy to do that.

MAKAR. See MAKAR IVANOVICH DOLGORUKY.

MAKAR IVANOV. See MAKAR IVANOVICH DOLGORUKY.

MAKAR IVANOVICH. See MAKAR IVANOVICH DOLGORUKY.

MAKAR IVANYCH. See MAKAR IVANOVICH DOLGORUKY.

SAVIN MAKAROV. An elder on MALGASOV's estate who is comically afraid to look through his master's microscope.

MAKARUSHKA. See MAKAR IVANOVICH DOLGORUKY.

MAKSIM IVANOVICH. See MAKSIM IVANOVICH SKOTOBOYNI-KOV.

ALEKSANDR VLADIMIROVICH MALGASOV. VERSILOV's maternal uncle who bequeathes his holdings to VERSILOV. As MAKAR discusses science and God with ARKADY, he recalls having looked through MALGASOV's microscope 35 years earlier.

MARS. In Roman mythology, the god of war whose status was next to that of JUPITER. VERSILOV ironically refers to a drunken lieutenant who stops him on the street and asks for a handout as a son of MARS.

MARYA. TATYANA PAVLOVNA's cook, a somber, proud, and foul-tempered woman who will go for weeks without speaking to her mistress. She takes TATYANA PAVLOVNA to court for striking her and wins a small settlement, but they are immediately reconciled and she continues to cook for her. She accepts a bribe from LAMBERT and assists in arranging the confrontation between him and KATERINA AKHMAKOVA at TATYANA PAVLOVNA's apartment.

MARYA IVANOVNA. NIKOLAY SEMYONOVICH's wife and a relative of ANDRONIKOV. Following ANDRONIKOV's death she arranges to have KRAFT give STOLBEEV's letter to ARKADY. She sews AKHMAKOVA's letter into ARKADY's coat.

MATVEY. A coachman who serves ARKADY.

MAURICE. See MAURICE LAMBERT.

MILITRISA. See KATERINA NIKOLAEVNA AKHMAKOVA. TATYANA PAVLOVNA refers to AKHMAKOVA as MILITRISA.

MILYUTIN. Count Aleksey Yakovlevich MILYUTIN, who built an area of commercial establishments in St. Petersburg. ANDREEV mentions MILYUTIN's shop as a place to get champagne and oysters.

"MINE OWN CLOTHES SHALL ABHOR ME" ["SAMYE ODEZHDY MOI VOZGNUSHALIS MNOYU"]. Citation from JOB 9:31 in the Old Testament in which JOB reflects on the inability of a wicked man to answer God. He insists that masking wickedness is futile and notes that even "MINE OWN CLOTHES SHALL ABHOR ME." MAKAR relates a tale about one PYOTR STEPANOVICH who laments that he should be a professor in a university. He emphasizes that fate seems to be against him by using this quotation. He drinks a lot but is good in the sciences.

MINERVA. In Roman mythology the goddess of learning and handicrafts who corresponds to the Greek Athena. STEBELKOV refers to ANNA ANDREEVNA as an ancient statue of MINERVA in modern dress.

MISERABLES. *Les MISERABLES,* a novel published by VICTOR HUGO in 1862. The work traces the life of Jean Valjean, unjustly accused of being a criminal, as he confronts individual and social injustice and labors to help others. VERSILOV observes that there are certain scenes in literature that are striking and even painful to remember, and he includes among them the meeting of the fugitive with the young girl in *MISERABLES.* The meeting in question is between Jean Valjean and Cosette, a mistreated illegitimate girl whom he tries to help.

MONTFERRAND [MONFERAN]. Auguste Richard MONTFERRAND (1786-1858), French architect who worked in Russia for most of his career and who is noted for his work on St. Isaac's Cathedral in St. Petersburg. In an anecdote related by PYOTR IPPOLITOVICH, the tsar wants a huge boulder removed from the road, and MONTFERRAND is the person considered for the task.

MADIER DE MONTJAU [MADIE DE MONZHO]. Noel François Alfred MADIER DE MONTJAU (1814-92), French lawyer and politician. In a restaurant ANDREEV overhears two Poles speaking about Parisian affairs and hears them pronounce MADIER DE MONTJAU with a Polish accent. He then gives the same pronunciation to make fun of them.

MOTHER SUPERIOR MITROFANIA [MATUSHKA IGUMENYA MITROFANIA]. The baroness Praskovya Grigorievna Rozen, mother superior of the Vladychne-Pokrovsky Monastery in Serpukhov who was brought to trial for illegally using notes to benefit the monastery. NIKOLAY SEMYONOVICH compares ANNA ANDREEVNA to MITROFANIA.

NAPOLEON. NAPOLEON I Bonaparte (1769-1821), emperor of France following the French Revolution and temporary conqueror of much of Europe. (1) See GALILEO. (2) STEBELKOV insists that on occasion first things become second and vice versa, and he uses the French Revolution and NAPOLEON as an example by pointing out that NAPOLEON was second but became first. (3) VERSILOV discusses a photo of SOFYA and comments how difficult it is to get one that looks like the person. He adds that in photos NAPOLEON could appear stupid and BISMARCK gentle.

IPPOLIT ALEKSANDROVICH NASHCHOKIN. A very self-confident, wealthy, and respected member of high society who is an acquaintance of SERGEY.

NASTASYA. A servant girl in the home in which VASIN has a room.

NASTASYA YEGOROVNA. See DARYA ONISIMOVNA.

ST. NICHOLAS [NIKOLAY UGODNIK]. The bishop of Myra who died about 345 A.D. In a dream-like reflection upon his life in TOUCHARD's school, ARKADY imagines his mother coming to him and bestowing a tearful blessing in which she asks that angels, the Holy Mother, and ST. NICHOLAS watch over him.

NIHILIST [NIGILIST]. A term used by Ivan Sergeevich Turgenev (1818-83) to describe Russian revolutionary attitudes in the late middle 19th century. NIHILISTS advocated the destruction of existing institutions irrespective of the tactics or the future effect. When ARKADY accosts two women on the street and objects to their clothing and behavior, they respond with threats and name-calling and refer to him as a NIHILIST.

NIKOLA. In a semi-delirium ARKADY hears the bell of a church that he thinks sounds like the church of NIKOLA in Moscow built during the reign of ALEKSEY MIKHAYLOVICH.

PRINCE NIKOLAY IVANOVICH. See PRINCE NIKOLAY IVANOVICH SOKOLSKY.

NIKOLAY SEMYONOVICH. See NIKOLAY SEMYONOVICH AN-DREEV.

NIKOLAY SEMYONOVICH. MARYA IVANOVNA's husband. AR-KADY stays with him for a time and considers him cold, egotistic, and very intelligent. ARKADY sends him his manuscript for an opinion and receives a less than laudatory response.

"OHE, LAMBERT! OU EST LAMBERT, AS-TU VU LAMBERT?" "Oh, LAMBERT! Where is LAMBERT; have you seen LAMBERT?" comic French expression designed to create a humorous effect. As ANDREEV leaves LAMBERT, he mocks him with these words.

THE OLD CURIOSITY SHOP [LAVKA DREVNOSTEY]. A novel written by Charles DICKENS in 1840-41. The novel is the sentimental tale of an orphan, Little Nell Trent, and her grandfather, the owner of a curiosity shop, who gambles away their means in an attempt to make a better life for Nell. The two are harrassed by unscrupulous characters, including a cruel dwarf named Quilp, until they succeed in disappearing to work as caretakers of a church. They both die before a potential benefactor, the grandfather's younger brother, can find them and ease their lives. TRISHATOV relates a scene from the novel to ARKADY and recalls that he had vowed to be as good as the young girl who ran away with her crazy grandfather.

OLECHKA. See OLYA.

OLIMPIADA (OLYMPE). A distant relative of PRINCE NIKOLAY IVANOVICH to whom he had given a dowry. She is 19, mediocre, and rather like a pillow.

OLYA (OLECHKA). A thin, pretty, and sickly girl of 20. She struggles through propositions from SAFRONOV and other unscrupulous men and solicitations to turn to prostitution to combat her poverty. In the midst of her struggles VERSILOV offers her a position, leaves her an advance, and throughout acts quite nobly. OLYA is tormented that she has received charity, and her pride causes her to question VERSILOV's motives. STEBELKOV's libelous assertions about VERSILOV prompts her to return VERSILOV's money and to accuse him of pursuing newspaper ads placed by poor teachers and governesses and of offering them money in order to achieve his own improper aims. Having turned away from this final hope, she hangs herself.

OLYMPE. See OLIMPIADA.

OSETROV. A retired navy man who aids TATYANA PAVLOVNA's cook when she sues her mistress for striking her.

OTHELLO [OTELLO]. The central character of *OTHELLO, the Moor of Venice*, a tragedy written by William SHAKESPEARE about 1604. OTHELLO strangles his love DESDEMONA when IAGO intices him to suspect her of infidelity, and he then commits suicide when he learns that she is innocent. (1) See DESDEMONA. (2) See IAGO. (3) VERSILOV observes that there are certain scenes in literature that are striking and even painful to remember, and he includes among them OTHELLO's final monolog, in which he expressed grief over DESDEMONA and his intent to kill himself.

BORIS MIKHAYLOVICH PELISHCHEV. A friend of PRINCE NIKO-LAY IVANOVICH since childhood. ANNA ANDREEVNA hopes to employ him and PRINCE V—to help secure her position with PRINCE NIKOLAY IVANOVICH. She wants them to reconcile the prince with AKHMAKOVA after her letter is made public and then to help her gain financial security with the prince.

THE PELISHCHEVS. The family with which AKHMAKOVA goes abroad following the action of the novel.

PETER [PYOTR]. PETER I or PETER the Great (1672-1725), tsar of Russia 1689-1725. His reign saw the construction of St. Petersburg and the opening of active contact with the West. SERGEY notes that during the reforms of PETER he had a great great grandfather named PYOTR who became an Old Believer and who fathered the SOKOLSKY line through which PRINCE NIKOLAY IVANOVICH was born.

ST. PETER'S DAY [PETROVKI]. June 29, the day on the Russian Orthodox calendar which commemorates the apostles Peter and Paul. MAKAR relates to ARKADY that he paid a visit to PYOTR VALER-YANYCH on ST. PETER'S DAY.

PETYA. See PETYA TRISHATOV.

PILATE [PILAT]. Pontius PILATE, Roman procurator of Judea ca. 26-36 whose desire to appease the Jews resulted in the crucifixion of CHRIST. Legend asserts that PILATE ultimately committed suicide. VERSILOV reports that PYOTR IPPOLITOVICH once insisted that the English parliament reenacted the trial of CHRIST before PILATE under current law and that the jury was compelled to uphold the original verdict.

PIRON. Alexis PIRON (1689-1773), French poet and dramatist noted for his witty epigrams. ARKADY observes that if he were ROTHSCHILD, then TALLEYRAND and PIRON would be nothing in comparison to him.

PLYUSHKIN. The miser in *Dead Souls (Myortvye dushi),* a novel written by Nikolay Vasilievich Gogol (1809-52). The first part of the novel was published in 1842, but subsequent parts were never finished. The novel traces the attempt by Chichikov to purchase the right to use dead serfs in a mortgage scheme and emphasizes human and social foibles. PLYUSHKIN is a grotesque character who hoards everything and makes use of nothing. See HARPAGON.

POLINKA SAKS. A novel written in 1847 by Aleksandr Vasilievich Druzhinin (1824-64). The work treats the theme of the emancipated woman and relates how a husband willingly permits his wife to join her young lover. (1) ARKADY observes that *POLINKA SAKS* and *ANTON GOREMY-KA* had a civilizing influence on the generation of the 1840s. (2) VERSILOV reads *POLINKA SAKS* before moving to the country. ARKADY, in wondering how VERSILOV and his mother could have had a liaison, notes that it must have been a direct beginning, because VERSILOV would not have begun with something like explaining *POLINKA SAKS* to her.

POLYAKOV. Samuil Solomonovich POLYAKOV (1837-88), Russian railroad magnate. See KOKOREV.

"LA PROPRIETE C'EST LE VOL." "Property is theft," inaccurate rendering of a phrase coined by French political figure Jacques Pierre Brissot de Warville (1754-93) and popularized by Pierre Joseph Proudhon (1809-65), French socialist, anarchist, and opponent of private property in his *Qu'est-ce que la Propriété (What Property Is)* written in 1840. Brissot de Warville's original statement was "La propriété exclusive est un vol dans la nature" ("Exclusive property is a theft against the natural order"). As ARKADY drunkenly walks the streets, he recalls that there are thieves in the area but muses that he may even give them his coat. With these thoughts he quotes these words.

TATYANA PAVLOVNA PRUTKOVA. A landowner living near the VERSILOV estate who keeps unofficial watch over his property. She is a small, bird-like, dry figure who is very independent and universally respected. After SOFYA is orphaned, she assumes her care and helps to arrange her marriage to MAKAR. At the time of the novel's action she is living in St. Petersburg near the VERSILOVS and continues to serve them faithfully. She and ARKADY often exchange harsh remarks, sometimes because of his immaturity and foolish actions but most often when he casts aspersions on VERSILOV. During one argument she in effect admits to ARKADY that she has loved VERSILOV for years, and thereafter she and ARKADY are much closer. Her apartment plays an important role in the novel and is the meeting place for ARKADY and AKHMAKOVA and the scene of LAMBERT's attempt to bribe AKHMAKOVA and of VERSILOV's attempted suicide. After VERSILOV recovers from his wound, he, SOFYA, and the family are maintained by TATYANA PAVLOVNA, who also offers to support ARKADY at the university.

PSALTER [PSALTYR]. The Biblical book of Psalms. An old man reads the PSALTER over MAKAR's body prior to the funeral.

PUSHKIN. Aleksandr Sergeevich PUSHKIN (1799-1837), the leading Russian writer of his age who is widely regarded as the father of modern Russian literature. (1) ARKADY notes that he memorized the monolog of PUSHKIN's THE COVETOUS KNIGHT when he was a child and considers that the author created no higher idea. (2) See GALILEO. (3) On a foggy, damp St. Petersburg morning ARKADY observes that it is the kind of morning on which the wild dream of PUSHKIN's HERMANN in *THE QUEEN OF SPADES* could be portrayed. (4) In characterizing ANNA ANDREEVNA's position as FANARIOTOVA's ward, ARKADY notes that it is not the same position that is depicted in literature, for example, the ward of the old countess in *THE QUEEN OF SPADES* by PUSHKIN. (5) In reflecting upon his proposed marriage to ANNA ANDREEVNA, PRINCE NIKOLAY IVANOVICH ponders his age and wonders why life is so short. He comments that his life is in the final perfect form of a PUSHKIN poem in which brevity is considered to be the first requirement in art. He alludes here to PUSHKIN's 1822 statement that "Precision and brevity, these are the prime merits of prose" ("Tochnost i kratkost, vot pervye dostoinstva prozy"). (6) After reading ARKADY's manuscript, NIKOLAY SEMYONOVICH comments that if he were a novelist, he would select representatives of the nobility for his characters because of their order and impressionability. He cites PUSHKIN's choosing subjects of future novels from "THE TRADITIONS OF THE RUSSIAN FAMILY" as an example.

PYOTR. SERGEY's great great grandfather. See PETER.

PYOTR. SERGEY's manservant.

PYOTR IPPOLITOVICH (IPPOLIT). ARKADY's landlord. He is a poor, pockmarked man of 40 who has a sickly child and a wife with tuberculosis. He tells VERSILOVA and ARKADY an amusing tale about a peasant who buries a boulder in the ground in order to dispose of it.

PYOTR STEPANOVICH. In MAKAR's story the teacher that SKOTO-BOYNIKOV hires for the boy he takes into his home. Despite his incompetence and alcoholism, his vanity prompts him to think that he should be a professor. SKOTOBOYNIKOV commissions him to paint a picture of the boy next to the river where he committed suicide. After completing the painting and being paid, PYOTR STEPANOVICH boasts, shows off his money, and is subsequently murdered and robbed.

PYOTR VALERYANYCH. MAKAR tells ARKADY about PYOTR VALERYANYCH, a man who lives in the wilderness of GENNADY under strict self-imposed rules but who has not taken upon himself monastic vows because he cannot give up his pipe. He, however, has expressed willingness to give up his wealth and rank. He later obtains a microscope and comes to wrestle a bit with religion and reason.

"QUAE MEDICAMENTA NON SANANT—FERRUM SANAT, QUA-E FERRUM NON SANAT—IGNIS SANAT!" "That which medicines will not heal—iron heals, that which iron will not heal—fire does!" statement attributed to Hippocrates (ca. 460-370 B.C.), Greek physician recognized as the father of medicine. As ARKADY enters DERGACHEV's apartment during a fiery debate, he hears these words shouted out, and he senses that the statement is made from the point of view of political unrest rather than medicine.

THE QUEEN OF SPADES [PIKOVAYA DAMA]. Short story written by Aleksandr PUSHKIN in 1833 and regarded as a classic of world literature. The story traces the attempts of HERMANN to gain the secret of winning at cards from an old vain countess. He uses her ward Lizaveta Ivanovna to gain access to her room, but fails to obtain the secret, and the countess dies of fright. In drunken nocturnal distress HERMANN is given the cards by the dead countess in an ostensible vision. He plays them only to be foiled by the queen of spades, which he associates with the countess, and he subsequently goes mad. See PUSHKIN (3,4).

"QUITE UNEXPECTEDLY AND QUICKLY" ["KAK NEVZN ACHAY I KAK PROVORNO"]. Inexact rendering of lines from *WOE FROM WIT* spoken by Khlyostova about CHATSKY to the effect that "He's gone quite mad! I ask you now!/So unexpectedly and quickly!" ("S uma soshyol! proshu pokorno!/Da nevznachay! da kak provorno!"). As he observes VERSILOV's actions following MAKAR's death, PRINCE NIKOLAY IVANOVICH states his opinion that VERSILOV has gone mad and quotes these lines. The lines reinforce the association between CHATSKY and VERSILOV.

BARON R. One of THE BARONS R., a tall, strong colonel of about 40. Following VERSILOV's insulting letters to AKHMAKOVA and BOERING, he visits VERSILOV and threatens him with appropriate measures to prevent any further insults. He and BOERING forcibly remove PRINCE NIKOLAY IVANOVICH from ANNA ANDREEVNA's clasp and roundly insult her in the process.

THE BARONS R. According to ARKADY, a line of barons of Germanic origin who have served in the Russian military. They have no means and live on their salary.

RECHBERG [REKHBERG]. A motley gambler whom ARKADY accuses of taking some of his winnings.

ABBE RIGAUD [ABBAT RIGO]. A man involved with LAMBERT's mother.

RINOCHKA. See ARINA.

THE ROHANS [ROGANY]. Ancient European noble line that is linked with many of Europe's ruling houses. SERGEY observes to ARKADY that the SOKOLSKY line has a long heritage like THE ROHANS, but adds that they are unfortunately impoverished.

JAMES ROTHSCHILD [DZHEMS ROTSHILD]. One of the five sons of Mayer Amschel Rothschild, the founder of a large European banking conglomerate that played an important role in European politics. He lived 1792-1858. (1) ARKADY attends an auction of MADAME LEBRECHT's effects, buys a worthless album for two rubles, and sells it for ten rubles. He compares himself with JAMES ROTHSCHILD, who, ARKADY insists, made several million francs when he conveyed the news of the death of the DUKE DE BERRY to the proper quarters. (2) When ARKADY puts his idea in writing for the first time, he states that his goal is to become exactly like JAMES ROTHSCHILD in attributes and wealth. He feels that the keys to this are determination and persistence. (3) ARKADY comments that over the centuries many have tried to become like ROTHSCHILD, but as yet he stands by himself. (4) ARKADY insists that one does not become ROTHSCHILD by living like other people and having normal expenditures and obligations. He asserts that this creates only average people. (5) ARKADY notes that to be ROTHSCHILD he must at the same time leave society. (6) ARKADY cites the example of two wealthy beggars who concealed their wealth and begged to accumulate more. He notes that they did not want to become ROTHSCHILD and were nothing more than HARPAGONS and PLYUSHKINS. (7) ARKADY states that his goal is isolation and that the idea of ROTHSCHILD plays a role because he needs power as well. (8) ARKADY indicates that his face is not an asset to him, but adds that if he were ROTHSCHILD, it would not matter because women would consider him handsome. He notes that even the man with curls on his brow would not be regarded so well. (9) ARKADY notes that if he were ROTHSCHILD, then TALLEYRAND and PIRON would be nothing beside him. (10) ARKADY asserts that if the talented and intelligent people of the world suddenly had ROTHSCHILD's millions, they would act quite like petty mediocrity and would likely be crushed. (11) ARKADY states that if he were ROTHSCHILD, he would wear old clothes and would not mind the weather or what he ate. The knowledge that he is ROTHSCHILD would be sufficient. (12) ARKADY wonders how JAMES ROTHSCHILD could have agreed to be a baron when he was already superior to everyone else. (13) ARKADY insists that if ROTHSCHILD has an open home, receives guests, and has a wife, he will become ordinary like other men, and the whole charm of his idea will be lost. (14) ARKADY notes that some may think that he is not capable of enduring ROTHSCHILD's millions, not because they would crush him, but because he may give them all away and become as he was before. He acknowledges that if he did acquire as much wealth as ROTHSCHILD, he may well give it all away, but in doing so would become thereby twice as wealthy as ROTHSCHILD. (15) During an argument with ARKADY, VERSILOV says that he is certain that ARKADY is beset by the idea of becoming ROTHSCHILD or someone similar and then going off by himself into his own grandeur. This observation crushes and humiliates ARKADY. (16) Even though VERSILOV has mentioned ROTHSCHILD, ARKADY feels certain that it is accidental and that he cannot possibly know about his idea.

JEAN JACQUES ROUSSEAU [ZHAN-ZHAK RUSSO]. French author, philosopher, and liberal political theorist who lived 1712-78. See *LES*

CONFESSIONS.

RYURIK. Semi-legendary founder of the ruling house of Novgorod to whom the Russian state traces its roots. He died in 879. VASIN says that SERGEY is the kind of person who while stating that he descends from RYURIK would be quite content to become a cobbler if that were necessary for him to eat. He would display a sign bearing his name as a cobbler and would find that quite noble.

SAFRONOV. A merchant who withholds money from OLYA and her mother. He ignores their pleas and deeply hurts OLYA by coarsely propositioning her.

NASTASYA STEPANOVNA SALOMEEVA. PRINCE NIKOLAY IVANOVICH mentions that he heard that ARKADY was dabbling in spiritism and comments that NASTASYA STEPANOVNA SALOMEEVA indulges herself in the same things.

MADEMOISELLE SAPOZHKOVA. See ANFISA KONSTANTINOVNA SAPOZHKOVA.

ANFISA KONSTANTINOVNA SAPOZHKOVA (MADEMOISELLE SAPOZHKOVA). An unmarried serf on VERSILOV's estate. ARKADY wonders how VERSILOV could have become involved with SOFYA, who is not beautiful, and notes that VERSILOV could have had a liaison with SAPOZHKOVA, who was pretty and available.

SASHA. SERGEY's brother, who dies as a child.

SCHILLER [SHILLER]. Johann Christoph Friedrich von SCHILLER (1759-1805), German dramatist, poet, and historian noted for his romantic idealism. (1) ARKADY disputes with two women in the street on account of their clothing and demeanor, and then to demonstrate that he is unafraid of their men he follows them home and waits outside of the house. VERSILOV responds that there is something of SCHILLER in this. (2) ARKADY drunkenly reflects that women represent vice and seduction while men suggest nobility and magnanimity. He notes that his contemplated use of AKHMAKOVA's letter does not destroy this generalization in the least and that pure SCHILLERS, at any rate, do not exist.

SEMYON SIDOROVICH (SEMYON SIDORYCH). A pompous, middle-aged, evil-looking man who has had extensive dealings with LAM-

BERT. He warns PETYA TRISHATOV of LAMBERT's plot on AKH-MAKOVA, thereby enabling ARKADY to foil the plot. He determines to betray LAMBERT and counts on the generosity and gratitude of BOER-ING, who expects to marry AKHMAKOVA.

SEMYON SIDORYCH. See SEMYON SIDOROVICH.

SERGEY. See PRINCE SERGEY PETROVICH SOKOLSKY.

SERGEY PETROVICH. See PRINCE SERGEY PETROVICH SO-KOLSKY.

SERYOZHA. See PRINCE SERGEY PETROVICH SOKOLSKY.

SHAKESPEARE [SHEKSPIR]. William SHAKESPEARE (1564-1616), the most eminent of English dramatists. (1) See GALILEO. (2) See OTHELLO.

ALEKSANDRA PETROVNA SINITSKAYA. An acquaintance of VER-SILOV who insultingly tells him that if he were to marry, he is the kind of person who would undoubtedly have children in the first year.

MAKSIM IVANOVICH SKOTOBOYNIKOV. The central character of one of MAKAR's stories, a wealthy merchant who dominates the small town of Afimievsk. He is a widower who is haughty, cruel, and drinks alot. When a rival merchant dies leaving a young widow and five small children, SKOTOBOYNIKOV casts the family out of their home. The four daughters die, leaving only the eldest child, a son, whom SKOTOBOY-NIKOV had on one occasion beaten. He experiences some contrition and invites the boy to come live with him. The boy lives in perpetual fear, and when he inadvertently breaks a china lamp one day, he flees the house and drowns himself in the river. The suicide weighs heavily upon SKOTO-BOYNIKOV and he comes to consider himself a curse on humanity who has offended little children. He proposes marriage to the widow after the boy appears to him in a dream and says that the two should marry and have a child. After much persuasion from many sources and SKOTOBOY-NIKOV's promise to build a church in the boy's memory, she agrees to the marriage. After the marriage his life changes—he becomes very charitable and regularly gives money away. She gives birth to a son, but her dead son comes to her also in a dream, and shortly thereafter the new child dies. SKOTOBOYNIKOV then transfers everything to his wife and goes off to save his soul. He returns to visit her once per year.

SOFYA. See SOFYA ANDREEVNA.

SOFYA ANDREEVNA (SOFYA, SOFYA ANDREVNA, SONYA). A serf on the VERSILOV estate. After her father's death leaves her an orphan, she marries MAKAR at her father's request when he is 55 and she but 18. After her marriage she begins a liaison with VERSILOV, despite the fact that she is described as not pretty and as one of the defenseless people in life whom one pities rather than loves. She goes away with VERSILOV and bears him ARKADY, LIZA, and a sickly son who dies in infancy. With the action of the novel she is living with VERSILOV in St. Petersburg and is about 39, thin, pale, and graying. She is a religious person and has always considered herself to be below VERSILOV. After VERSILOV wounds himself, she nurses him back to health and the two become quite close. She even gets to the point that she dares to speak with him about certain subjects. There is, however, no further mention of their possible marriage, which VERSILOV promised after MAKAR's death.

SOFYA ANDREVNA. See SOFYA ANDREEVNA.

VON SOHN [FON ZON]. An old debauchee who was the victim of a notorious murder in St. Petersburg in 1869. He was enticed into a brothel where he was poisoned, robbed, chopped into pieces and sent to Moscow. (1) PRINCE NIKOLAY IVANOVICH asks ARKADY if he knows the account of VON SOHN. (2) PRINCE NIKOLAY IVANOVICH reports that PYOTR IPPOLITOVICH showed him some pornographic pictures, and the prince notes that such women were brought to one poor fellow to get him drunk. ARKADY states that the prince is speaking of the case of VON SOHN.

THE SOKOLSKYS. SERGEY notes that during the reign of PETER he had a great great grandfather named PYOTR, who became an Old Believer and who fathered THE SOKOLSKYS, through which lineage PRINCE NIKOLAY IVANOVICH came.

THE SOKOLSKY PRINCES. Muscovite princes with whom VERSILOV is in litigation over an inheritance. They have a long noble line and are not the same family to which PRINCE NIKOLAY IVANOVICH belongs. VERSILOV ultimately wins the court battle.

OLD PRINCE SOKOLSKY. See PRINCE NIKOLAY IVANOVICH SOKOLSKY.

PRINCE NIKOLAY IVANOVICH SOKOLSKY (OLD PRINCE SO-KOLSKY). AKHMAKOVA's father. A wealthy official of 60 who has been a widower for twenty years. He is fond of taking destitute girls into his home, where he raises and educates them and then provides a dowry so that they might marry. The rumor that he had an attack of mental illness causes him to distrust others' feelings about him, and he becomes a bit paranoid. When ARKADY comes to St. Petersburg to pursue his idea, he is initially placed in rooms owned by the prince, and they often have occasion to discuss various matters. He is a former believer who has had a crisis of faith, and he and ARKADY discuss such topics as women and the existence of God. He takes a liking to ANNA ANDREEVNA and considers providing her with a dowry and marrying her to SERGEY. She refuses to marry SERGEY, however, and instead offers herself to the prince, who quickly accepts. After he is informed of the existence of his daughter's letter alluding to mental problems, he is brought to some rooms next to ARKADY by ANNA ANDREEVNA, who hopes that the move will insure her marriage and her obtaining some means. Fear and senility combine to make the prince think that he is in an asylum, and he becomes quite childlike. His hope is that ANNA ANDREEVNA and AKHMA-KOVA can be reconciled and that the situation will disappear. After BOERING and BARON R. forcibly remove him from these quarters and return him to AKHMAKOVA, he is relieved and makes his daughter the center of his life. He does not mention ANNA ANDREEVNA again until shortly before his death when he wills her 60,000 rubles, which she refuses to accept. Prior to his death he severs relations with ARKADY and the VERSILOVS.

PRINCE SERGEY PETROVICH SOKOLSKY (YOUNG PRINCE SOKOLSKY, SERGEY, SERYOZHA). A young, handsome retired army officer. Two events abroad prior to the action of the novel link him with the VERSILOVS. While in Ems he becomes involved with LIDIA AKHMA-KOVA and fathers a child by her. This leads him into conflict with VERSILOV, whom he publicly slaps following LIDIA's suicide. His conflict with VERSILOV is further aggravated by the fact that they are in litigation. While in Luga he falsely tells STEPANOV that the colonel's daughter is interested in him. When the story is circulated, the colonel summons SERGEY for an explanation, but SERGEY calls STEPANOV a liar, is cleared, and then retires. He is beset by guilt because of his conduct, but he meets LIZA and finds a refuge in her. When he and ARKADY finally meet in St. Petersburg, ARKADY notes that he contemplated challenging SERGEY to a duel to avenge VERSILOV. SERGEY admits sorrow for insulting VERSILOV and adds that he has tried to apologize.

This meeting leads to an emotionally intense association between the two. SERGEY is beset by debt and has turned to gambling in an attempt to extricate himself. Despite his interst in LIZA and the vision of life that she provides, he maintains an interest in AKHMAKOVA and in ANNA ANDREEVNA, who, it is rumored, may receive a large dowry from PRINCE NIKOLAY IVANOVICH. LIZA had instilled in him the concept of abandoning society and working the land, but he retains dreams of the social whirl and a favorable match that would solve his financial problems. He lies to LIZA about his intentions toward other women and fears that he may not be able to meet the requirements of her new vision. His disgust with himself, with VERSILOV's treatment of AKHMA-KOVA, and with ARKADY's gambling successes as compared to his own failures cause him to heatedly announce that LIZA is pregnant by him and that he has persuaded her to marry him. He also acknowledges to ARKADY that while in Europe he accepted money from STEBELKOV in exchange for contact with an emigrant who could help STEBELKOV counterfeit stock. STEBELKOV insists that ZHIBELSKY can incriminate SERGEY in the venture, and he demands money from SERGEY to offer ZHIBELSKY a bribe. SERGEY considers PRINCE NIKOLAY IVAN-OVICH his final hope to raise money, but when he hears of the prince's proposed marriage to ANNA ANDREEVNA, he feels that his last chance has evaporated. A final attempt at gambling fails and he then has an explanation with LIZA in which he confesses everything. He writes a letter to his former regiment clearing STEPANOV, writes a letter of apology to ARKADY, and finally surrenders to the authorities and confesses his involvement in the counterfeiting scheme. SERGEY's health fails him after these intense experiences—he is often disturbed and frequently dreams of spiders. He further admits that he showed the authorities a manuscript that VASIN had entrusted to LIZA, with the result that VASIN is arrested. Despite all of this he retains plans to marry LIZA in the prison church, but he falls ill with an inflammation of the brain and dies before he can be married or brought to trial.

YOUNG PRINCE SOKOLSKY. See PRINCE SERGEY PETROVICH SOKOLSKY.

SOLOMON. The son of DAVID and Bathsheba who succeeded his father as the last king of a united Israel. His reign (ca. 973-933 B.C.) was characterized by lavish spending and heavy taxation. He gained a reputation for wisdom and the just treatment of judicial matters. ARKA-DY insists that he will learn all about banking and stock exchanges without much effort, and he adds that he will not need the wisdom of SOLOMON so long as he has character and maintains his desire.

SONYA. See SOFYA ANDREEVNA.

SPORTSMAN'S SKETCHES [ZAPISKI OKHOTNIKA]. A series of sketches of peasant life written by Ivan Sergeevich Turgenev (1818-83) in the 1840s and early 1850s. The sketches give a balanced portrayal of peasant life and are characterized by understatement. They were very popular with liberal Western-oriented thinkers who viewed them as socially progressive. When ARKADY first meets VERSILOV, he observes that the ANDRONIKOV home is a literary one where *SPORTSMAN'S SKETCHES* were read aloud in the evenings.

STEBELKOV. VASIN's stepfather, a large, loud, overbearing man of some means who is regarded as a thoroughly revolting person by ARKADY. While in Europe he paid SERGEY to place him in contact with an emigrant who could help him counterfeit stock. Sometime later in St. Petersburg he insists that SERGEY provide money to bribe ZHIBELSKY, who, he insists, is capable of implicating SERGEY in the affair. SERGEY's position is doubly difficult because he is in debt to STEBELKOV, who is most anxious for SERGEY to marry ANNA ANDREEVNA so that he can recover his money. He frequently spreads rumors and is not above using and deceiving people, as evidenced by his telling ARKADY that VERSILOV had a child by LIDIA AKHMAKOVA. He is ultimately jailed because of the counterfeiting scheme and is still in prison when ARKADY concludes his writing.

STEPAN. ANDREY ANDREEVICH VERSILOV's lackey, who treats ARKADY very insultingly.

STEPANOV. An insignificant cornet in SERGEY's regiment. SERGEY falsely boasts that the colonel's daughter is interested in him, and when the allegation surfaces, the colonel summons the two for an explanation. SERGEY extricates himself by calling STEPANOV a liar. SERGEY then retires from the service while STEPANOV remains. He is subsequently cleared through a letter of confession from a contrite SERGEY.

STOLBEEV. The man whose will results in a lawsuit between VERSILOV and THE SOKOLSKY PRINCES. A letter is given to ARKADY following ANDRONIKOV's death that intimates that STOLBEEV sided with THE SOKOLSKY PRINCES, but the law ultimately favors VERSILOV.

ANNA FYODOROVNA STOLBEEVA. A distant relative of VERSI-LOV and of THE SOKOLSKY PRINCES. She maintains close relations with LIZA and SOFYA. SERGEY lives in her apartment.

STRADELLA. Alessandro STRADELLA (ca. 1645-82), Italian composer of operas, cantatas, and oratorios. See FAUST.

SUVOROV. In an anecdote related by PYOTR IPPOLITOVICH, the tsar wants a large boulder removed from the road, and a person first identified as SUVOROV, a descendent of the famous general, speaks with a simple peasant about the job. PYOTR IPPOLITOVICH then decides that it was not SUVOROV after all. The general referred to is Aleksandr Vasilievich SUVOROV (1729-1800), the most celebrated Russian military man of his age. The descendant alluded to is likely Aleksandr Arkadievich SUVO-ROV (1804-82), a grandson of the general.

TALLEYRAND [TALEYRAN]. Charles Maurice de TALLEYRAND-Périgord (1754-1838), French statesman who helped to restore the Bourbon monarchy following NAPOLEON's fall and who represented his country at the Congress of Vienna. ARKADY observes that if he were ROTHSCHILD, then TALLEYRAND and PIRON would be nothing in comparison with him.

TATYANA. See TATYANA PAVLOVNA PRUTKOVA.

TATYANA. TATYANA Larina, the heroine in PUSHKIN's novel in verse *YEVGENY Onegin*. She progresses from a naive, romantically inclined country girl infatuated with YEVGENY to the socially adept wife of a prominent general. Though she professes continued love for YEV-GENY, she refuses his advances in the final complete chapter of the novel by insisting that she will be faithful to her husband. VERSILOV observes that there are certain scenes in literature that are striking and even painful to remember, and he includes among them YEVGENY at the feet of TATYANA. VERSILOV has in mind YEVGENY's rejected appeal for TATYANA's love in the concluding scene.

TATYANA PAVLOVNA. See TATYANA PAVLOVNA PRUTKOVA.

TEN COMMANDMENTS [DESYAT ZAPOVEDEY]. As recorded initially in Exodus 20 in the Old Testament, the divine laws given to Moses by Jehovah. They form the basis of the Judeo-Christian ethic. (1) In answer to ARKADY's question about how he should live, VERSILOV responds that he should be honest, not lie, not envy his neighbor's house, in short, abide by the TEN COMMANDMENTS. (2) ARKADY wonders what he can do alone simply by keeping the TEN COMMANDMENTS, and VERSILOV responds that he will become great.

"THERE IS NO CRIME IN THAT" ["TUT NET YESHCHYO GRE-KHA"]. See "THE MAID HER SUITOR SHREWDLY EYED,/THERE IS NO CRIME IN THAT." VERSILOV is particularly amused when ARKADY recites this line from "THE DISCRIMINATING BRIDE."

"THERE IS NOTHING HID, WHICH SHALL NOT BE MANI-FESTED" ["NICHEGO NET TAYNOGO, CHTO BY NE SDALALOS YAVNYM"]. Slightly altered version of Mark 4:22 in the New Testament which reads in the original with no change in the translation "Net nichego taynogo, chto ne sdelalos by yavnym." When VERSILOV tells ARKADY that he will be great if he lives the TEN COMMANDMENTS, ARKADY complains that he will still be unknown. VERSILOV responds by quoting this Scripture.

TIKHOMIROV. A 27 year old teacher whom ARKADY meets at DERGACHEV's apartment. In response to KRAFT's suggestion that Russia is a second-rate nation, TIKHOMIROV notes that man must work for humanity and for a future nation.

TOUCHARD [TUSHAR]. A proud, uneducated Parisian of 45 who heads a Moscow school that ARKADY attends. Despite the fact that he has only six students, he objects to ARKADY's studying there because of his origin. VERSILOV's refusal to pay him more money causes him to abuse ARKADY.

"TOUS LES GENRES." Part of a phrase coined by Voltaire, pen name of Francois Marie Arouet (1694-1778), in his *Préface à l'Enfant Prodigue (Preface to the Prodigal Son)* written in 1738. The original is "TOUS LES GENRES sont bons hors le genre ennuyeux" ("All genres are good except the boring one"). As ARKADY prepares to relate to VERSILOV, TATYANA PAVLOVNA, LIZA and SOFYA the details of his son-father relationship, VERSILOV uses these introductory words to allude to the possibility that he may be very bored.

"TRADITIONS OF THE RUSSIAN FAMILY" ["PREDANIA RUSS-KOGO SEMEYSTVA"]. Line from the thirteenth stanza of the third chapter of *YEVGENY Onegin,* a novel in verse written by Aleksandr

PUSHKIN in 1823-31. The stanza expresses how PUSHKIN intends to use "TRADITIONS OF THE RUSSIAN FAMILY" as the basis of his writing. See PUSHKIN (6).

TRIFON. In MAKAR's tale SKOTOBOYNIKOV commissions PYOTR STEPANOVICH to paint a portrait of the young boy who committed suicide. He insists that he could hire anyone he cares to, but has hired a TRIFON like PYOTR STEPANOVICH because he remembers the boy's face. TRIFON is a name used here to imply dullness and lack of respect.

PETYA TRISHATOV. ANDREEV's young, well-dressed companion, whom ARKADY meets at LAMBERT's. He is the son of a general and has been saved from embarrassment in court by LAMBERT, with whom he participates in some shady dealings. When SEMYON SIDOROVICH informs him of LAMBERT's plot against AKHMAKOVA, he in turn tells ARKADY, and the two of them return to TATYANA PAVLOVNA's apartment where PETYA struggles with VERSILOV to prevent a murder-suicide. After this episode and ANDREEV's suicide, he vanishes.

"TUE-LA." "Kill her," words coined by Alexandre Dumas fils (1824-95), French dramatist and novelist, in his pamphlet *L'Homme-Femme (Man and Woman),* written in 1872. The work critically examines the role of women in society. ALPHONSINE complains to ARKADY that LAMBERT is cruel to her and then generalizes that woman is nothing in society, merely "TUE-LA," which is the last word of the French Academy. She alludes here to the fact that Dumas was elected to the Academy and presupposes that because of that the Academy did not favor the rights of women.

TUILERIES [TYUILRI]. Parisian royal palace which was bombed and burned by the Commune of Paris in 1871. VERSILOV reflects on his feelings about Europe's imminent demise and notes that he does not speak only about war or the burning of TUILERIES. He insists that as a Russian liberal and a true European he has the right to tell European insurgents that the burning was a mistake.

"TURN STONES INTO BREAD" ["OBRATIT KAMNI V KHLEBY"]. A reference to one of the temptations of CHRIST by Satan as recorded in Matthew 4:1-11, Mark 1:12-13, and LUKE 4:1-13 in the New Testament. Satan tempted the fasting CHRIST to turn stones into bread if He were the Son of God. In answer to ARKADY's question as to what constitutes a great idea, VERSILOV responds "TURN STONES INTO BREAD."

URIAH [URIA]. URIAH the Hittite, the husband of Bathsheba. See DAVID.

V. See ANDREY PETROVICH VERSILOV.

PRINCE V. A friend of PRINCE NIKOLAY IVANOVICH since childhood. ANNA ANDREEVNA hopes to employ him and BORIS MI-KHAYLOVICH PELISHCHEV to secure her position with PRINCE NIKOLAY IVANOVICH. She wants them to reconcile the prince with AKHMAKOVA after her letter is made public and then to help her gain financial security by marrying the prince.

PRINCE V-SKY. ARKADY recalls a meeting with ANDREY ANDREE-VICH VERSILOV at the apartment of PRINCE V-SKY. Rather than being received he is merely given money through a lackey. This mortifies ARKADY, and he often ponders revenge.

V—V. PETYA comments about how *INDEPENDANCE* often reports Russian names incorrectly and notes that V—V always comes out WALLONIEFF.

VARVARA STEPANOVNA. VERSILOV's late aunt, who cared for ARKADY in the country.

GRISHA VASIN. STEBELKOV's stepson, an intelligent man about whom ARKADY has heard much and whom he wants to meet. They meet at DERGACHEV's apartment, where VASIN objects to KRAFT's idea that Russia is a second-rate country. ARKADY comes to respect him highly although ARKADY's pride makes it difficult for him to respect anyone. VERSILOV contacts him about being his second, should he challenge SERGEY to a duel, but VASIN quickly and firmly refuses. He knew the VERSILOV family and SERGEY in Luga, and following SERGEY's surrender and imprisonment, LIZA often consults him for advice. He discounts the basis of her love for SERGEY, demeans him, and finally proposes himself, but LIZA refuses. When SERGEY shows a manuscript that VASIN entrusted to LIZA to the authorities, VASIN is arrested. When the manuscript is found to be merely a translation from French, he is released from prison and leaves the area.

ALPHONSINE DE VERDEN (ALPHONSINE, ALFONSINKA, AL-FONSINA KARLOVNA). LAMBERT's rather affected companion who was previously linked with ANDRIEUX. She is tall, thin, and much the worse for wear. She despises and fears LAMBERT and cites her position with him as typical of the place of women in society. She helps LAMBERT steal AKHMAKOVA's letter from ARKADY and then attempts to lead TATYANA PAVLOVNA and ARKADY away so that LAMBERT can carry out his intention to bribe AKHMAKOVA. After the ruse is discovered by PETYA and the scene with AKHMAKOVA, LAMBERT, and VERSILOV is brought to a close, ALPHONSINE disappears and ARKADY never sees her again.

COUNTESS VERIGINA. DARZAN comments that he has often seen NASHCHOKIN at the home of COUNTESS VERIGINA.

VERSILOFF. See ANDREY PETROVICH VERSILOV. ALPHON-SINE refers to him with the French VERSILOFF.

ANDREY ANDREEVICH VERSILOV. ANNA ANDREEVNA's brother and VERSILOV's son, who sees his father about twice per year. He comes to St. Petersburg to aid ANNA ANDREEVNA in her attempt to marry PRINCE NIKOLAY IVANOVICH, but breaks with her completely when she refuses the prince's inheritance. He treats ARKADY with disdain.

ANDREY PETROVICH VERSILOV (V., VERSILOFF). ARKADY's father. As a young man of means he attended the university, served in the cavalry, and then married FANARIOTOVA by whom he had two children, ANDREY ANDREEVICH and ANNA ANDREEVNA. He maintains a frantic social pace until FANARIOTOVA prematurely dies, and he finds himself a widower at age 25. At this stage of his life he is handsome, refined, and affects French airs. His financial affairs are continually in turmoil, and he manages to waste three fortunes in his lifetime. Following the death of his wife and his move to the country he initiates a liaison with SOFYA and then quickly and tearfully apologizes to her husband MAKAR. To his great surprise MAKAR accepts his offer of money for SOFYA and the two leave together. VERSILOV continually professes the highest respect for SOFYA's character and also that of MAKAR. He leaves SOFYA frequently and spends much time abroad but always returns to her. Three children are born to the two—a son ARKADY, a daughter LIZA, and a second son who dies in infancy. He gives his children to others to raise and sees them rarely; for example, prior to his inviting ARKADY to come to St. Petersburg, he has seen his son only once when the boy was ten. Until his difficult financial circumstances dictate otherwise, he maintains SOFYA in separate quarters, and throughout he promises to marry her once MAKAR dies. During one of his stays abroad he lives with the AKHMAKOVS and contemplates marriage to the general's 17 year old daughter LIDIA, who is pregnant by SERGEY. His intentions are noble and protective, but the AKHMAKOVS violently object to the proposal, and VERSILOV finds himself ostracized and publicly slapped by SERGEY following LIDIA's suicide. He does manage to save the child and has it placed in Russia following its mother's death. It is at this time that he begins his stormy involvement with LIDIA's stepmother KATERINA NIKOLAEVNA AKHMAKOVA. Their love/hate relationship extends back into Russia and greatly effects the course of events. Other important dimensions of VERSILOV are his liberalism and his feelings for religion. He is identified with CHATSKY in the play *WOE FROM WIT* and is thereby stamped as one of the rational liberal thinkers of the early and middle 19th century. This identification does not preclude his being critical of Europe or of having his roots in Russian soil, and he foresees the imminent collapse of Europe both materially and spiritually. He illustrates his feelings by recounting to ARKADY a dream about *ACIS AND GALATEA* in which he senses the demise of Europe and laments the passing of the old. His pride prompts him to state that he alone can tell Europe her mistakes and that he is one of the few men that Russian history has produced who can stand as a thinker and a doer and who can suffer (CHRIST-like) for all. He laments the passing of the idea of God from Europe and adds that although he was happy there and loved mankind he must yet make one person happy and love someone on a practical level. His statements about religion are equally double-edged. It is rumored, for example, that he converts to Catholicism, advocates salvation through monasticism and asceticism, and frightens people with statements about the FINAL JUDGMENT. At the same time he can encourage ARKADY to live the TEN COMMANDMENTS and to believe in God and also assert that it is impossible to love one's neighbor and that a Russian atheist is the best of men. He also adds that humanity without CHRIST is meaningless. As the action of the novel commences VERSILOV is 45, no longer refined, shining, or handsome, and beset with financial problems despite the fact that his litigation with THE SOKOLSKY PRINCES is successful. He is a proud man whose actions and statements reinforce the duality evident in his liberalism and feelings about religion. He incurs the ire of the equally proud OLYA, who accuses him in front of his family of pursuing newspaper ads placed by poor teachers and governesses in order to take advantage of them, but despite appearances he insists that giving her money is the only noble thing that he has done in some time. When ARKADY arrives in St. Petersburg at his invitation, he places him with PRINCE NIKOLAY IVANOVICH and spends much time with him despite the fact that he considers his son to be quite immature. During one conversation he acknowledges to ARKADY that he can entertain two opposite ideas at the same time. This is nowhere better evidenced than in his love/hate relationship with AKHMAKOVA. He writes her letters calling her debauched, comments to others that he considers her to be the noblest of women, and deliberately tries to infuriate BOERING, who is rumored to be planning marriage to her. At this same time, when MAKAR comes to spend some time with them, VERSILOV recommits to marry SOFYA following MAKAR's death and laments that even though he loves her very much he has brought her only evil. On the day that MAKAR dies he formally proposes to AKHMAKOVA through ANNA ANDREEVNA and then returns to SOFYA to call her an angel, announces that he is again leaving to wander, laments that he has a double, and breaks an icon that MAKAR desired to leave to him. After LAMBERT steals AKHMA-KOVA's letter from ARKADY, VERSILOV quickly joins forces with him and conjures up the ruse to have ALPHONSINE lure TATYANA PAVLOVNA and ARKADY away from the apartment so that AKHMA-KOVA can be accosted there. VERSILOV watches while LAMBERT confronts her, but when LAMBERT produces a revolver, VERSILOV rushes into the room, disarms him, and knocks him unconscious. When AKHMAKOVA faints, he picks her up and carries her about like a child. He kisses her and attempts to shoot her and himself, but ARKADY and PETYA TRISHATOV burst upon the scene, and in the ensuing struggle VERSILOV succeeds only in wounding himself. ARKADY feels that during these moments his father is insane because of his dual personality. SOFYA nurses him back to health, and he becomes very devoted and affectionate. Nothing more is said about his marrying SOFYA, but he seems to forget AKHMAKOVA. He asserts that he loves God but is unable to endure it.

ANNA ANDREEVNA VERSILOVA (ANNA). VERSILOV's daughter by his first wife FANARIOTOVA. She has lived with her grandmother FANARIOTOVA for years and has received no support at all from VERSILOV. She is 22, tall, very independent, has dark eyes and hair, and has an almost monastic element about her. Prior to the action of the novel she has met ARKADY only once. PRINCE NIKOLAY IVANOVICH attempts to provide her with a dowry and marry her to SERGEY, but she refuses such a match and then offers herself to the prince. LAMBERT offers to discredit AKHMAKOVA by exposing her letter about her father, thus enabling ANNA to arrange a lucrative match with the prince, but she decides upon her own ploy. She moves the prince near to ARKADY thinking that that will solidify her position and then plans to make the letter public and to reconcile AKHMAKOVA and the prince thinking that such steps will insure the marriage. Her plot fails however when ARKADY refuses to cooperate in any way and when BOERING and BARON R. forcibly remove the prince and take him to AKHMAKOVA. Sometime later the prince dies and leaves her 60,000 rubles in his will, but ANNA refuses to accept it. In a conciliatory gesture AKHMAKOVA leaves the money on deposit in ANNA's name. She comes to accept ARKADY as a friend and vows to enter a convent, but ARKADY suspects that she will not do this. TATYANA PAVLOVNA justifies ANNA's actions by noting that she has been insulted all of her life.

ALEKSANDRA PETROVNA VITOVTOVA. VERSILOV comments that he once played the role of CHATSKY in the amateur theater of ALEKSANDRA PETROVNA VITOVTOVA when the regular actor ZHILEYKO became ill. ARKADY views this performance and is most impressed.

WALLONIEFF. PETYA comments about how *INDEPENDANCE* often reports Russian names incorrectly and notes that V—V always comes out as WALLONIEFF.

"WAS DEAD, AND IS ALIVE AGAIN; HE WAS LOST, AND IS FOUND" ["BYL MYORTV I OZHIL, PROPADAL I NASHYOL-SYA"]. Part of LUKE 15:24 in the New Testament, the words of the rejoicing father upon the return of the prodigal son. VASIN tells ARKADY that VERSILOV has taken his letter of inheritance to SOKOLSKY's attorney and has renounced all claim to the money in their litigation. ARKADY perceives this as a noble, selfless act and literally falls in love again with his father, to whom he so desires to be close. He then quotes this passage of Scripture to illustrate his feeling that his "lost" father is back in his favor.

WOE FROM WIT [GORE OT UMA]. An immensely popular play in verse written 1822-24 by Aleksandr Sergeevich Griboedov (1795-1829). The play portrays the social and amorous failures of CHATSKY, a progressive in a backward society. (1) VERSILOV recalls that when he and ARKADY first met, ARKADY recited to him either a fable or something from *WOE FROM WIT.* (2) ARKADY comments that the ladies at ANDRONIKOV's home know alot of verse and often do scenes from *WOE FROM WIT.* (3) ARKADY attends the performance of *WOE FROM WIT* at VITOVTOVA's theater in which VERSILOV plays the role of CHATSKY.

YEFIM. See YEFIM ZVEREV.

YELISEEV. Owner of large food and wine outlets in 19th century Russia. When ARKADY wins his litigation with THE SOKOLSKY PRINCES, he brings home food and drink from the YELISEEV and BALLE establishments to celebrate.

YEVGENY. YEVGENY Onegin, the male lead in PUSHKIN's novel in verse by the same name. He is a liberal and progressive who is fashionably bored and who is representative of the young generation of his time. He refuses the love of the naive TATYANA under the guise that life has already passed him by, kills his token friend Lensky in a meaningless duel, and then is rebuffed years later by the more mature and now married TATYANA as he seeks a liaison. See TATYANA.

ZAVYALOV. Noted Russian knife craftsman in the middle 19th century. While discussing popular anecdotes with ARKADY, VERSILOV mentions one story in circulation to the effect that the English offered ZAVYALOV a million rubles if he would not affix his stamp to his products.

ZERSHCHIKOV. A retired military man who operates a gambling salon. ARKADY begins to frequent the establishment with SERGEY, and on one occasion ZERSHCHIKOV implies that ARKADY may be a thief. The allegation contributes to ARKADY's illness and a subsequent coma. ZERSHCHIKOV discovers his mistake and writes ARKADY a letter of apology.

ZHIBELSKY. An attorney's assistant who is involved in STEBELKOV's scheme to counterfeit railroad stock. He has two notes that implicate SERGEY in the venture and demands to be bribed so that he can emigrate. STEBELKOV insists that such a bribe come from SERGEY, and this situation contributes to SERGEY's general demise.

ZHILEYKO. An actor whom VERSILOV replaces in the role of CHAT-SKY in an amateur production of *WOE FROM WIT* in VITOVTOVA's theater.

YEFIM ZVEREV. A nineteen year old former classmate of ARKADY who is considering going to America. He quickly refuses ARKADY's request to serve as a second in a projected duel with SERGEY.

A GENTLE CREATURE (KROTKAYA) 1876

A—V. A hussar who impugns CAPTAIN BEZUMTSEV's reputation at a buffet during an intermission at the theater. A—V insists that the captain is drunk and is causing a scandal in the corridor. BEZUMTSEV's soldiers feel that the allegations reflect upon the entire company, and the men condemn the PAWNBROKER, the only one of their number present at the buffet, for not defending the captain's honor.

ARCHBISHOP OF GRANADA [ARKHIEPISKOP GRENADSKY]. One of the persons that GIL BLAS serves. His task is to write out the homilies that the archbishop composes. When the archbishop comes to trust him, he makes GIL BLAS promise to inform him when his homilies deteriorate in quality. Following a stroke the archbishop fails mentally, and GIL BLAS suggests that his homilies do not meet previous standards. The archbishop dismisses him in a rage, and GIL BLAS learns the lesson of being too truthful with those who cannot bear it. The GENTLE CREATURE laughingly tells the PAWNBROKER that she remembers the scene of the meeting of GIL BLAS and the ARCHBISHOP OF GRANADA. She mentions this to her husband after he castigates himself, expresses reverence for her, and tearfully begs her to begin a new life with him.

AUNTS [TYOTKI]. The women who raise the GENTLE CREATURE. They are cruel to her, resent that she is an extra mouth to feed, and even consider selling her into prostitution.

AUTHOR [AVTOR]. Dostoevsky explains to the reader in a brief preface that he is substituting this story for the usual entries in his *DIARY* because the subject matter has been heavily on his mind. He indicates that he has subtitled the work "fantastic" because of its form rather than its content and that he himself considers it quite realistic. The fantastic stems from the fact that the PAWNBROKER practically dictates his thoughts and feelings to an unseen stenographer following the GENTLE CREATURE's suicide in an attempt to explain what happened and to focus his thoughts. He notes that essentially this same technique is used in VICTOR HUGO's *THE LAST DAY OF A MAN CONDEMNED TO DEATH*, although he insists that in this work there is less reality since the assumption is made that the victim writes his notes until the very moment of execution.

CAPTAIN BEZUMTSEV. The captain of the PAWNBROKER's company. After the hussar A—V insists that BEZUMTSEV is drunk and causes a scandal in the theater, the PAWNBROKER is condemned by the company for not defending BEZUMTSEV's honor.

GIL BLAS [ZHIL-BLAZ]. The main character in *L'Histoire de GIL BLAS de Santillane* (1715-35), a picaresque novel written by Alain René Lesage (1668-1747). GIL BLAS is a rather lovable rogue who capers through a series of adventures, intrigues, and schemes before settling down for good in the country. The GENTLE CREATURE tells the PAWNBROKER that she read the scene of GIL BLAS with the ARCHBISHOP OF GRANADA and enjoyed it very much.

"BOILING BLOOD AND A SURPLUS OF ENERGY" ["KROV KIPIT I SIL IZBYTOK"]. Part of a line from "Don't Trust Yourself" ("Ne ver sebe"), a poem written by Mikhail Yurievich Lermontov (1814-41) in 1839. The poem is addressed to young dreamers, who are cautioned not to trust inspiration or to conceive of it as a sign of heaven, since it is likely "BOILING BLOOD AND A SURPLUS OF ENERGY." The PAWN-BROKER pontificates to the GENTLE CREATURE that cheap generosity is always easy because it is only "BOILING BLOOD AND A SURPLUS OF ENERGY." He says this to avoid being charitable.

CAPTAIN'S WIFE [KAPITANSHA]. An impoverished widow who brings a medallion, obviously a valued gift from her late husband, as a pledge to the PAWNBROKER in exchange for 30 rubles. She later attempts to replace it with a bracelet, but the PAWNBROKER refuses because the bracelet is worth much less. The GENTLE CREATURE later makes the exchange out of compassion and defiance of her husband and the matter results in her first argument with the PAWNBROKER.

DIARY [DNEVNIK]. *DIARY of a Writer (DNEVNIK pisatelya)*, diary-like work, primarily of a publicistic nature but containing some fiction, written by Dostoevsky and published 1873-81. See AUTHOR.

DOBRONRAVOV. A pawnbroker and an acquaintance of the PAWN-BROKER. The GENTLE CREATURE appeals to him, but he will not accept her worthless articles. The PAWNBROKER vows to sell out to DOBRONRAVOV and take his wife abroad so that she can recuperate.

FAUST. A play in two parts (1808, 1832) written by GOETHE. The play chronicles the career of FAUST, who sells his soul to MEPHISTOPHE-LES in exchange for the promise to comprehend all experience. See "I—I BELONG TO THAT PART OF THE UNIVERSE THAT WANTS TO

DO EVIL BUT DOES GOOD."

FAUST. A seeker of all knowledge, the central character in GOETHE's *FAUST.* He sells his soul to MEPHISTOPHELES in exchange for the promise to comprehend all experience. See "I—I BELONG TO THAT PART OF THE UNIVERSE THAT WANTS TO DO EVIL BUT DOES GOOD."

"FIRST IMPRESSIONS OF LIFE" ["PERVYE VPECHATLENIA BYTIA"]. Slight distortion of a line from "The Demon" ("Demon"), a poem written by Aleksandr Sergeevich Pushkin (1799-1837) in 1823. The original reads "all IMPRESSIONS OF LIFE" ("vse VPECHATLENIA BYTIA"). The poem notes that a demonic influence that discounted the beautiful and the elevated in life came to him and destroyed his feelings at a time when the "FIRST IMPRESSIONS OF LIFE" were still new and fresh. The PAWNBROKER tells the GENTLE CREATURE that youthful generosity is nice but is worth little because such magnanimity costs youth nothing and comes from a lack of experience as in the "FIRST IMPRESSIONS OF LIFE."

GENTLE CREATURE [KROTKAYA]. A 16 year old orphan of three years who is raised in virtual slavery by her AUNTS. They abuse her, resent her, and even consider selling her into prostitution. She comes to the PAWNBROKER to pledge her final possessions in order to pay for an ad in *THE VOICE* advertising her services as a governess. Her pride causes her to flare up at his efforts to dominate her but her poverty makes it necessary to control herself. When a neighboring merchant, much older and rather fat, wants her for his third wife, the PAWNBROKER intercedes and proposes. Overcome by her position, she accepts his offer but only after thoughtful consideration. The marriage is an agonizing one for her as the PAWN-BROKER attempts to dominate and control her in every way. She cannot even leave the apartment without him. She finally revolts over the issue of the CAPTAIN's WIFE's medallion and begins go out in the evenings to visit YULIA SAMSONOVNA. On one occasion upon returning home she confronts the PAWNBROKER with his past—his dismissal from the service for cowardice and his begging in the streets of St. Petersburg for three years. She has evidently sought knowledge about her husband and his past and objects that he never told her about any of these things before they were married. She confronts him on these matters with some derision and with injured pride. On one of her visits to YULIA SAMSONOVNA's apartment she has a rendezvous with YEFIMOVICH, whose propositions she skillfully and playfully rebuffs. Unknown to her the PAWNBROKER listens to the entire scene from the next room. When he suddenly enters the room and takes her home, she is severe and challenging, yet rather overcome. She does not sleep in the same bed with him that evening for the first time. Early that morning she picks up his revolver and holds it at his temple for a few tense moments. He opens his eyes, meets her gaze, and then closes them again; and after a short while she puts the gun down and leaves the room. That same day he buys a separate bed and screen to create a separate room, and without exchanging words she understands that she is to sleep there. That night she becomes delirious, has a high fever, and remains ill for six weeks, during which time the PAWNBROKER dutifully and solicitiously attends her. Following a partial recovery and while sewing one morning, she begins to sing, and her husband construes this to mean that she no longer thinks or cares about him. When he falls at her feet and begs to begin a new life, she is overwhelmed by his attention, his professed worship of her, and his self-incrimination. She expresses surprise at his conduct since she had feared that he would continue their relationship as it was. She experiences periods of sobbing and delirium and has difficulty accepting his praise and the intensity of his feelings. She insists that she is a criminal, that she is quite guilty before him, but that she will be faithful and will respect him. When he goes to secure their passports in order to take her abroad, she jumps from the window of their apartment clutching the icon that she had originally pawned with him, unable to come to terms with her guilt or the intensity of his feelings.

GOETHE [GYOTE]. Johann Wolfgang von GOETHE (1749-1832), German poet, playwright, novelist, and scientist, who is one of the giants of world literature. (1) The PAWNBROKER notes that even though one stands on a precipice in life, the words of GOETHE can be a ray of light. See MEPHISTOPHELES. (2) When the PAWNBROKER proposes and the GENTLE CREATURE hesitates, he becomes somewhat miffed by her delay and wonders if she is having a difficult time choosing between the fat old merchant and a pawnbroker who quotes GOETHE.

VICTOR HUGO [VIKTOR GYUGO]. VICTOR Marie HUGO (1802-85), French poet, novelist, and dramatist who became the leader and most authoritative writer of the French Romantic School. See AUTHOR.

"I—I BELONG TO THAT PART OF THE UNIVERSE THAT WANTS TO DO EVIL BUT DOES GOOD" ["YA—YA YESM CHAST TOY CHASTI TSELOGO, KOTORAYA KHOCHET DELAT ZLO, A TVORIT DOBRO"]. Adaptation of the words of MEPHISTOPHELES as he introduces himself to FAUST in GOETHE's *FAUST*. The original reads

"Ein Teil von jener Kraft/ /Die stets das Böse will und stets das Gute schafft" ("Part of that power that always desires evil but always does good"). When the PAWNBROKER first becomes acquainted with the GENTLE CREATURE, he quotes these words to her, indicates that they are the words with which MEPHISTOPHELES identifies himself to FAUST, and recommends that she read *FAUST*. He does this to demonstrate that even though he is a pawnbroker he is learned.

THE LAST DAY OF A MAN CONDEMNED TO DEATH [POSLEDNY DEN PRIGOVORENNOGO K SMERTNOY KAZNI]. *Le Dernier jour d'un condamné*, a tale written by VICTOR HUGO in 1829. See AUTHOR.

LUKERYA. A servant girl who attends the GENTLE CREATURE while she lives with her AUNTS and also later when she marries the PAWNBROKER.

MEPHISTOPHELES [MEFISTOFEL]. The demon-like tempter in *FAUST*. (1) See "I—I BELONG TO THAT PART OF THE UNIVERSE THAT WANTS TO DO EVIL BUT DOES GOOD." (2) The PAWNBROKER recalls that the details of the GENTLE CREATURE's life are so bad that he is surprised that she could express interest in the words of MEPHISTOPHELES.

MILL. John Stuart MILL (1806-73), British philosopher, economist, and reformer who tempered the theories of utilitarianism with a more libertarian and humanitarian outlook. He insisted that the empirical approach to truth was the only valid one. The PAWNBROKER insists that it is axiomatic that women have no originality and that even MILL cannot dispute that because it is the truth.

MOSER. A pawnbroker whom the GENTLE CREATURE consults. He will not accept most of her worthless articles.

PAWNBROKER [ZAKLADCHIK]. The narrator of the story who, confronted with his wife's suicide, attempts to bring his thoughts into focus and to solve the mystery of the situation. His efforts are fraught with contradictions and mistakes in logic, and are largely an attempt to blame her and to justify his own actions. He meets the GENTLE CREATURE when she comes to him to pawn her worthless articles in order to get money to place an employment ad in *THE VOICE*. He treats her stiffly and coolly on these visits in order to achieve dominance, and when she continues to come, he determines to test her. He considers her to be good and meek, and respects her. He has assumed his position as a pawnbroker after a difficult life, and she correctly perceives that his purpose is to revenge himself upon society. When the GENTLE CREATURE's position with her AUNTS becomes untenable, he proudly and rather condescendingly proposes marriage. He is very pleased with his gesture and recalls with evident pleasure the learned air and originality with which he spoke. He views himself as her liberator and is a bit peeved that she accepts his proposal only after some consideration. The fact that he is 41 and she 16 pleases him, and he enjoys their inequality and the feelings of dominance that he has. To enhance this he tries to stimulate in her a feeling that the two of them are very different and that he is a mystery. He emphasizes his superior mysterious quality by remaining aloof, communicating only rarely, withholding affection, and treating her coolly. He determines not to need her in any way and to suffer in silence. In addition to the emotional wasteland he imposes upon her he also maintains an austere life style with the goal of saving 30,000 rubles with which to retire to the Crimea. He keeps her in a degree of submission until they have an argument over the medallion of the CAPTAIN'S WIFE, and for the first time she revolts and disobeys him by leaving their apartment by herself. She returns from these sorties and confronts him with details of his past. He had been dismissed from the service for cowardice for refusing to fight a duel to defend CAPTAIN BEZUMTSEV and the honor of his company. He claims that refusing to fight was a courageous act on his part in that he refused to submit to the tyranny and false values of his fellow officers. He subsequently acknowledges that he had indeed been afraid and had acted cowardly. Following his dismissal he walked the streets of St. Petersburg, begged, and lived in degrading circumstances in such places as VYAZEMSKY's house. He admits these things with a perverse relish, and his assuming the role of a pawnbroker is his way of proudly revenging himself on a society that has debased such a person as himself. When he hears that his wife is visiting the home of YULIA SAMSONOVNA and even meeting YEFIMOVICH there, he arranges to eavesdrop from an adjoining room on their conversation. Despite the fact that he takes a revolver with him, he is proud to say that her virtuous behavior with YEFIMOVICH is precisely what he expected. He interrupts the scene by entering the room and escorting her away in total silence. Early that morning he awakes to find her standing over him with his revolver pointed at his temple. He meets her glance and then shuts his eyes determined not to open them or make any movement even though he expects to die. He senses that he is fighting a duel with her and is exultant and elated when he opens his eyes and finds her gone. This convinces him that he is victorious and that she is forever beaten but not forgiven. He buys her a bed and a screen to separate them and silently gives her to understand that she is to sleep there. These events result in his wife's serious illness, and he quickly assumes her devoted care. He spares nothing and even wants to waste money on her in a dual gesture of caring and of emphasizing his dominance. Hereafter he muses that no one has ever loved him and indeed probably cannot. When he marries her he wants to find a friend but senses that he must conquer her first and then prepare her to be a friend. This lack of emotional security together with his lost reputation as a result of being dismissed from the service torment him most, but he feels that he has overcome his past through his conquering of her and the revolver. He views her as his hope for the future, and her knowledge of his victory is sufficient for him. Despite the fact that he regards her highly and even pities her on occasion, he continues to be stiff and silent and is captivated primarily by their inequality. When she suddenly sings a few notes one morning, he becomes convinced that she no longer cares for or thinks about him, and he comes to her on his knees, kisses her feet, and declares his love. He kisses her dress and the place on the floor where she stood, vows to take her abroad so that she can get well, and looks forward to a new life. He is in ecstacy and demeans himself while praising her. While he makes preparations to sell his business and travel abroad, she commits suicide. He expresses conviction that the major reason for her act is that she could not endure the intensity of his love. He despondently wonders what he will do now and feels resentment and disinterest at society and its institutions and regulations.

"PEOPLE, LOVE ONE ANOTHER" ["LYUDI, LYUBITE DRUG DRUGA"]. Adaptation of several statements found in the New Testatment, most notably John 13:34: "A new commandment I give unto you, That ye love one another; as I have loved you, that ye also love one another." Similar statements are found in John 15:12, John 15:17, 1 John 3:23, and 2 John 5. Following the suicide of the GENTLE CREATURE the PAWNBROKER ponders its significance and wonders what will happen to him. In his grief he cites these words and wonders who said them.

SHRADER [SHREDER]. The doctor the PAWNBROKER engages to treat his wife when she becomes ill.

SONG BIRDS [PTITSY PEVCHIE]. *La Périchole*, a three act operetta written by Jacques Offenbach (1819-80), the creator of the French operetta, in 1868. The operetta portrays the love of a Peruvian street singer for another singer and her success in outwitting the improper designs of the Spanish viceroy. The PAWNBROKER notes that he took his wife to the theater to see *SONG BIRDS* or something like it.

THE VOICE [GOLOS]. Widely circulated St. Petersburg political and literary newspaper published 1863-84. Its liberal views resulted in its being closed. The GENTLE CREATURE attempts to pawn her possessions in order to place an ad in *THE VOICE* advertising her services as a governess.

VYAZEMSKY. The owner of a building where derelicts often slept, located in the center of the pub and vice section of St. Petersburg. The PAWN-BROKER admits to having wandered the streets of St. Petersburg and begging for three years. He adds that he even slept in the VYAZEMSKY building.

YEFIMOVICH. An officer acquaintance from the PAWNBROKER's military past. Their poor relations are aggravated when he attempts to launch a liaison with the GENTLE CREATURE. She rebuffs him while the PAWNBROKER eavesdrops on the scene.

YULIA SAMSONOVNA. A widow friend of the AUNTS whom the GENTLE CREATURE begins to visit when she rebells against her husband. Her apartment is the scene of the PAWNBROKER's eavesdropping on YEFIMOVICH and the GENTLE CREATURE.

THE PEASANT MAREY (MUZHIK MAREY) 1876

KONSTANTIN AKSAKOV. KONSTANTIN Sergeevich AKSAKOV (1817-60), Russian writer, critic, and thinker. He was a leader of the conservative Slavophile movement and advocated an idealized peasant commune and the need for close ties with the common man. The AUTHOR extolls the virtues of MAREY and the great love that he demonstrated and notes that this is the high education that KONSTANTIN AKSAKOV attributed to the peasants.

AUTHOR [AVTOR]. Dostoevsky reflects back to when he was 29 years old and in penal exile and recalls some of the barbarous things he saw and experienced. He then remembers his fondness for pretending he was asleep and reminiscing about his childhood and recalls an instance when he was 9 years old. He remembers playing in the forest and experiencing fascination with the plant and animal life and then suddenly hearing a voice warning of a wolf. He runs to a peasant named MAREY, who is plowing in an adjacent field, and is comforted with love and the same concern that MAREY would show to his own son. He realizes that he imagined the call about the wolf and is overcome with the love he was shown by the simple peasant. After recalling this incident he views his fellow prisoners with more compassion and pities people like M-TSKY who express only hatred for them. He adds that KONSTANTIN AKSAKOV must have had people like MAREY in mind when he praised the high education of the peasants.

CHRIST [KHRISTOS]. Jesus CHRIST, in Christianity the Son of God. MAREY comforts the AUTHOR and asks that CHRIST be with him.

GAZIN. A Tatar prisoner who becomes violent when he drinks. Six fellow prisoners beat him into submission when he becomes unruly, and they do so unmercifully because he is such a HERCULES. GAZIN is also mentioned in *NOTES FROM THE HOUSE OF THE DEAD.*

HERCULES [GERKULES]. Mythical Greek hero of fabulous strength. GAZIN is referred to as a HERCULES.

MAREY. A fifty year old peasant on the AUTHOR's boyhood estate. The nine year old AUTHOR runs to him for comfort when he imagines that someone shouts a warning of a wolf and is received with kindness and comfort. The AUTHOR notes that MAREY could not have treated him with more love had he been his own son.

M-TSKY. A Polish political prisoner. He refers to the peasant prisoners in the camp as brigands and has only disgust for them. When the AUTHOR, after reflecting upon his boyhood experience with MAREY, gains increased compassion for his fellow prisoners, he expresses pity for those like M-TSKY, who can only hate others. M-TSKY is also mentioned in *NOTES FROM THE HOUSE OF THE DEAD.*

NOTES FROM THE HOUSE OF THE DEAD [ZAPISKI IZ MY-ORTVOGO DOMA]. A somewhat fictionalized account of the AUTHOR's life in Siberian exile (1850-54), written in 1860. The AUTHOR notes that he has not written about his incarceration with the exception of *NOTES FROM THE HOUSE OF THE DEAD,* which was written from the point of view of a fictionalized criminal who was exiled for murdering his wife. He adds that because of that, many have felt that he himself was exiled for murdering his wife.

VOLCHOK. A dog on the AUTHOR's boyhood estate that gives him comfort and security after he is frightened by the imagined wolf.

DREAM OF A RIDICULOUS MAN (SON SMESHNOGO CHELOVEKA) 1877

CAPTAIN [KAPITAN]. A crude, intimidating man who rents a room next to THE RIDICULOUS MAN. There is a virtual SODOM in his room.

GIRL [DEVOCHKA]. A poorly dressed, shivering, and sickly girl of about eight who stops THE RIDICULOUS MAN on a miserable rainy evening and asks for help. She is rebuffed but becomes a focal point of his subsequent guilt and insight that people should love one another.

THE RIDICULOUS MAN [SMESHNOY CHELOVEK]. A self-described braggart and liar who acknowledges that he is ridiculous and has been so all of his life. He has always been proud and this has prevented him from admitting to others that he more than anyone else is aware of his nature. His attitude leads him to a feeling of indifference toward everything until he experiences a sudden conversion to the truth. This occurs on November 3 on a miserable, cold, rainy St. Petersburg day. On his way home in the uncomfortable weather he notices a star in the heavens amidst the clouds and determines to proceed with his plans of committing suicide, for which purpose he had purchased a revolver two months prior. In the midst of these thoughts a GIRL stops him on the street and begs for help for her mother, but he refuses her and continues home. Once home he holds the revolver and ponders the guilt he feels for not helping the GIRL, convinced that it is she who has delayed if not prevented his suicide. Troubled with these and other thoughts he falls asleep and has a dream that he claims brings him insight into truth. He dreams that he shoots himself in the heart, rather than in the head as he had planned, and is buried. After complaining to the Ultimate about water dripping on his face, he is suddenly swept from his grave and conveyed into the darkness of space by an undefined being. He is transported past a duplicate of the sun and placed upon what appears to be a replica of the earth. His response is great love for the earth that he has left and a refusal to live anywhere else. His surroundings quickly change his mind, however, and he views a paradise in which people, nature, and all of creation are united in love. He recognizes the circumstances as similar to those prior to the fall of man. He is impressed that the people know how to live and have the knowledge they need intuitively without the aid, or perhaps the impediment, of science. This state of love, unity, and innocence gradually becomes one of lies, passion, jealousy, cruelty, slavery, and war, and he blames himself for leading the people astray. Only in their fallen state do the people discover the intellectual concepts of science, brotherhood, humanitarianism, justice, and law, and they have no desire to return to innocence. They come to view science and knowledge as higher states than living and feeling. He feels very guilty but finds himself loving the people even more, and this causes him to suggest that they take his life on a cross. When they refuse and threaten to put him in an asylum, he awakens. Thereafter he finds suicide repugnant and wants to live and to preach. He comes to love all people, particularly those who mock him, and understands that people can be beautiful and happy even on the earth. He cannot accept the premise that evil is the nature of man. He begins to question whether he in fact led the people astray and concludes that the key is to love others as oneself. Such love will lead to specifics on how to build happiness. His concluding sentiments express a great desire to find the GIRL.

SIRIUS. Also called the Dog Star, the brightest star in the heavens located in the constellation Canis Major. As THE RIDICULOUS MAN is taken from his grave through space by the undefined being, he notices a star and wonders if it is SIRIUS. His companion answers that it is the star that he saw on the evening that he determined to commit suicide.

SODOM. As recorded in Genesis 18-19 in the Old Testament, a city which together with Gomorrah was destroyed by Jehovah because of its wickedness. The word implies wickedness and chaos. The drinking, fighting, and card playing that take place in the CAPTAIN's room are described as SODOM by THE RIDICULOUS MAN.

VOLTAIRE [VOLTER]. Pen name of François Marie Arouet (1694-1778), noted French satirist, philosopher, and historian. His name connotes a freethinking approach to issues and philosophy. THE RIDICULOUS MAN has a VOLTAIRE armchair in his room.

THE BROTHERS KARAMAZOV (BRATYA KARAMAZOVY) 1879

"ABOUT HIS MEEK EYES" ["PO KROTKIM GLAZAM"]. Slight distortion of a line from the poem "Before Twilight" ("Do sumerek") published in 1859 by Nikolay NEKRASOV. The poem portrays a peasant who brutally beats his half-dead horse in the street "About his crying, meek eyes" ("I po plachushchim, krotkim glazam!"). In discussing man's inhumanity to man IVAN cites NEKRASOV's poem and quotes this line.

"ABOUT THAT DAY AND HOUR NO ONE KNOWS, EVEN THE SON, ONLY MY FATHER IN HEAVEN" ["O DNE ZHE SYOM I CHASE NE ZNAET DAZHE I SYN, TOKMO LISH OTETS MOY NEBESNY"]. Slight distortion of Matthew 24:36 ("But of that day and hour knoweth no man, no, not the angels of heaven, but my Father only") and Mark 13:32 ("But of that day and that hour knoweth no man, no, not the angels which are in heaven, neither the Son, but the Father"). As IVAN reads his poem "The Legend of the GRAND INQUISITOR" to ALYOSHA he quotes this line and complains that it has been fifteen centuries, according to the time of the poem's action, since these words were spoken, and the faithful are still waiting.

ABRAHAM [AVRAAM]. As recorded in Genesis 12-25, an OLD TESTAMENT patriarch who was led by Jehovah out of Ur of the Chaldees into another land so that he could worship properly. Jehovah made a covenant with him to the effect that ABRAHAM would found a great nation that would bless the world. (1) ZOSIMA states that the Scriptures can be received by the Orthodox heart with understanding and cites as an example the story of ABRAHAM and SARAH, who were blessed with their only child, a son named ISAAC, in their advanced years. (2) ZOSIMA teaches that men are placed upon earth to have the opportunity to love. If men do not take advantage of this opportunity, they may still return to ABRAHAM's bosom (that is, obtain their rest in the heavens) as portrayed in the PARABLE OF LAZARUS AND THE RICH MAN, but they will feel the torment of not having loved. ZOSIMA adds that ABRAHAM will not bring a drop of water to quench the desire for spiritual love.

ACTS OF THE APOSTLES [DEYANIA APOSTOLSKIE]. The fifth book of the New Testament written most probably by LUKE. ZOSIMA refers to the conversion of SAUL as recorded in Chapter 9 of the ACTS OF THE APOSTLES and praises its effect on the people.

"AD MAJOREM GLORIAM DEI." "To the Greater Glory of God," the JESUIT motto. In his poem "The legend of the GRAND INQUISITOR" IVAN portrays CHRIST's entering Seville shortly after 100 heretics have been burned "AD MAJOREM GLORIAM DEI."

ADAM. As recorded in Genesis 1 in the OLD TESTAMENT, the first man on earth who dwelt in the Garden of Eden. SMERDYAKOV observes to IVAN that physical beating and torture are a reality in all countries, just as they were at the time of ADAM and EVE.

AESOP [EZOP, YEZOP]. Greek writer of fables (ca. 620-560 B.C.) who created a new class of animal tales which taught a popularized moral. Biographical legends portray him as a hunchback and a buffoon in addition to a storyteller. (1) MIUSOV, frustrated by FYODOR PAVLOVICH's behavior, determines that it is beneath him to be overly upset with such a person. He decides to prove to all concerned that he is not at all like FYODOR PAVLOVICH, whom he refers to as an AESOP, buffoon, and PIERROT. (2) DMITRY discusses with ALYOSHA the possibility of getting 3000 rubles from FYODOR PAVLOVICH in order to pay his debt to KATERINA IVANOVNA. When he fears that GRUSHENKA may be in his father's house, however, he bursts in, beats him, and instructs ALYOSHA not to mention anything about the money to such an AESOP as his father. (3) After DMITRY enters his father's house in search of GRUSHENKA and beats him, IVAN reflects upon the scene and also refers to FYODOR PAVLOVICH as AESOP. (4) IVAN asks ALYOSHA if he considers him capable of murdering an old AESOP like FYODOR PAVLOVICH. (5) At his trial for his father's murder DMITRY refers to FYODOR PAVLOVICH as an AESOP and PIERROT but admits that he was cruel to him.

AFANASY. See AFANASY PAVLOVICH.

AFANASY PAVLOVICH (AFANASY). ZOSIMA's valet. After ZOSIMA challenges his former sweetheart's husband to a duel, he returns to his quarters very angry and in his frustration brutally hits AFANASY. He is overcome by guilt for his conduct, and the next morning he begs AFANASY's forgiveness and initiates a new course in life.

AFIMYA. One of ZOSIMA's mother's servants who was ultimately sold.

AGAFYA. KRASOTKINA's servant.

AGAFYA. See AGAFYA IVANOVNA.

AGAFYA IVANOVNA (AGAFYA, AGASHA). KATERINA IVAN-OVNA's older sister by her father's first wife. She is talented and rather attractive.

AGASHA. See AGAFYA IVANOVNA.

AGRAFYONA. See AGRAFYONA ALEKSANDROVNA SVETLOVA.

AGRAFYONA ALEKSANDROVNA. See AGRAFYONA ALEKSAN-DROVNA SVETLOVA.

AGRIPPINA. See AGRAFYONA ALEKSANDROVNA SVETLOVA. MUSSYALOVICH refers to her as AGRIPPINA. The name recalls two notable Roman women: Vipsania Agrippina (13 B.C.-33 A.D.), who starved to death because of court intrigue and who gave birth to the future emperor Caligula, and Julia Agrippina (15-59), the daughter of Vipsania, who gave birth to the future emperor Nero and who led a life full of treachery and intrigue.

AKIM. A peasant at Mokroe.

ALEKSANDR ALEKSANDROVICH. A person mentioned by the mentally deficient ARINA PETROVNA.

ALEKSEY. The three year old son of NASTASYUSHKA and NIKI-TUSHKA who has recently died.

ALEKSEY. See ALEKSEY FYODOROVICH KARAMAZOV.

ALEKSEY FYODOROVICH. See ALEKSEY FYODOROVICH KA-RAMAZOV.

ALEKSEY THE MAN OF GOD [ALEKSEY CHELOVEK BOZHY]. The main figure of *The Life of Aleksey the Man of God (Zhitie Alekseya cheloveka bozhiya),* an important work of Russian hagiography. The saintly hero leaves home to seek salvation but ultimately returns to lead an exemplary life. The figure is one of the hagiographic and folkloristic sources for ALYOSHA. (1) ALEKSEY, the three year old son of NASTASYU-SHKA and NIKITUSHKA, is named after ALEKSEY THE MAN OF GOD. (2) ZOSIMA lauds the effect that reading the accounts of ALEKSEY

THE MAN OF GOD and SAINT MARY OF EGYPT have on the common people.

ALEKSEYCHIK. See ALEKSEY FYODOROVICH KARAMAZOV.

ALEXANDER THE GREAT [ALEKSANDR MAKEDONSKY]. Emperor Alexander III of Macedon (356-323 B.C.), who conquered the civilized world, extended Greek civilization into the East, and ushered in the Hellenistic Age. Following his scandalous row with DMITRY in the presence of ZOSIMA, FYODOR PAVLOVICH is greatly embarrassed, and he notes that some people have the heart of an ALEXANDER THE GREAT while others have the heart of the dog FIDELKA. He ruefully admits to possessing the latter.

ALYOSHA. See ALEKSEY FYODOROVICH KARAMAZOV.

ALYOSHECHKA. See ALEKSEY FYODOROVICH KARAMAZOV.

ALYOSHENKA. See ALEKSEY FYODOROVICH KARAMAZOV.

ALYOSHKA. See ALEKSEY FYODOROVICH KARAMAZOV.

"AN DIE FREUDE." "To Joy," a poem written by Friedrich SCHILLER in 1785 which celebrates the powers and virtue of love and joy that can direct man to God. On one of the occasions that DMITRY unburdens himself to ALYOSHA, he observes that he wants to begin his confession with SCHILLER's "AN DIE FREUDE."

"AND IN ALL NATURE THERE WAS NOUGHT/ /THAT COULD FIND FAVOR IN HIS EYES" ["I NICHEGO VO VSEY PRIRODE/ /BLAGOSLOVIT ON NE KHOTEL"]. A citation from the poem "The Demon" ("Demon") written by Aleksandr PUSHKIN in 1823. When his daughter VARVARA NIKOLAEVNA objects to his shaming himself in front of ALYOSHA, SNEGIRYOV quotes this couplet and admits that it characterizes the orientation of his family.

"AND ONLY SILENCE WHISPERS" ["I TOLKO SHEPCHET TISHI-NA"]. A slightly distorted line from Aleksandr PUSHKIN's narrative poem *Ruslan and Lyudmila (Ruslan i Lyudmila)* published in 1820. The original reads "And it seems...the silence whispers..." ("I mnitsya...shepchet tishina..."). When DMITRY fears that GRUSHENKA has come to visit FYODOR PAVLOVICH, he carefully approaches his father's bedroom window at night and listens carefully. When he is greeted only by a deathly silence, he recalls this line of verse.

"AND THE GIRL AROSE" ["I VOSSTA DEVITSA"]. Inaccurate rendition of the New Testament account of CHRIST's raising the daughter of Jairus from the dead. Mark 5:42 reads "And straightway the damsel arose" ("I devitsa totchas vstala"). In IVAN's "Legend of the GRAND INQUISITOR" CHRIST returns to Seville and raises a seven year old girl from the dead, and the event is described in these words.

"AND THE THIRD DAY THERE WAS A MARRIAGE IN CANA OF GALILEE; AND THE MOTHER OF JESUS WAS THERE" ["I V TRETY DEN BRAK BYST V KANE GALILEYSTEY, I BE MATI IISUSOVA TU"]. The first verse of ten verses quoted from JOHN 2:1-10 in the New Testament. The passage relates CHRIST's first miracle of turning water into wine at a marriage feast in Cana of Galilee. As ALYOSHA prays following ZOSIMA's death, he overhears PAISY reading these verses over ZOSIMA's body.

ANDREY. The coach driver who takes DMITRY and a large cargo of provisions to Mokroe for a rendezvous with GRUSHENKA and MUS-SYALOVICH.

ANFIM. A poverty-ridden old monk whom ZOSIMA greatly loves. Years ago they went on pilgrimages together throughout Russia.

ANTIQUITY [STARINA]. Russian *ANTIQUITY (Russkaya STAR-INA),* a monthly journal devoted largely to Russian history of the eighteenth and nineteenth centuries published 1870-1918. As IVAN relates tales of child abuse, he notes that one incident is recorded in either *THE ARCHIVE* or *ANTIQUITY,* but he cannot recall in which journal.

APOCRYPHA [APOKRIFICHESKIE YEVANGELIA]. Noncanonical Old and New Testament writing generally viewed as quasi-Scripture of spurious origin. The warden of the prison in which DMITRY is incarcerated for patricide becomes very interested in the APOCRYPHA and goes to the monastery to discuss it. There he becomes acquainted with ALYOSHA and willingly extends him access to DMITRY in prison.

APOSTLE [APOSTOL]. A collection of New Testament books containing the ACTS OF THE APOSTLES, the Pauline and other Epistles, and the Apocalypse. The *APOSTLE* is read at ILYUSHA's funeral.

"APRES MOI LE DELUGE." "After me the deluge," adaptation of a reply to King Louis XV (1710-74) of France following the defeat of the French and Austrian armies by Frederick the Great of Prussia in 1757 during the Seven Years War. The remark is attributed to Madame de Pompadour (1721-64), who is reputed to have said, "Après nous le déluge" ("After us the deluge"). In his concluding remarks to the jury at DMITRY's trial the prosecutor IPPOLIT KIRILLOVICH characterizes the moral life of FYODOR PAVLOVICH with this phrase.

ARBENIN. Yevgeny Aleksandrovich ARBENIN, the romantically demonic central protagonist of *The Masquerade (Maskarad),* a melodramatic drama in verse by Mikhail Yurievich Lermontov (1814-41) first published in 1842. FYODOR PAVLOVICH notes that he respects ZOSIMA but insists that he is akin to MEPHISTOPHELES or perhaps to *A HERO OF OUR TIME* and its central character ARBENIN. FYODOR PAVLOVICH is drunk when he makes the statement, but it is likely that he intentionally confuses ARBENIN with Pechorin, the central figure of *A HERO OF OUR TIME.*

THE ARCHIVE [ARKHIV]. The Russian *ARCHIVE (Russky AR-KHIV),* an historical-literary monthly published 1863-1917 and devoted largely to Russian history of the eighteenth and nineteenth centuries. As IVAN relates tales of child abuse, he notes that one incident is recorded in either *THE ARCHIVE* or *ANTIQUITY,* but he cannot recall which.

ARINA. When DMITRY arrives in Mokroe in his pursuit of GRUSHEN-KA, he asks TRIFON BORISYCH to secure gypsies and several girls, especially MARYA, STEPANIDA, and ARINA.

ARINA PETROVNA. See ARINA PETROVNA SNEGIRYOVA.

BAKUNIN. Mikhail Aleksandrovich BAKUNIN (1814-76), Russian radical thinker who was one of the founders of modern political anarchism. PYOTR ALEKSANDROVICH MIUSOV professes to know BAKUNIN and PROUDHON personally.

BALAAM [VALAAM]. As recorded in Numbers 22-24 in the OLD TESTAMENT, a prophet from Pethor by the Euphrates who was bribed by the Moabite King Balak to curse the invading Israelites. As BALAAM proceeded to Moab upon his ass, God was angry and placed a destroying angel in his path. The ass perceived the angel and balked at continuing but was rewarded by blows from BALAAM's staff and threats of death. The ass, given the gift of speech, spoke to BALAAM, who then saw the angel, repented, and blessed rather than cursed Israel. FYODOR PAVLOVICH refers to SMERDYAKOV as BALAAM's ass and expresses wonderment at his sayings.

BARBARA THE MARTYR [VARVARA VELIKOMUCHENITSA]. A third or fourth century Christian saint of questionable authenticity. She was ostensibly murdered by her pagan father for Christian beliefs and was venerated as the patroness of artillerymen, miners, gunsmiths, etc., until her feast day was dropped from the saints' calendar. When DMITRY approaches KHOKHLAKOVA to borrow 3000 rubles, she offers to solve his financial problems by encouraging him to mine for gold. She then solemnly gives him an icon of BARBARA THE MARTYR to bless him in his future life.

"BE NOBLE, OH MAN!" ["BUD, CHELOVEK, BLAGORODEN!"]. Translation of "Edel sei der Mensch," a line from "Das Göttliche" ("The Godlike"), a poem written in 1783 by Johann Wolfgang von Goethe (1749-1832). DMITRY quotes this line to ALYOSHA as he discusses his turbulent involvement with FYODOR PAVLOVICH, GRUSHENKA, and KATERINA IVANOVNA.

STEPANIDA ILYINISHNA BEDRYAGINA. When VASENKA does not write his mother PROKHOROVNA for some time, STEPANIDA ILYINISHNA, the wealthy wife of a merchant, counsels her to submit his name to the church to be prayed for as if he were dead. She states that these prayers will trouble his soul and prompt him to write. When PROKHOROVNA consults ZOSIMA on the matter, he rejects this counsel completely.

"BEHOLD, I COME QUICKLY" ["SE GRYADU SKORO"]. New Testament citation from Revelation 3:11, repeated in slightly different language in Revelation 22:7, 12, 20, which has reference to the SECOND COMING of CHRIST. In his "Legend of the GRAND INQUISITOR" IVAN notes that it has been fifteen centuries since these words were spoken, and he sarcastically adds that the people are still waiting.

"BELIEVE WHAT THE HEART WILL SAY,//THERE ARE NO VOICES FROM HEAVEN" ["VER TOMU, CHTO SERDTSE SKAZHET,//NET ZALOGOV OT NEBES"]. The concluding words from Friedrich SCHILLER's poem "Sehnsucht" ("Desire"), written in 1801, as translated by Vasily Andreevich Zhukovsky (1783-1852). The original reads: "Du musst glauben, du musst wagen,//Denn die Götter leihn kein

Pfand,//Nur ein Wunder kann dich tragen//In das schöne Wunderland" ("You must believe, you must risk all,//For Gods Themselves will not extend,//A miracle only can bear you there,//Into the beautiful wonderland"). In his "Legend of the GRAND INQUISITOR" IVAN notes that the faithful have been waiting for the SECOND COMING for fifteen centuries and that during these years the heavens have been closed. To illustrate his point he quotes these lines of verse.

BELINSKY. Vissarion Grigorievich BELINSKY (1811-48), Russian literary critic and journalist. He wrote for both *Fatherland Notes* and *The Contemporary* and insisted that literature realistically expose the seamy side of life with the intent of social reform. He was the first and most eminent of the so-called Radical Critics, and his ideas helped to stimulate the Natural School. (1) KOLYA insists to ALYOSHA that he is a confirmed socialist and acknowledges that many of his ideas come from RAKITIN and BELINSKY. As an example of his socialistic stance he states that CHRIST was a humanitarian and would be involved in the revolutionary movement if He were alive. KOLYA admits, however, that he has read from BELINSKY only the article which describes how TATYANA does not go with ONEGIN. The article referred to is the ninth of BELINSKY's "Articles on PUSHKIN" ("Statyi o PUSHKINE") published in 1845. (2) When IVAN is visibly disappointed at his devil's shabby appearance and manner, the devil attributes the response to IVAN's pride and aesthetic sense and notes that IVAN has the romantic elements demeaned by BELINSKY.

THE BELL [KOLOKOL]. A biweekly revolutionary journal published in London by Aleksandr Ivanovich Herzen (1812-70), a leading Russian revolutionary thinker, from 1857 to 1867. It was smuggled into Russia where it had a large readership. *THE BELL* was very critical of the social and political order in Russia. KOLYA fears that ALYOSHA might discover that he has only one issue of *THE BELL* and that he has read little of it, which would unmask him as a socialist.

BELMESOV. When DMITRY comes to KHOKHLAKOVA in hope of borrowing 3000 rubles, she vows to save him just as she saved BELMESOV, whom she encouraged to take up horsebreeding.

BELMESOVA. KHOKHLAKOVA's cousin and BELMESOV's wife.

BELYAVSKY. A handsome, wealthy young man who once courted FYODOR PAVLOVICH's second wife. When on one occasion he strikes FYODOR PAVLOVICH, she considers herself thoroughly insulted and insists that her husband challenge him to a duel.

BENJAMIN [VENIAMIN]. A son of JACOB and RACHEL. He was the youngest of the sons and the progenitor of the smallest of the Twelve Tribes of Israel. As recorded in Genesis 37-50 in the OLD TESTAMENT in the account of JOSEPH who was sold into Egypt, BENJAMIN was brought to Egypt at JOSEPH's insistence when the other brothers came to buy corn during the famine. Ultimately all the sons and their father were reunited and reconciled. ZOSIMA praises the effect of the Scriptures upon the Russian soul and as an example cites the account of JOSEPH, BENJAMIN, and his brothers.

CLAUDE BERNARD [KLOD BERNAR]. Celebrated French natural scientist and experimental physiologist (1813-78). (1) Following a visit by RAKITIN, DMITRY questions ALYOSHA about BERNARD and wonders who he is. BERNARD comes to symbolize the free-thinking, progressive outlook that DMITRY finds suspect. (2) DMITRY disgustedly refers to his lawyer as BERNARD and notes that even the lawyer thinks that he is guilty of patricide. (3) DMITRY wonders aloud to ALYOSHA whether he is a new man after his experiences or a despicable BERNARD, and he fears that he is the latter. (4) Upset at RAKITIN's demeanor and testimony at his trial, DMITRY angrily refers to him as BERNARD. (5) At DMITRY's trial a Moscow doctor testifies that DMITRY is in a strange mental condition, and the narrator observes that the doctor says unexpected words characteristic of BERNARD. (6) In his concluding words to the jury at DMITRY's trial the prosecutor IPPOLIT KIRILLOVICH refers to RAKITIN's unflattering opinion of GRUSHENKA, and DMITRY, visibly upset, audibly refers to them both as BERNARD.

KARL BERNARD [BERNAR]. See CLAUDE BERNARD. DMITRY mistakenly refers to CLAUDE BERNARD as KARL.

BIBLE [YEVANGELIE, BIBLIA]. A collection of books organized into the OLD TESTAMENT, a religious history from ADAM through the Twelve Tribes of Israel with emphasis on Judah, and the New Testament, the life and ministry of CHRIST. (1) PAISY objects to a cleric's use of a phrase from the BIBLE in what he feels is a secular and unintended meaning. See "THE CHURCH IS A KINGDOM NOT OF THIS WORLD." (2) ZOSIMA keeps a copy of the BIBLE in his private room. (3) ZOSIMA encourages all the monks to continually teach the people the BIBLE. (4) In IVAN's anecdote about RICHARD he notes that the seven year old boy was poorly fed and clothed and that while he worked he often hungered for the swine's food just as the PRODIGAL SON in the BIBLE. (5) In IVAN's anecdote about RICHARD he is arrested for murder and when imprisoned is quickly beset by various preachers and benefactors who instruct him in the BIBLE. (6) On the evening of his death ZOSIMA relates much of his life and teachings, and when he rests briefly during his exposition, PAISY reads from the BIBLE. (7) ZOSIMA relates that during his worldly cadet school years he hardly ever read the BIBLE but always had it with him "FOR A DAY AND AN HOUR, FOR A MONTH AND A YEAR." (8) In trying to convince the MYSTERIOUS VISITOR to confess his crimes and put his life in order, ZOSIMA reads him JOHN 12:24 from the BIBLE: "VERILY, VERILY, I SAY UNTO YOU, EXCEPT A CORN OF WHEAT FALL INTO THE GROUND AND DIE, IT ABIDETH ALONE: BUT IF IT DIE, IT BRINGETH FORTH MUCH FRUIT." (9) ZOSIMA observes that he looks forward to the day when men will seek to be the servants of others as in the BIBLE. (10) Since ZOSIMA was a priest and monk of the strictest order, those who attend his corpse read from the BIBLE over him rather than the PSALTER. (11) IOSIF and PAISY alternate reading the BIBLE over ZOSIMA's body. (12) When SNEGIRYOV, in grief over the impending death of his son ILYUSHA, quotes "IF I FORGET THEE, O JERUSALEM, LET CLEAVE...," KOLYA questions ALYOSHA about the passage. ALYOSHA explains that it is from the BIBLE and elaborates on its meaning. (13) In his summation to the jury at DMITRY's trial FETYUKOVICH quotes from the BIBLE in his attempt to discredit FYODOR PAVLOVICH as a father. See "WITH WHAT-SOEVER MEASURE YOU MEASURE, IT WILL BE MEASURED TO YOU." (14) The prosecutor IPPOLIT KIRILLOVICH objects that FETYU-KOVICH in his summation to the jury tries to correct the BIBLE and establish his own Christianity based upon analysis and common sense. He accuses FETYUKOVICH of looking in the BIBLE just before his summation in order to make a good impression upon the jury.

"BLESSED BE THE WOMB THAT BARE THEE, AND THE PAPS WHICH THOU HAST SUCKED—THE PAPS ESPECIALLY" ["BLA-ZHENNO CHREVO, NOSIVSHEE TEBYA, I SOSTSY, TEBYA PI-TAVSHIE,—SOSTSY OSOBENNO"]. Blasphemous rendering of LUKE 11:27 in the New Testament which recalls the words of an adoring woman addressed to CHRIST. FYODOR PAVLOVICH, playing the buffoon, addresses these words in mock solemn praise to ZOSIMA.

BOILEAU [BUALO]. Nicolas BOILEAU (1636-1711), French polemicist, satirist, and critic whose most famous work *L'Art Poétique* (1674) played an important part in upholding literature's classical doctrines. MAKSIMOV claims to have drunk with PIRON and BOILEAU and to have commented to the latter via an epigram "IS THAT YOU, BOILEAU? WHAT A FUNNY OUTFIT!" BOILEAU is supposed to have answered that he is going to a masquerade, or rather, to the baths.

BOROVIKOV. KOLYA notes that BOROVIKOV has learned a formula for making powder for his toy cannon.

BOURBON [BURBON]. The ruling family of France (1589-1793, 1814-30), Spain (1700-1808, 1814-33, 1874-1931), Naples (1735-1805, 1815-60), and Parma (1748-1859) which was noted for political and social conservatism. The term was sometimes used to designate rude, coarse individuals in Russia. (1) When DMITRY decides to revenge himself upon KATERINA IVANOVNA for her haughty manner when they first become acquainted, he describes his actions as that of a BOURBON. (2) When KATERINA IVANOVNA offers DMITRY her hand in marriage, DMITRY to his own dismay makes reference to her wealth and refers to himself as a poverty-stricken BOURBON.

"BREAD AND CIRCUSES!" ["KHLEBA I ZRELISHCH!"] A reference to lines from Satire X by Juvenal (Decimus Junius Juvenalis, ca. 60-140), the most eminent Roman satirist, who was noted for his express indignation. The lines read "Two things only the people anxiously desire—bread and circuses" ("Duas tantum res anxius optat,// Panem et circenses"). While testifying at DMITRY's trial IVAN condemns the public which has come to observe and sarcastically comments, "BREAD AND CIRCUSES!"

"BROTHERS, I AM JOSEPH, YOUR BROTHER" ["BRATYA, YA IOSIF, BRAT VASH"]. Inexact rendering of part of Genesis 45:4 from the OLD TESTAMENT: "I am Joseph your brother" ("Ya Iosif, brat vash"). See JOSEPH.

BULKIN. In talking about the home-made powder used in a toy cannon, KOLYA notes that BULKIN was thrashed by his father when he found a whole bottle of the mixture under his son's bed.

"BURDOCK WILL GROW ON MY GRAVE" ["VYRASTYOT LOP-UKH NA MOGILE"]. Inexact rendering of the words of Bazarov in Ivan TURGENEV's novel *Fathers and Sons (Ottsy i deti)* published in 1862. Bazarov complains about his possible fate after death and ruefully notes that "burdock will grow out of me" ("iz menya lopukh rasti budet"). In discussing with ZOSIMA her crisis of unbelief in an afterlife, KHOKHLA-

KOVA quotes these words from a forgotten source. She greatly fears that there may be nothing hereafter.

"BUT THERE SHALL BE MORE JOY IN HEAVEN OVER ONE THAT REPENTETH THAN OVER NINETY AND NINE JUST PERSONS, IT WAS SAID LONG AGO" [A OB ODNOM KAYUSHCHEMSYA BOLSHE RADOSTI V NEBE, CHEM O DESYATI PRAVEDNYKH, SKAZANO DAVNO"]. Inexact rendering of LUKE 15:7 in the New Testament: "I say unto you, that likewise joy shall be in heaven over one sinner that repenteth, more than over ninety and nine just persons, which need no repentance." ZOSIMA comforts a penitent woman with these words.

"BY THE MEASURE THAT IS MEASURED, IT WILL BE MEASURED IN RETURN" ["V TU ZHE MERU MERITSYA, V TU ZHE I VOZMERITSYA"]. Inexact rendering of part of LUKE 6:38 in the New Testament: "For with the same measure that ye mete withal it shall be measured to you again." Compare also Matthew 7:2 and Mark 4:24. FYODOR PAVLOVICH expresses his disgust for the peasants and notes that even though people no longer abuse or fight with them, they still fight among themselves. He then quotes these words with evident relish.

BYRON [BAYRON]. George Gordon Lord BYRON (1788-1824), English romantic poet who created the "BYRONIC hero," a defiant, brooding young man obsessed by some mysterious past sin. At DMITRY's trial the prosecutor IPPOLIT KIRILLOVICH objects that FETYUKOVICH in his summation to the jury attempted to portray SMERDYAKOV as a BYRONIC hero.

CAESAR [TSEZAR]. Julius CAESAR (100-44 B.C.), Roman general, statesman, and orator who after a distinguished military career forcibly assumed the role of emperor. DMITRY insists to ALYOSHA that every proper man is under some woman's heel but must nonetheless retain his nobility. He insists that this condition should not efface a real man or a hero like CAESAR.

CAIN [KAIN]. As recorded in Genesis 4 in the OLD TESTAMENT, a son of ADAM and EVE who murdered his brother Abel and as a result was cursed by God. IVAN complains that ALYOSHA is continually worrying about the conflict between FYODOR PAVLOVICH and DMITRY and insists that he is not his brother's keeper. He then comments that this statement recalls CAIN's answer to God's question about the whereabouts of Abel: "Am I my brother's keeper?" as recorded in Genesis 4:9.

CANDIDE [KANDID]. A popular philosophical novel written in 1759 by VOLTAIRE. The novel satirizes the naively optimistic view of life and takes direct issue with the German philosopher Gottfried Wilhelm Leibniz (1646-1716), who felt that this is the best of all possible worlds. The hero CANDIDE goes from one revolting situation to another with nothing ever working out right. When ALYOSHA questions KOLYA about whether he has read VOLTAIRE, he replies that he has read *CANDIDE* in a terrible Russian translation.

CATHERINE [YEKATERINA]. Empress CATHERINE the Great (1729-96), who ruled Russia 1762-96. Her reign marked an increase in contact with the West. See DIDEROT.

CERES [TSERERA]. The Roman goddess of agriculture who parallels the Greek Demeter. (1) In DMITRY's impassioned discussion with ALYO-SHA he quotes three stanzas beginning "WILD AND FEARFUL IN HIS CAVE//HID THE NAKED TROGLODYTE," which contains two references to CERES. (2) DMITRY notes to ALYOSHA that whenever he sinks to the depths of debauchery he reads this poem about CERES and man, but he admits that it does not reform him because he is a KARAMAZOV.

CHATSKY. Aleksandr Andreevich CHATSKY, the progressive young hero of *Woe From Wit (Gore ot uma)*, the satirical masterpiece which exposes the foibles of the semieducated gentry. The play was written by Aleksandr Sergeevich Griboedov (1795-1829) during the years 1822-24. See FAMUSOV.

CHERNOMAZOV. ARINA PETROVNA mistakenly refers to ALYO-SHA as CHERNOMAZOV, a name which ironically reproduces his name semantically since *kara* in Tatar and *chern-* in Russian both mean black.

"THE CHERUBIM" ["KHERUVIMSKAYA"]. An Orthodox liturgical song which is sung at ILYUSHA's funeral.

CHETYI-MENEI. An ecclesiastical calendar containing lives of saints and martyrs. (1) PYOTR PAVLOVICH reports that MIUSOV told him a story about a beheaded martyr who took up his severed head and walked away kissing it. He asks ZOSIMA if this story in the *CHETYI-MINEI* is true, but ZOSIMA and the monastery librarian insist that there is no such story.

FYODOR PAVLOVICH asserts that this story and not DIDEROT was the reason for his losing his faith. (2) MIUSOV admits that he has repeated the story of the beheaded martyr, possibly in FYODOR PAVLOVICH's presence, and recalls that he was told by a Frenchman that such a tale is in the *CHETYI-MINEI* and is read during Mass. He adds that he himself does read the *CHETYI-MINEI*. (3) After the death of his deformed child, GRIGORY turns to religious activity and often reads the *CHETYI-MINEI*. (4) ZOSIMA praises the effect the *CHETYI-MINEI* has on the people and cites the examples of ALEKSEY THE MAN OF GOD and SAINT MARY OF EGYPT.

CHICHIKOV. Pavel Ivanovich CHICHIKOV, the scheming central character of Nikolay GOGOL's *DEAD SOULS*. (1) KALGANOV insists that MAKSIMOV cannot be the MAKSIMOV of *DEAD SOULS* because CHICHIKOV flourished in the 1820s, and thus the years do not match. (2) See "OH, TROYKA, BIRD-LIKE TROYKA, WHO INVENTED YOU!"

CHILDREN'S READING [DETSKOE CHTENIE]. CHILDREN'S READING For the Heart and the Mind (DETSKOE CHTENIE dlya serdtsa i razuma), the first Russian children's journal published between 1785 and 1789 by Nikolay Ivanovich Novikov (1744-1818). The MYSTERIOUS VISITOR has difficulty confessing his murder even after he determines to do so because of his wife and precious children, who want him to read *CHILDREN'S READING* with them.

ALEKSEY IVANOVICH CHIZHOV. When KOLYA mentions SABANEEV, there arises a dispute about who that person really is, and one woman suggests that he is actually CHIZHOV.

CHRIST [KHRISTOS, IISUS KHRISTOS, IISUS, SPASITEL]. Jesus CHRIST, in Christianity the Son of God. (1) ALYOSHA feels that ZOSIMA's goodness will have such far-reaching effect that all men will become God's children and that the actual Kingdom of CHRIST will be ushered in. (2) In explaining his theory about ecclesiastical and civil courts, IVAN recalls the history of early Christianity and notes that when the Church of CHRIST came into the Roman Empire, it could not sacrifice its tenets but rather had to encompass and convert the Empire. (3) See "THE CHURCH IS A KINGDOM NOT OF THIS WORLD." (4) In reflecting upon church and state and civil and ecclesiastical courts, IVAN notes that if the church were the government, then when one was cut off from the church for crime, he would also be cut off from CHRIST. The crime would be against both the people and the Church of CHRIST, and men could no longer commit crimes and still attend church or claim that CHRIST was their friend. (5) ZOSIMA notes that without the Church of CHRIST there would be no restraint on the criminal and that only CHRIST's law can protect society from the criminal and make the criminal a new man. He adds that only by recognizing his guilt as a son of CHRIST's society can a criminal accept his guilt before society. (6) See "SHE LOVED MUCH." (7) When ZOSIMA tells ALYOSHA that he should leave the monastery and overcome the world, he adds that CHRIST will be with him. (8) As FYODOR PAVLOVICH berates faith and monastic life, the father superior comments that he accepts the comments as the corrections of CHRIST sent to heal their vain souls and bows to FYODOR PAVLO-VICH. (9) LUKYANOV relates the story of a soldier who was tortured to death because he would not renounce Christianity for Islam and adds that he died praising CHRIST. (10) In responding to LUKYANOV's story of the soldier who refused to renounce Christianity, SMERDYAKOV counters that it would not have been bad to have renounced CHRIST, saved his life, and lived to do good deeds in the years to come. He adds that if he renounces baptism, he is then no longer a Christian and therefore can not reject CHRIST. (11). DMITRY insists that as sure as CHRIST is the Lord, the virtues of KATERINA IVANOVNA are angelic and he is far beneath her. (12) FYODOR PAVLOVICH complains that he has asked IVAN in the name of CHRIST to go to Chermashnya and transact some business, but that as yet he has not gone. (13) FERAPONT mentions that the tree outside his cell sometimes at night appears to him to be CHRIST reaching out for him with two branch-arms. (14) PAISY tells ALYOSHA that the learned ones who revolt against Christianity are in the image of CHRIST and have never created a more elevated concept than that of CHRIST. (15) After LIZA and ALYOSHA declare their love for each other and exchange promises and kisses, she sends him back to be with the dying ZOSIMA and asks that CHRIST be with him. (16) When IVAN insists that man cannot love those close to him but only those not seen, ALYOSHA counters that there is much love in mankind that is like CHRIST's love. IVAN retorts that CHRIST's love is an impossible earthly miracle because He was God and men are not. (17) After RICHARD is arrested for murder, he is beset by clergy, members of various brotherhoods of CHRIST, and benefactors who try to teach him the Scriptures and reform him. (18) See DANTE. (19) After listening to IVAN's "Legend of the GRAND INQUISITOR," ALYOSHA observes that it is a tribute to CHRIST rather than a condemnation. (20) ZOSIMA states that the people will perish without the word of CHRIST. (21) ZOSIMA recalls admiring nature on one occasion and reflecting that not only men but also animals and all of life have CHRIST. (22) ZOSIMA praises monks as the salvation of Russia and asserts that they preserve the image of CHRIST in their quiet and pure isolation. (23) ZOSIMA indicts the leaders of Russian society who build on science and the mind instead of CHRIST. Such leaders claim that there is no crime and no sin. (24) ZOSIMA discusses the possibility of the wealthy and poor becoming brothers and notes that wealth must cease to be a hindrance and that men must see that true equality is in spiritual worthiness. With such an attitude the brotherhood of CHRIST, a thing precious to all the world, will become a reality. (25) ZOSIMA anticipates the day when men will seek to be servants to others and states that CHRIST will determine the time. (26) ZOSIMA, in renouncing reason as a basis for life, says that without the promises of CHRIST all would become violent and slay each other. (27) ZOSIMA insists that men are lost without the image of CHRIST before them. (28) ZOSIMA discusses the grief of those who commit suicide and states that even though the church teaches that they should not be prayed for, he personally feels it appropriate to pray for them. He adds that CHRIST will not be angry because men have shown love and concern. (29) As ZOSIMA's body is prepared for burial, an icon of CHRIST is placed in his hands. (30) When PAISY sees ALYOSHA sobbing after ZOSIMA's death, he tries to comfort him and observes that his tears are probably sent from CHRIST. (31) After FERAPONT denounces the deceased ZOSIMA, he falls sobbing to the ground and says that CHRIST has triumphed over the setting sun. (32) RAKITIN angrily asks if ALYOSHA hates him for delivering him to GRUSHENKA in exchange for twenty five rubles. He insists that he is not JUDAS and that ALYOSHA is not CHRIST. (33) When ALYOSHA returns to the monastery after visiting GRUSHENKA following ZOSIMA's death, he begins to pray. While he prays, his thoughts often turn to PAISY's reading the BIBLE over ZOSIMA's body, and he hears excerpts from the story of Cana of Galilee and of CHRIST's turning the water into wine. (34) While listening to PAISY read the account of Cana of Galilee, ALYOSHA reflects that CHRIST brought joy rather than sadness to man. (35) After GRUSHENKA escapes to Mokroe, DMITRY begs FENYA and MATRYONA in the name of CHRIST to tell him where she has gone. (36) When KOLYA and ALYOSHA discuss KOLYA's ostensibly socialist persuasions, he comes to admit that he has nothing against CHRIST, that He was a humanitarian, and that if He lived today He would be part of the revolutionary movement. (37) IVAN's devil insists that proofs, particularly material ones, do not contribute to faith, and he adds that THOMAS believed not because he saw the resurrected CHRIST but because he wanted to believe. (38) At DMITRY's trial FETYUKOVICH attempts to discredit GRIGORY's testimony by asking him how many years it has been since the birth of CHRIST. (39) In his summation to the jury at DMITRY's trial FETYUKOVICH discredits FYODOR PAVLOVICH as a father. He encourages all to live the teachings of CHRIST and insists that only then can fathers expect love from their sons. (40) IPPOLIT KIRIL—LOVICH objects that FETYUKOVICH in his summation to the jury presented a false picture of CHRIST through his quotations and appeals. He particularly objects to the misuse of CHRIST's teaching about doing unto others.

"THE CHURCH IS A KINGDOM NOT OF THIS WORLD" ["TSER-KOV EST TSARSTVO NE OT MIRA SEGO"]. Distortion of CHRIST's words to Pontius Pilate as recorded in JOHN 18:36 in the New Testament: "My kingdom is not of this world. " (1) In his article on ecclesiastical and civil courts IVAN takes issue with this concept and insists that the church and the world cannot be separate and that the ecclesiastical must encompass all of the civil. (2) PAISY objects to the cleric against whom IVAN wrote his article and states that the cleric's use of the above statement distorts the Scriptures. He insists that CHRIST came to found a church on earth.

"CI-GIT PIRON QUI NE FUT RIEN//PAS MEME ACADEMICIEN." "Here lies PIRON who was nothing//Not even a member of the Academy," "My Epitaph" ("Ma Epitaphe"), an epigram written by Alexis PIRON upon his failure to be elected to the French Academy. MAKSIMOV claims that he met PIRON and BOILEAU in a pub and exchanged epigrams and insults with them. He claims that when he insulted PIRON about his failure to be elected to the Academy, PIRON responded with this epitaph.

THE CONTEMPLATOR [SOZERTSATEL]. A painting by the Russian artist Ivan KRAMSKOY first exhibited in 1878. The narrator notes that SMERDYAKOV will often stand pensively for several minutes, but he insists that he has neither thoughts nor notions but only contemplates. He adds that such a scene reminds him of KRAMSKOY's *THE CON—TEMPLATOR.*

THE CONTEMPORARY [SOVREMENNIK]. Literary and political journal founded by Aleksandr PUSHKIN in 1836. It achieved its greatest influence after 1847 under the direction of Nikolay NEKRASOV when it published the work of some of the best writers and was a vocal advocate of liberal politics. Its increasingly liberal political bent subsequently drove many writers away and eventually resulted in its forcible closing in 1866. KHOKHLAKOVA insists to DMITRY that she is no novice in the women's question and that she has corresponded with SHCHEDRIN, from whom she learned a great deal about the significance of women. She notes that she sent him a short letter of thanks and wanted to sign it "a contemporary Mother," but she decided that such a signature might recall *THE CONTEMPORARY* and cause problems with the current censorship.

"CURSED BE THEIR ANGER, FOR IT WAS FIERCE"["PROKLYAT GNEV IKH, IBO ZHESTOK"]. JACOB's words of prophecy to his sons Simeon and Levi as recorded in Genesis 49:7 in the OLD TESTAMENT. The allusion is to Genesis 34 in which is recorded the brothers' vengeance upon the city of Shalem because of the violation of their sister Dinah. Simeon and Levi killed the offending man and spoiled the city. ZOSIMA notes that there are those in Europe who provoke the people against the wealthy and advocate force and revenge by saying that anger is justified. He then quotes this scripture to amplify his point of contention.

DANTE [DANT]. DANTE Alighieri (1265-1321), Italian poet who was the first prominent writer to write in Italian. One of the greatest of world writers, he is known principally for *The Divine Comedy*. (1) In explaining the origin of his "Legend of the GRAND INQUISITOR" IVAN observes that the action of the work takes place in the sixteenth century, when it was commonplace for writers to include heavenly beings in works of literature. He adds that he is not referring to DANTE but to several clerics and monks who brought the MADONNA, angels, saints, CHRIST, and God Himself on stage. (2) IVAN refers to *THE DESCENT OF THE VIRGIN INTO HELL* as a work which has scenes and daring on a par with DANTE.

DARDANELOV. KOLYA's teacher, a bachelor who unsuccessfully proposes marriage to KRASOTKINA. The students feel that KOLYA may be superior to him in arithmetic and world history.

DARDANUS [DARDAN]. In Greek mythology the father of the royal house of Troy and the son of Zeus and Electra. See TEUCER.

"THE DARK ALLEYS OF THE CITY" ["TYOMNYE STOGNA GRADA"]. Inexact quotation from "Recollection"("Vospominanie"), a poem by Aleksandr PUSHKIN written in 1828. The original reads "The silent alleys of the city ("Nemye stogna grada"). In IVAN's "The Legend of the GRAND INQUISITOR" the GRAND INQUISTOR ultimately releases CHRIST from prison and sends Him forth into "THE DARK ALLEYS OF THE CITY."

PRINCESS DASHKOVA. Yekaterina Romanovna DASHKOVA (1743-1810), an intimate confidante of the Empress CATHERINE the Great and the president of the Russian Academy 1783-96. She ultimately fell from the

Empress' favor despite having been closely involved in the plot to have her placed upon the throne in 1762. See DIDEROT.

DEAD SOULS [MYORTVYE DUSHI]. A novel by Nikolay GOGOL which chronicles the attempts of CHICHIKOV to buy deceased serfs from an array of grotesque landowners. The first volume was published in 1842, and GOGOL envisioned sequels in which the rakish hero would be reformed. He never completed the subsequent volumes and burned most of his material before his death. KALGANOV complains that MAKSIMOV continues to claim that he is the MAKSIMOV of *DEAD SOULS.*

DEMIDOV. FYODOR PAVLOVICH insists that ZOSIMA kept for himself 60,000 rubles entrusted to him by the merchant DEMIDOV. He is drunk when he makes his accusation and soon admits that he lied.

"DEN DANK, DAME, BEGEHR ICH NICHT." "I do not desire your thanks, madame," quotation from Friedrich SCHILLER's ballad "The Glove" ("Der Handschuh"), written in 1797. IVAN accuses KATERINA of consciously abusing him because she knows that he loves her and of loving her martyr's role in her relationship with DMITRY. He leaves saying that he does not need her hand and quotes this line from SCHILLER as a parting gesture.

THE DESCENT OF THE VIRGIN INTO HELL [KHOZHDENIE BOGORODITSY PO MUKAM]. Popular APOCRYPHAL tale of Byzantine origin which became part of Russian literature in its early development. The tale portrays the emotional response of the Virgin to the suffering of those in hell and her successful intercession in their behalf with the Father and Son. IVAN states that the force and daring of this work are in no way inferior to DANTÉ.

DIDEROT. Denis DIDEROT (1713-84), French philosopher, essayist, and dramatist best known for editing the massive *Encyclopédie* through which he attempted to further knowledge and neutralize reactionary forces. (1) When FYODOR PAVLOVICH discusses his inclination toward buffoonery with ZOSIMA, he contrives a scene in which DIDEROT appears before the metropolitan PLATON in the presence of CATHERINE. After first denying the existence of God, DIDEROT responds to PLATON's defense of deity by acknowledging his belief and requesting baptism. He is immediately baptised with PRINCESS DASHKOVA functioning as godmother and POTYOMKIN as godfather. FYODOR PAVLOVICH later confesses that he made up the anecdote. (2) When ZOSIMA cautions

FYODOR PAVLOVICH not to lie, he appeals for permission to continue talking about DIDEROT. ZOSIMA responds that it is lying to oneself that is truly harmful, and FYODOR PAVLOVICH is pleased to hear that he can talk a bit about DIDEROT without causing harm. (3) FYODOR PAVLOVICH insists that it was MIUSOV's story about the beheaded martyr from the *CHETYI-MINEI* that ruined his faith and not DIDEROT.

DIOGENES [DIOGEN]. Greek Cynic philosopher (ca. 400-325 B.C.). He lived an ascetic life and conducted a sarcastic daylight search with a lantern to find an honest man. During NIKOLAY PARFENOVICH's questioning DMITRY states that even though he has done many vile deeds in his life, he has also been a searcher for nobility with the lantern of DIOGENES.

DMITRY. See DMITRY FYODOROVICH KARAMAZOV.

DMITRY FYODOROVICH. See DMITRY FYODOROVICH KARA-MAZOV.

DMITRY FYODORYCH. See DMITRY FYODOROVICH KARA-MAZOV.

ANNA GRIGORIEVNA DOSTOEVSKAYA. Dostoevsky's second wife (1846-1918) whom he married in 1867. The novel is dedicated to her.

"DRIVE NATURE OUT THE DOOR AND SHE FLIES BACK THROUGH THE WINDOW" ["GONI PRIRODU V DVER, ONA VLETIT V OKNO"]. Translation of one couplet of "La Chatte méta-morphosée en Femme" ("The Cat Changed to a Woman"), a fable written by Jean de La Fontaine (1621-95), a prolific French writer most noted for his fables and tales. The original reads "Qu'on lui ferme la porte au nez,//Il reviendra par les fenêtres." The fable makes the point that one cannot change the nature of things and relates the tale of a man who so loved his cat that he transformed it into his wife. In his summation to the jury at DMITRY's trial FETYUKOVICH discredits FYODOR PAVLOVICH as a father and sets high standards for fatherhood. He admits that such statements may be harsh but quotes the above to substantiate his claims.

EISENSCHMIDT [EYZENSHMIDT]. An elderly German doctor who attends MARKEL.

ELIJAH [ILIA]. As recorded in I Kings 17-II Kings 2 in the OLD TESTAMENT, a ninth century B.C. prophet, called the Tishbite, whose ministry in Israel was to combat the spread of the worship of Baal. Following his ministry he was taken into heaven with a whirlwind and chariot of fire. FERAPONT mentions that at night the tree outside his cell looks like CHRIST reaching out for him with branch-like arms. He notes that CHRIST wants to take him away in the spirit and glory of ELIJAH.

"ENDURE, BE HUMBLE, AND KEEP STILL" ["TERPI, SMIRYAY-SYA I MOLCHI"]. Inexact citation from Fyodor TYUTCHEV's poem "Silentium!" written approximately 1830. The original reads "Be silent, hide yourself and conceal" ("Molchi, skryvaysya i tai"). During the interrogation following his arrest DMITRY ponders that NIKOLAY PARFENOVICH and IPPOLIT KIRILLOVICH may not be worthy to hear his confession. He does not want to reveal the details of his jealousy and of KATERINA's money, but quotes this line to himself and proceeds to answer.

ESTHER [ESFIR]. The central figure of a book by the same name in the OLD TESTAMENT, which records her marriage during the Babylonian Captivity to Ahasuerus, King of Persia. The king determined to divorce his wife VASHTI, when she would not appear in public to show her beauty, and married ESTHER in her place. ZOSIMA praises the effect of the touching story of ESTHER and VASHTI.

EUCLID. Fourth century B.C. Greek mathematician known for his clarity and incisiveness and his contributions to geometry. (1) In speaking with ALYOSHA about God, IVAN insists that if God exists and is the creator of the world, then He accomplished this through EUCLIDIAN geometry. He adds that many thinkers feel that the universe is based on EUCLIDEAN geometry while others disagree, and he complains that with this confusion he cannot understand God with his EUCLIDIAN mind. (2) IVAN laments that with his EUCLIDIAN mind he can see the suffering in the world but has no one to blame. This results in a EUCLIDIAN wilderness that he refuses to accept.

EVE [YEVA]. As recorded in Genesis I in the OLD TESTAMENT, the first woman on earth who dwelt with ADAM in the Garden of Eden. SMERDYAKOV observes to IVAN that physical beating and tortures are a reality in all countries, just as they were at the time of ADAM and EVE.

EVENINGS ON A FARM NEAR DIKANKA [VECHERA NA KHU-TORE BLIZ DIKANKI]. Nikolay GOGOL's first collection of tales, published 1831-32. The stories are set in the author's native Ukraine and feature extensive use of local color, folklore, and the supernatural.

FYODOR PAVLOVICH gives the book to SMERDYAKOV to read, but the latter does not even smile and claims that it is all falsehood.

FAMUSOV. Pavel Afanasievich FAMUSOV, comical conservative landowner in *Woe From Wit (Gore ot uma)*, a comedy in verse written by Aleksandr Sergeevich Griboedov (1795-1829) in 1822-24. KHOKHLAKOVA eavesdrops as LIZA and ALYOSHA exchange declarations of love, promises, and kisses. She confronts him as he leaves and draws a parallel with the final scene in *Woe From Wit*, in which she functions as FAMUSOV, ALYOSHA as CHATSKY, and LIZA as SOFYA. In the play FAMUSOV finds CHATSKY and SOFYA together and mistakenly suspects an involvement.

"FATHERS, DO NOT GRIEVE YOUR CHILDREN" ["OTTSY, NE OGORCHAYTE DETEY SVOIKH"]. Slightly inexact rendering of Colossians 3:21 in the New Testament, which reads "Fathers, provoke not your children to anger" ("Ottsy, ne razdrazhayte detey vashikh"). In his summation to the jury during DMITRY's trial, FETYUKOVICH insists that FYODOR PAVLOVICH was not deserving of the designation of father and quotes the above to substantiate his claim.

FAUST. The principal figure of *Faust*, a play in two parts (1808, 1832) written by Johann Wolfgang von Goethe (1749-1832), German poet, playwright, novelist, and scientist, and one of the major figures of world literature. The play chronicles the career of FAUST, who sells his soul to MEPHISTOPHELES in exchange for the promise to comprehend all experience. IVAN's devil alludes to MEPHISTOPHELES' visit to FAUST in which MEHPHISTOPHELES states that he desires evil but does only good. The devil says that he is quite the opposite.

FEDOSYA MARKOVNA. See FEDOSYA MARKOVA.

THE FEDOTOVS. KOLYA claims that he found the dog PEREZVON at the home of THE FEDOTOVS after it had run away.

"FELL UPON THE FOUNTAINS OF WATERS AND THEY BECAME BITTER" ["PALA NA ISTOCHNIKI VOD, I STALI ONI GORKI"]. Inexact quotation excerpted from The Revelation of John 8:10-11 from the New Testament, which discusses the falling of a great star upon the fountains of waters. The name of the star is Wormwood, and it makes the waters also become wormwood. In his "Legend of the GRAND INQUISITOR" IVAN states that a new heresy began in Germany and a large star, a metaphor for a church, "FELL UPON THE FOUNTAINS OF WATERS AND THEY BECAME BITTER." He identifies the heresy as one that discouraged belief in miracles among those waiting for the SECOND COMING.

"LES FEMMES TRICOTTENT." "Women are to knit." KOLYA insists to ALYOSHA that his allusion to TATYANA does not make him an advocate of women's emancipation, and he adds that he agrees with the thought behind the statement "LES FEMMES TRICOTTENT," which he attributes to NAPOLEON.

FENARDI. Acrobat and magician popular in Russia in the 1820s. MAKSIMOV, claiming to be the MAKSIMOV in GOGOL's *DEAD SOULS*, states that GOGOL used names allegorically but that his FENARDI was really meant to be FENARDI. He adds that FENARDI, however, was not Italian but a Russian named PETROV.

MADEMOISELLE FENARDI. MAKSIMOV notes that MADEMOISELLE FENARDI was beautiful in her tights and captivated all by her dancing. See FENARDI.

FENYA. See FEDOSYA MARKOVA.

FATHER FERAPONT. An aged ascetic who has taken vows of silence and great fasting and who lives in a small wooden cell in the monastery. He is large, rather athletic despite his seventy five years, heavily bearded, and reportedly wears heavy chains under his clothing in an attempt to mortify the flesh. He has the reputation of a holy fool and communicates to a visiting monk that he sees devils and communes with heaven. Actively opposed to ZOSIMA and the system of elders, he comes to the room where ZOSIMA's body is lying in state and denounces him for not having lived the way he should.

FETYUKOVICH. The St. Petersburg lawyer engaged to defend DMITRY. His fee amounts to 3000 rubles, and he usually demands more, but he consents to defend DMITRY, whom he considers guilty, because the case is known throughout Russia and he stands to receive much publicity. His strategy at the trial is to discredit the witnesses personally. In his concluding remarks to the jury he points out the absence of proof that there was any money to steal, attempts to show that SMERDYAKOV could be guilty, and discredits FYODOR PAVLOVICH as a father, thereby implying that the crime cannot be called patricide. His speech is met with thunderous applause from the gallery but has little effect upon the jury composed of the common people.

FIDELKA. After he quarrels with DMITRY in front of ZOSIMA, FYODOR PAVLOVICH professes embarrassment and notes that some have the heart of an ALEXANDER THE GREAT while others the heart of FIDELKA the dog. He admits to having the latter.

FINAL JUDGMENT [STRASHNY SUD]. In Christian teaching the final accounting every man must make to God. After DMITRY is adjudicated guilty at his trial, he swears by God and the LAST JUDGMENT that he is innocent.

FLAGELLANTS [KHLYSTY]. A Russian religious sect founded by Danilo Filippov (d. 1700) in the seventeenth century. The sect practiced violent physical behavior and mortification of the flesh to the extent of castration in order to obtain deliverance from evil. A principal doctrine is that man can become God on earth. (1) In an attempt to produce a scandal, FYODOR PAVLOVICH loudly demeans the monastery in an absurd demonstration of buffoonery. He claims that confessions are given publicly and that FLAGELLANT doctrines may be prevalent, and he threatens to remove ALYOSHA from the monastery. (2) After his deformed child dies, GRIGORY turns to religion and even investigates the FLAGELLANTS for a time.

FOMA. An acquaintance of DMITRY and a former soldier who rents a room from the owners of the house next to FYODOR PAVLOVICH. DMITRY stays with him for a time so that he can observe his father and prevent GRUSHENKA from coming to him.

"THE FOOL HATH SAID IN HIS HEART, THERE IS NO GOD" **["RECHE BEZUMETS V SERDTSE SVOYOM NEST BOG!"].** Citation from Psalms 14:1 and 53:1 (in the Russian BIBLE, Psalms 13:1 and 52:2) in the OLD TESTAMENT. FYODOR PAVLOVICH insists that this is PLATON's response to DIDEROT's denial of God. See DIDEROT.

"FOR A DAY AND AN HOUR, FOR A MONTH AND A YEAR"["NA DEN I CHAS, NA MESYATS I GOD"]. Seemingly a distortion of The Revelation of John 9:15 in the New Testament: "And the four angels were loosed, which were prepared for an hour, and a day, and a month, and a year, for to slay the third part of men." (1) ZOSIMA relates that during his cadet school years when he was living a very worldly life, he hardly ever read the BIBLE but always had it with him "FOR A DAY AND AN HOUR, FOR A MONTH AND A YEAR." (2) ZOSIMA praises the monks who may well be the salvation of Russia and who are prepared "FOR A DAY AND AN HOUR, FOR A MONTH AND A YEAR."

"FOR CONVEYING TO THE LANDOWNER MAKSIMOV A PER-SONAL INSULT WITH BIRCH RODS IN A DRUNKEN CONDI-TION" ["ZA NANESENIE POMESHCHIKU MAKSIMOVU LICH-NOY OBIDY ROZGAMI V PYANOM VIDE"]. Quotation from Nikolay GOGOL's *DEAD SOULS*. KALGANOV complains that MAKSIMOV has been insisting that he is the MAKSIMOV in *DEAD SOULS* who was struck by NOZDRYOV, who in turn was taken to court "FOR CONVEY-ING TO THE LANDOWNER MAKSIMOV A PERSONAL INSULT WITH BIRCH RODS IN A DRUNKEN CONDITION."

FUNDAMENTALS OF ECCLESIASTICAL-CIVIL COURTS [OSNO-VY TSERKOVNO-OBSHCHESTVENNOGO SUDA]. The title of a book that IVAN takes issue with in his discussion of the jurisdiction of ecclesiastical and civil courts. Many of the arguments cited originate with Mikhail Ivanovich Gorchakov (1838-?), professor of church law at St. Petersburg University, and his article "A Scientific Elaboration of Church Court Law" ("Nauchnaya postanovka tserkovno-sudnogo prava"), found in *An Almanac of National Knowledge* Vol. II. (*Sbornik gosudarstvennykh znany*) published in 1875.

FYODOR PAVLOVICH. See FYODOR PAVLOVICH KARAMAZOV.

GATTSUK. Aleksey Alekseevich GATTSUK (1832-91), Russian publisher most noted for his popular *A. GATTSUK's Politico-Literary, Artistic, and Industrialistic Newspaper (Gazeta A. GATTSUKA; politiko-literaturnaya, khudozhestvennaya i remeslennaya)* and *Calendar of the Cross (Kryostny Kalendar)* published in the 1870s and 1880s. During IVAN's conversation with his devil the latter envisions an ax orbiting the earth and astronomers carefully measuring its rising and setting. He adds that GATTSUK would surely include this in his calendar.

GENERAL'S WIFE [GENERALSHA]. GENERAL VOROKHOV's wi-dow. She assumes care of the orphaned SOFYA but so torments her that she tries to hang herself. She is an impatient tyrant who acts from idleness rather than from evil intent. When she notes how SOFYA suffers in her marriage to FYODOR PAVLOVICH, she rejoices and insists that God is punishing SOFYA for her ingratitude. After SOFYA's death she takes IVAN and

ALYOSHA away.

GENGHIS KHAN [CHINGIS KHAN]. Universal ruler, a title conferred upon Temüjin (ca. 1167-1227), the Mongol conqueror of an empire extending from eastern Europe to the Sea of Japan. The GRAND INQUISITOR insists that one of mankind's great needs is world unity and that conquerors like TIMUR and GENGHIS KHAN were unconsciously responding to this need. CHRIST's rejection of Satan's third temptation, a fusion of ecclesiastical and secular power, produces the GRAND INQUISITOR's comments.

"GIVE AWAY EVERYTHING AND FOLLOW ME IF YOU WANT TO BECOME PERFECT" ["RAZDAY VSYO I IDI ZA MNOY, YESLI KHOCHESH BYT SOVERSHEN"]. Adaptation of Matthew 10:21, Mark 10:21, and LUKE 18:22 in the New Testament. The quotation is closest to the version found in Matthew: "Jesus said unto him, If thou wilt be perfect, go and sell that thou hast, and give to the poor, and thou shalt have treasure in heaven: and come and follow me." In citing ALYOSHA's reasons for becoming a novice, the narrator notes that these quoted words were once spoken and that ALYOSHA could not but respond wholeheartedly.

GLAFIRA. One of KHOKHLAKOVA's servant girls.

GOGOL. Nikolay Vasilievich GOGOL (1809-52), popular Russian writer noted for his tragicomic portrayal of human foibles. He was viewed as the fountainhead of the Natural School and credited with critically describing reality with the idea of social reform. (1) KALGANOV complains that MAKSIMOV insists that he is the MAKSIMOV in GOGOL's *DEAD SOULS*. (2) In defending his claim to be the MAKSIMOV in *DEAD SOULS*, MAKSIMOV notes that GOGOL wrote allegorically and that all of the names he used are allegorical.

GORBUNOV. Ivan Fyodorovich GORBUNOV (1831-96), popular and talented actor, writer, and narrator. IVAN's devil asserts that he is trying to save IVAN's soul, and in their discussion he refers to those who can contemplate the depths of belief and disbelief at the same time. He notes that those who probe this deeply are almost turned upside down, and he attributes such a description to the actor GORBUNOV.

GORSTKIN. See LYAGAVY.

GRAND INQUISITOR [VELIKY INKVIZITOR]. In IVAN's poem, a ninety year old cardinal who directs the Inquisition of sixteenth century Seville. When CHRIST returns to the earth and raises a young girl from the dead, the GRAND INQUISITOR has Him arrested and then visits Him in prison to discuss His failures. He insists that CHRIST has no right to add anything to that which He has already spoken and that His SECOND COMING will only hinder the work. IVAN observes that he perceives this as the essence of Roman Catholicism. The cardinal notes that CHRIST's desire to make the people free has produced people miserable in their freedom and that his work is to correct this situation. After the work is corrected, people will continue to believe that they are free and perceive their situation as an even greater freedom. The need to correct the work is especially acute because, as the GRAND INQUISITOR insists, people cannot be both free and happy. The GRAND INQUISITOR takes particular issue with CHRIST's failure to submit to the temptations of Satan, thereby failing to leave a legacy of miracles accentuating His divinity. To compensate for this he insists that people will come to the church for bread because it was not provided by CHRIST or His angels. Soon people will gladly trade their freedom for bread, and the church will continue to mask the erection of a new TOWER OF BABEL as the work of CHRIST. Through this mass gravitation to the church all can be saved rather than only the few strong ones who are able to live by heavenly bread. People will revere the church hierarchy for ruling over them and will recognize them as gods. The GRAND INQUISITOR further insists that once the need for bread is met there remain only three forces that can capture the conscience of men—miracle, mystery, and authority. He indicts CHRIST for rejecting all of these by not succumbing to the temptations of Satan and notes that man seeks miracles more than God. He adds that by redoing CHRIST's work and founding it on miracle, mystery, and authority, they have shown a great love for mankind by accepting people in their weakness. The GRAND INQUISITOR admits that he does not love CHRIST and that the great secret of the church is that they have been with Satan for the past eight centuries. They have taken advantage of the last temptation by encompassing Rome and CAESAR's sword, and he insists that mankind has a need for a world union. In order to give all men peace, rather than only the elect, they will convince people that they can be free only when they reject CHRIST's freedom and subject themselves to the church. Also, in order to bless mankind and demonstrate their love for them, they will permit people to sin and will tell them that it is atoned for if done with their permission. They will take the punishment for these sins upon themselves so that the people will be happy, and they will suffer because of the curse of the knowledge of good and evil. After explaining these things to CHRIST, the GRAND INQUI-

SITOR dares Him to judge them in view of the millions of happy and sinless people they will produce. Following the tirade and threats of being burned at the stake, CHRIST simply kisses the GRAND INQUISITOR, who in turn tells Him to leave and never return. The GRAND INQUISITOR conveys much of the theology of the novel and in many ways validates CHRIST's program through his personal suffering and concern for mankind. He is an ironic symbol of IVAN's own concern for the masses as opposed to the individual.

POPE GREGORY VII [PAPA GRIGORY SEDMOY]. Hildebrand (ca. 1025-85) who served as pope 1073-85. He vigorously defended the papacy against secular power and insisted upon its primacy in religious matters. While ZOSIMA and others discuss the possibility of the ecclesiastical and civil government becoming one, MIUSOV observes that not even POPE GREGORY VII dreamed of such a thing.

GRIDENKA. A copy clerk who stole some money and concealed it in his clothing. Following DMITRY's arrest the investigators carefully search him, and remembering the case of GRIDENKA, they set aside various items of his clothing for further examination.

GRIGORY. See GRIGORY VASILIEVICH KUTUZOV.

GRIGORY VASILIEV. See GRIGORY VASILIEVICH KUTUZOV.

GRIGORY VASILIEVICH. See GRIGORY VASILIEVICH KUTU-ZOV.

GRIGORY VASILYICH. See GRIGORY VASILIEVICH KUTUZOV.

GRUSHA. See AGRAFYONA ALEKSANDROVNA SVETLOVA.

GRUSHENKA. See AGRAFYONA ALEKSANDROVNA SVETLOVA.

GRUSHKA. See AGRAFYONA ALEKSANDROVNA SVETLOVA.

HAMLET [GAMLET]. *HAMLET, Prince of Denmark,* a tragedy written about 1601 by William SHAKESPEARE. The play chronicles HAMLET's murderous revenge for the slaying of his father. While speaking of the horrors and inhumanity of men, IVAN notes that if the devil does not exist then man has created him in his own image. ALYOSHA counters that God too must have been created in the same way, and IVAN praises his ability to turn words, much like POLONIUS' in *HAMLET.*

HAMLET [GAMLET]. Central figure of *HAMLET.* (1) In a discussion with PERKHOTIN, DMITRY admits that he is melancholy because he so loves GRUSHENKA. In this mood he recalls the words of HAMLET: "I AM SO SAD, SO SAD, HORATIO—AH, POOR YORICK." (2) In his concluding remarks at DMITRY's trial the prosecutor IPPOLIT KIRIL-LOVICH reviews the terrible things happening in Russia and refers to the number of young people committing suicide. He notes that these young people commit suicide without posing to themselves the questions that HAMLET did about death and eternity. (3) In his concluding words to the jury at DMITRY's trial the prosecutor IPPOLIT KIRILLOVICH notes that as DMITRY contemplated suicide, he did not think of what life would be like after death, as did HAMLET. He insists that HAMLETS are beyond the grave while only KARAMAZOVS remain here. (4) Observers at DMITRY's trial praise IPPOLIT KIRILLOVICH's speech and find his words about HAMLETS and KARAMAZOVS particularly apt.

"HAVE YOU SEEN MY SERVANT JOB" ["A VIDEL LI RABA MOEGO IOVA?"]. Distortion of JOB 1:8 in the OLD TESTAMENT, which reads "Hast thou considered my servant JOB" ("obratil li ty vnimanie tvoyo na raba moego IOVA?"). The passage is part of a conversation between God and Satan in which God praises His servant JOB and Satan determines to try JOB's allegiance. ZOSIMA recalls being taken to church by his mother and hearing the story of JOB read. He quotes this line and others as he recounts the story.

"HE LIVED AMONG US" ["ON MEZHDU NAMI ZHIL"]. First line of a poem written by Aleksandr PUSHKIN in 1834 but never published during his lifetime. The poem was dedicated to the eminent Polish poet Adam Mickiewicz (1798-1855), who wrote invective verse against the Russian Empire following the abortive Polish revolution of 1830. In the poem PUSHKIN recalls him as a friend and expresses disenchantment with Mickiewicz's political posture. In his concluding remarks to the jury at DMITRY's trial the prosecutor IPPOLIT KIRILLOVICH refers to the deceased FYODOR PAVLOVICH with these words.

HEBREWS [K YEVREYAM]. The Epistle of Paul the Apostle to the HEBREWS, a letter written to some Christian Jews approximately 70 A.D. and included in the New Testament. While trying to encourage the MYSTERIOUS VISITOR to confess his crimes, ZOSIMA quotes him HEBREWS 10:31 "IT IS A FEARFUL THING TO FALL INTO THE

HANDS OF THE LIVING GOD."

HEINE [GEYNE]. Heinrich HEINE (1797-1856), German Romantic poet, journalist, and satirist. IVAN's devil admits that he hoped to entice IVAN with his literary ability and sarcasm à la HEINE.

HELPER AND DEFENDER [POMOSHCHNIK I POKROVITEL]. A canticle sung over the body of a monk if the deceased is also a priest. FERAPONT complains that *HELPER AND DEFENDER* will be sung over ZOSIMA's body but only *WHAT EARTHLY JOY* over himself when he dies because he is only a monk.

"HERMIT FATHERS AND CHASTE WOMEN" ["OTTSY PUSTYN-NIKI I V ZHYONY NEPOROCHNY"]. With the deletion of the preposition "V" the title of a poem written by Aleksandr PUSHKIN in 1836. The poem is a poetic rendition of a Lenten prayer. IVAN's devil observes that if he gives IVAN just a small seed of faith, it will grow into an oak. Then IVAN will want to become like "HERMIT FATHERS AND CHASTE WOMEN" because he secretly wants to save himself through an ascetic life in the wilderness.

A HERO OF OUR TIME [GEROY NASHEGO VREMENI]. A novel published by Mikhail Yurievich Lermontov (1814-41) in 1841 which chronicles the affairs of Pechorin, a moody, vain, and capricious figure who destroys lives. See ARBENIN.

HERRNHUTER [GERNGUTER]. Resident of the Saxony village of Herrnhut founded in 1722 by the MORAVIAN BRETHREN. HERZEN-STUBE is described as some kind of a HERRNHUTER or follower of the MORAVIAN BRETHREN by the narrator who records his testimony at DMITRY's trial.

HERZENSTUBE [GERTSENSHTUBE]. The local town doctor. He is seventy, well-liked, respected, very willing to help people, but quite incompetent. He treats LIZA but does little more than comment that he does not understand anything about her condition. He is quite amazed when she recovers following ZOSIMA's blessing. Also indicative of his incompetence is his suggestion that SNEGIRYOV's mad wife and hunchbacked daughter can be helped by mineral water and foot baths.

HOFF [GOFF]. IVAN's devil relates an anecdote in which his illness is cured by HOFF's malt extract.

HORATIO [GORATSIO]. HAMLET's loyal friend and confidant in William SHAKESPEARE's *HAMLET.* See "I AM SO SAD, SO SAD, HORA-TIO—AH, POOR YORICK."

VICTOR HUGO [VIKTOR GYUGO]. VICTOR Marie HUGO (1802-85), French poet, novelist, and dramatist who became the leader and most authoritative writer of the French Romantic School. See *NOTRE DAME DE PARIS.*

"I AM SO SAD, SO SAD, HORATIO—AH, POOR YORICK" ["MNE TAK GRUSTNO, TAK GRUSTNO, GORATSIO—AKH, BEDNY IOR-IK"]. Inexact citation from the first scene of the fifth act of *HAMLET.* In the original HAMLET exclaims "Let me see. Alas, poor YORICK!" when a gravedigger shows him a skull and indicates that it is the remnant of YORICK. See HAMLET.

"I AM THE GOOD SHEPHERD; THE GOOD SHEPHERD GIVETH HIS LIFE FOR THE SHEEP SO THAT NOT ONE OF THEM WILL BE LOST" ["AZ YESM PASTYR DOBRY, PASTYR DOBRY POLAGAET DUSHU SVOYU ZA OVTSY, DA NI ODNA NE POGIBNET"]. Rendering of JOHN 10:11 in the New Testament with "SO THAT NOT ONE OF THEM WILL BE LOST" being added to the original. In his summation to the jury at DMITRY's trial FETYUKOVICH quotes this passage as part of an appeal to save DMITRY's life. His nonscriptural addition to the verse illustrates his machinations to save his client.

"I LOVE YOU AND, LOVING YOU, I TORMENT YOU" ["LYUBLYU VAS I, LYUBYA, MUCHAYU"]. In discussing the positive effects of the Scriptures on the Orthodox heart, ZOSIMA cites the example of JOSEPH sold into Egypt, his service as Pharoah's steward, and his reunion with his family. ZOSIMA claims that these are JOSEPH's words to his brothers, but they are not found in the Biblical account.

"I TOO IN FACT WRITE VAUDEVILLES OF ALL KINDS" ["YA VED TOZHE RAZNYE VODEVILCHIKI"]. Partial quotation of KHLES-TAKOV's bombastic self-adulation in the sixth scene of the third act of Nikolay GOGOL's *The Inspector General (Revizor),* a comedy of human foibles published in 1836. The original reads in part "I am acquainted with charming actresses. I TOO IN FACT WRITE VAUDEVILLES OF ALL KINDS. I often meet with literary figures. I am good friends with PUSHKIN" ("S khoroshenkimi aktrisami znakom. YA VED TOZHE RAZNYE VODEVILCHIKI . . . Literatorov chasto vizhu. S Pushkinym na druzheskoy noge"). IVAN's devil complains to him that he is not taken seriously and often abused. He insists that he has a good heart and then quotes the above and refers to KHLESTAKOV.

"I WANT TO MAKE YOU FREE" ["KHOCHU SDELAT VAS SVO-BODNYMI"]. A distortion of some New Testament passages such as JOHN 8:32 ("And ye shall know the truth, and the truth shall make you free"). The GRAND INQUISITOR accuses CHRIST of frequently stating "I WANT TO MAKE YOU FREE," and he laments the effect that freedom has had upon the believers. He adds that he intends to finish the work that CHRIST started.

"I WILL NOT BELIEVE UNTIL I SEE" ["NE VERYU POKA NE UVIZHU"]. A distortion of the words of the apostle THOMAS to the news that CHRIST had been resurrected. As recorded in JOHN 20:25 in the New Testament, "Except I shall see in his hands the print of the nails, and put my finger into the print of the nails, and thrust my hand into his side, I will not believe." See THOMAS.

"IF GOD DID NOT EXIST, IT WOULD BE NECESSARY TO INVENT HIM" ["YESLI BY NE BYLO BOGA, TO YEGO NADO VYDUMAT"]. See "S'IL N'EXISTAIT PAS DIEU IL FAUDRAIT L'INVENTER." KOLYA makes this brash statement to ALYOSHA and admits that it was taken from a book. He acknowledges that he says such things to impress ALYOSHA because he prizes him so.

"IF I FORGET THEE, O JERUSALEM, LET CLEAVE" ["ASHCHE ZABUDU TEBE, IERUSALIME, DA PRILPNET"]. Distortion of Psalm 137:5-6 (Psalm 136 in the Russian BIBLE) in the OLD TESTAMENT—"IF I FORGET THEE, O JERUSALEM, let my right hand forget her cunning. If I do not remember thee, LET my tongue CLEAVE to the roof of my mouth." When ILYUSHA tells his father SNEGIRYOV that he is going to die and suggests that he find another son, SNEGIRYOV responds by quoting this passage to KOLYA and ALYOSHA.

"IL FAUDRAIT LES INVENTER." "It would be necessary to invent them," see "S'IL N'EXISTAIT PAS DIEU IL FAUDRAIT L'INVEN-TER." FYODOR PAVLOVICH discusses with ALYOSHA the existence of hooks of torture in hell and notes that they must exist in order to have truth on earth. He notes that if they are not there, "IL FAUDRAIT LES INVENTER" for his sake alone because he is such a shameless person.

ILUS [ILLYUS]. In Greek mythology the son of TROS and the great grandson of DARDANUS. See TEUCER.

ILYA. LIZAVETA SMERDYASHCHAYA's father. Homeless, ruined, and sickly, he is a bestial drunkard who brutally beats his daughter.

ILYINSKY. An acquaintance of FYODOR PAVLOVICH who writes to him that GORSTKIN, a merchant from another area, is prepared to offer him more for his timber than are the MASLOVS. He ultimately conducts DMITRY on his fruitless visit to GORSTKIN in search of money.

ILYUSHA (ILYUSHECHKA, ILYUSHKA). SNEGIRYOV's nine year old son. He is small, sickly, pale, beset by poverty, and fiercely devoted to his father. This devotion causes him extreme suffering when DMITRY physically humiliates and insults his father. Thereafter he finds himself in conflict with the other boys at school as he tries to defend his father's honor. Their taunts provoke a violent response and ravage his emotions. In revenge he attacks ALYOSHA with rocks, anxious to start a fight and be set upon himself. Abused by other boys, he is nonetheless befriended by the older KOLYA, who intends to develop him. Despite his own proud nature, which is very offended when his father plays the buffoon, he becomes very devoted to KOLYA. When he feeds his own dog ZHUCHKA a piece of bread with a pin in it (a cruel trick that SMERDYAKOV had taught him), KOLYA punishes him by withdrawing his friendship. ILYUSHA responds by attacking ALYOSHA and the other boys. He ultimately becomes terminally ill with consumption and states that God is punishing him for his actions toward ZHUCHKA. His death becomes the impetus for the reconciliation of the generations as focused in ALYOSHA and the twelve boys and has application to the epigraph of the novel: "VERILY, VERILY, I SAY UNTO YOU, EXCEPT A CORN OF WHEAT FALL INTO THE GROUND AND DIE, IT ABIDETH ALONE: BUT IF IT DIE, IT BRINGETH FORTH MUCH FRUIT."

ILYUSHECHKA. See ILYUSHA.

ILYUSHKA. See ILYUSHA.

"IN THE MAGNIFICENT AUTO DA FE//THEY BURNED THE WICKED HERETICS" ["V VELIKOLEPNYKH AVTODAFE//SZHI-GALI ZLYKH YERETIKOV"]. Slightly incorrect rendering of "Corio-lan," a poem written in 1834 by Aleksandr Ivanovich Polezhaev (1805-38). The original reads "In the magnificent auto da fé//They burned the wicked heretics" ("V velikolepnom avtodafe//Szhigali zlykh yeretikov"). The poem deals with the exploits of Caius Marcius, fifth and sixth century B.C. Roman patrician, who earned the nickname of Coriolanus for his heroism in conquering the city of Coriolo. In his "Legend of the GRAND INQUISITOR" IVAN notes that the action takes place in the sixteenth century at the height of the Inquisition, and he quotes this couplet as being illustrative of the times.

IN THE MEADOWS [VO LUZYAKH]. Popular folksong in which a girl asks her father not to give her in marriage to an older man but rather to one of the same age. Shortly after her marriage to GRIGORY, MARFA IGNATIEVNA takes part in some peasant dances to the tune of *IN THE MEADOWS* and other songs. GRIGORY beats her for the first and only time, and she never dances again.

IOSIF. A monk who serves as the monastery librarian.

IPPOLIT. See IPPOLIT KIRILLOVICH.

IPPOLIT KIRILLOVICH (IPPOLIT). The thirty five year old assistant prosecutor who prosecutes DMITRY's case. He is a consumptive with an unwarranted degree of self-esteem. He prosecutes DMITRY because he really believes in his guilt and also because he sees the opportunity to make a name for himself in contending with FETYUKOVICH, whom he once rivaled in St. Petersburg. His final summation to the jury is his life's masterpiece. In it he views the KARAMAZOV family as a prototype of the Russian intelligentsia in both its elevated and debased veins. He examines all the facts and possibilities of the case in great detail and finally systematically shows how SMERDYAKOV could not have been the murderer. Nine months after his greatest moment he dies of consumption.

"IS THAT YOU, BOILEAU? WHAT A FUNNY OUTFIT!" ["TY LETO, BUALO, KAKOY SMESHNOY NARYAD"]. First line of "Epigram on the Translation of the poem *L'Art poétique*" ("Epigramma na perevod poemy *L'Art poétique*") written by Ivan Andreevich Krylov (1768-1844), the famous Russian fabulist, in 1814. The "Epigram" is a caustic commentary on the translation of BOILEAU's epic work. MAKSIMOV claims that he had drinks with BOILEAU and PIRON and commented to the former "IS THAT YOU, BOILEAU? WHAT A FUNNY OUTFIT!" BOILEAU supposedly responded that he was going to a masquerade, as noted in the "Epigram," but quickly changed his mind to indicate that he is going to the baths instead.

ISAAC [ISAAK]. As recorded in Genesis 15-28 in the OLD TESTA-MENT, the son of ABRAHAM and SARAH. The main events in his life are his birth in the old age of his parents, his near sacrifice to God at the hands of his father upon Mount Moriah, his marriage to REBEKAH, and his bestowal of the birthright blessing upon JACOB rather than upon the firstborn Esau. ZOSIMA insists that the Orthodox heart responds with understanding to the Scriptures, and among other examples he cites the account of ISAAC and REBEKAH.

ISAAC THE SYRIAN [ISAAK SIRIN]. Seventh century church father who was born in Nineveh but who spent most of his life in the wilderness seeking the ascetic way to virtue. After the death of his deformed child, GRIGORY turns to religion and reads among other things the teachings of ISAAC THE SYRIAN. He understands next to nothing, but this causes him to value the writings even more! See *THE WORDS OF OUR HOLY FATHER ISAAC THE SYRIAN.*

FATHER ISIDOR. One of the monks at the monastery.

"IT IS A FEARFUL THING TO FALL INTO THE HANDS OF THE LIVING GOD" ["STRASHNO VPAST V RUKI BOGA ZHIVAGO"]. The words of Paul in HEBREWS 10:31 in the New Testament directed against those who fail to follow CHRIST and His teachings. In encouraging the MYSTERIOUS VISITOR to confess his crimes, ZOSIMA quotes this scripture.

"IT IS BETTER TO FREE TEN GUILTY PERSONS THAN TO PUNISH ONE INNOCENT" ["LUCHSHE OTPUSTIT DESYAT VI-NOVNYKH, CHEM NAKAZAT ODNOGO NEVINNOGO"]. Inaccurate allusion to the words of Tsar Peter the Great (1672-1725) in his "Short Exposition of Trials or Court Cases" ("Kratkoe izobrazhenie protsessov ili sudèbnykh tyazheb"), published in 1716. The original comment reads "it is better to free ten guilty persons than to condemn one innocent person to death" ("luchshe est 10 vinnykh osvobodit, nezheli odnogo nevinnogo k smerti prigovorit"). In his summation to the jury FETYUKOVICH cites this passage and attributes it to a "majestic voice from the past century" ("velichavy golos iz proshlogo stoletia").

"IT SMELLS OF LAUREL AND LEMON" ["LAVROM I LIMONOM PAKHNET"]. Slightly modified allusion to a passage in the second scene of PUSHKIN's tragedy *The Stone Guest (Kamenny gost),* written 1826-30 as an adaptation of the Don Juan legend. The original reads "the night smells of lemon and laurel" ("noch limonom//I lavrom pakhnet"). IVAN uses these words to describe the evening on which the GRAND INQUISITOR imprisons CHRIST.

IVAN. See IVAN FYODOROVICH KARAMAZOV.

IVAN FYODOROVICH. See IVAN FYODOROVICH KARAMAZOV.

"J'AI VU L'OMBRE D'UN COCHER, QUI AVEC L'OMBRE D'UNE BROSSE FROTTAIT L'OMBRE D'UNE CARROSSE." "I saw the shadow of a coachman, who with the shadow of a brush was rubbing the shadow of a coach," slightly adapted reference to a parody of the sixth song of Virgil's *Aeneid* written by the brothers Claude (1613-88), Charles (1628-1703), and Nicolas (1611-61) Perrault and a friend Beaurain about 1648. When ALYOSHA indicates to FYODOR PAVLOVICH that there are no hooks in hell upon which to hang the wicked, FYODOR PAVLOVICH responds that there are then likely only shadows of hooks. He then quotes these words and observes that this is how one Frenchman described hell.

JACOB [IAKOV]. ISAAC's youngest son whose name was changed to Israel and who fathered the twelve tribes of Israel. His story is recorded in Genesis 25-50 in the OLD TESTAMENT and he is believed to have lived about 1860-1715 B.C. ZOSIMA insists that the Orthodox heart responds with understanding to the Scriptures, and among other examples he cites JACOB's journey to his uncle LABAN in search of a wife (Genesis 29), his wrestling with an angel in search of a blessing (Genesis 32:24-32), and his joy in learning that his son JOSEPH's life had been spared (Genesis 45:25-28).

"JE PENSE DONC JE SUIS." "I think therefore I am," statement by the French philosopher and mathematician René Descartes (1596-1650) in his *Discours de la Méthode (A Discourse on Method),* published in 1637. In his ramblings IVAN's devil quotes these words.

JESUIT [IEZUIT]. The Society of Jesus, a religious order for Roman Catholic men founded by Ignatius Loyola (1491-1556) in 1534. The society is known for scholarship and missionary zeal and has been accused of secrecy and intrigue. (1) SMERDYAKOV reasons that it would be proper to deny being a Christian in order to save one's life. He notes that if one mentally rejects his baptism, then he cannot be said to reject CHRIST because he is then not a Christian. FYODOR PAVLOVICH responds by calling him a JESUIT. (2) A drunken FYODOR PAVLOVICH insists that ZOSIMA is quite witty and sly, and he refers to him as a PIRON and a

Russian JESUIT. (3) Following a discussion about rejecting Christianity, FYODOR PAVLOVICH refers to both SMERDYAKOV and GRIGORY as JESUITS. (4) IVAN notes that he has captured the essence of Roman Catholicism in the person of the GRAND INQUISITOR, that is, that CHRIST had no right to add anything to what He said while living on earth and that He has come again only to hinder the work of the church. He adds that the JESUITS even write such things. (5) After listening to IVAN's poem about the GRAND INQUISITOR, ALYOSHA comments that the general picture is a false one and portrays only the worst of Catholicism— the inquisitors and the JESUITS. (6) ALYOSHA questions IVAN as to whether JESUITS are really like he portrays them in his "Legend of the GRAND INQUISITOR." (7) After ALYOSHA objects that the JESUITS in the "Legend of the GRAND INQUISITOR" are distorted, IVAN retorts that his JESUITS always seek for material well-being, do not suffer, and do not love mankind. (8) In discussing his GRAND INQUISITOR, IVAN notes that it would require only one such man to make his ideas dominant in the Catholic Church because of all its armies and JESUITS. (9) When ALYOSHA questions IVAN about his personal beliefs after having listened to him read his "Legend of the GRAND INQUISITOR," IVAN responds sarcastically that he is not about to go join the JESUITS. (10) IVAN's devil cites an anecdote in which a marquis confesses to his JESUIT spiritual father that it is better to leave this life with a nose than without one. He later admits that the whole anecdote is JESUIT casuistry. (11) DMITRY observes to ALYOSHA that he will judge himself throughout his life and will thereby diminish his sins. He insists that this is how the JESUITS think, and he adds that he has always perceived ALYOSHA as a JESUIT.

JOB [IOV]. The narrator explains that following his death ZOSIMA's body rather quickly decays and gives off an odor. In contrast he cites the examples of JOB and VARSONOFY, who according to legend were buried with an almost living smile and whose bodies gave off a sweet odor.

JOB [IOV]. Central figure of the OLD TESTAMENT book of the same name who is tried mightily by Satan but who remains faithful to God despite losing everything. (1) After the death of his deformed child, GRIGORY turns to religion and holy books and particularly likes to read of JOB, who also lost his children. (2) IVAN's devil notes that he will continue to destroy people so that the few can be saved and adds that several were destroyed to produce one JOB. (3) ZOSIMA recalls being taken to church as a young boy by his mother and hearing the story of JOB read. He notes that he cannot read it without tears and adds that God must rejoice in His creation of JOB and that JOB in serving God also serves all creation.

JOHN [IOANN]. The Gospel of JOHN, the last of the four gospels in the New Testament, written by the apostle JOHN, called the Beloved, sometime between 80-95 A.D. In trying to encourage the MYSTERIOUS VISITOR to confess his crime, ZOSIMA reads him JOHN 12:24 from the BIBLE: "VERILY, VERILY, I SAY UNTO YOU, EXCEPT A CORN OF WHEAT FALL INTO THE GROUND AND DIE, IT ABIDETH ALONE: BUT IF IT DIE, IT BRINGETH FORTH MUCH FRUIT." This passage also serves as the epigraph to the novel.

JOHN THE GRACIOUS [IOANN MILOSTIVY]. Likely an allusion to the seventh century A.D. church father who served as bishop of Alexandria. IVAN notes that he cannot understand how one can love his neighbor and says that he once read an account of JOHN THE GRACIOUS, who took in a starving and freezing man, lay in bed with him to warm him, and breathed into his mouth, made foul by disease. IVAN asserts that JOHN THE GRACIOUS did this only because of a strained sense of love's duty and a lie. The specific details of the charitable act evidently orginate in *La Legende de Saint Julien l'Hospitalier (The Legend of Saint Julian the Hospitable)*, written by Gustave Flaubert (1821-80) in 1876.

FATHER JONAH [IONA]. An ascetic devoted to fasting and silence. He lives in a small cell in the monastery to age 105 and becomes famous for his deeds. Following his death FERAPONT moves into his cell.

JONAH [IONA]. OLD TESTAMENT prophet who preached approximately 790-775 B.C. The book in the OLD TESTAMENT that bears his name relates his unwillingness to travel to Nineveh to preach, his shipwreck, his being swallowed by a great fish, and his deliverance after spending three days in the fish's belly. Following his instructional experience JONAH completed his mission to Nineveh. (1) ZOSIMA praises the effect of the Scriptures on the Orthodox heart and cites the account of JONAH in the whale's belly as an example. (2) IVAN's devil tells him of a Russian thinker who is a combination of an enlightened atheist and the prophet JONAH who spent three days and three nights in the whale's belly.

JOSEPH [IOSIF]. The eleventh son of JACOB, who lived approximately 1770-1660 B.C. His story as recorded in Genesis 37-50 in the OLD TESTAMENT relates his being sold into Egypt as a slave by his jealous brothers, his rising to the stature of prime minister of Egypt under Pharaoh, and his ultimate reunion with his father and brothers during a great famine. ZOSIMA praises the effect of the scriptures upon the Orthodox heart and cites several examples from the life of JOSEPH.

JUDAH [IUDA]. The fourth son born to JACOB and Leah. It was promised that the future Messiah would come through his lineage. ZOSIMA praises the lasting effect of the Scriptures upon the Orthodox heart and cites the example of JUDAH through whom would come the CHRIST and the real hope of the world.

JUDAS [IUDA]. JUDAS Iscariot, one of the original twelve apostles of CHRIST who betrayed Him to His enemies in exchange for 30 pieces of silver. RAKITIN angrily asks if ALYOSHA hates him because he brought him to GRUSHENKA in exchange for 25 rubles. He insists he is not JUDAS and that ALYOSHA is not CHRIST.

JUPITER [YUPITER]. The supreme deity of Roman mythology who corresponds to the Greek Zeus. FETYUKOVICH mockingly refers to his rival IPPOLIT KIRILLOVICH as JUPITER.

K. See KATERINA IVANOVNA VERKHOVTSEVA.

SEMYON IVANOVICH KACHALNIKOV. A local justice of the peace.

PYOTR FOMICH KALGANOV (PETRUSHA). A distant relative of MIUSOV who accompanies him to the monastery to witness ZOSIMA's attempt to arbitrate the KARAMAZOV family dispute. He is 20 years old, a friend of ALYOSHA, and plans to enter the university. He is also associated with MAKSIMOV and is present with him at Mokroe when GRUSHENKA visits there.

KALMYKOVA. An old woman who lives with her elderly daughter in a poor rented hut near SNEGIRYOV and his family.

ALEKSEY FYODOROVICH KARAMAZOV (ALEKSEY, ALYOSHA, ALYOSHKA, LYOSHA, ALEKSEYCHIK, ALYOSHENKA, LYOSH-ECHKA, ALYOSHECHKA, ALEKSEY FYODOROVICH). The third son of FYODOR PAVLOVICH by his second wife SOFYA. He and IVAN are full brothers and represent a symbolic spirit and mind dichotomy. He is identified by the narrator as both his hero and an eccentric person. Following SOFYA's death he and IVAN are taken in by the GENERAL's WIFE and then by POLENOV, who takes a great interest in him and raises him in his family. Although only four when his mother dies, he remembers her throughout his life and feels her presence and influence continually. Because of his great love for ZOSIMA, he enters the monastery as a novice. He is a realist rather than a mystical dreamer and enters the monastery because he feels that he has found the truth and wholeheartedly wants to be part of it. His character is quite exemplary and much akin to that depicted in a saint's life: he is quiet, reflective, loves to read, has a great desire not to judge others, always earns people's respect and love, dislikes vulgarity, always forgives, and meekly accepts taunts. He alone among his brothers does not condemn his father because of his desire not to judge others, and this earns him FYODOR PAVLOVICH's love. As the action of the novel commences ALYOSHA is about twenty. Following the family row at the monastery and ZOSIMA's unsuccesful efforts to arbitrate, ZOSIMA tells ALYOSHA that he should not remain in the monastery but should go into the world, marry, and endure life's experiences before returning. Heeding this counsel, he "tours" the world through a series of meetings and interviews that dramatically portray many of the issues and themes of the novel: he meets DMITRY, discusses the family conflict, and admits that he too is a base KARAMAZOV; he meets the suffering ILYUSHA and is greeted with rocks and physical and verbal abuse; he meets KATERINA and IVAN and exposes her motives and feelings toward DMITRY, thereby focussing attention on the love/hate triangle of KATERINA/DMITRY/IVAN; he meets with LIZA, engages in a mutual declaration of love, kisses, and promises for the future, and implies to her that he might not believe in God; he meets IVAN and listens to his "Legend of the GRAND INQUISITOR," during which he comments that the questions of God and immortality are the real Russian questions, that he himself would not want to build paradise and harmony on the suffering of even one child, and that IVAN's literary work is really in praise rather than condemnation of CHRIST. He then kisses IVAN just as CHRIST does the GRAND INQUISITOR and returns to the monastery. He accepts ZOSIMA's charge to watch over DMITRY and prevent conflict with FYODOR PAVLO-VICH, but ZOSIMA's death intervenes. He is totally devoted to ZOSIMA and fully expects miracles at his death, but when the body stinks and positive signs are not forthcoming, he is crushed and leaves the monastery. Depressed that glory has not come to his mentor, he casts DMITRY from his mind and goes with RAKITIN to visit GRUSHENKA, with whom he fully expects to fall. She indulges in flirtation until she learns of ZOSIMA's death, and then she extends him compassion. With a totally changed conception of her, he returns to the monastery to pray, and during the prayer he imagines ZOSIMA's inviting him to participate in the marriage feast at Cana, the scene of CHRIST's first miracle, in which water is turned into wine. This experience prompts him to embrace the ground, kiss it tearfully, beg forgiveness for himself and others, and plead to be able to forgive others. He comes to acknowledge his own culpability in his father's murder since he did not watch DMITRY closely, and DMITRY's actions enabled SMERDYAKOV to murder FYODOR PAVLOVICH. Thereafter ALYOSHA begins to spend much time with children, particularly with ILYUSHA, and succeeds in converting KOLYA to his way of thinking. Following ILYUSHA's death and burial he lectures to twelve boys, charges them never to forget ILYUSHA or each other, and exhorts them to love each other. He tells them that there will be a resurrection and that they will see ILYUSHA again. This concluding scene in the novel portrays the reconciliation of the generations and the triumph of CHRIST and His principles. ALYOSHA's personal success in properly ordering his life is met with enthusiastic hurrahs on the part of the boys.

DMITRY FYODOROVICH KARAMAZOV (MITYA, MITENKA, DMITRY, MITKA, DMITRY FYODOROVICH, DMITRY FYODORYCH, MITRY FYODOROVICH, MITRY FYODORYCH). FYODOR PAVLOVICH's first son by his first wife ADELAIDA. He is abandoned by his mother at age three and quickly forgotten by his father, who consents to permit PYOTR ALEKSANDROVICH MIUSOV to assume charge of his upbringing. MIUSOV quickly returns to Paris and DMITRY is shunted to several people, never really knowing a home. After doing poorly in school he enters the military, where he experiences both success and failure, fights duels, incurs substantial debts, and lives a dissolute life. He lives under the assumption that he has adequate means from his father, but when he discovers that he has used it up, he becomes furious and suspects that FYODOR PAVLOVICH has deceived him. He files suit and is determined to regain his money. At the time of the novel's action he is 28, but shows the effects of a dissolute life. At the family conclave in the presence of ZOSIMA he violently argues with FYODOR PAVLOVICH, whereupon ZOSIMA bows down before him as an acknowledgement of his great suffering. Shortly thereafter in a conversation with ALYOSHA he reflects upon his baseness and his KARAMAZOV nature and notes that even though he acknowledges that he is debauched, he retains the idea that he is a son of God. He admits that he is torn between the exalted and the base and confesses that he has fallen in love with GRUSHENKA, whom he both loves and hates. His passionate obsession is to prevent her liaison with his father, who has offered her money if she will become his. DMITRY's relationship with GRUSHENKA is complicated by his prior relationship with KATERINA IVANOVNA. He had offered to replace the government money that her father had stolen, provided that she come to him alone to receive it. His original intent is to punish her virtue in exchange for the money, but when she comes to him ready to do his bidding, he simply bows and gives her the money following a dramatic inner struggle. Later at KATERINA IVANOVNA's prodding he agrees to marry her, and the two are formally betrothed. They too experience a stormy love/hate relationship that is aggravated by his spending on GRUSHENKA the 3000 rubles that KATERINA IVANOVNA had given him to send to her sister AGAFYA. The money issue torments DMITRY because he considers himself an honorable man, even though base, and paying back KATERINA IVANO-VNA becomes very important to him. He finds it impossible to envision life with GRUSHENKA until his debt is settled, and he unsuccessfully contacts SAMSONOV, LYAGAVY, and KHOKHLAKOVA to get the money. After brutally beating his father, when he suspects that GRUSHENKA may have visited him, and threatening to kill him, he later returns to the family home to see if she is perhaps there. With a pestle taken from GRUSHEN-KA's apartment in hand, he observes his father from the shadows outside his bedroom. Finally deciding to abandon his vigil in the yard, he is confronted by GRIGORY as he leaves, and knocks him unconscious with the pestle. He then continues his pursuit of GRUSHENKA. It is after this scuffle and DMITRY's self-incriminating presence in the yard that SMERDYAKOV murders FYODOR PAVLOVICH. After failing to find GRUSHENKA at his father's house and learning that she has left the city, DMITRY purchases many party supplies and travels to Mokroe, where he witnesses her reunion with her former lover, the Polish officer MUSSYALOVICH. He first attempts to bribe the Poles to leave and then contemplates suicide because of life's failures. GRUSHENKA, however, buoys him up with a declaration of love which is quickly followed by DMITRY's arrest for patricide and a lengthy interrogation. After the witnesses are questioned, DMITRY has a dream in which he travels with a peasant to a village with many black burned houses and sees a thin starving mother with a cold emaciated child. He is overcome by a desire to help them. The dream effectively demonstrates his virtues and human concern and starkly contrasts with his arrest and imprisonment. GRUSHENKA's vow to remain at his side forever sustains him in prison, and he insists that he has become a new person who loves God, longs for life, and is willing to suffer. He comes to teach actively that there cannot be virtue without God and that man cannot love his fellow man without God. His trial becomes a public spectacle, and despite his ultimate innocence and an eloquent if fallacious defense by FETYUKOVICH, he is convicted. Following the conviction he admits to ALYOSHA that he cannot tolerate the humiliation of prison and flogging and the absence of GRUSHENKA, and he seeks ALYOSHA's approval of IVAN's suggestion that he escape to America. Sensing that DMITRY is too weak to bear a martyr's burden and did not commit the actual murder, ALYOSHA endorses the escape plan. DMITRY insists that going to America is akin to going to prison because he is bound to his Russian homeland and the Russian God. He plans to stay there for only three years, farm the land, learn English, and then return to Russia as an American.

FYODOR PAVLOVICH KARAMAZOV. The patriarch of the KARA-
MAZOV family. He is a notorious debauchee, an evil buffoon who
deliberately debases himself before others because he is expected to act
inferior even though he feels superior, a confirmed liar, and at the same time
a crafty and successful money manager. He begins with nothing, but
through manipulation and toadying he eventually acquires ample means,
which he plans to use to attract girls after he is too old to attract them
himself. He is 55 at the time of the novel's action. He marries twice. He
chooses his first wife, ADELAIDA MIUSOVA, calculatingly as a way to
make his career. She bears him DMITRY, but after a period of continual
conflict during which she usually beats him, she leaves him with the three
year old child. At her death FYODOR PAVLOVICH responds with both
glee and tears and laments his abandonment and suffering. He simply
forgets about DMITRY and lets GRIGORY, MIUSOV, and others in
succession assume his upbringing. He sees DMITRY only much later in life
and then only due to a conflict over DMITRY's finances. His second wife,
SOFYA IVANOVNA, is a young, innocent, saintly woman whose attributes arouse his lust. Their eight year marriage is punctuated by his frequent
orgies with other women in their home and the birth of two sons, IVAN and
ALYOSHA. After her death FYODOR PAVLOVICH willingly gives his
sons to the GENERAL'S WIFE and then to POLENOV. Much later in life
IVAN returns home, and he and his father get along quite well even though
FYODOR PAVLOVICH professes a greater fear for IVAN than for
DMITRY, who threatens his life because of money and GRUSHENKA.
The only son he ever cares for is ALYOSHA, who gains his favor by not
judging or condemning him. The fourth "son," SMERDYAKOV, is
rumored to be the product of a grotesque liaison with LIZA SMERDYA-
SHCHAYA, a mentally deficient dwarf. FYODOR PAVLOVICH retains
SMERDYAKOV as a valet. When the family convenes at the monastery to
allow ZOSIMA to arbitrate the conflict between DMITRY and his father,
FYODOR PAVLOVICH plays the buffoon and causes a scene there and
later at a dinner offered by the Father Superior. Such excessive conduct is
deliberate and calculating, and FYODOR PAVLOVICH admits that the
insults he receives as a result of it are pleasant and desirable. He keeps a
packet of money in his bedroom as an enticement for GRUSHENKA, and
this leads to unpleasant scenes with DMITRY as the two compete for her.
He is ultimately murdered by SMERDYAKOV for the money, and the
blame is cast upon the impetuous DMITRY, who was attempting to guard
the house to prevent GRUSHENKA's entrance. FYODOR PAVLOVICH
expresses hatred for Russia and her people and insists that he would not

want to go to ALYOSHA's kind of paradise. These statements place him as an antagonist to Dostoevsky's ideals of the Russian land, Russian people, CHRIST, and brotherly love.

IVAN FYODOROVICH KARAMAZOV (IVAN, IVAN FYODORO-VICH, VANYA, VANECHKA, VANKA). FYODOR PAVLOVICH's second son and his first by his second wife SOFYA IVANOVNA. Following his mother's death he is taken in first by the GENERAL'S WIFE and shortly thereafter by POLENOV, whom he leaves at age thirteen to pursue his studies. Even in his youth he is characterized by brooding, pride, and hatred for his father. He successfully completes the university in natural sciences and gives lessons and writes for a newspaper to support himself. IVAN becomes known in certain literary circles largely through an article on ecclesiastical courts that captures the fancy of individuals of quite disparate opinions. He discusses this article with ZOSIMA and several monks and asserts that civil and ecclesiastical authority must be one, but, unlike the Roman model, the church should encompass and convert the state. He views the attempt on the part of Western European and Russian liberal dilettantes to mix socialism and Christianity as a serious mistake and rejects the concept. Such discussions are characteristic of IVAN, whom the author uses either to state or to extract from others many of the philosophical issues of the novel. Many of the issues IVAN raises are not really settled in his own mind, but he is prone to categorical judgments. His controversial and challenging comments include: (1) there is no virtue without immortality and if immortality does not exist one should put ego in it place; (2) there is no God, devil, or immortality; (3) Europe is a graveyard, but a very dear one whose thinkers and scientists one can admire; (4) one can accept God but not God's earth, which has so much suffering, particularly child abuse, and immediate revenge rather than recompence in the eternities is required; (5) the future paradise on earth cannot be purchased with the suffering of even one child; and (6) if there is no immortality then all is permitted. The quintessence of his thought is expressed in his "Legend of the GRAND INQUISITOR," which he recites to ALYOSHA in an attempt both to test his ideas and to try ALYOSHA, the believer. Following the recitation, which is more a panegyric to CHRIST than the intended deprecation, ALYOSHA kisses IVAN just as CHRIST does the GRAND INQUISI-TOR, and this gesture further establishes the novel's parallelism. IVAN admits that with such contradictions it is difficult to live, but he relies upon the strength of the KARAMAZOVS and on his dictum that if there is no immortality then all is permitted. In addition to extensive self-characteriza-tion IVAN is defined by others to the effect that he is not happy and does not believe much of what he says or writes (ZOSIMA), that he seeks torment

(ALYOSHA), and that he cannot love (FYODOR PAVLOVICH). IVAN's love interest is centered in KATERINA IVANOVNA, and the two of them form a love/hate triangle with DMITRY. He exposes her self-sacrificial pride and her emotional manipulation of him but nevertheless retains a semblance of love for her. The action of the novel finds IVAN living with his father and SMERDYAKOV and being considered his father's favorite son. He has a feeling of total aversion for SMERDYAKOV, whose intellectual pretentions parody his own. When SMERDYAKOV makes several allusions to the fact that FYODOR PAVLOVICH will be undefended the next day in view of his own announced epileptic fit and GRIGORY's incapacitation due to a radical home remedy, IVAN angrily indicates that he will leave the house early the next morning. He uneasily senses that SMERDYAKOV is implying that he will murder his father, and his leaving gives implicit approval. He leaves, but considers himself a scoundrel and returns after the murder. He recommends that DMITRY, who has been accused of the murder, flee to America with GRUSHENKA. Thereafter he exhibits strange behavior: he is visibly disturbed, frequently ill, prefers to be alone, and frequently mutters to himself that he is guilty. He visits SMERDYAKOV on three occasions and on the third learns conclusively that SMERDYAKOV is the murderer and that he too is guilty by virtue of implied permission. He takes the money SMERDYAKOV stole from FYODOR PAVLOVICH and vows to implicate both of them in court the next day at DMITRY's trial. Returning from this visit he helps a drunken peasant, that he had previously struck on his way to SMERDYAKOV, thereby symbolically extending himself to the individual that he finds so difficult to care for. Serving the individual as opposed to the abstract masses signifies IVAN's modicum of repentance and his suffering for guilt and indicates that he does indeed have a positive, if still rational, essence about him. Following his discussion with SMERDYAKOV and his aiding the peasant, IVAN returns home, where he is confronted by his devil, a bourgeois Russian "gentleman" of about fifty who is very shabbily and unstylishly dressed. The devil symbolizes the shabbiness of IVAN's rational orientation and of his intellectual questioning of the spiritual. IVAN confronts his devil with the fact that he is merely the embodiment of one aspect of himself, of his base and stupid thoughts, and in response the devil attacks the vanity and false intellectualism of his ideas. Such exposure enfuriates IVAN. Upon learning of SMERDYAKOV's death, IVAN's mind becomes still more unstable, and he relives much of his conversation with the devil. At the trial he produces the stolen money and in an almost delirious state implicates both himself and SMERDYAKOV. His testimony is not taken seriously, since he includes explanations of his devil, and he is carried from the courtroom very ill. KATERINA IVANOVNA takes him into her home to care for him, but the prognosis for his recovery is not encouraging.

KARP. A notorious criminal whom GRIGORY tries to blame for violating LIZAVETA SMERDYASHCHAYA. He does this in an attempt to shield FYODOR PAVLOVICH from flourishing rumors that identify him as the culprit.

KARTASHOV. An eleven year old boy who attends school with KOLYA. When KOLYA stumps DARDANELOV with the question of who founded Troy, KARTASHOV steals a peek in KOLYA's copy of SMARAGDOV's *WORLD HISTORY* to obtain the answer to this question which captures the interest of the whole school. He then proudly announces the answer at ILYUSHA's home but suffers KOLYA's proud wrath in response.

KATENKA. See KATERINA IVANOVNA VERKHOVTSEVA.

KATERINA. The servant of the doctor's wife who lives next to KRASOTKINA. She quite unexpectedly announces that she is about to deliver a baby.

KATERINA IVANOVNA. See KATERINA IVANOVNA VERKHOVTSEVA.

KATERINA OSIPOVNA. See KATERINA OSIPOVNA KHOKHLAKOVA.

KATKA. See KATERINA IVANOVNA VERKHOVTSEVA.

KATYA. See KATERINA IVANOVNA VERKHOVTSEVA.

KHLESTAKOV. Ivan Aleksandrovich KHLESTAKOV, the simple-minded buffoon who is mistaken for the government inspector in Nikolay GOGOL's play *The Inspector General (Revizor)*, written in 1836. IVAN's devil complains that IVAN considers him a KHLESTAKOV, and he insists that his fate is far more serious than that.

KATERINA OSIPOVNA KHOKHLAKOVA. An attractive widow of thirty three who brings her ill daughter LIZA to ZOSIMA for a cure. She is beset by a crisis of unbelief in the afterlife and is counseled by ZOSIMA to love others actively as a remedy. When she confesses that she cannot love selflessly and requires constant gratification, ZOSIMA encourages her to work and to endure rather than to seek great feats of love and promises that this will overcome her unbelief. Despite the seriousness of her religious problem, KHOKHLAKOVA is a scatterbrained woman who babbles at great length and whom others have difficulty taking seriously. She eavesdrops on the declarations of mutual love and life-long promises exchanged by ALYOSHA and LIZA and objects to him privately that he is not the kind of son-in-law that she desires. When DMITRY frantically tries to raise the money to repay KATERINA IVANOVNA, he appeals to KHOKHLAKOVA, whose Kharkov land holdings provide her with means. She vows to deliver him from his plight and suggests that he involve himself in gold prospecting, which promises great returns. She does not give him any money, however, and sends him on his way.

LIZA KHOKHLAKOVA (LISE). The fourteen year old daughter of KATERINA OSIPOVNA KHOKHLAKOVA whose health problems, particularly paralysis of the legs, greatly improve following a blessing from ZOSIMA. She is involved in a love/hate relationship with ALYOSHA, whom she belittles and loves in her own way. She confides to him that she desires disorder rather than happiness and prefers doing evil and seeking self-destruction to doing good. Her disturbed nature finds more kinship in IVAN on occasion than in ALYOSHA, and the three of them form a triangle which is not overly developed in the novel. She admits to ALYOSHA that she often has a dream in which she sees devils in her room. She alternately makes the sign of the cross to send them a short distance away and curses God to permit them to return. Such flirtation with temptation and inconsistency color much of her life, and it is noteworthy that ALYOSHA acknowledges having the same dream. Her state of mind is further characterized by her reference to an account of a Jewish father who cut off his four year old son's fingers and then crucified him. She notes that she envisions herself watching this scene while calmly eating pineapple compote. She feels guilty about her maltreatment of ALYOSHA, but she finds her confused response to him as enticing as the parallel vascillation between good and evil in her dreams.

A KINSMAN OF MUHAMMAD, OR CURATIVE TOMFOOLERY [RODSTVENNIK MAGOMETA, ILI TSELITELNOE DURACHEST-VO]. A book translated from French and published in Moscow in 1785 which deals with the amorous adventures of the French hero in Constantinople. KOYLA notes that he obtained his toy cannon from MOROZOV in exchange for this book.

"A KISS ON THE LIPS AND A KNIFE IN THE HEART" ["POTSE-LUY V GUBY I KINZHAL V SERDTSE"]. The words of KARL VON MOOR in Friedrich SCHILLER's *THE ROBBERS* upon receiving word that his father has disowned him and cast him out. The original edition reads "Küsse auf den Lippen! Schwerder im Busen!" When Father Superior NIKOLAY bows down to FYODOR PAVLOVICH and humbly thanks him for his rather rude criticism, FYODOR PAVLOVICH responds by saying that the gesture is mere sanctimoniousness, and he insists that it is just like this phrase from SCHILLER's *THE ROBBERS*.

PAUL DE KOCK [POL DE KOK]. French novelist (1793-1871) noted for his graphic portrayals of Parisian life. DMITRY confesses his baseness and debauchery to ALYOSHA and acknowledges that it is all like the work of PAUL DE KOCK.

KOLBASNIKOV. One of KOLYA's teachers, a classicist.

KOLYA. See NIKOLAY IVANOV KRASOTKIN.

KONDRATIEVA. A wealthy local widow who tries to give LIZAVETA SMERDYASHCHAYA a home until she delivers her illegitimate child. Despite her efforts LIZAVETA steals away on the day of her term and delivers her child in FYODOR PAVLOVICH's garden.

PAVEL PAVLOVICH KORNEPLODOV. A lawyer whom DMITRY consults about his financial disagreements with FYODOR PAVLOVICH.

KOROVKIN. When IVAN's devil relates an anecdote, IVAN recalls that he had thought it up himself when he was seventeen and had told it to a school chum named KOROVKIN. This incident confirms IVAN's contention that his devil is really only his own base side.

KOSTYA. The seven year old son of the doctor's wife who lives next to KRASOTKINA.

KRAMSKOY. Ivan Nikolaevich KRAMSKOY (1837-87), prominent Russian artist and leader of the Travellers (Peredvizhniki), a confederation of artists that took travelling exhibitions around the country. Much of the work of this group expressed social criticism. See *THE CONTEMPLA-TOR*.

KRASOTKIN. KOLYA's father, a rather nondescript civil servant who dies shortly after the birth of his son fourteen years prior to the action of the novel.

NIKOLAY IVANOV KRASOTKIN (KOLYA, NIKOLAY, NIKOLAY KRASOTKIN). A vain fourteen year old boy who thoroughly dominates his doting widowed mother. He is a superior student and potential intellectual who has gained notoriety by letting a train pass over him as he lies on the tracks. He proudly announces that he is a socialist and defines his belief as equality, common property, absence of marriage and religion, and laws that reflect whatever the people desire. In a somewhat condescending but basically genuine way he takes pity on the younger ILYUSHA and decides to befriend him and develop him. The equally proud ILYUSHA becomes absolutely devoted to him. When ILYUSHA perpetuates a trick taught to him by SMERDYAKOV by putting a pin in a piece of bread and feeding it to dogs, KOLYA breaks off relations with him. His intent is to humble ILYUSHA and then ultimately to again extend his hand of friendship, but the tormented ILYUSHA, abused by the other boys, attacks KOLYA with a knife. He repairs their relationship during ILYUSHA's final illness by bringing him a dog and a toy cannon. He long seeks to meet ALYOSHA and to learn from him. When they finally meet, he feels very comfortable around him as a virtual equal, and the two discuss KOLYA's beliefs. He initially insists that he is a confirmed socialist and notes that his ideas come from RAKITIN and BELINSKY, whom he has seldom read. He later acknowledges that he is beset with vanity, ego, and power and attributes much of what he says to these qualities. During their discussion he significantly comments that all of his circle are egoists and that they have become distant from the common people. He admits to ALYOSHA that he is very unhappy and sometimes fears that the whole world is laughing at him and that he appears funny. Much of the reason for his seeking an interview with ALYOSHA is to find relief from his fears and personality traits. ALYOSHA warns him that he could be very unhappy and counsels him to value life. KOLYA becomes totally converted to him.

ANNA FYODOROVNA KRASOTKINA. A thirty year old widow and KOLYA's mother. She lives with her husband for only about a year before he dies, and following his death she devotes herself so completely to KOLYA that he is taunted as a momma's boy. Her devotion to him is such that she refuses DARDANELOV's proposal of marriage so as not to "betray" her son.

KRAVCHENKO. A doctor in DMITRY's military battalion.

GRIGORY VASILIEVICH KUTUZOV (GRIGORY, GRIGORY VASI-LIEVICH, GRIGORY VASILYICH, GRIGORY VASILIEV, VASIL-IEV). FYODOR PAVLOVICH's faithful house servant. He is an honest, stubborn, rather cold, and dignified person who deeply loves his wife and children. After the freeing of the serfs he determines to stay with FYODOR PAVLOVICH because he perceives it as his duty. He assumes care of the three year old DMITRY when he is left by his mother ADELAIDA and forgotten by his father. His hatred for ADELAIDA is transformed into a loving defense of SOFYA, and he regularly argues with FYODOR PAVLOVICH and even forcibly breaks up some orgies. After SOFYA's death he assumes care of IVAN and ALYOSHA until they are taken by the GENERAL'S WIFE. His desire to have a family of his own is frustrated by the death of his first child and his rejection of the second that is born with six fingers. He is overcome by the deformity, refers to the child as a dragon, and does not even want it baptized. When the child dies at about two weeks of age, he is further crushed, never speaks of it, and finally turns to religion. On the day the child is buried, he takes in the newly-born SMERDYAKOV and raises him. Years later his utilization of a popular cure facilitates the murder of FYODOR PAVLOVICH. He and his wife drink a large amount of vodka mixed with a remedy and fall soundly asleep. When he suddenly awakes and goes into the garden to shut the gate, he is knocked out by the fleeing DMITRY. This sequence of events enables SMERDYAKOV to kill FYODOR PAVLOVICH and place the blame upon DMITRY.

KUVSHINNIKOV. A character in Nikolay GOGOL's *DEAD SOULS.* In discussing his claim to be the MAKSIMOV in *DEAD SOULS,* MAKSI-MOV notes that GOGOL specialized in allegory and that the names he used were allegorical. As an example he notes that KUVSHINNIKOV was actually SHKVORNEV.

KUZMA. See KUZMA KUZMICH SAMSONOV.

KUZMA. See KUZMICHEV.

KUZMA KUZMICH. See KUZMA KUZMICH SAMSONOV.

KUZMICHEV. After KOLYA mentions the name SABANEEV, several try to decide who SABANEEV might be. One woman suggests that he may be the person who worked for the KUZMICHEVS. One member of the KUZMICHEV family is later said to be named KUZMA.

LABAN [LAVAN]. The grandson of Nahor, ABRAHAM's brother, whose family remained in Haran when ABRAHAM moved to Canaan. He was the brother of REBEKAH, who married ISAAC, ABRAHAM's son, and the father of Leah and RACHEL, who married JACOB, ISAAC's son. As recorded in Genesis 28-31 in the OLD TESTAMENT, LABAN agreed to permit JACOB to marry RACHEL if he served him for seven years, but after the agreed-upon period he gave him Leah, his elder daughter, instead, and offered RACHEL only for an additional seven years of work. ZOSIMA insists that the Orthodox heart responds with understanding to the Scriptures, and cites as one example the story of JACOB and LABAN.

THE LAST OF THE MOHICANS [POSLEDNIE MOGIKANY]. A novel chronicling a frontiersman hero's exploits against the Huron Indians, published in 1826 by James Fenimore Cooper (1789-1851). Following the verdict rendered at his trial, DMITRY discusses his proposed flight to America and notes that he and GRUSHENKA will go deep into the country of *THE LAST OF THE MOHICANS.*

LAZARUS [LAZAR]. As recorded in LUKE 16:19-31 in the New Testament, a beggar who pleads daily at the gate of a rich man and who ultimately, unlike the rich man, receives an eternal reward in ABRAHAM's bosom. ZOSIMA teaches that men are put upon earth and given the opportunity to love. If men do not take advantage of it, they can still return to ABRAHAM's bosom as portrayed in THE PARABLE OF LAZARUS AND THE RICH MAN, but they feel the torment for not having loved.

LE BON JUGEMENT DE LA TRES SAINTE ET GRACIEUSE VIERGE MARIE. The Benevolent Judgment of the Most Holy and Gracious Virgin Mary. See *NOTRE DAME DE PARIS.*

"THE LEGS ARE SLIM, THE SIDES RING OUT,//THE TRAIN IS IN A FLOURISH" ["NOZHKI TONKI, BOKA ZVONKI,//KHVOSTIK ZAKORYUCHKOY"]. Folk riddle that like many others found its way into popular folk songs. As GRUSHENKA, quite drunk, prepares to dance at Mokroe, MAKSIMOV eagerly follows her about singing this little ditty.

LEPELLETIER [LEPELLETIE]. A St. Petersburg doctor suggests to SNEGIRYOV that his wife be sent to Paris to consult the psychiatrist LEPELLETIER.

"LET THE STOVE AND COTTAGE DANCE" ["KHODI IZBA, KHO-DI PECH"]. Words of a popular dance chorus which exist in various versions. After dismissing her former lover and his companion from Mokroe, GRUSHENKA insists upon drinking, singing, and dancing, and she quotes the above as an example of the kind of merriment she desires.

"LET THIS AWFUL CUP PASS FROM ME" ["PRONESI ETU STRASHNUYU CHASHU MIMO MENYA"]. Slightly distorted rendition of the words of CHRIST as He prayed in Gethsemane prior to His crucifixion. The words are recorded in varying versions in Mark 14:36, LUKE 22:42, and Matthew 26:39 in the New Testament. The closest approximation of the quotation is found in Mark 14:36, "Take this cup from me" ("Pronesi chashu siyu mimo Menya"). DMITRY muses on these words as he reflects upon his contemplated suicide.

LICHARDA. The servant of King Vidon in *The Tale of Bova Korolevich (Povest o Bove Koroleviche),* a widely adapted and translated tale that arose in France and found its way into Russia by the beginning of the seventeenth century. (1) SMERDYAKOV observes to IVAN that DMITRY has demanded that he watch his father's house and refuse to admit GRUSHENKA. He adds that DMITRY has called him his servant LICHARDA. (2) During IVAN's third visit to him, SMERDYAKOV admits that he murdered FYODOR PAVLOVICH, but he insists that he acted only with IVAN's approbation and as his servant LICHARDA.

"LIKE LIGHTNING FLASHING FROM THE EAST TO THE WEST" ["KAK MOLNIA, BLISTAYUSHCHAYA OT VOSTOKA DO ZAPA-DA"]. Distortion of the words of CHRIST to His disciples as He describes His SECOND COMING. The reference is likely to Matthew 24:27 in the New Testament, "For as the lightning cometh out of the east, and shineth even unto the west; so shall the coming of the Son of man be" ("Ibo, kak molnia iskhodit ot vostoka i vidna byvaet dazhe do zapada, tak budet prishestvie Syna Chelovecheskogo"). IVAN notes that the coming of CHRIST, which he depicts in his "Legend of the GRAND INQUISITOR," is not the one referred to in the Scriptures, which is sudden and is "LIKE LIGHTNING FLASHING FROM THE EAST TO THE WEST."

"LIKE THE SUN IN A SMALL DROP OF WATER" ["KAK SOLNTSE V MALOY KAPLE VODY"]. A line from "God" ("Bog"), an ode written in 1784 by Gavriil Romanovich Derzhavin (1743-1816). In his summation to the jury the prosecutor IPPOLIT KIRILLOVICH observes that the KARAMAZOV family exemplifies many traits of the contemporary intelligentsia as if seen under a microscope "LIKE THE SUN IN A SMALL DROP OF WATER."

LISE. See LIZA KHOKHLAKOVA.

"LITTLE PIG, OINK-OINK, OINK-OINK" ["SVINUSHKA KHRYU-KHRYU, KHRYU-KHRYU"]. Popular folk song chorus that MAKSI-MOV sings and dances to at Mokroe.

LIZAVETA. The infant daughter of a woman, who comes to ZOSIMA and donates sixty kopeks to the poor.

LIZAVETA. See LIZAVETA SMERDYASHCHAYA.

LIZAVETA SMERDYASHCHAYA (LIZAVETA, SMERDYASHCHA-YA). A very short, mentally deficient, mute woman, who is reverenced as a holy fool. She wears nothing but a shirt irrespective of the weather, eats only black bread and water, and gives away whatever food and clothing she is given. She is filthy, goes barefoot, and often sleeps outside. When she suddenly and surprisingly becomes pregnant, it is widely rumored that FYODOR PAVLOVICH is to blame. It is therefore significant that she delivers her son SMERDYAKOV in FYODOR PAVLOVICH's garden and then dies shortly thereafter. The child is born under the watchful eye of GRIGORY on the same day that GRIGORY's six-fingered son is buried, and he quickly assumes care of the new baby.

LOUIS XI [LYUDOVIK XI]. The son of Charles VII and king of France (1461-83). See *NOTRE DAME DE PARIS*.

LUKE [YEVANGELIE OT LUKI]. The third of the four gospels in the New Testament written by the physician LUKE. ZOSIMA praises the effect of the Scriptures upon the Orthodox heart and cites the parables in LUKE as an example.

LUKYANOV. A local merchant who relates to GRIGORY the story of a soldier who was tortured when he would not renounce Christianity in favor of Islam.

LUTHER [LYUTER]. Martin LUTHER (1483-1546), leader of the Reformation in Germany and translator of the Old and New Testaments into German. As IVAN's devil belittles his ideas and ego, IVAN throws a glass of tea at him in a rage and then alludes to LUTHER's inkwell. LUTHER recorded many personal experiences with the devil and one of them, likely of spurious origin, portrays his throwing an inkwell at the devil, who was tempting him during his translation of the BIBLE.

LUTHERAN [LYUTERAN]. The church which arose out of the contention between Martin LUTHER and the Roman Catholic Church. (1) FYODOR PAVLOVICH indicates that he prefers to believe in a delicate and enlightened hell as taught by the LUTHERANS. (2) ZOSIMA observes that church and state seem to be fusing into one in the LUTHERAN lands, that is, in Protestant Europe. (3) The pamphlet about RICHARD was supposedly translated from French by some LUTHERANS and then distributed free. (4) After recounting the story of JOB, ZOSIMA notes that even if LUTHERANS and heretics come in to take away the Orthodox flock, the people have so few possessions that they, like JOB, will be willing to part with them.

LYAGAVY (GORSTKIN). A merchant from another area, who offers to buy FYODOR PAVLOVICH's timber for more money than the local MASLOVS offer. He is embarrassed by his name, which refers to a pointer or setter, and prefers to be called GORSTKIN. He is known as a man of means, and DMITRY comes to him to get 3000 rubles for his interest in the Chermashnya Woods in an attempt to repay KATERINA IVANOVNA. LYAGAVY is so drunk, a frequent occurrence, that he dismisses DMITRY as a fraud.

LYOSHA. See ALEKSEY FYODOROVICH KARAMAZOV.

LYOSHECHKA. See ALEKSEY FYODOROVICH KARAMAZOV.

MADONNA. In Christianity the Virgin Mary, the mother of CHRIST. (1) In his confession to ALYOSHA, DMITRY laments the burdens man must bear and notes that even a sensitive and high-minded person can begin with the ideal of the MADONNA and conclude with the ideal of SODOM. He adds that it is still worse when he who has the ideal of SODOM does not abandon the ideal of the MADONNA. (2) In explaining the origin of his "Legend of the GRAND INQUISITOR" IVAN observes that the action of the work takes place in the sixteenth century, when it was commonplace for writers to include heavenly beings in works of literature. He adds that he is not referring to DANTE but to several clerics and monks who brought the MADONNA, angels, saints, CHRIST, and even God Himself on stage.

MIKHAIL MAKAROVICH MAKAROV (MIKHAIL MAKARYCH). A retired colonel and a widower who in his capacity as a district police officer comes to Mokroe to pick up DMITRY. He speaks very harshly to DMITRY and GRUSHENKA, but quickly perceives that she is a good woman with a Christian soul and changes his attitude toward them.

MAKSIMOV. A landowner in Nikolay GOGOL's *DEAD SOULS* who is beaten by NOZDRYOV. KALGANOV complains that MAKSIMOV has been saying that he is the MAKSIMOV in *DEAD SOULS,* and he strongly insists that this cannot be.

MAKSIMOV (MAKSIMUSHKA). A rather excitable, balding, sixty year old landowner of Tula who often plays the buffoon by telling stories about himself for others' amusement. When the KARAMAZOVS arrive at the monastery to let ZOSIMA arbitrate the dispute between ZOSIMA and FYODOR PAVLOVICH, MAKSIMOV escorts them to ZOSIMA's quarters. FYODOR PAVLOVICH observes that MAKSIMOV reminds him of VON SOHN and frequently calls him by that name in an attempt to belittle him. MAKSIMOV later appears at Mokroe with KALGANOV and joins in the strained revelling of GRUSHENKA and DMITRY. While there he relates tales in which he claims to be the MAKSIMOV in *DEAD SOULS* and claims to have met BOILEAU and PIRON. Following the events at Mokroe he stays with GRUSHENKA.

MAKSIMUSHKA. See MAKSIMOV.

MARFA. See MARFA IGNATIEVNA.

MARFA IGNATIEVA. See MARFA IGNATIEVNA.

MARFA IGNATIEVNA (MARFA, MARFA IGNATIEVA). GRIGO-RY's wife who has always submitted to him in everything. She bears him two children, both of which die shortly after birth, and then becomes mother to the abandoned DMITRY, IVAN, ALYOSHA, and SMERDYAKOV in succession.

MARIE. French name for the Virgin Mary. See *NOTRE DAME DE PARIS.*

MARKEL. ZOSIMA's brother, who is eight years older than he is. He has always been sickly and dies of consumption at age seventeen. Formerly critical of religion and under the influence of a professor and political exile, he changes radically as death approaches. He comes to teach that all should serve one another (he even wants to serve his own servants), that each is guilty before all others in all things, that because of this one should ask forgiveness of everyone and everything (he even asks forgiveness of the birds), and that mutual guilt and forgiveness can build paradise on earth. With these new attitudes he dies very happy. His thought strongly influences

ZOSIMA and becomes the core of the ethical and theological message of the novel.

FEDOSYA MARKOVA (FEDOSYA MARKOVNA, FENYA). MATRYONA's twenty year old granddaughter and one of GRUSHENKA's servants. She begs DMITRY not to hurt GRUSHENKA as he pursues her to Mokroe.

ST. MARY OF EGYPT [MARIA YEGIPTYANYNA]. Saint venerated in both the Eastern and Western churches. After a life of profligacy in Egypt she made vows to devote herself to mortification and penance in the wilderness, where she gained prophetic powers and sanctity. ZOSIMA praises the effect that reading the accounts of ALEKSEY THE MAN OF GOD and ST. MARY OF EGYPT have upon the common people.

MARYA (NATASHA). KOLYA speaks to one of the market-women in the street and condescendingly refers to her as NATASHA. She informs him that her name is MARYA.

MARYA (MARYUSHKA). When DMITRY arrives at Mokroe he asks TRIFON BORISYCH to send for gypsies and girls, especially MARYA, STEPANIDA, and ARINA.

MARYA KONDRATIEVNA. The daughter of the woman who lives in the house next to FYODOR PAVLOVICH. She plays the coquette with SMERDYAKOV.

MARYUSHKA. See MARYA.

MASLOV. A powerful merchant who dominates local commerce. He and his son negotiate to buy some timber from FYODOR PAVLOVICH, who in turn feels that he is not getting enough money and consults LYAGAVY.

MASLOV. MASLOV's son.

MASON. An oath-bound and secretive fraternal order of men originating probably in the fourteenth century among stonemasons. The order encourages belief in a Supreme Being and good moral and ethical character. (1) IVAN ponders that perhaps Catholics hate MASONS because they too are bound together by an internal mystery.(2) After listening to IVAN's dialectic and his "Legend of the GRAND INQUISITOR," ALYOSHA comments that IVAN himself could be a MASON. (3) DMITRY observes to ALYOSHA that he suspects IVAN of being a MASON.

"THE MASTER TRIED THE GIRLS" ["BARIN DEVUSHEK PY-TAL"]. The first of sixteen lines rendered by the singers and musicians at Mokroe. The song originates with Dostoevsky and is intended as an example of peasant art. The song proves obnoxious especially to KAL-GANOV.

"MASTER, WHAT SHALL I DO TO INHERIT ETERNAL LIFE?" ["UCHITEL, CHTO MNE DELAT, CHTOBY NASLEDOVAT ZHIZN VECHNUYU?"]. As recorded in LUKE 10:25 in the New Testament, the tempting words of a lawyer to CHRIST. When the KARAMAZOVS gather at the monastery to have ZOSIMA arbitrate the dispute between FYODOR PAVLOVICH and DMITRY, FYODOR PAVLOVICH suddenly falls upon his knees before ZOSIMA and addresses these both mocking and sincere words to him.

"MASTRYUK WAS ALL IN ALL, BUT CAME TO NAUGHT AT ALL!" ["BYL MASTRYUK VO VSYOM, STAL MASTRYUK NI VO CHYOM!"]. Line from a Russian historical folk song entitled "MAS-TRYUK Temryukovich." The original reads "Mastryuk lay sound asleep,/ / And did not hear his robe removed,/ / MASTRYUK WAS ALL IN ALL, BUT CAME TO NAUGHT AT ALL!" ("MASTRYUK bez pamyati lezhit,/ / Ne slykhal, kak platie snyali,/ / BYL MASTRYUK VO VSYOM, STAL MASTRYUK NI V CHYOM"). When PERKHOTIN expresses surprise that DMITRY is going to Mokroe at night and suddenly has much money, DMITRY responds with these words, thereby indicating that the loss of GRUSHENKA and his honor has literally stripped him of everything. It is also noteworthy that he is literally stripped of his clothing at Mokroe when arrested and searched.

MATRYONA. GRUSHENKA's aged cook and FEDOSYA MARKO-VA's grandmother.

COUNT MATTEI. IVAN's devil recounts an anecdote in which he becomes ill and writes to COUNT MATTEI for help.

MATVEY. A peasant with whom KOLYA has a brief conversation. KOLYA then proudly announces to SMUROV that he loves to speak with the common people.

MAVRA FOMINISHNA. MIUSOV's aunt. In admitting that he made up the story about DIDEROT, FYODOR PAVLOVICH nevertheless insists that he has heard several people, including MAVRA FOMINISHNA, say: "the fool says" ("reche bezumets"). See "THE FOOL HATH SAID IN HIS HEART, THERE IS NO GOD."

MAVRIKY MAVRIKICH. See MAVRIKY MAVRIKICH SHMERT-SOV.

"MEASURE WITH THAT MEASURE WHICH IS MEASURED UNTO YOU." See "WITH WHATSOEVER MEASURE YOU MEASURE, IT WILL BE MEASURED TO YOU."

MEPHISTOPHELES [MEFISTOFEL]. The demon-like tempter in the various versions of the FAUST legend. (1) When drunk FYODOR PAVLOVICH insists that he respects ZOSIMA despite the fact that there is something of MEPHISTOPHELES or perhaps more likely of *A HERO OF OUR TIME* in him. (2) IVAN's devil recalls MEPHISTOPHELES' visit to FAUST in which MEPHISTOPHELES claims that he wants to do evil but manages to do only good. The devil observes that he is quite the opposite.

MICHAEL [MIKHAIL]. In Christianity the chief angel and captain of God's host. IVAN recalls *THE DESCENT OF THE VIRGIN INTO HELL* and notes that the archangel MICHAEL conducts the Virgin on her tour of the underworld.

MIKHAIL. See MIKHAIL OSIPOVICH RAKITIN.

MIKHAIL. See THE MYSTERIOUS VISITOR.

MIKHAIL. A somewhat young and unlearned monk who serves as the prior of the small monastery that houses ZOSIMA.

MIKHAIL IVANOVICH. See MIKHAIL OSIPOVICH RAKITIN. KHO-KHLAKOVA mistakenly refers to RAKITIN as MIKHAIL IVANO-VICH.

MIKHAIL MAKARYCH. See MIKHAIL MAKARYCH MAKAROV.

MIKHAIL OSIPOVICH. See MIKHAIL OSIPOVICH RAKITIN.

MIKHAIL SEMYONOVICH. A town resident who eagerly discusses the imminent verdict at DMITRY's trial with several others.

THE MIKHAYLOVS. A local family. KOLBASNIKOV marries THE MIKHAYLOVS' daughter, whom KOLYA describes as being incredibly ugly, and his students write epigrams about it.

MISHA. PERKHOTIN's servant boy.

MISHA. See DMITRY FYODOROVICH KARAMAZOV.

MITENKA. See DMITRY FYODOROVICH KARAMAZOV.

MITKA. See DMITRY FYODOROVICH KARAMAZOV.

MITRY. When IVAN determines not to go to Chermashnya to see about the sale of his father's timber, he asks a driver named MITRY to inform FYODOR PAVLOVICH.

MITRY FYODOROVICH. See DMITRY FYODOROVICH KARA-MAZOV.

MITRY FYODORYCH. See DMITRY FYODOROVICH KARAMA-ZOV.

MITYA. See DMITRY FYODOROVICH KARAMAZOV.

MIUSOV. ADELAIDA IVANOVNA's father, who has been deceased for some time.

PYOTR ALEKSANDROVICH MIUSOV. ADELAIDA IVANOVNA's cousin, a proud man of about fifty. A liberal, free-thinker, and atheist exemplary of those of the 1840s and 1850s, he is well-educated and has lived in Europe for years. He knew PROUDHON and BAKUNIN personally and fondly recalls the French Revolution of 1848. Upon hearing of the death of his cousin ADELAIDA IVANOVNA, he determines to assume DMI-TRY's upbringing and succeeds in getting FYODOR PAVLOVICH to agree to this. He soon returns to Paris and forgets about DMITRY, and the child's upbringing is left first to an aunt and then to a married daughter. He is quite wealthy and owns an estate on the outskirts of the town, which has placed him in litigation with the monastery over fishing rights and timber cutting. He attends the meeting between ZOSIMA and the KARAMA-

ZOVS concerning the dispute between DMITRY and his father and becomes very offended at FYODOR PAVLOVICH's behavior. MIUSOV is ultimately exposed as the spreader of the tale of the beheaded martyr supposedly found in the *CHETYI-MINEI.*

ADELAIDA IVANOVNA MIUSOVA. FYODOR PAVLOVICH's first wife. She comes from a wealthy and noble family, and the narrator expresses his feeling that she married beneath herself to show her independence and caprice. She despises FYODOR PAVLOVICH, and the marriage is a farce punctuated with frequent arguments and mutual abuse. She runs away with a poverty-ridden seminarian and teacher, and leaves FYODOR PAVLOVICH with their three year old son DMITRY. She goes to St. Petersburg, where she lives a fully emancipated life and dies of either typhus or hunger depending upon the story one believes.

THE MIUSOVS. A local family of landowners with a noble lineage.

FRANZ MOOR [FRANTS MOR]. The greedy elder son of the GRAF VON MOOR, who conspires against his father and brother. FYODOR PAVLOVICH identifies DMITRY as his most dishonorable son, as FRANZ MOOR from SCHILLER's *THE ROBBERS.*

KARL VON MOOR [KARL FON MOR]. The noble and idealistic son of the GRAF VON MOOR who is wronged by his brother and turns to a life of robbery. FYODOR PAVLOVICH identifies IVAN as his most obedient and devoted son, as KARL VON MOOR from SCHILLER's *THE ROBBERS.* His faith in IVAN proves to be ill-placed as IVAN betrays both his father and DMITRY.

REGIERENDER GRAF VON MOOR. The Ruling Count VON MOOR, the father of FRANZ and KARL VON MOOR in Friedrich SCHILLER's *THE ROBBERS.* FYODOR PAVLOVICH compares himself to the old count and his sons DMITRY and IVAN to FRANZ and KARL VON MOOR respectively.

MORAVIAN BRETHREN [MORAVSKY BRAT]. An evangelical church originating with the Bohemian martyrs Jan Hus (1371-1415) and Jerome of Prague (1370-1416). HERZENSTUBE is described as some kind of a HERRNHUTER or follower of the MORAVIAN BRETHREN by the narrator during his testimony at DMITRY's trial.

MOROZOV. KOLYA claims that he traded MOROZOV a book entitled *A KINSMAN OF MUHAMMAD, OR CURATIVE TOMFOOLERY* for a toy cannon that he brings to entertain the dying ILYUSHA.

MOROZOVA. A merchant's widow and relative of SAMSONOV who rents an apartment to GRUSHENKA as a favor to SAMSONOV.

MUHAMMAD [MAGOMET]. In Arabic "the praised one," a name adopted by the founder of Islam (570-632). SMERDYAKOV notes that if one really believes in the Christian faith, then it would be a sin to embrace the cursed faith of MUHAMMAD.

MUSSYALOVICH. GRUSHENKA's former lover, a Polish officer who abandoned her five years prior to the action of the novel. He is short, unattractive, about fifty, and a civil servant of the twelfth rank who served in Siberia as a veterinarian. He returns after a failure there to meet GRUSHENKA at Mokroe with the intent of marrying her because he thinks she has money. He acts very pompously and teams with his companion VRUBLYOVSKY to cheat at cards. His conduct thoroughly distresses GRUSHENKA and extinguishes all her prior fond feelings for him. She then devotes herself to DMITRY.

"MY LORD AND MY GOD" ["GOSPOD MOY I BOG MOY!"]. As recorded in JOHN 20:28 in the New Testament, the words of the APOSTLE THOMAS upon seeing the wounds in the hands and side of the resurrected CHRIST. See APOSTLE THOMAS.

THE MYSTERIOUS VISITOR [TAINSTVENNY POSETITEL] (MI-KHAIL). A wealthy man of fifty who is active in various charitable organizations. He witnesses ZOSIMA's apology to his servant and then begins to visit him often. After several visits he confesses to ZOSIMA that fourteen years earlier he murdered the woman he loved when she announced that she intended to marry another. He initially justifies his action, but after he marries and fathers three children, the guilt becomes too much to bear, and he states that ZOSIMA's actions have given him the courage to confess. He struggles with himself and his contemplated confession because of his family, and on one occasion he intends to murder ZOSIMA because he cannot face him if he does not go through with the confession. He manages to restrain himself, however, and finally confesses the next day. This done, he becomes very ill and dies shortly thereafter, reconciled with himself and God.

"MYSTERY" ["TAYNA"]. As recorded in the Revelation of St. JOHN 17:5 in the New Testament, one of the names of abomination upon the head of the great harlot, who is portrayed sitting upon a great scarlet beast holding a golden cup of blasphemy and filthiness. The GRAND INQUISI- TOR admits that the church has submitted to the THIRD TEMPTATION OF SATAN by combining with Rome and that it will give mankind the unity it seeks in a comfortable fusion of church and state. He then adds that he and other church officials will sit upon the beast and raise a cup upon which is written "MYSTERY."

NAAFONIL. Neologism derived from Afon, the Russian word for Athos, a prominent ancient Grecian site of monastic activity. When quite drunk, FYODOR PAVLOVICH relates that ZOSIMA once told him that he was a good dancer and that he once danced the NAAFONIL quite regularly. FYODOR PAVLOVICH later admits that he lied.

"NAKED CAME I OUT OF MY MOTHER'S WOMB, NAKED SHALL I RETURN TO THE GROUND, THE LORD GAVE, AND THE LORD HATH TAKEN AWAY. BLESSED BE THE NAME OF THE LORD NOW AND FOREVER" ["NAG VYSHEL IZ CHREVA MATERI, NAG I VOZVRASHCHUS V ZEMLYU, BOG DAL, BOG I VZYAL. BUDI IMYA GOSPODNE BLAGOSLOVENNO OTNYNE I DO VEKA!"]. Distortion of JOB 1:21 in the OLD TESTAMENT, which actually reads: "And said, Naked came I out of my mother's womb, and naked shall I return thither: the Lord gave, and the Lord hath taken away; blessed be the name of the Lord" ("I skazal: nag ya vyshel iz chreva materi moey, nag i vozvra- shchus. Gospod dal, Gospod i vzyal; da budet imya Gospodne blagosloven- no!"). ZOSIMA recalls being taken to church by his mother when he was a child and hearing the story of JOB which he partially quotes.

NAPOLEON. NAPOLEON I Bonaparte (1769-1821), emperor of France following the French Revolution and temporary conqueror of much of Europe. (1) SMERDYAKOV wishes that NAPOLEON's invasion in 1812 would have been successful, because an intelligent nation would then have conquered an ignorant one. His attitude toward his native land and people and his preference for the West effectively demean him. (2) SMERDYA- KOV erroneously observes that NAPOLEON is the father of the current one in France. He has in mind Charles Louis Napoleon Bonaparte (1808- 73), who was actually NAPOLEON's nephew. (3) IVAN AND ALYOSHA agree that they meet not to discuss subjects such as KATERINA IVAN- OVNA, DMITRY, Russia, or NAPOLEON, but rather the eternal questions of life and their belief. Shortly thereafter IVAN recites to

ALYOSHA his "Legend of the GRAND INQUISITOR."(4) After alluding to PUSHKIN's TATYANA, KOLYA insists that this does not mean that he is an advocate of women's emancipation, and he quotes "LES FEMMES TRICOTTENT" and attributes it to NAPOLEON to prove his point.

NAPRAVNIK. Eduard Frantsovich NAPRAVNIK (1839-1916), Russian conductor and composer of opera. FYODOR PAVLOVICH excuses his buffoonery to ZOSIMA and then cites an example of his behavior. He relates that in a conversation with a district police captain, in Russian *ispravnik,* he made a pun by asking him to be their NAPRAVNIK. The man responds sullenly, fails to see the humor, and the whole affair is ruined.

NASTASYA PETROVNA. A woman mentioned by the mentally deficient ARINA PETROVNA SNEGIRYOVA.

NASTASYUSHKA. A woman who comes to see ZOSIMA. She has just buried her three year old son ALEKSEY and is going from monastery to monastery to pray. She has buried three other sons too and in her grief asks her husband NIKITUSHKA to permit her to go on a pilgrimage. ZOSIMA comforts her, assures her that ALEKSEY is an angel, and counsels her to return to her husband.

NASTYA. The eight year old daughter of the doctor's wife who lives next to KRASOTKINA.

NATASHA (MARYA). KOLYA speaks with one of the market women in the street and condescendingly refers to her as NATASHA. She informs him that her name is MARYA.

NAZAR IVANOVICH. The old doorman at the MOROZOVA house. FENYA asks him not to let DMITRY in again.

PROKHOR IVANOVICH NAZARIEV. A local merchant who serves on the jury during DMITRY's trial.

NEFEDOV. The justice of the peace who questions and then punishes KOLYA for his escapade with a goose. KOLYA had been with VISHNYAKOV when the latter ran over a goose's neck with a wagon wheel while it was eating oats.

NEKRASOV. Nikolay Alekseevich NEKRASOV (1821-78), Russian poet and editor prominent in radical literature. His poetry exhibits a concern for moral social values and liberal ideals. He edited both *THE CONTEMPO-RARY* and *Fatherland Notes*. In discussing man's inhumanity to man IVAN notes that NEKRASOV wrote a poem in which a horse is beaten "ABOUT HIS MEEK EYES" with a whip. He adds that this is a peculiarly Russian from of inhumanity.

NIKOLAY PARFENOVICH NELYUDOV (NIKOLAY PARFENYCH). A young police investigator recently arrived from St. Petersburg. He is among the group that arrests DMITRY at Mokroe, and it is he that conducts the interrogation.

NIKITUSHKA. NASTASYUSHKA's husband. He permits her to go on a pilgrimage to pray and recover following the death of their fourth son ALEKSEY.

FATHER NIKOLAY. The superior of the monastery.

NIKOLAY. See NIKOLAY IVANOV KRASOTKIN.

NIKOLAY ILYICH. See NIKOLAY ILYICH SNEGIRYOV.

NIKOLAY PARFENYCH. See NIKOLAY PARFENOVICH NELYU-DOV.

NINA NIKOLAEVNA (NINOCHKA). SNEGIRYOV's twenty year old daughter who suffers from a hump back and withered legs.

NINOCHKA. See NINA NIKOLAEVNA.

"NO SOCIAL ORGANIZATION CAN OR OUGHT TO ASSUME POWER OVER THE CIVIL AND POLITICAL RIGHTS OF ITS MEMBERS" ["NI ODIN OBSHCHESTVENNY SOYUZ NE MOZHET I NE DOLZHEN PRISVOIVAT SEBE VLAST—RASPORYAZHATS-YA GRAZHDANSKIMI I POLITICHESKIMI PRAVAMI SVOIKH CHLENOV"]. IOSIF, PAISY, and IVAN discuss IVAN's article on ecclesiastical and civil courts in which he objects to statements like the above taken from a book and author that remain nameless. IVAN's point of view is that church and state cannot be separate and that the ecclesiastical must encompass all of the civil. IVAN's unnamed adversary is likely Mikhail Ivanovich Gorchakov (b. 1838), professor of church law at St. Petersburg University. The quotation is a slightly distorted citation from his "Scientific Elaboration of Ecclesiastical Judicial Law" ("Nauchnaya postanovka tserkovno-sudnogo prava") printed in *A Collection of Public Knowledge, Vol. II (Sbornik gosudarstvennogo znania)* in 1875.

NOSOV. In discussing his claim to be the MAKSIMOV mentioned in GOGOL'S *DEAD SOULS*, MAKSIMOV notes that GOGOL wrote allegorically and that his names too were allegorical. As an example he states that NOZDRYOV was really NOSOV. His statement is a pun since NOZDRYOV refers to nostrils and NOSOV to nose.

NOTRE DAME DE PARIS. Commonly called *The Hunchback of Notre Dame*, a novel written by Victor HUGO in 1831. The novel deals with the defense of a gypsy dancer Esmerelda by Quasimodo, the hunchback bellringer of Notre Dame, who transcends his limitations and achieves a kind of greatness. In prefacing his "Legend of the GRAND INQUISITOR" IVAN observes that including heavenly figures in literature was common in the sixteenth century. He also cites the example of HUGO's *NOTRE DAME DE PARIS*, in which during the reign of LOUIS XI the birth of the heir to the throne was celebrated by a play *LE BON JUGEMENT DE LA TRES SAINTE ET GRACIEUSE VIERGE MARIE*, in which MARIE herself appears and offers judgment. There appears to be no such play.

"NOW LETTEST THOU DEPART" ["NYNE OTPUSHCHAESHI"]. Partial quotation from LUKE 2:29 in the New Testament. The passage deals with Simeon, a devout and just man, who was promised that he would not die until he had seen the CHRIST. After holding the baby Jesus he expresses thanks to God and then requests "NOW LETTEST THOU thy servant DEPART in peace, according to thy word." Upon hearing of the death of ADELAIDA IVANOVNA, FYODOR PAVLOVICH, quite drunk, reportedly races gleefully through the streets shouting these words.

NOZDRYOV. A character in Nikolay GOGOL's *DEAD SOULS* who is characterized by his coarse gaiety, bullying, and drinking. (1) KALGANOV complains that MAKSIMOV insists that he is the MAKSIMOV in *DEAD SOULS* who was beaten by NOZDRYOV. (2) In discussing his claim to be the MAKSIMOV of *DEAD SOULS*, MAKSIMOV observes that GOGOL did everything allegorically and that the names of his characters are allegorical. As an example he insists that NOZDRYOV was really NOSOV. (3) See "OH, TROYKA, BIRD-LIKE TROYKA, WHO INVENTED YOU!"

"OH, CHILDREN, CHILDREN, HOW DANGEROUS ARE YOUR YEARS" ["OKH, DETI, DETI, KAK OPASNY VASHI LETA"]. The first line (in the original the *okh* is simply *o*) of "The Rooster, the Cat and the Mouse" ("Petukh, kot i myshonok"), a fable published by Ivan Ivanovich Dmitriev (1760-1837) in 1802. The fable relates the tale of a young mouse that goes into the world most anxious to prove his manhood. He encounters a soft, indulgent cat, which he quickly considers a friend, and a ferocious-looking rooster that appears to be an enemy. The mouse's mother corrects his perceptions and warns him against making hasty judgments by appearances. When NASTYA and KOSTYA indicate that they will cry if KOLYA leaves them alone, he quotes these words to them. It is likely that the author intends that the words reflect ironically upon KOLYA himself, whose awakening years find him dabbling in socialism and Western thought and making incorrect perceptions.

"OH, TROYKA, BIRD-LIKE TROYKA, WHO INVENTED YOU!" ["AKH, TROYKA, PTITSA TROYKA, KTO TEBYA VYDUMAL!"]. Slight distortion (in the original the "OH" is rendered "ekh" rather than "AKH") of words at the conclusion of Nikolay GOGOL's *DEAD SOULS*. As CHICHIKOV rides away into the Russian vastness in a troyka, the author wonders rhetorically who could have invented such a means of transport other than an intelligent people in a land that takes things seriously. In his concluding remarks to the jury at DMITRY's trial the prosecutor IPPOLIT KIRILLOVICH reflects upon Russia's problems and alludes to the conclusion of *DEAD SOULS* with the above quote. He ponders aloud which direction the troyka of Russia will take, especially since it contains such types as SOBAKEVICH, NOZDRYOV, and CHICHIKOV.

"OH, YOU ATTIC, MY ATTIC" ["AKH, VY SENI, MOI SENI"]. Folk song that relates the involvement of a young woman with a handsome young man against the wishes of her father. As GRUSHENKA prepares to dance at Mokroe the chorus chimes in with this song.

OLD TESTAMENT [VETKHY ZAVET]. A collection of thirty nine books considered as Scripture by Jews and Christians. The books outline the religious history of the world from the creation of ADAM to the prophets of Israel before the coming of CHRIST. IVAN observes prior to his reciting "The Legend of the GRAND INQUISITOR" that in the years prior to PETER, mystery plays based upon the OLD TESTAMENT were common.

OLGA MIKHAYLOVNA. MIKHAIL MAKAROVICH MAKAROV's daughter.

OLSUFIEV. In discussing the likelihood that DMITRY killed his father, the prosecutor refers to the person who murdered the merchant OLSUFIEV. He notes that this person, like DMITRY, openly flaunted the money after the crime.

ONE HUNDRED FOUR SACRED STORIES OF THE OLD AND NEW TESTAMENT [STO CHETYRE SVYASHCHENNYE ISTORII VETKHOGO I NOVOGO ZAVETA]. A book edited by G. Gibner from which Dostoevsky learned to read. ZOSIMA indicates that he learned to read using this book.

ONEGIN. Yevgeny ONEGIN, the proud BYRONIC hero of Aleksandr PUSHKIN's novel of the same name. He is fashionably bored and is incapable of having a positive relationship with anyone. See BELINSKY (1).

ONEGIN. Yevgeny ONEGIN, a novel in verse published by Aleksandr PUSHKIN in 1831. The novel chronicles TATYANA's infatuation with ONEGIN, his pompous rejection of her, his killing a friend in a duel, his subsequent travels, and TATYANA's maturation and turnabout rejection of him. When KOLYA mentions TATYANA, ALYOSHA notes that he has obviously read PUSHKIN, specifically *ONEGIN.*

OPHELIA [OFELIA]. In William SHAKESPEARE's *HAMLET* the daughter of POLONIUS, who is romantically linked with HAMLET. At her father's request she spurns the romance. After HAMLET kills her father, OPHELIA goes mad and later drowns herself from grief and rejection. See SHAKESPEARE.

OTHELLO [OTELLO]. The central character of *OTHELLO, the Moor of Venice,* a tragedy written by William SHAKESPEARE about 1604. OTHELLO strangles his love Desdemona when he suspects her of infidelity and then commits suicide when he learns that she is innocent. See "OTHELLO IS NOT JEALOUS, HE IS TRUSTING."

"OTHELLO IS NOT JEALOUS, HE IS TRUSTING" ["OTELLO NE REVNIV, ON DOVERCHIV"]. Distortion of a remark by PUSHKIN in his *Table-talk* (1830s) to the effect that "Othello by nature is not jealous—on the contrary, he is trusting" ("Otello ot prirody ne revniv—naprotiv: on doverchiv"). While discussing DMITRY's jealousy with respect to GRU-SHENKA, the narrator digresses to discuss OTHELLO. He quotes PUSHKIN to the effect that OTHELLO is not a jealous person and praises the insight. He adds that OTHELLO would never spy on another or stoop to the levels that DMITRY does.

FATHER PAISY. A monk at the monastery. He is young, learned, and in poor health.

GENERAL PAKHATOV. RAKITIN observes that the monastery table is set more luxuriously for MIUSOV and the KARAMAZOVS than for anyone since the visit of GENERAL PAKHATOV.

PARABLE OF LAZARUS AND THE RICH MAN [PRITCHA O BOGATOM I LAZARE]. See LAZARUS.

PATER SERAPHICUS. Angelic Father, designation of spiritual stature and devotion applied to St. Francis of Assisi (1182-1226), who is purported to have seen an angel and received the crucifixion wounds of CHRIST. The term also appears in the last scene of the second part of *Faust*, in which PATER SERAPHICUS is one of three angelic figures who meet FAUST upon his death. After reciting his "Legend of the GRAND INQUISITOR" to ALYOSHA, IVAN sends him to see ZOSIMA, whom he dubs PATER SERAPHICUS.

PAVEL FYODOROVICH. See PAVEL FYODOROVICH SMERDYA-KOV.

"PENAL AND CIVIL PROSECUTION AUTHORITY MUST NOT BELONG TO THE CHURCH AND IS INCONSISTENT WITH THE CHURCH'S ROLE AS A DIVINE ESTABLISHMENT AND AS A PEOPLE GATHERED TOGETHER FOR RELIGIOUS PURPOSES" ["UGOLOVNAYA I SUDNO-GRAZHDANSKAYA VLAST NE DOL-ZHNA PRINADLEZHAT TSERKVI I NESOVMESTIMA S PRIRO-DOY YEYO I KAK BOZHESTVENNOGO USTANOVLENIA I KAK SOYUZA LYUDEY DLYA RELIGIOZNYKH TSELEY"]. See "NO SOCIAL ORGANIZATION CAN OR OUGHT TO ASSUME POWER OVER THE CIVIL AND POLITICAL RIGHTS OF ITS MEMBERS."

PEREZVON. KOLYA's dog. As an act of charity KOLYA brings it to the sick ILYUSHA, who is depressed over the loss of a dog he calls ZHUCHKA. The dogs are one and the same.

PYOTR ILYICH PERKHOTIN. The civil servant with whom DMITRY leaves his pistols as a pledge in exchange for ten rubles. When DMITRY returns covered with blood and with a lot of money, PYOTR ILYICH helps to clean him up and returns his pistols. After DMITRY leaves for Mokroe, PYOTR ILYICH becomes troubled over the situation and consults KHOKHLAKOVA, who admits that she did not give DMITRY any money. He then visits the district police captain MAKAROV and the two discuss the murder.

PETER [PYOTR]. PETER I the Great (1672-1725), who ruled Russia 1689-1725. He is noted for building a new capital at St. Petersburg and for turning Russia to the West to obtain the technical skills to enter Modern European life. Prior to reciting his "Legend of the GRAND INQUISI-TOR," IVAN notes that in the years before PETER, mystery plays based upon the OLD TESTAMENT were common.

PETROV. In discussing his claim to be the MAKSIMOV in *DEAD SOULS*, MAKSIMOV observes that GOGOL wrote in allegory and that the names of his characters are allegorical. He insists, however, that the FENARDI in *DEAD SOULS* was really FENARDI, only not an Italian, but rather a Russian named PETROV.

PETRUSHA. See PYOTR FOMICH KALGANOV.

PHAON [FAON]. According to legend a handsome seaman who rejected the love of SAPPHO and thereby caused her to throw herself into the sea. See "YOU ARE SAPPHO, I PHAON, THIS I DO NOT QUESTION."

PHOEBUS [FEB, FEB ZLATOKUDRY]. In Greek mythology a special name for Apollo, the god of light. (1) DMITRY jokingly asks PERKHOTIN to visit KHOKHLAKOVA and ask her if she gave him the 3000 rubles he requested. He encourages PERKHOTIN to visit as soon as the sun, the eternally young PHOEBUS, rises. (2) When PERKHOTIN expresses concern that DMITRY may commit suicide, DMITRY responds that he loves life, PHOEBUS, and its burning light, and wants to live very much. (3) In the PLOTNIKOVS' shop DMITRY encourages the boy MISHA to drink some champagne in honor of PHOEBUS, and he again reaffirms his love for life. (4) As DMITRY hurries to Mokroe at night to encounter GRUSHENKA and her former lover, he ponders what he will do and how he will act toward them with the first morning beams of PHOEBUS. (5) Following his interrogation DMITRY gazes into the rain and recalls that he intended to commit suicide upon the first appearance of PHOEBUS.

PIERROT [PIERO]. The clown in traditional comedy. (1) MIUSOV decides that it is beneath him to be put out with such a person as FYODOR PAVLOVICH, and he decides to prove to all that he is quite unlike such an AESOP, buffoon, and PIERROT. (2) At his trial DMITRY refers to his father as an AESOP and PIERROT and admits that he was cruel to him.

PIRON. Alexis PIRON (1689-1773), French poet and dramatist. (1) FYODOR PAVLOVICH drunkenly mentions that ZOSIMA has some wit and that one sees a bit of PIRON in him. (2) See BOILEAU. (3) SEE "CI-GIT PIRON QUI NE FUT RIEN//PAS MEME ACADEMICIEN."

TRIFON BORISYCH PLASTUNOV. The owner of an inn in Mokroe at which GRUSHENKA, her former lover MUSSYALOVICH, and DMITRY confront one another. He is quite greedy and after DMITRY's trial he literally dismantles his inn looking for the 1500 rubles that DMITRY supposedly had with him.

PLATON. Pyotr Yegorovich Levshin (1737-1812), metropolitan of Moscow 1775-1812 and a prolific writer of texts, saints lives, and sermons. See DIDEROT (1).

THE PLOTNIKOVS. The owners of the most prominent grocery store in the town founded by Pavel Ivanovich PLOTNIKOV. (1) DMITRY buys his supplies at this store on both occasions that he holds lavish parties at Mokroe. (2) When DMITRY tries to repay a ten ruble debt to PERKHO-TIN with a hundred ruble note, PERKHOTIN sends his servant boy MISHA to the PLOTNIKOV's store for change.

PODVYSOTSKY. (1) When DMITRY plays cards with the Poles MUS-SYALOVICH and VRUBLYOVSKY at Mokroe, an anecdote is related about a Pan PODVYSOTSKY who won a million dollar bank gambling in Warsaw. (2) Following GRUSHENKA's break with the Poles, DMITRY disgustedly refers to them as PODVYSOTSKY as he invites them to come watch them dance.

YEFIM PETROVICH POLENOV. The local master of the nobility who inherits the bulk of the GENERAL'S WIFE's fortune upon her death. A noble and humane man, he assumes the care of IVAN and ALYOSHA when it becomes clear that FYODOR PAVLOVICH will not. He becomes especially fond of ALYOSHA and raises him in his family.

POLONIUS [POLONY]. The lord chamberlain in William SHAKE-SPEARE's *HAMLET, Prince of Denmark.* He is a kindly but pompous person, the father of OPHELIA, and is murdered by HAMLET while eavesdropping. When IVAN comments that if the devil does not exist then man created him in his own image, ALYOSHA counters that God must then have been created in the same way. IVAN praises his ability to turn words much like POLONIUS in *HAMLET.* The reference could be to POLONIUS' assessment of HAMLET delivered to OPHELIA in which he cautions her not to believe the words of the clever HAMLET.

PORFIRY. A monk who serves ZOSIMA.

POTYOMKIN. Prince Grigory Aleksandrovich POTYOMKIN (1739-91), statesman and favorite of CATHERINE the Great. He served in various important capacities and supervised the annexation of the Crimea to Russia. See DIDEROT (1).

PRODIGAL SON [BLUDNY SYN]. As recorded in LUKE 15:11-32 in the New Testament, the central figure of a parable of the same name who leaves home, wastes his inheritance, and then returns home humbly to his father, who rejoices at his return. In IVAN's anecdote about RICHARD he asserts that the seven year old boy was not fed or clothed and often hungered after the swine's food, just like the PRODIGAL SON in the BIBLE.

PROKHOR. NAZAR IVANOVICH's twenty year old relative who watches the MOROZOVA house and informs DMITRY that GRUSHEN-KA has gone to Mokroe to meet her officer and former lover.

PROKHOROVNA. A grieving mother who comes to ZOSIMA for counsel. After her son VASENKA goes to Siberia, he stops writing home and causes his mother much concern. A friend STEPANIDA ILYINI-SHNA advises her to have prayers said for him in church as if he were dead. ZOSIMA insists that this is inappropriate and suggests that she should instead appeal to the Mother of God. He promises PROKHOROVNA that she will either see her son or receive a letter.

PROKHORYCH. SAMSONOV's elderly servant is on her way to see a man named PROKHORYCH when she is stopped by DMITRY and asked the whereabouts of GRUSHENKA.

"PROMPTNESS IS THE POLITENESS OF KINGS" ["TOCHNOST EST VEZHLIVOST KOROLEY"]. Popular saying attributed to King

Louis XVIII, who ruled France 1814-24. The original statement was "L'exactitude est la politesse des rois." When FYODOR PAVLOVICH arrives at the monastery to let ZOSIMA arbitrate his dispute with DMITRY, he uses these words to observe that he is on time whereas DMITRY is late.

PROSERPINA [PROZERPINA]. Also Persephone, in Greek mythology the wife of Hades and queen of the underworld. In his explanation to ALYOSHA, DMITRY quotes three verses of a poem which contains an allusion to PROSERPINA. See "WILD AND FEARFUL IN HIS CAVE//HID THE NAKED TROGLODYTE."

PROUDHON [PRUDON]. Pierre Joseph PROUDHON (1809-65), French socialist and anarchist. He was an ardent reformer and was very critical of private property, church, and state. PYOTR ALEKSANDROVICH MIU-SOV is said to have known PROUDHON personally.

PSALTER [PSALTYR]. The Book of Psalms in the OLD TESTAMENT authored largely by King David. Because of ZOSIMA's monastic rank those who attend him while his body lies in state read the BIBLE rather than the PSALTER.

PUSHKIN. Aleksandr Sergeevich PUSHKIN (1799-1837), the leading Russian writer of his age, who is widely regarded as the father of modern Russian literature. (1) While discussing DMITRY's passion and his captivation with GRUSHENKA's beauty, RAKITIN refers to PUSHKIN as the poet of women's feet and notes that while some like PUSHKIN sing their praises, others like DMITRY are overcome by them. PUSHKIN comments on women's feet in "City of Splendor, City of Need" ("Gorod pyshny, gorod bedny") written in 1828 and in *Yevgeny ONEGIN.* (2) See "OTHELLO IS NOT JEALOUS, HE IS TRUSTING." (3) ALYOSHA observes that since KOLYA mentioned TATYANA, he has obviously read PUSHKIN and specifically *ONEGIN.* (4) RAKITIN writes some verse about KHOKHLAKOVA's sore leg, and when PERKHOTIN criticizes it, he retorts that people want to build a monument to PUSHKIN because of women's legs and feet. (5) When RAKITIN writes verse about KHOKHLA-KOVA's sore leg, he claims it is better than PUSHKIN's verse on the subject because he has infused social consciousness into comic verse. (6) RAKITIN mentions PUSHKIN in his verse about KHOKHLAKOVA's sore leg.

PYOTR. The servant who is accused of murdering the woman that THE MYSTERIOUS VISITOR killed. He is arrested but dies of a fever before he can be tried.

PYOTR ILYICH. See PYOTR ILYICH PERKHOTIN.

RACHEL [RAKHIL]. As recorded in Genesis 29 in the OLD TESTA-
MENT, the younger of the daughters of LABAN, who married JACOB and
bore him JOSEPH and BENJAMIN. See "RACHEL WEEPING FOR
HER CHILDREN, AND WOULD NOT BE COMFORTED, BECAUSE
THEY ARE NOT."

**"RACHEL WEEPING FOR HER CHILDREN, AND WOULD NOT BE
COMFORTED, BECAUSE THEY ARE NOT" ["RAKHIL PLACHET
O DETYAKH SVOIKH I NE MOZHET UTESHITSYA, POTOMU
CHTO IKH NET"].** Slightly adjusted version of the prophecy of Jeremiah,
recorded in Jeremiah 31:15 in the OLD TESTAMENT, as found in
Matthew 2:18 in the New Testament. Matthew 2:18 reads "RACHEL
WEEPING FOR HER CHILDREN, AND WOULD NOT BE COM-
FORTED, BECAUSE THEY ARE NOT" ("RAKHIL PLACHET O
DETYAKH SVOIKH I NE MOZHET UTESHITSYA, ibo IKH NET"),
and Jeremiah 31:15 reads "Rahel (a variant of RACHEL) WEEPING FOR
HER CHILDREN, refused to BE COMFORTED for her children,
BECAUSE THEY ARE NOT" ("RAKHIL PLACHET O DETYAKH
SVOIKH I NE khochet UTESHITSYA o detyakh svoikh, ibo IKH NET").
The New Testament verse reports the fulfillment of a prophecy of grief when
King Herod slew all the children in Bethlehem under the age of two in an
attempt to slay the CHRIST child, who he feared would become king.
ZOSIMA quotes these words of Scripture while speaking with NASTAS-
YUSHKA, who has just buried her fourth son.

**MIKHAIL OSIPOVICH RAKITIN (MISHA, MIKHAIL, MIKHAIL
OSIPOVICH, RAKITKA, RAKITUSHKA, MIKHAIL IVANOVICH).**
GRUSHENKA's cousin, a twenty two year old seminarian and aspiring
theologian. He is tall, fresh-looking, maintains a look of propriety, and is
quite egocentric. He is a divided soul capable of both deeply religious
thinking and socialist leanings, and many of KOLYA's ideas come from
him. When he discovers ALYOSHA's great distress over ZOSIMA's
stinking body, he entices him to come with him to visit GRUSHENKA. He
delivers ALYOSHA to her because he is anxious to see the fall of a saintly
figure and to get the twenty five rubles she promised him for ALYOSHA.
He commences to visit KHOKHLAKOVA regularly until a row with
PERKHOTIN results in his dismissal. His visits are prompted by the hope
of marrying her and gaining control of her money in order to establish

himself in St. Petersburg and make a career as a critic. He intends to write a story about DMITRY to launch his career, and when an article appears in *RUMORS* on the KARAMAZOV affair with allusions to KHOKHLA-KOVA, she becomes very upset. The fact that he has written a brochure on ZOSIMA full of deeply religious thoughts and concepts emphasizes his divided personality.

RAKITKA. See MIKHAIL OSIPOVICH RAKITIN.

RAKITUSHKA. See MIKHAIL OSIPOVICH RAKITIN.

REBEKAH [REVEKKA]. As recorded in Genesis 22-28 in the OLD TESTAMENT, the daughter of Bethuel and the sister of LABAN who was given to ISAAC in marriage in exchange for fourteen years of service. She bore him JACOB and Esau and was instrumental in obtaining the birthright blessing for JACOB. ZOSIMA insists that the Orthodox heart responds with understanding to the Scriptures, and among other examples he cites the account of ISAAC and REBEKAH.

RICHARD [RISHAR]. IVAN relates the account of a Swiss child named RICHARD which he supposedly took from a French pamphlet. At age six the child is given to some Swiss shepherds who refuse to feed and clothe him and who put him to work at age seven to herd the sheep. IVAN compares this phase of his life to that of the PRODIGAL SON. RICHARD begins to steal and drink, and finally murders a man that he robbed. After his arrest he is beset by clergy and benefactors who convert him to religion, make him realize his baseness, and then help him to go willingly to the guillotine.

THE ROBBERS [RAZBOYNIKI]. Die Räuber, a tragedy written by Friedrich SCHILLER in 1781. The play records the perfidy of a scheming son, FRANZ MOOR, who maligns his brother KARL in an attempt to turn his father against him and have him disinherited. Frustrated with these developments and with mankind in general, KARL turns to crime but maintains a vestige of virtue and commitment to ideals, and he ultimately comes to understand that vengeance was not his province. FRANZ finally commits suicide, and his father dies after he learns of the life that KARL has been leading. KARL kills the woman devoted to him to demonstrate his allegiance to his robber band and then determines to surrender to the authorities. (1) FYODOR PAVLOVICH identifies IVAN as KARL VON MOOR, DMITRY as FRANZ MOOR, and himself as REGIERENDER GRAF VON MOOR from SCHILLER's *THE ROBBERS*. (2) When Father Superior NIKOLAY bows down to FYODOR PAVLOVICH and humbly thanks him for his rather rude criticism, FYODOR PAVLOVICH responds by saying that the gesture is mere sanctimoniousness, and he insists that it is just like the phrase "A KISS ON THE LIPS AND A KNIFE IN THE HEART" from SCHILLER's *THE ROBBERS*.

RUMORS [SLUKHI]. Probably the short-lived St. Petersburg newspaper *Molva (Rumor)* published 1879-81. (1) KHOKHLAKOVA informs AL-YOSHA that she has read about the murder of FYODOR PAVLOVICH and of her own connection in *RUMORS*, which started publication only that year. She adds that she loves rumors so much that she subscribed. (2) ALYOSHA relates to DMITRY that RAKITIN has revenged himself upon KHOKHLAKOVA by sending an article to *RUMORS*.

SABANEEV. When an unknown man confronts KOLYA about some improper activity, the brash KOLYA asks him if he knows SABANEEV, and receiving a negative response, he then simply walks away. The quick-thinking boy makes up the name.

MARQUIS DE SADE [MARKIZ DE SAD]. Donatien Alphonse François DE SADE (1740-1814), a prolific French writer who spent a good deal of his life in prison for his sexual escapades and for writing licentious books. His name has become synonimous with torturing the object of love and with depravity. FYODOR PAVLOVICH, after noting that he hates the peasants, mentions that in the vicinity of Mokroe they enjoy letting the young men violate the girls. It is customary for the men to return the next day and ask for the hand of the girls in marriage. FYODOR PAVLOVICH disgustedly refers to them all as MARQUIS DE SADE.

KUZMA KUZMICH SAMSONOV (KUZMA, KUMZA KUZMICH). A vindictive, cold, mocking, and debauched merchant who brings GRU-SHENKA to the city when she is eighteen and maintains her in his home. Even though he dominates his sons and many others, he becomes quite dependent upon GRUSHENKA, though he does not treat her very generously. When DMITRY offers to sell him his interest in the Chermash-nya woods, he refuses and sends him on a hopeless visit to LYAGAVY in an effort to demean him. He dies following DMITRY's trial after wishing GRUSHENKA the very best.

SAPPHO [SAFO]. Greek poetess who lived between 630 and 570 B.C. and who is widely regarded as the greatest poetess of antiquity. Despite the sentiments expressed in her poetry and testimonies to the contrary, legend involves her in lesbianism. Legend also claims that she cast herself into the sea after being rejected by a handsome seaman named PHAON. See "YOU ARE SAPPHO, I PHAON, THIS I DO NOT QUESTION."

SARAH [SARRA]. As recorded in Genesis 12-23 in the OLD TESTAMENT, the wife of ABRAHAM and the mother of ISAAC. ZOSIMA states that the Scriptures can be received by the Orthodox heart with understanding, and among other examples he cites the story of ABRAHAM and SARAH.

"SATANA SUM ET NIHIL HUMANUM A ME ALIENUM PUTO." "I am Satan and nothing human is strange to me," adaptation of a line from "The Self-Tormentor" ("Heauton Timorumenos"), a comedy written by the Roman comic poet Terence (ca. 195-159 B.C.) in 163 B.C. The original reads "Homo sum, humani nihil a me alienum puto" ("I am a man and nothing human is strange to me"). IVAN's devil insists that it is not strange at all that he should become embodied on occasion, and he quotes these lines to illustrate his point.

SAUL [SAVL]. The Jewish name of the apostle Paul. who as a Pharisee and member of the Sanhedrin actively persecuted the new Christian movement, until CHRIST appeared to him and wrought his conversion. Much of his activity is recorded in the ACTS OF THE APOSTLES, and his epistles comprise much of the New Testament. ZOSIMA refers to the conversion of SAUL as recorded in the ACTS OF THE APOSTLES and praises its effect on the people.

SCHILLER [SHILLER]. Johann Christoph Friedrich von SCHILLER (1759-1805), German dramatist, poet, and historian noted for his romantic idealism. (1) See *THE ROBBERS.* (2) When DMITRY explains himself at length to ALYOSHA in the form of a literary and self-exacerbating confession, he begins by citing SCHILLER's "AN DIE FREUDE." (3) IVAN quotes "DEN DANK, DAME, BEGEHR ICH NICHT" and demonstrates to ALYOSHA that he can read SCHILLER to the point of memorization. ALYOSHA had never considered IVAN capable of this. (4) In his summation to the jury at DMITRY's trial the prosecutor IPPOLIT KIRILLOVICH characterizes Russians both as devotees of the enlightenment of SCHILLER and also as rowdy frequenters of pubs. (5) In his summation to the jury at DMITRY's trial FETYUKOVICH castigates the prosecutor IPPOLIT KIRILLOVICH for laughing at DMITRY's love of SCHILLER and of the beautiful and sublime.

ALEKSANDR KARLOVICH VON SCHMIDT [FON SHMIDT]. The long-since deceased former owner of the house and land adjoining the property of FYODOR PAVLOVICH.

GOVERNOR SCHULZ [SHULTS]. FYODOR PAVLOVICH insists that ZOSIMA does not believe in God and that he admits this to intelligent people. He adds that ZOSIMA does believe in something, but he does not know what, and that he admits this to GOVERNOR SCHULZ.

SECOND COMING [VTOROE PRISHESTVIE]. The SECOND COMING of CHRIST prior to His reign upon the earth, an integral teaching of Christianity. The SECOND COMING is alluded to throughout the BIBLE and is to occur upon the destruction of the earth. MIUSOV complains that the union of church and state that IVAN and others discuss is an ideal that cannot be realized until the SECOND COMING.

SELIVESTR. See SILVESTR.

SEMYON. A peasant at Mokroe.

SHAKESPEARE [SHEKSPIR]. William SHAKESPEARE (1564-1616), the most eminent of English dramatists. In wondering how FYODOR PAVLOVICH's first wife could have ever married such a person, the narrator recalls the example of a woman who loved a gentleman for some time and could have married him in a perfectly normal manner but who suddenly imagined all kinds of barriers. She ultimately jumps to her death into a river out of her own caprice in order to be like SHAKESPEARE's OPHELIA.

SHCHEDRIN. Penname of Mikhail Yevgrafovich Saltykov (1826-89), Russian journalist, novelist, satirist, and political activist. KHOKHLAKO-VA insists to DMITRY that she is no stranger to the women's question and has even written SHCHEDRIN, who told her much about the status and significance of women.

"SHE LOVED MUCH" ["VOZLYUBILA MNOGO"]. Profanation of LUKE 7:47 in the New Testament. Verses 36-50 of the chapter record the story of a woman who washed CHRIST's feet with tears and ointment and wiped them with her hair in an act of reverence and humility as she sought forgiveness for her sins. CHRIST forgave her and commented that "SHE LOVED MUCH." FYODOR PAVLOVICH defends GRUSHENKA to a group of monks by saying that she is perhaps better than they and that even though she fell in her youth, "SHE LOVED MUCH" and because of that will be forgiven by CHRIST. IOSIF counters that CHRIST does not forgive because of that kind of love. It is significant that GRUSHENKA does come to love much in a more sisterly and self-sacrificial way and develops beyond what IOSIF perceives.

SHKVORNEV. See KUVSHINNIKOV.

MAVRIKY MAVRIKIEVICH SHMERTSOV (MAVRIKY MAVRI-KICH). A district police officer who is dispatched to Mokroe to watch DMITRY until other officials come to arrest him.

"SHOULD BE FULFILLED" ["VOSPOLNIT CHISLO"]. As recorded in The Revelation of St. John 6:9-11 in the New Testament, the souls of those martyred for God appeal to Him for vengeance. They are told to wait "until their fellowservants also and their brethren, that should be killed as they were, *SHOULD BE FULFILLED."* The GRAND INQUISITOR challenges CHRIST's right to judge him adversely because he has made millions happy and has suffered for them. He observes that he too has been in the wilderness, hungered, and prepared to become one of the chosen ones numbered among those that "SHOULD BE FULFILLED."

SHUSHERA. The widow of a general who attends DMITRY's trial.

"S'IL N'EXISTAIT PAS DIEU IL FAUDRAIT L'INVENTER." "If God did not exist it would be necessary to invent him," slight distortion of a statement made by VOLTAIRE in his "Epîtres XCVI. A l'Auteur du Livre des Trois Imposteurs" ("Epistle XCVI. To the Author of the Book About Three Imposters"), a verse diatribe written in 1770 against the spurious *Traité des Trois Imposteurs (The Treaty of the Three Imposters).* The original reads "Si Dieu n'existait pas, il faudrait l'inventer" with no appreciable change in the English translation. In discussing the existence of God with ALYOSHA, IVAN observes that there was an eighteenth century sinner who made the above comment.

SILENUS [SILEN]. Mythological diety usually viewed as the teacher of Dionysus and Bacchus. He is usually portrayed as drunk and riding on an ass with the help of other Satyrs. See "SILENUS WITH HIS ROSY FACE//UPON HIS STUMBLING ASS."

"SILENUS WITH HIS ROSY FACE//UPON HIS STUMBLING ASS"
["I SILEN RUMYANOROZY//NA SPOTKNUVSHEMSYA OSLE"].
The concluding couplet of the poem "Bas-relief" ("Barelief"), written by
Apollon Nikolaevich Maykov (1821-97) in 1842. The poem depicts the
author studying a bas-relief on which, among other signs of antiquity, is
depicted SILENUS upon his ass. As DMITRY begins his explanation to
ALYOSHA, he insists that he is not drunk and not SILENUS and quotes
these lines.

SILVESTR (SELIVESTR). An ascetic living in a far northern monastery
who sends a monk to visit with ZOSIMA.

SKOPTSY. A small secret offshoot of the Russian Orthodox Church that
practiced castration in order to renounce the body. (1) When SMERDYA-
KOV returns from his training in Moscow as a cook, he looks much older
than his twenty four years, has a yellow pallor, and looks rather like a
member of the SKOPTSY. (2) IVAN disgustedly notes that SMERDYA-
KOV has the haggard, wasted look of a member of the SKOPTSY. (3) On
his first visit to SMERDYAKOV following the murder of FYODOR
PAVLOVICH, IVAN notices SMERDYAKOV's dry, SKOPTSY-like
face.

SLOVOERSOV. Surname derived from the practice of adding an "s" to the
end of words in an attempt to convey respect and subservience. See
NIKOLAY ILYICH SNEGIRYOV.

SMARAGDOV. Sergey Nikolaevich SMARAGDOV (d. 1871), teacher of
history and geography at various St. Petersburg schools. (1) See *WORLD
HISTORY.* (2) When KOLYA stumps his teacher DARDANELOV with
the question of who founded Troy, all the students know that they must
consult SMARAGDOV's text to find the answer and that only KOLYA has
a copy. KARTASHOV steals a peek at the book and then proudly answers
the question about Troy at ILYUSHA's house.

PAVEL FYODOROVICH SMERDYAKOV. The son of LIZAVETA
SMERDYASHCHAYA and, according to rumor, FYODOR PAVLO-
VICH, from whom is derived his patronymic. Upon the death of his mother
he is raised by GRIGORY and becomes FYODOR PAVLOVICH's
servant. He had been sent to Moscow to be trained as a cook, and when he
returns he looks much older than his twenty four years, has yellowed, and
has the look of a member of the SKOPTSY. As a child he enjoyed hanging
cats and then ceremonially burying them, and he subsequently teaches

ILYUSHA how to put a pin into a piece of bread and feed it to dogs. He has rejected all religious instruction and is an avowed skeptic. At the time of the action of the novel he is epileptic, terribly antisocial, sullen, bereft of gratitude, and acts as if he despises everyone. He condemns the ignorance of the Russian peasant and observes that he hates Russia and Russians because his origin is belittled. He notes that he wishes that NAPOLEON's invasion in 1812 would have been successful, because then an intelligent nation would have conquered an ignorant one. Many of his ideas stem from IVAN, and much of the novel's dynamics center in the relationship of the two. Prior to FYODOR PAVLOVICH's murder he informs IVAN that he is certain that he will have a fit the next day and that GRIGORY and MARFA will be in a heavy sleep under the influence of a home remedy. He adds that FYODOR PAVLOVICH will therefore be unprotected and questions IVAN about going to Chermashnya. IVAN angrily states that he will leave for Chermashnya early in the morning, and SMERDYAKOV rightfully interprets this as carte blanche to proceed with the murder of his father. The next day he feigns epilepsy, commits the murder, and allows the blame to be placed upon DMITRY, who guards the entrance to his father's house in hope of intercepting GRUSHENKA. Following the murder IVAN visits him on three occasions, and on the final visit SMERDYAKOV shows him the money and explains how he committed the murder. He is quite insistent that he was only IVAN's servant in the whole affair. He intended to use the money to go abroad, and he labors with French in anticipation of leaving Russia. IVAN goes away after their third meeting with the intention of confessing in court, clearing DMITRY, and implicating SMERDYAKOV and himself, but SMERDYAKOV hangs himself.

SMERDYASHCHAYA. See LIZAVETA SMERDYASHCHAYA.

SMUROV. A friend of KOLYA and one of the young boys who throws rocks at ILYUSHA. He later visits him with KOLYA and is reconciled.

NIKOLAY ILYICH SNEGIRYOV (SLOVOERSOV). A retired captain, about forty five, frail, and slight. He is characterized by submissiveness and cowardice, yet also by a desire to stand up for himself. He is a buffoon and observes that during the latter years of his life he has begun to demean himself and to seek debasement, and he even refers to himself as SLOVOERSOV. He lives in abject poverty, yet is characterized by intense pride. On one occasion DMITRY drags him about by the beard in a fit of anger, and the laughter of the bystanders torments his young son ILYUSHA, who is very sensitive to his father's condition. When ALYOSHA delivers two hundred rubles from KATERINA to help the SNEGIR-

YOV family and to salve the captain's injured pride, SNEGIRYOV rejoices that he can provide for his family, but then tramples the money in the ground as if it were an attempt to purchase his honor. He indicates that he could not face ILYUSHA if he accepted money for his insult, but he is ultimately persuaded to accept the kindness. The illness and impending death of ILYUSHA torture him and he becomes thoroughly distraught upon his son's death.

ARINA PETROVNA SNEGIRYOVA. SNEGIRYOV's wife. She is emaciated, about forty three, has little use of her legs, and is weak-minded.

SOBAKEVICH. A comic figure from Nikolay GOGOL's *DEAD SOULS* who is characterized by brutishness, cunning, and gluttony. See "OH, TROYKA, BIRD-LIKE TROYKA, WHO INVENTED YOU!"

SODOM. As recorded in Genesis 18-19 in the OLD TESTAMENT, a city which together with Gomorrah was destroyed by Jehovah because of its wickedness. The word implies wickedness and chaos. (1) In his explanation to ALYOSHA, DMITRY laments that a sensitive and high-minded person can begin with the ideal of the MADONNA and conclude with the ideal of SODOM. He adds that it is even worse that he who has the ideal of SODOM does not abandon the ideal of the MADONNA. He concludes with the thought that for many beauty is centered in SODOM. (2) The scene in which GRUSHENKA orders her officer to leave and laments her five years of suffering is done to the accompaniment of singing by the girls that DMITRY hired and is angrily referred to by VRUBLYOVSKY as SODOM.

SOFYA. SOFYA Pavlovna, FAMUSOV's daughter in the comedy *Woe From Wit*. See FAMUSOV.

SOFYA IVANOVNA. FYODOR PAVLOVICH's second wife, who lives with him for eight years. An orphan, she is raised by the widow of GENERAL VOROKHOV, who tyrannizes her out of caprice rather than viciousness. Her meek, religious, and quiet nature falls victim to the widow's constant torments, and she even tries to hang herself. To escape her plight she runs away with FYODOR PAVLOVICH when she is only sixteen. His constant abuse and blatant orgies produce a nervous disorder in her which ultimately takes her life. She bears FYODOR PAVLOVICH two sons, IVAN and ALYOSHA, and dies when ALYOSHA is four. Her spiritual nature is reflected in the struggles and devotion of her sons.

VON SOHN [FON ZON]. An old debauchee who was the victim of a famous murder in St. Petersburg in 1869. He was enticed into a brothel where he was poisoned, robbed, chopped into pieces and sent to Moscow. (1) FYODOR PAVLOVICH observes that MAKSIMOV looks just like VON SOHN. (2) When FYODOR PAVLOVICH returns to the main building of the monastery to deliberately cause a scene after his meeting with ZOSIMA, he again refers to MAKSIMOV as VON SOHN. He explains how VON SOHN was murdered and robbed in a brothel and how his body was sent by rail from St. Petersburg to Moscow. Because of MAKSIMOV he announces that VON SOHN is now resurrected. (3) After scandalizing the monastery FYODOR PAVLOVICH again refers to MAKSIMOV as VON SOHN and invites him to come visit him for something to eat and a good time. He counsels MAKSIMOV not to miss his chance at happiness by staying around the monastery.

SPHINX [SFINKS]. In Greek mythology a creature with the body of a lion and the head of a woman who strangled all those who could not answer her riddles. The figure became common in Egyptian art with the body of a lion and the head of a man, hawk, or ram. The most famous rendition is the huge sculpture at Giza. The figure also refers to a person who seems deep and mysterious. (1) DMITRY refers to IVAN as a SPHINX who conceals his ideas. (2) The prosecutor IPPOLIT KIRILLOVICH objects to FETYU-KOVICH's trying to turn the trial and DMITRY into a SPHINX, by implication, a much more complicated issue than it really is.

STEPAN. A peasant at Mokroe.

STEPANIDA. When DMITRY arrives in Mokroe, he asks TRIFON BORISYCH to get gypsies and girls, especially MARYA, STEPANIDA, and ARINA.

STEPANIDA ILYINISHNA. See STEPANIDA ILYINISHNA BED-RYAGINA.

"STRIKE HEARTS WITH UNTOLD FORCE" ["UDARIT PO SER-DTSAM S NEVEDOMOYU SILOY"]. Line from "An Answer to Anonym" ("Otvet anonimu"), a poem written by Aleksandr PUSHKIN in 1830. The poem examines the relationship between the poet and the crowd, notes the power of the poet, and expresses gratitude for a warm reception from an unknown source. As FETYUKOVICH begins his summation to the jury, all recognize that he is the kind of orator who can ascend to the heights and "STRIKE HEARTS WITH UNTOLD FORCE."

AGRAFYONA ALEKSANDROVNA SVETLOVA (AGRAFYONA, AGRIPPINA, GRUSHA, GRUSHENKA, GRUSHKA). RAKITIN's twenty two year old cousin. She is beautiful, proud, brazen, rather tall, and has dark hair and blue-gray eyes. There is something childlike about her face and mannerisms despite the fact that she was deceived by a Polish officer MUSSYALOVICH when she was seventeen and that she has been SAMSONOV's kept woman. She is now quite emancipated from SAMSONOV, who has come to depend upon her and her business acumen. She is in conflict with KATERINA IVANOVNA over DMITRY, and each of them tries to win him out of pride and selfishness. On one occasion she visits KATERINA IVANOVNA and seemingly affects a reconciliation, but then insults her by saying that she might not want to forget DMITRY in favor of her officer and that she likes the idea that KATERINA IVANOVNA kissed her while she did not return the gesture. She succeeds in causing a terrible scene. She offers RAKITIN twenty five rubles to bring ALYOSHA to her so that she might ruin him, but when he comes and she learns that ZOSIMA's death has prompted his search for destruction, she removes herself from his lap and treats him with compassion. She has a confession-like conversation with ALYOSHA in which she insists that she is not good and does not want ALYOSHA to say that she is. She admits that she has loved her suffering and tears since her officer abandoned her, that she perhaps loves her insult more than him, and that despite several opportunities she has been involved with no one save SAMSONOV and the officer. She then kneels before ALYOSHA and admits that she has waited for someone like him to love her and to forgive her. When she finally meets her officer again at Mokroe, she is very disappointed in him and his conduct, for example, his cheating at cards, and she dismisses him completely, lamenting her wasted five years of suffering. Her tears express embarrassment for having loved him in the interim, and she quickly declares her love for DMITRY and expresses the need to be with him and to work. When DMITRY is arrested after her declaration of love, she insists that she is guilty and begs to be punished with him for the murder of FYODOR PAVLOVICH, whom she had tantalized with the possibility that she would come to him in exchange for money. After the experience at Mokroe, she becomes noticeably more serious about life and expresses concern for others. She intends to go to America with DMITRY and to stay with him so that she can regenerate him. His future almost exclusively depends upon her.

"TALITHA CUMI" ["TALIFA KUMI"]. "Damsel, I say unto thee, arise," as recorded in Mark 5:41 in the New Testament, the Aramaic words that CHRIST spoke to the daughter of Jairus as He called her forth from the dead. In IVAN's "Legend of the GRAND INQUISITOR" CHRIST returns to Seville and raises a seven year old girl with these words.

TATYANA. TATYANA Larina, the heroine of Aleksandr PUSHKIN's *Yevgeny ONEGIN.* She develops from girlish infatuation to a more mature and cautious outlook on life and love and is the prototype for the nineteenth century Russian novelistic heroine. (1) See BELINSKY. (2) ALYOSHA observes that since KOLYA mentions TATYANA, he has obviously read PUSHKIN and specifically *ONEGIN.*

TEUCER [TEVKR]. In Greek legend the most ancient king of Troy. When KOLYA puzzles his teacher DARDANELOV with the question of who founded Troy, all the young students become interested in the problem. They know that they will have to consult SMARAGDOV's history to find the answer and that only KOLYA has a copy. KARTASHOV steals a peek in the book and then at ILYUSHA's house proudly announces the answer to be DARDANUS, ILUS, TROS, and TEUCER.

"THERE WAS A MAN IN THE LAND OF UZ" ["BYL MUZH V ZEMLE UTS"]. The first phrase in the Book of JOB in the OLD TESTAMENT. ZOSIMA recalls being taken to church as a child, hearing these words, and understanding church language for the first time.

THIRD TEMPTATION OF SATAN [TRETIE DIAVOLOVO ISKU-SHENIE]. As recorded in Matthew 4:8-10 in the New Testament, the attempt of Satan to get CHRIST to worship him by offering Him "the kingdoms of the world, and the glory of them"(Matthew 4:8). (1) PAISY insists that the church will not turn to the state but rather the state will appeal to the church, otherwise the THIRD TEMPTATION OF SATAN would succeed. (2) See "MYSTERY."

"THIS PLACE IS AWFUL." ["STRASHNO MESTO SIE"]. ZOSIMA insists that the Othodox heart understands the Scriptures, and as an example he cites the OLD TESTAMENT account of JACOB's wrestling with an angel in search of a blessing (Genesis 32:24-32) and his pronouncement that "THIS PLACE IS AWFUL." The quotation is not part of the Biblical account of JACOB's search for a blessing, but a similar passage is found in Genesis 28:17, which is part of the account of JACOB's vision of the ladder ascending into heaven. Upon awakening JACOB exclaims "How awful is this place!" ("Kak strashno sie mesto!").

THOMAS [FOMA]. One of the original twelve apostles of CHRIST. (1) In discussing the fact that ALYOSHA believes in miracles but does not base his faith in them, the narrator cites the example of THOMAS, who really did believe and exercise faith even though he said that he had to see the resurrected CHRIST first. The narrator adds that THOMAS' faith was not a product of seeing. The allusion is to THOMAS' statement that he would not believe that CHRIST was resurrected until he saw Him and felt the wounds in His body. The account is recorded in JOHN 20:19-29 in the New Testament. (2) IVAN's devil insists that proofs, particularly material ones, do not contribute to faith, and he states that THOMAS believed not because he saw the resurrected CHRIST but because he wanted to believe.

"THOSE HAS GOD ALREADY FORGOTTEN" ["TEKH UZHE ZAB-YVAET BOG"]. IVAN alludes to *THE DESCENT OF THE VIRGIN INTO HELL* and its description of sinners suffering in a vast fiery lake. He paraphrases the words of MICHAEL to the Virgin to the effect that God has already forgotten some of the sufferers because of their transgressions.

TIMOFEY. A coach driver who takes GRUSHENKA to her rendezvous with her officer at Mokroe. He had previously taken DMITRY there for his first big party with GRUSHENKA.

TIMUR. TIMUR Lenk (1336-1405), also known as Tamerlane, a Mongol warrior who conquered the area from the Volga to the Persian Gulf. See GENGHIS KHAN.

LEV TOLSTOY. LEV Nikolaevich TOLSTOY (1828-1910), Russian novelist and thinker who was the most prominent writer of his age. IVAN's devil tries to convince him that he is a dream or a nightmare and insists that dreams can be so real and creative that even LEV TOLSTOY could not match them.

THE TOWER OF BABEL [VAVILONSKAYA BASHNYA]. As recorded in Genesis 11 in the OLD TESTAMENT, a tower begun by the descendants of Noah by means of which they intended to reach heaven. Jehovah prevented its completion by confounding the language of the builders. (1) The narrator states that atheism and socialism are part of the same phenomenon. He notes that socialism is like THE TOWER OF BABEL erected without the condescension of God for the lowering of heaven to the earth rather than the ascent to heaven from earth. (2) The GRAND INQUISITOR tells CHRIST that because of His refusal to succumb to Satan's temptation to provide earthly bread for His followers (the first temptation of Satan as recorded in Matthew 4:1-4 in the New Testament), He will lose disciples to Satan, who will supply men with bread. The result will be the replacement of the church with another TOWER OF BABEL. (3) The GRAND INQUISITOR mentions that those who have started to build THE TOWER OF BABEL, without the aid of those aligned with Satan to provide bread to the people, will ultimately come to cannibalism.

TRIFON BORISYCH. See TRIFON BORISYCH PLASTUNOV.

TRIFON NIKITICH. When accosted by a man on the street about something he had done, KOLYA calmly states that it is TRIFON NIKITICH's affair and not the stranger's.

TRIFONOV. An acquaintance of KATERINA IVANOVNA's father. He gives TRIFONOV forty five hundred rubles in government money to invest temporarily. Usually such money is quickly returned with interest, but on this occasion TRIFONOV denies that he was ever given any money, and KATERINA IVANOVNA's father finds himself in serious trouble. It is this occasion that involves her with DMITRY in her attempt to raise money to save her father from prosecution.

TROS. In Greek mythology sometimes identified as the father of ILUS, the founder of Troy. Compare DARDANUS. See TEUCER.

"TRUST NOT THE HOLLOW LYING CROWD//FORGET YOUR DOUBTS" ["NE VER TOLPE PUSTOY I LZHIVOY//ZABUD SOMNENIA SVOI"]. Lines from "When From the Darkness of Delusion" ("Kogda iz mraka zabluzhdenya"), a poem written by Nikolay NEKRASOV in 1845. The poem deals with the regeneration of the fallen woman through the aid of the man that loves her. DMITRY quotes these lines to ALYOSHA as he invites him to share a bottle of cognac with him. He tells ALYOSHA not to trust in the phantom of appearances.

TURGENEV. Ivan Sergeevich TURGENEV (1818-83), Russian novelist known for his poetic prose and portrayals of the personal and intellectual lives of the Russian nobility. KHOKHLAKOVA explains to DMITRY when he comes to borrow three thousand rubles from her that she is now a realist who intends to devote herself to practical ventures and that she is healed from previous attitudes. She adds "It is enough! as TURGENEV said" ("Dovolno! kak skazal TURGENEV"). The allusion is likely to TURGENEV's *It is Enough (Dovolno),* a tale written in 1865 that portrays a writer's farewell to literature.

TYUTCHEV. Fyodor Ivanovich TYUTCHEV (1803-73), one of the outstanding Russian poets and the foremost metaphysical poet of his age. In his "Legend of the GRAND INQUISTOR" IVAN discusses the long wait the faithful have had for the SECOND COMING of CHRIST, and he quotes TYUTCHEV's "WEIGHED DOWN BY THE BURDEN OF THE CROSS" as words penned by a believer.

UDOLPHO CASTLE [UDOLFSKY ZAMOK]. The location of the action for *The Mysteries of UDOLPHO,* a Gothic novel written in 1794 by Ann Radcliffe (1764-1823), who popularized the Gothic novel in England. In his summation to the jury FETYUKOVICH attempts to show that there was no money to be taken from FYODOR PAVLOVICH at the time of his murder. He cynically asks the jury where the money not found on DMITRY might be and suggests that it is perhaps in the basement of the UDOLPHO CASTLE.

ULTRAMONTANISM [ULTRAMONTANSTVO]. A movement characteristic of the Italian party of the Roman Catholic Church that advocated the fullest interpretation and the broadest use of the prerogatives and supremacy of the papacy. During IVAN's discussion of the role of church and state and the need for the church to be dominant, MIUSOV objects that the thrust of the discussion verges on ULTRAMONTANISM.

ULYSSES [ULISS]. The Roman version of Odysseus, who in Greek mythology is the king of Ithaca who participates in the siege of Troy. His adventures in returning from Troy are portrayed in Homer's *Odyssey.* See "WOMAN'S DISPOSITION IS GULLIBLE,//AND FICKLE, AND DEPRAVED."

VANECHKA. See IVAN FYODOROVICH KARAMAZOV.

VANKA. See IVAN FYODOROVICH KARAMAZOV.

VANYA. See IVAN FYODOROVICH KARAMAZOV.

VARSONOFY. A monk who was regarded almost as a holy fool and who introduced Zosima into the system of elders. The narrator explains that ZOSIMA's body rather quickly decays and gives off an odor, and he cites in contrast the examples of JOB and VARSONOFY, who according to legend were buried with an almost living smile and whose bodies gave off a sweet odor.

VARVARA ALEKSEEVNA. The mistress of the PLOTNIKOV store. DMITRY notices a dog there that belongs to her.

VARVARA NIKOLAEVNA (VARVARA NIKOLAVNA, VARYA). One of SNEGIRYOV's daughters. She objects to his playing the buffoon in front of ALYOSHA.

VARVARA NIKOLAVNA. See VARVARA NIKOLAEVNA.

VARVINSKY. A young local doctor who recently finished his course in a brilliant manner.

VARYA. See VARVARA NIKOLAEVNA.

VASENKA. PROKHOROVNA's son. He goes to Siberia, does not write his mother in over a year, and causes her great anxiety.

VASHTI [VASTIA]. As recorded in ESTHER 1-2 in the OLD TESTA-MENT, the wife of Ahasuerus, who deposed her in favor of ESTHER. See ESTHER.

VASILIEV. See GRIGORY VASILIEVICH KUTUZOV.

PAISY VELICHKOVSKY. Pyotr Ivanovich VELICHKOVSKY (1722-94), Russian Orthodox scholar and ascetic. As the narrator digresses to relate the history of elders in the monastic movement, he notes that since the end of the last century the system was renewed through the efforts of PAISY VELICHKOVSKY and his followers.

VENUS DE MILO [VENERA MILOSSKAYA]. A famous marble statue of VENUS, the Roman goddess of love associated with the Greek Aphrodite, discovered on the Aegean island of Melos and placed in the Louvre in Paris. In describing GRUSHENKA the narrator observes that she resembles VENUS DE MILO somewhat.

"VERILY I AM A LIE AND THE FATHER OF A LIE" ["VOISTINU LOZH YESM I OTETS LZHI"]. Distortion of part of JOHN 8:44 in the New Testament. The original, CHRIST's assessment of Satan and those who follow him, reads: "for he is a liar, and the father of it" ("ibo on lzhet i otets lzhi"). In a conversation with ZOSIMA, FYODOR PAVLOVICH quotes these words and applies them to himself. His words ironically do apply to himself and IVAN, who of all the sons is most like his father and who implicitly teaches SMERDYAKOV. The lies alluded to include the religious doubts characteristic of FYODOR PAVLOVICH and IVAN.

"VERILY, VERILY, I SAY UNTO YOU, EXCEPT A CORN OF
WHEAT FALL INTO THE GROUND AND DIE, IT ABIDETH
ALONE: BUT IF IT DIE, IT BRINGETH FORTH MUCH FRUIT"
["ISTINNO, ISTINNO GOVORYU VAM, YESLI PSHENICHNOE
ZERNO, PADSHI V ZEMLYU, NE UMRYOT, TO OSTANETSYA
ODNO, A YESLI UMRYOT, TO PRINESYOT MNOGO PLODA"].
Words recorded in JOHN 12:24 from the New Testament in which
CHRIST comments that it is time for Him to be glorified and to fulfill His
mission to the world by dying. (1) The Scripture serves as the epigraph to the
novel. (2) ZOSIMA quotes the passage in shortened form (beginning with
"EXCEPT A CORN") to ALYOSHA and charges him always to remember
it. The quotation follows a discussion of DMITRY and ZOSIMA's charge
to ALYOSHA to watch over him. (3) In trying to encourage the
MYSTERIOUS VISITOR to confess, ZOSIMA reads him this passage.

**KATERINA IVANOVNA VERKHOVTSEVA (K., KATENKA, KATYA,
KATKA).** The tall, beautiful, dark-eyed daughter of a noble lieutenant
colonel. When her father misappropriates government funds and is
threatened with prosecution, she learns from her sister AGAFYA that
DMITRY is willing to give the family the 4500 rubles her father needs,
provided that KATERINA IVANOVNA herself comes to get it. She goes to
DMITRY fully expecting to be required to exchange sexual favors for the
money, but DMITRY simply gives her the money and bows. She in turn
bows to the ground before him. Sometime later, when she unexpectedly
receives a large inheritance, she begs him to marry her. In a letter she
confesses her love, begs him to marry her even if he does not love her,
ironically and pridefully vows to be even a doormat for him, and expresses
her desire to love him forever and save him from himself. DMITRY
observes in response that she loves her virtue more than him. She becomes
involved in two love triangles when DMITRY falls in love with GRU-
SHENKA and she finds herself torn between IVAN and DMITRY. In
order to test DMITRY she gives him 3000 rubles to send to her sister
AGAFYA, fully expecting that he will spend the money on GRUSHENKA.
Like her initial offer to marry him, this gesture is an attempt to establish her
dominance over DMITRY, and she again expresses her desire to save him
and bear his many burdens. In an attempt at reconciliation she invites
GRUSHENKA to visit her and is exhilarated to hear that GRUSHENKA is
going to see her officer and former lover and will likely abandon DMITRY.
She kisses her and praises her rival until GRUSHENKA taunts her with the
possibility that she may not want to forget DMITRY after all. A terrible row
ensues, and KATERINA IVANOVNA calls GRUSHENKA several re-
proachful names. Her motives become clarified in a meeting with AL-

YOSHA in which he senses her need to dominate, and he determines that she could dominate DMITRY but not IVAN. In their conversation she expresses the desire to always be interested in DMITRY as a sister and friend and to be the source of his help. She vows to become a god to him and to make him realize his bad conduct. ALYOSHA suggests that she adopts this stance only to torment IVAN, whom she loves and whose love she acknowledges, and that she never really did love DMITRY. IVAN substantiates this feeling by exposing her pride and adding that she "loves" DMITRY because he insults her. After this experience she becomes hysterical and faints. These relationships are exposed still further at DMITRY's arrest and trial. After the events at Mokroe she engages expensive Moscow doctors for GRUSHENKA and the best lawyer for DMITRY. In the courtroom she initially testifies in behalf of DMITRY by referring to the time that he nobly gave her family money, but after IVAN testifies and implicates himself and SMERDYAKOV in the murder, she insists that DMITRY is the murderer and produces a letter he wrote to her in which he threatened to murder FYODOR PAVLOVICH. Her defense of IVAN reflects her deep offense at DMITRY's betrayal of her with GRUSHENKA. Following IVAN's collapse in the courtroom, she takes him into her home for care. She feels a sense of guilt for betraying DMITRY at his trial, but nevertheless expresses much hatred and resentment toward him. She comes to DMITRY to affect a reconciliation, but her gesture is deeply rooted in her desire to debase herself and to suffer. She vows to insure DMITRY's escape and to preserve him for GRUSHENKA in an act of professed self-sacrificial virture.

VISHNYAKOV. A twenty year old delivery boy for the PLOTNIKOVS. In company with KOLYA he runs over a goose's neck with a wagon wheel while it is eating oats.

"VIVOS VOCO!" "I call the living," the first part of the epigraph to SCHILLER's "Das Lied von der Glocke" ("The Ballad of the Bell"), written 1799-1800. The famous ballad deals with the making of the art object and the meaning of the object itself. These same words served as the slogan for *THE BELL.* In his summation to the jury at DMITRY's trial FETYUKO-VICH discredits FYODOR PAVLOVICH as a father and encourages all to be model fathers. With the words "VIVOS VOCO!" he calls all to live by these principles.

VOLTAIRE [VOLTER]. Pen name of François Marie Arouet (1694-1778), noted French satirist, philosopher, and historian. His name connotes a free-thinking approach to issues and philosophy. In discussing with ALYOSHA the possibility of loving mankind but not believing in God, KOLYA cites VOLTAIRE as a person who was able to do this. ALYOSHA counters that VOLTAIRE did believe in God somewhat and loved mankind only slightly. He pursues the matter by asking KOLYA if he has read VOLTAIRE, and KOLYA answers that he has read *CANDIDE.*

GENERAL VOROKHOV. The late husband of SOFYA IVANOVNA's benefactress.

VRUBLYOVSKY. A very tall Pole, a dentist by profession, who accompanies MUSSYALOVICH at his rendezvous with GRUSHENKA at Mokroe. The two use a marked deck of cards to bilk DMITRY and others of money.

"WEIGHED DOWN BY THE BURDEN OF THE CROSS,//THE KING OF HEAVEN IN SERVANT'S DRESS//HAS TRAVERSED ALL OF YOU, MY NATIVE LAND,//BLESSING ALL THE WAY" ["UDRU-CHYONNY NOSHEY KRESTNOY//VSYU TEBYA, ZEMLYA ROD-NAYA,//V RABSKOM VIDE TSAR NEBESNY//ISKHODIL BLA-GOSLOVLYAYA". The concluding quatrain of "These Poor Villages" ("Eti bednye selenia"), a short poem written by Fyodor TYUTCHEV in 1855. The poem depicts the poverty-ridden Russian landscape which conceals an inner spiritual light. In his "Legend of the GRAND INQUISI-TOR" IVAN discusses the long wait the faithful have had for the SECOND COMING and quotes these words from the believing TYUTCHEV.

"WHAT DO YOU BELIEVE OR DO YOU NOT BELIEVE AT ALL?" ["KAKO VERUESHI ALI VOVSE NE VERUESHI?"]. A question from the ritual of monastic consecration to which the respondent replies with a confession of faith. As ALYOSHA and IVAN converse prior to his recitation of the "Legend of the GRAND INQUISITOR," IVAN observes that the above is the question that they have come together to discuss.

WHAT EARTHLY JOY [KAYA ZHITEYSKAYA SLADOST]. A song based upon a Biblical theme sung over a monk following death. FERA-PONT complains that *HELPER AND DEFENDER* will be sung over ZOSIMA's body because he is a priest, but only *WHAT EARTHLY JOY* over himself when he dies because he is only a monk.

"WHO IS LIKE UNTO THIS BEAST, HE GAVE US FIRE FROM HEAVEN!" ["KTO PODOBEN ZVERYU SEMU, ON DAL NAM OGON S NEBESI!"]. Evidently a distortion of part of The Revelation of St.

John 13. The chapter portrays the appearance of two beasts given power by Satan. Part of the fourth verse, which describes the appearance of the first beast, reads "Who is like unto the beast?" ("Kto podoben zveryu semu"), while the thirteenth verse ascribes the power of making fire come down from heaven to the second beast—"he maketh fire come down from heaven" ("ogon nizvodit s neba"). The GRAND INQUISITOR assails CHRIST for not succumbing to the temptations of Satan and leaving behind a legacy of miracles for His followers. He adds that Satan will overcome Him because of this and that people will follow Satan quoting the above.

"WHO MADE ME A DIVIDER OVER THEM?" ["KTO MENYA POSTAVIL DELIT MEZHDU NIMI?"]. Distortion of LUKE 12:14 in the New Testament. The statement is provoked by one who wants CHRIST to persuade his brother to share his inheritance. The answer is "WHO MADE ME a judge or A DIVIDER OVER YOU?" ("KTO POSTAVIL MENYA sudit ili DELIT vas?"), and there follows some brief counsel on covetousness. ZOSIMA smilingly quotes these words to ALYOSHA after he agrees to arbitrate the dispute between DMITRY and FYODOR PAVLOVICH.

"WILD AND FEARFUL IN HIS CAVE//HID THE NAKED TROGLODYTE" ["ROBOK I DIK SKRYVALSYA//TROGLODIT V PESHCHERAKH SKAL"]. Words in Russian translation from the first stanza of Friedrich SCHILLER's "Das Eleusische Fest" ("The Eleusis Festival"), a poem written in 1798. The poem expresses disappointment with the state of civilization and then portrays the union of mother earth and man with the participation of the gods of Olympus. The result is that the earth produces, and earth's resources are used to build society and unite men. DMITRY begins his explanation to ALYOSHA about his character and problems by quoting several stanzas from this poem.

"WITH INVINCIBLE FORCE" ["NEPOBEDIMOY SILOY"]. The first line of a song sung intermittently by SMERDYAKOV. Other stanzas begin with "The tsar's crown" ("Tsarskaya korona") and "No matter what you try" ("Skolko ni staratsya"), and the song is based upon a lackey's song Dostoevsky himself heard. ALYOSHA overhears SMERDYAKOV sing the song that expresses his own superficial desires.

"WITH WHATSOEVER MEASURE YOU MEASURE, IT WILL BE MEASURED TO YOU" ["V NYU ZHE MERU MERITE, VOZMERITSYA I VAM"]. Distortion of Matthew 7:2 in the New Testament—"with what measure ye mete, it shall be measured to you again" ("Kakoyu meroyu merite takoyu i vam budut merit"). The same expression in a slightly different wording is found in Mark 4:24 and LUKE 6:38. In his summation to the jury at DMITRY's trial FETYUKOVICH discredits FYODOR PAVLOVICH as a father and encourages all to be exemplary fathers. He quotes these words to prove his point and states that they are from the BIBLE and not his own words. In his rebuttal the prosecutor IPPOLIT KIRILLOVICH objects that such words are from a false CHRIST, and he insists that the proper language should be "MEASURE WITH THAT MEASURE WHICH IS MEASURED UNTO YOU" ("MERIT V TU MERU, V KOTORUYU I VAM MERYAYUT").

"WOMAN'S DISPOSITION IS GULLIBLE,//AND FICKLE, AND DEPRAVED" ["LEGKOVEREN ZHENSKY NRAV,//I IZMENCHIV, I POROCHEN"]. Couplet from Fyodor TYUTCHEV's poem "The Funeral Feast" ("Pominki"), published in 1851. The poem is the poet's translation of Friedrich SCHILLER's "Das Siegesfest" ("The Feast of Victory"), written in 1803, which portrays the return from the siege of Troy. In the poem the words are ascribed to Odysseus, the equivalent of the Roman ULYSSES. With reference to his quoting "MASTRYUK WAS ALL IN ALL, BUT CAME TO NAUGHT AT ALL!" DMITRY observes that he is speaking about the harmful influence of women, and then adds these lines of verse to his indictment. He expresses this frustration after GRUSHENKA abandons him and flees to Mokroe to be reunited with MUSSYALOVICH.

THE WORD [SLOVO]. A term, most effectively expanded upon in JOHN 1 in the New Testament, that refers to CHRIST. (1) IVAN states that he is ready to believe many things, including THE WORD. (2) IVAN's devil states that he was present when THE WORD rose into heaven bearing with Him the soul of the penitent thief. The allusion is to LUKE 23:42-43 in the New Testament in which CHRIST promises one of the thieves crucified with Him that he will be with Him that day in paradise.

THE WORDS OF OUR HOLY FATHER ISAAC THE SYRIAN [SVYATOGO OTTSA NASHEGO ISAAKA SIRINA SLOVA]. On his third visit to SMERDYAKOV, IVAN notes this book lying near SMERD-YAKOV on a couch. SMERDYAKOV shows him the money he took from FYODOR PAVLOVICH following the murder and then places the book over it.

WORLD HISTORY [VSEOBSHCHAYA ISTORIA]. When SMERD-YAKOV complains that *EVENINGS ON A FARM NEAR DIKANKA* is based upon falsehood, FYODOR PAVLOVICH gives him SMARAG-

DOV's *WORLD HISTORY* to read instead. The reference is probably to *A Brief Outline of World History for Primary Schools (Kratkoe nachertanie vseobshchey istorii dlya pervonachalnykh uchilishch)*, first published in 1845 and appearing in several editions.

"YEA, O LORD, APPEAR TO US" ["BO GOSPODI YAVISYA NAM"]. A distortion of Psalms 118:27 (117:27 in the Russian version) from the OLD TESTAMENT. In his "Legend of the Grand INQUISITOR" IVAN asserts that the Lord's faithful have been praying for centuries for the appearance of the Lord and uses these words to express the feeling. The phrase as IVAN uses it does not make grammatical sense in the Slavonic original. The modern version reads "God is the Lord, which hath shewed us light" ("Bog—Gospod, i osiyal nas").

YEFIM PETROVICH. See YEFIM PETROVICH POLENOV.

YELISEEV BROTHERS. Wine merchants in nineteenth century Russia. (1) When FYODOR PAVLOVICH discovers YELISEEV BROTHERS wine on Father Superior NIKOLAY's table, he attacks the monks for taking financial advantage of the gospel. He deliberately attempts to perpetrate a scandal because he feels that he has demeaned himself before ZOSIMA. (2) It is mentioned that the store operated by the PLOTNIKOVS stocks YELISEEV BROTHERS wine.

YORICK [IORIK]. The king's jester in *HAMLET.* DMITRY says that he himself is YORICK and will ultimately become a skull, just as the dramatic character. See "I AM SO SAD, SO SAD, HORATIO... AH, POOR YORICK."

"YOU ARE SAPPHO, I PHAON, THIS I DO NOT QUESTION,//BUT TO MY UTTER GRIEF,//YOU CANNOT FIND THE SEA" ["TY SAFO, YA FAON, OB ETOM YA NE SPORYU,//NO, K MOEMU TY GORYU,//PUTI NE ZNAESH K MORYU"]. Slightly inaccurate rendering (the original has "and" ["i"] in place of "I" ["ya"] with no real change in translation) of "A Madrigal to the New Sappho" ("Madrigal novoy Safe"), written by Konstantin Nikolaevich Batyushkov (1787-1855) in 1809. The madrigal is one of thirteen brief entries numbered under the heading "Epigrams, Inscriptions, Etc." ("Epigrammy, nadpisi i pr."). MAKSIMOV claims that he encountered BOILEAU and PIRON in a pub and insulted them by quoting the above. See SAPPHO, PHAON.

"YOU WILL REMEMBER THE BUILDING//BY THE CHAIN BRIDGE" ["BUDESH POMNIT ZDANIE//U TSEPNOGO MOSTA!"]. Couplet from a political lyric entitled "An Epistle" ("Poslanie"), published in the journal *Polar Star (Polyarnaya zvezda)* in 1861. The poem describes the punishment meted out under the tsar's orders in the prison by the bridge. KOLYA observes to ALYOSHA that as a socialist he does not want to fall victim to the Third Section of the Secret Police and quotes these lines to illustrate his fear.

YULIA. A maid in the KHOKHLAKOVA house.

ZHUCHKA. See PEREZVON. Using SMERDYAKOV's trick, ILYU-SHA feeds the dog some bread with a pin concealed inside, and when the dog disappears, he contends that his suffering with consumption is punishment for what he has done.

ZINOVY. ZOSIMA's real name.

ZOSIMA (ZINOVY, PATER SERAPHICUS). The sixty five year old elder in the monastery. He is a devotee of the elder system, in which followers commit themselves to a mentor to perfect themselves through absolute obedience. ALYOSHA desires to attach himself to ZOSIMA in this manner, and it is he who provides a written history of ZOSIMA's life and teachings. In his youth, following the death of his brother MARKEL, he is sent to St. Petersburg by his mother in hope of making a career in the Cadets. While there he lives a very worldly existence and ultimately falls in love, but his pride prevents his acting and she marries another. This same pride prompts him to insult and challenge her new husband to a duel. On the eve of the duel he angrily strikes his valet AFANASY. During the night he recalls the teaching of his brother MARKEL to the effect that one should serve, love, and share the burdens of all men, and he arises from his bed a new person. He apologizes to AFANASY, begs forgiveness from his adversary at the duel, retires from the service, and intends to enter a monastery. His behavior at the duel leads to his acquaintance with MIKHAIL, the MYSTERIOUS VISITOR, whom he encourages to confess his crime and to order his life on the same principles that he now tries to live by. At the time of the novel's action he looks much older than sixty five years and is in poor health. He agrees to arbitrate the dispute between DMITRY and FYODOR PAVLOVICH and views with compassion FYODOR PAVLOVICH's buffoonery and personality problems. Follow-ing the scandalous encounter of father and son, ZOSIMA bows down before DMITRY, a gesture indicating that DMITRY will bear great suffering. He is frequently called upon to meet with the common people who come bearing various petitions, and he gives comfort and counsel where needed. Among the petitioners he has helped are the KHOKHLAKOVAS. He blesses LIZA, and when she recovers, Madame KHOKHLAKOVA pleads with him to cure her unbelief in immortality. He counsels her to love actively and makes a distinct difference between an active love and dream love (selfless love for one's neighbor vs. an abstract and superficial regard for humanity). His preachments and teachings are many: (1) He teaches the monks that they are no better and perhaps worse than those outside the monastery and encourages them to love others, accept responsibility for everyone's sins, and pray for all. He also praises the monk as a servant of the Russian people, the God-bearing people, and as one who enjoys true freedom. (2) He laments that some desire to build society with the mind rather than with CHRIST and that others claim that there is no crime and no sin. He insists that where there is no God there is no crime or sin. (3) He advocates that the wealthy and the common people can be united in brotherhood only when wealth is not a hindrance, and that this is accomplished when wealth is divided and people see that equality is based in spiritual worth. (4) Stimulated by MARKEL and his own past, he teaches that men should treat their servants as brothers. (5) He expounds that all should pray. (6) He insists that people should love others in their sins and correct them with love. Each should be responsible for everyone and everything, and men should judge only when they realize that they too are criminals. He even defines hell as the inability to love. His death is a pivotal point in the novel. When his moment comes, he kisses the earth in a symbolic gesture of unity and then willingly gives up the ghost. His body quickly begins to stink because of the heat and close quarters, and this produces a controversy among opponents and proponents of the elder system. The controversy is based upon legends ascribed to saints whose bodies emitted sweet odors at death, and several of ZOSIMA's enemies, notably FERAPONT, actively insist that the odor shows that he is not a saint and that the elder system is not divine. The death is most important because of the despondent reaction of ALYOSHA, who had expected miracles in connection with ZOSIMA's passing. His depression provokes a minor rebellion in which he visits GRUSHENKA and commences his odyssey in the world, an odyssey that ZOSIMA had counselled him to make.

INDEX

Aksyonov, 114
Akulina Kudimovna, 000
Akulina Panfilovna *(Uncle's Dream)*, 55
Akulina Panfilovna *(The Village of Stepanchikovo)*, 69
Akulka See Akulina Kudimovna
The Alarm Clock, 150
Albert, 152
Madame Albert, 90
Aleksandr *(Netochka Nezvanova)*, 44
Aleksandr *Notes From the House of the Dead)*, 114
Aleksandr I, 193, 318
Aleksandr II, 215
Aleksandr Aleksandrovich, 381
Aleksandr Demyanovich, 31
Aleksandr Filimonovich, 36
Aleksandr Grigorievich See Aleksandr Grigorievich Zamyotov
Aleksandr Ignatyich, 27
Aleksandr Petrovich, 90
Aleksandr Petrovich See Aleksandr Petrovich Goryanchikov
Aleksandr Semyonovich, 315
Aleksandr Semyonych See Aleksandr Semyonovich
Aleksandra See Aleksandr *(Notes From the House of the Dead)*
Aleksandra See Aleksandra Ivanovna Yepanchina
Aleksandra Ivanovna See Aleksandra Ivanovna Yepanchina
Aleksandra Mikhaylovna *(Netochka Nezvanova)*, 44
Aleksandra Mikhaylovna *(The Idiot)*, 193
Aleksandra Petrovna See Aleksandra Petrovna Sinitskaya
Aleksandra Semyonovna *(The Insulted and Injured)*, 91
Aleksandra Yegorovna See Aleksandra Yegorovna Rostanyova
Aleksandrina, 91
Aleksandrov, 36
Aleksasha See Aleksasha Likhachyov
Alekseich, 12
Aleksey *(The Idiot)*, 193
Aleksey *(The Brothers Karamazov)*, 381
Aleksey See Aleksey Fyodorovich Karamazov
Aleksey Ivanovich See Aleksey Ivanovich Velchaninov

Aleksey Ivanovich, 152
Aleksey Makarovich See Arkady Andreevich Dolgoruky
Tsar Aleksey Mikhaylovich, 91, 316
Aleksey Nikanorovich See Aleksey Nikanorovich Andronikov
Aleksey Nikiforych, 44
Aleksey Nilych See Aleksey Nilych Kirillov
Aleksey Petrovich See Aleksey Petrovich Valkovsky
Aleksey Semyonych, 161
Aleksey the Man of God, 381
Aleksey Yegorovich, 248
Aleksey Yegorych See Aleksey Yegorovich
Alekseychik See Aleksey Fyodorovich Karamazov
Alexander the Great, 69, 71, 91, 136, 382
"Alexander the Great was a hero, everyone knows that, but why break chairs?" 91
Alexis See Aleksey Ivanovich
Aley See Aley Semyonych
Aley Semyonych, 114
Alfonsina Karlovna See Alphonsine de Verden
Alfonsinka See Alphonsine de Verden
Alfred, 12
Alhambra, 55
"All ye that labor and are heavy laden," 248
Allah, 161, 193, 282, 316
Alma, 161
Almazov, 114
Alnaskar(-ov), 92
Alphonse and Dalinda, 91
Alphonsine See Alphonsine de Verden
Alyona Frolovna, 248
Alyona Ivanovna, 161
Alyosha, 27
Alyosha See Aleksey Fyodorovich Karamazov
Alyosha See Aleksey Petrovich Valkovsky
Alyoshechka See Aleksey Fyodorovich Karamazov
Alyoshenka See Aleksey Fyodorovich Karamazov
Alyoshka, 162
Alyoshka See Aleksey Fyodorovich Karamazov
Amal-Ivan See Amalia Fyodorvna Lippewechsel
Amalchen, 153
Amalia, 248